SOCIAL ISSUES IN AMERICA

AN ENCYCLOPEDIA

VOLUME THREE

JAMES CIMENT, EDITOR

SHARPE REFERENCE

an imprint of M.E. Sharpe, Inc.

RAP

SHARPE REFERENCE

Sharpe Reference is an imprint of M.E. Sharpe, Inc.

M.E. Sharpe, Inc.
80 Business Park Drive
Armonk, NY 10504

© 2006 by M.E. Sharpe, Inc.

Cover photos courtesy of ArtToday.com

Library of Congress Cataloging-in-Publication Data

Social issues in America : an encyclopedia / James Ciment, editor.
  p. cm.
Includes bibliographical references and index.
ISBN 0-7656-8061-0 (hc : set : alk. paper)
  1. Social problems—United States—Encyclopedias. 2. Social movements—United States—Encyclopedias.
3. United States—Social conditions—Encyclopedias. 4. United States—Social policy—Encyclopedias.
I. Ciment, James.

HN57.S624 2006
361.973'03—dc22   2005018778

Printed and bound in the United States of America

The paper used in this publication meets the minimum requirements of
American National Standard for Information Sciences
Permanence of Paper for Printed Library Materials,
ANSI Z 39.48.1984.

BM (c) 10 9 8 7 6 5 4 3 2

Publisher: Myron E. Sharpe
Vice President and Editorial Director: Patricia Kolb
Vice President and Production Director: Carmen Chetti
Executive Editor and Manager of Reference: Todd Hallman
Senior Development Editor: Jeff Hacker
Project Manager: Wendy E. Muto
Program Coordinator: Cathleen Prisco
Compositor: Nancy J. Connick
Text Design: Carmen Chetti
Cover Design: Jesse Sanchez

CONTENTS

TOPIC FINDER

Civil Rights and Civil Liberties Issues

Affirmative Action
Ageism
AIDS/HIV
Animal Rights
Anti-Muslim Discrimination and Violence
Anti-Semitism
Arts Funding and Censorship
Capital Punishment
Civil Liberties
Civil Rights
Criminal Rights
Disability Rights
Environmental Justice
Gay and Lesbian Rights
Hate Crimes
Hate Radio and Internet
Hate Speech
Native Americans and Government
  Policy
Police Abuse and Corruption
Prison Reform and Prisoner Rights
Privacy
Racial Profiling
Redlining, Loan Discrimination, and
  Predatory Lending
Secrecy, Government
Sexual Harassment
Students' Rights
Terrorism, War on
Voting Issues
Women's Rights

Economic and Class Issues

Affirmative Action
Air Travel: Safety, Security, and Service
Child Labor
Consumer Debt and Bankruptcy
Corporate Crime
Corporate Downsizing
Defense Spending and Preparedness

Energy Dependency
Farm Issues
Gambling
Gentrification
Homelessness
Housing, Affordable
Identity Theft
Infrastructure Deterioration
Media Consolidation
Migrant Workers
Minimum and Living Wages
Money Laundering
Not in My Backyard (NIMBY) Issues
Poverty and Wealth
Redlining, Loan Discrimination, and
  Predatory Lending
Social Security Reform
Superstores vs. Main Street
Sweatshops
Taxes and Tax Reform
Unemployment
Unions
Welfare and Welfare Reform

Educational Issues

Academic Freedom
Affirmative Action
At-Risk Students: Higher Education
Attention Deficit-Hyperactivity Disorder
Autism
Bilingualism
Cheating, Academic
Church-State Separation
College Sports
Corporal Punishment
Evolution Education
Hate Speech
Literacy
School Standards and Testing
School Violence
School Vouchers and Privatization

CROSS REFERENCE INDEX

Abortion and Reproductive Issues. *See also:* Adoption; AIDS/HIV; Birth Control; Sex Education; Single Parenting and Out-of-Wedlock Births; Women's Rights.

Academic Freedom. *See also:* Cheating, Academic; Hate Speech; Plagiarism, Literary and Artistic; Students' Rights.

Adoption. *See also:* Abortion and Reproductive Issues; Birth Control; Divorce and Child Custody; Foster Care; Single Parenting and Out-of-Wedlock Births.

Advertising, Children's. *See also:* Media Sex and Violence.

Affirmative Action. *See also:* Civil Rights; Racial Profiling.

Ageism. *See also:* Disability Rights; Social Security Reform.

AIDS/HIV. *See also:* Drug Abuse; Gay and Lesbian Rights; Infectious Disease and Epidemics; Medicine, Complementary and Alternative; Needle Exchange Programs; Sex Education.

Air Pollution. *See also:* Global Warming; Indoor Air Pollution.

Air Travel: Safety, Security, and Service. *See also:* Automobile and Highway Safety; Infrastructure Deterioration; Terrorism, Foreign; Terrorism, War on.

Alcohol and Alcoholism. *See also:* Domestic Violence; Drug Abuse; Tobacco.

Animal Rights. *See also:* Human Experimentation; Scientific Research Ethics.

Anti-Muslim Discrimination and Violence. *See also:* Civil Liberties; Civil Rights; Hate Crimes; Hate Radio and Internet; Hate Speech; Terrorism, War on; Xenophobia and Nativism.

Anti-Semitism. *See also:* Civil Rights; Hate Crimes; Hate Radio and Internet; Hate Speech.

Arson. *See also:* Crime; Rioting; Terrorism, Domestic.

Arts Funding and Censorship. *See also:* Media Bias; Plagiarism, Literary and Artistic.

At-Risk Students: Higher Education. *See also:* Cheating, Academic; School Standards and Testing; School Violence.

Attention Deficit-Hyperactivity Disorder. *See also:* Mental Illness; Special Education.

Autism. *See also:* Mental Illness; Special Education.

Automobile and Highway Safety. *See also:* Air Travel: Safety, Security, and Service; Mass Transit; Traffic Congestion.

Bilingualism. *See also:* Immigration Policy and Law; Special Education; Xenophobia and Nativism.

Birth Control. *See also:* Abortion and Reproductive Issues; Single Parenting and Out-of-Wedlock Births.

Campaign Finance Reform. *See also:* Public Opinion Polling; Voting Issues.

Cancer. *See also:* Environmentally Induced Illnesses; Medicine, Complementary and Alternative; Tobacco.

Capital Punishment. *See also:* Crime; Criminal Rights; Gun Violence and Gun Control; Prison Reform and Prisoner Rights.

Census Issues. *See also:* Public Opinion Polling; Voting Issues.

Cheating, Academic. *See also:* Plagiarism, Literary and Artistic; Students' Rights.

Child Abuse and Molestation. *See also:* Child Labor; Corporal Punishment; Divorce and Child Custody; Domestic Violence; Foster Care.

Child Labor. *See also:* Child Abuse and Molestation; Migrant Workers; Sweatshops.

Chronic Fatigue Syndrome. *See also:* Environmentally Induced Illnesses; Stress.

Church-State Separation. *See also:* Civil Liberties; "Cults" and Alternative Religions; Evolution Education; School Vouchers and Privatization.

Civil Liberties. *See also:* Civil Rights; Criminal Rights; Gun Violence and Gun Control; Hate Crimes; Hate Speech; Legal Services for the Poor; Police Abuse and Corruption; Prison Reform and Prisoner Rights; Secrecy, Government; Terrorism, War on.

Civil Rights. *See also:* Abortion and Reproductive Issues; Affirmative Action; Ageism; Anti-Muslim Discrimination and Violence; Anti-Semitism; Civil Liberties; Hate Crimes; Hate Speech; Police Abuse and Corruption; Racial Profiling; Redlining, Loan Discrimination, and Predatory Lending; Rioting; Women's Rights.

Coastal Pollution and Wetlands Protection. *See also:* Deforestation and Logging; Drought and Aquifer Depletion; Extinction and Species Loss: Biota Invasion and Habitat Destruction; Urban Sprawl; Water Pollution; Wilderness Protection.

College Sports. *See also:* Alcohol and Alcoholism; Gambling; Women's Rights.

Computer Crime and Hacking. *See also:* Hate Radio and Internet; Identity Theft; Intellectual Property Rights; Money Laundering; Organized Crime; Terrorism, Foreign; Terrorism, War on.

Consumer Debt and Bankruptcy. *See also:* Corporate Downsizing; Gambling; Minimum and Living Wages; Redlining, Loan Discrimination, and Predatory Lending; Superstores vs. Main Street; Taxes and Tax Reform; Unemployment.

Corporal Punishment. *See also:* Child Abuse and Molestation; Domestic Violence; Students' Rights.

Corporate Crime. *See also:* Crime; Money Laundering; Organized Crime.

Corporate Downsizing. *See also:* Consumer Debt and Bankruptcy; Media Consolidation; Minimum and Living Wages; Sweatshops; Unemployment; Unions.

Crime. *See also:* Arson; Capital Punishment; Civil Liberties; Computer Crime and Hacking; Corporate Crime; Criminal Rights; Domestic Violence; Drugs, War on; Gambling; Gun Violence and Gun Control; Hate Crimes; Identity Theft; Juvenile Justice; Legal Services for the Poor; Mandatory Sentencing; Money Laundering; Organized Crime; Police Abuse and Corruption; Prison Reform and Prisoner Rights; Prostitution; Rape; Terrorism, War on.

Criminal Rights. *See also:* Capital Punishment; Civil Liberties; Judicial Reform; Mandatory Sentencing; Police Abuse and Corruption; Prison Reform and Prisoner Rights.

"Cults" and Alternative Religions. *See also:* Militia Movement.

Defense Spending and Preparedness. *See also:* Drugs, War on; Energy Dependency; Nuclear Weapons; Terrorism, War on; Weapons of Mass Destruction.

Deforestation and Logging. *See also:* Coastal Pollution and Wetlands Protection; Extinction and Species Loss: Biota Invasion and Habitat Destruction; Global Warming; Urban Sprawl; Wilderness Protection.

Disability Rights. *See also:* Ageism; Civil Rights.

Divorce and Child Custody. *See also:* Adoption; Domestic Violence; Foster Care; Single Parenting and Out-of-Wedlock Births; Women's Rights.

Domestic Violence. *See also:* Alcohol and Alcoholism; Child Abuse and Molestation; Divorce and Child Custody; Drug Abuse; Foster Care; Rape; Single Parenting and Out-of-Wedlock Births.

Recycling and Conservation. *See also:* Coastal Pollution and Wetlands Protection; Deforestation and Logging; Drought and Aquifer Depletion; Energy Dependency; Waste Disposal.

Redlining, Loan Discrimination, and Predatory Lending. *See also:* Consumer Debt and Bankruptcy; Corporate Crime; Gentrification; Housing, Affordable; Poverty and Wealth.

Rioting. *See also:* Arson; Civil Rights; Crime; Police Abuse and Corruption; Racial Profiling.

School Standards and Testing. *See also:* Cheating, Academic; Special Education.

School Violence. *See also:* Corporal Punishment; Gangs; Gun Violence and Gun Control; Hate Crimes; Hate Speech; Juvenile Justice; Suicide.

School Vouchers and Privatization. *See also:* Church-State Separation; School Standards and Testing.

Scientific Research Ethics. *See also:* Abortion and Reproductive Issues; Academic Freedom; Animal Rights; Cheating, Academic; Genetic Engineering; Human Experimentation; Stem Cell Research.

Secrecy, Government. *See also:* Civil Liberties; Defense Spending and Preparedness; Privacy; Terrorism, War on.

Sex Education. *See also:* Abortion and Reproductive Issues; Birth Control; Child Abuse and Molestation; Single Parenting and Out-of-Wedlock Births.

Sexual Harassment. *See also:* Domestic Violence; Gay and Lesbian Rights; Hate Crimes; Pornography; Prostitution; Rape; Women's Rights.

Single Parenting and Out-of-Wedlock Births. *See also:* Abortion and Reproductive Issues; Birth Control; Divorce and Child Custody; Foster Care; Welfare and Welfare Reform.

Social Security Reform. *See also:* Ageism; Disability Rights; Medicare and Medicaid Reform; Taxes and Tax Reform; Welfare and Welfare Reform.

Space Exploration. *See also:* Defense Spending and Preparedness.

Special Education. *See also:* At-Risk Students: Higher Education; Attention Deficit-Hyperactivity Disorder; Autism; Bilingualism; Disability Rights; Literacy; School Standards and Testing.

Stem Cell Research. *See also:* Cancer; Genetic Engineering; Organ and Tissue Transplants; Scientific Research Ethics.

Stress. *See also:* Attention Deficit-Hyperactivity Disorder; Heart Disease and Cardiology; Occupational Safety and Health; Suicide; Traffic Congestion; Unemployment.

Students' Rights. *See also:* Academic Freedom; Cheating, Academic; Civil Liberties; Hate Speech.

Suicide. *See also:* Euthanasia; Gun Violence and Gun Control; Stress.

Superstores vs. Main Street. *See also:* Gentrification; Minimum and Living Wages; Traffic Congestion; Unions; Urban Sprawl.

Sweatshops. *See also:* Child Labor; Corporate Crime; Immigration, Illegal; Migrant Workers; Minimum and Living Wages; Occupational Safety and Health; Unions.

Taxes and Tax Reform. *See also:* Corporate Crime; Defense Spending and Preparedness; Medicare and Medicaid Reform; Poverty and Wealth.

Term Limits. *See also:* Campaign Finance Reform; Public Opinion Polling; Voting Issues.

Terrorism, Domestic. *See also:* Anti-Muslim Discrimination and Violence; Anti-Semitism; Arson; Crime; Hate Crimes; Militia Movement; Terrorism, War on; Xenophobia and Nativism.

Terrorism, Foreign. *See also:* Air Travel: Safety, Security, and Service; Anti-Muslim Discrimination and Violence; Terrorism, War on; Weapons of Mass Destruction; Xenophobia and Nativism.

Terrorism, War on. *See also:* Air Travel: Safety, Security, and Service; Anti-Muslim Discrimination and Violence; Civil Liberties; Defense Spending and Preparedness; Energy Dependency; Immigration Policy and Law; Money Laundering; Nuclear Weapons;

SOCIAL ISSUES
IN AMERICA

AN ENCYCLOPEDIA

VOLUME THREE

DIVORCE AND CHILD CUSTODY

The United States leads the industrialized world in the percentage of divorces granted per capita. Growing steadily through the nineteenth and twentieth centuries, divorce rates peaked in the 1970s at about four divorces annually per 1,000 persons, where they have remained ever since.

This increasing divorce rate has produced a certain acceptance of a social practice that was once frowned on. For example, popular culture is now full of positive portrayals of divorced individuals, whereas divorcés (divorced men) and divorcées (divorced women) were virtually nonexistent on television through the 1960s. Moreover, divorce is no longer fatal to political candidates. Despite the new level of acceptance, however, divorce remains controversial for many Americans. Underlying the controversy is the prevalence of "family values" in modern American culture. Few Western societies emphasize the importance of marriage and family to social cohesion more than the United States. Thus, to many Americans—especially members of conservative and evangelical communities—divorce is an affront to fundamental and long-enduring social values. In their minds, government authorities have made divorce too easy. In recent years, several southern states have passed "covenant marriage" laws, allowing couples to commit themselves to marriages that are more difficult to end, requiring counseling and cooling off periods before a legal divorce is granted.

Many of those who bemoan the impact of divorce on family values point to a time in the past when the practice was less common, implying that today's high divorce rates are at least partially responsible for the various woes of contemporary American society, including youth crime—because children do not have adequate parental supervision—and sexual promiscuity. Liberals, while bemoaning the impact of divorce on poverty rates among women and children, are generally more sanguine about the practice, saying it frees spouses (especially wives) from physically and emotionally abusive relationships.

Divorce rates in the early 2000s are far higher than they were in the early 1900s, or even the 1950s, but divorce has always been a part of American life. So, too, have controversies over the increasing prevalence of divorce and its negative impact on society existed since at least the mid-nineteenth century.

Closely related to divorce is the matter of child custody and support. The involvement of children complicates the issue of divorce not only for the couple in question, but also for society, which needs to ensure the children's safety and well-being. In the United States today, roughly 1 million children are affected by divorce annually. When couples with children get divorced, they face legal, financial, and emotional issues surrounding who gets the children, for what periods of time and on what terms, visitation rights for the parent who does not get custody, and financial support for the spouse raising the children. Moreover, divorce can have an emotional impact on children in two ways: the trauma of the breakup itself and the difficulties of growing up in a household with only one parent or, if the parent remarries, establishing a relationship with a new authority figure.

NUMBERS

In recent years, those who bemoan the prevalence of divorce often point to a single troubling statistic: for every two marriages in the United States, one ends in divorce. As statisticians quickly add, however, this should not be understood to mean that the divorce rate is 50 percent, since the people getting married each year are not the same ones getting divorced. In the early 2000s, there were roughly four divorces annually for every 1,000 persons in the United States. This figure is also deceptive, however, in that "persons" includes children below marrying age. Among women (or men) over the age of 18, the rate was roughly 20 divorces per 1,000 annually in the 1990s and early 2000s. These rates

CHRONOLOGY

1639 The first divorce in the British North American colonies is granted to a Massachusetts woman who charged her husband with bigamy.

1660 Massachusetts formalizes divorce by listing the grounds on which it can be granted.

1681 Pennsylvania founder William Penn formulates that colony's first divorce law.

1785 Pennsylvania turns over divorce-granting power from the legislature to the courts; Massachusetts follows a year later.

1835–50 Several southern states follow Pennsylvania's lead and place divorce in the state court system.

1881 The New England Divorce Reform League is organized to promote uniform divorce laws, thereby discouraging migratory divorce; the organization is renamed the National Divorce Reform League in 1885.

1928 The U.S. divorce rate reaches an all-time high, as one in six marriages ends in divorce.

1940 Some 3.1 million Americans tell census takers that they are living separately from their spouses.

1945 In *Williams et al. v. North Carolina*, the U.S. Supreme Court rules that only if a divorce-seeker's residence is authentic would a divorce be valid in the person's home state.

1949 South Carolina is the last state in the Union to shift authority over divorce from the legislature to the courts.

1968 New York State expands the grounds for divorce from adultery to include cruelty, abandonment, imprisonment, or separation for 2 years.

1970 California becomes the first state to grant no-fault divorce, as long as spouses can agree to divorce without stating such grounds as adultery or cruelty.

1971 In *Boddie v. Connecticut*, the U.S. Supreme Court rules that divorce is a constitutionally protected right of all Americans.

1976 In *Marvin v. Marvin*, the California Supreme Court rules that the more financially secure partner in a nonmarried relationship must provide financial support to the other partner if a contract or an implied contract is in effect; such compensation is called "palimony."

1984 The federal Child Support Enforcement Amendments to the Social Security Act require state child support enforcement agencies to garnish wages and withhold tax refunds of spouses whose child support payments are more than one month in arrears.

1996 The Personal Responsibility and Work Opportunity Reconciliation Act (better known as the Welfare Reform Act) further strengthens the ability of federal and state child support enforcement offices to garnish wages and tax refunds of so-called deadbeat dads who fail to provide child support payments; it also creates a nationwide databank to track down absconding parents who fail or refuse to provide legally obligated child support.

1998 The Deadbeat Parents Punishment Act makes it a federal felony offense to travel interstate or abroad to avoid child support obligations if those obligations have gone unpaid for a year or are greater than $5,000; it also becomes a felony under the act to willfully fail to pay support to a child residing in another state if the obligation has remained unpaid for 2 years or is greater than $10,000; both offenses are subject to a maximum prison term of 2 years.

2000 The U.S. Census finds that one out of every two marriages in the United States ends in divorce, the highest rate in the industrialized world.

allow for more telling comparisons. As Table 1 indicates, the number of divorced persons has grown astronomically over the course of the last century. In 1900, barely 0.3 percent of the adult (over 15 years) male population was divorced; by 2003, the figure was 8.8 percent, an increase of 2,900 percent. For women, the equivalent figures were 0.5 and 11.7, an increase of 2,300 percent.

Globally, the United States has the highest divorce rate in the Western industrialized world. According to U.S. Census Bureau statistics, the United States had 3.9 divorces per 1,000 persons in 2001. The next highest country in the Group of Seven industrialized nations (Canada, France, Germany, Italy, Japan, the United Kingdom, and the United States) was the United Kingdom at 2.6; Italy was the lowest at 0.6. Ignoring very small countries, where numbers can fluctuate greatly from year to year, the country with the highest rate of divorce is Russia at 4.3 divorces per 1,000 persons.

HISTORY

In 1533, King Henry VIII of England left the Catholic Church after the Pope refused to annul his marriage to Catherine of Aragon. Catherine had failed to produce a male heir and Henry wanted to remarry. (In fact, men are biologically responsible for the sex of the child, but this was unknown to sixteenth-century science.) Henry then founded the Anglican Church. Despite its origins, the Anglican Church, like the Church of Rome, considered marriage an irrevocable religious sacrament that could not be broken by divorce. Annulments were possible, but extremely rare.

Virginia, the first of England's mainland North American colonies, was dominated by the Anglican Church (as were the Carolinas and Georgia; as a Catholic colony, Maryland followed similar practices to those of Virginia). Not only were most colonists members, but the church enjoyed official sanction and was responsible for marriage, separation, and other family issues. As in England, the Anglican Church in the southern colonies never granted full divorce and rarely offered annulment. It did, however, offer what was called "divorces of bed and board," allowing a troubled couple to live apart; under a "separate maintenance agreement," the husband would continue to support his wife and children. Such "divorces" were quite rare, though more common than annulment, but the low number should not be taken to mean that marriages were rarely broken up in the colonial South. Instead, wives and particularly husbands often deserted their spouses, a much easier course of action in a barely settled society in which people could disappear into the frontier.

Having broken from the Church of England, the Puritan settlers of New England took a very different attitude toward divorce. Despite their reputation as religious extremists, the Puritans, in fact, did not frown on divorce nearly as severely as the Anglicans did. Instead, they saw it as a civil matter, a form of contract, which, like all contracts, could be legally broken. Divorce in colonial New England was permissible for a few reasons—notably adultery and desertion—but remained rare. Massachusetts witnessed just 101 divorces from 1692 to 1786. Moreover, a double standard existed, especially when it came to adultery. Of those 101 divorces, fully fifty were granted to men whose only complaint was adultery by their spouses; on the other hand, only six women were granted divorce for the same reason, and all of these were in the last dozen years of the period in question.

This last fact reflected changes wrought by the American Revolution. Among many other things that momentous event affected were attitudes toward marriage and divorce. Likening their husbands to the same tyrants against whom the patriots were fighting, women seeking divorce began to receive a more sympathetic hearing. State legislatures, particularly in the North, expanded the legal reasons for divorce to include cruelty and intemperance. The late eighteenth century also saw the origin of the "fault" divorce system, which would continue through the mid-twentieth century. Under this system, a divorce would be granted more easily if one spouse was innocent and the other guilty of the marital abuse in question. Moreover, if the wife was the innocent party, the husband would be forced to pay alimony (periodic payments to a wife for her financial support) or make a property settlement.

Equally important among the changes that came with American independence were those in the law concerning who could grant a divorce. In much of colonial America, that power was vested in the executive, usually the royal governor. First in the northern states and then in the South, the right to grant a divorce was turned over to the state legislatures. Before long, however, these bodies became overwhelmed by the sheer number of divorce cases coming before them. Therefore, beginning in Pennsylvania and Massachusetts in the 1780s, the legislatures gradually shifted the power to grant divorces to the courts (a change that did not occur in many southern states until well into the nineteenth century). In general, by shifting the power to grant divorces to the courts, lawmakers both expedited the process and turned it over to judges who were generally more sympathetic to those seeking a divorce. Unlike legislators, judges saw the petitioners in person and learned more of the details about the offending spouses' abuses.

The number of divorces grew steadily through the nineteenth century. This was partly a result of looser legal restrictions on the grounds for divorce and the process of obtaining one, even if divorce was still limited and difficult by modern standards. Just as important, perhaps, were changes in society at large. Urbanization and industrialization both put greater strains on married couples while offering new and greater temptations for wavering spouses. The city provided anonymity to those breaking marital vows, and the increasing mobility of the population allowed for more ways to desert. In addition, economic modernization increased financial insecurity for many, a common reason for divorce then and now.

War also had an effect. Hasty Civil War-era marriages were the least likely to last. From 1860 to 1866, the rate of marriages ending in divorce climbed by 50 percent, from 1.2 percent to 1.8 percent. The Gilded Age, with its quickening pace of urban life and economic change, saw further increases in the number of divorces, although it varied by region. From 1880 to 1906, the number of divorces per 1,000 person in the liberal and mobile West climbed from 0.83 to 1.31; those in the more stable and conservative Northeast went from 0.29 to 0.39. In addition, the percentage of divorces granted to women also rose; by the late 1880s, the wife was the petitioner in roughly two-thirds of all divorces granted.

This rising divorce rate led the Bureau of Labor and Commerce to start collecting statistics on the phenomenon by the 1880s. It also created a cultural and political backlash. Beginning in the 1850s, moral reformers such as Horace Greeley, editor of the influential New York *Tribune*, began to voice the opinion that divorce was a both a cause and symptom of social breakdown. What particularly worried Greeley and others was the growing ease of obtaining a divorce, especially in midwestern and western states. They began campaigning against so-called migratory divorces, whereby couples from stricter states established temporary residency in more lenient divorce states.

By the late 1870s, reformers were calling for a uniform national divorce law. (The framers of the Constitution had consciously decided to leave family law to the states.) In 1881, a Vermont minister named Samuel Dike founded the New England Divorce Reform League, called the National Divorce Reform League after 1885. Part of its mission was to

Table 1. Number and Percentages of Divorced Persons, 1900–2003

Year	Males (in 000s)	Percent of total population*	Females (in 000s)	Percent of total population*
1900	84	0.3	114	0.5
1910	156	0.5	185	0.6
1920	234	0.6	273	0.8
1930	489	1.1	572	1.3
1940	624	1.3	823	1.7
1950	1,070	2.0	1,373	2.4
1960	1,299	2.2	1,855	2.9
1970	1,925	2.8	3,002	4.0
1980	4,539	5.4	6,577	7.2
1990	6,957	7.4	9,627	9.5
1995	7,383	7.6	10,270	9.8
2000	8,572	8.3	11,309	10.2
2001	8,578	8.3	11,980	10.6
2002	8,686	8.1	12,268	10.7
2003	8,957	8.8	12,660	11.5

*Over the age of 15 years.
Source: U.S. Census Bureau. 2004 Statistical Abstract of the United States.

end migratory divorce. In reality, there were fewer of these than the league made out and states were reluctant to surrender their authority in family law matters. No national law was ever adopted, therefore, but the league was more successful in getting various states to pass reforms making divorce—migratory or otherwise—harder to get. Measures included waiting periods between application and hearing, longer time periods before a divorced person could remarry, and tighter restrictions on the reasons for which a divorce could be granted.

The reforms did little to slow the pace of divorce. Indeed, even as some states restricted the legal grounds for divorce, others—responding to the growing power of the women's movement in the late nineteenth and early twentieth centuries—expanded the grounds to include mental cruelty. At the same time, what some historians call the "dual system" of divorce began to emerge. That is, laws remained strict but the legal profession became increasingly adept at fabricating causes, as long as both spouses were willing to go along. Thus, between 1880 and 1916, the number of divorces per marriage rose from one in twenty-one to one in nine. Albeit with fluctuations, including a brief spurt in divorces after World War I, the rate rose to one in six by the end of the 1920s, where it remained through World War II. Depression-era economics made it difficult for many spouses to

Table 2. Divorce Rate, 1950–2002

Year	Divorces per 1,000 population
1950	2.6
1960	2.2
1970	3.5
1980	5.2
1990	4.7
1995	4.4
2000	4.1
2001	3.9
2002	4.0

Source: U.S. Census Bureau. 2004 Statistical Abstract of the United States.

get a legal divorce, though separations, especially as the result of financial stress, remained high.

Nor did migratory divorces disappear in the first half of the twentieth century, although they became increasingly restricted to one state—Nevada. Reno, then the only real city in the largely rural state, granted thousands of divorces annually. With a divorce rate of 49 per 1,000 persons, Nevada outstripped the other states by a wide margin. While clergy and others in the Silver State attempted to tighten the laws, entrepreneurs who made a living off the temporary residents seeking divorce blocked reforms. But Nevada's easy divorce laws created a constitutional problem. While the "full faith and credit" provision of the Constitution (Article IV, Section 8) requires states to recognize contracts from others states (a major issue in the current debate over a constitutional amendment to ban gay marriage), it also grants the states the right to control family legislation. In the 1945 case of *Williams v. North Carolina*, the U.S. Supreme Court split the difference, ruling that a Nevada divorce would be considered binding in North Carolina only if the latter state considered the couple's Nevada residency of legitimate duration and substance (had they rented habitations or gotten jobs there, for example).

By the post–World War II era, divorce laws based on "fault" seemed increasingly anachronistic, especially in the face of criticism from the newly reemerging feminist movement. The number of divorced persons rose from roughly 1.4 million in 1940 to nearly 5 million in 1970, a gain of more than 250 percent—far outstripping the roughly 55 percent growth in the overall population during the same period. With this rise in numbers came a gradual acceptance of divorce

as both a legitimate way to end an unhappy marriage and a normal part of American life. In 1949, South Carolina became the last state to turn over divorce proceedings to local courts, allowing judges to determine alimony, child custody, and child support.

In more liberal states, meanwhile, a new trend was growing in strength. In 1970, California became the first state in the Union to legalize "no-fault" divorce, ending the hypocrisy of the old "dual system." Under the California legislation, either spouse could get a divorce without having to state the reasons for it, although the other spouse could contest property allocation, alimony, child custody, and child support. By the end of the 1970s, virtually every state in the Union had followed California's lead. Meanwhile, in the 1971 case of *Boddie v. Connecticut*, the U.S. Supreme Court ruled that divorce was the right of every American. These changes in legislation and jurisprudence, along with evolving social attitudes, produced one of the greatest leaps in divorce rates in the nation's history. Between 1970 and 1980, the numbers of divorces per 1,000 persons jumped from 3.5 to 5.2, an almost 50 percent increase. In the decades since, the number has settled at about four per 1,000. Sociologists hypothesize that the peak of the 1970s represented pent-up demand, as couples long wanting a divorce finally were freed by the law and changing social mores.

CUSTODY AND SUPPORT ISSUES

Until the mid-nineteenth century, fathers were far more likely to win the custody of children in a divorce, even if they were deemed the guilty party. (The exceptions, of course, were desertion and sometimes adultery.) The reasons were both practical and socially determined. Fathers were better capable of financially supporting dependents. Children were also considered, at least in part, the property of their parents. The same laws and attitudes that gave men control over community property applied to custody of children. New attitudes about both childhood and motherhood changed that. Increasingly, children were seen less as property and more as innocent beings in need of nurturing and education. Gender attitudes of the nineteenth century also portrayed mothers as biologically more nurturing and caring. Thus, courts became increasingly willing to give the mother custody, and by the early twentieth century this had become the norm. That, of course, led to another problem—the need for child support.

As noted earlier, the fault system that took hold in the late eighteenth and early nineteenth centuries often required the offending husband to provide child support or a division of property with his divorced wife. Of course, if the wife shared in the guilt or was the offending party, she was entitled to nothing (this in an age when women earned far less than men—if they worked at all—and husbands enjoyed virtually total control over family property, even what the wife brought to the marriage).

Over the course of the nineteenth century, under increasing pressure from the women's movement, a number of states acted to give women more power over their own property. Still, in all but the rarest cases, single and divorced women were not economically independent. Even when the divorced woman was innocent, courts were often reluctant to force the husband to share property or pay child support or alimony. And when they did, it was not difficult in the time before modern recordkeeping methods to evade such obligations. Better policing and recordkeeping in the first half of the twentieth century made it more difficult to avoid paying support, just as courts became more sympathetic to the financial plight of divorced women, especially those caring for children.

It was the move to no-fault divorce in the 1970s that precipitated the major change in how the courts dealt with alimony and child support. Although no-fault laws did decrease the stigma of divorce and lowered court costs, it failed to equalize the economic circumstance between men and women. Under the no-fault system, dependent spouses, usually women, lost their bargaining power. If they accepted a no-fault divorce, they could not justify higher alimony or child support payments with their spouse's abusive or disrespectful behavior. Even in community property states, where the courts split assets evenly between husband and wife, the latter was at a disadvantage. That is, while the husband usually had a job and work experience, the wife did not, making it hard for a woman who had been a full-time homemaker throughout her married life to find well-paid employment. No-fault divorce, therefore, could leave a woman whose husband had committed adultery or even deserted the family in a worse financial situation than without no-fault or certainly poorer than her offending husband.

In place of "fault" determining the share of property or the size of alimony and child support payments, the courts increasingly substituted the notion of marriage as a "partnership." That is to say, regardless of who actually brought home the paycheck, both partners effectively had participated in earning it. By taking care of the home and children, the wife—or, more rarely, the husband—allowed the spouse to make money and buy property. Thus, the property and the increased earning potential of the spouse who received a paycheck was as much a product of the wife's work as the husband's, and she was thus entitled to half of the gain, and more if she had to raise the children after the divorce.

The courts also proved willing to apply the partnership concept to relationships with no formal marriage. In 1976, a California court ruled in the case of *Marvin v. Marvin* (the woman had legally changed her name to that of her partner, actor Lee Marvin, even though they never married) that Michelle Marvin was entitled to half of Lee's earnings—what came to be called "palimony"—during the years they cohabited, as they had an implied partnership contract.

Since the 1970s, two further developments have occurred in the financial arrangements subsequent to a divorce. One has been the decline of alimony. With women increasingly entering the workforce and earning greater pay—although still significantly less than men—the courts have held that divorced women are less entitled to alimony unless there is real financial need (the halving of property from the marriage-partnership is deemed both sufficient and just). Moreover, some women activists have come to see alimony as essentially demeaning, implying an ongoing dependency of an independent woman on her former husband.

Child support has evolved in the opposite direction. No matter what a court decides is fair and adequate, child support remains meaningless if the divorced husband or, more rarely, the wife refuses to pay it or absconds. Rising poverty rates among single women with children in recent decades have forced lawmakers to take action. In addition, the welfare reform bill of 1996, which strictly limited the period in which single mothers could collect payments (5 noncontinuous years), has added to the urgency in getting divorced or absent fathers to provide child support. Since the 1970s, states have moved to pass a series of laws making it possible for divorced mothers (and fathers) to garnishee wages and withhold tax refunds of the offending ex-spouse. At the same time, various states and the federal government have established agencies such as the Office of Child Support Enforcement and beefed up enforcement at existing agencies to help divorced mothers (and fathers) locate missing spouses. Still, despite these efforts, it is estimated that only one-fourth of all children of divorced or separated parents receive regular financial support from the non-cohabiting parent.

CONCLUSION

While divorce is nothing new in American history—the first divorce in New England was recorded just 9 years after the Puritans settled on Massachusetts Bay in 1630—its ubiquity is. And though some continue to bemoan that fact, few call for turning the laws back to the days—prior to the 1970s—when divorces were both difficult and expensive to get. Easy, no-fault divorce has become an integral part of American life and a right to which every American feels entitled.

While the increasing ease of divorce has no doubt spared many couples and their children expense and anguish, it has also created problems of its own. Experts continue to debate the emotional impact of divorce on children and whether children raised in single-parent households rather than two-parent households are emotionally well adjusted. Statistics on youth crime and dropout rates do point to a higher propensity for antisocial behavior in children experiencing the divorce of their parents or living in single-parent households.

According to many sociologists, however, the statistics do not prove a direct cause-and-effect relationship. The main problem with divorce and single parenting, they say, is not emotional but financial. Impoverished kids are more likely to drop out of school or live in neighborhoods where crime and drugs are prevalent. Solving the financial problem, they maintain, would eliminate the correlation between divorce and troubled children.

Glenda Riley

REFERENCES

Basch, Norma. *Framing American Divorce*. Berkeley: University of California Press, 2001.

Degler. Carl N. *At Odds: Women and the Family in America from the Revolution to the Present*. New York: Oxford University Press, 1980.

Gordon, Michael, ed. *The American Family in Social-Historical Perspective*. New York: St. Martin's, 1973.

Grossberg, Michael. *Governing the Hearth: Law and Family in Nineteenth-Century America*. Chapel Hill: University of North Carolina Press, 1988.

Hetherington, E. Mavis, ed. *Coping with Divorce, Single Parenting, and Remarriage: A Risk and Resiliency Perspective*. Mahwah, NJ: Lawrence Erlbaum, 1999.

Hetherington, E. Mavis, and John Kelly. *For Better or for Worse: Divorce Reconsidered*. New York: Norton, 2003.

Jacob, Herbert. *Silent Revolution: The Transformation of Divorce Law in the United States*. Chicago: University of Chicago Press, 1904.

May, Elaine Tyler. *Homeward Bound: American Families in the Cold War Era*. New York: Basic Books, 1988.

Mintz, Steven, and Susan Kellogg. *Domestic Revolutions: A Social History of American Family Life*. New York: Free Press, 1988.

Ricci, Isolina. *Mom's House, Dad's House: A Complete Guide for Parents Who Are Divorced or Remarried*. New York: Simon and Schuster, 1997.

Riley, Glenda. *Divorce: An American Tradition*. New York: Oxford University Press, 1991.

Wallerstein, Judith S., Sandra Blakeslee, and Julia M. Lewis. *The Unexpected Legacy of Divorce: The 25 Year Landmark Study*. New York: Hyperion, 2001.

Weitzman, Lenore J. *The Divorce Revolution: The Unexpected Social and Economic Consequences for Women and Children in America*. New York: Free Press, 1985.

WEB SITES

Divorce Magazine: www.divorcemag.com
Divorce Source: www.divorcesource.com
Office of Child Support Enforcement: www.acf.dhhs.gov/programs/cse/

GLOSSARY

Alimony. Court-ordered, regular financial payments made by the financially more secure spouse to the other following a divorce.

Child support. Court-ordered payments from a divorced spouse who does not have custody of the children to the spouse who does have custody for the purposes of providing financial support to children.

Community property. Assets belonging to both spouses in a marriage.

Covenant marriage. A type of marriage in which the partners agree to abide by rules making it more difficult to get a divorce.

Custody. Term for the right to have primary guardianship of the children of a divorce.

Deadbeat dads. Popular term for fathers who fail to provide child support to their divorced wives.

Fault divorce. The prevalent type of divorce from the early nineteenth to the mid-twentieth century; under its terms one spouse can get a divorce more easily if he or she is innocent of any wrongdoing within the marriage.

Migratory divorce. A divorce in which one or both spouses migrate to a state that has more liberal divorce laws.

No-fault divorce. A simplified type of divorce, first legalized in California in 1970, in which both partners agree that neither is at fault in the breakup of the marriage.

Palimony. Financial payments from the more financially secure partner to the less secure partner following the breakup of a nonmarriage relationship.

Visitation rights. The rights of the non-cohabiting parent to spend time with his or her children.

DOCUMENT

Marvin v. Marvin, 1976

In 1970, Hollywood actor Lee Marvin forced his lover, Michelle Marvin, to leave the house they had shared for 6 years. She subsequently sued for a share of his estate, saying they had an oral agreement to the effect that she had given up her own career to live with him. Lee's lawyers argued that such an agreement amounted to a form of prostitution. The California court ultimately ruled in Michelle's favor, as there was no explicit quid pro quo of sex for money. Instead, Michelle was Lee's wife in all but name and thus entitled to a share of his property under the state's community property rules. Judge Matthew Tobriner wrote the decision in this highly publicized case.

During the past 15 years, there has been a substantial increase in the number of couples living together without marrying. Such nonmarital relationships lead to legal controversy when one partner dies or the couple separates. Courts of Appeal, faced with the task of determining property rights in such cases, have arrived at conflicting positions: two cases have held that the Family Law Act requires division of the property according to community property principles, and one decision has rejected that holding. We take this opportunity to resolve that controversy and to declare the principles which should govern distribution of property acquired in a nonmarital relationship.

We conclude: (1) The provisions of the Family Law Act do not govern the distribution of property acquired during a nonmarital relationship; such a relationship remains subject solely to judicial decision. (2) The courts should enforce express contracts between nonmarital partners except to the extent that the contract is explicitly founded on the consideration of meretricious sexual services. (3) In the absence of an express contract, the courts should inquire into the conduct of the parties to determine whether that conduct demonstrates an implied contract, agreement of partnership or joint venture, or some other tacit understanding between the parties. The courts may also employ the doctrine of quantum meruit, or equitable remedies such

as constructive or resulting trusts, when warranted by the facts of the case.

In the instant case plaintiff and defendant lived together for seven years without marrying; all property acquired during this period was taken in defendant's name. When plaintiff sued to enforce a contract under which she was entitled to half the property and to support payments, the trial court granted judgment on the pleadings for defendant, thus leaving him with all property accumulated by the couple during their relationship. Since the trial court denied plaintiff a trial on the merits of her claim, its decision conflicts with the principles stated above, and must be reversed.

1. The factual setting of this appeal.

Since the trial court rendered judgment for defendant on the pleadings, we must accept the allegations of plaintiff's complaint as true, determining whether such allegations state, or can be amended to state, a cause of action. We turn therefore to the specific allegations of the complaint.

Plaintiff avers that in October of 1964 she and defendant "entered into an oral agreement" that while "the parties lived together they would combine their efforts and earnings and would share equally any and all property accumulated as a result of their efforts whether individual or combined." Furthermore, they agreed to "hold themselves out to the general public as husband and wife" and that "plaintiff would further render her services as a companion, homemaker, housekeeper and cook to . . . defendant."

Shortly thereafter plaintiff agreed to "give up her lucrative career as an entertainer [and] singer" in order to "devote her full time to defendant . . . as a companion, homemaker, housekeeper and cook"; in return defendant agreed to "provide for all of plaintiff's financial support and needs for the rest of her life."

Plaintiff alleges that she lived with defendant from October of 1964 through May of 1970 and fulfilled her obligations under the agreement. During this period the parties as a result of their efforts and earnings acquired in defendant's name substantial real and personal property, including motion picture rights worth over $1 million. In May of 1970, however, defendant compelled plaintiff to leave his household. He continued to support plaintiff until November of 1971, but thereafter refused to provide further support.

On the basis of these allegations plaintiff asserts two causes of action. The first, for declaratory relief, asks the court to determine her contract and property rights; the second seeks to impose a constructive trust upon one half of the property acquired during the course of the relationship.

Defendant demurred unsuccessfully, and then answered the complaint. Following extensive discovery and pretrial proceedings, the case came to trial. Defendant renewed his attack on the complaint by a motion to dismiss. Since the parties had stipulated that defendant's marriage to Betty Marvin did not terminate until the filing of a final decree of divorce in January 1967, the trial court treated defendant's motion as one for judgment on the pleadings augmented by the stipulation.

After hearing argument the court granted defendant's motion and entered judgment for defendant. Plaintiff moved to set aside the judgment and asked leave to amend her complaint to allege that she and defendant reaffirmed their agreement after defendant's divorce was final. The trial court denied plaintiff's motion, and she appealed from the judgment. . . .

Defendant first and principally relies on the contention that the alleged contract is so closely related to the supposed "immoral" character of the relationship between plaintiff and himself that the enforcement of the contract would violate public policy. He points to cases asserting that a contract between nonmarital partners is unenforceable if it is "involved in" an illicit relationship, or made in "contemplation" of such a relationship. A review of the numerous California decisions concerning contracts between nonmarital partners, however, reveals that the courts have not employed such broad and uncertain standards to strike down contracts. The decisions instead disclose a narrower and more precise standard: a contract between nonmarital partners is unenforceable only to the extent that it explicitly rests upon the immoral and illicit consideration of meretricious sexual services. . . .

Although the past decisions hover over the issue in the somewhat wispy form of the figures of a Chagall painting, we can abstract from those decisions a clear and simple rule. The fact that a man and woman live together without marriage, and engage in a sexual relationship, does not in itself invalidate agreements between them relating to their earnings, property, or expenses. Neither is such an agreement invalid merely because the parties may have contemplated the creation or continuation of a nonmarital relationship when they entered into it. Agreements between nonmarital partners fail only to the extent that they rest upon a consideration of meretricious sexual services. Thus the rule asserted by defendant, that a contract fails if it is "involved in" or made "in contemplation" of a nonmarital relationship, cannot be reconciled with the decisions. . . .

The decisions . . . thus demonstrate that a contract between nonmarital partners, even if expressly made in contemplation of a common living arrangement, is invalid only if sexual acts form an inseparable part of the consideration for the agreement. In sum, a court will not enforce a contract for the pooling of property and earnings if it is explicitly and inseparably based upon services as a paramour. The Court of Appeals opinion in Hill, however, indicates that even if sexual services are part of the contractual consideration, any severable portion of the contract supported by independent consideration will still be enforced. . . .

In summary, we base our opinion on the principle that adults who voluntarily live together and engage in sexual relations are nonetheless as competent as any other persons to contract respecting their earnings and property rights. Of course, they cannot lawfully contract to pay for the performance of sexual services, for such a contract is, in essence, an agreement for prostitution and unlawful for that reason. But they may agree to pool their earnings and to hold all property acquired during the relationship in accord with the law governing community property; conversely they may agree that each partner's earnings and the property acquired from those earnings remains the separate property of the earning partner. So long as the agreement does not rest upon illicit meretricious consideration, the parties may order their economic affairs as they choose, and no policy precludes the courts from enforcing such agreements.

In the present instance, plaintiff alleges that the parties agreed to pool their earnings, that they contracted to share equally in all property acquired, and that defendant agreed to support plaintiff. The terms of the contract as alleged do not rest upon any unlawful consideration. We therefore conclude that the complaint furnishes a suitable basis upon which the trial court can render declaratory relief. The trial court consequently erred in granting defendant's motion for judgment on the pleadings. . . .

In summary, we believe that the prevalence of nonmarital relationships in modern society and the social acceptance of them, marks this as a time when our courts should by no means apply the doctrine of the unlawfulness of the so-called meretricious relationship to the instant case. As we have explained, the nonenforceability of agreements expressly providing for meretricious conduct rested upon the fact that such conduct, as the word suggests, pertained to and encompassed prostitution. To equate the nonmarital relationship of today to such a subject matter is to do violence to an accepted and wholly different practice.

We are aware that many young couples live together without the solemnization of marriage, in order to make sure that they can successfully later undertake marriage. This trial period, preliminary to marriage, serves as some assurance that the marriage will not subsequently end in dissolution to the harm of both parties. We are aware, as we have stated, of the pervasiveness of nonmarital relationships in other situations.

The mores of the society have indeed changed so radically in regard to cohabitation that we cannot impose a standard based on alleged moral considerations that have apparently been so widely abandoned by so many. Lest we be misunderstood, however, we take this occasion to point out that the structure of society itself largely depends upon the institution of marriage, and nothing we have said in this opinion should be taken to derogate from that institution. The joining of the man and woman in marriage is at once the most socially productive and individually fulfilling relationship that one can enjoy in the course of a lifetime.

We conclude that the judicial barriers that may stand in the way of a policy based upon the fulfillment of the reasonable expectations of the parties to a nonmarital relationship should be removed. As we have explained, the courts now hold that express agreements will be enforced unless they rest on an unlawful meretricious consideration. We add that in the absence of an express agreement, the courts may look to a variety of other remedies in order to protect the parties' lawful expectations.

The courts may inquire into the conduct of the parties to determine whether that conduct demonstrates an implied contract or implied agreement of partnership or joint venture, or some other tacit understanding between the parties. The courts may, when appropriate, employ principles of constructive trust or resulting trust. Finally, a nonmarital partner may recover in quantum meruit for the reasonable value of household services rendered less the reasonable value of support received if he can show that he rendered services with the expectation of monetary reward.

Source: Marvin v. Marvin, 18 Cal. 3d 660 (Cal. 1976).

DOMESTIC VIOLENCE

Violence has been a feature of marriage since antiquity. The extent to which domestic violence is viewed as a problem or a matter for state intervention, however, has changed dramatically, especially in the last thirty years. There is little consensus about exactly what the phrase "domestic violence" encompasses, in part because there is significant disagreement about what constitutes domestic violence and who the perpetrators and victims are. In general, the term "domestic violence" is used to mean abuse of one's spouse. Researchers, activists, and legal and social service professionals prefer other terms such as woman abuse, wife battering, family violence, and intimate partner violence.

The phrases "woman abuse" and "wife battering" are preferred because most empirical evidence demonstrates women are much more likely to be battered by a male intimate than men are to be battered by female partners. Additionally, women suffer more severe injuries in battering incidents. Researchers who prefer the term "family violence" point out that spouse battering is often related to other forms of family violence such as child abuse, and it is important to understand why the family as a whole is such a violent institution. Some sociological research also suggests women batter male partners as often as men batter female partners. The "mutual violence" perspective is closely associated with the Family Violence Research Program and its studies using the Conflict Tactics Scale (CTS). This measure has many critics, however, most of whom cite the failure of the CTS to distinguish between acts of self-defense and acts intended to threaten or harm. While self-defense does not explain all of the violence women commit, the preponderance of the evidence indicates that domestic violence is mostly directed against women by men.

Finally, "intimate partner violence" is the most recent entry into the domestic violence lexicon. This term is currently preferred in U.S. government studies. The Centers of Disease Control and Prevention (CDC) includes, under "intimate partner violence," physical and sexual abuse between persons of either sex who have a current or former dating, marital, or cohabiting relationship. Here we use "domestic violence" and "intimate partner violence" interchangeably.

EARLY RESPONSES TO DOMESTIC VIOLENCE

Perhaps the first laws of marriage are attributed to the semimythical founder of Rome, Romulus, in 753 B.C.E. Married women were to be under the control of their husbands, and a wife's obligation to obey was matched by a husband's legal right and moral imperative to punish her for any "misbehavior." Founded in property rights, this right was justified because a woman became her husband's possession at marriage, ceasing to exist as a legal individual. From the end of the Punic Wars in 202 B.C.E. through the fourth century C.E., Roman family law underwent some liberalization. However, the rise of Christianity reestablished the older Roman tradition, as evidenced in the writings of St. Paul and Martin Luther. Not until the nineteenth century were property justifications for wife abuse legally abolished in the United States.

In the seventeenth century, the Massachusetts Bay and Plymouth colonies became the first communities in the Western world to pass laws against wife battering. But these laws were not absolute or uniformly enforced, as there were many accepted social justifications for a man to hit his wife. European settlers argued wife abuse was biblically sanctioned, drawing on passages such as Ephesians 5:22–23: "Wives, submit to your husbands as to the Lord; for the man is the head of the woman, just as Christ is the head of the Church." Some early American law also drew from continental European law which held husbands responsible for any crimes their wives committed; thus, abuse was permitted to keep women from committing crimes. Perhaps the most promi-

CHRONOLOGY

753 B.C.E. Romulus, the semimythical founder of Rome, is credited with formalizing the first known laws of marriage, which granted husbands the right to discipline their wives physically for a variety of offenses. These laws influenced later legal codes in many European nations and the English Common Law.

400 C.E. Roman law changes enough to make excessive violence by either spouse legally recognized grounds for divorce.

late 1400s Writings of Bernard of Siena and Friar Cherubino of Siena exemplify Christianity's ambivalent teachings about wife abuse throughout the Middle Ages; the former argues for moderation in correcting wives and the latter prompts, in his *Rules of Marriage,* "when you see your wife commit an offense, don't rush at her with insults and violent blows. . . . Scold her sharply, bully and terrify her. And if this still doesn't work . . . take up a stick and beat her soundly, for it is better to punish the body and correct the soul than to damage the soul and spare the body."

1824 In *Bradley v. State,* the Mississippi court rules that moderate corporeal punishment of one's wife is permissible.

1864 In *State v. Black,* the North Carolina court holds that, because a husband is responsible for his wife's actions, he has the right to chastise her. While physical violence might be unseemly, it is a greater good to protect the privacy and sanctity of the home from outside interference unless permanent injury is inflicted or excessive violence is used.

1868 In *State v. Rhodes,* a North Carolina appellate court rules men have no legal right to beat their wives, but agrees that the defendant is not guilty of assault. The court claims that the important legal question is not the method of chastisement (e.g., "rule of thumb") but the outcome. As with *State v. Black,* the privacy of the home is to be protected unless the outcome of the domestic violence is severe injury or death.

1871 Legal right of chastisement is overturned. *Fulgham v. State* (Alabama): "The husband has no right to inflict personal chastisement upon his wife." *Commonwealth v. McAfee* (Massachusetts): "Beating or striking a wife violently with the open hand is not one of the rights conferred on a husband by the marriage, even if the wife be drunk or insolent."

1882 Maryland becomes the first state to pass legislation outlawing wife beating.

1894 Mississippi court, in *Harris v. State,* overturns the "revolting precedent" of the 1824 case *Bradley v. State.*

1910 Supreme Court rules in *Thompson v. Thompson* that a woman cannot press civil charges against her husband for assault and battery.

1972 Women's Advocates, in St. Paul, Minnesota, start the first battered woman's hotline.

1974 The Comprehensive Employment and Training Act (CETA) is enacted.

U.S. battered women's movement opens its first shelters: Women's Advocates (St. Paul, Minnesota) and Transition House (Boston, Massachusetts).

1976 Pennsylvania establishes the first state coalition against domestic violence and creates the first state statute providing orders of protection for victims of domestic violence.

Scott v. Hart (Oakland, California) is a class action lawsuit filed against the police department for failing to respond adequately to domestic violence calls.

1977 Oregon Coalition Against Domestic and Sexual Violence proposes a bill requiring police officers to make arrests on probable cause of domestic assault or violating an order of protection. The bill is passed, making Oregon the first state to require police arrest in domestic violence cases. By 1994, fourteen states and the District of Columbia have mandatory arrest laws of some sort.

EMERGE is founded in Boston. It is the first male counseling and education collective founded by men to work cooperatively with battered women's shelters.

1978 **January 30–31.** U.S. Commission on Civil Rights hearings are held on whether battered women were receiving full and equal protection under the law.

National Coalition Against Domestic Violence (NCADV) is founded in January when battered women's advocates from across the United States met in Washington, D.C., for the U.S. Commission on Civil Rights hearing on battered women.

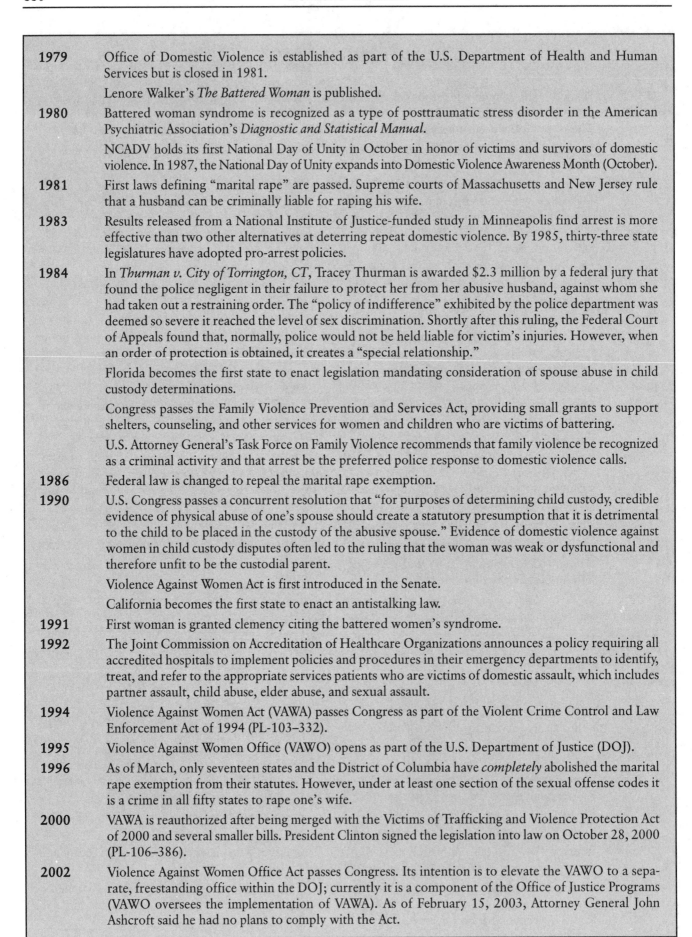

1979	Office of Domestic Violence is established as part of the U.S. Department of Health and Human Services but is closed in 1981.
	Lenore Walker's *The Battered Woman* is published.
1980	Battered woman syndrome is recognized as a type of posttraumatic stress disorder in the American Psychiatric Association's *Diagnostic and Statistical Manual*.
	NCADV holds its first National Day of Unity in October in honor of victims and survivors of domestic violence. In 1987, the National Day of Unity expands into Domestic Violence Awareness Month (October).
1981	First laws defining "marital rape" are passed. Supreme courts of Massachusetts and New Jersey rule that a husband can be criminally liable for raping his wife.
1983	Results released from a National Institute of Justice-funded study in Minneapolis find arrest is more effective than two other alternatives at deterring repeat domestic violence. By 1985, thirty-three state legislatures have adopted pro-arrest policies.
1984	In *Thurman v. City of Torrington, CT*, Tracey Thurman is awarded $2.3 million by a federal jury that found the police negligent in their failure to protect her from her abusive husband, against whom she had taken out a restraining order. The "policy of indifference" exhibited by the police department was deemed so severe it reached the level of sex discrimination. Shortly after this ruling, the Federal Court of Appeals found that, normally, police would not be held liable for victim's injuries. However, when an order of protection is obtained, it creates a "special relationship."
	Florida becomes the first state to enact legislation mandating consideration of spouse abuse in child custody determinations.
	Congress passes the Family Violence Prevention and Services Act, providing small grants to support shelters, counseling, and other services for women and children who are victims of battering.
	U.S. Attorney General's Task Force on Family Violence recommends that family violence be recognized as a criminal activity and that arrest be the preferred police response to domestic violence calls.
1986	Federal law is changed to repeal the marital rape exemption.
1990	U.S. Congress passes a concurrent resolution that "for purposes of determining child custody, credible evidence of physical abuse of one's spouse should create a statutory presumption that it is detrimental to the child to be placed in the custody of the abusive spouse." Evidence of domestic violence against women in child custody disputes often led to the ruling that the woman was weak or dysfunctional and therefore unfit to be the custodial parent.
	Violence Against Women Act is first introduced in the Senate.
	California becomes the first state to enact an antistalking law.
1991	First woman is granted clemency citing the battered women's syndrome.
1992	The Joint Commission on Accreditation of Healthcare Organizations announces a policy requiring all accredited hospitals to implement policies and procedures in their emergency departments to identify, treat, and refer to the appropriate services patients who are victims of domestic assault, which includes partner assault, child abuse, elder abuse, and sexual assault.
1994	Violence Against Women Act (VAWA) passes Congress as part of the Violent Crime Control and Law Enforcement Act of 1994 (PL-103–332).
1995	Violence Against Women Office (VAWO) opens as part of the U.S. Department of Justice (DOJ).
1996	As of March, only seventeen states and the District of Columbia have *completely* abolished the marital rape exemption from their statutes. However, under at least one section of the sexual offense codes it is a crime in all fifty states to rape one's wife.
2000	VAWA is reauthorized after being merged with the Victims of Trafficking and Violence Protection Act of 2000 and several smaller bills. President Clinton signed the legislation into law on October 28, 2000 (PL-106–386).
2002	Violence Against Women Office Act passes Congress. Its intention is to elevate the VAWO to a separate, freestanding office within the DOJ; currently it is a component of the Office of Justice Programs (VAWO oversees the implementation of VAWA). As of February 15, 2003, Attorney General John Ashcroft said he had no plans to comply with the Act.

nent influence on American law, though, was the tradition of English common law, which allowed husbands to "chastise" their wives.

The infamous "rule of thumb," holding that husbands could beat their wives with an instrument no thicker than their thumb, has been attributed to William Blackstone's *Commentaries on the Laws of England* (1765). Though no such rule is explicitly stated in the *Commentaries,* this did not preclude its appearance in some U.S. courts in the 1800s. (*Bradley v. State* in 1824 notes that the rule of thumb is part of the accepted legal tradition. *State v. Rhodes* [1868] and *State v. Oliver* [1873] refer to but reject this rule.) However, Blackstone did write about the law of chastisement: "The husband also (by the old law) might give his wife moderate correction. For, as he is to answer for her misbehaviour, the law thought it reasonable to intrust him with this power of restraining her, by domestic chastisement. . . ." This law was upheld explicitly through the mid-1800s and implicitly long after. In the United States, the legal right of chastisement was overturned in Alabama and Massachusetts in 1871; however, because the belief in men's right to chastise their wives persisted long after this date, the crime of domestic violence still was not often prosecuted successfully.

English law also established the precedent used in the United States of defining rape exclusively as sexual intercourse between a man and a female not his wife and without her consent. Sir Matthew Hale, a seventeenth-century English justice, wrote, "The husband cannot be guilty of a rape committed by himself upon his lawful wife, for by their mutual matrimonial consent and contract, the wife hath given herself in kind unto the husband which she cannot retract." This established the legal notion that a married woman does not have the right to refuse sex with her husband; thus, marital rape was not deemed a crime for most of this nation's history.

DOMESTIC VIOLENCE IN THE 1800s

Early organized protests against domestic violence were associated with the antebellum temperance movement and did not directly challenge the husband's legal prerogative to chastise his wife. Pointing to the violence of drunk husbands and fathers as one of the many social evils related to alcohol, temperance advocates argued that preventing the sale of alcohol would protect the family. Challenges to domestic violence also arose from the women's suffrage movement. When early feminist organizers, led by Elizabeth Cady Stanton and Lucy Stone, convened in Seneca Falls, New York, in 1848, their Declaration of Sentiments condemned common law doctrines of chastisement and coverture (the legal concept that a woman's existence as an individual in law disappeared into that of the husband).

Through the middle and late nineteenth century, coverture began to be rolled back with the passage of married women's property laws. The same period also saw significant legal reform of domestic violence law; case law reveals that wife battering became illegal in most jurisdictions during the second half of the nineteenth century. But while courts and legislatures were more willing to outlaw wife battering, they were still uncomfortable intervening in all but the most severe cases, on the grounds that opening the family to public scrutiny would inhibit the natural affection that could restore tranquility to the home.

The early decades of the twentieth century saw the advent of juvenile and family courts in most major cities. Here judges could ask about the workings of a marriage without being bound by rules of legal evidence. Dealing with abuse through family courts and social workers marked a shift in perception of domestic violence from a criminal problem to a family and personal problem best handled through social services or psychological solutions. The official policy of the courts was to urge family reconciliation; many family court cases were dismissed with a "go home" order.

REDISCOVERY OF DOMESTIC VIOLENCE AS A SOCIAL AND POLITICAL PROBLEM

After a long lull in significant social organizing and protest from the 1920s to the 1960s, wife battering again became a prominent public issue in the 1970s as a part of the feminist movement. The battered women's movement offered new analyses of violence and agitated for new laws and social services. As a result, domestic violence is no longer treated as a private matter but discussed in terms of equality, justice, and individual and social health.

The battered women's movement first provided refuges for battered women. These were not the earliest shelter services, but they were the first designed exclusively to provide a safe space and support for battered women. In the 1960s, Alcoholics Anonymous and Al-Anon opened shelters for the wives of men seeking treatment for drinking; these often became de facto community battered women's shelters even though they were not designed for that purpose. Other shelters grew out of the social service sector, which had access to more resources than small grassroots feminist groups. A 1981 survey of 127 shelters found, in fact, that feminist groups had established fewer than half of them.

Often in dire financial straits, feminist-run shelters began to form coalitions to increase their bargaining power with the state and federal governments and private funding sources. Feminist conferences such as the 1976 International Women's Year Conference in Houston served as networking and strategy-building opportunities. A certain percentage of shelters of all types were also financed by the Comprehensive Employment and Training Act (CETA) of 1974, a federal program that trained and paid salaries of many shelter employees. Some states implemented taxes on marriage licenses to fund shelters. Yet in 1979, fewer than fifteen states had such taxes, and fewer than half of the battered women's shelters received any money from the federal government. In 1981 and 1982, CETA funds for shelters were eliminated with the Reagan Administration's shift in funding priorities.

Another early target of feminist activism was inadequate police response to domestic violence calls. In the late 1970s, two class-action lawsuits were filed on behalf of battered women against police departments in New York City and Oakland, California, for failure to protect women from domestic assault. Both cases were settled out of court with the police departments agreeing to change their procedures; police would now arrest men who committed assault, respond to every call from battered women, inform battered women of their rights (including right of citizen arrest), and enforce civil restraining orders. These policies were not implemented immediately, nor did they spread quickly to other jurisdictions.

LEGAL AND SOCIAL REFORMS IN THE LATE TWENTIETH CENTURY

The legal and social resources available to victims of domestic violence have been strengthened and expanded over the last thirty years. Some of these changes have been the result of legislative actions; others are due to state and federal court rulings or bureaucratic changes in police and social service policies. While numerous laws and procedures have been introduced or altered, here we consider only some of the most sweeping.

The lawsuits against police departments for failure to protect battered women led to changes in arrest policies. By 1992, more than twenty states permitted "probable cause" arrests, which allow an officer to arrest someone without a warrant if there is reason to believe a domestic assault has occurred. Some jurisdictions have gone further and *require* arrests on domestic violence calls. As of 2003, nearly half of the states and the District of Columbia had implemented mandatory arrest laws. This has led to a sharp increase in dual arrests: if police cannot determine which party is the aggressor, or if the police believe domestic partners are battering each other, then they arrest both parties.

Mandatory arrest reforms were also fueled by a highly publicized study of the effect of arrest on recidivism. The Minneapolis Domestic Violence Experiment, whose results were published in 1984, found that arrest was the most effective means of deterring future violence. The same year, the U.S. Attorney General's Task Force on Family Violence recommended arrest as the standard approach to all misdemeanor domestic violence calls. However, six follow-up studies, funded by the National Institutes of Justice, have failed to replicate these findings. Independent researchers have also reached conflicting conclusions about the efficacy of mandatory arrest in deterring future violence.

Even when laws and arrest policies are reformed, many experts say broad social changes are needed as well to combat domestic violence. Heightened vigilance on the part of law enforcement officials, they argue, needs to be integrated with civil injunctions, mediation, diversion to social service agencies and shelters, and crisis intervention services. This kind of integrated approach, where the criminal justice system is *one part* of the overall response to domestic violence, seems to work better than mandatory arrest alone, these experts conclude.

One of the more significant and promising changes in the response of law enforcement, the courts, and the social service sector to domestic violence involves the advent of Coordinated Community Action. In 1981, Duluth, Minnesota, implemented the first and still best known coordinated approach: the Domestic Abuse Intervention Project (DAIP). This project coordinates the responses of the 911 center, the police, jail officials, prosecutors, probation departments, women's shelters, public health department, and mental health agencies. DAIP focuses on the male batterer/female victim domestic violence model, which has engendered some criticism from gay and lesbian activists and from men's groups who argue that women are also abusers. Despite these critiques, practitioners from the Duluth program have trained service providers in communities in all fifty states and fifteen foreign nations.

Another significant change in the legal system's response to domestic violence is the recognition of two widespread components of domestic violence as crimes: stalking and marital rape. Stalking was first recognized as a crime in 1990 with the passage of antistalking legislation in California. By 1998, all states and the District of Columbia had enacted antistalking laws. Legal definitions of stalking vary by state, but most define it as the willful, malicious, and repeated following and harassing of another person. Some states have more expansive definitions, including activities such as lying-in-wait, surveillance, telephone harassment, and vandalism.

The marital rape exemption was first successfully challenged in 1986 when courts in Massachusetts and New Jersey ruled that a husband could be held criminally liable for raping his wife. By 1996, marital rape was a crime under at least one code of the sex crimes statutes in every U.S. state. In more than half of the states, however, exemptions existed for husbands, excusing them from prosecution under certain conditions or trying them on lesser charges.

The 1980s and 1990s also saw significant changes in how courts dealt with battered women who kill. Before 1980, if a battered woman killed her spouse, she typically had to use an "excuse" defense in court. She could plead "temporary insanity" or claim a mental defect, for example, but could not argue justifiable homicide, regardless of how severe or prolonged the abuse. In 1980, some courts began to allow "battered woman syndrome" as part of a defense for battered women who kill. Battered woman syndrome is also used as a defense in cases of attempted homicide, child custody, child abuse, and being a party to a crime the abusive spouse committed. Finally, battered woman syndrome has been used with limited success in clemency pleas by women who are already imprisoned for killing their spouses. (Between 72 and 80 percent of battered women who kill their abusers are convicted or plead guilty, ending up with long prison terms.)

Perhaps the most significant legislative event in the history of the nation's response to domestic violence, and certainly the most comprehensive federal response to interpersonal violence, was the Violence Against Women Act (VAWA). On September 13,

1994, President Clinton signed the Violent Crime Control and Law Enforcement Act into law. Title IV of that bill, VAWA created training grants for law enforcement education to encourage arrest, rural domestic violence enforcement grants, the National Domestic Violence Hotline (launched in 1996), grants to battered women's shelters, and funding for domestic violence studies. The bill also made it a crime to cross state lines or enter or leave Native American reservations with the intention of injuring or harassing an intimate partner ("interstate domestic violence"). In October 2000 the bill was reauthorized; this act continued some of the original programs and created or strengthened others. Most notably, "dating violence" was included as a form of interpersonal violence to be studied and that qualifies for prevention grant programs; funding was included for coordinated community response programs (ten were being funded in 2001); and programs for battered immigrant women were greatly expanded. The 2000 bill authorized $3.3 billion over five years. It has yet to be fully appropriated. The $1.62 billion total authorized in 1994 had not been appropriated as of early 2004.

EXTENT OF THE PROBLEM

Domestic violence remains a significant social and legal problem today. Results from the U.S. Department of Justice's National Violence Against Women Survey (NVAWS) and National Crime Victimization Survey (NCVS) agree that women are more likely to be injured by someone they know than by a stranger and that men abuse women at a much higher rate than women abuse men. The NCVS reports that from 1992 to 1998, over half of reported attacks that caused injury were committed by an intimate partner. Women were found to be six times more likely to be attacked by an intimate than were male victims of violence. Nearly 30 percent of all female homicide victims are known to have been killed by husbands, former husbands, or boyfriends; in contrast, just over 3 percent of male homicide victims were killed by an intimate. Male intimates committed 26 percent of rapes and sexual assaults against women. The NVAWS also found that women living with female intimate partners experience less interpersonal violence than women living with male partners (11 percent versus 30.4 percent). Men who live with male partners experience higher levels of abuse than men living with female partners (15 percent versus 7.7 percent).

Table 1. Violence by Intimate Partners, by Type of Crime and Gender of Victims, 2001

| | Total | | Intimate partner violence | | | |
| | | | Female | | Male | |
	Number	Rate per 1,000 persons	Number	Rate per 1,000 persons	Number	Rate per 1,000 persons
Overall violent crime	691,710	3.0	588,490	5.0	103,220	0.9
Rape/sexual assault	41,740	0.2	41,740	0.4	—	—
Robbery	60,630	0.3	44,060	0.4	16,570	0.1
Aggravated assault	117,480	0.5	81,140	0.7	36,350	0.3
Simple assault	471,860	2.1	421,550	3.6	50,310	0.5

Source: National Crime Victimization Survey, Intimate Partner Violence, 1993–2001, NCJ 197838 (February 2003).

The data on how violence against women differs by race are mixed. There is little evidence that rates of violence against women differ among Hispanics, Asian Americans, and European Americans. NCVS studies seem to show that African American and Native American women experience higher rates of physical and sexual assault, but the NVAWS found that these differences diminished significantly when socioeconomic variables are controlled, making rates highly dependent on educational and economic levels. Thus, actual rates of domestic violence in different ethnic groups remain somewhat unclear, and racial and ethnic differences need to be studied further.

TYPES OF ABUSIVE BEHAVIOR

At least four categories of behavior occur in abusive relationships: emotional, physical, and sexual abuse, and stalking. (While some behaviors in each category overlap, the categories are distinct enough to be measured and discussed separately.) Emotional abuse also is referred to as psychological, verbal, or symbolic abuse. This includes verbal and nonverbal actions that hurt the partner, often by trying to destroy her self-esteem. Examples of emotional abuse include yelling; making one's partner do humiliating things; monitoring her activities; being excessively jealous about the partner's time, activities, and friends; restricting the partner's use of phone, e-mail, car, or money; destroying the partner's personal property; or threatening children or pets. Emotional abuse can include attempts to prevent one's partner from gaining financial self-sufficiency and socially isolating the partner so that she depends on her abuser for social interaction, access to information, and the satisfaction of all emotional needs. Emotional abuse early

in a relationship may lead to physical abuse once the relationship is more established.

In the case of physical abuse, the intention is to cause physical injury or pain. In some relationships, physical abuse is sporadic and infrequent. In most relationships involving physical abuse, however, the frequency and severity of abuse tends to increase the longer the relationship lasts. Examples of physical abuse include slapping, pushing, punching, kicking, pulling hair, throwing down stairs, throwing out of a vehicle, cutting, burning, locking into a room or closet, strangling, and using or threatening to use a weapon.

Sexual abuse includes acts that fall within the criminal definition of rape and sexual assault as well as physical assault on the sexual parts of a person's body and demands for sexual acts the partner does not wish to perform. Other forms of sexual abuse in domestic violence are interference with the partner's use of birth control, coercion to use or perform in pornography, or demands that one's partner have sexual relations with other persons.

The fourth category is stalking, also known as "obsessional following." Though it may occur at any point in a relationship, stalking is most frequently observed at the end of a relationship. Stalking behaviors include following the partner, sending her unwanted gifts, leaving threatening messages at home or work, damaging the partner's property, and stealing personal items from her.

CAUSES

A plethora of theories has been offered to explain the causes of domestic violence. Currently, the most widely accepted theories use some combination of

Table 2. Persons Victimized by an Intimate Partner in Lifetime, by Victim Gender, Type of Victimization, and White/Nonwhite Status of Victim

	Persons victimized in lifetime (%)	
Victim gender/type of victimization	White	Nonwhite*
Women	(n = 6,452)	(n = 1,398)
Rape	7.7	7.8
Physical assault	21.3	25.5
Stalking	4.7	5.0
Total victimized	24.8	28.6
Men	(n = 6,424)	(n = 1,335)
Rape	0.2	0.5**
Physical assault	7.2	9.1
Stalking	0.6	1.1
Total victimized	7.5	10.0

 * The nonwhite category consists of African American, Native American/Alaska Native, Asian/Pacific Islander, and mixed-race respondents.
 ** Relative standard error exceeds 30 percent; statistical tests not performed.
Source: Extent, Nature, and Consequences of Intimate Partner Violence: Findings from the National Violence Against Women Survey (July 2000).

approaches to explain why individuals abuse their partners. In 1979, well-known sociologists and family violence researchers Richard Gelles and Murray Straus noted at least fifteen theories on the causes of domestic violence, not counting the many feminist theories and some notable learning approaches. This section describes four broad categories of approaches to understanding and coping with domestic violence: psychoanalytic, learning, sociological, and feminist.

Once widely accepted, psychoanalytic theories of domestic violence have been rejected by almost all domestic violence researchers over the last thirty years. This approach is based on the work of Sigmund Freud (1856–1939), relying particularly on his belief in female masochism (the view that women derive pleasure from being dominated). While much of Freud's work has been denounced or seriously rethought, his underlying assumptions linger in some social attitudes toward domestic violence; for example, many still assume that women who stay in abusive relationships must enjoy the abuse.

Learning or behavioral theories are based on the psychological theories of stimulus-response conditioning and social learning. Proponents of this approach argue that when batterers receive positive reinforcement for their behavior (they get their way), they learn that violence is effective. One controversial social learning theory argues that battering is passed on from one generation to the next: that is, a child who sees abuse between his parents learns that this is appropriate behavior. The idea is compelling, but many batterers were not abused as children and did not witness violence in their homes; conversely, many children from abusive families do not grow up to become abusive adults. At best, we can say there is a *tendency* for violence to be passed from one generation to the next.

Behaviorists also explain why many battered partners stay with their abusers with operant conditioning study findings that random, unpredictable positive reinforcements are the most effective means of producing a desired behavior in another person. Lenore Walker, one of the most famous psychologists studying domestic violence, discusses three phases in the battering relationship: the tension-building phase, the acute battering incident, and the loving contrition stage. In her view, this third stage—a stage that may nearly disappear as the relationship evolves—provides the intermittent positive reinforcement that allows many battered women to believe the abuse will not happen again.

The "cycle of violence" theory is one of two main components of battered woman syndrome, a type of posttraumatic stress disorder recognized since 1981 as part of a legal self-defense claim for battered women who kill their partners. The second major component is "learned helplessness," a social learning theory concept. Drawing on behavioral psychologist Martin Seligman's work with caged dogs given electric shocks until they eventually stopped trying to escape, Walker found that people who believe they cannot leave a situation also "learn" helplessness and stop trying to get away. Walker's theory has been criticized for, among other things, failing to explain why many women do manage to leave abusive husbands.

Sociological theories of the root of spousal abuse focus on the high incidence of intrafamily conflict. Sociologists propose many reasons for such conflict, including the amount of time spent together, the range of sometimes conflicting interests in families, and the high level of emotional involvement among family members, which leads to greater frustration and a decreased likelihood that people will simply walk away from the source of the frustration. Murray Straus, by far the most influential sociologist of family violence, coined the phrase "the marriage license is a hitting license" to summarize his findings of the prevalence of marital violence. Straus runs the Family Violence

Research Program at the University of New Hampshire; he is best known for his work on "mutual violence" and his argument that women and men are nearly equally abusive in intimate relationships.

The sociological approach helps us understand why some families are violent, but it excludes the personal psychological factors at work in partner battering. Additionally, understanding domestic violence only in terms of family conflict fails to address the influence of anger and frustration from outside sources. Social psychology provides a more thorough and systematic approach, combining personal and systemic elements in its understanding of the causes of domestic violence and its strategies for combating the problem. Some social-psychological approaches are feminist, others are not.

There are a number of feminist analyses of the causes of and solutions to domestic violence. Most feminist theories focus on men battering their female partners, though more recent work considers situations in which women abuse their partners (whether male or female). Feminist theories of domestic violence may draw on elements of learning and sociological theories, but they also include a social and political analysis of sexism and women's lack of power relative to men in society, the law, and the economy. They focus more on this power imbalance as a cause of battering, downplaying the focus of psychological theories on factors such as lack of impulse control. Feminists also consider the contributing role of the legal legacy of coverture and, until the late 1970s, the seeming indifference of the courts, police, and legislatures to the serious prevalence and injuries of wife battering. Finally, they point to gender norms that equate masculinity with dominance and femininity with submission as another pernicious influence on the acceptance of domestic violence against women.

Many feminist theories link domestic violence to women's economic dependence on men. If more economic resources were available to women, they would be less likely to end up in or stay in abusive relationships; they could literally afford to leave. Feminists also connect wife battering to other forms of violence against women, including prostitution, pornography, and rape.

FUTURE OF RESEARCH AND LEGAL REFORM

Recent domestic violence legislation has focused on determining how expansive legal protections should be (allowing dating couples and homosexual couples to obtain orders of protection or access to shelters, for example). Social service workers who intervene in domestic violence situations are also attempting to provide more varied and inclusive treatment programs. Now that domestic violence has come to be seen and treated as a serious problem, the focus for the future will be on understanding better who is battering and why and implementing programs and strategies to prevent the violence and enforce existing laws. Indisputably, domestic violence has long been part of family life. What has changed is not the existence of family violence, but the social and legal meanings attached to the violence family members inflict on each other.

Carisa R. Showden

REFERENCES

American Medical Association. *Diagnostic and Treatment Guidelines on Domestic Violence.* 1992. www.ama-assn.org/ama1/pub/upload/mm/386/domesticviolence.pdf.

Balos, Beverly, and Mary Louise Fellows. *Law and Violence Against Women: Cases and Materials on Systems of Oppression.* Durham, NC: Carolina Academic Press, 1994.

Berger, Raquel Kennedy, ed. *Issues in Intimate Violence.* Thousand Oaks, CA: Sage, 1998.

Browne, Angela. *When Battered Women Kill.* New York: Free Press, 1987.

Buzawa, Eve S., and Carl G. Buzawa. *Domestic Violence: The Criminal Justice Response.* Thousand Oaks, CA: Sage, 1990.

Cook, Philip W. *Abused Men: The Hidden Side of Domestic Violence.* Westport, CT: Praeger, 1997.

Daniels, Cynthia, ed. *Feminists Negotiate the State: The Politics of Domestic Violence.* Lanham, MD: University Press of America, 1997.

DeKeseredy, Walter S., and Martin D. Schwartz. "Measuring the Extent of Woman Abuse in Intimate Heterosexual Relationships: A Critique of the Conflict Tactics Scales." Washington, DC: Department of Justice, 1998. www.vaw.umn.edu/Vawnet/ctscrit.htm.

Dobash, R. Emerson, and Russell P. Dobash. *Women, Violence, and Social Change.* New York: Routledge, 1992.

Dobash, Russell P., Emerson R. Dobash, Margo Wilson, and Martin Daly. 1992. "The Myth of Sexual Symmetry in Marital Violence." *Social Problems* 39, 1: 71–91.

Fagan, Jeffrey. *The Criminalization of Domestic Violence: Promises and Limits.* Washington, DC: National Institute of Justice Research Report, January, 1996.

Foshee, Vangie A., Karl E. Bauman, and G. Fletcher Linder. 1999. "Family Violence and the Perpetration of Adolescent Dating Violence: Examining Social Learning and Social Control Processes." *Journal of Marriage and the Family* 61, 2 (May): 331–42.

Gelles, Richard J., and Murray A. Straus. "Determinants of Violence in the Family: Toward a Theoretical Integration." In *Contemporary Theories about the Family*, ed. Wesley R. Burr, Reuben Hill, and Ivan Nye. New York: Free Press, 1979.

George, Malcolm J. 1994. "Riding the Donkey Backwards: Men as the Unacceptable Victims of Marital Violence." *Journal of Men's Studies* 3, 2: 137–59.

Goodyear-Smith, Felicity A., and Tannis M. Laidlaw. 1999. "Aggressive Acts and Assaults in Intimate Relationships: Towards an Understanding of the Literature." *Behavioral Sciences and the Law* 17: 285–304.

Gordon, Linda. *Heroes of Their Own Lives: The Politics and History of Family Violence, Boston 1880–1960.* New York: Viking, 1988.

Harvard Law Review. 1993. "Developments in the Law— Legal Responses to Domestic Violence." *Harvard Law Review* 106 (May): 1501–1620.

Jackson, Nicky Ali, and Giselé Casanova Oates, eds. *Violence in Intimate Relationships: Examining Sociological and Psychological Issues.* Boston: Butterworth-Heinemann, 1998.

Jasinski, Jana L., and Linda M. Williams, eds. *Partner Violence: A Comprehensive Review of 20 Years of Research.* Thousand Oaks, CA: Sage, 1998.

Loring, Marti Tamm. *Emotional Abuse.* New York: Lexington Books, 1994.

Mahoney, Martha R. 1991. "Legal Images of Battered Women: Redefining the Issue of Separation." *Michigan Law Review* 90, 1: 35–75.

Maschke, Karen J., ed. *The Legal Response to Violence Against Women.* New York: Garland, 1997.

Okun, Lewis. *Women Abuse: Facts Replacing Myths.* Albany: State University of New York Press, 1986.

Osthoff, Sue. 1992. "Restoring Justice: Clemency for Battered Women." *Response* 14: 2–3.

Pan, Helen S., Neidig, Peter H., and O'Leary, K. Daniel. 1994. "Male-Female and Aggressor-Victim Differences in the Factor Structure of the Modified Conflict Tactics Scale." *Journal of Interpersonal Violence* 9: 366–82.

Pleck, Elizabeth. *Domestic Tyranny: The Making of Social Policy Against Family Violence from Colonial Times to the Present.* New York: Oxford University Press, 1987.

Rennison, Callie Marie, and Sarah Welchans. "Intimate Partner Violence." Washington, DC: U.S. Department of Justice Bureau of Justice Statistics, 2000 (revised January 31, 2002).

Renzetti, Claire, and Charles Harvey Miley, eds. *Violence in Gay and Lesbian Domestic Partnerships.* New York: Haworth Press, 1996.

Russell, Diana E. H. *Rape in Marriage.* Bloomington: Indiana University Press, 1990.

Saunders, Daniel G. "Wife Abuse, Husband Abuse, or Mutual Combat?: A Feminist Perspective on the Empirical Findings." In *Feminist Perspectives on Wife Abuse*, ed. Kersti Yllö and Michele Bograd. Thousand Oaks, CA: Sage, 1988.

Schechter, Susan. *Women and Male Violence: The Visions and Struggles of the Battered Women's Movement.* Boston: South End Press, 1982.

Shepard, Melanie F., and Pence, Ellen L., eds. *Coordinating Community Responses to Domestic Violence: Lessons from Duluth and Beyond.* Thousand Oaks, CA: Sage, 1999.

Siegel, Reva B. 1996. "'The Rule of Love': Wife Beating as Prerogative and Privacy." *Yale Law Journal* 105 (June): 2117–2207.

Straus, Murray A. "The Marriage License as a Hitting License: Evidence from Popular Culture, Law, and Social Science." In *The Social Causes of Husband-Wife Violence*, ed. Murray A. Strauss and Gerald T. Hotaling. Minneapolis: University of Minnesota Press, 1980.

Straus, Murray A., and Richard J. Gelles, eds. *Physical Violence in American Families.* New Brunswick, NJ: Transaction Press, 1990.

Tjaden, Patricia, and Nancy Thoennes. *Extent, Nature, and Consequences of Intimate Partner Violence: Findings from the National Violence Against Women Survey.* Washington, DC: U.S. Department of Justice, 2000.

Viano, Emilio C., ed. *Intimate Violence: Interdisciplinary Perspectives.* Bristol, PA: Taylor and Francis, 1992.

Walker, Lenore E. *The Battered Woman.* New York: Harper and Row, 1979.

Zorza, Joan. 1992. "The Criminal Law of Misdemeanor Domestic Violence, 1970–1990." *Journal of Criminal Law and Criminology* 83, 1: 46–72.

WEB SITES

Domestic Abuse Intervention Project: www.duluth-model.org/daipmain.htm

Family Research Laboratory: www.unh.edu/frl

Family Violence Prevention Fund: http://endabuse.org

MenWeb Battered Men: www.batteredmen.com

Minnesota Center Against Violence and Abuse: www.mincava.umn.edu

National Coalition Against Domestic Violence: www.ncadv.org

National Coalition of Anti-Violence Programs: www.avp.org

Office on Violence Against Women: www.ojp.usdoj.gov/vawo

Violence Against Women NET: www.vawnet.org

GLOSSARY

Battered women's movement. General term for the social and political activism that started in the 1970s to recognize the abuse of wives by their husbands as a serious problem requiring public attention. Some in the battered women's movement were grassroots feminists; others were feminist and nonfeminist social service professionals.

Battered woman syndrome. A psychological condition used as a legal defense by some women who kill their abusive husbands. It was first named and described by psychologist Lenore Walker in her 1979 book, *The Battered Woman.* The two key components of battered woman syndrome are the "cycle of violence" in abusive relationships and the "learned helplessness" of many battered women. The American Psychiatric Association has recognized battered woman syndrome as a subtype of posttraumatic stress disorder since 1980.

Comprehensive Employment and Training Act (CETA). A U.S. Department of Labor job training program that provided staff for many shelters in the late 1970s. Without CETA-supplied staff and funds, many independent shelters could not have stayed open.

Conflict Tactics Scales (CTS). Widely used but much disputed measure of family violence. Developed by Murray Straus, this survey instrument asks respondents whether they have ever engaged in a variety of acts (e.g., "discussed issue calmly," "threw something," "choked him/her") to measure three things: reasoning, verbal aggression, and physical aggression (which is broken into minor and severe violence). The CTS is criticized because of certain methodological flaws, such as a reliance on self-reporting of behavior and poor performance on tests of interspousal reliability among responses. Importantly, it also fails to account for the context of violence or distinguish acts committed in self-defense from other forms of aggressive behavior.

Coordinated Community Action Models (CCAMs). Approaches to domestic violence that combine prevention and intervention, relying on a number of community resources including some or all of the following: stiff domestic violence laws with significant penalties for batterers, specialized education programs for batterers, shelters and legal advocates for victims, police training programs, domestic violence courts, training of emergency medical personnel, and clergy assistance. This approach to coping with domestic violence was first developed in Duluth, Minnesota, as the Domestic Abuse Intervention Project.

Coverture. A term in British and American law referring to a woman's status at marriage. After marriage, the husband and wife were treated as one entity, particularly in terms of property rights. The wife's separate legal existence disappeared, and she could not own or control her own property (unless a prenuptial provision had been arranged), nor could she file any lawsuits or execute contracts. In the United States, coverture was dismantled through state-level legislation between the 1840s and the 1880s.

Dual arrest. Police practice of arresting both parties in a domestic violence situation. Dual arrests increased with the implementation of mandatory arrest policies when arresting officers say they cannot determine which party is the "offending" party.

Duluth Model/Domestic Abuse Intervention Project (DAIP). This coordinated community intervention project was founded in Duluth, Minnesota, in 1981. The DAIP model has become one of the primary templates for communities around the world attempting to develop an integrated approach to dealing with domestic violence.

Family violence. A term sometimes substituted for domestic violence. It is considered to be a broader, more inclusive phrase denoting not just spousal abuse but also child and elder abuse. This term is also preferred by those who believe that domestic violence is "mutual" (partners violent toward each other) as opposed to one-sided (a batterer-victim relationship).

Family Violence Research Program. A research center at the University of New Hampshire run by Murray Straus and housing the Family Research Laboratory. The focus of the training, data collection, analyses, conferences, and other services in the program is on all types of family violence (partner abuse, child abuse, elder abuse, etc.).

Intimate partner violence (IPV). The new term the U.S. government uses to describe domestic violence. It is preferred because it captures the range of relationships in which battering can and does occur in a way that domestic violence, which for many connotes violence between heterosexual spouses living in a shared home, does not.

Mandatory arrest. Policy requiring police to arrest anyone believed to have committed assault or have an order of protection against him or her placed by someone in fear of imminent danger of physical injury. Not all jurisdictions with mandatory arrest policies also have mandatory prosecution policies. Thus, not all arrested batterers are charged with a crime (*see also* "Stitch Rule").

Mandatory prosecution (aka "No-drop prosecution"). Policy requiring government attorneys to bring charges against batterers who have been arrested, even if the complainant says she or he wants the charges dropped.

Mutual violence (sexual symmetry in relationship violence). The thesis that women and men are equally (or nearly equally) violent, and domestic violence most often occurs in a pattern of men and women abusing each other. The sexual symmetry thesis was first publicized in the late 1970s by Murray Straus, using his now famous phrase "the marriage license is a hitting license."

Order of protection (aka "civil protection order," "temporary restraining order," "temporary injunction," "stay-away order," "no-contact order"). A court-ordered injunction prohibiting violent or threatening acts of harassment against, contact or communication with, or physical proximity to another person. Such orders can be issued to be effective for a few days or up to a few years.

Separation assault. Refers to study findings demonstrating that the two years after one leaves an abusive relationship are the most dangerous and potentially lethal for the abused partner. Some, particularly Martha Mahoney, have argued that separation assault should

be a distinct criminal charge. Antistalking laws are designed in part to help address this phenomenon.

Stalking. Behavior defined by willfully, maliciously, and repeatedly following, threatening, and harassing another person in a way that makes the stalked person frightened for her life or safety. While it can occur at any point in a relationship, stalking often occurs when one partner tries to end the relationship (*see also* Separation assault).

Stitch Rule. Before mandatory arrest rules were implemented, some police departments used "stitch rules" as a guide for responding to domestic violence cases. An abused wife had to require a certain number of surgical sutures ("stitches") before a husband would be arrested for assault and battery.

Violence Against Women Act (VAWA). The most significant federal legislation to address directly the many components of domestic violence in one bill. First introduced to Congress in 1990, VAWA was passed as part of the 1994 Violent Crime Control and Law Enforcement Act (PL-103–332). In 2000, VAWA was modified slightly and reauthorized for five years.

DOCUMENTS

Document 1. Excerpt from *State v. A. B. Rhodes* (1868)

State v. Rhodes *is often cited as a case upholding the "rule of thumb"—the notion that a husband is allowed to beat or "chastise" his wife with a rod no thicker than his thumb. Yet in his ruling, Judge Reade expressly denies the legality of the rule of thumb, instead rendering a verdict of "not guilty" on the grounds that the courts should only intervene in family government in the cases of extreme violence. The import of the ruling is thus that domestic violence is a private family matter, not that the "rule of thumb" is valid.*

SUPREME COURT OF NORTH CAROLINA, RALEIGH

January, 1868, Decided

PRIOR HISTORY: ASSAULT AND BATTERY, tried before Little, J., at Fall Term, 1867, of the Superior Court of WILKES.

The defendant was indicted for an assault and battery upon his wife, Elizabeth Rhodes. Upon the evidence submitted to them the jury returned the following special verdict:

"We find that the defendant struck Elizabeth Rhodes, his wife, three licks, with a switch about the size of one of

his fingers (but not as large as a man's thumb), without any provocation except some words uttered by her and not recollected by the witness."

His Honor was of opinion that the defendant had a right to whip his wife with a switch no larger than his thumb, and that upon the facts found in the special verdict he was not guilty in law. Judgment in favor of the defendant was accordingly entered and the State appealed. . . .

OPINION: READE, J. The violence complained of would without question have constituted a battery if the subject of it had not been the defendant's wife. The question is how far that fact affects the case.

The courts have been loath to take cognizance of trivial complaints arising out of the domestic relations—such as master and apprentice, teacher and pupil, parent and child, husband and wife. Not because those relations are not subject to the law, but because the evil of publicity would be greater than the evil involved in the trifles complained of; and because they ought to be left to family government. . . .

In this case no provocation worth the name was proved. The fact found was that it was "without any provocation except some words which were not recollected by the witness." The words must have been of the slightest import to have made no impression on the memory. We must therefore consider the violence as unprovoked. The question is therefore plainly presented, whether the court will allow a conviction of the husband for moderate correction of the wife without provocation. . . .

We have sought the aid of the experience and wisdom of other times and of other countries.

Blackstone says "that the husband, by the old law, might give the wife moderate correction, for as he was to answer for her misbehavior, he ought to have the power to control her; but that in the polite reign of Charles the Second, this power of correction began to be doubted." 1 Black 444. Wharton says, that by the ancient common law the husband possessed the power to chastise his wife; but that the tendency of criminal courts in the present day is to regard the marital relation as no defense to a battery. Cr. L., secs. 1259–60. Chancellor Walworth says of such correction, that it is not authorized by the law of any civilized country; not indeed meaning that England is not civilized, but referring to the anomalous relics of barbarism which cleave to her jurisprudence. Bish. M. & D., 446, n. The old law of moderate correction has been questioned even in England, and has been repudiated in Ireland and Scotland. The old rule is approved in Mississippi, but it has met with but little favor elsewhere in the United States. *Ibid.*, 485. In looking into the discussions of the other States we find but little uniformity.

From what has been said it will be seen how much the subject is at sea. And, probably, it will ever be so: for it will always be influenced by the habits, manners and condition of every community. Yet it is necessary that we should lay down something as precise and practical as the nature of the subject will admit of, for the guidance of our courts.

Our conclusion is that family government is recognized by law as being as complete in itself as the State government is in itself, and yet subordinate to it; and that we will not interfere with or attempt to control it, in favor of either husband or wife, unless in cases where permanent or malicious injury is inflicted or threatened, or the condition of the party is intolerable. For, however great are the evils of ill temper, quarrels, and even personal conflicts inflicting only temporary pain, they are not comparable with the evils which would result from raising the curtain, and exposing to public curiosity and criticism, the nursery and the bed chamber. Every household has and must have, a government of its own, modeled to suit the temper, disposition and condition of its inmates. Mere ebullitions of passion, impulsive violence, and temporary pain, affection will soon forget and forgive, and each member will find excuse for the other in his own frailties. But when trifles are taken hold of by the public, and the parties are exposed and disgraced, and each endeavors to justify himself or herself by criminating the other, that which ought to be forgotten in a day, will be remembered for life. . . .

It will be observed that the ground upon which we have put this decision is not that the husband has the *right* to whip his wife much or little; but that we will not interfere with family government in trifling cases. We will no more interfere where the husband whips the wife than where the wife whips the husband; and yet we would hardly be supposed to hold that a wife has a *right* to whip her husband. We will not inflict upon society the greater evil of raising the curtain upon domestic privacy, to punish the lesser evil of trifling violence. Two boys under fourteen years of age fight upon the playground, and yet the courts will take no notice of it, not for the reason that boys have the *right* to fight, but because the interests of society require that they should be left to the more appropriate discipline of the school room and of home. It is not true that boys have a right to fight; nor is it true that a husband has a right to whip his wife. And if he had, it is not easily seen how *the thumb* is the standard of size for the instrument which he may use, as some of the old authorities have said; and in deference to which was his Honor's charge. A light blow, or many light blows, with a stick larger than the thumb, might produce no injury; but a switch half the size might be so used as to produce death. The standard is the *effect produced*, and not the manner of producing it, or the instrument used.

Because our opinion is not in unison with the decisions of some of the sister States, or with the philosophy of some very respectable law writers, and could not be in unison with all, because of their contrariety—a decent respect for the opinions of others has induced us to be very full in stating the reasons for our conclusion. There is no error.

Source: 61 N.C. 453 1868 N.C. LEXIS 38; 1 Phil. Law 453.

Document 2. Remarks of Senator Joseph Biden (D-DE) on Introducing the Violence Against Women Act to the 103rd Congress, 1993

The Violence Against Women Act is the most comprehensive piece of U.S. federal legislation addressing the problem of domestic violence against women. Senator Biden introduced the legislation on June 19, 1990. The following are excerpts from his speech reintroducing the act in the legislative session in which it was passed into law.

REFERENCE: Vol. 139 No. 5
TITLE: STATEMENTS ON INTRODUCED
BILLS AND JOINT RESOLUTIONS
VIOLENCE AGAINST WOMEN ACT

Mr. BIDEN: Mr. President, I rise today to introduce Senate bill number 11, the Violence Against Women Act of 1993—the first comprehensive legislation to address the growing problem of violent crime confronting American women.

Since I first introduced this legislation in 1990, the Judiciary Committee has held a series of four hearings; we have refined the legislation and issued reports; we have garnered the support of prominent groups and individuals with widely differing interests—from law enforcement, women's groups, and victims' advocates. The bill has twice received the unanimous approval of the Judiciary Committee. Now, it is time to complete our efforts. . . .

We have waited in my view too long, already, to recognize the horror and the sweep of this violence. For too many years, our idea of crime has left no room for violence against women. We now face a problem that has become doubly dangerous, as invisible to policymakers as it is terrifying to its victims.

Our blindness costs us dearly:

Every week, 21,000 women report to police that they have been beaten in their own homes;

Every day, over 2,500 women visit an emergency room because of a violent act perpetrated against their persons;

Every hour, as many as 70 women across the Nation will be attacked by rapist[s]—every hour.

Today, I believe more firmly than ever before, that this Nation will be powerless to change this course of violent crime against women unless the Congress takes a leadership role with the cooperation of the President of the United States. Only then can we as a Nation inscribe this violence with a name so that it will never be mistaken or dismissed as anything other than brutal, a brutal series of crimes and unconditionally, whether in the home or out of the home—wrong.

It bothers me when we talk about domestic violence, Mr. President. It implies somehow it is like a domesticated cat or a domesticated dog—that domestic violence is less violent than any other type.

The women who suffer the consequence of domestic violence are women who are shot, murdered, killed, beaten, deformed. This violence is of a most coarse nature. It is perpetrated and committed by someone who a person in that household trusts; had at one time, at least, loved; in fact lives with. It is the worst of all violence.

The bill I introduce today attacks violent crime against women at all levels—from our streets to our homes, from squad cars to courtrooms, from schoolrooms to hospitals. In large measure, it is the same bill that was introduced in the 102d Congress, with the addition of minor and technical amendments and a special new provision authored by Senator Kennedy to provide Federal funds for a national domestic violence hotline.

Let me briefly review the principal parts of the legislation.

TITLE I—SAFE STREETS FOR WOMEN ACT

Title I focuses on making our streets safer by boosting funding for police, prosecutors, and victim advocates, promoting rape education, and changing evidentiary rules to make our justice system fairer for the victims of this violence—to make our courts more user-friendly.

TITLE II—SAFE HOMES FOR WOMEN

Title II—The Safe Homes for Women Act—acknowledges, for the first time, the role of the Federal Government in fighting spouse abuse. It creates the first Federal laws against battering, provides nationwide coverage for stay-away orders, encourages arrest of spouse abusers, and boosts funding for battered women's shelters.

TITLE III—CIVIL RIGHTS FOR WOMEN

Title III—the most innovative provision of this bill—recognizes that violence against women presents questions not only of criminal justice, but also of equal justice. It takes a dramatic step forward by defining gender-motivated crime as bias crime and declaring, for the first time, that civil rights remedies should be available to victims of such crimes.

TITLE IV—SAFE CAMPUSES FOR WOMEN

Title IV, much of which passed in the higher education amendments of 1992, now authorizes increased funding for campus rape education efforts.

TITLE V—EQUAL JUSTICE FOR WOMEN IN THE COURTS ACT

Finally, Title V of the bill recognizes the crucial role played by the judicial branch in forming an effective response to violence against women, authorizing comprehensive training programs for State and Federal judges.

Let me close by urging my colleagues to join me in supporting this desperately needed legislation. Already, 40 Senators have indicated their support as original cosponsors. I hope that a significant number of others will join us so that we can ensure swift consideration and debate in the full Senate. Let us not wait another year as millions more suffer the pain of violence against women.

I will not take any further time to describe the contents of the bill. I ask unanimous consent that a summary and the complete text of the legislation appear in the Record following my remarks.

Source: Congressional Record, Thursday, January 21, 1993 (Legislative day of Tuesday, January 5, 1993), 103rd Cong. 1st Sess.,139 Cong Rec S 345.

DROUGHT AND AQUIFER DEPLETION

Climate variability and weather patterns affect the accessibility of water, even in locations with abundant moisture. Drought is defined as a protracted period of deficient precipitation, which contributes to the decline of water supplies. When replenishment of the groundwater slows, water tables drop below the bottom level of wells. If surface water is not available, subsurface supplies enhance the capacity of a growing population to sustain agricultural, municipal, and industrial development. However, droughts and depleted aquifers not only reduce the water supply but also generate public anxiety about the possibilities for economic growth.

Technological mastery and control of water secures a crucial resource for modern societies. Hydrotechnology enables societies to tap into water deep beneath the earth's surface within a permeable, water-bearing rock layer called the aquifer.

Although modern societies attempt to insulate populations from the discomforts of weather and the extremes of climate, droughts and aquifer depletions have continued to plague both rural and urban realms throughout the world. Cities in the United States consume, on average, 200 gallons per person each day, while producing a bushel of corn typically required 10 to 20 tons of water, including 2.5 tons lost through transpiration (moisture lost through stomata, or the tiny pores of leaves) and even more through evaporation. Accounting for indirect costs, a single pound of beef requires up 15 to 30 tons of water to produce. In fact, beef producers consume 400 gallons of water just to slaughter and process one animal. Every year, the 1 million head of cattle raised in the Great Plains use 600 million gallons of water. As beef production climbs with economic growth, so does water consumption, because—pound for pound—beef requires far more water than do grains or vegetables.

Of course, rainfall naturally replenishes groundwater, percolating through the layers of soil at a velocity ranging from approximately half a meter a day to several meters per year. Then again, an extended period of deficient precipitation can result in short-term water shortages for the population and its usual activities.

HYDROLOGIC IMBALANCE

Droughts begin when abnormally dry weather persists long enough to disrupt the flow of water. The immediate cause of a drought is the predominant sinking motion of air that results in compressional warming, that is, high pressure. In fact, regions under the influence of intense high pressure during a significant portion of the year become deserts, such as the Sahara and Kalahari Deserts of Africa and the Gobi Desert of Asia. A drought occurs when the normal balance between precipitation, on the one hand, and evaporation and transpiration, on the other, shifts in favor of the latter processes. The severity of the imbalance depends on the duration of the lack of precipitation and the size and population of the affected area. The extent of the imbalance correlates to the timing of rainfall, which is indicated by the principal rainy season, delays in its start, occurrence of rains in relation to principal crop growth stages, and the degree of saturation of the ground. Additional climatic factors such as high winds and low humidity correspond with rising temperatures and significantly aggravate the severity of a drought.

Most climatic regions experience varying changes in precipitation, but other climatic factors tend to modulate the impact. When large-scale anomalies in atmospheric circulation patterns persist over time, the simmering heat brings the dryness in the upper atmosphere down to earth. Meteorological drought is usually defined by a high degree of aridity compared to the average amount of moisture needed to maintain the area's hydrologic balance. Its definition reflects specific regional expectations, because the atmospheric conditions that result in precipita-

Table 1. Costliest Weather Disasters in the United States Since 1980

Disaster	Economic cost	Region	Year
Drought/heat wave	$40 billion	Midwest and east	1988
Hurricane (Katrina)	$35 billion*	Gulf coast	2005
Flood	$21 billion	Midwest	1993
Drought/heat wave	$20 billion	Southeast	1980

* Estimated insured losses.
Source: National Oceanic and Atmospheric Administration.

Figure 1. Relative Cost of Weather or Weather-Related Disasters in the United States, 1980–2001

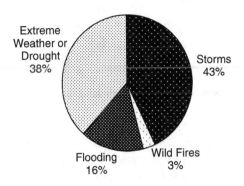

Source: National Oceanic and Atmospheric Administration.

tion deficiencies are highly variable. For example, drought may be defined on the basis of the number of days with less than the normal amount of precipitation. This measure is used in places with year-round precipitation regimes such as tropical rainforests, humid subtropical climates, or humid mid-latitude climates. In other areas, drought may be related to below-average precipitation over monthly, seasonal, or annual time scales. Regardless, the absence of normal rainfall has an impact on the flow rates for recharging the water table.

Agricultural drought correlates hydrologic imbalance to lowered crop yields, particularly in terms of precipitation shortages, actual versus potential evaporation and transpiration, soil water deficits, and reduced groundwater and reservoir levels. Water demand for cultivated crops depends on prevailing weather conditions, the specific crop's biological characteristics and stage of growth, and the physical and biological properties of the soil. Deficient topsoil moisture at planting hinders germination, which reduces crop production per acre and final yield. Without appropriate saturation, fields become desiccated and harvests eventually fail. If subsoil moisture is replenished as the growing season starts, however, the surface impact of agricultural drought is attenuated.

Hydrological drought is related to the particular effects of precipitation shortfalls on surface or subsurface water supplies. The frequency and severity of hydrological drought are often measured on a watershed or river basin scale. The effects of precipitation deficiencies on soil moisture depletion may be almost immediately discernible to agriculturalists, but the effects of disrupted stream flow, water tables, and reservoir levels may take longer to notice. The impact of reduced reservoir levels may not affect livestock industries or recreational areas for several sea-

sons. In fact, the increasing demand placed on water storage systems complicates the sequencing and quantification of environmental impacts. Multiple uses of a water storage system reduce its capacity to sustain high levels of development, particularly during periods of greatest demand.

A drought may be defined in socioeconomic terms even if precipitation levels do not fall to drought levels if the shortfall has an economic impact or growing demand causes a shortage. Socioeconomic drought occurs when the change in saturation level causes disequilibrium in the supply and demand of goods and services such as water, forage, food grains, fish, and hydroelectric power. For example, dryness significantly reduces hydroelectric power production because power plants depend on stream flow rather than stored water for power generation. In response to reduced hydroelectric power production, the government may be forced to convert to imported petroleum or initiate stringent energy conservation measures to curb power consumption. A multitude of social and economic functions are entangled with the water supply, resulting in panic, depression, and trauma when unseasonable shifts in weather persist.

A hydrologic imbalance in the United States during the 1930s affected 50 million acres of grassland, rendering the communities of the Great Plains helpless to meteorological, hydrological, agricultural, and socioeconomic drought. Unable to tap into alternative sources of groundwater, residents of the Dust Bowl states turned to the federal government for assistance. Government experts studied the region during its most traumatic period, issuing a comprehensive report in 1937 entitled *The Future of the Great Plains.* The "dirty thirties," as the Dust Bowl years were called, corresponded in magnitude with the Great Depression, leading to unprecedented government relief efforts and costly subsidy programs. The New Deal marked the beginning of farm aid and also initiated the first long-term, proactive programs to reduce future vulnerability to the fluctuations of the environment. For example, the Soil Conservation Service (SCS), which later became the Natural Resources Conservation Service, began to stress measures to reduce the perils of drought. The service designed the first soil conservation districts and promoted demonstration projects underscoring the benefits of dry farming practices such as tilling and drilling with a lister, a double plow with a divided moldboard that left furrows trapping water. In addition, terracing decreased the length of hillside slope, thereby reducing erosion, preventing the formation of gullies, and increasing water infiltration in the soil by retaining runoff. Other federal programs facilitated the planting of tree shelterbelts, or rows of trees that prevent wind erosion. In fact, the hydrologic imbalance taught hard lessons about survival in the Dust Bowl while raising national awareness of the potential for ecological disaster.

Thus, hydrologic imbalances remain entangled with our perception of how much economic activity and population a given environment can support. Depending on time and place, dry weather initiates scientific, political, or even religious turning points for societies.

Its effects on society result from the interplay between a phenomenological event, the available water supply, and population pressures. Annual rainfall below 190 millimeters might constitute a hydrologic imbalance in Ethiopia, whereas in Indonesia authorities define a drought as a week without rain. Whatever the definition, drought represents more than simply a physiographic constraint. The abundance of moisture remains contingent on air-sea interactions, soil moisture and land surface processes, topography, internal dynamics, and the accumulated influence of dynamically unstable large-scale weather systems. In other words, the Earth's natural climatic processes contain an uncertain amount of water, requiring sophisticated planning and elaborate systems to properly manage its use.

SUBSURFACE WATER

The depletion of an aquifer constitutes a lapse in an ecosystem's subsurface supplies of water. Water bal-

ance refers to all sources of moisture, but an aquifer exists deep below the ground forming a rock configuration, or regolith, that is saturated with water from moisture percolation. Aquifers provide a significant source of water when and where subsurface supplies are sufficiently replenished by precipitation and surface water flow. The rate of extraction, however, may exceed the rate of natural replenishment. In alluvial plains, reduced stream flow due to human diversion or dry weather decreases the rate of natural aquifer replenishment. Without curbs on usage, aquifer depletion ultimately exhausts a natural resource. In other words, continuous extraction of the subsurface supplies is comparable to mining water at a faster rate than nature can replenish it.

Water mining threatens to deplete the enormous Ogallala aquifer, composed of more than 3 billion acre-feet of groundwater. The subsurface water exists below 174,000 square miles of grasslands in the mid-latitudes of North America, mostly within the boundaries of present-day Texas, Oklahoma, Kansas, and Nebraska. What residents once dubbed the "underground rain" is irreplaceable because its sources of replenishment were cut off thousands of years ago. Unlike many of the world's aquifers, the Ogallala aquifer contains essentially "fossil water," or paleo-water, that seeped beneath the grasslands more than 10,000 years ago from the glacier-laden Rocky Mountains before geological forces diverted the melting ice and snow. The water table slopes gently eastward, and the underground water from earlier eras of wetter climate flows through the aquifer at a rate of 30 centimeters per day. The water-saturated gravel bed lies 50 to 300 feet beneath the surface.

Although no one could dig a well to reach such depths before the twentieth century, Progressive Era idealism stirred advocates to tap the Ogallala aquifer. William Smythe, a Nebraska journalist, opined that hydrotechnology enabled populations to master aridity and turn the subsurface water to the advantage of residents of dry land. In his book *The Conquest of Arid America* (1905), Smythe posited that "the essence of the industrial life which springs from irrigation is its democracy." Alarmed by frequent droughts and agricultural failure, he came to believe that irrigation provided the means to save modern societies from ruin and create a better place to live. Promoting the irrigation crusade before the Great Depression, Smythe contributed to the agitation for federal government programs dedicated to reclaiming land for farmers. In arid zones, reclamation nudged residents to seek their salvation by tapping the supplies of subsurface water.

After a recovery in agricultural prices following World War II, turbine impeller pumps and automobile engines enabled farmers to pull aquifer water from deep levels. At the turn of a valve or flip of a switch, the machinery extended their production whatever the weather conditions. Impeller pumps generated pressure to push the flow to the surface, where it was deployed to flood fields, sprinkle crops, or drip moisture. Expensive equipment to tap the subsurface water necessitated high crop prices or volume production to generate revenue streams. It was a capital-intensive form of food production that required increasing aquifer depletion at a rate directly proportional to the demands of the marketplace. On the Texas High Plains, where the self-regulating mechanical "center-pivot irrigator" was deployed, the number of irrigation wells rose from about 2,500 in 1941 to more than 42,200 by 1957. Thus, the Great Plains emerged as one of the most extensively irrigated areas in the United States.

As agribusiness became dependent on subsurface water, a "hydraulic society" developed in which control of the aquifer concentrated power into the hands of a small circle of elites. Seduced by the miracle of hydrotechnology, large operators who embraced irrigation soon abandoned dry farming practices and the habits of groundwater conservation. Irrigation allowed crops of wheat, corn, alfalfa, and sorghum to survive the droughts of the 1950s and 1970s. Unfortunately, irrigation depleted the aquifer at ten times the rate of replenishment. The aquifer also supports large numbers of ranchers, feedlots, and processors. With a billion acre-feet consumed between 1960 and 1990, the aquifer's saturated thickness declined by more than 50 percent in certain places. Studies suggest subsurface water supplies for irrigation are running dry and the Ogallala aquifer will be exhausted within the first few decades of the twenty-first century.

The dissipation of subsurface water raises troubling questions about aquifer use. Water tables in the arid Southwest have fallen more than 120 meters. The expansion of Las Vegas, Nevada, appropriated so much of the surrounding region's scarce water that springs and wetlands have disappeared, dooming wildlife and straining aquifers. According to the U.S. Geological Survey, intensive use of groundwater in southern California contributed to the intru-

sion of saltwater into the Los Angeles area coastal aquifer. Withdrawal in the African Sahara currently amounts to about 10 billion cubic meters a year, and water tables in India and China have declined significantly. In Bangladesh, local groundwater levels have dropped nearly 3 meters because of upstream dams and diversions of the Ganges River. Botswana and Namibia have reached their internal water supply limits. Almost all the states of the Arabian Peninsula consume much more water than their annual replenishment rates. As supplies of subsurface water dwindle, populations face greater risks to both the quantity and the quality of their groundwater.

RISK MANAGEMENT

In the future, the direct and indirect effects of climate change on water resources will require careful management of the risks. The greenhouse effect, for instance, is a naturally occurring phenomenon necessary to sustain life on earth. In a greenhouse, solar radiation passes through the mostly transparent glass or plastic structure, warming the inside air, surface, and plants with the trapped heat. On a global scale, greater quantities of carbon dioxide (produced by industrial and transportation emissions), methane (expelled by livestock), and ozone trap heat within the atmosphere and threaten to increase temperatures worldwide. Although future prospects of long-term climate change are uncertain, global warming resulting from the greenhouse effect points toward an increased risk of dryness in the short term. Other risks from global warming include declining water tables, increasing saltiness of water and topsoil, fewer sources of surface water, unusually high rates of soil erosion, and destruction of native vegetation.

A hotter climate threatens to make droughts and aquifer depletion more frequent, severe, and irreversible. In the United States, the droughts of the late 1980s foreshadowed the economic impacts of climate change with potentially more severe droughts. From 1987 to 1989, losses from drought in the United States totaled $39 billion. Moreover, though deserts expand and contract in discernable cycles, desiccated soils in transition zones contribute to permanent erosion. For instance, the African Sahara expanded into the Sahel during the 1970s when overgrazing in semiarid locales eradicated the grassy ground cover. As a result, more than 300,000 people and 5 million livestock died. In 2000, the United Nations Environment Program estimated that desertification threatens

60 percent of the 8.25 billion acres of arid or semi-arid zones around the globe. In densely populated regions of the world, desertification results from human activities as well as climate change.

Proactive strategies optimizing water supplies are the best measures to curb desertification. As the primary agency for water-resource information, the U.S. Geological Survey monitors the quantity and quality of water in the nation's rivers and aquifers. It assesses the sources and fate of contaminants in aquatic systems, develops tools to improve the application of hydrologic information, and ensures that its information and tools are available to all potential users. At the international level, the settlement of cross-border water rights requires diplomacy, especially where aquifer replenishment and groundwater extraction occur in different areas. In some locales, engineers and scientists are devising schemes for artificially recharging groundwater. Of course, large-scale interbasin water transfers may not be politically and socially practical. Despite experimentation and planning, populations confronting water shortages continue to dwell on the edge of disaster.

The debate over managing the threat of water shortages is permeated with the issue of discounting the future. The choice confronting modern societies is whether to consume a natural resource immediately or save it for future generations. External factors such as higher energy prices, lower crop prices, or larger surpluses of moisture may reduce the risks. Nevertheless, fairness to future generations presumes that risks taken today regarding consumption of resources will be informed and ethical. Without a national or international strategy for responding to drought and aquifer depletion, consumers must choose to avoid wasting water.

Water is vital to human existence, and modern societies endanger their survival by taking it for granted. Worldwide water use doubled at least twice during the twentieth century and appears likely to double again in just the first ten years of the twenty-first century. Developing countries continue to be severely strained by water shortages, and water's strategic value makes it a potential source of international conflict. Directly related to pollution, demographic growth, and climate change, this natural resource is even more likely than oil to cause wars. As metropolitan cultures spread and consume more natural resources, hydrotechnology becomes increasingly crucial to capture the flow of water. Droughts and aquifer depletion significantly affect the human condition and threaten to undermine long-term sustainability.

Brad D. Lookingbill

REFERENCES

Black, Peter E. *Conservation of Water and Related Land Resources*. Totowa, NJ: Rowman and Littlefield, 1987.

Brown, Lester, et al., eds. *State of the World: A Worldwatch Institute Report on Progress Toward a Sustainable World*. New York: Norton, 2000.

Bryson, Reid A., and Thomas J. Murray. *Climates of Hunger: Mankind and the World's Changing Weather*. Madison: University of Wisconsin Press, 1977.

Collier, Michael, and Robert H. Webb. *Floods, Droughts, and Climate Change*. Tucson: University of Arizona Press, 2002.

De Villiers, Marq. *Water: The Fate of Our Most Precious Resource*. Boston: Houghton Mifflin, 2001.

Donahue, John M., and Barbara Rose Johnston, eds. *Water, Culture, and Power: Local Struggles in a Global Context*. Washington, DC: Island Press, 1998.

Douglas, Mary, and Aaron Wildavsky. *Risk and Culture: An Essay on the Selection of Technological and Environmental Dangers*. Berkeley: University of California Press, 1982.

Fetter, C. W. *Applied Hydrogeology*. Upper Saddle River, NJ: Prentice-Hall, 2001.

Flannery, Tim F. *The Eternal Frontier: An Ecological History of North America and Its Peoples*. New York: Atlantic Monthly Press, 2001.

Glantz, Michael H. *Drought Follows the Plow: Cultivating Marginal Areas*. Cambridge: Cambridge University Press, 1994.

Glennon, Robert Jerome. *Water Follies: Groundwater Pumping and the Fate of America's Freshwaters*. Washington, DC: Island Press, 2002.

Great Plains Committee (Harlan H. Barrows; H. H. Bennett; Morris L. Cooke, Chairman; L. C. Gray; F. C. Harrington; Richard C. Moore; John C. Page; Harlow S. Person). *The Future of the Great Plains*. Washington, DC: U.S. Government Printing Office, 1937.

Hoyt, John C. *Drought of 1936*. U.S. Department of Interior. Water Supply Paper 820. Washington, DC: U.S. Government Printing Office, 1938.

Hundley, Norris. *The Great Thirst: Californians and Water, 1770–1990*. Berkeley: University of California Press, 1992.

Hwang, Ned H. C. *Fundamentals of Hydraulic Engineering Systems*. Upper Saddle River, NJ: Prentice-Hall, 1996.

Kromm, David E., and Stephen F. White, eds. *Groundwater Exploitation in the High Plains*. Lawrence: University Press of Kansas, 1992.

Lookingbill, Brad D. *Dust Bowl, USA: Depression America*

and the Ecological Imagination, 1929–1941. Athens: Ohio University Press, 2001.

Mortimore, Michael. *Adapting to Drought: Farmers, Famines, and Desertification in West Africa.* Cambridge: Cambridge University Press, 1989.

Opie, John. *Nature's Nation: An Environmental History of the United States.* Fort Worth, TX: Harcourt College, 1998.

———. *Ogallala: Water for a Dry Land.* 2nd ed. Lincoln: University of Nebraska Press, 2000.

Price, Michael. *Introducing Groundwater.* London: Chapman and Hall, 1996.

Riney-Kehrberg, Pamela. *Rooted in Dust: Surviving Drought and Depression in Southwestern Kansas.* Lawrence: University Press of Kansas, 1994.

Smith, Norman. *Man and Water: A History of Hydro-technology.* New York: Scribner, 1975.

Smythe, William E. *The Conquest of Arid America.* New York: Macmillan, 1905.

Steinberg, Ted. *Down to Earth: Nature's Role in American History.* New York: Oxford University Press, 2002.

Thomas, David S. G., and Nichalas J. Middleton. *Desertification: Exploding the Myth.* New York: John Wiley and Sons, 1994.

Tuan, Yi-Fu. *Landscapes of Fear.* New York: Pantheon Books, 1979.

Turner, B. L., et al., eds. *The Earth as Transformed by Human Action: Global and Regional Changes in the Biosphere over the Past 300 Years.* Cambridge: Cambridge University Press, 1990.

Ward, Diane Raines. *Water Wars: Drought, Flood, Folly, and the Politics of Thirst.* New York: Riverhead Books, 2002.

Wilhite, Donald A., ed. *Drought: A Global Assessment.* London: Routledge, 2000.

Wilhite, Donald A., and William E. Easterling, eds. *Planning for Drought: Toward a Reduction of Societal Vulnerability.* Boulder, CO: Westview, 1987.

Worster, Donald. *Rivers of Empire: Water, Aridity, and the Growth of the American West.* New York: Pantheon Books, 1985.

WEB SITES

National Drought Mitigation Center: www.drought.unl.edu
United Nations Environment Programme: www.unep.org
U.S. Geological Survey: http://water.usgs.gov
U.S. Water News: www.usawaternews.com

GLOSSARY

Aquifer. A water-bearing layer of rock, rock formations, sand, or gravel.

Climate models. Forecasting tools with which researchers represent the results of several factors on climatic trends.

Compressional warming. A process in which an air parcel's temperature rises as pressure increases during its descent within the atmosphere.

Desertification. Process that turns productive land into nonproductive desert as a result of poor land management.

Dust Bowl. A region in the mid-latitude grasslands of North America reduced to aridity by dust storms and drought.

Evaporation. Process of turning water into gas form, leaving behind only moisture.

Fossil water. Groundwater with no source of renewal.

Global warming. Increase in the average temperature of the earth's atmosphere sufficient to cause change in climate.

Greenhouse effect. Phenomenon whereby the earth's atmosphere traps solar radiation; gases such as carbon dioxide allow incoming sunlight to pass through but prevent heat radiated back from earth's surface from escaping.

Irrigation. Supplying dry land with water by means of ditches, pipes, or streams.

Meteorology. Study of weather and weather conditions.

Precipitation. Condensed moisture from atmospheric water vapor that is massive enough to fall to the earth's surface: rain, snow.

Regolith. Layer of loose rock material resting on bedrock; the surface of most land.

Reservoir. Water collected and stored for future use in a natural or artificial lake.

Shelterbelt. A barrier of planted trees and shrubs that reduces erosion and protects against wind and storms.

Soil Conservation Service. A U.S. government agency promoting the conservation of soil resources to mitigate erosion.

Transpiration. Process by which moisture is released through the stomata of plants or skin pores.

Water table. Depth or level below which the ground is saturated with water.

DOCUMENT

Excerpt of *The Future of the Great Plains, 1937*

Submitted by the Great Plains Committee, a group of experts President Franklin D. Roosevelt appointed to look into drought conditions on the Great Plains, the report called on federal authorities to work with state and local leaders to conserve water for future generations. Although many of the report's proposals stimulated debate, the risks to the region continued to increase in subsequent years.

Paucity of water is the most striking characteristic of the Great Plains. Husbandry and intelligent use of available supplies of water are necessary if the Plains are to sustain an economic development permanent in character, free from violent fluctuations, and conducive to some conditions of life.

Surface Waters—The principal streams of the Great Plains originate in the Rocky Mountains and flow east and southeast from the Continental Divide toward the Mississippi River. The largest drainage basin is that of the Missouri River, the chief tributaries of which are the Yellowstone, the Platte, and the Kansas.

Such rivers as the Missouri, the Arkansas, and the Canadian are perennial in character though subject to great fluctuation in volume. Many of the Plains streams are not perennial; many carry flash floods in spring and dwindle or disappear in summer.

The character of the flow of a stream will largely indicate the type of use to which it may be put. Streams of strong perennial flow are a dependable source of water for irrigation, but in the basins of most such rivers additional storage would be required for the reclamation of new lands. For the most part streams which originate in the Plains area are not dependable sources of water for highly developed irrigation practice unless large amounts of storage are provided. Moreover, the low water flow of such streams may be so highly impregnated with salts that it is unsuitable for irrigation.

Irrigation in the Great Plains has been undertaken chiefly along the perennial streams and has been carried to a point where the minimum flow is scarcely sufficient to provide the required water. Since the only large source of water in the Great Plains which might be used for additional irrigation is the Missouri River, further development would have to depend largely upon importing water from other watersheds. On the other hand, storage has not been developed to its maximum in most sections. Moreover, because of infrequent requirements, irrigation with surface waters

has not been practiced generally in the eastern portion of the Great Plains, although the flow of various streams increases to the eastward and dependable supplies of water could be obtained in some instances.

Ground Waters—Ground waters supplied in the Great Plains are found both near the surface and at considerable depths. The shallow deposits generally are found in alluvial valley bottoms, buried valleys, and glacial drift. The deep deposits are in rock formations most of which outcrop along the eastern flank of the Rocky Mountains; they are extensively used for domestic, municipal, and stockwater purposes in some portions of the Region. Although deep waters have not been used much for irrigation, shallow waters have been so utilized in the southern part of the Great Plains. Future irrigation with water from alluvial sands in river valleys can be anticipated in all areas where pumping is now taking place. In addition, irrigation with ground waters as well as surface waters may prove feasible in some areas along the eastern margin and in the northern portion of the Great Plains. However, most of the new large-scale projects are of doubtful feasibility, if that be measured in accordance with requirements of the national reclamation law, under which construction costs must be repaid without interest in forty years. Water for livestock can be obtained generally over the southern half of the Region from deep wells, but over great areas of the northern half the depth to water-bearing formations is prohibitive under present conditions.

Lack of Coordination of Water Uses and of Water with Land Resources—In few places have studies been made of preferences in the use of water, or of the possibilities and conditions of multiple use. For example, in some instances the use of water for generating power during the nonirrigation season involves a loss of water which otherwise could be stored for use in irrigation. In other instances, water is used for the production of cash crops to be shipped from a given area, while adjacent range resources cannot be used adequately in all years because of lack of supplemental forage.

Use of High Cost Water for Cash Crop Production on Lands of Low Productivity—In many places water is used on poor land at the expense of more productive land that might be served. Such misuse of resources may lower the productivity of an entire irrigation district and may result in the inability of the enterprise providing water to maintain its system properly. Standards of living may be depressed on both the well watered poor land and the inadequately watered good land. Wastage of water even on productive soils may result from the fact that in many stream basins its most efficient use is determined by climate and the length of the growing season, both of which may be unfavorable. It is therefore obvious that use of water for the irrigation of cash crops on inferior soils or under unpropitious climatic conditions may involve not only a waste of water, but also a waste of human effort. In such instances the adjustment of water use to fit other critical conditions would permit a better usage of all resources and increased returns for the effort expended.

Unbalanced Appropriation Resulting in Inequitable Distribution of Water Within a Stream Basin—In some instances lands which are inadequately supplied with water during part of the growing season receive a surplus of water during other periods of the year. Efforts to build up soil moisture by artificial application of water during periods of surplus supply often result in waste of water, increase of alkali in the soil, and an impairment of soil productivity. Occasional failures of crops in areas having inadequate or unseasonable supplies of water have led, in some instances, to the adoption of ineffective expedients, to defaults in financial obligations incurred in the construction of irrigation works, and to long litigation. Sometimes drainage problems resulting from unbalanced water appropriations require additional drainage works which add to the financial burden of the areas.

Poorly Designed Irrigation Systems—Storage reservoirs may be shallow, and thus contribute to high evaporation losses; silting may be heavy; some diversion works may be inadequate to secure water during periods of low run-off, and conversely other diversion works, canals, and ditches may not be capable of diverting or carrying the available supply during periods of high water. When the water rights of poor systems are senior to those of good systems, a loss of aggregate benefits to the users along the stream invariably results. The financial loss from such factors has been severe in many instances.

Improper Financing of Irrigation Works—Burdening of irrigated land with heavy investment costs which were presumably to be met within relatively short periods, or deterioration of irrigation systems because of inadequate maintenance funds, or both, have resulted in many foreclosures and even in the abandonment of the lands involved. The financial loss sustained by both settlers and investors has been severe. In other instances, wastage of water through transportation to scattered areas has resulted in bad financial conditions throughout an entire community. In most areas the owners of the lands to be irrigated have borne the entire cost of construction, although many benefits have accrued to others. The spreading of costs to all beneficiaries, both direct and indirect, in proportion to the benefits received—for instance, to include the urban market center of an irrigation district— would have transformed many unsuccessful projects into successful enterprises.

Depletion of Ground-Water Supplies—There has been excessive withdrawal of ground water from certain areas, notably in the eastern half of North Dakota and South Dakota, and in the Roswell artesian basin in eastern New Mexico, where in consequence thousands of acres, formerly highly productive, have reverted to native vegetation. There are few areas in which the recharge of ground waters is sufficiently rapid to warrant large-scale development of irrigated land dependent on them. Where the rate of withdrawal from the underground reservoir is greater than the rate at which recharge takes place, the falling water table causes the lift and cost of pumping to mount constantly. Soon[er] or later, a point must be reached where it is no longer economically feasible to recover the ground water for the use to which it had been applied. The industries and communities built around this decreasing and receding resource must then either undergo readjustments or disappear. Natural recharge of an underground water reservoir in the Great Plains is a slow process. The development of an economy around an exhaustible but renewable resource should take into account the effect of withdrawal from that resource, and should be adjusted to a permanent yield basis.

Source: Great Plains Committee. *The Future of the Great Plains.* Washington, DC: U.S. Government Printing Office, 1937, 33, 50–51.

DRUG ABUSE

Illicit drug abuse has devastated millions of people and their families since the mid-twentieth century. In 2001, the National Institutes of Health (NIH) estimated that, in the United States alone, 3.1 million persons age 12 years and older (1.4 percent of the population) received some kind of treatment for a drug- or alcohol-related problem. Drug abuse has been linked to social issues as varied as homelessness, poverty, petty crime, decreased workplace productivity, and drug-related illness, including human immunodeficiency virus/acquired immune deficiency syndrome (HIV/AIDS). For example, the NIH states that behavior associated with drug abuse is now the single largest factor in the spread of HIV infection in the United States.

This chapter examines the abuse of the most popular drugs in the United States, whether prescription drugs or illegal substances. Frequently abused prescription drugs include pain relievers (e.g., codeine, opiates, Vicodin, and OxyContin), sedatives (e.g., Ambien and Halcion), and hypnotics (e.g., Clonidine, Valium, and Xanax). Illegal substances include cocaine, heroin, psychedelics, and various other pharmaceuticals. Alcohol and marijuana are covered in separate chapters.

DEFINITIONS

Global health organizations—including the World Health Organization (WHO), the NIH, and the European Monitoring Centre for Drugs and Drug Addiction (EMCDDA)—have independently developed several definitions of drug use, substance abuse, and addiction.

Drug use is typically defined as any use of psychoactive drugs. The term "substance abuse" encompasses a broad range of substances (including alcohol and inhalants) to which users can become addicted. Drug abuse and drug addiction consist of habitual or chronic use of psychoactive drug to alter states of mind for other than medically acceptable purposes.

Nonscientific and traditional definitions characterizing drug abuse as depraved and sinful have little value in understanding addiction and are largely discounted by medical experts. Today, the term "addiction" is more often defined as the continuing, compulsive use of drugs, both licit and illicit, despite physical and psychological harm to the user and society. Most definitions include a discussion of psychological and physical dependence as components of addiction. Psychological dependence is the subjective need for a drug to maintain a feeling of well-being. Physical dependence is characterized by tolerance of the drug and the need for increasingly larger doses to avoid the usually severe withdrawal symptoms.

The National Institute on Drug Abuse (NIDA), a part of the NIH, helps clarify this terminology by maintaining that addiction is not just "a lot of drug use." The NIDA fact sheet, *Understanding Drug Abuse and Addiction*, states, "Recent scientific research provides overwhelming evidence that not only do drugs interfere with normal brain functioning creating powerful feelings of pleasure, but they also have long-term effects on brain metabolism and activity. At some point, changes occur in the brain that can turn drug abuse into addiction. . . . Those addicted to drugs suffer from a compulsive drug craving and usage and cannot quit by themselves. Treatment is necessary to end this compulsive behavior."

The Diagnostic and Statistical Manual of Mental Disorders, Fourth Edition (DSM-IV) of the American Psychiatric Association (APA) defines psychoactive substance abuse as a "maladaptive pattern of use indicated by . . . continued use despite knowledge of having a persistent or recurrent social, occupational, psychological or physical problem that is caused or exacerbated by the use [or by] recurrent use in situations in which it is physically hazardous." This residual diagnosis typically follows a less serious diagnosis of "substance dependence."

CHRONOLOGY

8000 B.C.E. Wine and beer production and trade occur in the Mediterranean.

3000 B.C.E. Chinese use marijuana in medicine.

1100 C.E. Distillation is discovered by Arab scientists.

1800–90 The chemical process for extracting the alkaloids morphine, cocaine, and heroin is perfected by an organic chemist in Europe.

1806 Friedrich Wilhelm Saturner, a German chemist, isolates morphine from opium.

1853 The hypodermic syringe is developed by Charles Gabriel Pravaz and Alexander Wood. The syringe has a needle fine enough to pierce the skin.

1859 Albert Niemann, a German chemist, isolates cocaine from the coca leaves.

1869 National Woman Suffrage Association is founded.

1874 The Woman's Christian Temperance Union (WCTU) is founded.

1875 San Francisco outlaws opium dens.

1884 Cocaine is used as an anesthetic.

1890 Heroin is extracted from morphine.

1895 The Anti-Saloon League of America joins the WCTU crusade.

1906 The first national drug law, the Pure Food and Drug Act, is enacted.

1914 The Harrison Narcotic Act, regulating the distribution of opiates and other drugs, becomes law.

1918 The Eighteenth Amendment is ratified by forty-six states to prohibit the "manufacture, sale, or transportation of intoxicating liquors."

1919 The Volstead Act (also known as the Prohibition Act) is passed, providing funding to enforce the law prohibiting the production and sale of alcohol.

1932 The Benzedrine Inhaler is first marketed to treat congestion. It is also used to treat hyperactive children. The inhaler becomes a major source of amphetamine for drug abusers.

1933 The Twenty-first Amendment repeals the Eighteenth Amendment.

1937 The Marijuana Tax Act is passed by Congress.

1943 Albert Hoffman, a Swiss chemist, discovers the hallucinogenic drug LSD.

1954 Aldous Huxley publishes *The Doors of Perception,* in which he relates his hallucinogenic experience using mescaline.

1965 Timothy Leary, a Harvard psychologist, publishes *The Psychedelic Reader,* which describes the use of LSD. His call for the younger generation to "Turn on, tune in, drop out" speaks to thousands of young people calling themselves hippies.

1960–80 The hippie generation initiates a new wave of drug use and abuse.

1971 The U.S. army begins testing U.S. military personnel in Vietnam for heroin use.

The *drug war* is declared during the Nixon administration.

1972 The National Commission on Marijuana recommends decriminalizing private use of marijuana in the United States.

1973 The State of Oregon decriminalizes the possession of small amounts of marijuana. Other states decriminalize marijuana and lower the drinking age to 18.

1975 The Alaska Supreme Court rules that personal possession and cultivation of marijuana is protected by the state constitution.

1980s All states increase the drinking age to 21 years of age and introduce stricter laws on marijuana and designer drugs.

1980s	The Colombian drug cartels and drug lords such as Pablo Escobor Gavíria take control of the cocaine drug business in Colombia.
1982	The National Academy of Sciences notes widespread use of marijuana in the United States and warns of its harmful effects.
1983	Crack cocaine is first developed in the Bahamas.
1980s–90s	The cocaine and crack cocaine epidemic sweeps the United States.
1990s	The use of ecstasy and date rape drugs becomes a widespread problem.
1996	California passes Proposition 215 (the Compassionate Use Act of 1996), approving the Medical Marijuana Initiative.
2004	Office of National Drug Control Policy estimates that drug abuse will soon top $200 billion in the United States.

The term "abuse" is so misused and ambiguous that WHO's International Statistical Classification of Diseases and Related Health Problems (ICD-10) prefers the terms "harmful" or "hazardous use," which are defined as "persistent or sporadic excessive drug use inconsistent with or unrelated to acceptable medical practice."

TYPICAL DRUGS OF ABUSE

Commonly abused psychoactive drugs have chemical structures similar to those of human neurotransmitters such as dopamine and serotonin, allowing them to attach to neurotransmitter receptors in the brain to produce a euphoric experience at low doses but causing death at high doses.

Amphetamines

The Drug Abuse Warning Network (funded by the Department of Health and Human Services, Substance Abuse and Mental Health Services Administration program) lists and describes amphetamines such as levamphetamine (Benzedrine), dextroamphetamine (Dexedrine), and methamphetamine (Methedrine; also called "speed," "crystal," and "ice," for its clear crystal appearance). These powerful central nervous system (CNS) stimulants are synthetic compounds designed to produce cocainelike reactions. They stimulate the release of the neurotransmitters dopamine and noradrenalin (norepinephrine) from CNS vesicles, or small cavities. Elevated dopamine levels are associated with feelings of pleasure and increased energy— the "high" reported by amphetamine abusers.

Amphetamines can be injected, sniffed, snorted, swallowed, and even smoked. The feelings of exhila-ration, strength, and energy and a false sense of self-assurance can last as long as 24 hours, depending on the drug's strength. Appetite and the need for sleep are also suppressed. The high is followed by depression and fatigue resulting from the rapid depletion of dopamine as the body eliminates the drug.

The physical effects of amphetamine include constricted peripheral blood vessels, dilated pupils, and increased temperature, heart rate, and blood pressure. Severe stress to the cardiovascular system can result in cardiac arrest. One of the more troublesome side effects of amphetamine abuse is violent, antisocial behavior. Long-term use can also reduce mental acuity, cause paranoia, and induce psychosis.

Cocaine

Cocaine, like the synthetic amphetamines, is a strong CNS stimulant that interferes with the normal release of dopamine in the CNS. Elevated dopamine is associated with feelings of pleasure and energy followed by depression when the blood level of the dopamine falls below normal.

Prolonged cocaine snorting can cause ulceration of the nasal mucous membrane and damage the nasal septum. And as with amphetamines, long-term use reduces mental clarity, triggers paranoia, and induces psychosis. Death results from cardiac arrest or seizures.

"Crack" cocaine is the street name for cocaine processed to be smoked without loss of potency. Cocaine hydrochloride is usually processed with sodium bicarbonate (baking soda), water, and heat to remove the hydrochloride. "Crack" refers to the sound the processed cocaine makes when it is smoked, caused by the baking soda remaining in the compound.

Heroin

Heroin is a derivative of opium, a naturally occurring substance produced by the Asian poppy's seedpod. Like morphine and opium, heroin (also known as "smack," "H," "skag," and "junk") is highly addictive. Over time, users develop a tolerance to the drug, requiring ever-increasing dosages to obtain a high. Heroin addiction has been considered a serious problem in the United States since the beginning of the twentieth century. The Harrison Narcotics Act passed in 1914 was the first major legislative attempt to control drug abuse and reduce the number of addicts by restricting the use of controlled drugs in medical treatment.

Heroin can be injected, snorted, or smoked, slowing metabolism and producing euphoria, described as a "rush" that can last for several hours. In the early stage of heroin intoxication users often "nod out" for a short period, and their skin develops a warm flush as small blood vessels under the skin dilate.

Chronic heroin abuse results in serious health problems, including collapsed veins from frequent injections, infection of the heart lining and valves, abscesses, liver disease, infectious diseases (including HIV/AIDS and hepatitis from sharing unsterilized needles), and sometimes fatal overdoses. The U.S. Drug Abuse Warning Network listed heroin and morphine among the top three drugs most often associated with drug-related deaths in 2001.

Withdrawal symptoms begin several hours after the last dose. Physical indicators are drug craving, restlessness, muscle cramps and pain, insomnia, diarrhea and vomiting, and cold flashes. Heroin detoxification peaks within 48 to 72 hours of the last dose and subsides in about a week. Unlike sudden alcohol or barbiturate withdrawal that can result in death, sudden heroin withdrawal is not life threatening unless the user is in extremely poor heath.

Like alcoholism, heroin abuse during pregnancy causes birth defects and a higher risk of infant mortality. Children exposed during gestation to drugs such as heroin tend to have learning disabilities and social and behavioral problems.

Psychedelics

Psychedelic or hallucinogenic drugs are alkaloid chemical compounds that affect users' subjective experiences of emotions, perception, and thought. Typically, users experience sensory distortions such as warping of surfaces, shape suggestibility, blurred vision, prisms of color, color variations, and time distortions. The drugs also produce euphoria and introspection. Lysergic acid, commonly known as LSD or acid, was first synthesized in 1937 by the Swiss chemist Dr. Albert Hoffmann. This class of hallucinogens has no sedative effects, so users have vivid and clear memories of the psychedelic experience.

Naturally occurring hallucinogens are typically ingested, by chewing the peyote plant, for example, or drinking a tea made from psilocybin mushrooms. LSD (also found in ergot or the wheat rust fungus) has been produced in pill form, and liquid doses can be applied to paper that is chewed and swallowed. MDMA (ecstasy) is a synthetic compound with hallucinogenic properties. Humphrey Osmond and his colleagues used hallucinogens in experimental psychotherapy in the 1950s, because of their capacity to induce introspective states of mind.

Sedative-Hypnotics

Barbiturates and benzodiazepines are the two major categories of sedative-hypnotics. Some of the better-known barbiturates are Nembutal (pentobarbital) and Seconal (secobarbital); Valium (diazepam), Librium (chlordiazepoxide), Clonidine (hydrochloride), and Xanax (alprazolam) are examples of benzodiazepines. Both drug groups are dangerous at high doses.

Typically taken in pill form, these drugs slow the CNS, affecting thought, emotions, body control, and physiological function. In low doses, their actions are similar to mild alcohol intoxication, producing drowsiness and relaxation. Users experience reduced tension and increased feelings of well-being. Benzodiazepines reduce feeling of anxiety and increase a sense of inner calm, and are often used along with counseling to treat anxiety disorders.

High doses of sedative-hypnotics can affect the autonomic nervous system that innervates muscles and internal organs, producing sleep, hampered breathing, unconsciousness, and even death. The body develops tolerance of these extremely addictive drugs, requiring higher doses to achieve the same effect. Treatment for barbiturate addiction begins with medical detoxification. Sudden withdrawal from barbiturates can result in death.

Sedative-hypnotics combined with alcohol are extremely dangerous and frequently result in death. This deadly combination is commonly used in suicides.

Narcotic analgesics act on the CNS to relieve pain or combined with anesthetics before or during surgery. Codeine and hydrocodone also relieve coughing. Narcotics may become habit-forming, causing mental or physical dependence. Physical dependence results in pain, sleeplessness, and depression on withdrawal. Anesthesia, or induced unconsciousness, involves three phases: *analgesia* (pain relief), *amnesia* (loss of memory), and *immobilization.*

DEMOGRAPHICS, SOCIAL FACTORS, AND ECONOMICS

In 2001, 41.7 percent of Americans 12 years old and older reported having used an illegal drug at least once in their lives. Over 12 percent reported illicit drug use during the year before the SAMHSA survey. Some 15.9 million (7.1 percent) were estimated to have used an illicit drug 30 days before responding to the SAMHSA 2001 National Household Survey on Drug Abuse. By comparison, in the same year, an estimated 50 percent (approximately 140 million people) of the population 12 years or older regularly drank alcohol.

The same NHSDA survey showed the most commonly used illegal drug was marijuana, with 12.1 million users (5.4 percent of the population). Cocaine was the second most used illegal drug with 1.7 million users (0.7 percent of the population). Some 1.3 million people (0.6 percent of the population) used hallucinogens (LSD; PCP, or "Angel Dust"; and ecstasy). Approximately, 12.3 percent said they had used cocaine during their lifetime, and 12.5 percent reported using hallucinogens at least once in their lives.

These numbers do not reveal the full extent of the problem, however, as many of those who abuse illegal drugs both in the United States are young persons. The National Institute on Drug Abuse's 2002 Monitoring the Future Study found that 53 percent of high school seniors in the United States said they had used an illegal drug at least once, and approximately 41 percent in the past year. Over 25 percent said they had used an illegal drug in the past month. Of course, these numbers include alcohol, which is generally illegal for people under 21 years old. Underage alcohol consumption greatly exceeds illegal drug use.

The use of illicit drugs varies significantly among major racial and ethnic groups. For whites, illicit drug use (in the year previous to the 2002 study) was 8.5 percent. For African Americans and Hispanics, the

Table 1. Estimated Number (in thousands) **of Persons Who First Used Marijuana from 1965 to 2000, and Their Mean Age at First Use**

Year	Number of initiates (1000s)			Mean age
	All ages	12–17 years	18–25 years	
1965	585	194	308	19.7
1970	2,477	1,075	1,133	18.6
1975	2,847	1,538	965	18.4
1980	2,639	1,471	796	19.1
1985	1,860	1,103	610	17.8
1990	1,448	789	508	18.4
1995	2,439	1,539	766	16.6
2000	2,440	1,622	621	17.5

Source: Substance Abuse and Mental Health Services Administration (SAMHSA), Office of Applied Studies, National Household Survey on Drug Abuse, 1999–2001, Table H.42.

Table 2. Estimated Number (in thousands) **of Persons Who First Used Cocaine from 1965 to 2000, and Their Mean Age at First Use**

Year	Number of initiates (1000s)			Mean age
	All ages	12–17 years	18–25 years	
1965	18	*	*	*
1970	258	34	189	21.0
1975	776	171	497	21.4
1980	1,280	284	733	21.7
1985	1,222	231	733	22.1
1990	703	111	384	22.9
1995	648	194	348	21.1
2000	926	314	503	20.0

*Low precision; no estimate reported.
Source: Substance Abuse and Mental Health Services Administration (SAMHSA), Office of Applied Studies, National Household Survey on Drug Abuse, 1999–2001, Table H.43.

rates were 9.7 and 7.2 percent, respectively. Native Americans reported the highest usage, at 10.1 percent, and Asian Americans the lowest at 3.5 percent.

Over the years the NHSDA has been taken, illegal drug use has been about twice has high among males than among females. In 2002, illicit drug use among men was 10.3 percent and 6.4 percent for women. Use of prescription drugs for nonmedical purposes, however, was roughly the same for males (2.7 percent) and females (2.6 percent).

Researchers in the field of substance abuse and geriatrics are noting the pervasiveness of substance abuse among people age 60 and older. According to a study conducted by the Drug and Alcohol Services

Table 3. Estimated Percentage of Past-Month Drug Use Among 12–17-Year-Olds in the United States

7%	Youth ages 12–17 years have smoked marijuana in the past month (2000)
22.4%	High school seniors have smoked marijuana in the past month (2001)
2.1%	High school seniors have used cocaine in the past month (2001)
1.7%	High school seniors have used inhalants in the past month (2001)
175,000	Cocaine-related emergency room episodes in 1999 (2000)

Source: National Center for Health Statistics. *Health, United States, 2002.* With Chartbook on Trends in the Health of Americans. Data from Tables 64, 65, and 66.

Information System, between 1995 and 1999 alcohol was the primary problem for the majority of more than 55,000 people over the age of 55 who sought help from publicly funded drug treatment facilities. Also during that four-year period, alcohol admissions declined by 9 percent, while admissions for illicit drugs increased by 25 percent for men and 43 percent for women. Prescription drug abuse is prevalent among seniors because more medications are prescribed to older individuals and because age-related physiological changes make the body more vulnerable to drugs' effects.

Studies have linked drug addiction to various social factors, including exposure to HIV/AIDS, susceptibility to disease and illness, homelessness, crime, drug trafficking, rising gang violence, and decreased workplace productivity.

The use of illegal drugs is associated with a range of diseases, including tuberculosis, hepatitis, sexually transmitted diseases, and HIV/AIDS. Addicts who inject drugs risk exposure to HIV/AIDS and other bloodborne pathogens, and women also put their future children at risk. AIDS has become the fourth leading cause of death among women 15 to 44 years of age, while approximately 54 percent of pediatric AIDS cases in the United States result from the mother injecting drugs or having sexual relations with a drug-injecting male partner. In 2002, the rate of illicit drug use among pregnant women 15 to 44 years old within a month of the NHSDA survey was 3.3 percent; among nonpregnant women in the same age group the rate was 10.3 percent. Among nonpregnant women who gave birth in the last 2 years, 5.5 percent used illicit drugs. These findings suggest that a majority of women stop their drug use when they become pregnant, but many resume use after giving birth.

The NIDA has explored the connection between drug abuse and homelessness, especially homeless youth. In one NIDA study of 432 homeless youths in Los Angeles, 71 percent reported an alcohol or drug abuse disorder or both. In a nationwide survey of 600 youths living on the streets, 50 percent of those who had tried to kill themselves said that using alcohol or drugs had led to their suicide attempt. In an analysis of three national surveys of substance abuse among youths ages 12 to 21 who had run away or been homeless at some point in their lives, Dr. Christopher Ringwalt, Jody Greene, and their colleagues at Research Triangle Institute in North Carolina found that some 75 percent of street youths were using marijuana; approximately one-third were using hallucinogens, stimulants, and analgesics; and 25 percent were using crack, other forms of cocaine, inhalants, and sedatives.

With the exception of drug-related homicides, which have declined in recent years, drug-related crime is on the rise. In a 1996 profile of jail inmates, the U.S. Department of Justice, Bureau of Justice Statistics, reported about one in four convicted drug offenders had committed their crimes to get money for drugs. A higher percentage of drug offenders in 1996 (24 percent) than in 1989 (14 percent) were in jail for a crime committed to raise money for drugs. According to the Bureau, in a 1997 Survey of Inmates in State and Federal Correctional Facilities, 33 percent of state prisoners and 22 percent of federal prisoners said they had committed their current offense while under the influence of drugs. Inner-city neighborhoods where illegal drug markets flourish are accompanied by increased rates of crime and violence.

Researchers have linked drug abuse with decreased work productivity. An ongoing, nationwide study conducted by the U.S. Postal Service compared the job performance of drug users versus nonusers. Among drug users, absenteeism is 66 percent higher, health benefit utilization is 84 percent greater in dollar terms, disciplinary actions are 90 percent higher, and there is significantly higher employee turnover. Companies in the private sector have concluded that employee drug abuse affects performance, absenteeism, and turnover rates. Given these statistics, the workplace often functions as a source of information on substance-abuse prevention and identification to adults who are not being reached through more traditional means, as well as to youth who are employed while attending school. Many employers sponsor employee-assistance programs, conduct drug testing, or use procedures for detecting substance abuse and promoting early treatment.

The Economic Costs of Drug Abuse in the United States 1992–1998, published by the Office of National Drug Control Policy (ONDCP) in 2001, reported an economic cost in the United States of $143.4 billion in 1998. The overall cost of drug abuse between 1992 and 1998 increased 5.9 percent annually from $102.2 to $143.4 billion, and is expected to continue rising at 5.9 percent per year, reaching over $200 billion by 2005. These numbers include the direct costs of health and law enforcement, as well as such indirect costs as lost worker productivity and drug-related crime. By contrast, alcohol abuse accounts for roughly $90 billion per year in direct and indirect costs.

The ONDCP 2001 report breaks costs down into three categories: healthcare costs, productivity losses, and "other" costs. Productivity losses account for 69 percent of the economic costs, including time lost to drug abuse-related illness, incarceration, and early death. Healthcare accounts for about 9 percent of total cost, and the remaining 22 percent of economic costs are identified as "other." This category includes police protection, incarceration, and criminal justice costs as well as property damage and the social welfare programs that represent 2.4 percent of total costs.

HISTORY

Use of drugs to alter one's state of consciousness goes back to the time of cave dwellers, when shamans used hallucinogenic drugs to communicate with the spirits and gods. Alfred R. Lindesmith, in his book *Addiction and Opiates* (1969), cites evidence that by 5000 B.C.E., the Sumerians' ideogram for the use of opium translates as "a thing of joy." Historian Ashley Montague, in his article in *Reflections,* "The Long Search for Euphoria," suggests that by 2500 B.C.E. the Lake Dwellers of Switzerland were eating poppy seeds for their euphoric effect. He also claims that Greek naturalist and philospher Theophrastus (371–287 B.C.E.) made the first undisputed reference to the use of poppies as a potion with medicinal properties.

Before the 1800s, there was little change in the drugs people used (e.g., opium, herbs, plants, cacti), primarily in religious rituals or for medicine. Many plants such as mushrooms and cacti have been used around the world for their hallucinogenic properties. Native Americans in the southwestern United States and Mexico used the peyote cactus in various religious rituals long before the Europeans arrived. Tribes in the Central and South American rain forests made and continue to use a number of hallucinogenic plants (including strong tobacco) in religious ceremonies.

Because of the unrestricted availability of drugs of all types in the 1800s, historian Edward Brecher, in his highly respected book, *Licit and Illicit Drugs* (1964), refers to nineteenth-century America and Europe as a "dope-fiend's paradise." With no legal restrictions, drugstores, dry goods stores, grocery stores, and mail order houses sold patent medicines containing opiates, morphine, and later heroin without a prescription. Concoctions called Cherry Pectoral, Mrs. Winslow's Soothing Syrups, and Godfrey's Cordial (a mixture of opium, molasses, and sassafras) and hundreds of others were sold as pain relievers, tranquillizers, and even teething syrups for babies.

Syrups made with cocaine were also popular toward the end of the nineteenth century. "Mariani's wine," an elixir of red wine and coca leaf made in Italy, was popular in both Europe and the United States. John Styth Pemberton in 1885 first sold a cocaine elixir called "French Wine Coca—Ideal Nerve and Tonic Stimulant." The following year, he dropped the wine and added syrup made from the African kola nut in another syrup he called Coca-Cola. The widely popular syrup was the target of reformers because of its cocaine content. The Pure Food and Drug Act of 1906 was, in fact, passed in part to restrict the sale of Coca-Cola, but by this time the cocaine had been dropped from the recipe. The company was sued nonetheless by the Bureau of Food and Drugs because caffeine had been added, an ingredient prohibited by the act. The suit was settled when the Coca-Cola Company agreed to change its manufacturing process.

In the mid-1800s, patterns of drug abuse changed abruptly. German chemist Friedrich W.A. Serturner isolated the pure alkaloids from opium called *morphia* (morphine). In 1844, cocaine was isolated in its pure form from the leaf of the coca plant. This was followed by German scientist Johann von Baeyer's (1864) discovery of the molecular structure of benzene, a synthesized barbituric acid that was the first barbiturate. Over the century, barbiturates became the drug of choice for many addicts.

Finally, in 1898, *diacetylmorphine* (heroin) was synthesized. Morphine addicts switched from morphine to heroin, changing the pattern of drug abuse and addiction. In his article "The Long Search for Euphoria," Montague pointed out that, at the time of its discovery, heroin was extolled as a "safe preparation free from addiction-forming properties." These almost pure alkaloid drugs were far more powerful than the organic substances they came from and produced a stronger dependency in the abusers.

When the hypodermic syringe was invented during the Civil War, morphine injections were used to prevent patients from dying of shock during amputations and surgery. Powerful *anesthetic* drugs such as morphine and cocaine allowed surgeons to operate slowly and carefully. But the hypodermic also ushered in a new pattern of drug abuse. After the Civil War, so many soldiers were addicted that morphine addiction was called the "soldier's disease." Later in 1890, when heroin was extracted from morphine, the heroin injection syringe led to the heroin epidemics of the twentieth century. By the early 1900s, an estimated 250,000 people were addicted to morphine and opium in the United States.

Most Protestant religious leaders, politicians, and social reformers in the United States opposed the use, sale, and production of alcohol and most psychoactive drugs that were being abused in the late 1800s. Post–Civil War Prohibitionists convinced a majority of citizens that alcohol and drugs damaged the mind and body and were directly correlated with crime, poverty, and violence. Temperance societies sprang up in the United States and across Europe demanding abolition of the "devil rum" and the "drunkard-makers" (the liquor industry, saloonkeepers, and drug stores), as slavery had been abolished.

The Woman's Christian Temperance Union (WCTU), founded in 1874, campaigned nationally against the use and sale of alcohol. The Anti-Saloon League of America joined the WCTU crusade in 1895. One strategy of the temperance societies was civil disobedience, made famous in Kansas by Carry Amelia Moore Nation (1846–1911). She and her followers attacked saloons and taverns with axes, breaking the wooden barrels used in saloons to dispense beer.

Less familiar are the attacks on drugstores, where elixirs similar to Godfrey's Cordial were sold from the soda fountains. Prohibitionists considered these narcotic mixtures, predecessors to cocaine-laced drinks such as Coca-Cola, as harmful as alcohol.

Temperance reformers were pushing legal measures to stop the indiscriminate sale of addictive drugs in the United States. The first law restricting drug use was passed in San Francisco in 1875. Largely aimed at the city's Chinese population, the law banned opium dens. The first national drug law, the Pure Food and Drug Act (1906), required accurate labeling of patent medicines containing opium and other drugs. In 1914, the Harrison Narcotic Act forbade sale of substantial doses of opiates or cocaine except by licensed doctors and pharmacies. Heroin was later totally banned, and subsequent Supreme Court decisions made it illegal for doctors to prescribe narcotics to addicts. After several high-profile cases in which physicians were imprisoned for prescribing narcotics, the practice ended. Once drugs such as opium, heroin, and cocaine were illegal, the Federal Bureau of Narcotics (now the Drug Enforcement Administration) began campaigning against marijuana. The Marijuana Tax Act (1937) made the untaxed possession and sale of marijuana illegal.

The use of marijuana, amphetamines, and heroin, which had been low during the 1930s and 1940s, began to increase in the 1950s. But it was the social upheaval and counterculture of the 1960s that brought a dramatic increase in and a degree of social acceptance to drug use. By the early 1970s, some states and localities had decriminalized marijuana and lowered the drinking age to 18.

The 1960s was a period when the young were questioning social standards of all kinds. They pointed to a double standard, making marijuana and psychedelic drugs illegal but not alcohol. Experimenting with "mind-expanding" drugs such as LSD was viewed as beneficial compared to dulling perception with medically prescribed sedatives and tranquilizers. These attitudes led to a dramatic increase in drug experimentation with LSD, mescaline, and psilocybin mushrooms. The recreational use of hallucinogens became a *cause célèbre* for the hippie generation. Former Harvard psychology professor Timothy Leary, advocated psychedelics as a tool for opening the mind to emotional and spiritual growth and exploration, advising young people to "Turn on, tune in, drop out."

During the last half of the 1960s, illegal drug use spread from the hippie community to suburban youth, making drug use a middle-class problem. The national response was swift and strict.

The Nixon administration's "war on drugs" was successful in reducing the drug trafficking (mostly marijuana) from Mexico. But an unanticipated consequence of this interdiction program at the Mexican border was increased trafficking from other countries such as Jamaica and Colombia by sea and air routes. Later, as the Coast Guard made smuggling of bulky marijuana more costly, drug smugglers turned to the more profitable cocaine. The ONDCP estimated that the "war on drugs" cost about $50 billion in 2000.

The importing of Colombian cocaine in large quantities—combined with the false but common belief that cocaine is nonaddictive and popular among the rich and famous—resulted a cocaine "epidemic" in the United States by the end of the 1970s. A new, cheaper form of cocaine, crack cocaine, appeared on the market in the 1980s and gained popularity because of its quick high. Crack was first reported in the Dutch Antilles about 1980 and, in 1983, came through the Bahamas to the United States, where it was being sold in Florida and New York City by the mid-1980s. The availability of this cheap, highly addictive drug resulted in devastating addiction in poor, inner-city communities where it was aggressively marketed in the late 1980s.

By the mid-1990s, cocaine was declining somewhat in popularity, particularly its smokable, crack form. But methamphetamine was growing in popularity. By 2004, "meth labs" were so widespread in the Midwest that their discarded toxic waste constituted an environmental threat in some communities. The labs were easy to set up and dismantle, and the ingredients are available in over-the-counter cold and allergy medications. This led many states to restrict the sale of over-the-counter medications with the active ingredients ephedrine or pseudoephedrine.

TREATMENT REGIMENS

Substance abuse treatment is based on the philosophy, supported by scientific evidence, that addictive disorders are very treatable. The NIH recognizes a number of effective treatment options for people addicted to an illegal drug, including medications, behavioral therapies, inpatient and outpatient treatment, counseling, psychosocial therapies, and other supportive services. Behavioral therapies can include counseling, psychotherapy, support groups, or family therapy. Of the 3.1 million persons age 12 years and older who received treatment for a drug- or alcohol-related problem, 1.6 million received treatment at a self-help group.

According to the NIH, treatment medications offer assistance in suppressing the withdrawal syndrome and drug craving and in blocking the effects of drugs. Studies show that treatment for heroin addiction using methadone at an adequate dosage level combined with behavioral therapy reduces death rates and many health problems associated with heroin abuse.

In treatment programs, positive outcome is discontinued use and return to a stable and productive life. Over the last 25 years, studies show that treatment works to reduce drug intake and crimes committed by drug-dependent people. Researchers also have found that drug abusers who have been through treatment are more likely to hold jobs. Social scientists contend that motivational and cognitive-behavioral interventions appear to be the most effective counseling approaches, but lack of access to treatment remains a serious problem. In 2001 an estimated 5 million people were unable to receive needed treatment.

TREATMENT VERSUS PUNISHMENT

The role of criminal law versus prevention and treatment programs in reducing illegal drug use has been debated for more than 150 years in the United States. Many argue that punishment is the only way to reduce illegal drug use, prevent future use, and stop the damage illegal drugs has on the country's moral fabric. This approach includes interdiction policies to reduce the supply of illegal drugs into the country. The "war on drugs" started by President Richard Nixon in the 1970s and continuing into the twenty-first century relies on criminal law and punishment to eliminate illegal drug trafficking. Criminal justice advocates claim treatment is often ineffective and leniency only encourages those drawn to the vast profits to be made by selling illegal drugs.

By the end of the twentieth century, however, scientific evidence was favoring drug treatment. In 1996, the Bureau of Justice Statistics estimated that $30 billion of the $38 billion spent on corrections went to incarcerating individuals with histories of drug or alcohol abuse, convicted of drug- or alcohol-related violations.

The 1999 National Treatment Improvement Evaluation Study from the Center for Substance Abuse Treatment reported that each alcohol or drug treatment episode cost an average of $2,941. The cost of incarcerating a person in a federal or state prison was slightly over $20,000 per year in 1999. The estimated benefit to society of treatment programs was $9,177 per client, an average savings of $3 for every $1 dollar spent on substance abuse treatment from the reduced crime-related and healthcare costs and the increased earnings by recovering addicts. The evidence supporting treatment is so compelling that the Violent Crime Control and Law Enforcement Act of 1994 was passed to ensure that all inmates who need it have drug treatment prior to their release.

Despite the billons of dollars spent on interdiction efforts and drug treatment over the past half-century, and their failure to stop illegal drug use, the public continues to support the war on drugs. The majority of Americans still believe all psychoactive drugs should be illegal except for alcohol, tobacco, caffeine, and prescription drugs. A staunch minority, however, argues for decriminalization. Attitudes toward eliminating or reducing criminal penalties for use or sale of such drugs as marijuana have changed with the times and the perceived dangers of illegal drugs. Many localities decriminalized marijuana in the 1970s—and many reinstituted stricter laws in the 1980s. In the 1990s, the movement to legalize marijuana for medical use began to gain ground. The Netherlands, Switzerland, Britain, and Canada decriminalized marijuana and other drugs in the 1980s and 1990s, increasing pressure on the United States.

The people who support decriminalization believe it would greatly reduce drug trafficking and the violence it promotes. In additional, government regulation of dosage and purity would make drugs safer for the users, while lower prices for drugs such as cocaine, marijuana, and heroin would take the profit out of drug trafficking. Decriminalization would also save the $20 billion to $30 billion the federal government spends every year to stop drug trafficking. Opponents of decriminalization counter that removal of deterrents would encourage drug use, addicts would continue to steal to buy drugs, and many drugs are so inexpensive to make that there would still be a black market for them.

CONCLUSION

Illegal drug production and trafficking have also destroyed communities in the United States and led to upheavals in supplier countries. Billions of dollars have been spent to stop drug use and trafficking with little evidence of success. A minority of medical, legal, and sociological experts are increasingly concluding that the government's criminological approach to drug abuse may be doing more harm than good. The flow of illegal drugs into the United States has not declined, and ever-increasing numbers of Americans are being imprisoned for simple possession of illegal substances.

While no model or set of policies will rid America of drug abuse, other approaches have shown some promise in reducing the damage it causes. "Harm reduction," for example, assumes some drug abuse is inevitable and the "zero tolerance" approach is impossible to achieve. Harm reduction advocates instead argue that the best that society can achieve is to limit the damage that drugs cause individuals, families, and society in general. Thus, treatment replaces incarceration. Many experts and public officials, however, still insist that showing any sign of lenience only encourages more abuse. No doubt the debate—and drug abuse itself—will continue.

Andrew L. Cherry

REFERENCES

Amaro, H., S. M. Blake, P. M. Schwartz, and L. J. Flinchbaugh. "Developing Theory-Based Substance Abuse Prevention Programs for Young Adolescent Girls." *Journal of Early Adolescence* 21, 3 (2001): 256–93.

Brecher, E. *Licit and Illicit Drugs.* Boston: Little, Brown, 1972.

Cherry, Andrew. *A Research Primer for the Helping Professions: Methods Statistics and Writing.* Pacific Grove, CA: Brooks/Cole, 2000.

———. *Examining Global Social Welfare Issues Using MicroCase.* Pacific Grove, CA: Brooks/Cole, 2003.

Cherry, Andrew, Mary Dillon, and Douglas Rugh. *Abuse of Alcohol and Other Drugs: A Global View.* Westport, CT: Greenwood, 2002.

DeHaas, R. A., J. E. Calamari, J. P. Bair, and E. D. Martin. "Anxiety Sensitivity and Drug or Alcohol Use in Individuals with Anxiety and Substance Use Disorders." *Addictive Behaviors* 26, 6 (2001): 787–801.

Gfroerer, J. "Correlation between Drug Use by Teenagers and Drug Use by Older Family Members." *American Journal of Drug and Alcohol Abuse* 13 (1987): 95–108.

Gorman, D. M., and J. H. Derzon. "Behavioral Traits and Marijuana Use and Abuse—A Meta-analysis of Longitudinal Studies." *Addictive Behaviors* 27, 2 (2002): 193–206.

Gray, J. P. *Why Our Drug Laws Have Failed and What We Can Do about It: A Judicial Indictment of the War on Drugs.* Philadelphia: Temple University Press, 2001.

Hallfors, D., H. Cho, D. Livert, and C. Kadushin. "Fighting Back against Substance Abuse—Are Community Coalitions Winning?" *American Journal of Preventive Medicine* 23, 4 (2002): 237–45.

Hanson, G. R., A. E. Fleckenstein, and Peter J. Venturelli. *Drugs and Society.* Sudbury, MA: Jones and Bartlett, 2002.

Human Rights Watch. *Punishment and Prejudice: Racial Disparities in the War on Drugs.* New York: Human Rights Watch, 2000.

Irvin, J. E., C. A. Bowers, M. E. Dunn, and M. C. Wang. "Efficacy of Relapse Prevention: A Meta-analytic Review." *Journal of Consulting and Clinical Psychology* 67, 4 (1999): 563–70.

Jacobson, S. W., and J. L. Jacobson. "Alcohol and Drug-Related Effects on Development: A New Emphasis on Contextual Factors." *Infant Mental Health Journal* 22, 3 (2001): 416–30.

Johnson, K., D. D. Bryant, D. A. Collins, T. D. Noe, T. N. Strader, and M. Berbaum. "Preventing and Reducing Alcohol and Other Drug Use among High-Risk Youths by Increasing Family Resilience." *Social Work* 43, 4 (1998): 297–308.

Karch, Steven B. *Karch's Pathology of Drug Abuse.* Boca Raton, FL: CRC Press, 2001.

Moberg, D. P., and D. L. Piper. "The Healthy for Life Project: Sexual Risk Behavior Outcomes." *AIDS Education and Prevention* 10, 2 (1998): 128–48.

Montague, Ashley. "The Long Search for Euphoria." *Reflections* 1, 62–69 (May–June 1966): 66.

National Institute on Drug Abuse. *Understanding Drug Abuse and Addiction.* Available online at the National Institutes of Health Web site, www.nida.nih.gov/Infofax/understand.html.

———. "Drug Abuse Among Runaway and Homeless Youth Calls for Focused Outreach Solutions." *Children on the Brink: Youths at Risk of Drug Abuse* 12, 3 (May/June 1997).

ODCCP. *Global Illicit Drugs Trends.* United Nations Office for Drug Control and Crime Prevention. Vienna, Austria: United Nations, 1999.

———. *World Drug Report.* United Nations Office for Drug Control and Crime Prevention. Vienna, Austria: United Nations, 2000.

Shulamith Straussner, S. *Ethnocultural Factors in Substance Abuse Treatment.* New York: Guilford, 2001.

United Nations. *World Drug Report.* New York: United Nations, 2000.

Wilson, R. W., and C. Kolander. *Drug Abuse Prevention.* 2nd ed. Sudbury, MA: Jones and Bartlett, 2003.

WEB SITES

Bureau of Justice Statistics: www.ojp.usdoj.gov/bjs
Centers for Disease Control: www.cdc.gov
Drug Enforcement Administration: www.dea.gov
National Center for Health Statistics: www.cdc.gov/nchs
National Drug Intelligence Center: www.usdoj.gov/ndic
National Drug Strategy Network: www.ndsn.org
National Institutes of Health: www.nih.gov
National Institute on Drug Abuse: www.nida.nih.gov
Office of National Drug Control Policy: www.whitehousedrugpolicy.gov
Substance Abuse and Mental Health Services Administration (SAMHSA): www.samhsa.gov

GLOSSARY

Addictive personality. A concept based on the disease model, referring to people who are prone to addiction.

Antagonist. A chemical or drug that interferes with the physiological action of another drug, typically by blocking its nerve receptor. Antabuse (Disulfiram), for example, causes alcohol intolerance, producing an intensely noxious reaction when a person drinks alcoholic beverages.

Detoxification. A normal metabolic process that rids the body of toxins.

Detoxification center. A medical program in which alcoholics and other addicts are monitored during detoxification. Typically, this type intervention is the first phase of a comprehensive drug treatment program for physiological addictions.

Drug abuse and drug addiction. A habitual or chronic use of any psychoactive drug to alter states of the mind for other than a medically acceptable purpose.

Employee assistance program (EAP). A program for employees who have a drug or alcohol problem designed to restore employees to full productivity.

Endorphins. Peptide hormones that bind to opiate receptors in the brain. High levels of endorphins enhance emotional states and reduce physical pain.

Gateway drugs. A drug that tends to lead to the abuse of other, more addictive and harmful drugs.

Hallucinogens. A substance such as lysergic acid diethylamide (LSD) that induces hallucination and causes distortion of perception and altered states of awareness.

Harm reduction. A public health concept focusing on reducing the harm caused by drug use.

Intoxication. Physical state in which drugs or alcohol affect mental and bodily control. Legally defined in most states as a 0.08 blood level of alcohol. Blood tests measure the number of grams of alcohol per 100 milliliters of blood.

Mescaline. An alkaloid drug obtained from the peyote cactus *(Lophophora williamsii)*. Found in Mexico and the Southwest United States, it produces hallucinations when eaten.

Narcotic. An addictive drug such as heroin and morphine. Narcotics are extremely useful in controlling pain.

Neurotransmitter. A chemical in the body (i.e., acetylcholine and dopamine) that transmits nerve impulses across synapses.

Physical dependence. A condition characterized by tolerance of a drug and the need for increasingly larger doses to avoid the almost unbearable withdrawal symptoms.

Psychedelic. A drug that causes hallucinations such as LSD and mescaline.

Psychoactive drug. A class of drugs that alters mood, behavior, perception, or mental function.

Psychological dependence. The subjective feeling that a drug is needed to maintain a feeling of well-being.

Serotonin. An organic compound found in animal and human tissue, with highest concentrations in the brain and blood. An active ingredient in antidepressant drugs such as Prozac and Zoloft, it facilitates the impulses between nerve cells and regulates other physiological processes.

Stimulant. A drug such as cocaine or caffeine that increases physiological activity.

Substance abuse. A term referring to addiction to or abuse of a broad range of substances (including alcohol and inhalants) that can fit the addictive profile.

Syndrome. A set of physical and behavioral characteristics that typically denote a psychological disorder such as alcohol addiction.

Therapeutic community. The Therapeutic Community Model was an outgrowth of the Synanon program started in 1958 by a former alcoholic, Charles Dederich, in California.

Therapeutic dose. The amount of a drug needed to have a specific therapeutic effect on a person.

Tolerance. The ability of the body to absorb large doses of a drug without harmful effect.

DOCUMENT

Schedule of Controlled Substances, 1970

Under the Federal Controlled Substances Act, passed by Congress in 1970, illegal drugs were classified in five schedules, depending on their potential for beneficial medical use, their addictiveness, and the harm they can cause. Penalties for possession and sale of controlled substances depend largely on which schedule they fall under. This excerpt concludes with a list of well-known controlled substances by schedule.

Sec. 812. - Schedules of controlled substances

(a) Establishment. There are established five schedules of controlled substances, to be known as schedules I, II, III, IV, and V. Such schedules shall initially consist of the substances listed in this section. The schedules established by this section shall be updated and republished on a semiannual basis during the two-year period beginning one year after October 27, 1970, and shall be updated and republished on an annual basis thereafter.

(b) Placement on schedules; findings required. Except where control is required by United States obligations under an international treaty, convention, or protocol, in effect on October 27, 1970, and except in the case of an immediate precursor, a drug or other substance may not be placed in any schedule unless the findings required for such schedule are made with respect to such drug or other substance. The findings required for each of the schedules are as follows:

(1) Schedule I.
(A) The drug or other substance has a high potential for abuse.
(B) The drug or other substance has no currently accepted medical use in treatment in the United States.
(C) There is a lack of accepted safety for use of the drug or other substance under medical supervision.

(2) Schedule II.
(A) The drug or other substance has a high potential for abuse.
(B) The drug or other substance has a currently accepted medical use in treatment in the United States or a currently accepted medical use with severe restrictions.
(C) Abuse of the drug or other substances may lead to severe psychological or physical dependence.

(3) Schedule III.
(A) The drug or other substance has a potential for abuse less than the drugs or other substances in schedules I and II.
(B) The drug or other substance has a currently accepted medical use in treatment in the United States.
(C) Abuse of the drug or other substance may lead to moderate or low physical dependence or high psychological dependence.

(4) Schedule IV.
(A) The drug or other substance has a low potential for abuse relative to the drugs or other substances in schedule III.
(B) The drug or other substance has a currently accepted medical use in treatment in the United States.
(C) Abuse of the drug or other substance may lead to limited physical dependence or psychological dependence relative to the drugs or other substances in schedule III.

(5) Schedule V.
(A) The drug or other substance has a low potential for abuse relative to the drugs or other substances in schedule IV.
(B) The drug or other substance has a currently accepted medical use in treatment in the United States.
(C) Abuse of the drug or other substance may lead to limited physical dependence or psychological dependence relative to the drugs or other substances in schedule IV.

(c) Initial schedules of controlled substances. Schedules I, II, III, IV, and V shall, unless and until amended following drugs or other substances, by whatever official name, common or usual name, chemical name, or brand name designated:

SCHEDULE I

(a) Unless specifically excepted or unless listed in another schedule, any of the following opium derivatives, their isomers, esters, ethers, salts, and salts of isomers, esters, and ethers, whenever the existence of such isomers, esters, ethers, and salts is possible within the specific chemical designation:

. . .
Codeine methylbromide.
Codeine-N-Oxide.
Heroin.
Morphine methylbromide.
Morphine methylsulfonate.
Morphine-N-Oxide.
. . .
(b) Unless specifically excepted or unless listed in another schedule, any material, compound, mixture, or preparation, which contains any quantity of the following hallu-cinogenic substances, or which contains any of their salts, isomers, and salts of isomers whenever the existence of such salts, isomers, and salts of isomers is possible within the specific chemical designation:
. . .
3,4-methylenedioxy amphetamine.
5-methoxy-3,4-methylenedioxy amphetamine.
3,4,5-trimethoxy amphetamine.
4-methyl-2,5-diamethoxyamphetamine.
Ibogaine.
Lysergic acid diethylamide. [LSD]
Marihuana.
Mescaline.
Peyote.
Psilocybin.
Psilocyn.
Tetrahydrocannabinols
. . .

SCHEDULE II

(a) Unless specifically excepted or unless listed in another schedule, any of the following substances whether produced directly or indirectly by extraction from substances of vegetable origin, or independently by means of chemical synthesis, or by a combination of extraction and chemical synthesis:

(1) Opium and opiate, and any salt, compound, derivative, or preparation of opium or opiate.

(2) Any salt, compound, derivative, or preparation thereof which is chemically equivalent or identical with any of the substances referred to in clause (1), except that these substances shall not include the isoquinoline alkaloids of opium.

(3) Opium poppy and poppy straw.

(4) Coca leaves, except coca leaves and extracts of coca leaves from which cocaine, ecgonine, and derivatives of ecgonine or their salts have been removed; cocaine, its salts, optical and geometric isomers, and salts of isomers; ecgonine, its derivatives, their salts, isomers, and salts of isomers; or any compound, mixture, or preparation which contains any quantity of any of the substances referred to in this paragraph.

(b) Unless specifically excepted or unless listed in another schedule, any of the following opiates, including their isomers, esters, ethers, salts, and salts of isomers, esters and ethers, whenever the existence of such isomers, esters, ethers, and salts is possible within the specific chemical designation:

Methadone.

SCHEDULE III

(a) Unless specifically excepted or unless listed in another schedule, any material, compound, mixture, or preparation which contains any quantity of the following substances having a stimulant effect on the central nervous system:

(1) Amphetamine, its salts, optical isomers, and salts of its optical isomers.

(2) Phenmetrazine and its salts.

(3) Any substance (except an injectable liquid) which contains any quantity of methamphetamine, including its salts, isomers, and salts of isomers.

(4) Methylphenidate.

(b) Unless specifically excepted or unless listed in another schedule, any material, compound, mixture, or preparation which contains any quantity of the following substances having a depressant effect on the central nervous system:

Any substance which contains any quantity of a derivative of barbituric acid, or any salt of a derivative of barbituric acid.

. . .

Lysergic acid.

Lysergic acid amide.

. . .

(d) Unless specifically excepted or unless listed in another schedule, any material, compound, mixture, or preparation containing limited quantities of any of the following narcotic drugs, or any salts thereof:

(1) Not more than 1.8 grams of codeine per 100 milliliters or not more than 90 milligrams per dosage unit, with an equal or greater quantity of an isoquinoline alkaloid of opium.

(2) Not more than 1.8 grams of codeine per 100 milliliters or not more than 90 milligrams per dosage unit, with one or more active, non-narcotic ingredients in recognized therapeutic amounts.

(3) Not more than 300 milligrams of dihydrocodeinone per 100 milliliters or not more than 15 milligrams per dosage unit, with a fourfold or greater quantity of an isoquinoline alkaloid of opium.

(4) Not more than 300 milligrams of dihydrocodeinone per 100 milliliters or not more than 15 milligrams per dosage unit, with one or more active, nonnarcotic ingredients in recognized therapeutic amounts.

(5) Not more than 1.8 grams of dihydrocodeine per 100 milliliters or not more than 90 milligrams per dosage unit, with one or more active, nonnarcotic ingredients in recognized therapeutic amounts.

(6) Not more than 300 milligrams of ethylmorphine per 100 milliliters or not more than 15 milligrams per dosage unit, with one or more active, nonnarcotic ingredients in recognized therapeutic amounts.

(7) Not more than 500 milligrams of opium per 100 milliliters or per 100 grams, or not more than 25 milligrams per dosage unit, with one or more active, nonnarcotic ingredients in recognized therapeutic amounts.

(8) Not more than 50 milligrams of morphine per 100 milliliters or per 100 grams with one or more active, nonnarcotic ingredients in recognized therapeutic amounts.

(e) Anabolic steroids.

SCHEDULE IV

Barbital.

. . .

Phenobarbital.

SCHEDULE V

Any compound, mixture, or preparation containing any of the following limited quantities of narcotic drugs, which shall include one or more nonnarcotic active medicinal ingredients in sufficient proportion to confer upon the compound, mixture, or preparation valuable medicinal qualities other than those possessed by the narcotic drug alone:

(1) Not more than 200 milligrams of codeine per 100 milliliters or per 100 grams.

(2) Not more than 100 milligrams of dihydrocodeine per 100 milliliters or per 100 grams.

(3) Not more than 100 milligrams of ethylmorphine per 100 milliliters or per 100 grams.

(4) Not more than 2.5 milligrams of diphenoxylate and not less than 25 micrograms of atropine sulfate per dosage unit.

(5) Not more than 100 milligrams of opium per 100 milliliters or per 100 grams

Source: 21 U.S.C. 812.

DRUGS, WAR ON

At the start of the twenty-first century, international drug trafficking was the world's most profitable illicit business, with criminals taking in an estimated $400 to $500 billion annually, according to UN Drug Control Program estimates. Indeed, some experts argued that illegal drugs were the second most valuable internationally traded commodity, legal or illegal, exceeded only by petroleum.

Every year thousands of unfortunate people of all ages and classes die or have their lives ruined because of international drug trafficking. Meanwhile, governments from all parts of the globe spend billions of dollars annually combating the illicit trade. What has come to be known as the War on Drugs, however, is a relatively recent phenomenon. In fact, only since the late nineteenth century have governments been concerned about the harmful effects of illegal drugs.

THE DRUG TRADE BEFORE WORLD WAR II

In the early nineteenth century, governments did not just turn a blind eye to the drug trade—they encouraged it. Beginning in about 1840, Great Britain dominated and the United States participated in lucrative opium trade with China. Trading opium helped the West overcome its traditional trade deficit with China. Concerned about the drug's effect on their society, however, the Chinese laid siege to the port of Canton (now Guangzhou), confiscating and destroying the opium waiting to be unloaded from the foreign ships. The British retaliated by sending an expeditionary force to China and routing the nation's poor military, forcing China to pay $2 million in compensation for the seized opium and another $6 million in punitive damages. By 1856, however, the balance of trade once again favored the Chinese, and a second Opium War was launched. This time, the Americans, Russians, and French aided the English, and after sacking the city of Canton, the alliance demanded even more in payments from the

Chinese to offset the trade imbalance. The British then appointed a committee that legalized and regulated the opium trade with China.

In America, meanwhile, the use of opium, as well as cocaine and marijuana, was both legal and widely prevalent during the late nineteenth century. The opium poppy was grown legally in many states, and doctors prescribed a variety of drugs that are strictly illegal today (such as opium, marijuana, cocaine, and heroin) for the treatment of such ailments as tetanus, dysentery, fever, migraine headaches, and even broken bones.

When cocaine began arriving in the United States in the 1870s, a number of famous personalities hailed it as a "wonder drug." President William McKinley, the inventor Thomas Edison, and a number of other notables enjoyed a drink called Vin Mariani, which consisted of wine mixed with cocaine. In 1898, Bayer Laboratories in Germany introduced heroin as a supposedly nonaddictive substitute for morphine, and doctors began prescribing the drug as a treatment for the worst coughs and chest pains. The American Medical Association endorsed the drug as safe for treating respiratory problems.

In the late nineteenth century, however, easy access to narcotic drugs led to rising incidents of drug abuse, which caused public concern. Sigmund Freud, an early champion of cocaine in medical treatment, began to have second thoughts and warned the public that use of the drug could lead to addiction. By the early 1900s, doctors were abandoning heroin because of concerns that many patients were requiring stronger and stronger doses.

The attitude toward the use of narcotics began to change significantly in 1899, when the United States acquired the Philippines after the Spanish-American war the previous year. The Spanish had allowed local Chinese residents to purchase opium and taxed its sale, but the non-Chinese population had also begun to use the drug to relieve a variety of disorders. The result was a growing problem of drug ad-

CHRONOLOGY

1840 Opium imports to the United States begin to increase significantly; Opium Wars begin.

1865 Morphine administered to soldiers during the Civil War is believed to create an estimated 400,000 addicts.

1875 San Francisco passes first significant U.S. antidrug law; "hashish houses" modeled on opium dens begin to appear.

1880 United States bans smoking of opium by Asian immigrants.

1905 United States bans opium use in Philippines.

1909 Shanghai Congress is held to examine opium trade; U.S. Congress passes Opium Exclusion Act.

1914 U.S. Congress passes Harrison Act, requiring those who sell or distribute narcotics to register with the government.

1919 The League of Nations establishes Committee on Traffic in Opium and Other Dangerous Drugs; League of Nations creates Advisory Committee on Traffic in Opium and Other Dangerous Drugs; United Kingdom passes Dangerous Drug Act.

1925 The Geneva International Opium Convention of 1925 is held.

1937 U.S. Congress passes Marijuana Tax Law, effectively outlawing the drug.

1939 The Convention for the Suppression of the Illicit Traffic in Dangerous Drugs goes into force.

1942 U.S. Congress passes Opium Control Act.

1943 UN Commission on Narcotic Drugs is established.

1956 U.S. Congress passes Narcotics Control Act, substantially increasing the penalties for trafficking in marijuana and heroin.

1961 UN Single Convention on Narcotic Drugs is signed; the document calls for coordinated action against drug cultivation and trafficking, as well as better treatment programs for addicts.

1962 First White House Conference on Narcotics and Drug Abuse is held.

1963 UN Protocol for Limiting and Regulating the Cultivation of the Poppy Plant is passed.

1966 President Lyndon Johnson creates Bureau of Drug Abuse Control (BDAC).

1967 UN Conference on Drug Abuse Control is held to help coordinate international action against drug abuse.

1968 International Narcotics Board of the United Nations is established; U.S. Bureau of Narcotics and Dangerous Drugs is established to coordinate federal law enforcement efforts against illegal drug trafficking and abuse.

1970 U.S. Congress establishes the National Commission on Marijuana and Drug Abuse; the Comprehensive Drug Abuse Prevention and Control Act reduces the penalty for first-time possession of marijuana from a felony to a misdemeanor punishable by less than a year in jail.

1971 UN Convention on Psychotropic Substances is ratified; convention is designed to allow for legal uses of such substances while preventing trafficking and abuse of illegally obtained psychotropic substances.

1972 U.S. Congress passes Drug Abuse and Treatment Act to finance research into drug abuse and treatment by the National Institutes of Health and other federal agencies.

1973 Oregon becomes first state to legalize marijuana; French Connection drug distribution network is smashed.

1974 U.S. Congress enacts Narcotic Addict Treatment Act of 1974, to coordinate federal efforts at providing drug treatment to addicts.

1981 South Florida Task Force is established to coordinate efforts to prevent cocaine smuggling in that state.

1984 Colombian Justice Minister Rodrigo Lara Bonilla is assassinated by drug cartel leaders, and Colombian President Belasario Bentacourt declares "War without Quarter" on the country's drug traffickers; U.S. Army and Transportation Department initiate drug-testing programs.

1985 U.S. Senate approves a bill requiring random drug testing of airline pilots; Nancy Reagan starts Just Say No campaign.

1986	Colombian President Virgilio Barco implements extradition treaty with United States; U.S. Congress passes the Controlled Substance Analogue Act of 1986; U.S. Congress passes Comprehensive Methamphetamine Control Act; Organization of American States (OAS) ratifies Hemisphere antidrug plan.
1987	OAS establishes Inter-American Drug Abuse Commission; United Nations passes UN Convention Against Illicit Traffic in Narcotics Drugs and Psychotropic Substances; William Bennett is appointed first U.S. drug czar; U.S. government issues first National Drug Control Strategy report; U.S. Supreme Court upholds government's right to demand urine tests; the European Committee to Combat Drugs is organized.
1990	Decade Against Drug Abuse (1991–2000) is proclaimed by United Nations; UN International Drug Control Program is established; Colombian drug lord Pablo Escobar is killed; Colombian President Ernesto Samper's presidential campaign is accused of accepting money from Cali Cartel.
1995	Colombia is decertified as a partner in the U.S. war on drug smuggling; Colombian authorities capture Gilberto Rodriguez Orejuela, Cali Cartel kingpin; U.S. Supreme Court upholds legality of drug testing of student athletes in public schools.
1997	Colombia passes extradition law.
2002	Gilberto Rodriguez, Cali Cartel godfather, is released from jail.
2003	UN reports that opium cultivation in Afghanistan is at an all-time high; Gilberto Rodriguez is rearrested on drug trafficking charges.

diction. Concerned American missionaries and clergy in the Philippines petitioned Governor William Taft to investigate the matter, and he organized a commission that concluded the opium trade was one of the most serious problems in the Philippines and East Asia generally. The findings led Congress to ban opium use in the Philippines in 1905.

Developments in the Philippines sparked an international crusade that led to a series of treaties regulating the opium trade. In 1912, the signatories of the International Opium Convention committed themselves to enacting laws that would "suppress the abuse of opium, morphine, cocaine, as well as drugs prepared or derived from these substances." While the United States strongly supported international laws controlling opium, a popular consensus against drug use and abuse was also building at home. In 1914, Congress passed the Harrison Narcotic Act, one of the most important drug laws in U.S. history. The legislation made it mandatory for anyone selling, importing, or dispensing drugs to register with the federal government. Now no one could obtain heroin or cocaine legally without a doctor's prescription. The Harrison Act became the cornerstone of U.S. domestic drug policy for the next 65 years. The legislation, however, excluded marijuana, which was not brought under control until 1937.

The tough U.S. stance reflected the international mood. In the 1920s and 1930s, the League of Nations sponsored several opium treaties that many

countries ratified. As the international community adopted tougher drug control measures, criminal syndicates in the major cities of Asia and the West began to organize the underground traffic in illegal drugs. By the 1920s, heroin had become big business in the United States. A decade later, the Italian Cosa Nostra had joined Jewish organized crime groups in the narcotics trade and was importing opium and heroin from Asia, France, and the Middle East. During World War II, however, the problem of international drug trafficking was put on hold, as the United States and its allies concentrated their resources and attention on defeating the Axis powers. U.S. forces even worked with the Cosa Nostra during the invasion of Sicily in 1943.

THE DRUG TRADE AFTER WORLD WAR II

With the defeat of the Axis powers in 1945, international attention once again focused on drug trafficking, and the newly formed United Nations took over the drug-control function of the defunct League of Nations. Meanwhile, the Federal Bureau of Narcotics (FBN), the chief U.S. antidrug agency at the time, expanded its operations to Europe and the Middle East.

In the immediate postwar period, a few key events helped further the expansion of international drug trafficking. In 1948 the Chinese Revolution deposed General Chiang Kai-shek and brought the communist leader Mao Tse-tung to power, forcing Chiang Kai-shek's Fifth Kuomintang Army (KMT) to flee China, crossing the border into Burma (now Myanmar). The KMT quickly got involved in the local heroin trade to obtain arms and other matériel, helping turn the Golden Triangle in southern China and Southeast Asia into one of world's biggest producers of opium.

During the war, drug traffickers had a difficult time smuggling heroin into the United States; without access to the drug, many addicts were forced to withdraw. The FBN estimated there were no more than 20,000 addicts in the entire country at the time—a meager 0.13 percent of the entire population.

The addiction rate changed dramatically after the war, however, when U.S. authorities deported Cosa Nostra leader Charles "Lucky" Luciano to Italy in 1945. Luciano had been serving an extended prison term for crimes relating to extortion and prostitution, but the government granted the mobster's release for reported "services" on behalf of the U.S. war effort—though it never fully explained the nature of his services. In any event, Luciano's deportation was to have a major impact on the growth of international drug trafficking.

The organized crime leader already had much experience in the heroin trade. In the 1930s, he and other mob figures had imported the drug to get their prostitutes addicted and dependent on them for more. After his release in 1945, Luciano quickly took control of the local Mafia in Italy and developed a plan of action to ship heroin into the United States and Europe. His organization began buying raw opium from the poppy fields in Turkey, Lebanon, and other Middle Eastern countries, setting up heroin processing labs in Sicily, and developing a sophisticated drug-smuggling network. By 1952 the FBN had revised its estimate of the number of addicts in the United States, putting the figure at three times the prewar level.

By the early 1950s, Luciano's crime syndicate had a system in which supplies of morphine base were refined into heroin in Marseilles, shipped to Montreal or Sicily, and then sent directly to the United States, the world's biggest market for the illegal drug. This arrangement became known as the French Connection, and it allowed the Mafia to dominate the heroin trade from the 1950s into the early 1970s. At its peak, the French Connection smuggled an estimated 95 percent of the heroin distributed in the United States. *Newsweek* magazine had declared the drug issue dead in 1946, but 3 years later it was publishing articles about heroin use among young people in urban areas, warning that the youngsters were "turning their arms and legs into pin cushions."

By the end of the 1950s, statistics once again showed an apparent decline in drug abuse, and governments became smug in their belief that they had the problem under control. That attitude changed radically in the 1960s, when illicit drug use exploded in the United States and Western Europe. Opiates, more than any other narcotic substance, had dominated the attention of the U.S. antidrug movement during the first half of the twentieth century, but that focus also changed in the 1960s, as the demand for heroin, marijuana, and cocaine transformed the international drug trade. Americans from all walks of life began experimenting with a variety of illegal drugs and using them regularly for recreation.

The enormous appetite for illegal drugs during this politically turbulent and culturally transformative decade created the conditions that allowed international drug trafficking to expand and flourish. Widespread marijuana use helped to make drug trafficking a booming multibillion-dollar business, while heroin use was once again on the rise, especially in the United States. Between 1960 and 1970 the number of heroin users in the United States rose from 40,000 to 500,000. Among them were many GIs who had become addicted while serving in Vietnam. By 1971 an estimated 25,000 to 37,000 American soldiers in Vietnam were using heroin; about 14 percent were believed to be addicted to the drug. Heroin traffic in Southeast Asia centered in the Golden Triangle, an area of rugged terrain spanning parts of Laos, Thailand, and Burma that by the late 1990s, according to the DEA, supplied 70 percent of the world's heroin and opium. That changed with the fall of the Taliban government to U.S. forces in late 2002. Since that time, the various warlords who control much of the countryside have ramped up opium production. By early 2005, according to the UN, Afghanistan was producing roughly 90 percent of the world's opium crop.

Until the 1960s, the cost of cocaine was such that it became known as the "champagne of drugs." Nevertheless, it became increasingly popular during the course of the decade, and traffickers were able to increase the supply by persuading coca growers in Latin America to plant more leaves. This, in turn, spawned powerful organization such as the Medellín and Cali Cartels, named after the Colombian cities in which they were based. As the supply of cocaine increased, its price decreased, and the drug became more affordable for more people. By the early 1970s, cocaine had become the drug of choice for literally millions of Americans, and the United States had a new epidemic on its hands.

The U.S. government under the leadership of President Richard Nixon adopted several measures to deal with the growing drug problem. At the international level, Nixon summoned his ambassadors to France, Turkey, and Mexico and told them to help their foreign counterparts move more aggressively against international drug trafficking. He also signed the 1971 Convention on Psychotropic Substances, which extended existing international policing, information-sharing, and enforcement measures to hallucinogens, amphetamines, barbiturates, and tranquillizers not previously covered by international drug treaties.

The Gerald Ford administration continued the interdiction strategy Nixon had begun, but the federal antidrug policy underwent a sea change after President Jimmy Carter took office in 1977. In March 1977, the U.S. House of Representatives held hearings on the decriminalization of marijuana, and incoming Attorney General Griffin Bell testified that the government could no longer effectively prosecute use of the drug. The administration also softened its position on cocaine, which Dr. Peter Bourne, the president's director of the Office of Drug Abuse Policy (ODAP), described as "probably the most benign of illicit drugs currently in widespread use."

REAGAN ADMINISTRATION

The inauguration of President Ronald Reagan in January 1981 led to another about-face in U.S. drug policy, resuming a hard-line antidrug agenda. In launching his "War on Drugs," Reagan reorganized the chain of command and ordered an impressive array of military hardware, intelligence, and other resources to south Florida and the frontline of the campaign. It was not a unilateral decision. Congress strongly supported the administration's efforts, and a variety of legislative sources, including the powerful House Foreign Affairs Committee, called for a tougher stance on drugs smugglers and dealers.

By the end of Reagan's first term in 1984, U.S. authorities were seizing more illegal drugs than ever before, according to DEA statistics. In 1984 law enforcement confiscated a reported 27,525 pounds of cocaine and 664 pounds of heroin, compared to 1,438 pounds of cocaine and 123 pounds of heroin in 1979—twentyfold and fivefold increases, respec-

Table 1. Arrests by the U.S. Drug Enforcement Administration, 1986–2002

Calendar year	Number of arrests
2002	27,635
2001	33,539
2000	38,957
1999	39,500
1998	37,762
1997	33,628
1996	28,922
1995	24,931
1994	22,858
1993	21,432
1992	24,219
1991	23,396
1990	22,611
1989	24,881
1988	24,728
1987	22,543
1986	19,693
Total	443,600

Source: Drug Enforcement Administration.

tively, in 5 years. The statistics looked impressive, but U.S. Customs officials admitted they were confiscating only about 15 percent of the drugs pouring into the United States.

During the Reagan administration, the focus of the War on Drugs shifted from heroin to cocaine and marijuana—the drugs the administration believed Americans were using the most—and the interdiction of drugs in Latin America became its major priority. By the mid-1980s, however, the United States and eventually Europe had to deal with another dangerous drug. Crack, the most potent, most addictive, and by far the cheapest form of cocaine, had begun appearing in Miami, Los Angeles, and New York and was spreading to inner cities across America. The result was gang warfare among drug dealers determined to protect their turf in the lucrative drug trade. Violent crime rates soared.

This new development heightened the public's concern about the impact of illegal drugs, and President Reagan responded by increasing the funding for the drug war from $1.5 billion in 1981 to $2.75 billion in 1986. He signed the Anti Drug Abuse Act of 1986, which authorized $1.7 billion in additional money to fight drug abuse and provided for stiff prison sentences for drug dealers who sold drugs near schools or recruited young people to peddle them.

Table 2. Drug Seizures by the U.S. Drug Enforcement Administration, 1986–2002

Year	Cocaine (kg)	Heroin (kg)	Marijuana (kg)	Methamphetamine (dosage units)	Hallucinogens (dosage units)
2002	61,594	705	195,644	118,049,279	11,532,704
2001	59,426	752	271,785	124,532,740	13,756,939
2000	58,627	546	331,964	129,622,961	29,306,453
1999	36,167	351	337,832	76,621,124	1,716,954
1998	34,448	371	262,176	62,907,212	1,075,257
1997	28,630	399	215,348	116,143,493	1,100,912
1996	44,765	320	190,453	74,648,735	1,719,096
1995	45,326	876	219,830	139,540,464	2,768,165
1994	75,051	491	157,182	139,500,284	1,366,817
1993	55,158	616	143,030	92,608,266	2,710,063
1992	69,323	722	201,507	48,498,483	1,305,177
1991	67,016	1,170	98,601	21,882,289	1,295,874
1990	57,031	532	127,694	46,358,120	2,826,966
1989	73,592	758	286,167	174,849,333	13,125,010
1988	60,826	730	347,306	108,919,418	16,706,442
1987	49,668	512	629,892	24,179,401	6,556,884
1986	30,333	371	599,166	32,602,774	4,146,224

Source: Drug Enforcement Administration.

As the United States intensified its antidrug effort at home, the War on Drugs heated up overseas as well. During the 1970s, drug traffickers had operated throughout Colombia without much interference from local authorities, but by 1984 the Colombian government was under pressure from the United States to change its laissez-faire ways and begin to get tough on the traffickers. Justice Minister Rodrigo Lara Bonilla authorized a spectacular raid on a major cocaine processing plant known as Tranquilandia, located in the desolate southeast Llanos region of the Amazon. The surprise raid resulted in the arrest of forty workers, the seizure of 10,000 barrels of chemicals, and the confiscation of over $1 billion in cocaine. But the raid caused considerable anger in the powerful Medellín Cartel, and its godfather, Pablo Escobar, had Lara Bonilla assassinated in 1984. Colombian President Belasario Betancour Cuertas declared "a war without quarter" on all Colombian drug traffickers in the early 1980s. The battle between the Colombian government and the country's powerful drug traffickers led to the era of so-called narcoterrorism in Colombia that extended through the late 1980s and into the early 1990s. Hundreds of politicians, judges, police journalists, and ordinary citizens were killed in the violence and mayhem.

The militarization of the War on Drugs begun under President Reagan continued under Presidents George H.W. Bush and Bill Clinton. The United States and its allies in the war could claim a number of high-profile successes. In 1987, Colombian authorities captured cartel godfather Carlos Lehder and then extradited him to the United States, where he is currently serving a life term in prison. In 1989, the United States invaded Panama and captured General Manuel Antonio Noriega, who had been indicted in a U.S. federal court for alleged participation in international drug trafficking; the former Panamanian leader is now also serving an extended term in a U.S prison. In December 1992, Pablo Escobar was killed after one of the biggest manhunts in the annals of international law enforcement. In 1995 the brothers Gilberto and Miguel Rodriguez Orejuela, leaders of Colombia's Cali Cartel, were captured. And later in the decade, the legendary Golden Triangle heroin drug trafficker Khu Sa of Burma retired from the trade.

Despite the aggressiveness and successes of the War on Drugs, international trafficking continued to grow. Two important events in the early 1990s dramatically increased the potential for expanding the drug trade, especially to Europe. The first was the collapse of the Communist bloc and the dissolution of the Soviet Union in December 1991. The second was the lowering of trade barriers and border restrictions among members of the European Community (now the European Union) in accordance with the terms of the Single Europe Act of 1987. After the fall of the Berlin Wall in 1989, the first links between East and West were those established by organized crime syndicates. Major crime groups, such as the Russian Mafia, the Colombian drug cartels, and the Italian Mafia began holding summits in the early 1990s to see how they could better cooperate to further their criminal interests.

Law enforcement expressed concerns about developments in Russia and Eastern Europe after the fall of communism. In testimony before Congress on May 25, 1994, Hans Ludwig Zachert, president of the German Criminal Police, noted the growing significance of Eastern Europe in international cocaine trafficking. "The traffickers come . . . taking advantage of the political process and fundamental economic restructuring in order to transport drugs to Western Europe, circumventing the former transit routes and transit countries," he said. "At the same time that these Eastern European states are increasingly being used as transit countries for drug deliveries to Western Europe, the consumption of all kinds of drugs in these countries has risen considerably."

The proof of Russia's and Eastern Europe's growing involvement as trans-shipment centers for illegal drugs was evident in the type and amount of cocaine seizures in the region. On February 21, 1993, for example, some 1,092 kilograms of cocaine were seized and seven people arrested near St. Petersburg, Russia. In September and October 1991, Czechoslovakian and Polish authorities seized two 100-kilogram loads of cocaine hidden in beer shipments. The following year, Russian officials announced the seizure of 4.6 kilograms of cocaine. A year later, the amount seized had increased to 1,000 kilograms. There seemed to be no limits to the level of international criminal cooperation. European traffickers were even traveling to Colombia to exchange information with local traffickers on methods of refining and producing heroin.

CHANGING NATURE OF DRUG TRAFFICKING

By the turn of the century, the War on Drugs had many critics calling for more creative approaches to the drug problem. The dissenters came from across the political spectrum and a variety of backgrounds, including such notable personalities as economist Milton Friedman, the conservative commentator William F. Buckley, former Baltimore Mayor Kurt Schmoke, the editors of the influential British news magazine *The Economist*, and former Colombian Pros-

ecuting Attorney General Gustavo de Greiff. Each criticized different aspects of the War on Drugs, but all agreed it was expensive, it diverted resources from treatment and domestic crime prevention, it was ineffectual—drug use was not going down—and it was a destabilizing factor in many drug-producing developing countries. Meanwhile, it was also becoming apparent to many of America's allies in the War on Drugs that ground was being lost: neither the quantity of smuggled drugs nor the number of drug users was declining appreciably. They started to call for a global effort to combat international drug trafficking.

By the late 1990s, the nature of international drug trafficking had changed dramatically, as the drug traffickers learned well from the past. One of the big lessons they had learned was that criminal organizations that became too big and complex were more vulnerable to a law enforcement takedown. As a result, a radically different type of drug trafficking organization exists today. Gone is the huge drug trafficking organization represented by the Medellín and Cali Cartels, which employed thousands, had the global reach of a multinational corporation, smuggled large-scale shipments of drugs to the United States and earned Fortune 500-like revenues reaching $7 billion annually. These traffickers have been replaced by the so-called *cartelitos*, or baby cartels, of Colombia, Mexico, and other Latin American countries, which try to operate discretely but do not rely on the sophisticated organizational structure and communications systems of the cartels.

The *cartelitos* have changed the modus operandi. In the days of the big cartels, drug traffickers relied on the cell phone to manage their day-to-day business activities. Today's drug traffickers use the Internet as the primary means of communication. They sell directly to the Mexicans so the United States won't be able to make extradition cases against them, no matter where the cocaine ends up. They prefer face-to-face meetings, which makes it more difficult for law enforcement authorities to tap their communications.

Yet the downsizing has not diminished the international flow of illegal drugs. Though the U.S. government provided billions of dollars in aid to Colombia during the 1990s, for example, it still became the premier coca-cultivating—as opposed to coca-processing—country in the world, growing more coca leaf than Peru and Bolivia combined.

The drug traffickers have not only downsized, they have also diversified. For example, cocaine is not the only drug trafficked from Colombia today. As early as 1995, Colombia became the largest producer of poppy in the Western Hemisphere, producing a third more of the crop than Mexico. By 1999, 85 percent of the heroin seized by federal authorities in the Northeast United States originated in Colombia. Meanwhile, law enforcement officials are increasingly concerned about the growing role of Colombia in the trafficking of the popular drug ecstasy, especially to European markets. Putting the Colombian cartels out of business caused only minor disruptions in the flow of illicit drugs from Colombia to the U.S. and European markets.

One could easily assume that, because of their small size, the *cartelitos* have more difficulty moving their product to market than the large cartels did. That assumption is wrong. Their use of the Internet, cell phones, and other anonymous means of communications and the strategic alliances they have built around the world have helped them thrive. As late as the fall of 1997, Interpol reported the Cali Cartel had forged alliances with the Russian mafia, which was supplying it with military equipment, including MK-47 rifles and grenades and helicopters, in exchange for cocaine. In a predawn raid on a warehouse in Bogotá on September 7, 2000, Colombian police were shocked to find a 100-foot submarine under construction. A joint project of the Colombian drug traffickers and the Russian mob, the plan was to use the submarine to smuggle tons of narcotics out of Colombia.

According to the *Los Angeles Times*, the discovery of the submarine was the first solid evidence of a close partnership between Colombia's new smaller cartels and the Russian mob. Intelligence analysts report, however, that Colombian drug traffickers had held summit meetings with Russian, Chinese, Japanese, and Russian criminal groups at least three times between 1994 and 1998 to discuss ways to coordinate smuggling, marketing, and distributing of illicit drug shipments.

In another important international development, the Colombian drug traffickers have been willing to cede more control and responsibility to Mexican drug traffickers for smuggling drugs to its biggest market, the United States. This trend began during the Medellín and Cali Cartel era of the early 1990s, when law enforcement disrupted the cartels' distribution routes through the Caribbean, and they turned to their Mexican colleagues to help move the drugs. Today, Mexicans no longer merely transport cocaine across the Colombian-Mexican border for the Co-

lombians for a fee. They now move the drugs to the point of sale, and, in return, receive a commission from their Colombian suppliers.

GLOBALIZATION AND THE DRUG TRADE

The North American Free Trade Agreement (NAFTA) of 1994 has made it easier for Mexicans to move drugs across the U.S.-Mexico border. Ironically, perhaps, the trend toward globalization in finance and trade has spurred the growth of international drug trafficking.

With the creation and growth of free-trade organizations such as NAFTA and the European Community, national borders have declined in importance and customs and security safeguards were reduced—trends that the events of September 11 have not entirely reversed. This made it easier for international organized crime to move into new markets, distribute illegal goods and services, and shift their profits to countries around the world, eager to serve as safe havens for cash deposits and the laundering of drug money. It is no wonder that some DEA and customs agents working the U.S.-Mexican border have jokingly referred to NAFTA as the North American Free Drug Trafficking Agreement.

Adding to the difficulties of stopping drug traffickers is the sheer volume of immigration, legal and illegal, in recent years. Millions of people from all parts of the world continue to arrive in the United States searching for a better life or trying to escape ethnic or political conflict. With them come criminals seeking to exploit immigrant communities for illegal means and use them as a base for their criminal activities.

These developments suggest that the current strategy in the War in Drugs—focusing on single targets—may ignore the reality that when one drug trafficking organization is dismantled, another fills the void. The truth of the observation that as long as there is a demand for an illegal product, criminals will try to market it is well illustrated by the rise and fall of the Colombian cartels. But while governments may not be able to stop drugs from reaching the marketplace, many experts argue they can develop a more effective strategy that makes this more difficult. For starters, say experts, the United States and its allies in the War on Drugs can take a lesson from the criminals' tactics and make a more concerted effort to establish effective strategic alliances. Countries can develop partnerships to deal with what is an international problem and with its root causes, by providing alternatives to farmers and others in Third World countries for whom the drug trade is the only lifeline.

Colombia is a telling example of how enterprising groups, traditional criminal or otherwise, will always be willing to enter a lucrative market such as illegal drugs if the opportunity presents itself. The guerrillas and paramilitaries in Colombia, such as the Revolutionary Armed Forces of Colombia (FARC, its Spanish acronym) on the left and the United Self-Defense Forces of Colombia (AUC) on the right, have expanded their roles in the drug trade and helped fill the void created by the takedown of the major cartels. Guerrillas are involved in the Colombian drug trade, mainly in protecting drug traffickers' crops, labs, and airfields for a fee and taxing peasants who grow crops in areas under their control. By the year 2000, the guerrillas' total annual take from the drug trade was estimated as high as $400 million.

The 10,000-strong paramilitary group AUC has also financed its operations through the drug trade. In January 2000, paramilitary leader Carlos Castano admitted on Colombian television that his organization routinely charges a tax on the coca and poppy crops that Colombians farmers grow. Fueled by the drug trade, the brutal struggle between guerrillas and paramilitaries has contributed to at least 3,500 murders annually in Colombia.

The U.S. government indicted the leaders of FARC and the AUC in 2002 on drug trafficking charges, while putting their organizations on its official list of terrorist organizations. In its pursuit of the War on Terrorism after the events of September 11, 2001, the government has downgraded the War on Drugs as a priority but linked it to the War on Terrorism. In August 2002, the Office of National Drug Control Policy began running advertisements urging Americans to stop buying illegal drugs like cocaine and heroin, which they claim helps fund the terrorists trying to destroy America. "If you quit drugs, you join the fight against terror in America," President George W. Bush declared.

The focus on the global War on Terrorism leaves uncertain the future direction of the War on Drugs. There is concern, though, that a connection exists between the two. In 2000, the Taliban rulers of Afghanistan banned the growing of poppy, a move that garnered much praise from the United Nations Drug Control Program. Statistics show that during the Taliban era, poppy production dropped from 90,583 hectares in 1999 to 82,171 in 2000 and just 7,600 in 2001. After the ouster of the Taliban in 2001, however, poppy cultivation began to increase dramatically, and Afghanistan once again became the world's leading producer of that crop. Since the September 11 attacks, the U.S. government has claimed that al Qaeda supports its terrorist activities through heroin trafficking.

CONCLUSION

Although most experts agree there is still a long way to go, the world community believes it has made some progress in fighting the international narcotics trade since President Ronald Reagan declared the War on Drugs in 1982. Skeptics contend there is little to show for the policy initiatives, political efforts, and billions of dollars spent on the effort. The fact is that a century after the worldwide antidrug movement began, international drug trafficking remains both vast and complex, with a myriad criminal factions working together in the relentless pursuit of fabulous riches and power. For the Drug War to become more effective, most experts believe far more cooperation is needed among the more than 100 countries around the world connected in some way to international drug trafficking.

Ron Chepesiuk

REFERENCES

Baum, Dan. *Smoke and Mirrors: The War on Drugs and Policy of Failure.* Boston: Little, Brown, 1996.

Bowden, Mark. *Killing Pablo.* Boston: Atlantic Monthly Press, 2002.

Bugliosi, Vincent. *The Phoenix Solution.* New York: Star Press, 1996.

Crandall, Russell. *Driven by Drugs: U.S. Policy Toward Colombia.* Boulder, CO: Lynne Rienner, 2002.

Chepesiuk, Ron. *Hard Target: The U.S. War on International Drug Trafficking, 1982–1997.* Jefferson, NC: McFarland, 1997.

Cooper, Mary H. *The Business of Drugs.* Washington, DC: Congressional Quarterly, 1990.

Ehrenfeld, Rachel. *Narco-Terrorism.* New York: Basic Books, 1990.

Falco, Mathew. *Re-thinking International Drug Control: New Directions for Foreign Policy.* New York: Council on Foreign Relations, 1997.

Friman, H. Richard. *Narco Diplomacy: Exporting the U.S. War on Drugs.* Ithaca, NY: Cornell University Press, 1996.

Grosse, Robert E. *Drugs and Money: Laundering Latin America's Cocaine Dollars.* Westport, CT: Praeger, 2001.

Gugliotta, Guy, and Jeff Leen. *The Kings of Cocaine.* New York: Simon and Schuster, 1989.

Lee, Rennselaer. *White Labyrinth: Cocaine and Political Power.* Brunswick, NJ: Transaction, 1989.

Mills, James. *The Underground Empire: Where Crime and Justice Embrace.* New York: Doubleday, 1986.

Poppa, Terrance E. *The Life and Death of a Mexican Kingpin.* Seattle: Demand, 1998.

Riley, Kevin Jack. *Snow Job?: The War Against International Cocaine Trafficking.* New Brunswick, NJ: Transaction, 1996.

Simon, David, and Edward Burns. *A Year in the Life of an Inner City Neighborhood.* New York: Broadway Books, 1998.

Sterling, Claire. *Octopus: The Long Reach of the Sicilian Mafia.* New York: Norton, 1991.

Streitfeld, Dominic. *Cocaine: An Unauthorized Biography.* New York: St. Martin's, 2002.

Strong, Simon. *Whitewash: Pablo Escobar and the Cocaine Wars.* New York: Macmillan, 1995.

U.S. Congress. House. Select Committee on Narcotics Abuse and Control, Hearings. 95th Cong., 1st sess., April 9–23, 1977.

U.S. General Accounting Office. "Money Laundering: The U.S. Government Response to the Problem." Washington, DC: U.S. Government Printing Office, 1991.

WEB SITES

Drug Library: www.druglibrary.org
Drug Policy Alliance: www.drugpolicy.org
Narco News Bulletin: www.narconews.com
Observatoire Geopolitique Des Drogues: www.ogd.org
United Nations Drug Control Program: www.undcp.un
U.S. Drug Enforcement Agency: www.dea.gov
U.S. Office of National Drug Control Policy: www.whitehousedrugpolicy.org

GLOSSARY

Cartelitos. Spanish for "baby cartels," the smaller organizations that replaced the cartels after the latter were broken by Colombian authorities in the late 1980s.

Cartels. During the 1970s and 1980s, cartels, or major drug production and smuggling rings, were based in the Colombian cities of Cali and Medellín.

French Connection. A mid-twentieth-century heroin ring that funneled illegal drugs into the United States through the French port of Marseilles.

Golden Triangle. A region of Southeast Asia where much of the world's heroin was grown in the second half of the twentieth century.

Heroin. A synthetic form of the painkilling drug morphine.

Morphine. A painkilling drug derived from the opium poppy.

Narcoterrorism. A drug cartel–led campaign of assassination, kidnapping, and other violent crimes designed to intimidate Colombian authorities in the latter's war against the cartels.

Opium Wars. Mid-nineteenth-century wars between China and Britain; China wanted to close its borders to opium while Britain wanted to sell the drug there.

Psychotropic drugs. Drugs that alter a person's ability to perceive reality; their use is often accompanied by hallucinations.

War on Drugs. A term first used by the administration of President Richard Nixon in 1971 to describe coordinated governmental efforts to combat the smuggling, production, sales, and abuse of illegal drugs.

DOCUMENTS

Document 1. Narcotic Control Act of 1956

Public concern about illegal drug use was rising during the 1950s, a result of a media focus on the link between drug trafficking and organized crime. In early 1956, a special subcommittee of the Judiciary Committee was organized under Senator Price Daniel (D-TX) to investigate the problem of trafficking, sale, and abuse of marijuana and narcotics. Out of these hearings came the Narcotic Control Act of 1956, which substantially increased the penalties for selling or smuggling illegal drugs such as marijuana and heroin.

Sec. 7237. VIOLATION OF LAWS RELATING TO NARCOTIC RINGS AND TO MARIHUANA.

(a) ... Whoever commits an offense, or conspires to commit an offense, described in part I or part II of subchapter A of chapter 39 for which no specific penalty is otherwise provided, shall be imprisoned not less than 2 or more than 10 years and, in addition, may be fined not more than $20,000. For a second offense, the offender shall be imprisoned not less than 5 or more than 20 years and, in addition, may be fined not more than $20,000. For a third or subsequent offense, the offender shall be imprisoned not less than 10 or more than 40 years and, in addition, may be fined not more than $20,000.

(b) ... Whoever commits an offense, or conspires to commit an offense, ... shall be imprisoned not less than 5 or more than 20 years and, in addition, may be fined not more than $20,000. For a second or subsequent offense, the offender shall be imprisoned not less than 10 or more than 40 years and, in addition, may be fined not more than $20,000. If the offender attained the age of 18 before the offense and—

(1) the offense consisted of the sale, barter, exchange, giving away, or transfer of any narcotic drug or marihuana to a person who had not attained the age of 18 at the time of such offense, or

(2) the offense consisted of a conspiracy to commit an offense described in paragraph (1), the offender shall be imprisoned not less than 10 or more than 40 years and, in addition, may be fined not more than $20,000.

Sec. 7607. ADDITIONAL AUTHORITY FOR BUREAU OF NARCOTICS AND BUREAU OF CUSTOMS.

The Commissioner, Deputy Commissioner, Assistant to the Commissioner, and agents, of the Bureau of Narcotics of the Department of the Treasury, and officers of the customs . . . may—

(1) carry firearms, execute and serve search warrants and arrest warrants, and serve subpoenas and summonses issued under the authority of the United States, and

(2) make arrests without warrant for violations of any law of the United States relating to narcotic drugs . . . or marihuana . . . where the violation is committed in the presence of the person making the arrest or where such person has reasonable grounds to believe that the person to be arrested has committed or is committing such violation.

Sec. 107. SALE OF HEROIN TO JUVENILES—PENALTIES.

Section 2 of the Narcotic Drugs Import and Export Act, as amended, is further amended by adding at the end thereof the following:

(1) Not withstanding any other provision of law, whoever, having attained the age of eighteen years, knowingly sells, gives away, furnishes, or dispenses, facilitates the sale, giving, furnishing, or dispensing, or conspires to sell, give away, furnish, or dispense, any heroin unlawfully imported or otherwise brought into the United States, to any person who has not attained the age of eighteen years, may be fined not more than $20,000, shall be imprisoned for life, or for not less than ten years, except that the offender shall suffer death if the jury in its discretion shall so direct.

Sec. 1407. BORDER CROSSINGS—NARCOTIC ADDICTS AND VIOLATORS.

(a) In order further to give effect to the obligations of the United States pursuant to the Hague convention of 1912, proclaimed as a treaty on March 3, 1915, and the limitation convention of 1931, proclaimed as a treaty on July 10, 1933, and in order to facilitate more effective control of the international traffic in narcotic drugs, and to prevent the spread of drug addiction, no citizen of the United States who is addicted to or uses narcotic drugs . . . (except a person using such narcotic drugs as a result of sickness or accident or injury and to whom such narcotic drug is being furnished, prescribed, or administered in good faith by a duly licensed physician in attendance upon such person, in the course of his professional practice) or who has been convicted of a violation of any of the narcotic or marihuana laws of the United States, or of any State thereof, the penalty for which is imprisonment for more than one year, shall depart from or enter into or attempt to depart from or enter into the United States, unless such person registers, under such rules and regulations as may be prescribed by the Secretary of the Treasury with a customs official, agent, or employee at a point of entry or a border customs station. Unless otherwise prohibited by law or Federal regulation such customs official, agent or employee shall issue a certificate to any such person departing from the United States; and such person shall, upon returning to the United States, surrender such certificate to the customs official, agent, or employee present at the port of entry or border customs station.

(b) Whoever violates any of the provisions of this section shall be punished for each such violation by a fine of not more than $1,000 or imprisonment for not less than one nor more than three years, or both.

Source: Public Law 84–728 (Narcotic Control Act), July 18, 1956.

Document 2. Drug-Free America Policy, Subtitle F, 1995

During the 1980s and 1990s, federal and state governments took an increasingly tough position against the sale, possession, and use of illegal drugs. The goal of the government became nothing less than the complete elimination of illicit drugs from American life. The following is a set of findings by Congress in a 1995 federal law that increased the penalties for involvement with illegal drugs.

SEC. 5251. UNITED STATES POLICY FOR A DRUG-FREE AMERICA BY 1995.
21 USC 1502

(a) FINDINGS.—The Congress finds that—note.

(1) approximately 37 million Americans used an illegal drug in the past year and more than 23 million Americans use illicit drugs at least monthly, including more than 6 million who use cocaine;

(2) half of all high school seniors have used illegal drugs at least once, and over 25 percent use drugs at least monthly;

(3) illicit drug use adds enormously to the national cost of health care and rehabilitation services;

(4) illegal drug use can result in a wide spectrum of extremely serious health problems, including disruption of normal heart rhythm, small lesions of the heart, high blood pressure, leaks of blood vessels in the brain, bleeding and destruction of brain cells, permanent memory loss, infertility, impotency, immune system impairment, kidney failure, and pulmonary damage, and in the most serious instances, heart attack, stroke, and sudden death;

(5) approximately 25 percent of all victims of AIDS acquired the disease through intravenous drug use;

(6) over 30,000 people were admitted to emergency rooms in 1986 with drug-related health problems, including nearly 10,000 for cocaine alone;

(7) there is a strong link between teenage suicide and use of illegal drugs;

(8) 10 to 15 percent of all highway fatalities involve drug use;

(9) illegal drug use is prevalent in the workplace and endangers fellow workers, national security, public safety, company morale, and production;

(10) it is estimated that 1 of every 10 American workers have their productivity impaired by substance abuse;

(11) it is estimated that drug users are 3 times as likely to be involved in on-the-job accidents, are absent from work twice as often, and incur 3 times the average level of sickness costs as non-users;

(12) the total cost to the economy of drug use is estimated to be over $100,000,000,000 annually;

(13) the connection between drugs and crime is also well-proven;

(14) the use of illicit drugs affects moods and emotions, chemically alters the brain, and causes loss of control, paranoia, reduction of inhibition, and unprovoked anger;

(15) drug-related homicides are increasing dramatically across the Nation;

(16) 8 of 10 men arrested for serious crimes in New York City test positive for cocaine use;

(17) illicit drug use is responsible for a substantially higher tax rate to pay for local enforcement protection, interdiction, border control, and the cost of investigation, prosecution, confinement and treatment;

(18) substantial increases in funding and resources have been made available in recent years to combat the drug problem, with spending for interdiction, law enforcement, and prevention programs up by 100 to 400 percent and these programs are producing results—

(A) seizures of cocaine are up from 1.7 tons in 1981 to 70 tons in 1987;

(B) seizures of heroin are up from 460 pounds in 1981 to 1,400 pounds in 1987;

(C) Drug Enforcement Administration drug convictions doubled between 1982 and 1986; and

(D) the average sentence for Federal cocaine convictions rose by 35 percent during this same period;

(19) despite the impressive rise in law enforcement efforts, the supply of illegal drugs has increased in recent years;

(20) the demand for drugs creates and sustains the illegal drug trade and;

(21) winning the drug war not only requires that we do more to limit supply, but that we focus our efforts to reduce demand.

(b) DECLARATION.—It is the declared policy of the United States Government to create a Drug-Free America by 1995.

Source: 102 Stat. 4310, Public Law 100–690.

EATING DISORDERS

ating disorders are complex, chronic illnesses that are poorly understood and often misdiagnosed. Approximately 8 million people in the United States—90 percent of them adolescent and young adult women—suffer from eating disorders, according to the National Association of Anorexia Nervosa and Associated Disorders. The three most common eating disorders—anorexia nervosa, bulimia nervosa, and binge-eating disorder—are all on the rise in the United States and worldwide.

The American Anorexia and Bulimia Association (AA/BA) estimates that 1 million women develop eating disorders every year. Adolescent and young adult females appear to be particularly vulnerable because of their tendency to go on strict diets to achieve an "ideal" figure. Researchers have found dieting to be a risk factor for triggering eating disorders. The consequences of eating disorders can be severe: one in ten cases of anorexia nervosa leads to death from starvation, cardiac arrest, or suicide—making it one of the nation's leading causes of mortality.

Although no exact cause of eating disorders has been found, most experts believe it takes multiple factors to set the behaviors in motion. Among these are personality, biological makeup, and sociocultural factors (e.g., family, peer pressures, and media). Specific neurochemical factors may also be important in the etiology of eating disorders, as is stress. Changing demographic factors that contribute to stress include increases in the number of dual-career families and the divorce rate, both of which challenge the development of a strong personal identity and sense of competence in young people. Eating disorders often emerge during a period of change in a woman's life, such as mid-adolescence and young adulthood, indicating difficulty dealing with these transitions. All socioeconomic, ethnic, and cultural groups are at risk for eating disorders.

The tragic death of pop singer Karen Carpenter in 1983 due to heart failure associated with prolonged starvation and years of suffering with anorexia nervosa increased public awareness of the potentially fatal consequences of eating disorders.

Although anorexia nervosa, bulimia nervosa, and binge-eating disorders are the most common eating disorders, there are several lesser-known forms. Some of these disorders have existed for decades and are considered formal diagnoses, while others need continued research and clinical evaluation to be fully recognized as medical diagnoses. Among these are muscle dysmorphia, nocturnal sleep-related eating disorder, pica, gourmand syndrome, Prader-Willi syndrome, cyclic-vomiting syndrome, and obesity. Simple obesity is included as a general medical condition in the International Classification of Diseases (ICD) but does not appear in the Diagnostic and Statistical Manual of Mental Disorders (DSM-IV). Disorders of feeding and eating are usually first diagnosed in infancy or early childhood (i.e., pica, rumination disorder, and feeding disorder of infancy and early childhood). This essay focuses on anorexia nervosa, bulimia nervosa, and binge-eating disorder.

Figure 1. Age of Onset of Eating Disorders, 2004

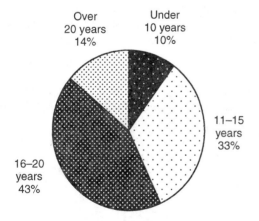

Source: Adapted from the National Association of Anorexia Nervosa and Associated Disorders Web site, www.anad.org.

CHRONOLOGY

1694   Dr. Richard Morton is credited as the first to identify anorexia nervosa, which he refers to as a form of "nervous consumption" caused by "sadness and anxious cares."

1821   The use of the tape measure and manufacture of ready-made clothes allows regulation of the posture of American men and women.

1859   Medical doctor William Stout Chipley publishes the first American description of sitomania, characterized by "insane dread of food." Chipley pushes for these patients to be institutionalized for medical supervision.

1865   Robley Dunglison's medical dictionary defines anorexia as *absence of appetite*: "Anorexia is a simple and obvious sign of disease or general medical condition" (not a disease or disorder in itself).

1868   Physician William Withey Gull first conceives of anorexia nervosa as a coherent disease distinct from starvation among the insane and unrelated to such organic diseases as tuberculosis, diabetes, or cancer; Gull describes anorexia nervosa as essentially a mental disorder rather than a medical condition.

1873   Charles Lasegue, a French psychiatrist, provides the description of *l'anorexie mysterique* that provides the first real glimpse of the pressured family environment as a factor in anorexia nervosa.

1883   Anorexia patients begin to be put in asylums.

1900   Oscar H. Rogers, a physician with New York Life Insurance Company, reports that the mortality rate of fat policyholders is higher than average; in 1901 the hypothesis that obesity shortened human life is substantiated, contradicting the previous notion that "being thin was a sign of ill health."

1918   The appearance of America's first best-selling weight-control book, *Diet and Health with a Key to the Calories* by Lulu Hunt Peters, confirms that weight is a source of anxiety among women and fat is out of fashion. Peters's book is popular because it is personal and timely with the food shortages of the war in Europe. Peters portrays calorie counting as an act of both patriotism and humanitarianism—saving a child from starving.

1920s   American doctors used two terms interchangeably: "hysterical anorexia" (a neurological conception) and "anorexia nervosa." In the 1920s, the need to diet intensifies not only because of medical advice and the "flapper" style. Advertising and movies stimulate the development of a new mass culture that sets styles and sells goods, especially among youth.

1930s   During the 1930s, anorexia nervosa is established as a female psychological or "neurotic" disorder. Biomedical treatment continues, but the growing reputation and influence of Freudian psychoanalysis and its emphasis on the unconscious becomes increasingly popular. By the 1930s the scientific study of emotions and the bodily changes that accompany emotional states is the focus of a new field called *psychosomatic medicine*. For the first time, physicians routinely incorporate psychotherapy in the treatment of anorexia nervosa.

1939   Psychiatrists following Freud postulate that the refusal to eat is related to psychosexual dysfunction. A 1939 report by George H. Alexander from Butler Hospital, a psychiatric facility in Providence, Rhode Island, makes the first and most complete report of the discovery of a psychosexual mechanism in anorexia nervosa.

1940s–50s   Psychotherapists report that women with anorexia nervosa fear eating as "impregnation" and regard obesity as pregnancy. The anorexics' sexuality (or lack of it) takes center stage, focusing on their sexual repression or puritanical attitudes.

1960s   As in the 1920s, anthropologist Mary Douglas theorizes that rapid social change and disintegrating social boundaries stimulate both great external and internal control of the physical body.

1973   Psychiatrist Hilde Bruch provides a new view of eating disorders, encouraging a broader and more complex view of the significance of food behavior and its relation to the individual's developmental history. In *Eating Disorders* she stresses the formation of individual personality and factors within the family that precondition the patient to respond to problems by undereating or overeating.

1978	In *The Golden Cage*, Hilde Bruch suggests that social change affects the development of anorexia nervosa, particularly with increased educational, occupational, and sexual options for women.
1979	Gerald Russell, a psychiatrist who worked at the Royal Free Hospital in London, is the first to define bulimia as a specific set of behaviors.
1980	*The Beverly Hills Diet*, a best-seller, openly suggests some people "compensate for their binges" by eating enormous amounts of raw fruit to induce diarrhea, a form of bulimia.
1981	A made-for-television movie about anorexia nervosa, *The Best Little Girl in the World,* is shown in prime time on a major network. *The International Journal of Eating Disorders* is founded to foster and publish research on eating disorders.
1983	The 32-year-old popular pop singer Karen Carpenter dies of heart failure associated with anorexia nervosa. Her death triggers increased public awareness of the fatal consequences of eating disorders.
1984	Bulimia nervosa obtains independent disease status. In DSM-II-R, anorexia and bulimia are described as separate but related disorders.
1994	A new hormone, leptin, is discovered to be produced by fat cells and involved in the regulation of weight and the feeling of satiety. Patients with anorexia nervosa have very low blood levels of leptin, which rise to normal quickly with normal food intake.
1995	A nutrition monitoring report finds young girls 7 to 12 years old showing signs of severe malnutrition and obsessed with their size, shape, and weight. Data collected over 10 years prior to the study reveal that eating disorders rarely affect girls under 15.
2000s	Researchers in neurobiology use an integrative, interdisciplinary approach to study the multiple determinants of eating behaviors, energy balance, and body weight. The determinants being explored are simple nutrients in the blood, classical neurotransmitter molecules, neuropeptides, circulating hormones, neurochemical signals in the central nervous system, and the role of the hypothalamus.
2003	Approximately 8 million people in the United States suffer from eating disorders; 90 percent are adolescent and young adult women. More than half of the women and girls in the United States are trying to lose weight at any one time.

DEFINITIONS

Anorexia nervosa is defined as a chronic and debilitating illness characterized by a significant weight loss due to a purposeful attempt to stop eating. Its essential features are refusal to maintain a minimally normal body weight, intense fear of gaining weight, and significant disturbance in the perception of the shape or size of the individual's body. Anorexics (or anorectics) have an intense fear of becoming obese and typically consider themselves fat, no matter what their actual weight. They have what is referred to as a distorted body image.

To be diagnosed with anorexia nervosa one must be 15 percent below his or her normal body weight and have lost weight through induced starvation. Thus, if 100 pounds is considered normal weight for someone 5 feet tall, the individual would be considered anorexic if his or her weight dropped to 85 pounds. Many anorexics attempt to accelerate weight loss or undo the damage of occasional binges by vomiting, taking laxatives, using diuretics, or exercising rigorously. Amenorrhea always occurs in female anorexics, often before a significant amount of weight has been lost. A halt in menstruation, combined with attempts at dieting and an intense fear of becoming fat, are signs that anorexia is the problem. The typical patient with anorexia nervosa is an adolescent female who is a perfectionist, high achiever, and good student. She usually has successful parents and feels compelled to excel. Approximately 1 percent of all adolescent girls in America develop anorexia nervosa.

Bulimia nervosa, more commonly called bulimia, has only recently been seen as a separate eating disorder. Bulimia (from the Greek meaning "ox hungry") involves episodes of eating large amounts of food in a short time ("binge"), followed by an attempt to get rid of the food and calories in "purge episodes." Purging may include self-induced vomiting, misusing laxatives or enemas, or taking other medications to induce vomiting. Diagnostic criteria now distinguish patients who compensate for binge eating by purging (e.g., by vomiting and/or misusing laxatives and diuretics) from those who use nonpurging behaviors (e.g., fasting or excessive exercising). A binge-eating/purging subtype of anorexia also exists. Similar to bulimics, anorexics in this subtype consume huge amounts of food, claiming that they can't stop eating once they begin. According to the established diagnostic criteria, patients who are 15 percent below natural body weight and binge eat are considered anorexic.

To meet the diagnosis of bulimia, the binge eating and the compensatory behavior must occur at least twice per week for at least 3 months. Bulimics generally have normal body weight, but typically are never satisfied with their weight or shape and have an ideal weight in mind, which drives their goal to become thinner. Approximately 3 percent of young women develop bulimia. Both anorexia nervosa and bulimia have a peak onset between ages 13 and 20 years. The long-term outcome of bulimia nervosa is not known. About 30 percent of patients with bulimia rapidly recover, but up to 40 percent remain chronically symptomatic.

Binge-eating disorder (BED), a newly defined condition, was added to the DSM-IV in 1994 on a provisional basis with the criteria described in Appendix B. BED patients, unlike those with bulimia, do not demonstrate compensatory behaviors for the binge eating by purging (e.g., vomiting or laxatives and diuretics) or use nonpurging behaviors (e.g., fasting or excessive exercising). The essential features of BED include recurrent episodes of binge eating associated with a subjective sense of impaired control over the binges, a significant level of distress about the binge eating, and an absence of inappropriate compensatory behaviors. The marked distress required for the diagnosis includes feelings of disgust, guilt, or depression after overeating along with concerns about the long-term effect of the recurrent binge episodes on body weight and shape.

To meet BED criteria, binge episodes must occur, on average, at least 2 days a week for at least 6 months. The duration of a binge-eating episode varies greatly, and many individuals have difficulty separating their binge eating into discrete episodes. BED patients can usually recall whether or not they binged on a given day, however, so clinicians count the number of days the binge eating occurs instead of the number of episodes (as in bulimia).

As many as 4 percent of Americans suffer from BED. Among women in weight-control programs, the prevalence of BED may be as high as 50 percent, and these BED patients on average are more obese than those not seeking help. Patients in weight-control programs also have more weight fluctuations than individuals without BED. Those seen in clinical settings have varying degrees of obesity, typically have a long history of repeated efforts to lose weight, and feel desperate about their difficulty in controlling food intake. Some persons who meet the BED criteria continue trying to restrict calorie intake, whereas others have quit dieting because of repeated failures. In nonpatient community samples, most individuals with BED are overweight. Individuals with BED often report that their eating or weight interferes with relationships, their work, and their ability to feel good about themselves.

HISTORICAL PERSPECTIVES

Anorexia was first described in medical literature three centuries ago with the same symptoms as today. Before this, food avoidance and emaciation were described as common symptoms of well-known diseases such as hysteria, mania, melancholy, and a variety of psychotic disorders. At the end of the seventeenth century, the English physician Richard Morton described "nervous consumption," caused by emotional turmoil, which had a wasting different from tuberculosis. In the nineteenth century, the Parisian clinician Ernest-Charles Lasegue and the London physician Sir William Withey Gull were the first to explicitly describe anorexia nervosa as a coherent disease distinct from starvation among the insane and unrelated to organic diseases such a tuberculosis, diabetes, or cancer. In April 1873, Lasegue published his article on *anorexie hysterique,* which appeared in English translation shortly before Gull presented his paper on "anorexia hysteria" in October of the same year. Gull reported that his disease had a very specific victim: young women between the ages of 16 and 23.

Between 1900 and the 1920s, the field of medicine developed its first standards of weight and height based on insurance industry data. Beginning in the mid-nineteenth century, insurance companies began using body weight as one indicator of risk. The hypothesis that obesity shortened human life was substantiated by data analyzed by doctors and statisticians. By 1910, a growing number of Americans wanted to know their exact weight, as determined by a weigh-in at the doctor's office or on recently marketed home scales.

In 1908, Paul Poiret, a French fashion designer whose new ideal figure was "slim and straight," revolutionized the world of women's fashion. The slenderized fashion image was picked up and promoted by America's new ready-to-wear garment industry. The ready-to-wear production in the United States accelerated during the first two decades of the twentieth century. To market ready-to-wear clothing in the 1920s, the industry turned to standardized sizes, which seemed to heighten concerns about body size. Female figure flaws became a source of frustration and embarrassment as thinness became an even more popularized ideal.

In the period from 1945 to 1960, psychiatry was increasingly dominated by psychoanalytic views, traces of which can be seen in contemporary theories of anorexia nervosa. The analysts focused on the fear of food intake, for example, as linked to the unconscious fears of oral impregnation. But interest in anorexia was not great until after 1960, when the pioneering work of (German-born) American psychiatrist Hilda Bruch drastically changed the focus of anorexia's etiology and treatment to the anorexic's lack of self-esteem and distorted body. Throughout her work, Bruch stressed the formation of individual personality and factors within the family that preconditioned the patient to respond to his or her problems by undereating or overeating. The clinical emphasis on assessing how particular families managed food and eating linked individuals who ate excessively and those who restricted their intake to the point of dangerous emaciation as part of a therapeutic puzzle for the first time.

In the 1950s and 1960s, physicians began to use antidepressants and antipsychotic medications to alleviate some psychological issues, such as depression. Antidepressant medications are still the most commonly used to treat eating disorders today.

The American public discovered anorexia nervosa relatively recently. Although the disease was known to physicians as early as the 1870s, the general public knew virtually nothing about the "starving disease" until the 1970s, when the popular press began to feature stories about young women who refused to eat despite the availability of plentiful food. In 1974, the "starving disease" made its first appearance as an independent subject heading in the *Readers' Guide to Periodical Literature*, a standard library reference tool that identifies the subjects of mainstream magazine articles. In 1979, Gerald Russell first defined a specific set of behaviors for bulimia as a separate disorder from anorexia nervosa while working at the Royal Free Hospital in London. Researchers have been unable to find any documentation that bulimia was recognized prior to Dr. Russell's description.

As in other areas of research, there are definite "trends" in attributing cause. For example, during the 1960s and 1970s, an "anorexogenic family environment" was thought to be crucial in the development of anorexia nervosa. During the 1980s and 1990s, childhood trauma, in particular childhood sexual abuse, was promoted as crucial—mainly for bulimia. With the advent of new biotechnologies (molecular biology, brain scanning), we are seeing a revival of interest in biological factors.

ETIOLOGY

As researchers and clinicians struggle to understand the devastating impact of disturbed eating, the complicated picture of predisposing factors in the development of eating disorders continues to be studied and discussed. The cause of eating disorders is widely thought to be "multifactorial," including a number of risk factors. These factors include predispositions based on personality, biological, environmental, and sociocultural influences.

Personality Factors

Researchers and clinicians have found that most persons with eating disorders share certain personality traits: low self-esteem, feelings of helplessness, perfectionism, and a fear of becoming fat. These eating disorders have also been found to be coping strategies for individuals to manage stress and anxieties.

Eating disorders often begin with dieting. A person with low self-esteem attempts to feel better by dieting, to look slimmer, perhaps to conform to current societal ideals (slender for women; lean and muscular for men). These diets get out of control, as the dieter feels "thin" is never enough and continues restricting food intake.

Biological and Environmental Factors

Eating disorders appear to run in families, most often affecting female relatives. Studies have shown an increased risk of anorexia nervosa in first-degree relatives (parents, siblings, or children) of individuals with the disorder. Persons with a family history of mood disorders (anxiety, depression) or chemical dependency are also at higher risk for developing eating disorders. Such relatives have a ten times higher incidence of anorexia nervosa than the general population.

Inhibiting food intake has consequences those attempting such restriction may not have anticipated. Starvation and self-imposed dieting appear to result in binge eating once food is available. There are also psychological manifestations such as preoccupation with food and eating, increased emotional sensitivity, dysphoria, distractibility, and a tendency to binge after restrictive eating. A similar tendency to overeat after food deprivation has been observed repeatedly in humans and animals.

Another biological factor in eating disorders is found within the neuroendocrine system. This system regulates multiple functions of the mind and body including sexual function, physical growth and development, appetite and digestion, sleep, heart and kidney functions, emotions, thinking, and memory. Many of these regulatory mechanisms are seriously disturbed in people with eating disorders. In the central nervous system—particularly the brain—key chemical messengers known as neurotransmitters control the production of hormones. The neurotransmitters serotonin and norepinephrine function abnormally in people affected by depression. Recently, researchers funded by the National Institutes of Mental Health (NIMH) have discovered these neurotransmitters are also decreased in acutely ill anorectic and bulimic patients and long-term recovered anorectic patients. Because many people with eating disorders also appear to suffer from depression, some scientists believe there is a link between the biological factors associated with clinical depression and the development of anorexia and bulimia.

Gender differences have been found in eating disorders, with greater prevalence in females than males. Recent studies, however, show the incidence of eating disorders is increasing among males. Currently an estimated 5 to 15 percent of people with anorexia nervosa and bulimia are male, as are 35 percent of those with BED. Further, up to one in four children referred to an eating disorders professional for anorexia is a boy. Many boys with eating disorders share the same characteristics as their female counterparts, including low self-esteem, the need to be accepted, an inability to cope with emotional pressures, and family and relationship problems. Eating

disorders occur most commonly in specific subgroups of males. For instance, males who wrestle show rates of eating disorders seven to ten times the normal rate. Male runners have also been cited as a vulnerable group. Additionally, homosexual males have an increased rate of eating disorders.

Sociocultural Factors

The sociocultural factors center on the idealization of thinness and physical fitness and disparagement of those who are overweight, primarily originating with the mass media, family, and peers. Evidence is mounting that the mass media, in particular television, magazines, and movies, promote a negative body image and eating disturbances. Body dimensions of female models, actresses, and other female icons have become thinner over the last several decades. One-fourth of the models in some magazines, for example, satisfy the weight criteria for anorexia nervosa. Young women are constantly bombarded by images of thinness, vitality, and youth that, for many, are irresistible, though completely unattainable and unrealistic. The average person sees between 400 and 600 advertisements per day. Sometimes these images are not even of real women but composite photos combining the head of an adult woman, the torso of a young girl, and the legs of a boy. Randomized experiments have documented that constant exposure to media-portrayed thin-ideal images results in increased body dissatisfaction and negative affect (e.g., depression, shame, anger).

With each passing year, the task of looking perfect becomes more difficult for the American woman. Since 1950, Miss Americas have grown thinner while the average American has grown heavier. The average model is now 5 feet 10 inches tall and weighs 111 pounds (normal weight range based on the Milwaukee weight charts is 150 to 160 pounds). The average Playboy model weighs nearly 20 percent less than an average woman the same height. As the disparity between real and ideal increases, the average woman's self-esteem and satisfaction with her body drops. Many of the most celebrated—and emulated—female stars of television and movies are below the normal weight range for their height and body type. When adolescent girls compare their own bodies to these women, it is not surprising many perceive themselves as fat, hate their bodies, and attempt to diminish themselves in a deadly competition to be slimmest.

During the 1980s a series of case studies and media reports began to emerge about eating disorders among individuals in specific "high-risk" populations, such as athletes, dancers, and fashion models. An increasing amount of research has explored the extent and nature of eating disorders in these groups. In addition to the sociocultural pressure to conform to an unrealistically thin body ideal, athletes and dancers may come under specific pressure from within their highly competitive subcultures to manipulate eating and weight to maximize performance and improve aesthetic appeal. This pressure is likely to be particularly intense for athletes competing in sports that have weight restrictions (such as rowing or wrestling) or require a lean body shape or low body weight for reasons of performance or appearance (such as distance running, gymnastics, ballet, and figure skating).

Research estimates as many as 22 percent of young women athletes and dancers have an eating disorder. Delayed menarche, as late as age 19 or 20 for very thin female athletes and ballet dancers, is linked to osteoporosis and bone fractures later in life. Avoiding meat, common for women athletes, is also linked to menstrual abnormalities. Female runners who eat less than 100 grams of red meat per week have significantly lower iron levels. Obsession with a sport may be a "red flag" that the athlete is overtraining in unhealthy ways. Male runners and wrestlers with weight restrictions are also vulnerable groups.

The American College of Sports Medicine, USA Gymnastics Task Force on Eating Disorders has called for mandatory training to make coaches aware of exercise dependence and eating disorders, and alert them to warning signs. In particular, female athletes who call themselves vegetarians should be screened for disordered eating and amenorrhea and, if either is found, for osteoporosis.

Sociocultural pressures emanating from the family environment may promote body image and eating disturbances. Parental pressure to lose weight, family criticism regarding weight, and parental investment in a daughter's slenderness are positively correlated with adolescent eating disorders. There is some indication that general disturbances in family functioning are related to eating pathology: individuals with eating disorders have reported their families are more conflicted, disorganized, and critical, and less cohesive than non-eating disordered individuals. The National Institutes of Mental Health has reported that girls who live in strict families who emphasize physical attractiveness and weight control are at increased risk for inappropriate eating behaviors and eating disorders.

There is also growing evidence that peers can impact the development of eating disorders by emphasizing thinness and weight control and engaging in weight-related teasing. Individuals with bulimia, for example, report perceiving greater pressure from their peers to be thin than do non-eating disordered adolescent girls. Many indicated they initiated bulimic behavior following pressure from a friend to lose weight.

MEDICAL COMPLICATIONS

If not stopped, starving, bingeing, and purging can lead to irreversible physical damage and even death. Eating disorders affect every cell, tissue, and organ in the body. The following is a partial list of the medical dangers associated with anorexia, bulimia, and binge-eating disorder:

- Irregular heart beat, cardiac arrest, death
- Kidney damage, death
- Liver damage (made worse by substance abuse), death
- Disruption of menstrual cycle, infertility
- Destruction of teeth, rupture of esophagus, loss of muscle mass
- Weakened immune system
- Icy hands and feet
- Swollen glands in neck; stones in salivary duct; "chipmunk cheeks"
- Excess hair on face, arms, and body
- Anemia, malnutrition; disruption of body fluid/mineral imbalance
- Fainting spells, sleep disruption, bad dreams, mental fuzziness
- Permanent loss of bone mass, fractures, and lifelong skeletal problems
- Increased risk of cardiovascular disease
- Increased risk of bowel, breast, and reproductive cancers
- Increased risk of diabetes
- Arthritic damage to joints

One common consequence of restrictive eating, as with anorexia nervosa, is slowed gastric motility. Food stays in the stomach and intestines longer than it did before the person began to diet. The dieting person's gastrointestinal tract does not pass digesting food along as rapidly as it did before, which makes the person feel stuffed. If the person subsequently eats normally, his or her GI tract should gradually return to normal.

EATING DISORDERS TODAY

Living in a female body today is more complicated than it was 100 years ago. The popularity of diet and exercise programs, body sculpturing, liposuction, and breast augmentation indicate that women have internalized the contemporary obsession with a perfect body. While society tells females their gender role is not a barrier to achievement, girls learn very early that their power is linked to how attractive and sexy they are.

According to the National Center for Health Statistics, more than half of women and girls in the United States are trying to lose weight at any one time, often with hazardous methods. To be overweight is to fail in the diet wars. The need-to-be-thin messages are so pervasive in contemporary culture that larger women face severe discrimination in healthcare, career, college, and personal relationships. Indeed, an international crisis exists in four weight and eating problems: dysfunctional eating, eating disorders, overweight, and size prejudice. Eating problems are growing more disruptive as people try harder to lose weight.

As recently as the 1980s, eating disorders rarely affected girls under the age of 15. Today, they are fast becoming a normative epidemic in girls aged 7 through 12. A nutrition monitoring report in the late 1990s found that girls in this age group show severe malnutrition and are obsessed with their size, shape, and weight. A study published in the March 1999 issue of the *Journal of Pediatrics* found that two-thirds of girls in grades 5 through 12 said magazine photos influenced their notion of the ideal figure. Only 29 percent of the 548 girls in the study were actually considered overweight, but 66 percent wanted to lose weight. Those who consistently read the fashion magazines were three times more likely to exercise and lose weight than infrequent readers, and three times more likely to have unrealistic body expectations.

Scientists have studied the biochemical functions of people with eating disorders, focusing recently on the neuroendocrine system, a combination of the central nervous and hormonal systems. Through complex but carefully balanced feedback mechanisms, the neuroendocrine system regulates sexual function, physical growth and development, appetite and digestion, sleep, heart and kidney function, emotions, thinking, and memory. Many of these regulatory mechanisms are seriously disturbed in people with eating disorders.

Scientists have found a biochemical connection between people with eating disorders and obsessive-compulsive disorder (OCD) similar to that between depression and eating disorders. Many patients with bulimia have obsessive-compulsive behaviors as severe as those with only OCD; conversely, patients with OCD frequently have abnormal eating behaviors.

Several family and twin studies suggest high heritability of anorexia nervosa and bulimia. Researchers have been searching for genes that confer susceptibility to these disorders. Scientists suspect that multiple genes may interact with environmental and other factors to increase the risk of developing an eating disorder.

Another sociocultural factor that may trigger eating disorders is physical or sexual abuse. Some clinicians have found a high percentage of their clients with eating disorders also have histories of physical or sexual abuse. Current research, however, suggests abuse victims have the same incidence of eating disorders as those who have not been mistreated. Although not statistically significant, abuse effects on a developing teen or young adult can be very damaging. The loss of control and power involved in victimization can set the stage for the development of an eating disorder.

PREVENTION AND TREATMENT

Early intervention and treatment can save the life of someone with an eating disorder. The longer the abnormal eating behaviors persist, the more difficult it is to overcome the disorder and its effects on the body. The complex interaction of emotional and physiological problems in eating disorders necessitates a multidisciplinary team approach involving a physician, therapist, and nutritionist.

Many eating disorder patients need individual, group, and family therapy as well as nutrition and body image information. Individual psychotherapy, including cognitive-behavioral therapy (a form of psychotherapy that teaches patients how to change abnormal thoughts and behavior), has been the most productive type of treatment. Cognitive-behavioral therapists focus on changing eating behaviors, usually by rewarding or modeling wanted behavior. These therapists also help patients change the distorted and rigid thinking patterns associated with eating disorders. In a recent study of bulimia, researchers found intensive group therapy and antidepressant medications, combined or alone, benefited patients. In another study, the combined use of cognitive-behavioral therapy and antidepressant medications was most effective.

Prevention programs that make individuals more resilient to the adverse effects of sociocultural influences are beneficial. Brief interventions helping women become more critical consumers of the media may buffer them from the influence of "thin-ideal" images. Interventions that reduce family and peer pressures might also reduce body-image disturbances and eating disorders.

The Office on Women's Health sponsors an education and prevention program called "BodyWise," whose goal is to increase knowledge about eating disorders, including the signs, symptoms, and preventive steps to take when at-risk women or girls are identified. The BodyWise campaign also includes information on promoting healthy eating and reducing preoccupation with body weight and size.

CONCLUSION

People die from eating disorders. In fact, the death rate from eating disorders ranks as one of the leading causes of death and the highest death rate of all psychiatric disorders. At the heart of the three most common eating disorders (anorexia nervosa, bulimia, and binge-eating disorder) lies an intense fear of becoming overweight. Although no exact cause has been found, most experts believe a combination of factors trigger eating disorders. Dieting, now at epidemic levels in the United States, appears to be one contributing factor to the increase in eating disorders. As the historical Minnesota Starvation Study suggests, restrictive eating leads to irrational thoughts and a greater obsession with food. Likewise, those who restrict food intake over a long period of time will eventually binge. These negative consequences of dieting and restricted eating to lose weight may outweigh the benefits of restraining one's eating. Healthful, balanced eating without specific food restrictions should be recommended as a long-term strategy for weight control.

Sociocultural pressures to have an unrealistically thin body is one of the central causes of eating disorders in children, adolescents, and young adults. In addition to this pressure (particularly on females),

athletes and dancers may be subjected to specific pressure within their highly competitive subcultures to manipulate their eating and weight to maximize their performance or improve their aesthetic appeal. Eating disorders also tend to run in families, suggesting both genetic and personality predispositions. Ongoing research on etiology includes exciting molecular genetics and twins studies.

Although eating disorders are deadly and create numerous medical complications, they are treatable, and people recover from them. The sooner treatment begins, the sooner the person can develop personal strength and have a productive life. Recovery from eating disorders is a long-term process, and while a small number of individuals develop chronic problems and others struggle with periodic lapses in eating disorder symptoms, many persons fully recover.

Richelle Moen Moore

REFERENCES

Abraham, S. *Eating Disorders: The Facts*. New York: Oxford University Press, 2001.

American Psychiatric Association. *Diagnostic and Statistical Manual for Mental Disorders*. 4th edition *(DSM-IV)*. Washington, DC: American Psychiatric Press, 1994.

Berg, F. M. *Women Afraid to Eat: Breaking Free in Today's Weight Obsessed World*. Hettinger, ND: Healthy Weight Network, 2001.

Brumberg, J. J. *Fasting Girls: The History of Anorexia Nervosa*. New York: Penguin Books, 1989.

Claude-Pierre, P. *The Secret Language of Eating Disorders: The Revolutionary New Approach to Understanding and Curing Anorexia and Bulimia*. New York: Times Books, 1997.

Fairburn, C. *Overcoming Binge Eating*. New York: Guilford, 1995.

Harris, E. C., and B. Barraclough. "Excess Mortality of Mental Disorder." *British Journal of Psychiatry* 173 (1998): 11–53.

Immell, M. *Eating Disorders*. San Diego: Greenhaven, 1999.

Keenan, B. *The Women We Wanted to Look Like*. New York: St. Martin's, 1977.

Keys, A., et al. *The Biology of Human Starvation*, 2 vols. Minneapolis: University of Minnesota Press, 1950.

Kirkpatrick, J., and P. Caldwell. *Eating Disorders: Anorexia Nervosa, Bulimia, Binge-Eating and Others*. New York: Firefly Books, 2001.

Leone, D. A. *Anorexia*. San Diego: Greenhaven, 2001.

Levenkron, S. *Treating and Overcoming Anorexia Nervosa*. New York: Warner Books, 1997.

Matthews, D. D. *Eating Disorders Sourcebook*. Detroit: Omnigraphics, 2001.

Medina, L. M. *Bulimia*. San Diego: Greenhaven, 2001.

Siegel, M., J. Brisman, and M. Weinshel. *Surviving an Eating Disorder: Strategies for Family and Friends*. New York: Harper Perennial, 1997.

WEB SITES

American Anorexia and Bulimia Association: www.aabbinc.org

Eating Disorders Awareness and Prevention Inc.: www.member.aol.com/edapinc/home.html

Eating Disorders Referral and Information Center: http://edreferral.com

National Association of Anorexia Nervosa and Associated Disorders: www.anad.org

National Eating Disorder Information Center: www.nedic.on.ca

National Eating Disorders Organization: www.kid.org

GLOSSARY

Amenorrhea. Absence of normal menstrual cycle.

Anorexia. Loss of appetite for food, a secondary symptom in many medical and psychiatric disorders.

Anorexia nervosa. An eating disorder characterized by refusal to eat, an intense desire to be thin, repeated dieting, and excessive weight loss with a weight 15 percent below normal for height. To maintain an abnormally low weight, people may diet, fast, overexercise, or engage in self-induced vomiting or the misuse of laxatives, diuretics, or enemas.

Binge. A period of rapid, uncontrolled overeating.

Binge-eating disorder (BED). A disorder primarily identified by repeated episodes of uncontrolled overeating or binges. The person also feels a sense of guilt or embarrassment over these binges.

Body Mass Index (BMI). A measure devised over 100 years ago to determine whether a person is of normal weight, underweight, or obese. A person's BMI score is calculated by this equation: (weight/height) x 2. The normal BMI range is approximately 19 to 24.9.

Bulimia nervosa. An eating disorder involving uncontrolled eating or binges followed by behaviors to rid the body of food consumed. These compensatory behaviors include self-induced vomiting and the misuse of laxatives, diet pills, diuretics (water pills), excessive exercise, or fasting. As with anorexia nervosa, bulimics are overly concerned with food, body weight, and shape.

Calorie. The energy content of food as measured by the heat it generates.

Cognitive-behavioral therapy. Psychological therapy intended to change maladaptive ways of thinking and thereby improve psychological disorders. A technique used to help people think differently in order to behave differently.

Compulsion. The recurring urge to perform a particular behavior.

Cyclic vomiting syndrome. Cyclic vomiting is usually found in children between 2 and 16. Symptoms include recurrent episodes of stomach pain, nausea, vomiting up to ten times or more per day, and headaches.

***Diagnostic and Statistical Manual of Mental Disorders,* fourth edition (DSM-IV).** Manual published by the American Psychological Association that includes the definitions, diagnostic criteria, and symptoms of all mental health disorders and syndromes.

Disordered eating. Chaotic and irregular eating—dieting, fasting, bingeing, skipping meals, or consistently undereating or overeating much more than the body needs or wants.

Diuretic. A chemical that increases urine production.

Dyspepsia. A term used prior to the Civil War for the condition of being overweight.

Edema. Swelling caused by accumulated excess fluid in a part of the body.

Electrolytes. Essential chemicals (such as sodium and potassium) found in body fluids; often thrown out of balance in eating disorders.

Emaciation. A condition of extreme thinness.

Emetic. A substance swallowed to induce vomiting.

Esophagus. The tube connecting the mouth to the stomach.

Gourmand syndrome. Preoccupation with fine food, including purchase, preparation, presentation, and consumption. It is caused by injury to the right side of the brain.

Hyperphagia. Overeating.

Lanugo. Fine, downlike hairs that appear on the face and body as a result of anorexia nervosa.

Laxatives. Medicines to relieve long-term constipation. Used only if other methods fail.

Malnutrition. A condition caused by not eating enough food or not eating a balanced diet.

Metabolic rate. A measure of how actively and efficiently the body produces energy.

Metabolism. The chemical and physical processes involved in the body's production of energy.

Neurasthenia. A social disease on the rise after the Civil War, described as "nervous consumption" and "indigestive thinness."

Neurotransmitters. Key chemical messengers in the brain that control hormone production. Serotonin and norepinephrine function abnormally in people with depression.

Obesity. Extra body fat of 20 percent (or more) for their age, height, sex, and bone structure. BMI greater than 25.

Obsessive-compulsive disorder (OCD). A psychiatric disorder the essential features of which are recurrent obsessions or compulsions severe enough to be time-consuming, cause marked distress in an individual, or significantly interfere with normal functioning.

Osteoporosis. A disease of thinning or loss of density in the bones.

Pica. An eating disorder characterized by craving inedible substances not normally eaten, such as clay, dirt, chalk, dried paint, and toothpaste.

Prader-Willi syndrome. A rare congenital problem affecting children. Prader-Willi syndrome includes the following characteristics: mental retardation, behavioral and speech problems, abnormal growth, muscle weakness, and constant hunger; sometimes confused with bulimia but the person shows little concern about body image and gorges because the physiological brakes controlling appetite and hunger are missing.

Purge. In eating disorders, deliberately eliminating food from the stomach or bowel by vomiting, taking laxatives, or other means.

Refeeding. Increasing someone's food intake to help establish a more normal eating pattern.

Restricting. In eating disorders, severely limiting choices and amounts of food.

Satiation. A normal feeling of stomach fullness.

Satiety. The feeling of not being hungry, which results from a number of factors.

DOCUMENTS

Document 1. *Diagnostic and Statistical Manual for Mental Disorders*, 4th edition (DSM-IV)

Diagnostic criteria for anorexia nervosa, bulimia nervosa, and binge-eating disorder (BED) are found in Appendix B of the American Psychiatric Association's DSM-IV. The criteria are still in the research phase and do not yet constitute an independent diagnosis.

Anorexia Nervosa Diagnostic Criteria

A. Refusal to maintain body weight at or above a minimally normal weight for age and height (e.g., weight loss leading to maintenance of body weight less than 85 percent of that expected; or failure to make expected weight gain during period of growth, leading to body weight less than 85 percent of that expected).

B. Intense fear of gaining weight or becoming fat, even though underweight.

C. Disturbance in the way in which one's body weight or shape is experienced, undue influence of body weight or shape on self-evaluation, or denial of the seriousness of the current low body weight.

D. In postmenarcheal females, amenorrhea, i.e., the absence of at least three consecutive menstrual cycles. (A woman is considered to have amenorrhea if her periods occur only following hormone, e.g., estrogen, administration.)

Specify type:

Restricting Type: during the current episode of Anorexia Nervosa, the person has not regularly engaged in binge-eating or purging behavior (i.e., self-induced vomiting or the misuse of laxatives, diuretics, or enemas)

Binge-Eating/Purging Type: during the current episode of Anorexia Nervosa, the person has regularly engaged in binge-eating or purging behavior (i.e., self-induced vomiting or the misuse of laxatives, diuretics, or enemas)

Bulimia Nervosa Diagnostic Criteria

A. Recurrent episodes of binge eating. An episode of binge eating is characterized by both of the following:

(1) eating, in a discrete period of time (e.g., within any 2-hour period), an amount of food that is definitely larger than most people would eat during a similar period of time and under similar circumstances.

(2) sense of lack of control over eating during the episode (e.g., a feeling that one cannot stop eating or control what or how much one is eating)

B. Recurrent inappropriate compensatory behavior in order to prevent weight gain, such as self-induced vomiting; misuse of laxatives, diuretics, enemas, or other medications; fasting; or excessive exercise.

C. The binge eating and inappropriate compensatory behaviors both occur, on average, at least twice a week for 3 months.

D. Self-evaluation is unduly influenced by body shape and weight.

E. The disturbance does not occur exclusively during episodes of Anorexia Nervosa.

Specify type:

Purging Type: during the current episode of Bulimia Nervosa, the person has regularly engaged in self-induced vomiting or the misuse of laxatives, diuretics, or enemas

Nonpurging Type: during the current episode of Bulimia Nervosa, the person has used other inappropriate compensatory behaviors, such as fasting or excessive exercise, but has not regularly engaged in self-induced vomiting or the misuse of laxatives, diuretics, or enemas

Research Criteria for Binge-Eating Disorder

Pending validated research studies to support the official diagnostic criteria for binge-eating disorder. Currently persons that meet this criteria are diagnosed Eating Disorder Not Otherwise Specified (NOS)

A. Recurrent episodes of binge eating. An episode of binge eating is characterized by both of the following:

(1) eating in a discrete period of time (e.g., within any 2-hour period), eating in a similar period of time under similar circumstances

(2) a sense of lack of control over eating during the episode (e.g., a feeling that one cannot stop eating or control what or how much one is eating)

B. The binge-eating episodes are associated with three (or more) of the following:

(1) eating much more rapidly than normal

(2) eating until feeling uncomfortably full

(3) eating large amounts of food when not feeling physically hunger

(4) eating alone because of being embarrassed by how much one is eating

(5) feeling disgusted with oneself, depressed, or very guilty after overeating

C. Marked distress regarding binge eating is present.

D. The binge eating occurs, on average, at least 2 days a week for 6 months.

E. The binge eating is not associated with the regular use of inappropriate compensatory behaviors (e.g., purging, fasting, excessive exercise) and does not occur exclusively during the course of Anorexia Nervosa or Bulimia Nervosa.

Source: American Psychiatric Association. *Diagnostic and Statistical Manual of Mental Disorders*, 4th ed. (Washington, DC: American Psychiatric Association, 1994).

Document 2. Excerpt from the Minnesota Starvation Study, 1950

Ancel Keys and his associates, from November 19, 1944, through October 20, 1945, conducted a Biology of Human Starvation study, known as the Minnesota Starvation Study. Designed to increase understanding of wartime starvation, the experiment was a response to the prevalence of famine edema among prisoners of war during World War I and starvation conditions throughout the world caused by World War II. It focused on the condition of human starvation as it occurs most commonly under natural conditions, typically involving prolonged caloric deficit resulting in chronic undernutrition or "semistarvation." Most human beings can tolerate a weight loss of 5 to 10 percent with little physical or mental disorganization. The study also compares wartime starvation with such types of semistarvation as anorexia nervosa.

In planning the Minnesota Experiment it was recognized that to obtain the most generally applicable data on the effects of semi-starvation and subsequent rehabilitation, the use of a well-defined sample of the general population would be highly desirable. . . . A potential source of subjects for such an experiment were the conscientious objectors who, as drafted civilians, were under the direction and control of the Selective Service System for the duration of the war. . . . The 32 subjects (selected) were in continuous residence at the Laboratory of Physiological Hygiene from November 19, 1944, through October 20, 1945, including the 12-week control period, 24 weeks of semi-starvation, and 12 weeks of restricted rehabilitation. Twelve of the subjects remained for an additional 8 weeks of unrestricted rehabilitation, and follow-up examinations were made on more than half the subjects after about 8 and 12 months of post-starvation recovery.

. . . During the semi-starvation period only two meals a day were served, at 8:30 a.m. and 5:00 p.m. The semi-starvation diet consisted of 3 basic menus repeated in rotation. The major food items served were whole-wheat bread, potatoes, cereals, and considerable amounts of turnips and cabbage. Only token amounts of meats and dairy products were provided. The diet was designed to represent as nearly as possible the type of foods used in European famine areas. . . . The average daily intake was 1,570 Calories and included about 50 grams of protein and 30 grams of fat. . . . Each subject was assigned to a specific project job that required about 15 hours per week doing tasks as general maintenance of the Laboratory and living quarters, laundry, laboratory assistance, shop duties, and clerical and statistical work. In addition to the project work, each subject was required to walk 22 miles out-of-doors per week and for a half-hour each week on a motor-driven treadmill at 3.5 miles per hour on a 10 per cent grade. Walking to and from the dining hall added an extra 2 to 3 miles per day.

. . . As semi-starvation progressed in the Minnesota Experiment, complaints of inability to concentrate for any period of time and of difficulty in developing thoughts became numerous. By the end of the semi-starvation period a large proportion of the men felt that their judgment had been impaired. They reported further that their general alertness and comprehension had declined. . . . The men exhibited symptoms of depression, irritability, "nervousness," and general emotional instability. Social withdrawal, narrowing of interests, obliteration of sexual drive, and difficulty in concentration were prominent. Food and eating became their dominant concern. In conversation, speech was slow but did not show evidences of faults in memory or logic.

Source: American Psychiatric Association. *Diagnostic and Statistical Manual of Mental Disorders*, 4th ed. (Washington, DC: American Psychiatric Association, 1994).

ENERGY DEPENDENCY

America's high standard of living, unparalleled industrial output, and preeminent economic position are in large measure the result of its successful development of energy resources. The key to understanding America's current energy issues is its history. Many of the nation's current environmental problems and foreign relations difficulties are closely tied to its ever-increasing demand for energy and dependency on imported fuel.

The first energy source Americans relied on was wood. Although Hopi Indians are known to have used coal for cooking as early as 1350, wood was the most important energy source in colonial America. Wood was primarily used as firewood, and water power provided most of the energy used in sawmills as wood production increased. Until the advent of the railroads, animals provided transportation, but even as late as the 1870s, wood was the primary fuel for railroads (although charcoal was used in iron production). After 1875, the use of wood declined as forest resources became scarcer and coal became more readily available. This change coincided with America's growing need for energy to fuel the Industrial Revolution. Coal use peaked by 1899, providing 89 percent of the nation's power.

Coal consists of hydrocarbons, fixed carbon, water, sulfur, and ash, and it is formed by compression of plant matter in swamps. In about a hundred years, one foot of peat forms in a swamp, but up to 8 feet of peat is needed to produce a foot of coal.

There are many kinds of coal. Bituminous coal is the most important in industry and transport, and anthracite is the best for domestic heating use. Some coal is removed by relatively inexpensive surface mining, but some coal mines are up to 2,000 feet deep. Underground mining methods include drill, shaft, and slant mining. The first recorded coal mine in the United States was opened near Richmond, Virginia, in 1701. The mined coal is crushed and then shipped to consumers via truck, boat, railroad, barge, or pipeline (where it is mixed with water and oil to form a slurry).

Until World War I, coal was the source of energy in America, but as people gained more access to petroleum, between 1918 and 1947, coal production decreased. As oil and natural gas provided most of the energy in World War II, however, domestic coal use rose during that period. To deal with the economic decline during the Great Depression, a regional cartel called Appalachian Coal Inc. was formed, and the Supreme Court ruled that it did not violate the Sherman Antitrust Act. Unfortunately, it was not very effective at stabilizing market prices, and the New Deal's National Recovery Administration was likewise unsuccessful. With passage of the Bituminous Coal Act in 1937, a regulatory system to set minimum prices for coal sale was established, but the result was to make alternative fuels more competitive, reducing demand for coal even further.

From the 1940s to the 1970s prices finally stabilized and production increased. This was partly the result of an alliance between the large coal companies and the United Mine Workers. In the 1970s, during the Nixon and Carter administrations, the Arab oil embargo resulted in increased coal production. During the oil crisis, people even referred to America as the "great black hope," with coal as the source of energy until renewable sources could be further developed.

Between 1969 and 1970, two major federal acts were passed to regulate the coal industry: the Mine Health and Safety Act of 1969 and the Clean Air Act of 1970. The Mine Health and Safety Act established safety procedures to protect miners. Unfortunately, one result of this policy was a decline in production, and some small mines were forced to close. The act encouraged surface mining, and old techniques such as the pillar systems gave way to the long wall mining method and larger, more technically advanced mines. The Clean Air Act, along with the Environmental Protection Agency's (EPA's) clean air emission standards, worked to control the amount of nitrogen, sulfur dioxide, and particulates (ash) in the air.

CHRONOLOGY

1701   First recorded coal mine in the United States begins production near Richmond, Virginia.

1850   Wood provides 85 percent of the energy used in the United States.

1859   First U.S. oil well in Titusville, Pennsylvania, begins production.

1882   The first hydropower turbine is attached to a generator in Wisconsin.

1899   Coal use peaks in the United States.

1904   Steam power is used to make electricity.

1911   Supreme Court orders the dissolution of the Standard Oil Trust.

1914–18   Oil supply is an issue during World War I.

1934   Iran and Iraq become the largest Middle Eastern oil exporters.

1938   Foreign oil companies in Mexico are nationalized; massive oil deposits are discovered in Saudi Arabia and Kuwait.

1939–45   Control of the oil supply from the Middle East plays a major role in the events of World War II.

1948   For the first time, America has to import more oil than it exports.

1951   Iran nationalizes the Anglo Iranian Oil Company.

1954   Atomic Energy Act passes, advocating use of nuclear power.

1957   Development of nuclear energy begins in the United States.

1959   Arab Oil Congress in Cairo is the first major attempt by Arab companies to gain control over oil marketing and production.

1960   Organization of Petroleum Exporting Countries (OPEC) is created.

1968   The *Ocean Eagle* spill occurs off of the coast of Puerto Rico.

1969   National Environmental Policy Act passes; an oil platform explodes off Santa Barbara, California, producing major oil spill; Mine Health and Safety Act is passed.

1970   The Clean Air Act is passed; U.S. oil production peaks.

1971   OPEC countries start nationalizing oil companies.

1973   Because of the oil embargo/energy crisis, oil prices rise from $2.90 to $11.65 per barrel; Endangered Species Act is passed; last completed nuclear power plant is licensed in the United States.

1974   Energy Research and Development Administration is created.

1977   Alaska oil pipeline is finished; Clean Water Act is passed.

1978   The Solar Energy Research Institute is founded; Public Utilities Regulatory Policies Act passes, encouraging competition in electricity industry.

1978–79   Windfall Profit Tax on oil industry profits is implemented.

1979   First major nuclear disaster in United States occurs at the Three Mile Island plant near Harrisburg, Pennsylvania; Iranian revolution overthrows pro-U.S. government of Shah, leading to another oil crisis.

1979–81   Oil prices rise from $13.00 to $34.00 per barrel.

1980   Iraq goes to war against Iran, war continues through 1988; Crude Oil Windfall Profits Tax helps renewables.

1980s   Federal Regulatory Commission furthered competition in wholesale power markets.

1982   OPEC creates oil quotas.

1986   Chernobyl nuclear accident occurs; oil prices collapse; the Tax Reform Act has positive implications for alternative energy sources; amendments to the Price-Anderson Act provisions of the Atomic Energy Act are passed.

1989   Exxon Valdez oil spill occurs near Alaska; California energy crisis and blackouts occur.

1990	Oil Pollution Act decreases marine oil spills from about 8 million gallons a year to 1 million in 1999; Iraq invades Kuwait and the UN responds with an embargo on Iraq.
1991	Gulf War starts; Kuwait oilfields are set on fire during Operation Desert Storm.
1992	Energy Policy Act gives a 10 percent credit to businesses for using solar or geothermal power; wind, biomass, and solar energy are subsidized; the United States signs the Rio Agreement on Climate.
1995	UN lets Iraq export some oil in the "oil for food" deal.
1997	Kyoto Agreement on climate protection is drafted.
1999	The U.S. Environmental Protection Agency (EPA) issues the Regional Haze Rule.
2001	September 11th, terrorists attack the United States.
2002	United States backs out of the Kyoto Protocol.
2003	U.S. Senate rejects proposal to allow drilling in the Alaskan Arctic National Wildlife Refuge; United States invades Iraq and overthrows regime of Saddam Hussein.

Encouraging the use of low sulfur coals, these policies have produced about $6 billion of research investments and technology to reduce the pollutants in coal. The 1985 clean coal technology program contributed greatly to this progress. A major innovation was the discovery that coal preparation plants could significantly reduce the sulfur in coal simply by washing it; another was flue gas desulferization units or scrubbers. These scrubbers filter the coal smoke through limestone before releasing it into the atmosphere. In addition, coal-burning technology has improved. Burning coal in stages improves emissions, and fluidized burners allow more limestone to mix with coal, reducing sulfur emissions. The coal also burns at cooler temperatures (1400°F rather than 3000°F) and thus releases fewer nitrogen oxides. Pressurized fluidized bed boilers and a process called gasification further improve coal burning technology.

Since the decline in U.S. oil production in the 1970s, coal production has increased 80 percent and contributes $21 billion annually to the economy. Coal is plentiful in the United States as America has one-fourth of the world's coal reserves. In fact, the nation has more mineable coal than the rest of the world has remaining oil deposits. Nonetheless, there are still some worries about the environmental impacts of coal use. According to the Environmental Media Services, a nonprofit clearinghouse for environmental journalists, "power plants are the number one industrial source of the air pollution responsible for ozone-smog, acid rain, global warming, deadly particulate matter and toxic mercury," and "coal-fired power plants produce 55 percent of the electricity in the United States, but they are responsible for 80–99

percent of the pollution from the electric power industry."

These environmental problems affect everyone, especially agriculture. The sulfur dioxide and nitrogen oxides emitted from coal-fired power plants not only contribute to ground-level ozone (or smog), acid rain, and degradation of natural forest, but also reduce the yield of many important agricultural crops. Pollution from these chemicals makes crops more susceptible to disease and contributes to overfertilization and eutrophication of marine environments. This results in a loss of habitat for economically valuable plants, fish, and other aquatic species.

There may also be reason to worry about the human health impacts of coal technology. For example, mercury pollution may be a problem with the current technology for producing energy from coal. According to EPA estimates, 60 to 75 percent of the mercury in American waters is from pollution, and coal-fired power plants are both the largest and only unregulated source of this pollution. In addition, coal-based power plants emit more than sixty toxic chemicals, some of which have been shown to cause cancer, impair reproduction, and hinder normal development in children, while others affect the nervous and immune systems, and contribute to respiratory illness.

Although coal is important in America's economy, the rise of petroleum production after 1900, coupled with the increasing demands for energy, helped establish petroleum as America's primary fuel source. Petroleum, composed of hydrocarbons (carbon and hydrogen molecules), is found in a liquid, gas, or solid state. Crude oil is the most common form of petroleum, but natural gas, methane, ethane, pro-

Figure 1. Composition (by energy source) of America's Electricity Consumption (2000)

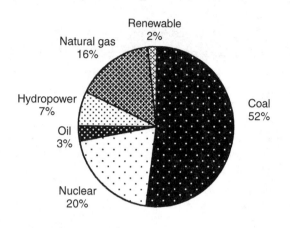

Note: Renewable sources include primarily solar, wind, and biomass.
Source: U.S. Department of Energy, Energy Information Administration.

pane, and butane are petroleum products as well. Most scientists agree that petroleum products are formed from heat and pressure on organic matter that has been deposited over centuries or even millions of years. But the abiogenic theory posits that petroleum was trapped beneath the surface of the earth when the earth was formed and is slowly surfacing. The reservoirs of petroleum products that remain trapped underground can be located thousands of meters below the surface of the earth.

The first oil well was drilled in Titusville, Pennsylvania, in 1859. By 1970, U.S. oil production reached its peak, producing 11.3 million barrels of oil a day, but our oil needs had also increased and are still increasing. In 1990, the average consumption was 12 million barrels a day. Producing two-thirds of the world's oil during the First World War, the United States today is the world's third largest oil producer. Because oil is expensive to produce, large corporations in America came to control the oil industry soon after its inception. In the early years of development, U.S. companies were able to invest heavily not only in domestic production, but also abroad. At first, American oil companies were able to set the world's oil prices. They invested heavily in Mexican oil. Furthermore, between 1930 and 1950, the United States obtained about a quarter of the Iraq Petroleum Company as well as several companies in Kuwait, Bahrain, and Saudi Arabia. While Iran and Iraq had become the largest Middle Eastern oil ex-

porters by 1934, by 1938 Mexico had nationalized all foreign oil companies.

Some American companies made questionable deals with Middle Eastern countries in the 1940s and 1950s. Some of these oil deals entailed effectively giving American tax money to foreign governments (e.g., Saudi Arabia). One of the most interesting events in the 1950s was the Iranian Prime Minister Mohammed Mosaddegh's attempt to nationalize oil properties. This resulted in U.S. oil companies boycotting Iranian oil, with the U.S. government's support. The boycott contributed to the fall of Mosaddegh's regime, and the U.S. "arbitrated" the dispute, thus reinstating the influence of U.S. companies.

However, U.S. control over the foreign oil industry was soon to be diminished. By the end of the 1950s and the early 1960s, a group of Middle Eastern countries, in an attempt to gain some control over the oil market, created the Organization of Petroleum Exporting Countries (OPEC). Instigated by Iraq, this cartel soon expanded beyond the Middle East. It gained more power over world affairs as demand for oil continued to rise and U.S. supplies dwindled in the 1970s. By decreasing production, exacting higher taxes on foreign companies operating within their borders, establishing requirements for profit sharing, and raising oil prices, OPEC soon demonstrated its ability to control the world's oil supply. This also allowed OPEC members to discriminate among consumers and show their distaste for American support of Israel in the 1970s, leading to the first oil crisis of 1973. When the Arab world, displeased with American foreign policy, stopped supplying the United States with oil, gas prices immediately tripled, and oil prices rose again in 1979 when the Ayatollah Khomeini forced the Shah of Iran to leave.

In response to the embargo and oil crisis of 1973, the Nixon administration instituted regulatory procedures, entitlements, allocation of supplies, and price controls on oil. Henry Kissinger led in the creation of the International Energy Program and International Energy Agency to lessen the effects of the embargos through an oil-sharing insurance policy. President Nixon also implemented the Emergency Petroleum Allocation Act to govern petroleum distribution in a short-term crisis. Yet, not until President Jimmy Carter's National Energy Plan was a long-term strategy for dealing with energy crises suggested. Although Congress did implement parts of this plan, including a gas-guzzler tax and subsidy for

Figure 2. Known Oil Reserves (2000)

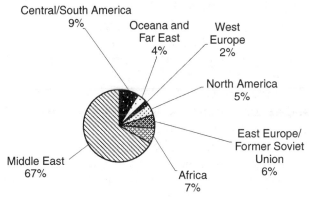

Source: U.S. Department of Energy, Energy Information Administration.

gasohol (a fuel mixing ethanol with gasoline), it took the oil shock of 1978–1979 to stimulate more changes. These changes included the 1980 Windfall Profit Tax—a tax intended to protect low-income groups—and the unsuccessful Energy Security Act, which was discontinued in the late 1980s.

While OPEC member countries could nationalize oil companies by 1980 if they so desired, their influence was weakened in part by the development of alternative energy sources in the 1980s and poor internal cooperation. Soon oil prices dropped from $41 to $17 a barrel. Unfortunately, this was the end of America's oil-related energy crisis. When Iraq invaded Kuwait in 1990 (Kuwait was rumored to be one of the countries most exceeding OPEC-established oil quotas and thus driving down oil prices), Operation Desert Storm was launched. George H.W. Bush convinced a large coalition of nations to join America in ousting Saddam Hussein from Kuwait partly by asserting hostile nations such as Iraq should not be allowed to control too much of the Persian Gulf's oil reserves.

No one contests that the world's oil resources are running out. Oil is a nonrenewable resource and will eventually disappear if consumption continues to climb at the present rate. The question is when. Pessimistic experts say it could be in a few decades; optimists assert it might take 100 years or more. If the less sanguine forecasts are true, the situation could be especially grim for the United States, which consumes more than 25 percent of the oil produced worldwide and imports more than half of this amount. Tensions between the United States and Middle Eastern countries continue to be exacerbated by concerns over oil and "by 2020 the Middle East is projected to supply between 54 and 67 percent of

the world's oil," says a White House report. Because of this, George W. Bush administration's National Energy Policy Development (NEPD) Group has suggested reviewing sanctions against Middle Eastern countries, increasing communication with these countries, and upping direct foreign investment in the Middle East.

The group also recommends increasing free trade and expanding investment in energy-related goods. While such policies may help protect American economic interests, their effects on Middle Eastern countries (and thus American foreign relations) will not necessarily be good. The NEPD made similar recommendations regarding other parts of the world, emphasizing diversified avenues of supply and expanded control over energy resources, a policy some worry contributed to America's decision to initiate Operation Iraqi Freedom in 2003.

There are other reasons to worry about America's oil use. Like coal, oil is a fossil fuel, and pollution from burning fossil fuels contributes to health and environmental problems. Even with this knowledge, however, Americans do not seem to be making a great effort to conserve oil resources. Partly because car sizes increased in the 1950s and 1960s, gas mileage dropped to an average of 13.5 miles per gallon (mpg). Improved efficiency raised the average number of miles per gallon to an unprecedented high of about 22 miles per gallon for passenger cars in 1998, but the recent popularity of sports utility vehicles has again lowered that average to about 20 mpg.

In addition to causing air pollution and global climate change, oil has other negative impacts on the environment. The most memorable in recent history was the 1989 Exxon Valdez oil spill near Alaska. The effects of such spills on everything from bacteria to birds to humans are devastating. For example, 15,000 otters are estimated to have died as a result of the Exxon spill. But worse still, only 20 percent of the oil tankers release into the ocean comes from spills; the rest is the result of normal tanker operations. Most experts agree that more efficiency and responsibility in oil consumption would benefit America in both the international and domestic arenas.

Though coal and oil continue to be important energy resources for America, the forecast for their future is poor. Existing reserves are fast being depleted—especially as China and other developing countries rapidly increase consumption—and new ones tend to be in difficult-to-access or environmentally sensitive regions. Thus, for economic or politi-

Table 1. Largest Tanker Oil Spills in the United States Since 1968

Tanker	Year	Location	Size of spill (tons)
Ocean Eagle	1968	U.S., Puerto Rico	21,000
Texaco Oklahoma	1971	U.S., East Coast	29,000
Corinthos	1975	U.S., Delaware River	36,000
Argo Merchant	1976	U.S., East Coast	28,000
Hawaiian Patriot	1977	Hawaiian Islands	101,000
Exxon Valdez	1989	U.S., Alaska	36,000

Source: Energy Educators of Ontario.

cal reasons, it may be difficult to bring new reserves on line. While far more plentiful, coal presents other problems—notably it is far dirtier to burn than oil. A vast expansion of coal-burning may prove to present unacceptable health and environmental costs. And both fuels, of course, produce large quantities of carbon dioxide when burned, thus contributing to global warming.

The growing realization that the future of oil and coal as the world's main energy source is in jeopardy has led to research into cleaner fuels. Historically, this research has resulted in the development of nuclear energy from uranium and other radioactive materials. Production of nuclear energy beginning after World War II (in 1957) was heralded as a cheap, efficient, safe, and clean source of energy. Unlike traditional fossil fuels, nuclear energy does not directly pollute the air. However, indirectly, the enrichment process creates pollution with large energy inputs usually generated from coal burning plants. In addition, nuclear energy is not as safe as people supposed. By 1965, six nuclear power generating plants operated in the United States, and eighteen such power plants by 1970. Throughout this time hundreds of small nuclear accidents occurred. The first major disaster, however, was a nuclear meltdown in 1979 at the Three Mile Island plant near Harrisburg, Pennsylvania. Although there were no direct casualties, the accident undermined public opinion regarding nuclear power, and the fear increased with the Chernobyl accident in 1986.

Another problem with nuclear power is that the radioactive materials, like coal and oil, often lie far underground. Their removal is both dangerous and often contentious. For example, some lands containing uranium are still owned by Native Americans, and conflicting economic, cultural, and environmental considerations create tension both within and between communities. In addition, between the 1930s and 1960s over 6,000 miners were exposed to cancer-causing radiation in obtaining the uranium required for nuclear weapons and power. But not until the 1960s were radon control programs implemented to reduce the risks associated with mining. Nuclear power also has other environmental impacts and negative health consequences. For example, the enrichment of uranium requires a large amount of water for cooling. The heated water that is released negatively affects marine environments, and some radioactive material can be released into the water and air.

The worst risks associated with nuclear energy involve generated waste (or tailings). These nuclear tailings pose environmental and health risks and can be found all over the United States. The estimated cost of removing the tailings from homes and offices is over $100 million. Waste disposal is also a problem because no one wants to live near a nuclear waste site. In the early 1990s, the country had an estimated 16,000 tons of nuclear wastes in temporary facilities. Plans currently being developed for a more permanent nuclear waste depository at the Yucca Mountain site in southern Nevada carry an estimated $2 billion dollar price tag. "Though some of the waste that would be deposited could be hazardous for millions of years, predictions are being limited to 10,000 years. Beyond this time span, most questions of safety are simply unanswerable," say Miller and Miller.

The amount of energy produced by nuclear power can be significant (since 1980, efficiency of power generation has increased from 70 percent to about 90 percent), but the costs of nuclear energy are large. Under the current upgraded regulations, no new plants have been economically viable in America since 1973. From the nuclear power industry's creation, the Congressional Research Service reports, it has received over $66 billion dollars in taxpayer research and development subsidies. The Price-Anderson Act, a taxpayer-financed insurance policy, gives additional support.

But other sources of energy have become important to America that are less risky than nuclear energy and are renewable. Unfortunately, with the exception of hydropower, the development of renewable energy resources has been slow. Reasons for this include the high initial cost of equipment, storage costs (as many such energy sources provide only intermittent power), reliability issues, and federal tax policies. The fact that social and environmental costs of standard fuels have not traditionally been taken into account in economic decisions may also contribute to the reluctance to change energy sources. Other factors are subsidies for competing energy resources (especially nuclear energy), promotional programs such as the rural electrification project, market constraints, and resistance to change from the building industry, in conjunction with lack of information and legal uncertainties.

Until the 1970s' oil crisis, people did not seem to realize that fossil fuels would not last forever, and until then energy conservation was not even considered. When the Energy Research and Development Administration was created in 1974, renewable energy was one of its six programs, but the funding for such programs was only about one thousandth of the total energy budget. By 1978, the Solar Energy Research Institute was created, and tax credits were one of several policy changes favoring renewable energy. This contributed to the growth of renewables in the 1970s and 1980s. In the 1980s, Congress tried to increase the funding for renewable energy, but President Reagan stymied these efforts. More recently, renewable energy programs have been minimal with perhaps a slight increase in funding in the late 1990s. Nonetheless, a short look at the alternatives available, and their potential as energy resources, will be useful in understanding America's energy issues and possible solutions to future energy crises.

Bioenergy, one type of renewable energy, is generated by waste recycling or biomass power and has been used in small amounts for thousands of years. Examples of bioenergy include ethanol motor fuel, gas from landfills, wood burned in fireplaces and stoves, and plant matter used to create energy in power plants. Currently, the most important sources of bioenergy in America are ethanol and plant matter. Ethanol is created from corn products and can yield 50 percent more total energy than is used to grow the corn and make ethanol. However, plant groups such as grasses and trees can produce up to four to five times the energy required to make the ethanol. The highest energy yields from biomass occur in generating electricity, with energy outputs up to ten times greater than the energy inputs. The Department of Energy (DOE) suggests that up to 50 percent of our transportation fuels could be produced from biomass by 2050. Significant increases are also possible in electricity generation. But the Union of Concerned Scientists reports that government subsidy programs for both food crops and fossil fuels make increasing energy crops difficult. In addition, transportation costs for biomass are large, so plants need to be located near the production source.

However, though ethanol use has the potential to decrease harmful environmental effects such as global warming, its benefits are not guaranteed. Environmentalist support for biomass energy depends on the types of crops used, the methods of farming, and the proportion of fuel mixed with gasoline. Scientists have found only gas mixtures with over 80 percent ethanol reduce smog and mixes with less than 80 percent ethanol may be worse than regular gasoline products, releasing other smog-forming chemicals. So, while biomass energy may be less harmful to the environment and less risky than some traditional power sources, there may be better options.

Other possibly more sustainable alternatives include hydroelectric and geothermal power sources, which unfortunately still have some negative environmental impacts. Hydroelectric power is generated by water and has been used since the beginning of civilization for such tasks as grinding grain. In 1882, the first turbine was attached to a generator in Wisconsin, and hydropower is now the most reliable, lowest cost electricity source in America. Ocean energy is a possible hydropower source, as well as river energy, but it is still in the development stage. Most of the hydropower plants still functioning today were created by federal government irrigation and energy projects in the 1930s. These plants use turbines and dams on rivers. Many of these are still federally owned, although independent developers became more prominent after the Public Utility Regulatory Policies Act was passed in 1978. An estimated 1,750 old or idle dams might be able to produce energy, but growth of hydropower has been modest because of environmental, political, and regulatory obstacles. Hydropower dams can have negative impacts on wildlife and river ecosystems. The flooding of river habitat destroys some natural environments, and dams may block fish migratory routes, endangering some species. Water quality may also be affected.

Fortunately, the impacts of dams can be lessened by creating minimum instream flows. This decreases the dam's total power-generating ability, but may greatly improve the health of rivers, fish, and wildlife. The Federal Energy Regulatory Commission is responsible for overseeing the licenses of hydropower dams; as the licenses for old dams come up for renewal, the Commission ensures that the dams meet regulations imposed by the 1977 Clean Water Act, the 1973 Endangered Species Act, and the 1969 National Environmental Policy Act. Based on environmental and safety risks, some environmental groups argue against renewing dam licenses and federal subsidies for hydropower. Instead they suggest giving tax incentive packages to more sustainable energy sources such as wind and solar power. They advocate a market approach in which projects can apply for "low-impact" certification by the Low Impact Hydropower Institute. This program creates incentives, according to the Environmental Media Services, "for dam owners to meet modern environmental standards by rewarding well-sited and well-operated projects with certification that can be used in the market place to sell power at a premium."

Geothermal energy, like hydropower, is a minor supplier of energy in the United States. Geothermal energy has been used for centuries by harnessing the energy of the earth in the form of steam and hot water. Steam power was first used to make electricity in 1904. Advantages of geothermal energy include its reliability and enormous energy reserves. Currently the United States has 1,300 geothermal direct-use systems in operation with a capacity to produce about 2,700 megawatts of geothermal energy. About equal to the energy generated from 58 million barrels of oil, it can provide for the energy needs of 3.7 million people. The DOE has suggested that geothermal energy might provide 10 percent of the West's energy needs within a generation. The cost of geothermal energy is very low (in the range of 4 to 8 cents per kilowatt with further cost reductions possible). This makes geothermal energy a competitive alternative to new coal-fired power plants.

Other sustainable alternatives include solar, wind, and hydrogen energy. Wind energy, like geothermal power, has been used for centuries. In the 1980s, wind power became the fourth largest renewable energy electricity source in the United States. Wind power is now relatively cheap to produce, at 3 to 6 cents per kilowatt-hour. Improved technology has reduced the cost of making electricity from wind power by 90 percent since the 1980s, making it competitive with energy from fossil fuels. There are over 3,000 megawatts of wind power in the country, and 6 percent of contiguous U.S. land is considered good wind area, which could supply more than 4.4 billion megawatt hours if it were all used for energy production. This is more than a third of the electricity used in the United States in 1999. Perhaps more realistically, DOE has suggested that wind energy might be expanded to provide the electricity for 10 million homes.

The use of solar power, or energy generated from the sun, is also expanding rapidly in the United States as over 200,000 homes use some sort of solar energy. The sun provides more than 650 times the actual amount of energy the country used in the early 1990s, and 100 square miles in Nevada could yield all its annual needs. Photovoltaic (PV) panels are the primary means of capturing this energy and creating electricity. This technology was developed as a result of the 1970s energy crisis, and greatly improved in the 1980s, but during the 1990s the technology's growth slowed for two reasons. First, oil prices stabilized; second, tax incentives for solar energy were removed. But PV panels have great potential for ameliorating today's energy problems, because they can produce energy when the electricity grid is most in demand. Solar energy may help prevent supply problems such as those that caused California's blackouts in 1989. The best thing about PV systems is that they produce electricity without polluting. Within three years, according to the Environmental Media Services, they also pay back "the energy used in producing them and the CO_2 generated in doing so."

When hydrogen is used in fuel cells, only heat and water are produced as by-products, but the process of producing the hydrogen can create pollution. Hydrogen can be extracted from water, natural gas, or even some bacteria and algae. As of the early 2000s there were problems in storing and transporting the vast amounts of gas required. It is worth mentioning, however, that if hydrogen energy can be made sustainable, it may be palatable to the current energy industry because the inputs must be gathered regularly and can be sold in small amounts in the same way that oil or gas can be sold. Thus it may be more widely accepted than other alternative energy sources.

AMERICA'S ENERGY POLICY

Given the current energy crisis, the decline of oil availability, and the environmental and health impact of traditional energy resources, it seems clear to many that America's energy policy should focus on sustainable energy resources. Especially promising resources are geothermal, solar, and wind power. There are some signs that the United States is moving in this direction. President Bush's energy policy department, the NEPD, for example, has proposed further research and development of these technologies for America's future policy (currently being debated in Congress). But reaction to their proposal, like the recent policy suggestions of other government bodies, was mixed. Some argue that recent trends do not bode well for America's energy future. In the following paragraphs we discuss a few of the recommendations by various government and social agencies.

The NEPD's goal was to create a balanced energy plan for America's future. In addition to renewable energy research, the department suggested increased funding for power from coal and nuclear energy, opening up access to federal land to drill for oil, drilling in Alaska and the Artic for natural gas and oil, and making it easier for companies to get licenses for nuclear power plants. According to energy expert Eric Oatman, the rationale is that "the nation owes its misfortunes with energy not just to a shortage of cheap oil but to a host of causes, including disarray in the nuclear power industry, environmental roadblocks to coal exploitation, and the inability or unwillingness of Americans to use energy more efficiently." Nonetheless, the NEPD has come under attack for many of these policies. Many environmentalists argue that an energy policy based on vast subsidies for coal and rolling back the Clean Air Act will have negative impacts on both public health and the environment.

Partly because of these worries, not all of the NEPD's suggestions are being implemented. For instance, the U.S. Senate, in 2003, rejected the bill passed in the House of Representatives proposing drilling in the Alaskan Arctic National Wildlife Refuge. Other NEPD's proposals are environmentally friendly, such as increasing funding for renewable energy use and development. Specifically, the NEPD suggests using geothermal energy, biomass, and solar energy and emphasizes the importance of alternative fuel vehicles that use methanol, ethanol, compressed natural gas, propane, biodiesel, and natural gas. Hydrogen energy and fusion are also mentioned as possible avenues for further research. The NEPD further advised increasing energy efficiency and conservation.

The NEPD also indicated that increased regulation of pollutants including sulfur dioxide, nitrogen oxides, and mercury would be desirable if appropriate market-based incentives were used.

Unfortunately, some specific NEPD proposals regarding renewable energy resources are controversial and yet to be implemented. For example, the NEPD advocated increasing the use of ethanol. As discussed earlier, ethanol is not the best energy alternative and environmentalists worry about the impact of hydropower dams. Political allegiances to corn growers may be a factor in this decision. The NEPD has stated that "[t]he most important barrier to increased renewable energy production remains economic: Non-hydropower renewable energy generation costs are greater than other traditional energy sources." However, this conclusion is questionable given the current costs of solar, geothermal, and wind power and their amazing energy-generating potential. Perhaps the NEPD and U.S. government should focus on encouraging the use of more sustainable rather than just renewable energy resources and the maintenance of current methods of energy production.

Concerns with the NEPD policy might be addressed by following the Union for Concerned Scientists' recommendation to implement a "Renewable Portfolio Standard." This standard market-oriented policy gradually increases the required percentage of electricity coming from renewable energy resources. A goal of 20 percent by 2020 would help stabilize carbon dioxide emissions and cut pollution from nitrogen oxides, sodium dioxides, and mercury associated with coal burning. It would also slowly increase natural gas prices, shield consumers from the price volatility of current energy markets, and create jobs.

Net metering is another promising policy that would eliminate penalties for homes and small businesses generating power from renewable sources, as they would pay utility companies only for their net usage, receiving a discount against their utility bills for the electrical energy they put back into the grid. This provides an incentive to use such resources, reduces the strain on the electricity transmission and distribution system, and establishes simple and consistent rules for the entire grid.

A Public Benefits Trust Fund for investment in renewables, created by taxing electricity to generate $6 billion annually, has also been suggested. This fund would establish energy efficiency and low-income assistance programs to help guarantee universal access to energy. Finally, tax incentives for renewables might be furthered by permanently extending the 1.5 cents per kilowatt-hour production tax credit for energy created by wind power and closed-loop biomass, and broadening the credit to include open-loop biomass, solar energy, and geothermal energy. Tax credits might also be created for homes and businesses that install small solar or wind energy-generating systems. Alternately, requiring companies and consumers to absorb the community costs of pollution (i.e., take responsibility for the external costs of burning fossil fuels) would help make renewables competitive. The full costs of fossil fuels are much higher than people realize.

OTHER POLICIES AND SUGGESTIONS OF INTEREST

Implementing these recommended changes will not be easy. The United States signed the Rio Agreement on Climate in 1992, and the EPA implemented the Regional Haze Rule of 1999 to control air pollution near national parks. But in 2002, the United States backed out of the Kyoto Protocol agreements, which were intended to supplement the Rio Agreement provisions. The Rio Agreement was an attempt by the international community to control air pollution and reduce carbon dioxide emissions and other greenhouse gases that lead to global climate change. It provided for technology and funds to help developing countries reduce their emissions.

One reason President Bush refused to sign the Kyoto Protocol was its requirement that the United States cut its emissions by approximately 40 percent. The president was also concerned that the agreement required only that developing countries stabilize (not reduce) their emissions. However, a clause in the agreement allowed countries to trade permissible pollution levels. This would have helped stabilize world pollution levels as developed countries supported developing countries in becoming more environmentally sound by purchasing the rights to produce more pollution. Presumably, the reasoning was that the developed countries (who have created most of the pollution in the process of development) ought to bear the costs of cleanup. Instead, President Bush proposed policy changes focused on "develop[ing] technologies, market incentives, and other creative ways to address climate change," according to the Center for Energy and Economic Development, a pro-coal industry organization.

This does not, however, appear to be happening, as the Bush administration's 2001 budget cut spending on renewable energy technology and research by 37 percent. "Even more drastically—photovoltaics, solar buildings, concentrated solar power, wind energy, and geothermal programs are being cut by half or more," according to an Environmental Media Services report, while some claim that "they should be receiving large infusions of new funding to take advantage of the unique contribution they can make to increasing and diversifying our energy supply."

The twenty-first century will require significant changes in America's energy consumption. To be successful, America will have to make good policy decisions in dealing with energy issues. Because oil reserves are running out and alternative energy sources must be found, the environmentalists appear to be right that now is the time for America to make the change to more sustainable energy alternatives.

N. Hassoun

REFERENCES

Ball, Howard. *Justice Downwind: America's Atomic Testing Program in the 1950's.* New York: Oxford University Press, 1986.

Banks, Ferdinand. *The Political Economy of Coal.* Lanham, MD: Lexington Books, 1985.

Blackburn, John. *The Renewable Energy Alternative: How the United States and the World Can Prosper Without Nuclear Energy or Coal.* Durham, NC: Duke University Press, 1987.

Bromley, Simon. *American Hegemony and World Oil: The Industry, the State System and the World Economy.* University Park: The Pennsylvania State University Press, 1991.

Brower, Michael. *Cool Energy: Renewable Solutions to Environmental Problems.* Cambridge, MA: MIT Press, 1994.

Campbell, John. *Collapse of an Industry: Nuclear Power and the Contradictions of U.S. Policy.* Ithaca, NY: Cornell University Press, 1988.

Ender, Richard, and John Kin, eds. *Energy Resources Development: Politics and Policies.* New York: Quantum Books, 1987.

Flavin, Christopher. *Electricity for a Developing World: New Directions.* Worldwatch Paper, 70. Washington, DC: Worldwatch Institute, 1986.

Flavin, Christopher, Rick Plitz, and Nichols Chris. *Sustainable Energy.* Washington, DC: Renew America, 1989.

Ghanem, Skuti. *OPEC: The Rise and Fall of an Exclusive Club.* New York: Methuen, 1986.

Hunt, Daniel. *The Gasohol Handbook.* New York: Industrial Press, 1981.

Karlsson, Svante. *Oil and the World Order: American Foreign Oil Policy.* Totowa, NJ: Barnes and Noble, 1986.

Katsouros, Mary. "Oil Spills." In *The Energy Environment Connection,* ed. Jack M. Hollander. Washington, DC: Island Press, 1992.

Knoepfel, Heinz. *Energy 2000: An Overview of the World's Energy Resources in the Decades to Come.* New York: Gordon and Breach Science Publishers, 1986.

Knowles, Ruth. *America's Energy Famine: Its Cause and Cure.* Norman: Oklahoma Press, 1980.

Miller, E. Willard, and Ruby Miller. *Energy and American Society: A Reference Handbook.* Santa Barbara, CA: ABC-CLIO, 1993.

Murray, Raymond. *Nuclear Energy.* 3rd ed. Pergamon Unified Engineering Series, Vol. 22. Elmsford, NY: Pergamon Press, 1988.

Oatman, Eric. *Prospects for Energy in America.* The Reference Shelf. Volume 52, No. 3. New York: H. W. Wilson, 1980.

Roberts, Paul. *The End of Oil: On the Edge of a Perilous New World.* Boston: Houghton Mifflin, 2004.

Rudolph, Richard, and Scott Ridley. *Power Struggle: The Hundred-Year War over Electricity.* New York: Harper and Row, 1986.

Seymour, Richard, and Richard Geyer. "Fates and Effects of Oil Spills." In *Annual Review of Energy and the Environment,* ed. Jack M. Hollander. Palo Alto, CA: Annual Review Inc., 1992.

Shea, Cynthia. *Renewable Energy: Today's Contribution, Tomorrow's Promise.* Worldwatch Paper, 81. Washington, DC: Worldwatch Institute, 1988.

Smil, Vaclav. *Energy in World History.* Boulder, CO: Westview, 1994.

———. *Energy at the Crossroads: Global Perspectives and Uncertainties.* Cambridge, MA: MIT Press, 2003.

Swan, Christopher. *Suncell: Energy, Economy and Photovoltaics.* San Francisco: Sierra Club Books, 1986.

Tsai, Hui-Liang. *Energy Shocks and the World Economy: Adjustment Policies and Problems.* Westport, CT: Praeger, 1989.

Union of Concerned Scientists. *The Nuclear Fuel Cycle.* MIT Press Environmental Studies Series. Cambridge, MA: MIT Press, 1975.

Yergin, Daniel. *The Prize: The Epic Quest of Oil, Money and Power.* New York: Touchstone Books, 1992.

WEB SITES

American Council for an Energy-Efficient Economy: www.aceee.org/energy/index.htm

Coalition for Affordable and Reliable Energy: www.carenergy.com

Department of Energy: www.doe.gov

Environmental Media Service: www.ems.org

European Commission web site on Energy Research: http://europa.eu.int/comm/research/energy/index_en.html

Low Impact Hydropower Institute: www.lowimpacthydro.org

National Energy Policy Development Group: www.whitehouse.gov/energy/

New Energy Partners: www.newenergypartners.com

Petroleum World: www.petroleumworld.com

Union of Concerned Scientists: www.ucsusa.org/clean_energy/renewable_energy/

GLOSSARY

Abiogenic Theory. The theory that petroleum was trapped beneath the surface of the earth when the earth was formed and is slowly surfacing.

Bioenergy. Energy generated from ethanol motor fuel, gas from landfills, wood burned in fireplaces and stoves, and plant matter used to create energy in power plants.

Bitumen. A petroleum product extracted from oil sands that can be turned into crude oil and natural gas.

CO_2. Carbon dioxide, a compound that contributes to global warming and climate change.

Coal. A type of fossil fuel composed of hydrocarbons. Types of coal include lignite, sub-bituminous, bituminous, semi-bituminous, semi-anthracite, and anthracite.

Combustion. Burning.

Eutrophication. Pollution of marine environments by excessive nutrient inputs, especially phosphorus and nitrogen.

Fluidized burners. Used for burning coal, these burners allow large amounts of limestone to mix with coal and reduce sulfur emissions; they also burn at cooler temperatures (1400°F rather than 3000°F), and thus release fewer nitrogen oxides.

Gasification. A process that occurs when coal is turned into carbon monoxide and hydrogen gas. These gases can then be burned or turned into everything from liquid fuels like methanol to plastic products.

Hydrocarbons. Carbon and hydrogen molecules.

Infrared radiation. A type of light wave between the visible and microwave parts of the electromagnetic spectrum.

Instream flows. Water maintained in a river to help preserve wildlife, habitat, and aesthetic value.

Kilowatt-hours. A measure of energy that is generated by a single-kilowatt source in one hour.

Megawatt-hours. One common measure of energy generation and consumption frequently used in talking about large power plants.

Mercury. A toxic chemical released from coal-burning power plants.

Nitrogen oxides. Chemicals emitted from coal-fired power plants that not only contribute to ground-level ozone (or smog), acid rain, and degradation of natural forest, but also reduce the yield of many important agricultural crops.

Nuclear power. Power generated from uranium and other radioactive materials.

OPEC. Organization of Petroleum Exporting Countries.

Particulate matter. Ash and other sooty materials in the air.

Petroleum. A term that includes crude oil, natural gas, and bitumen collected from oil sands.

Photovoltaic panels. The primary means of capturing solar energy and creating electricity. These panels consist of mirrored surfaces that focus light onto a receiver to heat a liquid and drive a turbine in the panel.

Renewable energy. Types include water power, geothermal energy, biomass energy, wind, and solar energy.

Scrubbers. Also known as flue gas desulferization units, scrubbers use limestone to filter noxious chemicals from coal smoke before it is released into the atmosphere.

Slurry. A mixture of coal, water, and oil created to aid in transporting coal through pipelines.

Sulfur dioxide. Chemicals emitted from coal-fired power plants that not only contribute to ground-level ozone (or smog), acid rain, and degradation of natural forest, but also reduce the yield of many important agricultural crops.

Tailings. Nuclear waste deposits.

Ultrasound. High-frequency soundwaves.

Yucca Mountain. Site for nuclear waste deposits in southern Nevada.

DOCUMENTS

Document 1. Excerpts from Report of the National Energy Policy Development Group, Overview, 2001

In January 2001 the George W. Bush administration established the National Energy Policy Development Group, chaired by Vice-President Dick Cheney. While admitting the importance of energy conservation, the Report of the National Energy Policy Development Group *emphasized the need to develop more domestic energy supplies of oil, gas, and coal. The plan also calls for a renewed development of nuclear energy.*

Overview: Reliable, Affordable, and Environmentally Sound Energy for America's Future

Components of the National Energy Policy

The National Energy Policy we propose follows three basic principles:

- The Policy is a long-term, comprehensive strategy. Our energy crisis has been years in the making, and will take years to put fully behind us.
- The Policy will advance new, environmentally friendly technologies to increase energy supplies and encourage cleaner, more efficient energy use.

- The Policy seeks to raise the living standards of the American people, recognizing that to do so our country must fully integrate its energy, environmental, and economic policies.

Applying these principles, we urge action to meet five specific national goals. America must modernize conservation, modernize our energy infrastructure, increase energy supplies, accelerate the protection and improvement of the environment, and increase our nation's energy security. . . .

Modernize Our Energy Infrastructure

The energy we use passes through a vast nationwide network of generating facilities, transmission lines, pipelines, and refineries that converts raw resources into usable fuel and power. That system is deteriorating, and is now strained to capacity.

One reason for this is government regulation, often excessive and redundant. Regulation is needed in such a complex field, but it has become overly burdensome. Regulatory hurdles, delays in issuing permits, and economic uncertainty are limiting investment in new facilities, making our energy markets more vulnerable to transmission bottlenecks, price spikes and supply disruptions. America needs more environmentally-sound energy projects to connect supply sources to growing markets and to deliver energy to homes and business.

To reduce the incidence of electricity blackouts, we must greatly enhance our ability to transmit electric power between geographic regions, that is, sending power to where it is needed from where it is produced. Most of America's transmission lines, substations, and transformers were built when utilities were tightly regulated and provided service only within their assigned regions. The system is simply unequipped for large-scale swapping of power in the highly competitive market of the 21st century.

The National Energy Policy will modernize and expand our energy infrastructure in order to ensure that energy supplies can be safely, reliably, and affordably transported to homes and businesses. This report includes recommendations to:

- Direct agencies to improve pipeline safety and expedite pipeline permitting.
- Issue an Executive Order directing federal agencies to expedite permits and coordinate federal, state, and local actions necessary for energy-related project approvals on a national basis in an environmentally sound manner, and establish an interagency task force chaired by the Council on Environmental Quality. The task force will ensure that federal agencies set up appropriate mechanisms to coordinate federal, state and local permitting activity in particular regions where increased activity is expected.
- Grant authority to obtain rights-of-way for electricity transmission lines with the goal of creating a reliable national transmission grid. Similar authority already exists for natural gas pipelines and highways.
- Enact comprehensive electricity legislation that promotes competition, encourages new generation, protects consumers, enhances reliability, and promotes renewable energy.
- Implement administrative and regulatory changes to improve the reliability of the interstate transmission system and enact legislation to provide for enforcement of electricity reliability standards.
- Expand the Energy Department's research and development on transmission reliability and superconductivity.

Increase Energy Supplies

A primary goal of the National Energy Policy is to add supply from diverse sources. This means domestic oil, gas, and coal. It also means hydropower and nuclear power. And it means making greater use of non-hydro renewable sources now available.

One aspect of the present crisis is an increased dependence, not only on foreign oil, but on a narrow range of energy options. For example, about 90 percent of all new electricity plants currently under construction will be fueled by natural gas. While natural gas has many advantages, an over-reliance on any one fuel source leaves consumers vulnerable to price spikes and supply disruptions. There are several other fuel sources available that can help meet our needs.

Currently, the U.S. has enough coal to last for another 250 years. Yet very few coal-powered electric plants are now under construction. Research into clean coal technologies may increase the attractiveness of coal as a source for new generation plants.

Nuclear power plants serve millions of American homes and businesses, have a dependable record for safety and efficiency, and discharge no greenhouse gases into the atmosphere. As noted earlier, these facilities currently generate 20 percent of all electricity in America, and more than 40 percent of electricity generated in 10 states in the Northeast, South, and Midwest. Other nations, such as Japan and France, generate a much higher percentage of their electricity from nuclear power. Yet the number of nuclear plants in America is actually projected to decline in coming years, as old plants close and none are built to replace them.

Enormous advances in technology have made oil and natural gas exploration and production both more efficient and more environmentally sound. Better technology means fewer rigs, more accurate drilling, greater resource recovery and environmentally friendly exploration. Drilling pads are 80 percent smaller than a generation ago. High-tech drilling allows us to access supplies five to six miles away from a single compact drilling site, leaving sensitive wetlands and wildlife habitats undisturbed. Yet the current regulatory structure fails to take sufficient account of these extraordinary advances, excessively restricting the environmentally safe production of energy from many known sources.

Our policy will increase and diversify our nation's sources of traditional and alternative fuels in order to furnish families and businesses with reliable and affordable energy, to enhance national security, and to improve the environment. This report includes recommendations to:

- Issue an Executive Order directing all federal agencies to include in any regulatory action that could significantly and adversely affect energy supplies a detailed statement on the energy impact of the proposed action.
- Open a small fraction of the Arctic National Wildlife Refuge to environmentally regulated exploration and production using leading-edge technology. Examine the potential for the regulated increase in oil and natural gas development on other federal lands.
- Earmark $1.2 billion of bid bonuses from the environmentally responsible leasing of ANWR to fund research into alternative and renewable energy resources including wind, solar, biomass, and geothermal.

- Enact legislation to expand existing alternative fuels tax incentives to include landfills that capture methane gas emissions for electricity generation and to electricity produced from wind and biomass. Extend the number of eligible biomass sources to include forest-related sources, agricultural sources, and certain urban sources.
- Provide $2 billion over 10 years to fund clean coal technology research and a new credit for electricity produced from biomass co-fired with coal.
- Direct federal agencies to streamline the hydropower relicensing process with proper regard given to environmental factors.
- Provide for the safe expansion of nuclear energy by establishing a national repository for nuclear waste, and by streamlining the licensing of nuclear power plants.

Accelerate Protection and Improvement of the Environment

America's commitment to environmental protection runs deep. We are all aware of past excesses in our use of the natural world and its resources. No one wishes to see them repeated. In the 21st century, the ethic of good stewardship is well established in American life and law.

We do not accept the false choice between environmental protection and energy production. An integrated approach to policy can yield a cleaner environment, a stronger economy, and a sufficient supply of energy for our future. The primary reason for that has been steady advances in the technology of locating, producing, and using energy. Since 1970, emissions of key air emissions are down 31 percent. Cars today emit 85 percent less carbon monoxide than 30 years ago. Lead emissions are down 90 percent. Lead levels in ambient air today are 98 percent lower than they were in 1970. America is using more, and polluting less.

One of the factors harming the environment today is the very lack of a comprehensive, long-term national energy policy. States confronting blackouts must take desperate measures, often at the expense of environmental standards, requesting waivers of environmental rules, and delaying the implementation of anti-pollution efforts. Shortfalls in electricity generating capacity and shortsighted policies have blocked construction of new, cleaner plants, leaving no choice but to rely on older, inefficient plants to meet demand. The increased use of emergency power sources, such as diesel generators, results in greater air pollution.

New anti-pollution technologies hold great promise for the environment. The same can be said of 21st century power generators that must soon replace older models; significant new resources for land conservation efforts; and continued research into renewable energy sources. All have a place in the National Energy Policy.

The National Energy Policy will build upon our nation's successful track record and will promote further improvements in the productive and efficient use of energy. This report includes recommendations to:

- Enact "multi-pollutant" legislation to establish a flexible, market-based program to significantly reduce and cap emissions of sulfur dioxide, nitrogen oxides, and mercury from electric power generators.
- Increase exports of environmentally friendly, market-ready U.S. technologies that generate a clean environment and increase energy efficiency.
- Establish a new "Royalties Conservation Fund" and earmark royalties from new, clean oil and gas exploration in ANWR to fund land conservation efforts.
- Implement new guidelines to reduce truck idling emissions at truck stops.

Increase Energy Security

The National Energy Policy seeks to lessen the impact on Americans of energy price volatility and supply uncertainty. Such uncertainty increases as we reduce America's dependence on foreign sources of energy. At the same time, however, we recognize that a significant percentage of our resources will come from overseas. Energy security must be a priority of U.S. trade and foreign policy.

We must look beyond our borders and restore America's credibility with overseas suppliers. In addition, we must build strong relationships with energy-producing nations in our own hemisphere, improving the outlook for trade, investment, and reliable supplies.

Energy security also requires preparing our nation for supply emergencies, and assisting low-income Americans who are most vulnerable in times of supply disruption, price spikes, and extreme weather.

To ensure energy security for our nation and its families, our report includes these recommendations:

- Dedicate new funds to the Low Income Home Energy Assistance Program by funneling a portion of oil and gas royalty payments to LIHEAP when oil and natural gas prices exceed a certain amount.
- Double funding for the Department of Energy's Weatherization Assistance Program, increasing funding by $1.4 billion over 10 years.
- Direct the Federal Emergency Management Administration to prepare for potential energy-related emergencies.
- Support a North American Energy Framework to expand and accelerate cross-border energy investment, oil and gas pipelines, and electricity grid connections by streamlining and expediting permitting procedures with Mexico and Canada. Direct federal agencies to expedite necessary permits for a gas pipeline route from Alaska to the lower 48 states.

Looking Toward the Future

The President's goal of reliable, affordable, and environmentally sound energy supplies will not be reached overnight. It will call forth innovations in science, research, and engineering. It will require time and the best efforts of leaders in both political parties. It will require also that we deal with the facts as they are, meeting serious problems in a serious way. The complacency of the past decade must now give way to swift but well-considered action.

Present trends are not encouraging, but they are not immutable. They are among today's most urgent challenges, and well within our power to overcome. Our country has met many great tests. Some have imposed extreme hardship and sacrifice. Others have demanded only resolve, ingenuity, and clarity of purpose. Such is the case with energy today.

We submit these recommendations with optimism. We believe that the tasks ahead, while great, are achievable. The energy crisis is a call to put to good use the resources around us, and the talents within us. It summons the best of America, and offers the best of rewards—in new jobs, a healthier environment, a stronger economy, and a brighter future for our people.

Source: National Energy Policy Development Group, Overview of "Report of the National Energy Policy Development Group," 2001.

Document 2. Excerpts from the Sierra Club's "America's Future Under the Bush Energy Plan," 2001

In this critique of the George W. Bush administration's approach to America's energy future, the environmental organization, the Sierra Club, argues that the administration-created National Energy Policy Development Group's plan overemphasizes development of new oil, gas, and coal sources on environmentally threatened land as well as nuclear energy, and fails to push strongly enough for conservation and the development of environmentally friendly renewable energy sources such as solar and wind power.

President Bush says we need to drill for oil and gas on America's public lands, build 1,300 new power plants and increase our reliance on nuclear power. But there's a better way to meet America's energy needs. We must increase our energy efficiency, expand our use of clean, renewable energy and switch from dirty coal power to cleaner natural gas. At the same time, we can and must protect our public lands.

The president's plan calls for oil and gas exploration on public lands. The *Energy Map* that accompanies this report shows 21 wild areas that could be irreversibly damaged if his plan were implemented. We don't have to sacrifice these lands to meet our nation's energy needs.

The president's plan calls for 1,300 new power plants by 2020. Where will he put all these plants? This map shows how the country could look if we spread the new power plants evenly around the country. We can choose a better future. A Department of Energy study shows that we can avoid the need for approximately 610 of the new power plants with energy-efficiency measures and avoid another 180 plants by using renewable energy. We could meet remaining demand by replacing old, dirty coal-fired power plants with new, cleaner, high-efficiency natural gas plants.

The president's plan calls for an expansion of nuclear power. But there is no safe way to store the dangerous radioactive waste from existing nuclear plants, and nuclear energy could only be expanded with huge federal subsidies. We should instead invest those monies in wind, solar, geothermal and other renewable technologies that can help meet our energy needs and protect the environment.

Dig, Drill and Destroy

President Bush's "dig, drill and destroy" approach to energy policy puts some of America's most treasured wildlands at risk in a shortsighted attempt to address energy needs. Wildlands from the remote coastal plain of the Arctic National Wildlife Refuge to the waters off the California shore could be threatened by oil spills and the inevitable degradation that large-scale operations cause. In addition, neighborhoods all across the United States would be at risk of increased air pollution and resulting health problems from new power plants.

Multinational oil companies already have access to the bulk of public lands in the West—95 percent of lands managed by the Bureau of Land Management in the Rocky Mountain West are available for oil and gas leasing. Yet Bush's energy plan would target for industrial development the few remaining pristine wild areas of the West, as well as fragile coastal waters currently protected from industrial development.

Fortunately, we have other choices: There are quicker, cleaner, cheaper and safer ways to solve our energy problems. By making our appliances and cars more energy efficient and switching our focus to renewable energy options like solar and wind power and cleaner natural gas, we make an immediate impact, save money, maintain the quality of life in our neighborhoods and preserve our wild places for generations to come.

Lands at Risk

Among the special places at risk from Bush's energy plan are our national monuments. His plan would "review public lands withdrawals" and "impediments to oil and gas leasing" on our public lands. Both President Bush and Interior Secretary Gale Norton have indicated they would exploit our national monuments for oil and gas extraction and coal mining, despite overwhelming public opposition. In fact, 68 percent of Americans oppose oil drilling in national monuments. . . .

America's Coasts at Risk

America's coastlines provide outstanding tourism and recreation opportunities, as well as crucial wildlife habitat for a host of coastal and marine species. A moratorium on offshore oil and gas drilling has protected the bulk of our sensitive coastlines for almost two decades. The ban has been renewed year after year due to the support of an overwhelming majority of citizens in coastal states, who oppose the adverse effects that offshore development will have on critical shoreline habitat and regional economies that depend largely on tourism.

The Bush energy plan threatens to undo this protection for some coastal areas, threatening our shorelines and rich coastal waters with devastating oil spills as well as the routine but substantial pollution associated with oil and gas development.

Wild Forests Vulnerable to Drilling

Wild roadless forests purify our drinking water, provide our families with places to hike, hunt, fish and camp, and give homes to fish and wildlife, including endangered species like grizzly bear and salmon. In January 2001, following years of public debate in which the majority of the American public expressed strong support for permanently protecting our wild forests, President Clinton created a rule that would protect nearly 60 million acres of wild national forests from new and damaging roadbuilding and oil and gas development. But President Bush has derailed this plan, leaving our most pristine forests vulnerable to development.

For instance, several wild areas of the San Juan National Forest at the heart of Colorado's Rocky Mountains are at risk. The Hermosa area contains perhaps the most diverse array of forest habitats on the entire San Juan National Forest, with numerous superb examples of old-growth ponderosa pine stands, and two significant proposed Research Natural Areas. Hermosa also harbors thriving populations of Colorado River cutthroat trout. In addition, the HD Mountains area includes some of the highest quality old-growth ponderosa pine left in the San Juan Mountains, and in Colorado for that matter.

But the oil and gas industry have their sights set on the San Juan, with numerous proposals to drill for coalbed methane in the HD Mountains, as well as other development.

It's not just oil and gas development that threatens our wildlands. The Bush energy plan will undoubtedly push for new uranium mining in many states. The Bush plan to expand nuclear power poses a distinct threat to places like the Kaibab National Forest in Arizona and New Mexico's Crown Point, where proposed uranium mines would threaten the groundwater and the health of 10,000 local people, mostly Navajos.

Building 1,300 new power plants will also require massive construction of new transmission lines. Arizona is especially threatened by this construction. One power line is slated to cut through the Ironwood National Monument, another is to be built just outside the boundaries.

A Balanced Energy Plan: Quicker, Cleaner, Cheaper, Safer

President Bush's energy plan relies heavily on drilling for oil, mining for coal and expanding nuclear power. The president's plan won't work. We need a plan that is quicker, cheaper, cleaner and safer. Instead of relying on 20th-century energy sources, we need a plan that will move us into the 21st century, and that will shift our focus from coal and nuclear to renewable energy sources and energy efficiency.

The president has included $2 billion in his budget for the coal industry, and he supports so-called "clean coal." The fact is that coal is not clean. In the electric-utility sector, coal-fired power plants are responsible for 88 percent of carbon-dioxide emissions, which contribute to global warming; 93 percent of smog-forming nitrogen-oxide emissions; and 99 percent of mercury emissions, which contaminate our water and land.

The president also wants to expand our nation's nuclear industry. This move would increase stockpiles of high-level radioactive nuclear waste that remain dangerous for tens of thousands of years. Right now, this waste is piling up around the country with nowhere to go, because there is no acceptable place to store it. To make matters worse, nuclear power requires huge government subsidies that force taxpayers to support this dangerous industry.

Instead of depending on big oil, dirty coal and dangerous

nuclear power for our energy needs, we should be adopting an energy policy that is based on energy efficiency, renewable energy and responsible supply. Increasing energy efficiency guarantees that we won't waste as much energy in the first place. For example, raising our automobile fuel-economy standards to an average of 40 miles per gallon would cut global warming pollution by 600 million metric tons, save consumers at least $45 billion at the gas pump and save 1 billion barrels of oil per year. Increasing the energy efficiency of our residential air conditioners by 30 percent, versus the 20 percent increase that the president proposed, could eliminate the need for 43 new power plants.

We also need to substantially increase our use of renewable energy. Wind power has become competitive with natural gas, and the Department of Energy has estimated that wind power could be expanded to serve the electricity needs of 10 million homes. In addition, 200,000 homes in the United States use some type of photovoltaic solar technology and the market is expanding by 15 percent annually. We need to supplement these clean options with responsible use of fossil fuels, replacing our coal-fired power plants with cleaner-burning natural gas.

Source: Sierra Club, "America's Future Under the Bush Energy Plan," 2001.

ENVIRONMENTAL JUSTICE

Environmental justice (EJ) is the term for a relatively new idea in U.S. public affairs: that all people should be free from environmental inequality and have equal access to resources and the decision-making processes that govern their physical, cultural, and biological communities. The U.S. Environmental Protection Agency (EPA) defines EJ as the "fair treatment for people of all races, cultures, and incomes, regarding the development of environmental laws, regulations, and policies." The desire of individuals and communities to be "free from environmental inequality" and the movement to establish "fair treatment" have resulted from the historically disproportionate environmental burden minorities and low-income communities endure.

ORIGINS OF THE MOVEMENT

In 1978, oil contaminated with polychlorinated biphenyls (PCBs) was sprayed from a truck along the roadside of fourteen counties in North Carolina. Some 32,000 cubic yards of soil on the shoulder of 210 miles of road were illegally contaminated with the substance. State officials determined that the perpetrator of this unlawful act was the Ward Transformer Company, a Raleigh company owned and operated by Robert Earl Ward, Jr.

The State of North Carolina prosecuted Ward on charges of malicious damage to property, but the trial resulted in an acquittal. Ward was then charged and convicted in federal court on eight counts of unlawful disposal of toxic substances under the Toxic Substance Control Act (15 U.S.C. 2601–2629). Although the conviction was affirmed by the Fourth Circuit U.S. Court of Appeals, nothing in it resolved what to do with the contaminated soil.

Seeking a safe place to store the contaminated soil, the State of North Carolina proposed a 5-acre tract of land in a predominantly poor African American community in Warren County. In 1979, the EPA maintained that appropriate engineering would make the proposed landfill safe. Warren County took the state to court over the proposed landfill, believing that there were more ecologically suitable places to place the toxic soil. The federal court, however, rejected the suit (*Warren County v. North Carolina*).

The rejection prompted county officials and community members to question the political motives for selecting Warren County as the state's PCB dumping ground, because the county was the third poorest in North Carolina and 63 percent African American. A second lawsuit was filed by Warren County on grounds that the selection of the landfill site was discriminatory. That suit was unsuccessful as well, and in 1982 the state of North Carolina began trucking the PCB-contaminated soil to the Warren County location.

For 6 weeks, citizens and activists, along with Representative Walter Fauntroy (D-DC), Dr. Joseph Lowery of the Southern Christian Leadership Conference, and Dr. Benjamin F. Chavis, leader of the Commission for Racial Justice (CRJ) of the United Church of Christ, engaged in peaceful civil disobedience in an attempt to stop the dumping. One demonstration resulted in the arrest of more than 500 activists. The many protests and publicity campaigns by civil rights leaders focused attention on the plight of the Warren County residents, whose struggle became a nationwide news story and political issue in Washington.

Representative Fauntroy requested that the U.S. General Accounting Office (GAO) conduct a study of the relationship between hazardous waste landfills and the race and socioeconomic status of the communities in which they are located. The report, "Siting of Hazardous Waste Landfills and Their Correlation with Racial and Economic Status of Surrounding Communities," was completed and published in 1983. Based on 1980 U.S. Census data in eight southern states, the report found that three out of every four hazardous waste landfills were located in close proximity to minority communities. Dr. Chavis referred to the pat-

CHRONOLOGY

1964 Civil Rights Act passed; under Title VI, federal funds cannot be used to discriminate based on race, creed, color, sex, or national origin.

1969 The most comprehensive U.S. environmental legislation to date, the National Environmental Policy Act (NEPA), or "Environmental Bill of Rights," is passed by Congress and signed into law on January 1, 1970.

1970 The Environmental Protection Agency (EPA) is created. The Clean Air Act is adopted.

1971 The annual report of the President's Council on Environmental Quality (CEQ) determines that racial discrimination negatively affects the environment of the urban poor.

1976 The Toxic Substances Control Act is adopted to protect citizens' health and the environment by testing hazardous chemicals, establishing regulations, and restricting or banning harmful chemical production. The Resource Conservation and Recovery Act (RCRA) is adopted to monitor and manage solid and hazardous waste from production to disposal.

1978 Residents of Love Canal, New York, near Niagara Falls, find buried toxic waste seeping into their houses and lawns. The community of Glen Avon, California, becomes aware of the Stringfellow Acid Pits after heavy rains damage the containment wall of a dam holding back 34 million gallons of toxic waste.

1979 Linda McKeever Bullard files a complaint in *Bean v. Southwestern Waste Management Corporation* on behalf of the Northeast Community Action Group of Houston.

1980 The Comprehensive Environmental Response, Compensation and Liability Act (CERCLA), or Superfund Act, is passed.

1982 For 6 weeks, the citizens of Warren County, North Carolina, and civil rights leaders engage in peaceful civil disobedience in an attempt to stop a PCB landfill. The federal government orders the evacuation of Times Beach, Missouri, because of dioxin contamination.

1983 The GAO report, "Siting of Hazardous Waste Landfills and Their Correlation with Racial and Economic Status of Surrounding Communities," is published. The document, based on 1980 census data in eight southern states, finds that three out of four hazardous waste landfills are located in close proximity to minority communities.

1986 The West Harlem Environmental Action (WEACT) community is organized to contest the harmful effects of the North River Sewage Treatment Plant on their community.

1987 The predominantly poor and black community of Reveilletown, Louisiana, is found to be so contaminated by waste from the Georgia Pacific Company (now Georgia Gulf) that all 106 residents have to be relocated and all structures torn down. The United Church of Christ Commission for Racial Justice releases the report "Toxic Wastes and Race in the United States: A National Report on the Racial and Socioeconomic Characteristic of Communities with Hazardous Waste Sites."

1989 Residents of the lower Mississippi River area (also known as "Cancer Alley") lead the Great Louisiana Toxic March from New Orleans and Baton Rouge to draw national attention to polluted living conditions.

1990 EPA Administrator William Reilly institutes the Environmental Equity Workgroup, a collaboration of twelve federal agencies that look into issues of environmental injustice. Greenpeace publishes research findings that communities with persons of color are 89 percent more likely to have an existing hazardous waste incinerator than the general population.

1992 The EPA makes public one of the most comprehensive governmental reports on environmental justice, "Environmental Equity: Reducing Risk for All Communities." The EPA establishes the Office of Environmental Equity. St. Francis Prayer Center of Flint, Michigan, files an administrative complaint with the EPA against Genessee Power under Title VI. The complaint was misplaced by the EPA for 2 years.

1993 Representative Collins (D-IL) introduces the Environmental Health Equity Information Act to amend CERCLA of 1980. The legislation was largely unsuccessful.

1994 President Clinton issues Executive Order 12898, stating that "all federal agencies [must] insure that their programs do not inflict disproportionate environmental harm" on poor and minority communities.

1995 An environmental justice delegation participates in the Fourth World Conference on Women, in Beijing, China. Various EJ groups join together in forming the Environmental Justice Fund.

1996 Grassroots organizing by Margaret Williams results in the relocation of 358 blacks and low-income persons from the Pensacola, Florida, area due to the contamination of the Escambia Wood Treatment Plant.

1997 President Clinton issues Executive Order 13045, aimed at protecting children from environmental health and safety risks.

1998 After 8 years of litigation, the Citizens Against Nuclear Trash (CANT) wins its case against the Nuclear Regulatory Commission Atomic Safety and Licensing Board; the court finds racial bias in the selection process.

1999 Groups from thirty-seven states attend a meeting in New Orleans that leads to formation of the National Black Environmental Justice Network. The Indigenous Environmental Network (IEN) partners with the Alaska Community Against Toxins (ACAT) to establish the Persistent Organic Pesticides (POPs) campaign.

2000 End to the Toxic Terror in Black Communities national press conference is organized by the National Black Environmental Justice Network in Washington.

2001 The North Carolina legislature appropriates $7 million for the initial detoxification of the Warren County PCB landfill.

In a landmark ruling, a New Jersey court finds that the state violated Title VI of the Civil Rights Act (*South Camden Citizens in Action v. New Jersey Department of Environmental Protection*); the decision is overturned in federal court. Residents of Anniston, Alabama, win a $42.8 million settlement against Monsanto for PCB contamination. The Celebrity Tour of Cancer Alley draws national attention to the toxic corridor in the Mississippi Delta.

2002 Alaska Community Against Toxins (ACAT) publishes preliminary research findings that Siberian Yupik natives on St. Lawrence Island, Alaska, have blood PCB levels ten times higher than those of the average American.

2003 The U.S. Commission on Civil Rights publishes "Not in My Backyard: Executive Order 12,898 and Title VI as Tools for Achieving Environmental Justice," detailing the progress and shortcomings of four federal departments and agencies (Department of the Interior, Department of Housing and Urban Development, Department of Transportation, and Environmental Protection Agency) in achieving EJ.

tern of policies, practices, and directives that inordinately affected communities of race and poverty as "environmental racism and injustice."

The Warren County experience was much more than a news story about a community opposed to a locally unwanted land use (LULU) or a fashionable research topic on race relations. The civil disobedience demonstrations and GAO research captured national media attention, which in turn compelled others to examine the social circumstances of hazardous waste sitings. Specifically, Warren County became the epicenter for those at the state and federal levels determined to challenge and correct the unfair and discriminatory use of community lands. Most important, the protests of the Warren County citizenry helped create a new social class- and race-oriented perspective on environmental issues. In short, the Warren County struggle bridged two movements and principles: social justice and environmentalism.

Before the Warren County protests, environmentalism was regarded by people of color as a "white people's movement" that sought to preserve endangered wildlife, wilderness areas, and natural habitats. The events in Warren County, however, awakened poor and minority communities across the country to a new awareness of unequal environmental health risks, which they came to view as a civil rights issue.

A LONG-STANDING ISSUE

There were, of course, many instances of environmental inequality prior to the Warren County landfill case. U.S. Public Health Service (USPHS) research dating back to 1970, for example, revealed that lead poisoning from old paint disproportionately affected black and Hispanic inner-city children. In 1971, the annual report of the President's Council on Environmental Quality (CEQ) revealed that low-income and minority groups were more likely to inhabit areas with environmental pollutants and thus receive higher exposure levels. The CEQ also found that urban environmental problems are closely correlated to the lower socioeconomic status of community members.

Lower-income rural whites were also struggling against environmental injustice at Love Canal in New York, Times Beach in Missouri, and the Stringfellow Acid Pits in California, all during the 1970s and 1980s. In each of these incidents, the toxic pollution and potential for human harm was so great the towns had to be evacuated—albeit only after a long, concerted struggle on the part of citizens in each community.

Shortly after the Love Canal, Times Beach, and Stringfellow Acid Pit incidents, the U.S. government passed the Comprehensive Environmental Response, Compensation and Liability Act of 1980 (CERCLA), or the Superfund Act. The legislation made temporary emergency federal funding available for the cleanup of derelict chemical waste dumps when the parties responsible cannot be located or are unable to meet their financial obligation for cleanup. CERCLA provided one of the key pieces of federal legislation environmental justice advocates have used over the years to rectify toxic waste hazards in poor and minority areas.

The EJ movement is based on other federal legislation, such as the Civil Rights Act of 1964, which under Title VI prohibits discrimination based on race, color, religion, sex, or national origin in federally funded projects. Another federal law on which the EJ movement is based is the National Environmental Policy Act (NEPA) of 1969, frequently referred to as the "Environmental Bill of Rights." NEPA endeavors to "encourage productive and enjoyable harmony between man and his environment . . . and stimulates the health and welfare of man" (Sec. 2 [USC § 4321]). Still another federal act important to the EJ movement is the Resource Conservation and Recovery Act (RCRA) of 1976, which granted the EPA "cradle-to-grave" authority over "generation, transportation, treatment, storage, and disposal of hazardous waste" (EPA 2003). Since then, the EJ movement has focused on protecting the environment of minority and low-income communities, thereby enhancing the central aims of the Civil Rights Act, NEPA, and RCRA. Thus, the EJ movement acts as a direct agent for all communities to address civil liberty violations under these three federal acts.

RESEARCH: RACE AND SOCIOECONOMIC STATUS

After the Warren County case, the EJ movement grew rapidly across the United States, as many groups actively challenged the social structure that disproportionately burdens people of color and the rural poor with hazardous waste and pollution. Since 1982, the EJ perspective has inspired numerous research studies documenting the unequal burden of hazardous waste and plants, which have been used to help effect change through grassroots organizing and legal challenges.

Studies in the years following the Warren County struggle closely examined the relationship between race and location of hazardous waste in poor and minority communities, and GAO research in 1983 demonstrated that race was indeed a critical variable in predicting the location of hazardous waste facilities. The 1987 CRJ research report titled "Toxic Wastes and Race in the United States: A National Report on the Racial and Socioeconomic Characteristic of Communities with Hazardous Waste Sites" found that (1) the racial and socioeconomic composition of the community were reliable indicators of toxic sitings, (2) African Americans were overrepresented in areas with toxic waste sites, and (3) three out of every five African Americans and Hispanics were in communities adjacent to unregulated toxic waste sites. The CRJ findings were later supported by Robert Bullard's 1990 book *Dumping in Dixie: Race, Class, and Environmental Quality.* The 1992 National Law Journal report, "Unequal Protection: The Racial Divide in Environmental Law," found that it took the EPA 20 percent longer to cite derelict properties in minority communities and the polluters responsible paid 54 percent less in fines than in nonminority communities.

Separating race from socioeconomic status, migration patterns, economic circumstances, and other factors in the locating of toxic waste sites has been a contentious issue in the scientific community. It may not be explicit or overt racism that drives the decisions to locate toxic waste dumps in poor and minority areas. Bullard suggests that hazardous waste facilities were historically located in low-income and minority communities not because they were poor or black per se, but because these communities represented the bureaucratic "paths of least resistance." Simply put, these communities have less political, social, and economic influence and are less able to challenge the powerful economic interests that desire to dispose of their toxic waste. The result is environmental policies, directives, regulations, enforcement, and zoning laws that place poor and minority communities at a greater health risk from hazardous or toxic waste dumps.

Although these communities are at a political and economic disadvantage, they do have the means to counter LULUs. In fact, victims of environmental injustice have discovered two useful ways of countering the status quo: legal challenges and grassroots activism.

LEGAL CHALLENGES

The main legal challenges by the EJ movement have been based on the Fourteenth Amendment of the U.S. Constitution and Title VI of the Civil Rights Act of 1964. Specifically, EJ court complaints cite the Equal Protection Clause of the Fourteenth Amendment in alleging discriminatory siting of hazardous waste facilities. The first civil rights complaint to challenge the siting of a waste facility was *Bean v. Southwestern Waste Management Corporation* (1979), in which it was argued that the site locations were racially motivated and thus in violation of 42 USC §1983. But the court ultimately ruled against the plaintiff, Northeast Community Action Group of Houston, contending that the locations of the waste sites were not selected because of the minority population but because of their proximity to industrial plants.

A series of other cases based on the Equal Protection Clause of the Fourteenth Amendment followed *Bean v. Southwestern*. The state court in Georgia heard the case of *East Bibb Twiggs Neighborhood Association v. Macon-Bibb County Planning and Zoning Commission*, in which it was alleged that the Macon-Bibb County zoning commission had selected the East Bibb Twiggs community for a landfill because it was predominantly black and the citizens therefore had been denied equal protection under the constitution. Housing discrimination was acknowledged in the zoning hearing, but since the landfill siting was not a zoning issue, the discrimination was deemed inadmissible in the state court proceedings. To date, the Equal Protection Clause has been an unsuccessful legal avenue because it is difficult to prove discriminatory intent on the part of those who locate LULUs in poor and minority communities.

Environmental justice cases have also focused on Title VI of the Civil Rights Act of 1964. Specifically,

these cases have sought to prove "disparate impact"— that the neighborhoods in question assume a disproportionate burden or health risk from a hazardous facility located in their neighborhood. Two early cases based on the "disparate impact" theory—*R.I.S.E v. Kay* (1991) in Virginia and *Boyd v. Browner* (1995) in the U.S. District Court for the District of Columbia—were dismissed because the plaintiffs were unsuccessful in proving intentional environmental discrimination.

In 2001, a landmark ruling was handed down when a New Jersey district court in *South Camden Citizens in Action v. New Jersey Department of Environmental Protection* found the state had violated the "disparate impact" regulations under Section 602 of Title VI. Specifically, the New Jersey Department of Environmental Protection had violated the civil rights of South Camden citizens by granting an air permit to the St. Lawrence Cement Company. Residents convinced the court to prevent construction of the cement factory because it would have a discriminatory outcome (i.e., would likely cause adverse health affects) on the predominately African American and Hispanic community. The court injunction was dissolved, however, in a split-panel decision by the federal Third Circuit Court of Appeals on the grounds that "no private cause of action" under Section 602 of the Title VI could be used in an environmental justice claim. Hence, the court asserted that permit decisions for hazardous facilities need only comply with the EPA's "disparate impact" guidelines.

GRASSROOTS ACTIVISM

EJ court cases have been closely linked to the actions of grassroots organizations. Since the Warren County case, thousands of community actions across the United States and other countries have protested the disproportionate environmental burden endured by minority and low-income communities. Many cases are filed on behalf of a particular group struggling against a LULU. Specifically, grassroots activists and community leaders have used the research data and theories of the scientific community to challenge industrial polluters, policymakers, and state and federal officials' decisions to place toxic dumps and other environmentally hazardous facilities in poor and minority communities.

Native Americans, especially on reservations, have been involved in the EJ movement virtually from the outset. Currently in Nevada, members of the Shundahai Network, a Western Shoshone group, are actively opposing the proposed placement of the Yucca Mountain nuclear storage facility on their ancestral lands.

Because of the remoteness of and persistent economic disadvantages on Indian reservations—as well as the weak sovereignty of some tribal governments—federal and state environmental protection laws are generally less stringent and less vigorously enforced. As a result, tribes are enticed by the polluters' capital to consider toxic and hazardous waste storage and disposal facilities to solve the persistent economic problems of the reservation community. Native EJ groups, however, have long been opposed to the disposal of hazardous waste on their traditional lands.

At the same time, however, grassroots Native American groups have challenged polluters and sometimes their own tribal governments and corporations. The Native grassroots groups are typically small but committed—among them are the Native Americans for Clean Environment (NACE), Eyak Preservation Council (EPC), and Diné CARE—and have a common agenda: to stop the siting of hazardous waste dumps and environmentally destructive logging and mining operations on their lands, as well as cleanup of polluted areas.

One of the best known of these struggles involves Grace Thorpe, a Sac (Asakiwaki) and Fox (Meshkwahkihaki) native from Oklahoma. In 1992, Thorpe became concerned about her tribal government's decision to accept $2.8 million in exchange for allowing tribal land to be used as a Department of Energy (DOE) repository for high-level radioactive material. After researching the potential adverse health affects (e.g., cancer and genetic deformities) from human exposure to radioactive rods, she circulated a petition urging members of the reservation to oppose the facility. In 1993, the Sac and Fox Nation joined with her and the nuclear repository was rejected. Her success inspired other groups, and in 1993 she established the National Environmental Coalition of Native Americans (NECONA), which has convinced more than a dozen tribes to withdraw their nuclear waste zoning applications.

Other minority groups have also been active in the EJ movement, with some notable successes. In 1993, the predominantly Hispanic community of Sunset Park in Brooklyn, New York, successfully pressured Mayor David Dinkins to withdraw the siting of a sludge composting plant in their neighborhood. In 1986, the West Harlem Environmental Action (WEACT) organized a successful campaign to con-

test the harmful effects of the North River Sewage Treatment Plant on their community. In 1985, the Erie County (NY) Department of Environment concluded that there were dangerously high levels of arsenic in the soil of the Kingsley Park playground, located in a predominately African American neighborhood of Buffalo. Before being made into a playground, the site had been the home of Diarsenol, a pharmaceutical and manufacturing company that made an arsenic-based medication. Local residents protested for years, but the park was not closed down until 1988.

Since 1993, Asian and Pacific Islanders have been represented in a variety of EJ activities by the Asian-Pacific Environmental Network (APEN). In 1995, the organization joined with the Southwest Network for Environmental and Economic Justice (SNEEJ), the Indigenous Environmental Network (IEN), the Farmworker Network for Economic and Environmental Justice (FNEEJ), the Southern Organizing Committee for Economic and Social Justice (SOCESJ), and the Northeast Environmental Justice Network (NEJN) in establishing the Environmental Justice Fund. More recently, APEN has advocated on behalf of the Contra Costa County community in the San Francisco Bay area, where residents have been exposed to toxic emissions and various refinery accidents at Chevron's Richmond refinery.

Perhaps the best-known EJ struggle, however, is that among the impoverished African American communities of the Mississippi Delta. In 1989, residents of the lower Mississippi River area, often referred to as "Cancer Alley" for its high number of carcinogen-producing petrochemical plants, organized the Great Louisiana Toxic March. Participants marched from New Orleans and Baton Rouge to draw national attention to their polluted living conditions. Similar events have included an Institute of Medicine fact-finding trip to the area in 1996; the Toxic Tour of Cancer Alley, a march organized by religious leaders (bishops and church leaders from the Council of Black Churches) in 1998; and the Celebrity Tour of Cancer Alley, which included writer Alice Walker, in 2001.

Before such efforts could be marshaled, however, citizens of two Cancer Alley towns, both established by freed slaves after the Civil War, had to be relocated because of the excessive pollution. In 1987, Reveilletown, Louisiana, was found to be so contaminated by waste from a facility of the Georgia Pacific Company (now Georgia Gulf) that all 106 town residents—most of them poor and black—had to be relocated and all structures torn down. Two year later, the Dow Chemical Company was forced to buy out and relocate most of the residents of the town of Morrisonville, Louisiana, because of dangerous pollution levels.

The success of the grassroots campaign has brought national attention to the problem of pollution in Mississippi Delta communities. Years of grassroots activism have focused on the plight of those living in Cancer Alley and spurred a variety of efforts to challenge the status quo. The Tulane Environmental Law Clinic, for example, has filed a number of court cases on behalf of residents. In 1994 it succeeded in barring Shintech, Inc., from opening a polyvinyl chemical (PVC) factory in Convent, Louisiana. In another successful litigation, the residents of Anniston, Alabama, in 2001 won a $42.8 million settlement against Monsanto for excessive PCB contamination. And in 2002, after a 15-year struggle, citizens of the Diamond district in Norco, Louisiana, forced the Shell Company to buy out their property and relocate them because of toxic chemicals spewing from a nearby plant.

All in all, grassroots activism has helped transform the EJ movement into a major domestic force and an international phenomenon. In 1991, more than 1,000 people attended the First National People of Color Environmental Leadership Summit in Washington, D.C. Delegates to the meeting drafted and adopted a document titled "Principles of Environmental Justice," which outlined the objectives, goals, and demands of the EJ movement. The following year, an EJ delegation participated in the Earth Summit in Rio de Janeiro, Brazil, and in 1995 an EJ delegation attended the Fourth World Conference on Women, in Beijing, China.

FEDERAL RESPONSE

Collectively, the scientific research, grassroots activism, and legal challenges have placed increasing pressure on government—local, state, and federal—to address EJ concerns. In 1990, EPA head William Reilly established the Environmental Equity Workgroup to investigate the greater environmental burdens on poor and minority communities and assess what the EPA could do about it. Two years later, the EPA released a comprehensive report called "Environmental Equity: Reducing Risk for All Communities." According to the document, minority and low-income communities indeed have a higher level of exposure to environmental pollution (e.g., emissions from hazard waste facilities, air pollution, pesticides) and mortality (death) and morbidity (disease/illness) rates than the general population. Also in 1992, the EPA founded the Office of Environmental Equity, later renamed the Office of Environmental Justice, whose mission was to assess environmental risks and health disparities in minority and lower-income communities.

In 1994, President Clinton issued Executive Order 12898, "Federal Actions to Address Environmental Justice in Minority Populations and Low-Income Populations," requiring that "all federal agencies insure that their programs do not inflict disproportionate environmental harm" on poor and minority groups. The order called on federal agencies to comply with Title VI but was not, strictly speaking, an enforcement directive. Instead, it was a procedural order for federal agencies or programs receiving federal funding for environmental or public health activities; it established guidelines for managing and reducing environmental discrimination in compliance with Title VI regulations.

Throughout the 1990s, the EJ movement in America has worked to strengthen its domestic and international networks. Leaders have voiced their concerns about environmental injustice at numerous international conventions, such as the World Conference against Racism (WCAR) in Durban, South Africa, and the Climate Justice Summit in The Hague, Netherlands. The EJ movement has also been expanding its efforts into new areas of concern at home, such as deteriorating infrastructure and transportation inequality issues.

At the same time, the EJ movement has struggled to maintain the gains achieved in the past and thwart policy rollbacks amid shifts in prevailing political ideology. Specifically, the pro-industry stance of the George W. Bush administration has resulted in several setbacks for the EJ movement. For example, lax enforcement of environmental regulations has made it more difficult for farmers to sue the pesticide industry over product labels, and the oil and gas industries have been exempted from regulations regarding runoff pollution. According to the advocacy group Public Employees for Environmental Responsibility (PEER), cases referred to the EPA by the Department of Justice declined by 20 percent in 2001. Also, under the Bush administration, the fines for polluters breaking environmental laws declined

64 percent in 2001 and 2002. In addition to the lax enforcement of existing laws and regulations, leaders of the EJ movement point to a general reduction or softening of federal pollution regulations by the Bush administration, as well as heavy budget cuts in cleanup programs.

Andrew J. Hund

REFERENCES

Adamson, Joni, Mei Mei Evans, and Rachel Stein. *The Environmental Justice Reader: Politics, Poetics, and Pedagogy*. Tucson: University of Arizona Press, 2001.

Barnett, Harold C. *Toxic Debts and the Superfund Dilemma*. Chapel Hill: The University of North Carolina Press, 1994.

Been, V. "Unpopular Neighbors: Are Dumps and Landfills Sited Equitably?" *Resources* 115 (Spring 1994): 16–19.

Bryant, Bunyan, and Paul Mohai, eds. *Race and the Incidence of Environmental Hazards: A Time for Discourse*. Boulder, CO: Westview, 1992.

Bullard, Robert. *Dumping in Dixie: Race, Class, and Environmental Quality*. Boulder, CO: Westview, 1990.

———, ed. *Confronting Environmental Racism: Voices from the Grassroots*. Boston: South End Press, 1993.

———. *A New "Chicken-or-Egg" Debate: Which Came First—The Neighborhood, or the Toxic Dump? The Workbook*. Albuquerque, NM: Southwest Research and Information Center 19 no. 2, 1994, 60–62.

———, ed. *Unequal Protection: Environmental Justice and Communities of Color*. San Francisco: Sierra Club Books, 1996.

Camacho, David, ed. *Environmental Injustices, Political Struggles: Race, Class, and the Environment*. Durham, NC: Duke University Press, 1998.

Dunlap, Riley E., and Angela G. Mertig, eds. *American Environmentalism: The U.S. Environmental Movement, 1970–1990*. Philadelphia: Taylor and Francis, 1992.

Edelstein, Michael R. *Contaminated Communities: Psychosocial Impacts from the Contamination of Home and Place*. Boulder, CO: Westview, 1988.

Foreman, Christopher H. *The Promise and Peril of Environmental Justice*. Washington, DC: Brookings Institution, 1998.

Freudenburg, William R., and Robert Gramling. *Oil in Troubled Waters: Perceptions, Politics, and the Battle Over Offshore Drilling*. Albany: State University of New York Press, 1994.

Hamilton, J. "Testing for Environmental Racism: Prejudice, Profits, Political Power?" *Journal of Policy Analysis and Management* 14, 1 (1995): 107–32.

Mohai, P., and B. Bryant. "Environmental Racism: Reviewing the Evidence." *University of Michigan Law School Symposium on Race, Poverty, and the Environment*. Ann Arbor, Michigan, 1992.

National Law Journal. *Special Issue-Unequal Protection: The Racial Divide in Environmental Law*. September 21, 1992.

Petrikin, Jonathan. *Environmental Justice*. San Diego, CA: Greenhaven, 1995.

Roberts, J. Timmons, and Melissa M. Toffolon-Weiss. *Chronicles from the Environmental Justice Frontline*. New York: Cambridge University Press, 2001.

U.S. Environmental Protection Agency. *Environmental Equity: Reducing Risk for All Communities*. EPA-230-R-92–008 Vol. 1: Workgroup Report to the Administrator. Office of Policy, Planning and Evaluation (PM-221). Washington, DC, 1992.

U.S. States General Accounting Office. *Report, Siting of Hazardous Waste Landfills Their Correlation with Racial and Economic Status of Surrounding Communities*. AO/RCED-83–168, B-211461 (June 1, 1983).

Wapner, Paul. *Environmental Activism and World Civic Politics*. Albany: State University of New York Press, 1996.

Wells, Donald T. *Environmental Policy: A Global Perspective for the 21st Century*. Upper Saddle River, NJ: Prentice-Hall, 1996.

Zimmerman, R. "Social Equity and Environmental Risk." *Risk Analysis* 13, 6 (1993): 649–66.

WEB SITES

Deep South Center for Environmental Justice: www.xula.edu/dscej

Environmental Justice Database: www.msue.msu.edu/msue/imp/modej/masterej.html

Environmental Justice Foundation: www.ejfoundation.org

Environmental Justice Resource Center at Clark Atlanta University: www.ejrc.cau.edu/Welcome.html

Indigenous Environmental Network: www.ienearth.org

Northeast Environmental Justice Network: www.weact.org/nejn

U.S. Environmental Protection Agency (EPA)—Environmental Justice: www.epa.gov/compliance/environmentaljustice/index.html

GLOSSARY

Big 10. The ten largest environmental organizations in the United States: Defenders of Wildlife, Environmental Defense Fund, Environmental Policy Institute, Friends of the Earth, Izaak Walton League, National Audubon Society, National Wildlife Federation, Natural Resources Defense Council, Sierra Club, and the Wilderness Society.

Cancer Alley. An 80-mile stretch of Louisiana road from Baton Rouge to New Orleans that has elevated cancer rates and one of the highest concentrations of chemical factories and oil refineries (more than 100) in the United States.

CERCLA, or Superfund Act. The Comprehensive Environmental Response, Compensation and Liability Act (CERCLA) of 1980 made temporary emergency federal funding available for cleanup of derelict chemical waste properties. Specifically, this act covered parties responsible for the environmental damage in the event they cannot be located or are unable to meet their financial obligation for the cleanup.

Diné CARE. An environmental group formed in 1988 after a toxic waste dump was proposed in Dilkon on the Southwest part of the Navajo Nation. Comprised chiefly of Navajo, Diné CARE operates according to the traditional Diné philosophy of "Beauty Way."

El Pueblo para el Aire y Agua Limpio (i.e., People for Clean Air and Water) v. County of Kings. A 1991 case filed on behalf of Mexican farm workers of Kettleman City, California, by the Center on Race, Poverty and the Environment. The judge ruled that the permit process for a toxic waste incinerator was flawed because the documents were in English and community members were predominately non-English-speaking. Thus, the community members were not "meaningfully involved" in the permit process.

Environmental classism. Policies, practices, or directives, regardless of intention, that differentially affect individuals or groups from the lower social class and their communities.

Environmental equity. The equal treatment and protection, regardless of a person's race, gender, ethnicity, or social class, under existing environmental laws, policies, directives, regulations, and practices.

Environmental justice. The recognition that all people should be free from environmental inequality and have equal access to resources and the decision-making processes that govern their physical, cultural, and biological community.

Environmental racism. Policies, practices, and directives, regardless of intention, that differentially affect minority individuals, groups, and their communities.

Locally unwanted land use (LULU). A construction or land development project that local residents oppose.

Love Canal. Town in New York near Niagara Falls where residents in 1978 found buried toxic waste seeping into their homes and lawns. From 1942 to 1953, Hooker Chemicals and Plastic Corporation (presently Occidental Chemical) buried 22,000 tons of chemical waste in Love Canal. Lois Gibbs, a 27-year-old housewife, organized a 3-year community struggle for environmental justice, ultimately resulting in the relocation of 833 families. The effort also pioneered strategies and methods for educating people, challenging corporations, government officials, and scientific findings, and organizing local residents.

National Environment Coalition of Native Americans (NECONA). An antinuclear group formed by Grace Thorpe in 1992. It seeks to educate the public about the adverse health effects of radioactivity, the dangers of transporting nuclear waste, and how to organize against and challenge the nuclear industry.

National Environmental Policy Act (NEPA). Popularly known as the "Environmental Bill of Rights," the National Environmental Policy Act of 1969 is the most comprehensive environmental legislative act passed by Congress.

Not in my backyard (NIMBY). An attitude or response of individuals or community members to a LULU—such as a toxic landfill, incinerator, or nuclear dump—that they feel is dangerous to the community.

Resource Conservation and Recovery Act (RCRA). Federal legislation adopted in 1976 and designed to monitor and manage solid and hazardous waste from production to disposal.

Shundahai Network. Formed in 1994, this Western Shoshone group is actively opposed to the production, distribution, storage, and use of nuclear weapons and by-products. Under the guidance of the Corbin Harney, the Shundahai Network works in partnership with other environmental and peace groups in "breaking the nuclear chain."

Stringfellow Acid Pits. Toxic dump site discovered by residents of Glen Avon, California, in 1978 after heavy rains damaged the containment wall of a dam housing 34 million gallons of waste. Without consulting surrounding communities and under the supervision of the Regional Water Quality Control Board (RWQCB), 1 million gallons of hazardous waste had been released into local canals and creeks to relieve pressure on dam walls. Community members noticed that their children's clothing was eroding at an unusual rate, which triggered a NIMBY response and a multiyear struggle. Ultimately, the government paid to relocate the families living near the Stringfellow Acid Pits.

Title VI of the Civil Rights Act of 1964. Prohibits the use of federal funds to discriminate based on race, color, religion, sex, or national origin.

Toxic Substances Control Act. Federal legislation passed in 1976 to protect citizens' health and the environment by testing hazardous chemicals, establishing regulations, and restricting or banning the harmful chemical production.

DOCUMENTS

Document 1. Principles of Environmental Justice, 1991

In October 1991, more than 1,000 people attended the First National People of Color Environmental Leadership Summit in Washington, D.C. Delegates drafted and adopted the Principles of Environmental Justice, which listed seventeen principles that outlined the objectives, goals, and demands of the environmental justice movement.

PREAMBLE

WE, THE PEOPLE OF COLOR, gathered together at this multinational People of Color Environmental Leadership Summit, to begin to build a national and international movement of all peoples of color to fight the destruction and taking of our lands and communities, do hereby re-establish our spiritual interdependence to the sacredness of our Mother Earth; to respect and celebrate each of our cultures, languages and beliefs about the natural world and our roles in healing ourselves; to insure environmental justice; to promote economic alternatives which would contribute to the development of environmentally safe livelihoods; and, to secure our political, economic and cultural liberation that has been denied for over 500 years of colonization and oppression, resulting in the poisoning of our communities and land and the genocide of our peoples, do affirm and adopt these Principles of Environmental Justice:

Principles

1) Environmental Justice affirms the sacredness of Mother Earth, ecological unity and the interdependence of all species, and the right to be free from ecological destruction.

2) Environmental Justice demands that public policy be based on mutual respect and justice for all peoples, free from any form of discrimination or bias.

3) Environmental Justice mandates the right to ethical, balanced and responsible uses of land and renewable resources in the interest of a sustainable planet for humans and other living things.

4) Environmental Justice calls for universal protection from nuclear testing, extraction, production and disposal of toxic/hazardous wastes and poisons and nuclear testing that threaten the fundamental right to clean air, land, water, and food.

5) Environmental Justice affirms the fundamental right to political, economic, cultural and environmental self-determination of all peoples.

6) Environmental Justice demands the cessation of the production of all toxins, hazardous wastes, and radioactive materials, and that all past and current producers be held strictly accountable to the people for detoxification and the containment at the point of production.

7) Environmental Justice demands the right to participate as equal partners at every level of decision-making, including needs assessment, planning, implementation, enforcement and evaluation.

8) Environmental Justice affirms the right of all workers to a safe and healthy work environment without being forced to choose between an unsafe livelihood and unemployment. It also affirms the right of those who work at home to be free from environmental hazards.

9) Environmental Justice protects the right of victims of environmental injustice to receive full compensation and reparations for damages as well as quality health care.

10) Environmental Justice considers governmental acts of environmental injustice a violation of international law, the Universal Declaration on Human Rights, and the United Nations Convention on Genocide.

11) Environmental Justice must recognize a special legal and natural relationship of Native Peoples to the U.S. government through treaties, agreements, compacts, and covenants affirming sovereignty and self-determination.

12) Environmental Justice affirms the need for urban and rural ecological policies to clean up and rebuild our cities and rural areas in balance with nature, honoring the cultural integrity of all our communities, and provided fair access for all to the full range of resources.

13) Environmental Justice calls for the strict enforcement of principles of informed consent, and a halt to the testing of experimental reproductive and medical procedures and vaccinations on people of color.

14) Environmental Justice opposes the destructive operations of multi-national corporations.

15) Environmental Justice opposes military occupation, repression and exploitation of lands, peoples and cultures, and other life forms.

16) Environmental Justice calls for the education of present and future generations which emphasizes social and environmental issues, based on our experience and an appreciation of our diverse cultural perspectives.

17) Environmental Justice requires that we, as individuals, make personal and consumer choices to consume as little of Mother Earth's resources and to produce as little waste as possible; and make the conscious decision to challenge and reprioritize our lifestyles to insure the health of the natural world for present and future generations.

Source: Washington Office of Environmental Justice.

Document 2. The Albuquerque Declaration, 1998

In 1998, the Indigenous Environmental Network (IEN) organized a meeting of 180 delegates from North American indigenous communities for "Circles of Wisdom: Native Peoples/Native Homelands Climate Change Workshops," sponsored by NASA. Dozens of elders shared their knowledge and ideas on climate change with the Circles of Wisdom workshop participants. As a result of this gathering, "The Albuquerque Declaration" was drafted and sent to the United Nations Framework Convention on Climate Change in Buenos Aires, Argentina. The document called for a more inclusive partnership between indigenous leaders and national/international policymakers and researchers.

As indigenous peoples, we are to begin each day with a prayer, bringing our minds together in thanks for every part of the natural world. We are grateful that each part of our natural world continues to fulfill the responsibilities set for it by our Creator, in an unbreakable relationship to each other. As the roles and responsibilities are fulfilled, we are allowed to live our lives in peace. We are grateful for the natural order put in place and regulated by natural laws.

Mother Earth, Father Sky, and all of Creation, from microorganisms to human, plant, trees, fish, bird, and animal relatives are part of the natural order and regulated by natural laws. Each has a unique role and is a critical part of the whole that is Creation. Each is sacred, respected, and a unique living being with its own right to survive, and each plays an essential role in the survival and health of the natural world.

Because of our relationship with the lands and waters of our natural surroundings, which have sustained us since time immemorial, we carry knowledge and ideas that the world needs today. We know how to live with this land: we have done so for thousands of years.

We express profound concern for the well being of our sacred Mother Earth and Father Sky and the potential consequences of climate imbalance for our indigenous peoples and the significance of these consequences for our communities, our environment, our economies, our cultures and our relationships to the natural order and laws. A growing body of Western scientific evidence now suggests what indigenous peoples have expressed for a long time: life as we know it is in danger. We can no longer afford to ignore the consequences of this evidence.

In June 1997, more than 2,000 U.S. scientists, from over 150 countries, including Nobel Laureates, signed the Scientists Statement on Global Climate Disruption which reads, in part, the "accumulation of greenhouses gases commits the sacred Earth irreversibly to further global climate change and consequent ecological, economic, social and spiritual disruption" (Intergovernmental Panel on Climate Change, December 1995). Climate imbalance will cause the greatest suffering to the indigenous peoples and most pristine ecosystems globally. According to this overwhelming consensus of international scientists, the burning of oil, gas, and coal (fossil fuels) is the primary source of human-induced climate change.

The increasing effects of the indiscriminate use of fossil fuels adds to other adverse impacts on natural forests. Natural forests are critical parts of the ecosystems that maintain global climate stability. The mining and drilling for coal, oil, and gas, as well as other mineral extractions, results in substantial local environmental consequences, including severe degradation of air, forests, rivers, oceans and farmlands. Fossil fuel extraction areas are home to some of Mother Earth's last and most vulnerable indigenous populations, resulting in accelerated losses of biodiversity, traditional knowledge, and ultimately in ethnocide and genocide.

For the future of all the children, for the future of Mother Earth and Father Sky, we call upon the leaders of the world, at all levels of governments, to accept responsibility for the welfare of future generations. Their decisions must reflect their consciousness of this responsibility and they must act on it.

We request that the potential consequences of climate imbalance for indigenous peoples and our environments, economies, culture, place and role in the natural order be addressed by:

1. Establishing and funding an Inter-sessional Open-ended Working Group for indigenous peoples within the Conference of the Parties of the UN Framework Convention on Climate Change.

2. Provisions for case studies be established within the framework of that Working Group that would allow for assessing how climate changes affect different regions of indigenous peoples and local communities, assessing climate changes on flora and fauna, freshwater and oceans, forestry, traditional agricultural practices, medicinal plants and other biodiversity that impact subsistence and land-based cultures of indigenous peoples, and other case studies that would provide a clearer understanding of all effects and impacts of climate change and warming upon indigenous peoples and local communities.

3. Indigenous participation. Indigenous peoples of North America were invited by neither the United States nor Canada to participate in the negotiations of the United Nations Convention on Climate Change. We demand a place at the table of this important international discussion.

Indigenous peoples have the right, responsibility and expertise to participate as equal partners at every level of decision-making including needs assessments, case studies, within national and international policy-making activities concerning climate change impacts, causes and solutions. They need to help establish protocols that would actively promote international energy efficient and sustainable forms of development, including the widespread use of appropriately scaled solar energy and renewable energy technologies as well as sustainable agricultural and forestry practice models; exploration and development in the traditional territories of indigenous peoples of the world must be done with the full consent of indigenous peoples, respecting their right to decline a project that may adversely impact them. Where destruction has already occurred, there should be a legally binding obligation to restore all areas already affected by oil, gas, and coal exploration and exploitation. This restoration must be done such that indigenous peoples can continue traditional uses of their lands.

Source: Indigenous Environmental Network.

ENVIRONMENTALLY INDUCED ILLNESSES

One of the most challenging controversies of the early twenty-first century concerns the proliferation of thousands of synthetic chemicals and their effects on human health. A range of human illnesses have been linked to environmental factors such as toxic waste, cigarette smoke, acid rain, smog, and chemical compounds. Demonstrated disorders include cancers, reproductive problems, birth defects, respiratory illnesses, immune system deficiencies, allergies and hypersensitivity conditions, nervous system abnormalities, cerebral dysfunction, sleep disorders, gastrointestinal tract malfunctions (nausea, gastritis, and diarrhea), endocrine system dysregulation (disruption), and such newly emerging toxicant-induced illnesses as chronic fatigue syndrome, fibromyalgia (chronic pain syndrome), and chemical hypersensitivity. A major challenge in limiting the incidence of environmentally induced illnesses is the sheer quantity of chemicals dispersed into the environment every year.

The industrial manufacturing and development that drives economic growth also disperses vast quantities of potentially dangerous materials into the air, land, and water. Every year, tens of billions of pounds of chemicals designated by the U.S. Environmental Protection Agency (EPA) as hazardous chemicals, irritants, and known carcinogens are released into the environment. The creation, manufacture, dispersal, and use of these toxicants are a legal—if regulated—practice in the United States. One known consequence of these practices is an increase in the incidence of human illness, including fatalities, among both children and adults.

A toxicant is defined as an element or compound with a harmful or lethal effect on the physiology, behavior, reproduction, or survival of a living organism. Exposure to even minute doses of ambient environmental toxicants can have significant biological effects on an organism as complex and sensitive as the human body. Chlorine is one example. Since the 1780s, the chemical has been used as a central ingredient in thousands of common consumer products, including those used in household cleansers, water treatment, paper products, and plastics (like pipes and a variety of products), as well as medical technology. It is a naturally occurring chemical considered safe for human use at smaller doses but very dangerous in larger quantities. In a gaseous state, stored in a railroad car, for instance, chlorine gas is deadly and a ruptured tank can release a cloud capable of killing a person in a matter of moments. After use for more than 200 years in industrial applications, chlorine is now present in natural ecosystems around the world. At higher doses, it contributes to birth defects, cancerous cell growth, and the elimination of various biological organisms—an effect called chlorine contamination. A contaminant is a substance that, in sufficient concentration, can adversely alter the environment, including organisms living in it.

PROLIFERATION OF COMPLEX CHEMICALS

After World War II, the United States underwent an unprecedented population growth and economic expansion. Consumers sought products and goods to make life easier. These included broader choices of food and clothing, a diversity of home appliances and electronics, larger houses, and the highest quality healthcare money could buy. A rapidly expanding economy also called for the development of larger farms, bigger factories, and expanded transportation and other infrastructure systems.

By the late 1940s, the growth of the consumer economy had led to the accelerated development of scientific research on new chemicals and chemical processes. Additional factories were built to produce an array of products. New chemical manufacturing facilities were also constructed, many of them adjacent to larger cities in Illinois, California, New Jersey, Mississippi, Louisiana, and other states. Company names such as Dow Chemical and Monsanto became synonymous with progress, as advances in chemical science brought major benefits including new medicines to prevent diseases or unblock clogged arteries, pesticides to protect plants and fruits from insects, and preservatives to make food and other commodities last longer.

With such advances, however, came a greater incidence of toxicant-induced illnesses. As the economy expanded, chemicals became more pervasive and new threats were identified. Building materials contained formaldehyde and asbestos; personal body products contained aluminum, urine, and petroleum distillates; water had chlorine; gasoline and paint had lead; and food was filled with dozens of chemical preservatives. Widespread use revealed the damaging effects of certain chemicals, including acute sickness and sudden death. Neighborhoods were contaminated by mercury through trash incineration, causing various cancers and neurological disorders; side effects of inadequately tested medications were severe enough to kill; and the diagnosis of "chemical hypersensitivity," resulting in acute allergic reactions including respiratory distress, was becoming increasingly common with exposure to certain chemicals.

Some of the more harmful substances—such as toxaphene (an insecticide) in 1982 and polychlorinated biphenyls (PCBs, organic synthetic chemicals) in 1978—were removed from the market. In the case of PCBs, however, major cleanup efforts sometimes took decades to begin. In New York, for example, it was not until 2003 that the EPA reached agreement with General Electric—which had been responsible for dumping PCBs for years—on paying for cleaning up contaminated sediment in the Hudson River. The cost to the company for the environmental remediation was expected to soar into the hundreds of millions of dollars. Meanwhile, however, the U.S. chemical industry produced more than 10 billion tons of toxic chemicals in 2003 alone, at an estimated 3,646 chemical manufacturing facilities across the country. By that year, U.S. chemical production since 1940 had grown 32-fold. Although health concerns were expressed as early as 1950, growth of the industry was little hampered.

By the late 1950s, the effects of new synthetic chemicals on human health increasingly drew the attention of scientists and medical professionals. In her groundbreaking 1962 book, *Silent Spring*, Rachel Carson reported alarming evidence of the harm chemicals were causing to the health of wildlife: herring gulls were forming same sex-pairs and abandoning their eggs; deformed beaks were found in bald eagles; immune systems were damaged in seals; and eggshells from certain bird species were too thin to allow for development and survival. Carson's work raised awareness and public concern over the proliferation and use of chemicals, highlighting the effects on animals as a precursor to serious human damage. Her efforts led to an increase in government oversight and the banning of such dangerous chemicals as the insecticide dichlorodiphenyltrichloroethane, or DDT, in 1972. Today, more than four decades after Carson's work, new discoveries prove that manmade chemicals have infiltrated the farthest reaches of the planet.

In 1970, the U.S. government responded to public outcry over harm to people and the environment by forming a new authority, the Environmental Protection Agency (EPA). President Richard Nixon, in creating this unprecedented regulatory agency, acknowledged that,

> It has become increasingly clear that we need to know more about the total environment—land, water, and air. . . . Our national government today is not structured to make a coordinated attack on the pollutants which debase the air we breathe, the water we drink, and the land that grows our food. . . . Despite its complexity, for pollution control purposes the environment must be perceived as a single, interrelated system.

EXAMPLES OF ENVIRONMENTALLY INDUCED ILLNESSES

Nearly 800,000 Americans a year become sick as a result of exposure to toxic chemicals. Although commercial and industrial chemicals are beneficial in many respects, damage to the environment and all forms of life may occur when the product (or by-product) is improperly used and disposed of. The result has often put the scientific community, regulators, environmentalists, and the public at large in a complex position. To what degree should chemicals be managed and studied before they are made available for public use? How harmful must a substance be before it is banned? Specific examples show that human illness occurs in a variety of situations and settings.

Water and Air Pollution

Since the 1960s, the increasing evidence of environmental contamination includes elevated concentrations of carbon dioxide in the air, posing a threat to human respiration, and several types of pesticides in the water that can cause cancers and birth defects. Well water has been found laced with dry-cleaning fluids (which are cancer-causing) and gasoline, and communities downwind of power plants or industrial facilities have shown high concentrations of illness-inducing pollutants such as acid rain, dioxins, heavy metals, and chlorofluorocarbons.

The EPA relies on several pieces of legislation to regulate the use and dispersal of hazardous pollutants into the air and water: the Clean Air Act (1963), Clean Water Act (1972), and Resource Conservation and Recovery Act (1976), among others. Most air and water toxins originate from human activities, including mobile (e.g., cars, trucks, buses), stationary (e.g., factories, refineries, power plants), and indoor (e.g., building materials and activities such as cleaning) sources. To better understand toxic pollution, the EPA created a clearinghouse of dangerous sites across the country. This National Priorities List is organized by threat level, and currently includes more than 1,000 hazardous waste sites.

Many environmental pollutants are complex substances that do not coexist well within the chemistry of natural ecosystems. This means that a synthetic chemical has difficulty being absorbed into natural chemical processes, in either the environment or living tissue. One example is the family of organochlorines, a wide variety of chemicals containing carbon, chlorine, and, in some cases, several other elements. A range of organochlorine compounds is found in cleaning agents, herbicides, insecticides, and fungicides as well as industrial chemicals such as PCBs. These complex synthetic chemicals form a strong molecular bond when chlorine combines with carbon. They are highly stable and persist for long periods of time. Scientists have discovered that when a chlorine product interacts with a natural system, it can create new chemicals that are more toxic and live longer than the original product. Organochlorines are more soluble in fats than in water and, once in the environment, can migrate into living tissue. Fish from polluted rivers often contain organochlorides, lead, mercury, and a number of dioxins. When eaten, these fish have a number of health effects on humans, including miscarriages, cancers, and nervous system damage. Contaminant levels also multiply as the chemicals move up the food chain, in a process known as bioaccumulation. Species near the top of the food chain, such as humans, have the greatest risk.

Asthma is an environmentally induced respiratory illness that has been growing in the U.S. population

Table 1. Asthma Rates, by Race and Ethnicity, All Ages, 2002

	Whites (non-Hispanic)	Blacks (non-Hispanic)	Hispanic
Lifetime asthma prevalence (per 1,000 persons)	111	138	83
Current asthma prevalence (per 1,000 persons)	72	95	49
Asthma attack prevalence (per 1,000 persons)	42	55	31
Deaths per 100,000 persons	1.2	3.7	1.4

Source: National Center for Health Statistics.

steadily since the 1960s. According to the U.S. Centers for Disease Control (CDC), over 15 million people currently experience asthma-related conditions. Asthma is a chronic lung disease characterized by temporary obstruction of airflow that leads to breathing difficulty, coughing, inflammation of the airways, and an increased sensitivity to a variety of triggers that cause breathing difficulty. Triggers include industrial pollution, chemical products, and allergens (dust, dander, pollen).

To better understand this health problem, the CDC studied asthma cases between 1960 and 1995. CDC researchers found that, historically, a common diagnosis for asthma was allergy to natural items such as pollen or dust. As the population has grown over the years, the most common cause has changed considerably as a large number of asthma cases today have been linked to industrial pollution. As more potent chemicals emanate from factories, a greater number of respiratory difficulties are occurring. The CDC also found that the number of asthma cases is continuing to climb and younger and younger people are being affected each year. Minorities living in urban areas have the highest rates of asthma nationwide.

One of the worst cases of environmental contamination in the United States occurred in New York in 1978. At the Love Canal site, located on 100 acres of land on the eastern edge of Niagara Falls, nearly 200 houses and a school were built in the 1950s adjacent to an abandoned canal. What no one knew was that, beginning in 1942, the Hooker Chemical Company had used the site as an industrial landfill, depositing nearly 20,000 gallons of hazardous waste into the trench. The working-class suburb soon became a nightmare for residents. Children were born with an inordinate number of birth defects (deafness, missing eyes, extra rows of teeth, missing limbs, retardation), leukemia rates exceeded national averages, and there were high incidences of cancer and other ailments.

Government response to the Love Canal tragedy ultimately set the standard for many environmental disasters to follow. In 1978, state and federal authorities moved residents off the development property and began a thorough scientific investigation. Months of testing identified the cause of the medical problems—a chemical dump found to contain high concentrations of 82 hazardous chemical compounds, 11 of them known carcinogens. The chemicals had leached into garages, basements, pools, living rooms, schools, and other private and public buildings in the area. The government purchased all of the homes, spending $7 million to relocate residents and millions more to clean up the site. A fund was set up to help the victims pay for medical care. The incident raised awareness and forced state and federal agencies to modify industrial development citing requirements. The disaster also led the U.S. Congress, in 1980, to enact the Superfund law, which established cleanup requirements for toxic waste sites around the nation and required waste dumpers to pay cleanup costs. At Love Canal, Hooker Chemical eventually settled with the federal government for $130 million, and by 1987 a $101 million Superfund cleanup was underway at the site.

OCCUPATIONAL RISKS

Employees spend a considerable amount of time at their workplaces, 2,000 hours or more per year for full-time workers. Exposure to toxicants, including pesticides and pollutants emitted by office machinery and other toxicants, has become a significant issue. For years, workplace hazards were "assumed" to be a common risk of employment in certain fields. In 1971, Congress created the Occupational Safety and Health Administration (OSHA) to enforce federal standards at the workplace.

Since its inception, OSHA has helped to cut workplace fatalities by more than 60 percent and occupational injury rates by 40 percent. Meanwhile, the number of employees injured by environmental illness has been growing steadily. In 1992, there were 457,000 cases of environmental injuries, including respiratory damage, toxic exposure, and poisoning. By 2003, the number had grown to 802,900 illnesses. Of that number, 130,200 were skin disorders, 55,000 were respiratory conditions, and 11,000 were poisonings; the category of other illnesses, accounting for 606,700 of the cases, included such injuries as

chemical exposure, "sick building" disorders, and chronic injuries related to the work environment.

Occupational illnesses vary broadly. Hazards at an automotive repair shop are different from those at a postal sorting facility or a chemical manufacturing plant. Common hazards in a mine or manufacturing setting include exposure to asbestos, lead and other heavy metals, chemical solvents, and hazardous waste. Persons exposed to these and other materials suffer from several types of environmental illnesses, including asthma and other lung diseases, nervous system problems, gastrointestinal disorders, reproductive problems, latex allergies, repetitive strain injuries (carpal tunnel syndrome, tendonitis), hearing loss, multiple chemical sensitivity (severe intolerance of complex environmental chemicals), and building-related illnesses (such as Legionnaires disease, hypersensitivity pneumonitis, and others directly attributed to airborne pollutants in the building).

Certain environmental illnesses have become more common, and thus better diagnosed, over the years. These include silicosis, a lung disease common among miners, industrial workers, and potters exposed to silica dust; scrotal-skin cancer in chimney sweeps and furnace repairmen exposed to soot; neurologic disorders in potters exposed to lead glazes; brain cancer in boat builders who use liquid fiberglass; and bone disease in workers exposed to phosphorus in the manufacture of matches. There are also more emergent illnesses in human populations, including multiple chemical sensitivity and Gulf War syndrome, a medical condition of uncertain origin (characterized by fatigue, headache, dizziness, nausea, rashes, joint pain, and respiratory disorders) affecting many veterans of the 1991 Persian Gulf War.

One of the most serious occupational environmental illnesses occurred at a military facility in Colorado, the Rocky Mountain Flats Arsenal northeast of Denver. The 6-square-mile facility, heralded when it opened in 1951 for all the high-paying jobs it would provide, was designed to manufacture a variety of weapons systems. A major product was a plutonium trigger for nuclear missiles; other manufactured items included sarin, mustard gas, and napalm. After many years of discharges, fires, and complaints about poor upkeep of the facility, a grand jury in 1989 found multiple criminal offenses at the facility; the company that maintained the site, Rockwell International, settled for millions of dollars in cleanup costs. Also in 1989, the Federal Bureau of Investigation raided the site and found numerous environmental crimes,

Table 2. Cancer Rates, by Residence Area, Adults over 18 Years Old, 2002

Residence area	Cancer frequency (in 000s of persons)
Metropolitan areas (1 million plus)	5,496
Metropolitan areas (under 1 million)	5,310
Rural	3,576
Northeast	2,667
Midwest	3,692
South	5,390
West	2,633

Source: Department of Health and Human Services. Summary: Health Statistics for U.S. Adults, National Health Interview Survey, 2002.

and the plant was forced to close. Massive amounts of chemicals (many radioactive) had been illegally dumped across the sprawling, grassland site.

The employees' toxic exposure was severe. By the 1960s, the first Rocky Flats workers were diagnosed with chronic beryllium disease, a nuclear-plant version of black lung, caused by inhalation of the strong, lightweight metal used in manufacturing nuclear weapons. Others suffered from various degrees of uranium exposure, which is essentially radiation poisoning. By the 1980s, nearly twenty-two other types of cancer were diagnosed in dozens of former employees of the facility. The Rocky Flats property required one of the largest environmental cleanups in U.S. history, with an $8 billion price tag. In 2004, the site was designated as a federal wildlife refuge.

Cancer in humans can be attributed to genetic predisposition (inherited) or lifestyle choices (food, occupational exposure, living conditions). Occupational exposure plays a central role in this type of illness. In 2005, cancer was identified as the second leading cause of death in the United States; more than 570,000 Americans (about 1,500 per day) were expected to die of cancer that year. Of that total, the majority of cases were directly attributable to occupational conditions. Cancer in the workplace is often manifested in clusters, with several employees getting sick simultaneously. A cancer cluster is defined as a greater-than-expected number of cases occurring within a group of people in a geographic area over a period of time. In 1910, a cluster of women was diagnosed with a cancer of the jaw (osteosarcoma) while employed as wristwatch dial painters in New Jersey and Connecticut; the women, it was revealed, had been exposed to ionizing radiation from radium in the paint when they used their lips to form a tip on their paintbrushes. In 1965, a

cluster of lung cancer (asbestosis) cases was found in factories that produced asbestos products (brake pads, insulation). And in 1974, there were several reported clusters of liver cancer (angiosarcoma) among plastics chemical workers exposed to vinyl chloride. One of the best-known cases—thanks chiefly to the motion picture *Erin Brockovich* (2000)—came to light in 1984, when Pacific Gas & Electric dumped millions of gallons of cancer-causing chemicals into unlined ponds in Hinkley, California, and employees and residents became sick with brain, liver, and stomach cancer; 648 individuals eventually filed and settled a class-action lawsuit against the company.

Environmental Pollutants in Food and Drugs

At the turn of the twentieth century, several high-profile food poisonings and drug fatalities motivated the federal government to assert regulatory control over food and drug products sold to the public. In 1906, Congress passed the Federal Food and Drugs Act, which relied on a new concept—labeling—to show product contents. Drugs were required to meet the standards of strength, quality, and purity defined in the United States Pharmacopoeia and National Formulary. Food producers were required to list ingredients that would substitute for the food, pose a health hazard, or constitute a dirty or decomposed substance. This landmark legislation also created a new agency, the Food and Drug Administration (FDA), to implement the various measures. In 1938, Congress replaced the 1906 law with the Food, Drug, and Cosmetic Act, which provided for tighter government control of cosmetics, drugs, food, and therapeutic devices. It required that new drugs be proven safe before distribution to the public and created standards for chemical use and exposure, or tolerances, for dangerous substances.

Twentieth-century federal law and the agencies it engendered have reduced exposure to many environmentally dangerous substances that cause damage to humans. This is done on both a proactive and reactive basis. Proactively, the FDA oversees a list of several thousand pharmaceutical drugs currently on the market. It requires research on pharmaceutical drugs and chemicals to explore links between exposures and health effects. One controversial aspect of the legislation is that the drug companies fund and conduct the review process themselves—albeit with strict reporting procedures. In 2003 alone, nearly 3.6 million Americans ended up in emergency rooms for injuries or illnesses related to prescription drug use. Working reactively, the FDA was given the power in 1938 to issue federal injunctions ordering a company to remove any food or drug item from the market. Indeed it has done so on dozens of occasions over the last six decades. The agency was granted this authority largely because of a single case the previous year. A Tennessee drug company marketed a so-called wonder drug (elixir sulfanilamide) that would appeal to pediatric patients to fight various infections. The untested liquid form of the drug turned out to be a highly toxic chemical, however, and more than 100 people—many of them young children—died from ingesting it. More recent examples of drugs pulled from the market include the popular anti-inflammatory medications Vioxx and Bextra, which were found to cause an increase in cardiovascular events (including fatal heart attacks). More than 5 million Americans were actively using these drugs when they were removed from the market in 2005.

For centuries, food preservation methods such as curing, canning, and freezing have allowed consumable products to be shipped great distances or to be stored for prolonged periods. In modern times, however, the use of chemicals has replaced these proven methods as the primary means of preserving food. Large-scale farming in the 1940s led to an expansion of food manufacturing and processing operations, and larger orders need to stay fresh longer for a wider geographic market. Historically regional food products now could be chemically treated to last for weeks as they travel across the country. Virtually every food group has been affected. Cheese has sodium citrate added as a plasticizer to soften it and chloramine added as a deodorant; potassium nitrate is added to sausage for color and sodium chloride as a preservative; cakes have diglycerides and aluminum phosphate additives to make them stay soft longer; and even canned peas have magnesium chloride to make them last longer and appear fresher.

Food preservation has caused serious health damage to humans. The nitrites used to preserve meat products, for example, convert to other chemicals when eaten and in laboratory research have stimulated the growth of cancers. Antioxidants are used to protect baked goods, dried goods, and other mixes. They allow shelf foods to last up to 2 years. Unfortunately, they also have been shown to promote cancerous cell growth. Sulfites include a broad family of chemicals intended to halt bacteria growth in food and slow the browning of fruits and vegetables. This additive was ordered removed from certain foods when it caused severe asthma reactions and even heart failure.

CONCLUSION

While toxic substances have been affecting human health since the use of fire in caves, industrialization in the nineteenth century and especially the development of the petrochemical industry since World War II have increased the volume of synthetic toxic substances released into the environment and exposed to humans. Modern chemical manufacturers have synthesized more than 70,000 different substances for commercial use, and many of the day-to-day products people use contain and emit such toxins. While the problem in the early years of the twenty-first century is vast, experts believe the impact of toxins on human health can be eased through regulation, research, education, and other ameliorative measures.

Human exposure to environmental toxins is a global problem, not one confined within national or state boundaries. Because toxins can drift on air or water currents for thousands of miles, pesticides and other hazardous materials are found everywhere on Earth, including both polar ice caps. Virtually every human being on the planet is regularly exposed to toxins that may have originated thousands of miles away. Epidemiologic research confirms that human populations, even in remote areas, carry dozens of synthetic chemicals in their blood. Recent studies have confirmed such toxins in the blood of Inuit natives as well as polar bears, whales, and seals in the North Pole region.

The rule of international law makes controlling synthetic chemicals a considerable challenge since policymaking and lawmaking are normally done within individual nation-states. Coordinating global solutions is often a drawn-out and difficult process. One such example is the 1997 UN-sponsored Kyoto Protocol (revised in 2002), which commits 141 industrial nations to sharply reduce greenhouse gas emissions, primarily carbon dioxide. The treaty took nearly a decade to draft and officially went into force in February 2005 after ratification by Russia. But the United States—the world's largest emitter—withdrew from the protocol in 2001, with the administration of President George W. Bush citing the heavy cuts being asked of industrialized nations and the economic costs of implementation.

Another example of international cooperation to control toxic chemicals came in 2001, when delegates from 127 countries formally adopted a global treaty banning twelve highly toxic chemicals from their soils. The Pact on Persistent Organic Pollutants was concluded in South Africa after 2 years of sometimes tense negotiations. The treaty was aimed at eventually eliminating all hazardous chemicals but committed particularly to targeting the twelve widely known as "the dirty dozen" for priority action. The chemicals include PCBs, dioxins, DDT, and other pesticides whose use and improper disposal have been shown to contribute to birth defects, cancers, and other health problems in humans and animals. The United States led the effort and resisted a campaign on the part of other countries to allow DDT. According to those nations, the damage caused by DDT is outweighed by the benefits of saving millions of lives a year by stopping waterborne diseases such as malaria, typhoid, and cholera. The final version of the treaty did include a ban on DDT.

Reliance on complex chemical products has been shown to guarantee a degree of benefit but also a host of environmental illnesses. Living in a large city with traffic congestion compromises respiratory functions but not as severely as asbestos compromises coal miners, who often develop asbestosis, a severe and often fatal lung disease. The regulatory framework that oversees chemical use in the United States relies on a patchwork of government and private forces. These entities attempt to manage individual pollutants using such scientific and engineering tools as risk assessment, pollution control technology, and toxicological tests. Much of the work is painstaking, time-consuming, and often debated by various parties.

The biggest question is what will happen in the next generation. As the consumer economy has grown, so has the number of environmentally induced illnesses every year. American society appears to have adjusted to this fact by instituting government regulatory oversight with an accepted level of chemical use. As we discover threats from a product that may harm humans or the environment, the government acts to remove it from use. Other countries experiencing rapid economic growth (their first priority) are just beginning to draft laws to protect the environment and human health. One factor driving many aspects of change is growing global awareness and the expectation that global companies must do business responsibly. Although awareness alone does not protect people and the environment, it may lead to institutions and mechanisms with the power to exact appropriate sums for cleanup, medical costs, and penalties.

James Fargo Balliett

REFERENCES

American Public Health Association. "Policy Statement 9606: The Precautionary Principle and Chemical Exposure Standards for the Work Place" *American Journal of Public Health* 87, 3 (March 1997): 500–01.

Ashford, Nicholas, and Claudia Miller. *Chemical Exposures: Low Levels and High Stakes*. New York: Van Nostrand Reinhold, 1998.

Barrett, Stephen, and Ronald E. Gots. *Chemical Sensitivity: The Truth about Environmental Illness*. Amherst, NY: Prometheus Books, 1998.

Carson, Rachel. *Silent Spring*. New York: Mariner Books, 1962.

Colburn, Theo, et al. *Our Stolen Future: Are We Threatening Our Fertility, Intelligence and Survival?—A Scientific Detective Story*. New York: Penguin Books, 1996.

Davis, Devra. *When Smoke Ran Like Water: Tales of Environmental Deception and the Battle Against Pollution*. New York: Basic Books, 2002.

Fagin, Dan, and Marianne Lavelle. *Toxic Deception: How the Chemical Industry Manipulates Science, Bends the Law, and Endangers Your Health*. Secaucus, NJ: Carol, 1997.

Harden, Garrett. "The Tragedy of the Commons." *Science* 162 (1968): 1243–48.

Harr, Jonathan. *A Civil Action*. New York: Random House, 1995.

Hill, A. B. "The Environment and Disease: Association or Causation?" *Proceedings of the Royal Society of Medicine* 58 (1965): 295–300.

Kerns, Thomas. *Environmentally Induced Illness: Ethics, Risk Assessment and Human Rights*. New York: McFarland, 2001.

Lappé, Marc. *Chemical Deception: The Toxic Threat to Health and the Environment*. San Francisco: Sierra Club Books, 1991.

Miller, Claudia. "White Paper: Chemical Sensitivity: History and Phenomenology." *Toxicology and Industrial Health* 10, 4/5 (1994): 253–76.

Millichap, Gordon. *Environmental Poisons in Our Food*. Chicago: PNB, 1993.

Montague, Peter. "History of Precaution, Part 2." *Rachel's Environment & Health Weekly* 540 (April 3, 1997).

Rea, William J. *Chemical Sensitivity*. Vol. 4. Boca Raton, FL: Lewis, 1992–97.

Rodale, J.I. *Our Poisoned Earth and Sky*. Emmaus, PA: Rodale Books, 1964.

Satcher, David. "CDC's First 50 Years: Lessons Learned and Relearned." *American Journal of Public Health* 86, 12 (December 1996): 1705–08.

Saunders, Thomas. *The Boiled Frog Syndrome: Your Health and the Built Environment*. Hoboken, NJ: Wiley-Academy, 2002.

Stauber, J. Rampton, and Sheldon Rampton. *Toxic Sludge Is Good for You: Lies, Damn Lies, and the Public Relations Industry*. Monroe, ME: Common Courage, 1995.

Steingraber, Sandra. *Living Downstream: An Ecologist Looks at Cancer and the Environment*. Reading, MA: Addison-Wesley, 1997.

Thornton, Joe. *Pandora's Poison: Chlorine, Health, and a New Environmental Strategy*. Cambridge, MA: MIT Press, 2000.

Wargo, John. *Our Children's Toxic Legacy: How Science and Law Fail to Protect Us from Pesticides*. New Haven, CT: Yale University Press, 1996.

WEB SITES

Centers for Disease Control: www.cdc.gov
Environmental Illness Resource: www.ei-resource.org
Environmental Protection Agency: www.epa.gov
Occupational Safety and Health Administration: www.osha.gov
United Nations Environmental Programme: www.unep.org
World Health Organization: www.who.org

GLOSSARY

Ambient toxicants. Toxicants disseminated in the air, water, and soil throughout the environment.

Anthropogenic chemicals. Chemicals created by human activity that do not occur, at least in substantial quantities, in the natural world.

Biological monitoring. Analyzing chemicals, hormone levels, or other substances in biological materials (blood, urine, breath, etc.) as a measure of chemical exposure and health status in humans or animals.

Carcinogen. An agent or substance that causes cancer in humans or animals.

Endocrine System. The system of glands responsible for hormone production.

Environmentally induced illnesses. Illnesses that biomedical and epidemiological research has shown environmental toxins to have played a causal role.

Epidemiology. The study of the causes of health effects in human populations. An epidemiologic study compares groups of people who are alike except for one factor, such as exposure to a chemical or the presence of a health effect.

Fibromyalgia. A chronic disorder characterized by fatigue and widespread pain in the muscles, ligaments, and tendons.

Maximum contaminant level (MCL). The maximum level of a contaminant federal or state regulations allow to go uncorrected by a public water system. Depending on the contaminant, allowable levels might be calculated as an average over time or based on individual test results.

Multiple chemical sensitivity. A condition in which a person reports sensitivity or intolerance (as distinct from allergy) to a number of chemicals and other irritants at very low concentrations. Medical professionals have different views as to the existence, causes, diagnosis, and treatment of this condition.

Organic. Originating from plants or animals, and made primarily of carbon and hydrogen. Scientists use the term to refer to chemical compounds based on carbon. An organic product is made without additives or pesticides.

Organochlorines. A wide range of chemicals that contain carbon, chlorine, and sometimes several other elements. A wide range of organochlorine compounds has been produced, including many herbicides, insecticides, fungicides, and such industrial chemicals as polychlorinated biphenyls (PCBs).

Pesticide. By convention, a chemical or chemical compound used primarily to kill undesirable organisms. Insecticides are designed to kill insects, herbicides to kill weeds, fungicides to kill fungi.

Precautionary principle. A principle of environmental decision making that recommends, in the face of insufficient data about a chemical's health effects, policymakers not allow the chemical to be deployed in the environment until they have sufficient data about its health effects.

Reactive airways disease syndrome. Asthma-like respiratory illness caused by a reaction to chemicals in the environment.

Remediation. Correction or improvement of a problem, such as work done to clean up or stop the release of chemicals from a contaminated site.

Risk assessment. A modern form of utilitarian thinking to help in environmental policymaking. According to risk assessment principles, we should promote policies that serve the interests of the largest number of stakeholders.

Superfund. U.S. federal and state programs to investigate and clean up inactive hazardous waste sites.

Toxicant. A synthetic anthropogenic chemical agent known to have toxic effects on tissues of living beings.

Volatile. Evaporating readily at normal temperatures and pressures. The air concentration of a highly volatile chemical can increase quickly in a closed room.

DOCUMENTS

Document 1. Environmental Protection Agency Mission Statement, 1970

In the wake of several environmental catastrophes and in response to the burgeoning environmental movement, President Richard Nixon established the Environmental Protection Agency in 1970 as a subcabinet-level agency responsible—according to its mission statement—for protecting human health and the environment from human-created pollutants.

The mission of the U.S. Environmental Protection Agency is to protect human health and to safeguard the natural environment—air, water, and land—upon which life depends.

EPA's purpose is to ensure that:

- All Americans are protected from significant risks to human health and the environment where they live, learn and work.
- National efforts to reduce environmental risk are based on the best available scientific information.
- Federal laws protecting human health and the environment are enforced fairly and effectively.
- Environmental protection is an integral consideration in U.S. policies concerning natural resources, human health, economic growth, energy, transportation, agriculture, industry, and international trade, and these factors are similarly considered in establishing environmental policy.
- All parts of society—communities, individuals, business, state and local governments, tribal governments—have access to accurate information sufficient to effectively participate in managing human health and environmental risks.
- Environmental protection contributes to making our communities and ecosystems diverse, sustainable and economically productive.
- The United States plays a leadership role in working with other nations to protect the global environment."

Source: Environmental Protection Agency.

Document 2. Draft Declaration of Human Rights and the Environment, 1994

Invited by the Sierra Club Legal Defense Fund, human rights advocates and environmental experts gathered in 1994 under United Nations auspices in Geneva, Switzerland, to draft the first-ever declaration of principles on the environment and human rights—reproduced here.

PREAMBLE

Guided by the United Nations Charter, the Universal Declaration of Human Rights, the International Covenant on Economic, Social and Cultural Rights, the International Covenant on Civil and Political Rights, the Vienna Declaration and Program of Action of the World Conference of Human Rights, and other relevant international human rights instruments,

Guided also by the Stockholm Declaration of the United Nations Conference on the Human Environment, the World Charter for Nature, the Rio Declaration on Environment and Development, Agenda 21: Programme of Action for Sustainable Development, and other relevant instruments of international environmental law,

Guided also by the Declaration on the Right to Development, which recognizes that the right to development is an essential human right and that the human person is the central subject of development,

Guided further by fundamental principles of international humanitarian law,

Reaffirming the universality, indivisibility and interdependence of all human rights,

Recognizing that sustainable development links the right to development and the right to a secure, healthy and ecologically sound environment,

Recalling the right of peoples to self-determination by virtue of which they have the right freely to determine their political status and to pursue their economic, social and cultural development,

Deeply concerned by the severe human rights consequences of environmental harm caused by poverty, structural adjustment and debt programmes and by international trade and intellectual property regimes,

Convinced that the potential irreversibility of environmental harm gives rise to special responsibility to prevent such harm,

Concerned that human rights violations lead to environmental degradation and that environmental degradation leads to human rights violations,

THE FOLLOWING PRINCIPLES ARE DECLARED:

Part I

1. Human rights, an ecologically sound environment, sustainable development and peace are interdependent and indivisible.

2. All persons have the right to a secure, healthy and ecologically sound environment. This right and other human rights, including civil, cultural, economic, political and social rights, are universal, interdependent and indivisible.

3. All persons shall be free from any form of discrimination in regard to actions and decisions that affect the environment.

4. All persons have the right to an environment adequate to meet equitably the needs of present generations and that does not impair the rights of future generations to meet equitably their needs.

Part II

5. All persons have the right to freedom from pollution, environmental degradation and activities that adversely affect the environment, threaten life, health, livelihood, well-being or sustainable development within, across or outside national boundaries.

6. All persons have the right to protection and preservation of the air, soil, water, sea-ice, flora and fauna, and the essential processes and areas necessary to maintain biological diversity and ecosystems.

7. All persons have the right to the highest attainable standard of health free from environmental

8. All persons have the right to safe and healthy food and water adequate to their well-being.

9. All persons have the right to a safe and healthy working environment.

10. All persons have the right to adequate housing, land tenure and living conditions in a secure, healthy and ecologically sound environment.

11. All persons have the right not to be evicted from their homes or land for the purpose of, or as a consequence of, decisions or actions affecting the environment, except in emergencies or due to a compelling purpose benefiting society as a whole and not attainable by other means. All persons have the right to participate effectively in decisions and to negotiate concerning their eviction and the right, if evicted, to timely and adequate restitution, compensation and/or appropriate and sufficient accommodation or land.

12. All persons have the right to timely assistance in the event of natural or technological or other human-caused catastrophes.

13. Everyone has the right to benefit equitably from the conservation and sustainable use of nature and natural resources for cultural, ecological, educational, health, livelihood, recreational, spiritual or other purposes. This includes ecologically sound access to nature.

Everyone has the right to preservation of unique sites, consistent with the fundamental rights of persons or groups living in the area.

14. Indigenous peoples have the right to control their lands, territories and natural resources and to maintain their traditional way of life. This includes the right to security in the enjoyment of their means of subsistence.

Indigenous peoples have the right to protection against any action or course of conduct that may result in the destruction or degradation of their territories, including land, air, water, sea-ice, wildlife or other resources.

Part III

15. All persons have the right to information concerning the environment. This includes information, howsoever compiled, on actions and courses of conduct that may affect the environment and information necessary to enable effective public participation in environmental decision-making. The information shall be timely, clear, understandable and available without undue financial burden to the applicant.

16. All persons have the right to hold and express opinions and to disseminate ideas and information regarding the environment.

17. All persons have the right to environmental and human rights education.

18. All persons have the right to active, free, and meaningful participation in planning and decision-making activities and processes that may have an impact on the environment and development. This includes the right to a prior assessment of the environmental, developmental and human rights consequences of proposed actions.

19. All persons have the right to associate freely and peacefully with others for purposes of protecting the environment or the rights of persons affected by environmental harm.

20. All persons have the right to effective remedies and redress in administrative or judicial proceedings for environmental harm or the threat of such harm.

Part IV

21. All persons, individually and in association with others, have a duty to protect and preserve the environment.

22. All States shall respect and ensure the right to a secure, healthy and ecologically sound environment. Accordingly, they shall adopt the administrative, legislative and other measures necessary to effectively implement the rights in this Declaration.

These measures shall aim at the prevention of environmental harm, at the provision of adequate remedies, and at the sustainable use of natural resources and shall include, inter alia,

- collection and dissemination of information concerning the environment
- prior assessment and control, licensing, regulation or prohibition of activities and substances potentially harmful to the environment;
- public participation in environmental decision-making;
- effective administrative and judicial remedies and redress for environmental harm and the threat of such harm;
- monitoring, management and equitable sharing of natural resources;
- measures to reduce wasteful processes of production and patterns of consumption;
- measures aimed at ensuring that transnational corporations, wherever they operate, carry out their duties of environmental protection, sustainable development and respect for human rights; and
- measures aimed at ensuring that the international organizations and agencies to which they belong observe the rights and duties in this Declaration.

23. States and all other parties shall avoid using the environment as a means of war or inflicting significant, long-term or widespread harm on the environment, and shall respect international law providing protection for the environment in times of armed conflict and cooperate in its further development.

24. All international organizations and agencies shall observe the rights and duties in this Declaration.

Part V

25. In implementing the rights and duties in this Declaration, special attention shall be given to vulnerable persons and groups.

26. The rights in this Declaration may be subject only to restrictions provided by law and which are necessary to protect public order, health and the fundamental rights and freedoms of others.

27. All persons are entitled to a social and international order in which the rights in this Declaration can be fully realized.

Source: United Nations Environment Programme.

EUTHANASIA

The term "euthanasia" comes from the combination of two Greek words: *eu,* meaning "well" or "good," and *thanos,* meaning "death." Coined in the seventeenth century, euthanasia refers to a "good death," that is, a dignified death or one freeing the person from a life deemed not worth living. Today, however, the term is used specifically to designate the intentional killing, by act or omission, of a dependent individual for his or her alleged benefit. Euthanasia is not limited to people; animals can be euthanized too, but this chapter focuses specifically on euthanasia of human beings.

There are three types of euthanasia. *Voluntary euthanasia* occurs when a person requests to be killed. *Nonvoluntary euthanasia* occurs when the person did not request to be killed or give his or her consent to the act. *Involuntary euthanasia* occurs when the person expressed the desire not to be killed.

In addition to the three major *types* of euthanasia, euthanasia can be active or passive. *Active euthanasia* involves intentionally bringing about of a person's death by performing a specific action, such as administering a lethal injection. *Passive euthanasia* involves the intentional withholding of necessary and ordinary (i.e., usual and customary) care or food and water.

These three main types of euthanasia and two primary means of performing the act create six distinct categories of euthanasia: voluntary active euthanasia, voluntary passive euthanasia, nonvoluntary active euthanasia, nonvoluntary passive euthanasia, involuntary active euthanasia, and involuntary passive euthanasia.

It is important to distinguish euthanasia from physician-assisted suicide, with which it is often confused. When a person is euthanized, someone else brings about the death. In physician-assisted suicide, death is inflicted by the individual with the *help* of a doctor. In other words, a person who dies by physician-assisted suicide kills himself or herself. Nor should euthanasia (especially passive euthanasia) be confused with certain common medical practices such as the refusal to begin treatment that would not benefit the patient; the discontinuation of treatment that has been ineffective, has onerous side effects, or is otherwise undesirable to the patient; or the administration of high doses of painkillers that may endanger the patient's life.

HISTORY OF EUTHANASIA

The Greek physician Hippocrates is often called the "father of medicine" for his formulation (in about 400 B.C.E.) of the code of medical practice known as the "Hippocratic Oath." In part, the oath expressly prohibits any type of active (although not passive) euthanasia, as the physician swears "I will give no deadly medicine to any one if asked, nor suggest such counsel."

The distinction between active and passive euthanasia—in which the former is prohibited but the latter is not—has been enshrined in Western law. Passive euthanasia has commonly been considered, in principle, both legally and morally permissible, while active euthanasia is legally and morally prohibited. The distinction is based on the view that intentionally or actively killing another person, even if the person requests it, is wrong, while intentionally failing to provide treatment or sustenance, even if it results in someone's death, is acceptable. In essence, physicians do not necessarily have a duty to assist in anyone's death, but they do have a duty to refrain from intentionally killing them.

Both colonial and early state legislators and courts in the United States codified this view that active (but not passive) euthanasia violated medical ethics. In the Massachusetts case of *Commonwealth v. Bowen* (1816), for example, in which one man killed another man at the latter's request, Chief Justice Parker informed the jury of the common law principle that "the consent of a homicide victim is wholly immaterial to the guilt of the person who caused his

CHRONOLOGY

400 B.C.E. Hippocratic Oath is formulated by Hippocrates.

1816 In *Commonwealth v. Bowen*, Chief Justice Parker articulates the common law principle that "the consent of a homicide victim is wholly immaterial to the guilt of the person who caused his death."

1920 *Permitting the Destruction of Life Not Worthy of Life* is published in Germany.

1939 Aktion T4 eugenics program is instituted in Germany.

1973 Voluntary Euthanasia Societies form in the Netherlands.

1981 Rotterdam court states conditions under which aiding suicide and administering voluntary euthanasia would not lead to prosecution in the Netherlands.

1984 The Supreme Court of the Netherlands declares that voluntary active euthanasia is acceptable provided that it meets ten clearly defined conditions.

1991 Notification procedure is established between the Royal Dutch Medical Association and the Dutch Ministry of Justice.

1994 New York State Task Force argues against legalizing active euthanasia in New York State.

1995 Study shows that that there were about 9,700 requests per year for either physician-assisted suicide or euthanasia, of which about 3,700 were honored.

Australia's Northern Territory legalizes euthanasia.

1997 Chief Justice Rehnquist decides in *Washington v. Glucksberg* that under American law there is no right to "determin[e] the time and manner of one's death," no "right to die," no protected "liberty to choose how to die," nor a right "to choose a humane, dignified death."

Colombia legalizes active euthanasia.

Australia's Northern Territory euthanasia bill is overturned by the Australian Parliament.

2000 The Netherlands fully legalizes active euthanasia.

death." Anglo-American law, then, expressly prohibited active euthanasia (whether voluntary, involuntary, or nonvoluntary). This view was later reaffirmed in the Ohio case of *Blackburn v. State* (1872) and the Virginia case of *Martin v. Commonwealth* (1946). The former held that the prohibitions against assisted suicide and euthanasia pertain even if the deceased requested to be killed and did so because he or she was suffering pain and close to death. The court ruled that "the life of those to whom life ha[d] become a burden—or those who [were] hopelessly diseased or fatally wounded—nay, even the lives of criminals condemned to death, [were] under the protection of the law, equally as the lives of those who [were] in the full tide of life's enjoyment, and anxious to continue to live." In *Martin v. Commonwealth,* the court held that "The right to life and personal security is not only sacred in the estimation of the common law, but it is inalienable."

The U.S. Supreme Court reaffirmed this in *Washington v. Glucksberg* (1997). Although the case ad-

dressed the issue of physician-assisted suicide rather than euthanasia, Chief Justice Rehnquist's decision is equally applicable to the continued legal prohibition of active euthanasia. In short, Rehnquist argued that the government has a legitimate interest in prohibiting intentional killing and preserving human life, and can enforce this interest by law. Moreover, he held that under American law there is no right to "determin[e] the time and manner of one's death," no "right to die," no protected "liberty to choose how to die," and no right "to choose a humane, dignified death." Just as the prohibition on physician-assisted suicide was deemed constitutional, so also was the ban on active euthanasia.

EUROPEAN EXPERIENCES WITH ACTIVE EUTHANASIA

The Anglo-American legal tradition of sharply distinguishing between active and passive euthanasia is not universally shared. In Germany, for example, in their

1920 landmark book *Permitting the Destruction of Life Not Worthy of Life,* Alfred Hoche, a professor of psychiatry at the University of Freiburg, and Karl Binding, a professor of law at the University of Leipzig, argue that persons who ask for "death assistance" should be able to obtain it from physicians in certain conditions. The book was ultimately used to justify widespread euthanasia in Nazi Germany after October 1939 under the eugenics program code-named "Aktion T4." The program focused at first on newborns and very young children; healthcare professionals were required to register children up to the age of three who showed signs of mental retardation, physical deformity, or other symptoms included on a questionnaire issued by the Reich Health Ministry. The program was soon expanded to include older disabled children and adults. In October 1939, Hitler enlarged the authority of certain physicians so that "persons who, according to human judgment, are incurable can, upon a most careful diagnosis of their condition of sickness, be accorded a mercy death."

The Nazi endorsement of euthanasia cast a dark shadow over its use and is frequently cited by the opponents of legalized active euthanasia as an example of what might happen were the laws prohibiting active euthanasia repealed. It must be remembered, however, that the Nazi laws were primarily concerned with active *nonvoluntary* and active *involuntary* euthanasia. In contrast to this, the countries that are now most interested in legalizing—or have already legalized—active euthanasia are concerned primarily with voluntary active euthanasia. Moreover, the motivation is concern for people whose lives are, *in their own eyes,* not worth living, rather than people whose lives the state or other individuals deem unworthy.

The most prominent country that has legally endorsed the practice of active euthanasia is the Netherlands. The Dutch trend toward the legalization of active euthanasia began in 1973, with the formation of voluntary euthanasia societies. Under pressure from these groups and others, and a growing national consensus that active euthanasia should be legalized, a Rotterdam court in 1981 stated conditions under which assisting suicide and voluntary euthanasia would not lead to prosecution in the Netherlands. This pronouncement was followed in 1984 by a declaration of the Dutch Supreme Court that voluntary active euthanasia is acceptable if it meets ten clearly defined conditions; the six most important were that (1) the patient made voluntary, persistent, and explicit requests for euthanasia; (2) the physician had a

close enough relationship with the patient to determine if the request was both voluntary and well considered; (3) the patient's suffering was unbearable and without prospect of improvement, according to prevailing medical opinion; (4) the physician and the patient discussed alternatives to euthanasia; (5) the physician consulted at least one other physician with an independent viewpoint; and (6) euthanasia was performed in accordance with good medical practice. Switzerland now has similar regulations.

With these guidelines established, a notification procedure was defined in 1991 between the Royal Dutch Medical Association and the Dutch Ministry of Justice requiring physicians who actively euthanize a patient to report the case to evaluate whether criminal prosecution is called for. The extent to which such legal acceptance of euthanasia altered the Dutch way of death is readily assessed. A 1995 study showed about 9,700 requests were made per year for either physician-assisted suicide or euthanasia, about 3,700 of which were honored. An additional 1,000 deaths were brought about by physicians in violation of official guidelines. The total number of physician-assisted deaths in the Netherlands in 1995 came to about 1.7 percent of all deaths for the year. That figure is believed to represent the percentage of total deaths due to active euthanasia in the Netherlands that year, but some 17.9 percent of all deaths in that country are the result of passive euthanasia.

The Netherlands fully legalized active euthanasia in 2000, but it was preceded by Colombia, which legalized active euthanasia in 1997, and succeeded by Belgium, which legalized it in 2002. In 1995, Australia's Northern Territory approved a bill legalizing euthanasia; the law went into effect the following year but was overturned by the Australian Parliament in 1997.

EUTHANASIA IN THE UNITED STATES

In policy statement E. 2210f, the American Medical Association reflects the distinction between active and passive euthanasia and the principle that only the latter is permissible, stating that "Euthanasia is fundamentally incompatible with the physician's role as healer, would be difficult or impossible to control, and would pose serious societal risks." Since *passive* euthanasia is considered acceptable, the debate over legal and moral acceptability of euthanasia is really a debate over whether or not *active* euthanasia is morally acceptable and should be legalized.

One of the most influential public bodies to address this question was the New York State Task Force on Life and the Law, which considered repealing the state's laws prohibiting euthanasia and physician-assisted suicide. The task force focused on the question of whether there are any relevant differences between a patient's right to refuse medical treatment knowing this would lead to death and the patient's claimed right to request a physician to actively carry out euthanasia or help commit suicide. A person's right to refuse medical treatment knowing that doing so would lead to death is firmly enshrined in Anglo-American law. That being the case, if the task force found no relevant differences between this right and the claimed right to request active euthanasia or assistance in suicide, there would be no legitimate legal basis for treating the two rights differently. Indeed, the task force would have discovered a legitimate reason for repealing laws prohibiting active voluntary euthanasia and physician-assisted suicide.

The task force issued its findings in 1994 in the form of eight "conclusory judgments." All but the first of these were directly related to the task force's ultimate conclusion that there *is* a significant difference between a patient's right to refuse treatment and the claimed right of a patient to request active euthanasia—and that there is *no* legal basis to alter the law prohibiting the recognition of this claimed right.

The task force's judgments expressed two main concerns. The first was that if active euthanasia were legalized, certain vulnerable members of the population might be unduly pressured into accepting it. The experience in the Netherlands corroborated this concern in the 1991 Remmelink Report on the practice of euthanasia, which noted that 0.8 percent of all reported deaths through active euthanasia that year were of persons who had not been legally competent to give their consent. The second concern of the New York Task Force was that legalizing active euthanasia might blunt the moral sensibilities of the population. Again, the Netherlands' experience appears to support this concern. The Remmelink Report noted that the percentage of all deaths in the Netherlands by active euthanasia rose from 1.7 percent in 1991 to 2.4 percent in 1995.

Although the task force's concerns are well-intentioned and may be supported by statistical evidence, the evidence is by no means incontrovertible. Nor does the evidence provide sufficient reason to continue the prohibition of active euthanasia in the United States. First of all, vulnerable members of society might need protection from passive euthanasia as much as from active euthanasia. The fact that passive euthanasia is legal, however, suggests that the level of concern expressed by the task force regarding active euthanasia is already accepted in law. Second, the increase in deaths by active euthanasia in the Netherlands after the practice was codified, in 1990, may be misleading. This rise from 1.7 percent in 1991 to 2.4 percent in 1995 may reflect less a shift in attitude toward death among the Dutch population than the aging of the population and the increased proportion of deaths from cancer versus heart disease. Cancer patients are more likely to request active euthanasia than those suffering from heart disease, because of cancer's chronic and painful nature. The figures may also reflect the increasing availability of life-prolonging medical procedures; these techniques sustain some individuals even though they no longer feel their lives are worth living.

By the same token, even if these explanations allay the New York Task Force's concerns, one should not generalize from the seemingly positive experience in the Netherlands nor leap to the conclusion that the American (or any other) legal system should follow suit. Dutch society is distinctive in several ways. First, the population of the Netherlands enjoys an unusually high standard of medical care; more than 95 percent of the people are covered by private health insurance, guaranteeing a solid core of basic healthcare, including long-term care. In addition, Dutch palliative care is highly advanced, with pain and palliation centers attached to all hospitals; this is not the case in other countries. Finally, Dutch patients place considerable trust in their healthcare providers, many of whom they have often known for a long period of time.

CONCLUSION

Clearly, the Anglo-American moral and legal tradition makes a sharp distinction between passive and active euthanasia. Active euthanasia is held to be morally and legally unacceptable, while passive euthanasia is regarded as both morally and legally acceptable. This distinction rests on a differentiation between killing and letting someone die; the former is impermissible but the latter is not.

Germany's Nazi experience cast a pall on the further use of active euthanasia. However, the fact that active euthanasia can be used for a clearly morally repugnant end does not make the practice itself morally repugnant. Active voluntary euthanasia is legal in the Netherlands, where the social ills opponents have predicted do not seem to have come to pass. Similar approaches have been taken in Belgium and Switzerland. The experiences of these countries seem to pave the way to a debate over legalization of the practice in other countries, such as the United States. But the debate may be moot. The different approaches to euthanasia may have less to do with either the purported moral distinction between active and passive euthanasia or the legal distinction than with such cultural factors as standards of public health care, access to pain relief and palliative care, and the patient-physician relationship.

James Stacey Taylor

REFERENCES

Admiraal, Piter V. "Euthanasia in the Netherlands." *Free Inquiry* 17, 1 (Winter 1997): 5–8.

Angell, Michael. "Euthanasia in the Netherlands—Good News or Bad?" *New England Journal of Medicine* 335, 22 (November 28, 1996): 1676–78.

Aries, Philippe. Trans. Patricia M. Ranum. *Western Attitudes Toward Death from the Middle Ages to the Present.* Baltimore: Johns Hopkins University Press, 1974.

Beauchamp, Tom. *Intending Death: The Ethics of Assisted Suicide and Euthanasia.* Upper Saddle River, NJ: Prentice-Hall, 1995.

Beauchamp, Tom, and James Childress. *Principles of Biomedical Ethics.* New York: Oxford University Press, 2001.

Berger, Arthur S., and Joyce Berger. *To Die or Not to Die?: Cross-Disciplinary, Cultural, and Legal Perspectives on the Right to Choose Death.* Westport, CT: Praeger, 1990.

Burleigh, Michael. *Death and Deliverance "Euthanasia" in Germany c. 1900–1945.* New York: Cambridge University Press, 1994.

De Hann, Jurriaan. "The Ethics of Euthanasia Advocates' Perspectives." *Bioethics* 16, 2 (April 2002): 154–72.

Dillman, R.J.M. "Euthanasia in the Netherlands: The Role of the Dutch Medical Profession." *Cambridge Quarterly of Healthcare Ethics* 5, 1 (Winter 1996): 100–106.

Dworkin, Gerald, R. G. Frey, Sissela Bok, eds. *Euthanasia and Physician-Assisted Suicide.* Cambridge: Cambridge University Press, 1998.

Dworkin, Ronald. *Life's Dominion: An Argument About Abortion, Euthanasia, and Individual Freedom.* New York: Vintage Books, 1994.

Emmanuel, Ezekiel. "Whose Right to Die?" *Atlantic Monthly* 279 (March 1997): 73–79.

Harris, John. *Bioethics.* New York: Oxford University Press, 2001.

Keown, John. *Euthanasia, Ethics, and Public Policy: An Argument Against Legislation.* Cambridge: Cambridge University Press, 2002.

McCarrick, Pat Milmoe. "Active Euthanasia and Assisted Suicide." *Kennedy Institute of Ethics Journal* 2, 1 (March 1992): 79–100.

New York State Task Force on Life and the Law. *When Death Is Sought: Assisted Suicide and Euthanasia in the Medical Context.* Albany: New York State Task Force on Life and the Law, May 1994.

Quill, Timothy, and Gerrit K. Kimsa. "End-of-Life Care in the Netherlands and the United States: A Comparison of Values, Justifications, and Practices." *Cambridge Quarterly of Healthcare Ethics* 6, 2 (Spring 1997): 189–204.

Torr, James. *Euthanasia: Opposing Viewpoints.* San Diego, CA: Greenhaven, 2000.

Urofsky, Melvin. *Lethal Judgments: Assisted Suicide and American Law.* Lawrence: University Press of Kansas, 2000.

Van der Maas, P. J., J. J. M. van Delden, L. Pijenborg. *Euthanasia and Other Medical Decisions Concerning the End of Life.* Amsterdam: Elsevier, 1992.

Van der Maas, P. J., et al. "Euthanasia, Physician-Assisted Suicide, and Other Medical Practices Involving the End of Life in the Netherlands, 1990–1995." *New England Journal of Medicine* 335, 22 (November 22, 1996): 1699–1705.

Yount, Lisa. *Euthanasia.* San Diego, CA: Lucent, 2000.

WEB SITES

American Medical Association: www.ama-assn.org

Compassion & Choices: www.compassionandchoices.org

Euthanasia.com: www.euthanasia.com

Euthanasia Research and Guidance Organization: www.finalexit.org

International Task Force on Euthanasia and Physician-Assisted Suicide: www.internationaltaskforce.org

GLOSSARY

Aktion T4. In the fall of 1939 the German government established the "Euthanasie Programme" The headquarters of the operation was at Tiergartenstrasse 4, Berlin, and the code name for the program (T4) was derived from that address.

American Medical Association. A professional association of physicians and medical students in America.

Hippocratic Oath. According to the American Medical Association's *Code of Medical Ethics* (1996 edition) this "has remained in Western civilization as an expression of ideal conduct for the physician."

Reich Health Ministry. The ministry in the Third Reich responsible for, among other things, the administration of Aktion T4.

Royal Dutch Medical Association. Established in January 1, 1999, this is a federation of medical practitioners' professional associations. It also has a limited number of individual members.

Voluntary euthanasia societies. Societies established in the Netherlands to lobby for the legalization of voluntary active euthanasia.

DOCUMENTS

Document 1. Excerpts from 2001 Dutch Legislation for the Review of Cases of Termination of Life on Request and Assistance with Suicide

Under Dutch law, termination of life on request is punishable but will not be prosecuted if due care requirements have been satisfied. This document outlines what conditions must be met for a physician who terminates the life of a patient to have exercised such due care.

Special provision on exemption from punishment

A physician who helps a patient to die must comply with two conditions to remain exempt from punishment:

1. He must practice due care as set forth in a separate law, the Termination of life on request and assisted suicide (Review) Act;

2. He must report the cause of death to the municipal coroner in accordance with the relevant provisions of the Burial and Cremation Act.

The incorporation of a special provision on exemption from punishment in Criminal Code (Article 293, paragraph two, and in Article 294, paragraph two, sentence two), does not decriminalise other forms of euthanasia and assisted suicide. Therefore, to say that euthanasia and assisted suicide are no longer punishable is not a correct presentation of the tenor of this bill.

Due care requirements

Under current legislation termination of life on request is punishable but will not be prosecuted if due care requirements have been complied with. The due care requirements stipulate, among other things, that the patient's request to die must be voluntary and well-considered, that his condition is hopeless and his pain unbearable, that a second doctor must be consulted and that the euthanasia or assisted suicide is performed with due medical care. Furthermore, the physician is obliged to report that the cause of death is euthanasia or assisted suicide. The physician's action is then examined by a regional review committee to determine whether it was performed with due care. The judgment of the review committee is then sent to the Public Prosecution Service, which uses it as a major argument to decide whether or not to institute proceedings against the physician in question.

The new legal regulations do not essentially change anything in the grounds permitting termination of life on request and assisted suicide. However, the due care requirements have been formulated somewhat more extensively. The due care requirements mentioned in Criminal Code Article 293, paragraph two, stipulate that the physician:

a. must be convinced that the patient has made a voluntary and well-considered request to die;

b. must be convinced that the patient is facing interminable and unendurable suffering;

c. has informed the patient about his situation and his prospects;

d. together with the patient, must be convinced that there is no other reasonable solution;

e. has consulted at least one other independent doctor of the patient;

f. has seen and given his written assessment of the due care requirements as referred to in points a to d;

g. has helped the patient to die with due medical care.

Regional review committees

The five regional review committees continue to exist under the new legislation but they will play a different role. They will continue to assess whether a case of termination of life on request or assisted suicide complies with the due care criteria. If the committee is of the opinion that the physician has practiced due care, the case is finished. But if that is not so, the case is brought to the attention of the Public Prosecutor. The Public Prosecutor does of course have the power to launch his own investigation if he suspects that a criminal act may have been committed. . . .

To monitor the uniformity of the assessments of the different review committees, the chairs of the committees will consult regularly in a meeting attended by representatives of the Council of Procurators-General and the Health Care Inspectorate of the State Supervisory Agency for Public Health.

Minors

The legislation also includes regulations regarding termination of life on request and assisted suicide involving minors. It is generally assumed that minors too have the discernment to arrive at a sound and well-considered request to end their life. Regarding the various age groups, the new legislation links up with the existing legislation concerning medical conduct towards minors. Children of 16 and 17 can, in principle, make their own decision. Their parents must, however, be involved in the decision-making process regarding the ending of their life. For children aged 12 to 16, the approval of parents or guardian is required.

Furthermore, the doctor must comply with the due care requirements mentioned above when he agrees to help a minor commit suicide.

Declaration of will

Finally, the legislation offers an explicit recognition of the validity of a written declaration of will regarding euthanasia (the so-called euthanasia declaration).

The presence of a written declaration of will means that the physician can regard such a declaration as being in accordance with the patient's will. The declaration has the same status as a concrete request for euthanasia. Both an oral and a written request legitimises the physician to accede to the request. However, he is not obliged to do so. And he may only accede to the request while taking into account the due care requirements mentioned in the bill. The due care requirements must be complied with, regardless of whether it involves a request from a lucid patient or a request from a non-lucid patient with a declaration of will. In each case the doctor must be convinced that the patient is facing interminable and unendurable suffering. If he believes that this is not so, he may not accede to the request for euthanasia, no matter what the declaration of will states.

The doctor may only provide information to the patient and discuss with him a reasonable alternative solution if the patient is able to communicate, and in many cases this will not be so.

It is important that the contents of the declaration should, if possible, be discussed by patient and doctor. In this way, the patient can make clear what he means by his declaration and what his precise wishes are. The doctor can, in his turn, make clear to the patient what the conditions are for acceding at any time to this written request for euthanasia.

Source: Euthanasia and Assisted Suicide Control Act, Official Summary, Department of Justice, the Netherlands.

Document 2. Oregon Death with Dignity Act

This document outlines the core sections of Oregon's controversial Death with Dignity Act. This citizens' initiative, which was first passed by Oregon voters in 1994 and went into effect in 1997, gave persons in the state the legal right to request life-ending medication.

GENERAL PROVISIONS

2.01. Who may initiate a written request for medication.

(1) An adult who is capable, is a resident of Oregon, and has been determined by the attending physician and consulting physician to be suffering from a terminal disease, and who has voluntarily expressed his or her wish to die, may make a written request for medication for the purpose of ending his or her life in a humane and dignified manner in accordance with this Act. . . .

3.01. Attending physician responsibilities.

(1) The attending physician shall:

(a) Make the initial determination of whether a patient has a terminal disease, is capable, and has made the request voluntarily; . . .

(c) . . . Inform the patient of:

(A) his or her medical diagnosis;

(B) his or her prognosis;

(C) the potential risks associated with taking the medication to be prescribed;

(D) the probable result of taking the medication to be prescribed;

(E) the feasible alternatives, including, but not limited to, comfort care, hospice care and pain control.

(d) Refer the patient to a consulting physician for medical confirmation of the diagnosis, and for determination that the patient is capable and acting voluntarily;

(e) Refer the patient for counseling if appropriate pursuant to Section 3.03;

(f) Request that the patient notify next of kin; . . .

(h) Inform the patient that he or she has an opportunity to rescind the request at any time and in any manner, and offer the patient an opportunity to rescind at the end of the 15 day waiting period pursuant to Section 3.06;

(i) Verify, immediately prior to writing the prescription for medication under this Act, that the patient is making an informed decision;

(j) Fulfill the medical record documentation requirements of Section 3.09;

(k) Ensure that all appropriate steps are carried out in accordance with this Act prior to writing a prescription for medication to enable a qualified patient to end his or her life in a humane and dignified manner.

3.02. Consulting Physician Confirmation

Before a patient is qualified under this Act, a consulting physician shall examine the patient and his or her relevant medical records and confirm, in writing, the attending physician's diagnosis that the patient is suffering from a terminal disease, and verify that the patient is capable, is acting voluntarily and has made an informed decision.

3.06. Written and oral requests

In order to receive a prescription for medication to end his or her life in a humane and dignified manner, a qualified patient shall have made an oral request and a written request, and reiterate the oral request to his or her attending physician no less than fifteen (15) days after making the initial oral request. At the time the qualified patient makes his or her second oral request, the attending physician shall offer the patient an opportunity to rescind the request.

3.08. Waiting periods

No less than fifteen (15) days shall elapse between the patient's initial and oral request and the writing of a prescription under this Act. No less than 48 hours shall elapse between the patient's written request and the writing of a prescription under this Act.

3.10. Residency requirements

Only requests made by Oregon residents, under this Act, shall be granted.

6.01. Form of the request

A request for a medication as authorized by this Act shall be in substantially the following form:

REQUEST FOR MEDICATION TO END MY LIFE IN A HUMANE AND DIGNIFIED MANNER

I, _____, am an adult of sound mind.

I am suffering from _____, which my attending physician has determined is a terminal disease and which has been medically confirmed by a consulting physician.

I have been fully informed of my diagnosis, prognosis, the nature of medication to be prescribed and potential associated risks, the expected result, and the feasible alternatives, including comfort care, hospice care and pain control.

I request that my attending physician prescribe medication that will end my life in a humane and dignified manner.

INITIAL ONE:

____ I have informed my family of my decision and taken their opinions into consideration.

____ I have decided not to inform my family of my decision.

____ I have no family to inform of my decision.

I understand that I have the right to rescind this request at any time.

I understand the full import of this request and I expect to die when I take the medication to be prescribed.

I make this request voluntarily and without reservation, and I accept full moral responsibility for my actions.

Signed: _____
Dated: _____

DECLARATION OF WITNESSES
We declare that the person signing this request:

(a) Is personally known to us or has provided proof of identity;

(b) Signed this request in our presence;

(c) Appears to be of sound mind and not under duress, fraud or undue influence;

(d) Is not a patient for whom either of us is attending physician.

_____ Witness 1/
Date
_____ Witness 2/
Date

Note: One witness shall not be a relative (by blood, marriage or adoption) of the person signing this request, shall not be entitled to any portion of the person's estate upon death and shall not own, operate or be employed at a health care facility where the person is a patient or resident. If the patient is an inpatient at a health care facility, one of the witnesses shall be an individual designated by the facility.

Source: The Oregon Death with Dignity Act, Oregon Revised Statutes, 127.800, 127.890, 127.895, 127.897.

Document 3. Excerpts from the Rights of the Terminally Ill Act, Northern Territory of Australia

This document contains the core of the Northern Territory of Australia Rights of the Terminally Ill Act, as in force in December 1997. The legislation conferred on the terminally ill within that jurisdiction the legal right to request physician-assisted suicide, but it was later overturned by the Australian federal government.

An Act to confirm the right of a terminally ill person to request assistance from a medically qualified person to voluntarily terminate his or her life in a humane manner; to allow for such assistance to be given in certain circumstances without legal impediment to the person rendering the assistance; to provide procedural protection against the possibility of abuse of the rights recognised by this Act; and for related purposes.

PART 2—REQUEST FOR AND GIVING OF ASSISTANCE

4. Request for assistance to voluntarily terminate life

A patient who, in the course of a terminal illness, is experiencing pain, suffering and/or distress to an extent unacceptable to the patient, may request the patient's medical practitioner to assist the patient to terminate the patient's life.

5. Response of medical practitioner

A medical practitioner who receives a request referred to in section 4, if satisfied that the conditions of section 7 have been met, but subject to section 8, may assist the patient to terminate the patient's life in accordance with this Act or, for any reason and at any time, refuse to give that assistance.

6. Response of medical practitioner, &c., not to be influenced by extraneous considerations

(1) A person shall not give or promise any reward or advantage (other than a reasonable payment for medical services), or by any means cause or threaten to cause any disadvantage, to a medical practitioner or other person for refusing to assist, or for the purpose of compelling or persuading the medical practitioner or other person to assist or refuse to assist, in the termination of a patient's life under this Act. . . .

(2) A person to whom a reward or advantage is promised or given, as referred to in subsection (1), does not have the legal right or capacity to receive or retain the reward or accept or exercise the advantage, whether or not, at the relevant time, he or she was aware of the promise or the intention to give the reward or advantage.

7. Conditions under which medical practitioner may assist

(1) A medical practitioner may assist a patient to end his or her life only if all of the following conditions are met:

(a) the patient has attained the age of 18 years;

(b) the medical practitioner is satisfied, on reasonable grounds, that—

(i) the patient is suffering from an illness that will, in the normal course and without the application of extraordinary measures, result in the death of the patient;

(ii) in reasonable medical judgment, there is no medical measure acceptable to the patient that can reasonably be undertaken in the hope of effecting a cure; and

(iii) any medical treatment reasonably available to the patient is confined to the relief of pain, suffering and/or distress with the object of allowing the patient to die a comfortable death;

(c) two other persons, neither of whom is a relative or employee of, or a member of the same medical practice as, the first medical practitioner or each other—

(i) one of whom is a medical practitioner who holds prescribed qualifications, or has prescribed experience, in the treatment of the terminal illness from which the patient is suffering; and

(ii) the other who is a qualified psychiatrist, have examined the patient and have—

(iii) in the case of the medical practitioner referred to in subparagraph (i), confirmed—

(A) the first medical practitioner's opinion as to the existence and seriousness of the illness;

(B) that the patient is likely to die as a result of the illness; and

(C) the first medical practitioner's prognosis; and

(d) the illness is causing the patient severe pain or suffering;

(e) the medical practitioner has informed the patient of the nature of the illness and its likely course, and the medical treatment, including palliative care, counselling and psychiatric support and extraordinary measures for keeping the patient alive, that might be available to the patient;

(f) after being informed as referred to in paragraph (e), the patient indicates to the medical practitioner that the patient has decided to end his or her life;

(g) the medical practitioner is satisfied that the patient has considered the possible implications of the patient's decision to his or her family;

(h) the medical practitioner is satisfied, on reasonable grounds, that the patient is of sound mind and that the patient's decision to end his or her life has been made freely, voluntarily and after due consideration;

(i) the patient, or a person acting on the patient's behalf in accordance with section 9, has, not earlier than 7 days after the patient has indicated to his or her medical practitioner as referred to in paragraph (f), signed that part of the certificate of request required to be completed by or on behalf of the patient;

(j) the medical practitioner has witnessed the patient's signature on the certificate of request or that of the person who signed on behalf of the patient, and has completed and signed the relevant declaration on the certificate;

(k) the certificate of request has been signed in the presence of the patient and the first medical practitioner by another medical practitioner (who may be the medical practitioner referred to in paragraph (c)(i) or any other medical practitioner) after that medical practitioner has discussed the case with the first medical practitioner and the patient and is satisfied, on reasonable grounds, that the certificate is in order, that the patient is of sound mind and the patient's decision to end his or her life has been made freely, voluntarily and after due consideration, and that the above conditions have been complied with;

(l) where, in accordance with subsection (4), an interpreter is required to be present at the signing of the certificate of request, the certificate of request has been signed by the interpreter confirming the patient's understanding of the request for assistance; . . .

(n) not less than 48 hours has elapsed since the signing of the petition. . . .

Source: Government of the Northern Territory of Australia.

Document 4. Hippocratic Oath— Modern Version

The Hippocratic Oath has defined the prevailing ethical precepts for Western physicians since the time of Ancient Greece. This version, however, differs from more traditional renderings in that it does not bind physicians to refrain from intentionally ending the lives of their patients. It was written in 1964 by Louis Lasagna, academic dean of the School of Medicine at Tufts University, and is used in many medical schools today.

I swear to fulfill, to the best of my ability and judgment, this covenant:

I will respect the hard-won scientific gains of those physicians in whose steps I walk, and gladly share such knowledge as is mine with those who are to follow.

I will apply, for the benefit of the sick, all measures which are required, avoiding those twin traps of overtreatment and therapeutic nihilism.

I will remember that there is art to medicine as well as science, and that warmth, sympathy, and understanding may outweigh the surgeon's knife or the chemist's drug.

I will not be ashamed to say "I know not," nor will I fail to call in my colleagues when the skills of another are needed for a patient's recovery.

I will respect the privacy of my patients, for their problems are not disclosed to me that the world may know. Most especially must I tread with care in matters of life and death. If it is given me to save a life, all thanks. But it may also be within my power to take a life; this awesome responsibility must be faced with great humbleness and awareness of my own frailty. Above all, I must not play at God.

I will remember that I do not treat a fever chart, a cancerous growth, but a sick human being, whose illness may affect the person's family and economic stability. My responsibility includes these related problems, if I am to care adequately for the sick.

I will prevent disease whenever I can, for prevention is preferable to cure.

I will remember that I remain a member of society, with special obligations to all my fellow human beings, those sound of mind and body as well as the infirm.

If I do not violate this oath, may I enjoy life and art, respected while I live and remembered with affection thereafter. May I always act so as to preserve the finest traditions of my calling and may I long experience the joy of healing those who seek my help.

Source: Louis Lasagna, Dean, Tufts University School of Medicine, 1964.

EVOLUTION EDUCATION

Evolution, referring to changes in the frequency of genetic traits in a population over time, is the scientific model explaining the diversity of life on earth. The theory is supported by an overwhelming body of scientific evidence from a variety of disciplines, including molecular biology, geology, paleontology, comparative anatomy, and developmental biology. Nevertheless, evolution education in public schools remains one of the most heated and enduring controversies in American society, as the Western religious tradition—at least in the eyes of many—adheres to countervailing biblical explanations of human origin. Advocates of the biblical view insist that public instruction in evolution alone, or at all, is both unfounded and prejudicial. A significant percentage of the population in the United States today, in contrast with most of the world, question or reject public instruction in evolution—and the theory itself. This opposition has spawned numerous lawsuits, protests, and well-funded organizations that seek to block, hinder, and vilify the teaching of evolution.

EARLY IDEAS ABOUT BIOLOGICAL DIVERSITY

In the early 1800s, several scientists proposed models for evolution. Among the most famous was the French naturalist Jean Baptiste Lamarck (1744–1829), who in 1809 proposed that "species have only a limited or temporary constancy in their characters." Lamarck, who coined the term *biology*, believed that evolution gradually complicates and perfects organisms, and that acquired traits can be inherited. Although Lamarck was one of the first scientists to propose that species changed as a result of natural law, not miraculous intervention, his ideas were quickly disproved and rejected. By the mid-1800s, most scientists and the public continued to believe that an all-powerful deity had created life on Earth out of nothing.

Charles Darwin's (1809–1882) masterpiece *On the*

Origin of Species by Means of Natural Selection, Or the Preservation of Favoured Races in the Struggle for Life (commonly known as *The Origin of Species*) provided the first plausible mechanism for evolution. Darwin's ideas were shaped by decades of scientific study—he had sailed as the de facto naturalist on a five-year scientific expedition of the HMS *Beagle* from 1831 to 1836—as well as application of Adam Smith's laissez-faire economic principles to nature. The tenets of Darwin's model for evolution by natural selection, all of which have been validated by innumerable scientific studies, are as follows:

- Species produce more offspring than can survive. This overreproduction creates a struggle for survival.
- There is an inherited variation among offspring.
- Some variations adapt organisms to local conditions. Individuals with these adaptations have a greater probability of surviving and reproducing than those without them. As a result, favorable traits accumulate over time, and the proportion of individuals in the population with adaptive traits increases.

The publication in 1859 of Darwin's *Origin of Species* provoked a storm of controversy because it (1) challenged the belief in a divine creation of species; (2) argued that humans descended from other organisms according to principles that guided the evolution of species; (3) removed the need for purpose in explaining life's diversity; and (4) documented that populations change but never "progress" or become perfect. In Darwin's world, nature is not peaceful and harmonious, as the Victorians believed, but brutal and amoral. Individuals struggle to increase the representation of their genes in future generations, nothing more.

By the 1870s, the controversy surrounding Darwin's ideas had subsided, and most people in the United Kingdom had accepted evolutionary theory. In the United States, there were isolated in-

CHRONOLOGY

ca. 310 B.C.E. Aristotle proposes that each form of life occupies a fixed position in a hierarchy that reflects the organism's degree of perfection.

1830 C.E. Charles Lyell argues convincingly that the Earth is very old, plants and animals are in flux, and species are constantly disappearing as others emerge.

1859 Charles Darwin publishes *On the Origin of Species by Means of Natural Selection; Or, The Preservation of Favoured Races in the Struggle for Life*, which describes natural selection as a mechanism for biological evolution. Darwin will publish six editions of the book before his death in 1882.

1871 Darwin's *The Descent of Man* eliminates the possibility that evolution does not apply to humans.

1923 Oklahoma becomes the first state to circumspect the teaching of evolution by offering free textbooks to public schools whose teachers will not mention evolution.

1925 In a trial that draws worldwide attention, John Scopes is convicted of violating Tennessee's newly passed law banning the teaching of evolution in public schools. Scopes's conviction prompts publishers to remove evolution from biology textbooks. The conviction is overturned on a technicality two years later, but bans on teaching evolution in Tennessee, Mississippi, and Arkansas remain in effect for more than forty years.

1960 The movie version of *Inherit the Wind* is released to widespread acclaim. The public accepts the largely fictitious movie as an accurate documentary of the Scopes trial.

1961 John Whitcomb and Henry Morris publish *The Genesis Flood: The Biblical Record and Its Scientific Implications*. This book becomes a foundation for creation science and claims for "equal time" in science classrooms.

1963 The Biological Sciences Curriculum Study (BSCS) uses federal funds to begin publishing biology textbooks that emphasize evolution as the unifying concept of biology. By 1970, almost half of all U.S. high schools use the BSCS books.

1968 In *Epperson v. Arkansas*, the U.S. Supreme Court rules unanimously that banning the teaching of evolution in public schools is unconstitutional. This ruling prompts creationists to begin devising other strategies to promote their religious agendas while ensuring that Darwin's ideas are ignored or downplayed in public schools.

1970 In the first lawsuit filed by creationists, Leona Wilson sues the Houston Independent School District on behalf of her daughter, Rita Wright, claiming that her constitutional rights are being violated by the teaching of evolution as fact without referring to other theories of origin. The lawsuit (*Wright v. Houston Independent School District*) is later dismissed.

The Mississippi Supreme Court declares that Mississippi's law banning the teaching of evolution—the last surviving law of its kind—is "void."

1972 William Willoughby sues to force the government to provide money for the publication of creationism-based books (i.e., as it had for the evolution-based books published by the Biological Sciences Curriculum Study). *Willoughby v. Stever* is dismissed the following year.

1973 Tennessee passes the Genesis Act, requiring that all biology textbooks give equal emphasis to "other theories, including, but not limited to, the Genesis account in the Bible." Two years later, the Sixth Circuit Court of Appeals declares in *Daniel v. Waters* that the Genesis Act is "patently unconstitutional."

1976 In *Hendren v. Campbell*, an Indiana Superior Court rules that the use of the pro-creationism textbook *Biology: A Search for Order in Complexity* in public schools violates constitutional bans on the advancement of religion. The decision is not appealed.

1978 In *Crowley v. Smithsonian Institution*, District Judge B.D. Parker rejects claims that the Smithsonian Institution should provide equal time to the biblical story of creation.

1981	Arkansas and Louisiana pass laws requiring that evolution and creationism be given equal time and "balanced treatment" in science classes of public schools. The ACLU immediately challenges the laws.
1982	In *McLean v. Arkansas*, Federal Judge William Overton rules that Arkansas' equal-time law is unconstitutional, that creation science is religion rather than science and has no scientific significance. Arkansas does not appeal Overton's blunt, forceful decision.
1987	In *Edwards v. Aguillard*, the U.S. Supreme Court rules seven to two that Louisiana's law mandating equal time for evolution and creationism is unconstitutional.
1990	In *Webster v. New Lenox School District #122*, the Seventh Circuit Court of Appeals rules that (1) a teacher does not have a First Amendment right to teach creationism in public schools, and (2) a school district can ban a teacher from teaching creationism.
1995	Alabama requires all biology textbooks used in public schools to include a disclaimer stating that evolution is a "theory, not fact."
1996	Republican parties in seven states adopt platforms calling for the teaching of creationism in public schools.
	Pope John Paul II describes evolution as "more than a hypothesis," announcing that he sees no conflict between religious teachings and the theory of evolution. The Pope's announcement outrages many creationists.
1997	In *Freiler v. Tangipahoa Parish Board of Education*, a U.S. District Court rules that (1) it is unlawful to require teachers to read aloud a disclaimer saying that the biblical version of creationism is the only concept "from which students [are] not to be dissuaded," and (2) proposals for teaching "intelligent design" are equivalent to proposals for teaching "creation science."
1998	The National Academy of Sciences reaffirms that evolution is "the most important concept to modern biology," that "there is no debate within the scientific community over whether evolution has occurred," and that "there is no evidence that evolution has not occurred."
1999	The Kansas Board of Education eliminates virtually all mention of evolution in the state's science standards. Most creationist members of the board are voted out of office in the next election, after which evolution returns to the Kansas educational standards.
	U.S. House of Representatives majority whip Tom DeLay continues creationists' long-standing practice of vilifying evolution when he blames the teaching of evolution for school violence.
2000	In *Rodney LeVake v. Independent School District #656*, District Court Judge B.E. Borene rules that a biology teacher's right to free speech does not override the right of the school district to require that teachers not corrupt the curriculum by teaching the alleged "evidence against evolution."
	A review of states' educational guidelines shows that (1) nineteen states' standards have a weak-to-reprehensible treatment of evolution, (2) twelve states shun the word *evolution* in their standards, and (3) four states avoid teaching evolution altogether. Creationism remains surprisingly popular among biology teachers, and many biology teachers in states with the highest standards for teaching evolution avoid or reject evolution.
2002	About one-third of biology teachers in public schools want creationism taught in their classes, and almost 20 percent of those teachers actually teach creationism.

cidents of opposition but no organized efforts to oppose Darwin's ideas, which were common in the best-selling biology textbooks of the early 1900s.

THE CONTROVERSY ERUPTS

Following World War I, the United States experienced a collective nostalgia for the seeming innocence of prewar life. This longing for an earlier time, combined with a perceived decline in morality, led many people to seek comfort and guidance in their religious faith. Religious fundamentalism, based on a literal interpretation of the Bible, became popular. Creationism is an important doctrine of theological perspective. Although it comes in several distinguishable varieties, most creationists endorse the following Genesis-based beliefs:

- The universe, life, and energy were formed suddenly from nothing by a Creator.
- Humans and apes do not share a common ancestry.
- Evolution cannot adequately account for life's diversity.
- Changes in species occur only within the originally created forms of life.
- Geological history is best explained by catastrophism, including a Noachian flood.
- The Earth is less than 10,000 years old.

After their successful campaign to outlaw alcoholic beverages, fundamentalists focused their attention on evolution. Religious leaders such as William Bell Riley, Aimee Semple McPherson, and William "Billy" Sunday blamed Darwin's ideas for the nation's societal ills such as crime, war, and communism. Longing for simpler times, Christian fundamentalists began in the early 1920s to try to save the nation's soul by banning discussions of evolution, especially in public schools. These efforts reached a spectacular climax in Dayton, Tennessee, in the summer of 1925, when the clash between science and fundamentalism took center stage in the Scopes "Monkey Trial." Although Scopes's misdemeanor trial accomplished nothing legally, it has profoundly influenced virtually all legislation, court decisions, and local actions involving the evolution-creationism controversy ever since.

In March 1925, fundamentalists in Tennessee—convinced that the United States had abandoned "old-fashioned faith"—passed the nation's first ban on the teaching of evolution in public schools. Neither the Tennessee legislature nor Governor Austin Peay actually intended to enforce the legislation, but the American Civil Liberties Union (ACLU) placed an advertisement in the *Chattanooga News* seeking a teacher to test the law, and business leaders in Dayton recognized that a high-profile case might boost the town's struggling economy. John T. Scopes, a young substitute biology teacher, agreed to test the law.

The Scopes trial became a national story in May, when three-time Democratic presidential candidate William Jennings Bryan volunteered to help prosecute the case. Bryan, who described the trial as "a duel to the death" between evolution and Christianity, rejected the theory that humans evolved from other animals and blamed the teaching of evolution

for World War I and the evils of society. Bryan's decision to participate in the trial immediately prompted Clarence Darrow, the country's leading criminal defense attorney, to volunteer for Scopes's defense.

Darrow attempted to turn the tables on Bryan by putting his alleged threat to individual liberty on trial, rather than Scopes's teaching of evolution. Bryan, for his part, appealed to religious faith and tradition: "Darrow is an atheist, I'm an upholder of Christianity," he maintained. "If evolution wins, Christianity loses." These and other inflammatory proclamations were reported by journalist H.L. Mencken (1880–1956) of the *Baltimore Sun*, whose coverage of the trial is recognized as one the great journalistic events of the twentieth century. The Scopes trial was the first in history to include daily radio updates.

State of Tennessee v. John Thomas Scopes reached its climax on July 20, 1925, when presiding judge John Raulston—concerned about the intense heat and fearing the throng of people would collapse the floor of the second-story courtroom—moved the proceedings to a dais under shade trees on the courthouse lawn. There, in front of almost 2,000 spectators, Darrow called Bryan to the witness stand, where he was forced to admit that he did not always believe in a literal interpretation of the Bible. Despite the drama of the moment and Darrow's forensic victory, Scopes was convicted the next day of the crime of teaching evolution. Although his conviction was overturned on a technicality two years later, the constitutionality of the Tennessee law was upheld. Legislation banning the teaching of evolution in public schools remained on the books in Tennessee, Mississippi, and Arkansas for more than forty additional years.

AFTERMATH OF THE SCOPES TRIAL

Bryan died in Dayton after a church service five days after the Scopes trial, becoming a martyr to the fundamentalist cause. Antievolution organizations such as The Bible Crusaders sprang up to carry on Bryan's work, and followers later established a private fundamentalist college in Dayton in his memory. The antievolution movement soon began to dissipate, however, as many Protestant fundamentalists redirected their attacks to Jews, Catholics, and the evils of alcohol.

The most dramatic effect of the Scopes trial was on biology textbooks. Although pre-Scopes textbooks had touted evolution as the unifying theme of biology, Darwin and the word *evolution* disappeared from all best-selling textbooks after the trial. The teaching of evolution in public schools declined dramatically.

In the 1940s and 1950s, evolution slowly began to reappear in high-school biology textbooks. The trend was hastened dramatically in 1957 by the Soviet Union's launch of *Sputnik I*, the first orbiting artificial satellite. *Sputnik* triggered widespread concern that the United States had fallen behind the Soviet Union in science and technology, and two years later the federal government funded the Biological Sciences Curriculum Study (BSCS), a nonprofit organization charged with developing science curricula and state-of-the-art textbooks. In 1963, BSCS published three textbooks that used evolution as a unifying theme of biology. All three became best-sellers, prompting other publishers to take a similar direction. Evolution was back in the curriculum.

The legend of the Scopes trial was revived in 1960 by the highly acclaimed motion picture, *Inherit the Wind*. Premiering in Dayton on the thirty-fifth anniversary of the trial, the film was meant to be a commentary on the dangers of McCarthyism but was interpreted by much of the public as a documentary on the trial itself and the issue of evolution education. Soon after *Inherit the Wind* was released, creationist theologians John Whitcomb and Henry Morris rescued antievolutionary thought from 35 years of dormancy with *The Genesis Flood: The Biblical Record and Its Scientific Implications* (1961). The book presents the flood geology of George McReady Price (1870–1963) as the only acceptable interpretation of *Genesis* and declares that the principles of biblical literacy can explain natural phenomena.

The Genesis Flood became a pillar of the new "creation science," and demands for "equal time" in the classroom proliferated during the 1970s and 1980s. Morris, who became the most influential antievolutionist of the late twentieth century, formed the Creation Research Society in 1963 to promote his beliefs that the Bible is a science book and the theory of evolution is guided by Satan.

THE CONTROVERSY RETURNS TO THE COURTROOM

The evolution-related events of the early 1960s—that is, the widespread return of evolution-based biology textbooks, the popularity of *Inherit the Wind*, and the appearance of *The Genesis Flood*—stirred new sentiments about evolution education. In Arkan-

sas, a newly hired biology teacher at Little Rock's Central High School named Susan Epperson was concerned about the Arkansas law banning the teaching of evolution. Epperson, a devout Christian and theistic evolutionist—she believed that God used evolution to create life—wanted to obey the law but also felt she could not be a responsible biology teacher if she did not teach evolution. And so she decided to challenge the law.

Epperson filed a lawsuit late in 1965. The first legal challenge of an antievolution statute since the Scopes trial, her suit was opposed by the governor and most other politicians in Arkansas. Although Epperson won the initial trial, the Arkansas Supreme Court reversed the lower court's decision. Finally, in 1968, the U.S. Supreme Court ruled unanimously in *Epperson v. Arkansas* that the Arkansas law banning the teaching of evolution was unconstitutional.

Epperson v. Arkansas forced creationists to change their tactics. Without a legal foundation for the outright banning of Darwin's ideas from the classroom, creationists—like other groups in the 1970s who felt their rights were being violated—attempted to use the legal system to impede or erode evolution education and promote creationism incrementally. Creationist lawsuits raised a variety of issues pertaining to evolution education, including the following:

1. Does a student have a right to be shielded from scientific findings such as evolution that are incompatible with their religious beliefs? No (*Wright v. Houston Independent School District*). This lawsuit was the first in the evolution-creationism controversy to be filed by a creationist.

2. Can states demand that teaching and textbooks be tailored to particular religious beliefs (such as biblical creationism)? No (*Willoughby v. Stever*; *Daniel v. Waters*).

3. Can a state mandate that creationism and evolution be given "equal emphasis" or "balanced treatment"? No (*Daniel v. Waters*; *Edwards v. Aguillard*). *Edwards v. Aguillard* was decided by a seven to two decision of the U.S. Supreme Court

4. Can creationism-based textbooks be adopted for use in public schools? No (*Hendren v. Campbell*).

5. Can federal institutions be banned from using tax money to promote evolution as science? No (*Crowley v. Smithsonian Institution*).

6. Do exhibits that promote evolution as science restrict the free exercise of religion? No (*Crowley v. Smithsonian Institution*).

7. Is creation science really science? No (*McLean v. Arkansas Board of Education*). Judge William Overton's blunt, forceful decision in *McLean v. Arkansas Board of Education* provides a legal analysis of what science is and what it is not, destroying the legal legitimacy of creation science popularized two decades earlier by *The Genesis Flood*.

8. Does creation science have any scientific or educational merit as science? No (*McLean v. Arkansas Board of Education*).

9. Is creation science anything but religion masquerading as science? No (*McLean v. Arkansas Board of Education*).

10. Does a teacher have a First Amendment right to teach creationism in a public school? No (*Webster v. New Lennox School District #122*).

11. Can a teacher teach creationism if it is not included in the state's educational guidelines? No (*Peloza v. Capistrano Unified School District*).

12. Does a teacher have a right to teach a curriculum that violates the state's educational guidelines? No (*Peloza v. Capistrano Unified School District*).

13. Can a teacher read aloud a disclaimer favoring the biblical version of creationism? No (*Freiler v. Tangipahoa Parish Board of Education*).

14. Are proposals for intelligent design different from those for creation science? No (*Freiler v. Tangipahoa Parish Board of Education*).

15. Does a teacher's right to free speech entitle him or her to teach the alleged "evidence against evolution"? No (*LeVake v. Independent School District #656*). LeVake's lawsuit, funded by an organization sponsored by televangelist and former Republican presidential candidate Pat Robertson, cited the phrase "evidence against evolution" from the minority opinion in *Edwards v. Aguillard*.

EMERGENCE OF "INTELLIGENT DESIGN"

After losing all of their legal challenges to evolution education, creationists again changed their tactics. By the 1990s a new type of creationism called "intelligent design," or ID, became increasingly popular. One of the earliest proponents of ID was William Paley (1743–1805), who argued in the early 1800s that God's existence could be proved by examining His works. Paley used a simple analogy to make his point: if someone finds a watch, it is obvious that the watch could not have come together by chance. The existence of the watch implies a watchmaker who has purposefully designed the watch. Similarly, the discovery of purpose, design, and order in the natural world is evidence of an omniscient designer. How, according to Paley, could a structure as complex as the vertebrate eye evolve?

The promoters of ID, most of whom are philosophers and historians rather than scientists, argue that many of life's mechanisms (e.g., flagella, propellerlike appendages found in some of the simplest forms of life) are too complex to be explained by natural phenomena and Darwinian evolution alone. According to advocates of ID, somewhere and somehow *something* must have intervened in evolution. For virtually all advocates of ID, that "something" is the Christian God.

Unlike biblical literalists and creation scientists, ID proponents accept most tenets of basic science (e.g., that the Earth is very old) as well as the fact that Darwin's postulates do explain *some* aspects of life's diversity. ID meshes comfortably with religion, and many people accept ID's seemingly undogmatic approach.

ID, like all other forms of creationism, is critical of evolution, yet it offers no testable ideas as a substitute for modern evolutionary principles. Moreover, its opponents claim ID stifles science because it attributes what is not yet understood to an unknowable and untestable cause.

EVOLUTION EDUCATION TODAY

In recent years, evolution education has become increasingly important—not just scientifically, but economically and socially. For example, the escalating use of pesticides and antibiotics has fostered the evolution of resistant pests and pathogens. Evolutionary theory is used to track infectious diseases (e.g., to infer sources of HIV transmission), and drug developers use some of nature's evolutionary mechanisms (e.g., recombination, mutation) in "directed evolution" to find molecules for specific functions.

Although society has become increasingly dependent on science and technology, evolution education

Table 1. What Americans Want Taught in Public Schools (in %)

Teach only evolution without mentioning creationism	20
Teach only evolution in science class, but discuss creationism outside of science class	17
Discuss creationism in science class, but as a "belief," not science	29
Teach evolution and creationism as "scientific theories" in science class	13
Teach only creationism without mentioning evolution	16
Not sure	5

Source: People for the American Way Foundation. *Evolution and Creationism in Public Education: An In-depth Reading of Public Opinion.* Washington, DC: People for the American Way Foundation, 1999.

remains controversial in the United States. Evolutionary theory is a foundation of science, yet the public overwhelmingly supports the inclusion of creationism in public schools, and many people view the teaching of evolution as a threat to cultural values. Although scientists are convinced of the validity of Darwin's basic ideas, the public is not.

Many of the people who question or reject evolution are biology teachers in public schools. Despite decades of science education reform and focus on evolution by biology textbooks and professional scientific organizations (such as the National Association of Biology Teachers, National Science Teachers Association, and American Association for the Advancement of Science), evolution is rejected, ignored, or mentioned only in passing by a large percentage of biology teachers. In some states, education officials classify evolution with gun control, witchcraft, the occult, and other topics that "may not be suitable for assessment items" on state educational exams. If students or their parents do not want to be exposed to evolution, students are given alternative assignments. In Kentucky, for example, the state legislature in 1990 reenacted a law passed in 1976 stipulating that teachers who cover evolution can also teach "creationism as presented in the Bible" and that students who adhere to biblical creationism should get credit on exams.

Taken together, these and other efforts by antievolutionists have been remarkably effective. According to one survey, almost 80 percent of Americans want both creationism and evolution to be taught in public schools, and more than one-third of Americans favor teaching creationism only. Similarly, many Americans simply reject evidence that humans developed from earlier species of animals, and almost half believe "God created man pretty much in his present form at one time within the last 10,000 years."

Randy Moore

REFERENCES

Darwin, Charles. *On the Origin of Species by Means of Natural Selection, Or the Preservation of Favoured Races in the Struggle for Life.* London: Murray, 1859.

———. *Descent of Man and Selection in Relation to Sex.* London: Murray, 1871.

de Camp, L. Sprague. *The Great Monkey Trial.* Garden City, NY: Doubleday, 1968.

Dobzhansky, T. "Nothing in Biology Makes Sense Except in the Light of Evolution." *The American Biology Teacher* 35 (1973): 125–29.

Falwell, Jerry. *The Fundamentalist Phenomenon: The Resurgence of Conservative Christianity.* Garden City, NY: Doubleday, 1981.

Gilkey, Langdon. *Creationism on Trial: Evolution and God at Little Rock.* New York: Harper and Row, 1985.

Gould, Stephen J. *Ever Since Darwin.* New York: Norton, 1977.

Grabiner, J. V., and P. D. Miller. "Effects of the Scopes Trial." *Science* 185 (1974): 832–36.

Grobman, Arnold B. *The Changing Classroom: The Role of the Biological Science Curriculum Study.* Garden City, NY: Doubleday, 1969.

La Follette, Marcel C., ed. *Creationism, Science and the Law: The Arkansas Case.* Cambridge: Massachusetts Institute of Technology Press, 1983.

Larson, Edward J. *Trial and Error: The American Controversy over Creation and Evolution.* Updated edition. New York: Oxford University Press, 1989.

———. *Summer for the Gods: The Scopes Trial and America's Continuing Debate over Science and Religion.* New York: Basic Books, 1997.

Lawrence, Jerome, and Robert E. Lee. *Inherit the Wind.* New York: Bantam Books, 1955.

Martin, William C. *With God on Our Side: The Rise of the Religious Right in America.* New York: Broadway Books, 1996.

Moore, Randy. "Creationism in the United States. VII. The lingering impact of *Inherit the Wind.*" *The American Biology Teacher* 61 (1999): 246–51.

———. "The Lingering Impact of the Scopes Trial on High School Biology Textbooks." *BioScience* 51 (2001): 790–96.

———. *Evolution in the Courtroom: A Reference Guide.* Santa Barbara, CA: ABC-CLIO, 2002.

———. "Teaching Evolution: Do State Standards Matter?" *BioScience* 52 (2002): 378–81.

Morris, Henry. *The Long War Against God. The History*

and Impact of the Creation/Evolution Conflict. Grand Rapids, MI: Baker, 1989.

Morris, Henry Madison. *History of Modern Creationism.* San Diego: Master Books, 1984.

Nelkin, Dorothy. *The Creation Controversy: Science or Scripture in the Schools?* New York: Norton, 1982.

Numbers, Ronald L. *The Creationists: The Evolution of Scientific Creationism.* Berkeley: University of California Press, 1992.

Paterson, F.R.A., and L. F. Rossow. "'Chained to the Devil's Throne': Evolution and Creation Science as a Religio-Political Issue." *The American Biology Teacher* 61 (1999): 358–64.

Rennie, J. "Fifteen Answers to Creationist Nonsense." *Scientific American* (July 2002): 78–85.

Scopes, John T., and James Presley. *Center of the Storm: Memoirs of John T. Scopes.* New York: Holt, Rinehart and Winston, 1967.

Scott, E. C. "Antievolution and Creationism in the United States." *Annual Review of Anthropology* 26 (1997): 263–89.

Whitcomb, John C., Jr., and Henry M. Morris. *The Genesis Flood: The Biblical Record and Its Scientific Implications.* Philadelphia: Presbyterian and Reformed, 1961.

WEB SITES

Americans United for Separation of Church and State: www.au.org

Institute for Creation Research: www.icr.org

National Academy of Sciences: www.nationalacademies .org/evolution

National Association of Biology Teachers: www.nabt.org

National Center for Science Education: www.ncseweb.org

PBS website for evolution: www.pbs.org/wgbh/evolution

Skeptic magazine: www.skeptic.com

Talk.Origins archive: www.talkorigins.org

Tennessee v. John Thomas Scopes: www.law.umkc.edu/ faculty/projects/ftrials/scopes/scopes.htm

GLOSSARY

Catastrophism. The belief that Earth's geological formations are best explained by rare, cataclysmic events. Catastrophism is a fundamental aspect of creation science and advocated by antievolutionists who are biblical literalists. Creation scientists believe that the most recent catastrophe was a Noachian flood.

Creationism. The belief that a deity formed the universe and all living things, including humans. There are many types of creationists, ranging from young-earth creationists (who believe that God created the universe in six 24-hour days and that the Earth is less than 10,000 years old) to theistic evolutionists (who believe that God used evolution to create life).

Creation science. A type of creationism that believes that a Noachian flood occurred and the Bible should be read as a book of science. Popularized in the 1960s by the book *The Genesis Flood,* creation science was declared to be a religion and to have no scientific significance in *McLean v. Arkansas,* but it remains the basis for well-funded antievolution organizations such as Answers in Genesis and The Institute for Creation Research. These organizations are dogmatic in their beliefs; for example, Answers in Genesis claims that "By definition, no apparent, perceived, or claimed evidence in any field . . . can be valid if it contradicts the Scriptural record."

Evolution. Changes in the frequency of genetic traits from one generation to the next. In more general terms, evolution refers to the descent of modern organisms with modification from earlier life forms. Charles Darwin proposed the first scientifically valid theory for evolution in 1859 in his book entitled *On the Origin of Species.*

Fundamentalism. A conservative theology that, among Christians, is often based on biblical literalism. Fundamentalists helped spawn the evolution-creationism controversy in the United States in the early 1900s.

Intelligent design. A type of creationism based on the belief that many aspects of life are too complex to have evolved by chance. This belief is taken as evidence of an "intelligent designer," which is virtually always a deity.

Natural selection. The differential survival and reproduction of organisms due to genetic differences among individuals, resulting in the preservation of favorable adaptations. Natural selection is the foundation of Charles Darwin's theory of evolution.

Noachian flood. In Christian theology, the worldwide flood described in the Bible. This flood is the basis of several types of creationism, including creation science.

Theistic evolution. The theological view that God creates through evolution. Theistic evolution is taught at most mainstream Protestant seminaries, and is the official position of the Catholic Church.

DOCUMENTS

Document 1. Excerpt from *McLean v. Arkansas Board of Education*

In 1981, Arkansas passed a law requiring teachers in public schools to give equal time to evolution and "creation science." The law was challenged by the American Civil Liberties Union, which argued that the law was an attempt to establish religion in public schools, and therefore violated the First Amendment. The following decision by Judge William Overton remains the only evolution-related decision to directly address the educational value and scientific merits of "creation science."

. . . The conclusion that creation science has no scientific merit or educational value as science has legal significance in light of the Court's previous conclusion that creation science has, as one major effect, the advancement of religion. The second part of the three-pronged test for establishment reaches only those statutes as having their *primary* effect the advancement of religion. Secondary effects which advance religion are not constitutionally fatal. Since creation science is not science, the conclusion is inescapable that the *only* real effect of Act 590 is the advancement of religion. . . .

V(D)

The application and content of First Amendment principles are not determined by public opinion polls or by a majority vote. Whether the proponents of Act 590 constitute the majority or the minority is quite irrelevant under a constitutional system of government. No group, no matter how large or small, may use the organs of government, of which the public schools are the most conspicuous and influential, to foist its religious beliefs on others.

The Court closes this opinion with a thought expressed eloquently by the great Justice Frankfurter:

We renew our conviction that "we have staked the very existence of our country on the faith that complete separation between the state and religion is best for the state and best for religion." *Everson v. Board of Education*, 330 U.S. at 59. If nowhere else, in the relation between Church and State, "good fences make good neighbors." [*McCollum v. Board of Education*, 333 U.S. 203, 232 (1948)]

An injunction will be entered permanently prohibiting enforcement of Act 590.

It is ordered this January 5, 1982.

—William R. Overton *in the U.S. District Court, Eastern District of Arkansas, Western Division*

Source: McLean v. Arkansas Board of Education. 529 F. Supp. 1255, 50 U.S. Law Week 2412 (1982).

Document 2. Excerpt from *Edwards v. Aguillard* (1987)

In 1981, Louisiana passed a law requiring that teachers in public schools who teach evolution also give "balanced treatment" to creationism. Don Aguillard, a young biology teacher in Louisiana, challenged the law because he believed that it was unconstitutional and undermined scientific education. Aguillard's case reached the U.S. Supreme Court, which issued the following decision.

OPINION: JUSTICE BRENNAN delivered the opinion of the Court.

The question for decision is whether Louisiana's "Balanced Treatment for Creation-Science and Evolution-Science in Public School Instruction" Act (Creationism Act), La. Rev. Stat. Ann. §§ 17:286.1–17:286.7, is facially invalid as violative of the Establishment Clause of the First Amendment.

III A

. . . The goal of basic "fairness" is hardly furthered by the Act's discriminatory preference for the teaching of creation science and against the teaching of evolution. While requiring that curriculum guides be developed for creation science, the Act says nothing of comparable guides for evolution. Similarly, resource services are supplied for creation science but not for evolution. Only "creation scientists" can serve on the panel that supplies the resource services. The Act forbids school boards to discriminate against anyone who "chooses to be a creation-scientist" or to teach "creationism," but fails to protect those who choose to teach evolution or any other noncreation science theory, or who refuse to teach creation science. . . .

III B

As in Stone and Abington, we need not be blind in this case to the legislature's preeminent religious purpose in enacting this statute. There is a historic and contemporaneous link between the teachings of certain religious denominations and the teaching of evolution. It was this link that concerned the Court in *Epperson v. Arkansas*, 393 U.S. 97 (1968), which also involved a facial challenge to a statute regulating the teaching of evolution. In that case, the Court reviewed an Arkansas statute that made it unlawful for an instructor to teach evolution or to use a textbook that referred to this scientific theory. Although the Arkansas antievolution law did not explicitly state its predominate religious purpose, the Court could not ignore that "[t]he statute was a product of the upsurge of 'fundamentalist' religious fervor" that has long viewed this particular scientific theory as contradicting the literal interpretation of the Bible. . . . After reviewing the history of antievolution statutes, the Court determined that "there can be no doubt that the motivation for the [Arkansas] law was the same [as other anti-evolution statutes]: to suppress the teaching of a theory which, it was thought, 'denied' the divine creation of man." . . . The Court found that there can be no legitimate state interest in protecting particular religions from scientific views "distasteful to them," . . . and concluded "that the First Amendment does not permit the State to require that teaching and learning must be tailored to the principles or prohibitions of any religious sect or dogma," . . .

Furthermore, it is not happenstance that the legislature required the teaching of a theory that coincided with this religious view. The legislative history documents that the Act's primary purpose was to change the science curriculum of public schools in order to provide persuasive advantage to a particular religious doctrine that rejects the factual basis of evolution in its entirety. The sponsor of the Creationism Act, Senator Keith, explained during the legislative hearings that his disdain for the theory of evolution resulted from the support that evolution supplied to views contrary to his own religious beliefs. According to Senator Keith, the theory of evolution was consonant with the "cardinal principle[s] of religious humanism, secular humanism, theological liberalism, aetheistism [sic]." . . . The state senator repeatedly stated that scientific evidence supporting his religious views should be included in the public school curriculum to redress the fact that the theory of evolution incidentally coincided with what he characterized as religious beliefs antithetical to his own. The legislation therefore sought to alter the science curriculum to reflect endorsement of a religious view that is antagonistic to the theory of evolution.

V

The Louisiana Creationism Act advances a religious doctrine by requiring either the banishment of the theory of evolution from public school classrooms or the presentation of a religious viewpoint that rejects evolution in its entirety. The Act violates the Establishment Clause of the First Amendment because it seeks to employ the symbolic and financial support of government to achieve a religious purpose. The judgment of the Court of Appeals therefore is Affirmed.

JUSTICE SCALIA, with whom THE CHIEF JUSTICE joins, dissenting.

Even if I agreed with the questionable premise that legislation can be invalidated under the Establishment Clause on the basis of its motivation alone, without regard to its effects, I would still find no justification for today's decision. The Louisiana legislators who passed the "Balanced Treatment for Creation-Science and Evolution-Science Act" (Balanced Treatment Act) . . . , each of whom had sworn to support the Constitution were well aware of the potential Establishment Clause problems and considered that aspect of the legislation with great care. After seven hearings and several months of study, resulting in substantial revision of the original proposal, they approved the Act overwhelmingly and specifically articulated the secular purpose they meant it to serve. Although the record contains abundant evidence of the sincerity of that purpose (the only issue pertinent to this case), the Court today holds, essentially on the basis of "its visceral knowledge regarding what must have motivated the legislators," that the members of the Louisiana Legislature knowingly violated their oaths and then lied about it. I dissent. Had requirements of the Balanced Treatment Act that are not apparent on its face been clarified by an interpretation of the Louisiana Supreme Court, or by the manner of its implementation, the Act might well be found unconstitutional; but the question of its constitutionality cannot rightly be disposed of on the gallop, by impugning the motives of its supporters.

Source: Edwards v. Aguillard, 482 U.S. 578; 107 S. Ct. 2573.

EXTINCTION AND SPECIES LOSS:
BIOTA INVASION AND HABITAT DESTRUCTION

No area of the globe or country among the community of nations can escape the problems created by the invasion of alien flora, fauna, and pathogens into their native biotas—the plants, animals, and other living organisms of a particular region. The invasion of non-native species into an existing biota often presents a natural system in which the invaders can flourish without the competition and natural enemies of their original environment. The decline in biodiversity created by bioinvasions is, along with habitat destruction, the major problem confronting the world's native biota.

ACCIDENTAL INTRODUCTIONS OF SPECIES

Bioinvasions occur through the agency of humans and by natural means. People share the biosphere with an estimated 14 million species and both directly and indirectly aid non-native species that are always seeking to maintain themselves and expand their populations and range. The problem these invaders create will become even more significant in the twenty-first century as trade between nations increases and transportation shrinks the globe, permitting even more rapid movement of people from continent to continent. Humans never travel alone; knowingly and unknowingly, they bring plants, animals, and microbes from the lands where their journeys began.

Since the rise of civilization in the world's great river valleys, men and women have been invasive species themselves; their movements throughout the world have not only set off wars of conquest and colonization, but also devastated native peoples with pandemics. Europeans in particular were agents of the "virgin soil epidemics"—measles, smallpox, malaria, and yellow fever epidemics that reduced the populations of the lands they settled. Global monitoring of such interchanges today would record the daily intrusion of exotic species into existing biota. Few areas of the globe are remote any longer, and their plants, animals, and other organisms only await transportation to the rest of the world.

The complexity of pathways by which they move from their native biota into that of other species is often either unknown or poorly understood. Surprises occur daily for scientists who study the diverse routes through which non-native species enter new ecosystems. Who could have predicted that the Asian Tiger mosquito would enter the Port of Houston on ships carrying tire carcasses from Asia in the early 1980s? Until their discovery in that city during the summer of 1985, the mosquitoes had not been found anywhere in North America. This mosquito reproduces in standing water, is difficult to kill, an aggressive biter, and an excellent vector (mechanism or agent for spreading a disease) for a number of viruses harmful to humans and animals. Now found in seventeen states, the Tiger mosquito has also been accidentally introduced into the Dominican Republic, Brazil, Bolivia, Colombia, Nigeria, Albania, Italy, New Zealand, and Australia.

Growing global human populations and per capita consumption require even more agricultural activity, industrial expansion, and construction of cities, highways, docks, and airports. All of these developments also disturbed natural habitats, increasing the success of invasive species within the resulting disturbed systems. Increasingly, millennia-old barriers of oceans, lakes, deserts, and mountain ranges that isolated, or buffered, various biota from the invasive species are being broached or reduced by human action. Nineteenth- and twentieth-century American canal building not only saved time and money in shipment of the nation's commerce but also introduced such invasive species into the Great Lakes as the sea lamprey, alewife, and white perch, to name but a few. These species devastated populations of sport and commercially significant fish. The continued improvement of lock systems permitting seagoing vessels to enter the Great Lakes has brought many invasive species in their ballasts.

CHRONOLOGY

12000–6000 B.C.E.	The rise of agriculture, growth of agricultural villages, and beginning of domestication of animals occurs.
6000–3000 B.C.E.	Civilizations rise in the great river valleys of the world with people living in cities in greater population densities. Concentrated populations, less hygienic conditions, and greater contact with animals stimulated the increase of human diseases. Growing production of cereals leads to agricultural monocultures, which are more susceptible to pests.
800–1300s C.E.	Polynesian settlement of New Zealand begins, and introduction of nonindigenous species, including dogs and rats, eliminates native species of flightless birds and other flora and fauna.
1348	Black Death, or bubonic plague, arriving from the east, breaks out in Europe in a pandemic that decimates that continent's population for centuries.
1500s–1800s	European exploration, discovery, and colonization take place, disseminating Europeans and their non-native animals, plants, pests, and diseases.
1520s–1600	Old World disease appears in the New World, bringing death to Mesoamerican natives. European diseases continue to devastate populations in Mexico, Peru, Brazil, and the South Pacific until the middle of the nineteenth century.
1630s–40s	Smallpox appears in New England, eastern Canada, and the Great Lakes, devastating the Native Americans of these regions.
1759–1900	Rabbits are released in Australia for sport, food, and fur; within 150 years they overrun much of the country—estimated to number over a half billion.
1770s–1900s	Prickly pear, *Opuntia ficus-indica*, is brought to South Africa, and by the early 1900s becomes a major limitation on farming and livestock raising. Some control over the prickly pear is obtained with the introduction of the biocontrol agent, the cochineal insect.
1788	Prickly pear cactus is brought to Australia with the First Fleet to serve as a host for the cochineal insect to start the red dye industry.
1790s–1830s	European whalers and settlers begin to arrive in New Zealand bringing, intentionally and unintentionally, animals, plants, and microorganisms from their native lands. Biodiversity has been reduced and nonindigenous species have established themselves. The biota, habitat, ecosystems, and extinctions of certain species in New Zealand are the result of bioinvasions precipitated by the arrivals of Polynesians and Europeans.
1800s	Prickly pear is reintroduced into Australia as fodder for livestock.
	Nonindigenous fish are cultured and placed in bodies of water around the world to provide food and sport for European settlers.
	Salt cedars (*Tamarix*) are introduced into the American southwest early in the century as ornamental trees and shrubs to stabilize eroding river drainage systems. Their many negative impacts on native ecosystems could be anticipated.
1870s–1926	Prickly pear grows unchecked in Australia despite the use of poison, fire, and mechanical means to control it. Introduction of the Cactoblastis moth in 1926 brings the prickly pear under control but does not eradicate it.
1800–1930	Acclimatization societies are organized in many nations—Australia, Java, India, Malaysia, United States, Great Britain, Sicily, New Zealand, Russia, and Argentina—to introduce new species of birds, fish, mammals, and plants into native ecosystems.
1800s–present	The fossil fuel age begins, permitting the industrial development of the modern world with its inexpensive forms of production, transportation, and energy.
1840s	Water ballast systems for ships are developed, dispersing marine life throughout the world's oceans, seas, and connected seaways.
1860s	The gypsy moth is brought into America from France.

1870s–80s	Rainbow trout, brown trout, and Chinook salmon are introduced into the Great Lakes. U.S. Fish and Fisheries Commission distributes from its railroad fish cars salmon, trout, carp, whitefish, bass, pike, and haddock into native biota, subsequently altering these ecosystems. The European carp now has the widest geographical distribution of any American fish.
1900–40s	The chestnut blight begins to be observed in American forests, creating a four-decade devastation of great stands of American chestnuts.
1906	Melaleuca trees are brought to the demanding environment of south Florida and the Everglades.
1918–present	Two species of South American fire ants (black and red) apparently enter the United States through the port of Mobile, Alabama, between 1918 and 1930 in soil used as ballast. Now found in ten states, they have established themselves over 275 million acres. Fire ants are also accidentally introduced into Australia, joining the rabbit as one of the most successful invaders, and can be found in other areas of the world. Effective control measures have not yet been developed.
1950	Australian rabbits are successfully exposed to a South American strain of the myxoma virus, substantially reducing rabbit populations. Still a significant pest in Australia, rabbits are developing an immunity to the virus.
1950–present	Brown tree snakes (*Boiga irregularis*) from New Guinea, either in ship or air cargo, establish themselves on the island of Guam. With populations of up to 13,000 per square mile in forested areas, they have caused the extinction of twelve species of birds, endangered other birds and animals, and caused more than 1,200 significant electrical power outages.
1958	Charles S. Elton publishes the first seminal study of bioinvasions, *The Ecology of Invasions by Animals and Plants.*
1973	Endangered Species Act is signed into law by President Richard Nixon; the law requires that species survival be considered in development decisions.
1982	Comb jellyfish from the coast of New England and the North Atlantic are observed in the Black Sea. Their successful invasion and domination of that biota seem unlikely at the time.
1988	Zebra mussels are first observed in Lake Erie. By the beginning of the twenty-first century, they are not only an uncontrollable problem in the Great Lakes, but have also spread into the Mississippi Valley.
1992	Captive-bred California condors are reintroduced into the wild.
1993	President Bill Clinton hosts a forest summit among environmentalists and loggers in Portland, triggered by concerns over the extinction of the northern spotted owl.
2000	The UN Environmental Programme reports more than 12,000 species worldwide are threatened with extinction.
2003	President George W. Bush proposes a series of changes in enforcement of the Endangered Species Act, which environmentalists say will weaken the act.

Zebra mussels were first observed in Lake Erie in 1988, probably discharged in the ballast from an oceangoing cargo carrier a year or two earlier. Although they seldom reach a length of more than an inch and a half, their ability to produce millions of eggs several times a year and their capacity to maintain themselves on underwater structures in densities of several thousand mussels per square yard have made zebra mussels not only competitors with other aquatic life in the Great Lakes but also a problem for water and cooling intake systems, boat hulls, rudders and propellers, and docks. They have also established themselves in the drainage system of the Mississippi River and its numerous tributaries.

Many invasive species are quite harmless in their native habitats. The comb jellyfish does not sting and appears to be just an unusual and attractive marine species in its native waters along the Atlantic coast from Maine to Argentina. In 1982, it was discovered in the Black Sea, however, where 6 years later, its population had grown dramatically and begun to devastate Black Sea fisheries. In less than a decade, the anchovy catch fell by 99 percent, while the horse mackerel catch disappeared, and the sprat catch was less than half its former levels. Almost 500 comb jellyfish can live in a cubic yard, consuming the zooplankton, eggs, and young fish larvae that supported the commercial species. At the peak of its growth, before its population declined as its food supply was exhausted, the species constituted almost 95 percent of the Black Sea's biomass. From there, the comb jellyfish has made its way into the Caspian Sea through the Volga-Don River Canal, severely reducing the food base of the Caspian's commercial fish species, including the sturgeon that produces the region's famous caviar.

Invasive species do not usually disrupt native ecosystems immediately, for their initial populations are too small to challenge the native plants and animals. Indeed, only around 1 percent of invaders ever become a serious problem. But as a species' population increases, so does the likelihood it will become a problem. No area is immune, but the more polar and distant from the equator a region is, the more difficult it is to invade that biota. More varieties of life are thus found in the tropics than in temperate zones. While the devastation to human economies and existing ecosystems may be profound, one should remember that the majority of bioinvasions fail. Fewer than 20 percent of alien species become a major problem in a new biota.

PURPOSEFUL INTRODUCTION OF SPECIES

While many non-native plants and animals create havoc with existing biota and ecosystems, the food supply of every nation is complemented by non-native animals and plants that have been introduced as food crops—rice, wheat, corn, and livestock (cattle, sheep, goats, and chickens). Indeed, most food consumed in the United States, Europe, China, South America, South Africa, New Zealand, Australia, and elsewhere comes from introduced species. It is because of this desire for new food and fiber resources that many exotic plants and animals have been moved from their native homes to new worlds. More than 25,000 species of non-native plants have been brought to America's shores to grace individual gardens, grow in arid regions, augment regional flora, provide food or fiber, be used as a cash crop, and add beauty to an existing landscape. Almost a fifth of these consciously

Table 1. Number of Known Invasive and Native Species in Select Geographical Areas

Country or region	Number of native species	Number of invasive species
New Zealand (plants)	1,790	1,570
Hawaii (plants)	956	861
Hawaii (all flora and fauna)	17,591	4,456
Tristan de Cunha Island	70	97
Campbell Island (plants)	128	81
South Georgia Island (plants)	26	54
California (freshwater fish)	83	50

Source: Jeffrey A. McNeely, "The Future of Alien Invasive Species: Changing Social Views," in *Invasive Species in a Changing World,* Harold A. Mooney and Richard J. Hobbs, eds. (Washington, DC: Island, 2000), p. 174.

introduced plants have escaped human control and become a threat to the nation's biotas.

By the end of the twentieth century, approximately 50,000 plants, animals, and microbes had invaded American ecosystems, some consciously introduced and others via hidden routes. The larger the animal or plant, the more likely it was deliberately introduced. Nonvertebrates and microorganisms often invade a new biota surreptitiously—on the hull or in the ballast of ships, inside automobile tires from Asia, in shipborne cargo containers, on the leaves and stems of imported plants, or by a variety of other means.

While the impact of bioinvasions is worldwide and has occurred since the origin of life itself, the rise of humankind has made its consequences more visible. The human species has most successfully colonized every continent on Earth and visited, if not settled, even the most remote islands. Never traveling alone, humans have always been accompanied by other species. By accident as well as by design, we have become primary agents in the spread of exotic plants, animals, and diseases. Recordkeeping varies from society to society, and the ability to trace the impacts of invasive species on a region and culture depends on the extant data that allow us to reconstruct this intrusion into the regional biota. The longer the tradition of literacy and recordkeeping in a society, the easier it is to trace the historic consequences of invasive species for a specific habitat. Nevertheless, the record is clear in one respect: early humans played a significant role in bringing plants, animals, and microbes to new lands. On the Pacific islands this led to the extinction of many native species. Hawaii, Australia, and New Zealand in particular bear witness to the devastations that non-native species introduced.

HISTORY

Biological invasions by prehistoric humans had profound and far-reaching consequences. Their skills as hunter-gatherers ultimately limited populations of the wild animals and altered the plant communities that nourished their growing numbers. While the role of humans in the extinction of large animals is difficult to document, there is no question we have placed enormous pressure on many animal populations in many areas of the world.

With the rise of agriculture and development of irrigation and river management systems, human alteration of established natural systems became pronounced in the river valleys of Mesopotamia, Egypt, India, and China. Concentrating single plants in well-defined areas made cereal crops particularly susceptible to the intrusion of the animals, insects, and diseases that fed on them. Famine resulted not only from shortages of rainfall and water for irrigation, but also from the loss of crops to invading insects and plant diseases. The benefits of emerging agriculture were compromised by the environmental consequences of early farmers' alterations of natural ecosystems and creation of attractive habitats for invasive species.

Alien plants, animals, and microbes dispersed at a dramatically increasing rate during the era of European exploration and colonization from the fifteenth through seventeenth centuries. Many invasive animal and plant species were consciously introduced around the globe to feed or transport European settlers and their livestock, but the pathogens that traveled with them devastated whole populations of native peoples, who had no immunity to European diseases.

In the United States, no region has escaped the habitat alteration, extinctions and declining biodiversity and economic effects of nineteenth- and twentieth-century biotic invasions. Beginning in the early 1900s, the great forests of American chestnuts that reached from the Canadian border southward to Louisiana and as far west as Michigan and the Great Lakes were decimated by the chestnut blight fungus imported from Asia on nursery stock to New York around 1900. Within four decades, it has been estimated, 3.5 billion chestnuts died from this disease, a decline unequaled in the history of the world's forests. Elm trees, which once shaded the streets of American cities in large numbers, have also fallen victim to a fungal wilt, Dutch elm disease, that was unknowingly imported from France in a shipment of elm logs around 1930. The fungus spread rapidly across the nation and by 1970 had devastated elm trees from the Atlantic Ocean to the Pacific.

American forests have often been susceptible to invaders, but few invasive species have had an easier entrance than the gypsy moth. The French émigré Etienne Leopold Trouvelot consciously introduced gypsy moth eggs in the late 1860s to place on trees in his Boston suburb backyard for acculturation. Escaping from his care, their population and range spread unchecked through the forests of the northeast, feeding on many North American trees, particularly oaks and aspens. The moth defoliated millions of trees. Although tree mortality is usually less than 20 percent from this pest, attempts by state and federal agents to eliminate it have been unsuccessful. Both the gypsy moth and Dutch elm disease altered existing biota, reduced native ecosystems, and promoted the decline of species linked to them.

Non-native trees have also played a significant role in the destruction of American ecosystems. Salt cedars began to be imported into America in the 1820s, but by the 1870s they had been carried beyond the Mississippi River to prevent erosion, stabilize riverbanks, and serve as ornamentals. Seldom reaching more than 20 feet high, they quickly established themselves along the arid banks of many western rivers. Originally found in the arid areas of southern Europe, North Africa, the Middle East, China, and Japan, these water-consuming, aggressive colonizers overwhelm competing native willows, cottonwoods, and other riverbank vegetation. Often drawing more than 200 gallons a day from the water table, 35 percent more than native species, they further establish themselves by secreting salt above and below ground, preventing the growth of competitors. Unchecked by any human intervention, this species has spread over more than a million acres in the American Southwest and is now well established in the states of Arizona, New Mexico, Utah, Texas, Nevada, California, Colorado, Oregon, Idaho, and Utah. In twenty-three states, it has lowered water tables, created fuel-laden fire hazards, increased sedimentation in creeks, rivers, and lakes, and altered habitats for native plants and animals.

In the last decades of the nineteenth century, water hyacinths became a problem in the waterways, lakes, and rivers of the southern United States as they were transported from their Amazon Valley home because of their beautiful lavender flowers.

With the capacity to double its area of coverage every 12 days, the plant has become a management problem for many nations including India, Thailand, Malaysia, Africa, China, and Australia. Mechanical, chemical, and biological agents have had some success in limiting its growth, but the expense and difficulties of totally eliminating this aquatic invader have prevented its eradication. In many cases, the expense is so excessive that only control measures can be undertaken.

In Florida, an attempt to solve one problem has led to an even greater problem. In 1906, a forestry professor at the University of Miami hoping to find a tree that would grow in south Florida imported the seeds of the melaleuca from Australia. Reaching heights of 80 feet, this tree was valued in Australian parks for its ornamental qualities and the habitat it provided for birds and bees. For the next five decades, it enjoyed varying degrees of popularity as it was sold throughout Florida as an ornamental tree for landscaping, fencerows, and windbreaks. In the 1960s, however, the melaleuca became a problem in the Everglades, covering hundreds of thousands of acres, degrading the "sea of grass," and altering the habitat of many native species. Countless other plants have helped shape the history of North America— among them the purple loosestrife, the leafy spurge, Johnson grass, kudzu, and hydrilla—and all large nations with diverse habitats and ecosystems can relate similar experiences with invading plants.

Many birds and mammals successfully introduced into non-native ecosystems have also become invasive species as their populations grew and their habitats expanded. Acclimation societies in the eastern United States introduced starlings and sparrows in the nineteenth century, displacing local species. Rabbits were brought to Australia more than thirty times for both sport and consumption by British settlers; the problems created by their rapid growth in a new world is well documented and frequently recited.

HABITAT DESTRUCTION AND FRAGMENTATION

Until the twentieth century, species that became extinct or saw their populations decline dramatically to endangered levels usually achieved this status because of invasive plants, animals, and microbes. Since the seventeenth century, at least 700 species have become extinct, and countless have others disappeared before they were even discovered. Once transported to new lands by canoe and sailing ship, invasive species now arrive in steam-powered cargo ships and jet aircraft. In the twenty-first century, habitat alteration, fragmentation, and destruction resulting from human activities are becoming the principal route to extinction, or its brink. Habitat loss, either through human activities or invasive species, reduces the stability of ecosystems. An ecosystem's vitality and future are based on its diversity, and in some cases the loss of one animal can undermine the entire ecosystem. Insects and hummingbirds pollinate 95 percent of the trees in some tropical forests; if these pollinators are displaced, the forest dies, habitats are destroyed, biodiversity is compromised, and the entire ecosystem is fractured.

Modern civilization, with its exponentially increasing demands on natural resources and alterations of the physical world, is becoming a geological force as rivers are dammed for energy and agriculture, mountains are leveled for mining, forest are clear-cut, and coastal estuaries are destroyed by pollution and silt. These diverse habitat-changing activities reduce native biota, creating smaller, fragmented ecosystems for native plants and animals. Invasive species not only profoundly affect native flora and fauna, but also have a major impact on, and in some cases even destroy, their habitats. Declining native species are reduced in range, becoming candidates for extinction.

Examples of such habitat destruction are found globally. Leafy spurge (*Euphorbia esula*) apparently entered the United States as an impurity in imported European seeds in the early nineteenth century. Able to survive in a variety of soil conditions, it spread westward to the northern plains and southern prairie provinces of Canada, aggressively invading both sides of the border. It is now found in twenty-six states, including Alaska, and has altered the indigenous floral habitat in all of them. The weed has driven out native plants, and the animals dependent on them; as grazing fields for cattle decline, land values drop.

To understand the impact of habitat intrusion, modification, and destruction on species of a given biota, it is necessary to understand how many species may live in that particular ecosystem. Precise assessments of the diverse forms of life found in a given area are difficult to make because unknown, and unclassified, species may exist or the methodology to precisely calculate their numbers may be lacking. The number of life forms that exist globally is still debatable, though methodologies and models for

Table 2. Endangered Habitats in the United States

Habitat location	Factors precipitating habitat decline	Consequences
American forests	Logging, road building, acid rain, air pollution, increased recreational activities, invasive species	Flora and fauna decline, habitat fragmentation, reduction in tree species, decline of Eastern songbirds
American coastal areas	Increased urbanization, pollution, dumping waste products, oil spills, recreational activities, invasive flora and fauna	Decline in marshes, estuaries, coastal wildlife, commercial fishing, erosion of coastline, decline of native biota
American agricultural lands	Conversion of cropland to suburbs, invasive flora, overutilization of pesticides, herbicides, and fertilizers, overgrazing of federal lands	decline in biodiversity, fragmentation of habitat, exhaustion of soil, rise of vulnerable monocultures
American river and lake systems	Invasive aquatic flora and fauna, federal dam, canal, and reservoir programs, increased recreational activities, industrial pollution, agricultural runoffs	Loss of biodiversity—particularly a decline in commercial and sport fisheries; decline in water quality
American arid lands	Invasive flora, overgrazing of livestock, destruction of watersheds, urbanization, mining, increased recreational activities	Loss of biodiversity, reduction of intervals between fires, less ground cover and more erosion

Source: Compiled by author.

determining or predicting the total number of species on Earth are constantly advancing. Approximately 1.75 million species have been identified to date, but evidence suggests millions of others are waiting to be discovered—estimates range from 2 million to 100 million. More than 10,000 new species are discovered each year, but many others become extinct before they can be discovered, classified, and named.

Paradoxically, estimates of the number of stars in our galaxy are more precise than those of the life forms on Earth. Many species of deep-sea marine life have yet to be collected and analyzed. In the tropical jungles of Panama a mere nineteen trees yielded 1,200 species of beetles, 80 percent of which were previously unknown. In a sampling of one square yard of tropical grasslands, an estimated 32 million nematodes (microscopic worms) can sustain themselves. Tropical forests, which support from 50 to 90 percent of the Earth's life forms, are being reduced at the rate of almost 42 million acres per year. Clear-cutting for agriculture is creating a profound environmental problem. Loss of tropical forest habitat as carbon sinks is also having a significant impact on attempts to lessen negative effects of global warming on the Earth's diverse biomes.

Though debate continues over the number of life forms on the planet, there is no disputing the unprecedented rate at which species are becoming endangered and extinct. Indeed, their present rate of disappearance has been compared to the mass ex-

tinctions of 65 million years ago when the dinosaurs disappeared. When non-native pests attack climax forests, making dead trees as common as live trees, and invasive weeds crowd out and replace native grasses, fires occur more frequently. Native biomes become fragmented as indigenous habitat and native species disappear.

Presently, habitat destruction and invasive species are the principle reasons for this rapid and unnatural decline of the Earth's biodiversity. Predicting which invasive species will become a threat to other species is very difficult. The overwhelming majority of flora, fauna, and microbes have little impact on the forms of life they find in new biota; only about 1 percent become a problem. The dilemma, of course, is how to predict and prevent that 1 percent from entering.

Generations of horticulturalists, botanists, and soil scientists have extolled the beneficial role of earthworms in bringing nutrients into the soil. Charles Darwin himself praised their role in nature, but he never witnessed the destruction they are wreaking on hardwood forests from New England to the Great Lakes. On both sides of the U.S.-Canadian border, forest habitats that had maintained their complexity and vitality since the last Ice Age some 10,000 years ago are now being invaded and altered by earthworms. Although these forests have some native earthworms, the destructive invaders came from Europe in the earthen balls of imported plants and the dirt ballasts of cargo ships. Gardeners practicing composting and fishermen emptying bait containers on the banks of rivers or lakes have contributed significantly to their geographic distribution into new ecosystems. Earthworms are particularly effective in destroying the spongy, moist, and rich organic duff beneath the leaves and broken limbs on the forest floor, which provides homes for the distinctive flora and fauna of a northern hardwood forest. These invaders remove this rich environment, leaving only a barren, inhospitable forest floor. Plants reestablishing themselves on this barren surface are usually invasive species that continue to reduce the habitat's diversity. Earthworms seldom advance more than 15 feet annually, but their advance is steady as long as the duff remains.

At first glance, the Earth's diverse topographies and climates seem adequate to provide habitats for its many species. On closer scrutiny, however, the Earth's finiteness and the competition for living space become more obvious. With 71 percent of the globe covered by oceans and 4 percent by glaciers and freshwater lakes, the remaining 25 percent serves as the habitat for all terrestrial flora and fauna. Mountains, deserts, and polar ice confine the living space for millions of species to specific biomes that are vulnerable to invasive species, habitat fragmentation, and the growing pressures of contemporary human activities. Fewer species exist the further one travels from the equator.

The rising demands on the Earth's resources of a global population, in 2003, of almost 6.5 billion people has eliminated or fragmented the habitats of native flora and fauna into patches of biome too small for the species' success. The study of invasive species and their impacts on native biota and habitat lack precision, but human impact is acknowledged as the most significant factor in the decline of native species. Contemporary civilization, with its increasing demands for more cropland, water, mineral resources, timber, and human settlement sites, places unsustainable pressures on the Earth's remaining natural habitats. Forests in the tropics are logged and converted into poorly producing farmland, while rich agricultural lands in America are plowed under for developing homes and shopping malls; 2 million acres of undeveloped land are built on each year, including marginal land exploited for grazing, crops, and dwelling sites in underdeveloped regions. Coastal wetlands are transformed by human settlements in North America and shrimp farming in Asia. These human activities degrade habitats and reduce living

space for many animals; more than 80 percent of endangered mammals and birds are threatened by human alterations to their habitats. We have become the keystone species shaping the future of all global ecosystems.

In the nineteenth century, the passenger pigeon was the most numerous bird in North American history. Over the course of decades, however, they were hunted to extinction. In the fog-covered, ice-clad islands off the coast of Newfoundland and Iceland, the great auk also vanished under the pressure of human harvesting. By the 1850s, only the paintings of John James Audubon and other naturalists, specimen skins in European museums, and eggs and feathers in the natural history cabinets of wealthy European collectors remained to remind the world of this flightless bird's tragic fate. Direct extinction of a species at the hands of humankind, though rare, can be chronicled for species around the globe; much more commonly flora and fauna disappear through the indirect means of human-generated habitat modification.

A modest new appreciation of nature and wildlife began to emerge in America in the latter half of the nineteenth century. Beginning in 1872 with the creation of Yellowstone Park, the world's first national park, the United States initiated a program of preserving areas of unique, unspoiled beauty throughout the nation. Today, approximately 11 percent of the nation's land receives some protection from habitat destruction. These preserved areas are only remnants of the natural biota that once existed, with the introduction of non-native fish and non-native plants invading the meadows and forests. Roads, parking lots, campgrounds, and concessionaire's stores fragment the habitats of the national parks. In federally designated wilderness areas, the grazing of sheep and cattle, elimination of predators, and overgrazing of native grasses have visibly changed native habitats in areas believed to be protected by federal laws. No national park or wilderness has escaped invasion by non-native flora and fauna.

To provide some protection for American wildlife, President Theodore Roosevelt created the first national wildlife refuge in 1903 on Pelican Island, in Florida. Every state now has at least one refuge to protect and manage native wildlife and their habitats. Many national parks have also reestablished native bison, moose, elk, and wolves.

More than 120 nations today seek to preserve areas where native ecosystems and indigenous habitats can be maintained. The World Conservation Moni-

Table 3. Extinction of Vertebrates of the United States, U.S. Territories, and Canada Since 1492

Common name	State or region	Date
Fish		
Longjaw cisco	Lakes Erie, Huron, Michigan	1970s
Yellowfin cutthroat trout	Colorado	1910
Phantom shiner	Texas, New Mexico, Mexico	1975
Silver trout	New Hampshire	1930s
Las Vegas dace	Nevada	1950s
Snake River sucker	Wyoming	1928
Blue pike	Lakes Erie and Ontario	1971
Birds		
Labrador duck	N.E. United States, S.E. Canada	1878
Heath hen	Eastern United States	1932
Laysan rail	Hawaii	1944
Hawaiian brown rail	Hawaii	1964
Wake Island rail	Wake Island	1945
Great auk	North Atlantic	1844
Passenger pigeon	Central and Eastern United States	1914
Carolina parakeet	Southeastern United States	1914
Oahu thrush	Hawaii	1825
Texas Henslow's sparrow	Texas	1983
Black mamo	Hawaii	1907
Greater kona finch	Hawaii	1894
Kona finch	Hawaii	1894
Kusaie starling	Caroline Islands	1828
Mammals		
Puerto Rican shrew	Puerto Rico	1500
Puerto Rican grand sloth	Puerto Rico	1500
Penasco chipmunk	New Mexico	1980
Goff's pocket gopher	Florida	1955
Gull Island vole	New York	1898
Louisiana vole	Louisiana, Texas	1905
Atlantic gray whale	Atlantic Coast	1750
Southern California kit fox	California	1903
Florida red wolf	Southeastern United States	1903
Texas red wolf	Texas, Oklahoma	1970
Newfoundland wolf	Newfoundland	1911
Banks Island wolf	Banks and Victoria Islands	1920
Northern Rocky Mountains wolf	Alberta, Idaho, Montana, Oregon, Wyoming	1940
Great Plains wolf	Great Plains	1926
Sea mink	New Brunswick, New England	1890
Caribbean monk seal	Florida, West Indies	1960
California grizzly bear	California	1925
Wisconsin cougar	North Central United States	1925
Steller's sea cow	Alaska	1768
Eastern elk	Central and Eastern United States	1880
Queen Charlotte caribou	Queen Charlotte Islands	1935
Badlands bighorn	Montana, Nebraska, North Dakota, South Dakota, Wyoming	1910
Reptiles		
Navassa iguana	Navassa Island, West Indies	1800s
St. Croix racer	St. Croix, U.S. Virgin Islands	1900s

Source: James D. Williams and Ronald M. Nowak, "Vanishing Species in Our Own Backyard: Extinct Fish and Wildlife of the United States and Canada." In *The Last Extinction,* Les Kaufman and Kenneth Mallory, eds. (Cambridge, MA: MIT University Press, 1986), pp. 133–39. Reprinted with permission of MIT Press.

toring Centre, which encourages and supports such stewardship, reports that approximately 6.25 percent of these nations' land is under nominal protection from habitat destruction and the invasion of foreign plants and animals. In 80 percent of the countries of Asia and Africa, at least half of the natural habitat has been destroyed. Until the latter half of the twentieth century, most conservation efforts focused on individual species rather than their habitats.

Future efforts need to focus on habitat preservation to maintain the Earth's biodiversity. The challenges are formidable. Even among the world's protected areas, only the remote coasts of Antarctica have thus far escaped detectible invasion from alien species. The emerging crisis of the southern polar region may require confronting global warming and the ultimate habitat destruction.

COSTS

The appearance of non-native plants and animals alters established habitats, creating an increasingly fragile global environment whose stability is constantly challenged. The invasions of exotic plants, animals, and pathogens not only modify existing ecosystems but also lead to the decline of native species and in some cases even extinction. They affect human societies, economies, physical well-being, and the future on a scale never before approached. In the United States alone, the cost is estimated between $123 billion and $135 billion a year. More than 4,600 acres a day are encroached on by invasive plants. Globally, nonindigenous plants and habitat destruction are the two principal causes of the decline of plant and animal species. The strains these invaders impose on the global ecosystem become increasingly profound as they grow more competitive with native flora and fauna. Their displacement of native species and interruption of native ecosystems have increased the rate of species extinction.

Nonindigenous species in native biota are thought to be responsible for more than 20 percent of mammal, bird, and fish extinctions and 40 percent of reptile extinctions. Almost 42 percent of endangered plant and animal life in the United States is endangered because of competition with nonindigenous species. In some areas of the world, the competition is even more pronounced, with up to 80 percent of endangered species being challenged by non-native species. Alien weeds reduce the productivity of range and cultivated land and diminish the genetic pool of

Table 4. Percentage and Number of Terrestrial Vertebrate Species Threatened by Biotic Invaders on Continents and Islands

Taxonomic group	Continental (mainland areas)		Insular (islands, isolated areas)	
	Percent	Number	Percent	Number
Mammals	19.4	283	11.5	61
Birds	5.2	250	38.2	144
Reptiles	15.5	84	32.9	76
Amphibians	3.3	30	30.8	13
Total for all species considered	12.7	647	31.0	294

Source: Jeffrey A. McNeely, "The Future of Alien Invasive Species: Changing Social Views." In *Invasive Species in a Changing World,* Harold A. Mooney and Richard J. Hobbs, eds. (Washington, DC: Island, 2000), p. 175.

native flora. As the Earth's flora and fauna become less diverse, the resulting homogeneity of the world's biota weakens their ability to respond to new challenges and diminishes not only the beauty of the web of life but also its viability.

Biotic invasions are complex, difficult to assess, and unpredictable in their behavior. Unfortunately, the consequences are often not appreciated, and lack of knowledge, resources, and political will prevents effective responses. Prevention of invasions of nonnative species is always more successful than efforts to control or eradicate them after the fact. Biological controls fail as often as they succeed, and often become problems in their own right.

RESPONSES

In the last three decades of the twentieth century, increasing knowledge of the decline in global biodiversity generated a more universal concern about the pace and nature of biotic invasions. Scientists, policymakers, and the Earth's citizens began to see the problems these invaders generated as issues that needed to be addressed on a global basis. Each decade since the United Nation Conference on Human Environment held at Stockholm in 1972 has seen the organization of international conventions, agreements, international working groups, and reports addressing in some manner the Earth's declining biodiversity, habitat destruction, and invasive species in native biota. International action culminated at Rio de Janeiro in June 1992, when 156 nations and the European Community agreed to the Convention on Biological Diversity. By August 2001,

181 international parties had agreed to the Convention, which seeks to maintain the diversity of life by conserving the planet's populations, species, habitats, and ecosystems. The Convention on Biological Diversity, with its diverse committees and reports, is the most holistic, international, and sustained attempt of the nations of the world to address one of the most pressing environmental problems confronting the twenty-first century.

Phillip Drennon Thomas

REFERENCES

Bright, Chris. *Life Out of Bounds.* New York: Norton, 1998.

Campbell, F. T., and S. E. Schlarbaum. *Fading Forests: North American Trees and the Threat of Exotic Pests.* New York: Natural Resources Defense Council, 1994.

Cox, George W. *Alien Species in North America and Hawaii, Impacts on Natural Ecosystems.* Washington, DC: Island, 1999.

Cronk, Quentin C. B., and Janice L. Fuller. *Plant Invaders, the Threat to Natural Ecosystems.* New York: Chapman and Hall, 1995.

Crosby, Alfred. *The Columbian Exchange, Biological and Cultural Consequences of 1492.* Westport, CT: Greenwood, 1972.

———. *Ecological Imperialism.* New York: Cambridge University Press, 1986.

Deither, V. G. *Man's Plague? Insects and Agriculture.* Princeton, NJ: Darwin, 1976.

Devine, Robert. *Alien Invasion, America's Battle with Non-Native Animals and Plants.* Washington, DC: National Geographic Society, 1998.

Elton, Charles S. *The Ecology of Invasions by Animals and Plants.* London: Methuen; New York: John Wiley & Sons, 1958.

Goudie, Andre. *The Human Impact on the Natural Environment.* 5th ed. Cambridge, MA: MIT Press, 2000.

Groves, R. H., and F. Di Castri. *Biogeography of Mediterranean Invasions.* New York: Cambridge University Press, 1991.

Jones, Gareth E. *The Conservation of Ecosystems and Species.* New York: Croom Helm, 1987.

Kaufman, Les, and Kenneth Mallory, eds. *The Last Extinction.* Cambridge, MA: MIT Press, 1986.

King, C. M. *Immigrant Killers: Introduced Predators and the Conservation of Birds in New Zealand.* Auckland: Oxford University Press, 1984.

McKnight, B. N., ed. *Biological Pollution: The Control and Impact of Invasive Exotic Species.* Indianapolis: Indiana Academy of Science, 1993.

McNeill, J. R. *An Environmental History of the Twentieth Century World.* New York: Norton, 2000.

Meyer, William B., and B. L. Turner II. *Changes in Land Use and Land Cover: A Global Perspective.* New York: Cambridge University Press, 1994.

Minckley, Wendal L., and James E. Deacon. *Battle Against Extinction: Native Fish Management in the American West.* Tucson: University of Arizona Press, 1991.

Mooney, Harold A., and Richard J. Hobbs. *Invasive Species in a Changing World.* Washington, DC: Island, 2000.

National Research Council. *Predicting Invasions of Nonindigenous Plants and Pests.* Washington, DC: National Academy Press, 2002.

Simberloff, Daniel, D. C. Schmitz, and T. C. Brown, eds. *Strangers in Paradise.* Washington, DC: Island Press, 1997.

Williamson, Mark. *Biological Invasions.* New York: Chapman and Hall, 1996.

Wilson, Edward O. *The Diversity of Life.* New York: Norton, 1999.

Woodwell, George M. *The Earth in Transition: Patterns and Processes of Biotic Impoverishment.* New York: Cambridge University Press, 1990.

Worster, Donald. *The Ends of the Earth, Perspectives on Modern Environmental History.* New York: Cambridge University Press, 1988.

WEB SITES

Heinz Center, State of the Nation's Ecosystems: www.heinzctr.org/ecosystems

Invasive and Exotic Species of North America: www.invasive.org

Invasivespecies.gov: www.invasivespecies.gov

UNEP World Conservation Monitoring Centre: www.unep-wcmc.org

U.S. Department of Agriculture and the Natural Resources Conservation Service: www.nrcs.usda.gov/technical/invasive.html

Wildlife Conservation Society: www.wcs.org

World Conservation Union, Global Invasive Species Database: www.issg.org/database/reference/countries.asp

World Resource Institute: www.wri.org

GLOSSARY

Alewife. Entering the Great Lakes in the 1950s, these small, silver, bony, oceanic fish, *Alosa pseudoharengus*, have established themselves in Lake Michigan and Lake Huron, reducing the populations of native herring, white fish, and perch.

Asian Tiger mosquito. *Aedes albopictus* is a mosquito from northern Asia that has successfully established itself in the United States and other areas of the world and become a vector for a number of diseases.

Ballast. To maintain stability at sea and lower their center of gravity when they are not loaded, ships fill their holds and tanks with water, stones, or earth. Before receiving their cargo, they discharge or unload their ballast into whatever body of water they are in. This discharge spreads diverse forms of life throughout the world's oceans and bays. Ballast discharge is a major dispersal route of invasive species.

Bioinvasion. The introduction of non-native plants and animals into native and established biota.

Biomass. The total weight of all living materials in a given area.

Biosphere. The Earth and its surrounding atmosphere, which supports life in its diverse forms.

Biota. All plant and animal life in a specified area.

Carbon sink. An ocean, lake, forest, or reservoir that withdraws carbon dioxide from the atmosphere and stores more than it releases. Forests are among the best carbon sinks.

Chestnut blight. The fungus *Endothia parasitic*, which destroys the great forests of American chestnut trees; attempts to control it have failed.

Climax forest. The final development of the natural succession of trees and plants in a forest community.

Comb jellyfish. This jellyfish, *Mnemiopsis leidy*, has devastated marine ecosystems in the Black Sea, Caspian Sea, and Sea of Azov.

Convention on Biological Diversity. UN agreement reached in 1992 among most of the world's nations; it coordinates global efforts to maintain biodiversity and limit unwanted species.

Duff. The level of decomposing organic materials found beneath the layer of leaves, fallen twigs, and needles on a forest floor.

Dutch elm disease. A fungus spread by the elm bark beetle that can kill a tree in 3 weeks.

Earthworm. There are more than 3,000 species of these burrowing terrestrial worms, some of which aerate the soil while others convert organic wastes into fertile soil.

Ecosystem. Dynamic interaction of plants, animals, and microorganisms with the nonliving, physical world that supports them.

Extinction. The complete disappearance of a living species from the Earth.

Fauna. Animal life, often with reference to a specific region.

Flora. Plant life, often with reference to a specific region.

Fungus. Primitive form of plant life that does not perform photosynthesis, including molds, yeasts, mildews, and mushrooms.

Genetic code. The information that orders the sequencing of protein synthesis in the DNA molecule, which in turn determines the development and individual characteristics of living entities.

Gypsy moth. Devastating eastern and southern forests of North America by devouring their foliage, this moth, *Lymantria dispar*, continues to expand its range. Some success has been achieved in reducing its population in specific areas.

Habitat. Specific area where a given animal or plant maintains itself by using the area's resources.

Invasive species. Non-native species of plants, animals, and microorganisms that establish themselves in a new, natural habitat—often at the expense of native flora and fauna.

Invertebrates. Animals without a vertebral or spinal column.

Leafy spurge. This rapidly growing perennial plant (*Euphorbia esula*) spreads quickly, reaching a height of 16 to 32 inches, driving out indigenous plants and destroying native grazing lands.

Melaleuca. The paperbark tea tree or punk tree, *Melaleuca quinquenervia*, is a fast-growing, rapidly spreading, successful competitor and intensely inflammable tree from Australia imported into Florida in the 1930s, now creating a significant problem for the Everglades.

Nematodes. With more than 12,000 known species, these round, unsegmented parasitic worms affect humans, other animals, and other plants.

Nonindigenous. Animals or plants that are not native to the biota within which they have established themselves or been observed.

Non-native species. Species that have entered, or been introduced, into the habitat of native species.

Pathogens. Disease-causing microorganisms—bacteria, virus, or parasite.

Pathways. Paths or mechanism by which invasive, alien, or exotic species enter a new habitat.

Salt cedars. These small trees and shrubs are members of the genus *Tamarix*, natives of Africa and Eurasia, and have successfully established themselves in great numbers along rivers and water courses in the American Southwest.

Tropical rain forest. Equatorial forests that receive more water from rainfall than they lose through evaporation; found in South America, Africa, and Asia and distinguished by numerous and diverse life forms.

Vector. Animal, insect, or other agent by which a disease (pathogen) is spread to another host.

Virgin soil epidemics. Outbreaks of disease among a people, usually in a newly discovered land, who have no experience with the disease and consequently have developed no immunity to it.

Water hyacinth. A beautiful aquatic plant from South America, *Eichhornia crassipes* has altered and reduced native plant and animal life in the United States and other countries since its introduction in the late nine-teenth century. It can be controlled at great expense but not eradicated.

Weed. An unwanted plant that flourishes at the expense of desired flora.

World Conservation Monitoring Centre. Organization charged by the United Nations Environment Programme (UNEP) to encourage nations to develop plants to maintain the world's biodiversity.

Zebra mussels. Natives of the Caspian Sea, these small mussels, *Dreissena polymorpha*, have successfully invaded the Great Lakes and Mississippi River Valley system and migrated northward into Canada. They are persistently expensive, only marginally controllable, and destructive.

DOCUMENTS

Document 1. Excerpt from Executive Order 13112

On February 3, 1999, President William Clinton signed Executive Order 13112, establishing the National Invasive Species Council. The measure called for the creation of a Council of Departments to address the issue of invasive species. Currently ten departments and agencies are represented on the Council.

Section 2. Federal Agency Duties.

(a) Each Federal agency whose actions may affect the status of invasive species shall, to the extent practicable and permitted by law,

(1) identify such actions;

(2) subject to the availability of appropriations, and within Administration budgetary limits, use relevant programs and authorities to: (i) prevent the introduction of invasive species; (ii) detect and respond rapidly to and control populations of such species in a cost-effective and environmentally sound manner; (iii) monitor invasive species populations accurately and reliably; (iv) provide for restoration of native species and habitat conditions in ecosystems that have been invaded; (v) conduct research on invasive species and develop technologies to prevent introduction and provide for environmentally sound control of invasive species; and (vi) promote public education on invasive species and the means to address them; and

(3) not authorize, fund, or carry out actions that it believes are likely to cause or promote the introduction or spread of invasive species in the United States or elsewhere unless, pursuant to guidelines that it has prescribed, the agency has determined and made public its determination that the benefits of such actions clearly outweigh the potential harm caused by invasive species; and that all feasible and prudent measures to minimize risk of harm will be taken in conjunction with the actions. . . .

Section 3. Invasive Species Council.

(a) An Invasive Species Council (Council) is hereby established whose members shall include the Secretary of State, the Secretary of the Treasury, the Secretary of Defense, the Secretary of the Interior, the Secretary of Agriculture, the Secretary of Commerce, the Secretary of Transportation, and the Administrator of the Environmental Protection Agency. The Council shall be Co-Chaired by the Secretary of the Interior, the Secretary of Agriculture, and the Secretary of Commerce. . . . (b) The Secretary of the Interior shall establish an advisory committee under the Federal Advisory Committee Act, 5 U.S.C. App., to provide information and advice for consideration by the Council, and shall, after consultation with other members of the Council, appoint members of the advisory committee representing stakeholders. Among other things, the advisory committee shall recommend plans and actions at local, tribal, State, regional, and ecosystem-based levels to achieve the goals and objectives of the Management Plan in section 5 of this order. The advisory committee shall act in cooperation with stakeholders and existing organizations addressing invasive species. The Department of the Interior shall provide the administrative and financial support for the advisory committee.

Section 4. Duties of the Invasive Species Council. The Invasive Species Council shall provide national leadership regarding invasive species, and shall:

(a) oversee the implementation of this order and see that the Federal agency activities concerning invasive species are coordinated, complementary, cost-efficient, and effective, relying to the extent feasible and appropriate on existing organizations addressing invasive species, such as the Aquatic Nuisance Species Task Force, the Federal Interagency Committee for the Management of Noxious and Exotic Weeds, and the Committee on Environment and Natural Resources;

(b) encourage planning and action at local, tribal, State, regional, and ecosystem-based levels to achieve the goals and objectives of the Management Plan in section 5 of this order, in cooperation with stakeholders and existing organizations addressing invasive species;

(c) develop recommendations for international cooperation in addressing invasive species;

(d) develop, in consultation with the Council on Environmental Quality, guidance to Federal agencies pursuant to the National Environmental Policy Act on prevention and control of invasive species, including the procurement, use, and maintenance of native species as they affect invasive species;

(e) facilitate development of a coordinated network among Federal agencies to document, evaluate, and monitor impacts from invasive species on the economy, the environment, and human health;

(f) facilitate establishment of a coordinated, up-to-date information-sharing system that utilizes, to the greatest extent practicable, the Internet; this system shall facilitate access to and exchange of information concerning invasive species, including, but not limited to, information on distribution and abundance of invasive species; life histories of such species and invasive characteristics; economic, environmental, and human health impacts; management techniques, and laws and programs for management, research, and public education; and

(g) prepare and issue a national Invasive Species Management Plan as set forth in section 5 of this order.

Section 5. Invasive Species Management Plan.

(a) Within 18 months after issuance of this order, the Council shall prepare and issue the first edition of a National Invasive Species Management Plan (Management Plan), which shall detail and recommend performance-oriented goals and objectives and specific measures of success for Federal agency efforts concerning invasive species.

(b) The first edition of the Management Plan shall include a review of existing and prospective approaches and authorities for preventing the introduction and spread of invasive species, including those for identifying pathways by which invasive species are introduced and for minimizing the risk of introductions via those pathways, and shall identify research needs and recommend measures to minimize the risk that introductions will occur. Such recommended measures shall provide for a science-based process to evaluate risks associated with introduction and spread of invasive species and a coordinated and systematic risk-based process to identify, monitor, and interdict pathways that may be involved in the introduction of invasive species. If recommended measures are not authorized by current law, the Council shall develop and recommend to the President through its Co-Chairs legislative proposals for necessary changes in authority.

(c) The Council shall update the Management Plan biennially and shall concurrently evaluate and report on success in achieving the goals and objectives set forth in the Management Plan. The Management Plan shall identify the personnel, other resources, and additional levels of coordination needed to achieve the Management Plan's identified goals and objectives, and the Council shall provide each edition of the Management Plan and each report on it to the Office of Management and Budget. Within 18 months after measures have been recommended by the Council in any edition of the Management Plan, each Federal agency whose action is required to implement such measures shall either take the action recommended or shall provide the Council with an explanation of why the action is not feasible. The Council shall assess the effectiveness of this order no less than once each 5 years after the order is issued and shall report to the Office of Management and Budget on whether the order should be revised.

Section 6. Judicial Review and Administration.

(a) This order is intended only to improve the internal management of the executive branch and is not intended to create any right, benefit, or trust responsibility, substantive or procedural, enforceable at law or equity by a party against the United States, its agencies, its officers, or any other person.

(b) Executive Order 11987 of May 24, 1977, is hereby revoked.

(c) The requirements of this order do not affect the obligations of Federal agencies under 16 U.S.C. 4713 with respect to ballast water programs.

(d) The requirements of section 2(a)(3) of this order shall not apply to any action of the Department of State or Department of Defense if the Secretary of State or the Secretary of Defense finds that exemption from such requirements is necessary for foreign policy or national security reasons.

Source: Office of the President of the United States.

Document 2. Excerpt from the Convention on Biological Diversity

At the 1992 Earth Summit in Rio de Janeiro, world leaders agreed on a comprehensive strategy for "sustainable development"—meeting current needs while ensuring a healthy and viable world for future generations. One of the key agreements adopted at Rio was the Convention on Biological Diversity. This pact among the vast majority of the world's governments set commitments for maintaining the world's ecological underpinnings amid the pursuit of economic development. The Convention establishes three main goals: conservation of biological diversity, sustainable use of its components, and fair and equitable sharing of genetic resources.

Preamble

The Contracting Parties,

Conscious of the intrinsic value of biological diversity and of the ecological, genetic, social, economic, scientific, educational, cultural, recreational and aesthetic values of biological diversity and its components,

Conscious also of the importance of biological diversity for evolution and for maintaining life sustaining systems of the biosphere,

Affirming that the conservation of biological diversity is a common concern of humankind,

Reaffirming that States have sovereign rights over their own biological resources,

Reaffirming also that States are responsible for conserving their biological diversity and for using their biological resources in a sustainable manner,

Concerned that biological diversity is being significantly reduced by certain human activities,

Aware of the general lack of information and knowledge regarding biological diversity and of the urgent need to develop scientific, technical and institutional capacities to provide the basic understanding upon which to plan and implement appropriate measures,

Noting that it is vital to anticipate, prevent and attack the causes of significant reduction or loss of biological diversity at source,

Noting also that where there is a threat of significant reduction or loss of biological diversity, lack of full scientific certainty should not be used as a reason for postponing measures to avoid or minimize such a threat,

Noting further that the fundamental requirement for the conservation of biological diversity is the in-situ conservation of ecosystems and natural habitats and the maintenance and recovery of viable populations of species in their natural surroundings,

Noting further that ex-situ measures, preferably in the country of origin, also have an important role to play,

Recognizing the close and traditional dependence of many indigenous and local communities embodying traditional lifestyles on biological resources, and the desirability of sharing equitably benefits arising from the use of traditional knowledge, innovations and practices relevant to the conservation of biological diversity and the sustainable use of its components,

Recognizing also the vital role that women play in the conservation and sustainable use of biological diversity and affirming the need for the full participation of women at all levels of policy-making and implementation for biological diversity conservation,

Stressing the importance of, and the need to promote, international, regional and global cooperation among States and intergovernmental organizations and the non-governmental sector for the conservation of biological diversity and the sustainable use of its components,

Acknowledging that the provision of new and additional financial resources and appropriate access to relevant technologies can be expected to make a substantial difference in the world's ability to address the loss of biological diversity,

Acknowledging further that special provision is required to meet the needs of developing countries, including the provision of new and additional financial resources and appropriate access to relevant technologies,

Noting in this regard the special conditions of the least developed countries and small island States,

Acknowledging that substantial investments are required to conserve biological diversity and that there is the expectation of a broad range of environmental, economic and social benefits from those investments,

Recognizing that economic and social development and poverty eradication are the first and overriding priorities of developing countries,

Aware that conservation and sustainable use of biological diversity is of critical importance for meeting the food, health and other needs of the growing world population, for which purpose access to and sharing of both genetic resources and technologies are essential,

Noting that, ultimately, the conservation and sustainable use of biological diversity will strengthen friendly relations among States and contribute to peace for humankind,

Desiring to enhance and complement existing international arrangements for the conservation of biological diversity and sustainable use of its components, and

Determined to conserve and sustainably use biological diversity for the benefit of present and future generations. . . .

Source: Convention on Biological Diversity.

FARM ISSUES

At first glance, American agriculture is one of the economic wonders of the modern world. Over the course of the twentieth century, the percentage of the labor force engaged in agricultural pursuits fell from 15 percent to less than 2 percent. Yet not only has the nation's farm sector been capable of feeding a population that has grown from 75 million to nearly 300 million over the same period, but it also has been capable of producing vast exports. By the early 2000s, American farmers were exporting more than $50 billion in goods annually, representing just under 10 percent of all U.S. exports.

Despite these impressive achievements, however, the American farmer—particularly the family farmer—has faced an economic squeeze, especially in the last few decades, a victim of fluctuating crop prices, rising land prices, and increased competition from corporate farms and overseas producers. Since 1950, the number of farms has fallen from roughly 7 million to just over 2 million. Many farmers and farm experts argue that the days of the family farmer—outside a narrow sector that specializes in truck and organic farming—may be a relic of the past.

COLONIAL AND ANTEBELLUM ERAS

From the beginning of European settlement in early seventeenth-century Virginia, agriculture was the mainstay of the American economy. Abundant fertile land and a largely temperate climate ensured good crop yields. Early colonial farmers also took advantage of Native American food crops that grew well in North America, including corn—which became the leading food crop of colonial America—squash, and beans.

Over the course of the seventeenth century, agricultural patterns began to vary from colony to colony. In New England, small farms specializing in food crops for local consumption prevailed. With its relatively cool climate and stony soil, the re-

gion was less suited for large-scale export agriculture than regions further south. The mid-Atlantic colonies focused on grain and livestock production, with a significant portion being exported to Europe and European slave colonies of the Caribbean. But it was to the south, from Maryland to Georgia, that commercial, export-oriented agriculture truly took hold. The key factors behind this were an abundance of fertile land, numerous waterways allowing for easy transportation, a long growing season, and the importation of cheap labor in the form of indentured servants from England at first, and then slaves from Africa and the Caribbean. Early commercial crops included rice, indigo, long-staple cotton, and, most notably, tobacco. By the time of the American Revolution, the Chesapeake Bay region of Maryland and Virginia was exporting some 756,000 pounds sterling (about $150 million in today's dollars) of tobacco, mostly to Great Britain.

The American Revolution had a profound effect on American agriculture. By eliminating British rule, the colonists also rid themselves of London's trade regulations that limited where they could sell their products. In addition, the end of British rule lifted British restrictions on expansion to the vast and fertile Mississippi and Ohio River valleys to the West. In the northern half of this region, small and medium-sized farms using paid labor produced large quantities of grain and livestock products for export. The southern half of the region replicated the plantation agriculture of the southern Atlantic seaboard states, but on a much vaster scale, with hardier short-staple cotton as the main crop. By 1860, the nation had more than 2 million farms and was producing over 800 million bushels of wheat, some 170 million bushels of corn, and more than 5 million bales of cotton.

This abundance was not due solely to the huge land resources of the country. American farmers, even those who relied on slave labor, displayed a

CHRONOLOGY

Pre-Columbian era to 1492   Native American farmers in the Americas domesticate crops such as corn, potatoes, tomatoes, and tobacco.

1610s   Tobacco is introduced as a successful cash crop in Virginia.

1619   The first African slaves are imported in Virginia and put to work on tobacco plantations.

1775–81   American patriots, mostly farmers and planters, overthrow British rule, eliminating imperial restrictions on where they can sell agricultural products overseas and on westward expansion.

1793   Eli Whitney, a New England inventor, creates the first cotton gin, allowing for expansion of cotton farming and slavery in the American South.

1825   The Erie Canal opens in New York State, allowing for a cheap all-water route from the agriculturally rich upper Midwest to the Atlantic trading world.

1861–65   The American Civil War temporarily disrupts cotton production and leads to the end of slavery.

1860s–70s   The sharecropping system, whereby landlords and tenants share in the output of the land, becomes widespread in the South.

1870s–90s   As railroads expand across the continent, farmers settle the Trans-Mississippi West.

1896   Faced with falling crop prices, Populists—primarily midwestern and southern farmers—take control of the Democratic Party and push for the monetization of silver, but are defeated by pro-business, pro-gold Republicans in national elections.

1914–18   World War I in Europe leads to higher crop prices, motivating farmers to increase their debt load to expand operations.

1920s   While urban America enjoys unprecedented prosperity, many farmers languish in poverty, burdened by low crop prices.

1930s   Farmers in the Midwest are struck by the twin blows of economic depression, which further lowers crop prices, and prolonged drought; dry conditions and windstorms strip away soil; many farmers in the southern Midwest and Great Plains go bankrupt and move to California.

1933   The administration of President Franklin Roosevelt pushes the Agricultural Adjustment Act through Congress, providing subsidies to farmers for not growing crops in an effort to cut supply and raise prices.

1939–45   World War II in Europe and Asia leads to unprecedented demands for American crops and prosperity for the American farmer.

1940s–50s   Petroleum-based synthetic fertilizers and pesticides are widely introduced on American farms.

1962   Environmental writer Rachel Carson publishes *Silent Spring*, a best-selling book that exposes the dangers the pesticide DDT to the nation's birds.

1970s–80s   High food prices lead farmers to go into debt to increase output in the 1970s; when prices fall in the 1980s, many farmers are forced into bankruptcy.

1972   Congress bans the use of DDT.

1985   Country music star Willie Nelson creates Farm Aid, an organization to help struggling American farmers.

1996   The first genetically modified crops are introduced in the United States; Congress passes the Freedom to Farm Act, giving farmers more control over what they grow.

1998   The European Union bans the import of genetically modified foods.

2003   The United States files a protest with the World Trade Organization, arguing that the European Union's ban on the importation of genetically modified foods is a restraint of trade banned by the organization's bylaws and rules.

propensity to use technology to enhance both output and distribution. Several innovations and inventions stand out, such as iron and steel plows and reaping and threshing machines, all powered by an ever increasing population of draft animals. Cotton continued to be cultivated and picked largely by hand, but the cotton gin—invented in the 1790s —allowed workers to remove the seeds from much larger quantities of cotton. On the distribution end, canals, the steamboat, and, most important, the railroad enabled shipping of ever greater amounts of farm produce across the nation and around the world.

POST–CIVIL WAR ERA THROUGH 1920s

The Civil War, a conflict sparked in large part by conflicting views between the North and the South over agricultural labor, temporarily disrupted American farm output, particularly in the embargoed and war-torn South. In the aftermath of the war, the South had to reorganize its agricultural system to accommodate the newly freed slaves. With land still abundant but capital in short supply, the South adopted a system of agricultural peonage known as sharecropping. Under this system, former slaves, as well as numerous poor whites, leased fields from landholders and shared the crop they produced. This saved the financially strapped landholders from having to pay for labor, but it often left the laborers in perpetual debt; half the crop often failed to pay for seed and supplies provided by the landholders at the beginning of the season.

Meanwhile, the post–Civil War decades saw a vast expansion of grain farming and livestock raising in the trans-Mississippi West. Railroads promoted settlement through advertising, to assure themselves of customers, and the government offered free land to homesteaders, that is, anyone willing to live on and improve the frontier for a set number of years. These enticements lured millions of Americans from the Eastern states, as well as immigrants from northern and western Europe, to settle on lands from the Mississippi to the Rocky Mountains. At the same time, the use of new steam- and animal-driven farm equipment— like Cyrus McCormick's mechanical reaper—raised output enormously. Between 1870 and 1910, the number of persons engaged in agriculture increased from roughly 6.8 million to an all-time high of just under 11.8 million, while the number of farms increased from 2 million to more than 6 million and acreage under cultivation from just over 400 million acres to over 800 million acres.

But this productive success was not without its problems. Even as the United States expanded its agricultural output, so did other areas of the world— notably Canada, Argentina, Australia, and Russia. While food consumption around the world was growing—a result of better diets and increasing population—it could not keep up with production, resulting in falling crop prices. Adding to the problem of supply and demand were monetary issues. Since the early 1870s, America had a gold-based currency. But gold was in limited supply before the end of the century when new discoveries were made in the Yukon and, more notably, South Africa. Dollars, pegged to increasingly scarce gold supplies, increased in value. Thus, a single dollar could buy far more in 1890 than in 1870, further deflating crop prices reduced by a glut in world agricultural output. This was advantageous for urban workers and creditors, as food became cheaper; every dollar earned from labor or investments bought more produce. But for farmers, perennially in debt to cover their expenses until the crops came in, the increasing value of the dollar was an economic catastrophe. By 1900, annual farm income was less than $300, while nonagricultural workers earned more than $600.

Farmers responded to the crisis politically, organizing the Populist Party to represent their interests. The Populists pushed for a number of political and economic reforms. Three planks in the party's platform were of particular interest to farmers. One called for the monetization of silver. Tying the dollar to abundant and cheap silver would have reduced its value, producing inflation and debt relief for farmers. The other plank advocated what was called the "subtreasury scheme," a plan to establish government warehouses to store farmers' crops until prices rose. Third, the Populists called for both nationalization of the railroads and the end of rebating, whereby big shippers got discounts while farmers paid full price to ship their crops.

Ultimately, the Populist Party failed politically. After fusing with the Democrats, it went down to defeat in the pivotal election of 1896. Nevertheless, some of the reforms Populists called for were eventually enacted by liberal progressives of the early twentieth century and the New Dealers of the Great Depression. The latter instituted price supports for farmers to make sure they received adequate payment for their crops.

GREAT DEPRESSION AND WORLD WAR II

In the meantime, market forces and new discoveries of gold in the early twentieth century alleviated some of the farmers' economic problems. World War I, in particular, produced sky-high prices for American crops, as European sources were disrupted by the conflict. But, as in the post–Civil War period, this encouraged farmers to expand their output, going into deeper debt to do so. A postwar slump in prices devastated rural areas so that, while the country's urban economy experienced a boom in the 1920s, farmers continued to struggle economically. The Great Crash of 1929 and the Great Depression that followed only made things worse, as prices for virtually all crops plummeted. Adding to farmers' woes were climatic conditions, including a prolonged drought in the Midwest. The drought, combined with poor farming practices, led to massive erosion and dust storms that stripped away fertile topsoil. Hundreds of thousands of indebted farmers were forced off the land, with many heading to California for agricultural work. These so-called Okies, because many came from Oklahoma, went to work for the huge factory farms of the Golden State, owned by large agricultural businesses whose size and efficiency allowed them to weather the hard times.

Catastrophic as it was, the Great Depression nevertheless saw the inauguration of the modern, government-supported agricultural system. Immediately following his election in 1932, reforming Democratic President Franklin Roosevelt pushed the Agricultural Adjustment Act (AAA) through Congress. To cut production, and thereby raise prices, the government began to pay farmers subsidies for *not* growing crops. While the AAA helped stabilize the nation's agricultural system, much of the program's subsidies went to larger farmers capable of understanding and negotiating the regulatory system. Indeed, because they could make more money off the subsidies, many southern landholders threw their sharecroppers off the land. Much as it did for the nation's urban unemployed, so World War II rescued the American farmer from economic depression, creating enormous demand for their products and raising crop prices.

POST–WORLD WAR II ERA

No era in American history has seen more dramatic agricultural change than the period following World War II. First was a dramatic decline in the number of

Table 1. Average Size of U.S. Farms, in Acres, 1940–2004

Year	Acreage
1940	174
1950	213
1960	297
1970	374
1980	426
1990	460
2000	434
2004	443

Source: National Agriculture Statistics Service, U.S. Department of Agriculture.

farms and farmers. At the end of the war, there were roughly 6 million farms in the United States, down by half from the peak early in the century, but still a substantial number. By 2000, that figure had dropped to just over 2 million. Even more substantial was the decline in the number of farmers. In 1945, fully one-fourth of the American workforce was engaged in agriculture. By 2000, that figure had fallen to well under 2 percent of the workforce. At the same time, the average size of the American farm increased from roughly 200 acres to about 430 acres. More dramatic was the gain in agricultural productivity. Whereas an hour of labor in the late 1930s produced about 2 bushels of wheat, 2.5 pounds of cotton, and 35 pounds of milk (about 4.4 gallons), by the late twentieth century an hour's worth of labor produced about 12 bushels, 60 pounds, and 250 pounds of wheat, cotton, and milk (about 31 gallons), respectively. To take just one example of what the increased productivity meant—in livestock, a 2000 farm population less than one-tenth the size of that in 1940 produced 2.5 times the quantity of red meat and 12 times the amount of poultry.

What explains this enormous growth in productivity? Technology and petroleum. New gasoline- and diesel-powered farm equipment meant that one farmer in the late twentieth century could produce what five or ten farmers had in the mid-century. At the same time, a host of synthetic fertilizers and pesticides—many derived from the same petroleum that ran the equipment—increased the land's fertility and eliminated many of the pests that had previously reduced farm output. The federal government helped as well. By the mid-1950s, Washington was subsidizing American farmers to the tune of $2.5 billion annually, through either crop price supports or payments for not growing crops. By the early 2000s, that figure had climbed to more than $20 billion.

Yet all was not ideal for the American farmer of the postwar era, as evidenced by the decreasing number of farms and farmers. Some of the decline was the result of social change. Increasing numbers of young rural Americans were attending college and taking less physically demanding jobs in cities, where they also enjoyed access to more cultural and entertainment outlets. But economic factors played an even greater role in the decline. To compete with large-scale industrial farms, family farmers not only had to increase the size of their holdings, but they also had to invest in ever more expensive farm equipment. The indebtedness of farmers skyrocketed in the postwar period. Farmers held about $20 billion in debt in 1960; by the early 2000s, that figure had climbed to nearly $200 billion—more than $60,000 per farmer.

As long as farm prices were stable or rising, the farmer could pay back the debt. Yet high farm prices could also represent a trap. In the 1970s, crop and food prices rose dramatically. To take advantage of this, farmers purchased new equipment and new land—the average farm size grew from 374 acres in 1970 to 426 in 1980, a 14 percent increase. Overall farm debt soared, from $27 billion to just over $100 billion over the decade. The emphasis on supply inevitably produced a glut, leading to dramatically lower food prices in the 1980s. As in the 1930s, indebted farmers were caught in an economic squeeze, leading to a wave of foreclosures on smaller operations.

The vast majority of urban Americans usually ignore farm issues, but this particular crisis gained much media attention. Popular musicians held fundraising concerts to help economically strapped farmers. Increasingly desperate farmers turned to violence, intimidating government and bank officials who tried to foreclose on farms. But neither the aid nor the violence did much good, as the number of farms continued to drop through 1990. More stable crop and food prices in the 1990s and early 2000s, however, helped reverse the decline of the family farm, whose overall numbers have since remained roughly stable at just over 2 million.

CURRENT ISSUES

While U.S. farmers in the twenty-first century continue to face the age-old uncertainties of climate and fluctuations in crop price, a series of new issues has arisen in recent years. Drought, frost, flood, and other deleterious weather phenomena are ancient prob-

lems, but global warming threatens to exacerbate them. Adding to the environmental issues facing farmers today are the negative effects of synthetic pesticides and fertilizers on the quality of the soil, as well as the waste created by large-scale concentration of livestock. Economic problems include high land prices and urban sprawl, particularly in farmlands adjacent to the growing cities of the Sunbelt, and competition from low-cost farmers around the world, who have greater access to U.S. markets in the age of globalization. Finally, two entirely new issues have arisen in recent years—genetically modified (GM) crops and mad cow disease.

Environmental Issues

U.S. farmers in the twenty-first century confront two major environmental problems: one local and largely of their own making (pesticide and fertilizer pollution and livestock waste), the other international and caused by forces from outside the agricultural community (global warming), although farmers contribute to it with petroleum-intensive practices and the methane produced by livestock.

Pesticides create two types of problems. The first is resistance. As early as the first half of the 1950s, farmers and agricultural experts noticed that ever-larger doses of pesticide were required to achieve the same insect-reduction result. The dilemma was caused by basic evolutionary factors. Synthetic pesticides were very effective, but not 100 percent. The bugs that survived passed on their pesticide-resistant genes, making it increasingly difficult to fight the insects. Farmers responded with several solutions: more careful application of pesticides (at key points in the insects' or crops' life cycles); planting more pest-resistant strains of crops; and using the insects themselves (by releasing either predator bugs or sterilized males that failed to breed). Beginning in the 1970s, some farmers opted out of synthetic pesticide use altogether and began practicing organic farming.

Unfortunately, while farmers have been able to maintain an upper hand over insect infestation through "integrated control"—the limited use of pesticides combined with predator or sterilized insects—other side effects of synthetic pesticides and fertilizers are not so easy to control. Synthetic insecticides were widely hailed on their introduction after World War II, but it did not take long to see that their toxic effects were being felt beyond the farm. Among the most effective of early postwar pesticides was dichlorodiphenyltrichloroethane, better known by its acronym DDT. In the late 1950s, scientists began to suspect that DDT was causing birds to lay eggs with thin and brittle shells, which failed to produce hatchlings. This phenomenon, highlighted in environmental writer Rachel Carson's path-breaking book *Silent Spring* (1962), led eventually to the banning of DDT in the United States a decade later. But a host of other pesticides remained in use, continuing to poison groundwater and produce toxic runoffs that flow into rivers and eventually the ocean. Scientists have noted large "dead zones" of several thousand square miles in the Gulf of Mexico—that is, zones in which little life exists—which they attribute to synthetic fertilizer and pesticide runoff from the Mississippi River. Sometimes the land itself is affected. Overuse of synthetic pesticides and fertilizers is blamed for the poisoning of hundreds of square miles of land in California's agriculturally rich Salinas Valley. Pesticides have also been cited as dangerous to farm workers. Meanwhile, industrial-style hog-farming in places such as North Carolina—where thousands of animals are raised in vast climate-controlled sheds—has resulted in huge concentrations of waste that have led to groundwater pollution and a stench that can be smelled for miles.

Global warming is another environmental phenomenon that bodes ill for farmers. With global temperatures expected to rise by as much as 10 or 12 degrees Fahrenheit by the end of the twenty-first century, climatologists argue that farmers may face increasingly unstable weather. Since global warming will not be evenly distributed—because of ocean current and jet stream patterns—earlier frosts may occur in some areas and longer periods of heat and drought in others. In addition, global warming will also give crop-damaging insects longer breeding periods and may result in the introduction of warm-weather insects into temperate regions.

Economic Issues

Two critical economic issues face U.S. farmers as they enter the twenty-first century. As with environmental problems, one is local and one is international. The local issue concerns urban sprawl and escalating land prices. On the one hand, rising land prices have been a boon to farmers, allowing many to retire in comfort on the land they have sold. But for those who want to stay in the business of farming, rising land prices and urban sprawl can have two serious

side effects. First, property taxes often rise as land values increase. Rising land prices also make it difficult for farmers located near urban areas, as well as those farming on scenic lands coveted by resort community developers, to expand their operations. Similarly, urban sprawl puts the interests of farmers at loggerheads with those of their new suburban and exurban neighbors. In places like California's rapidly expanding Central Valley, new residents on the fringe of urban areas like Fresno complain about the noise, dust, pesticide residues, and stench emanating from farming activities. As suburban dwellers outnumber farmers, they are able to influence the political process, leading to the passage of laws that control such "nuisances" and make it more difficult and more expensive to farm.

International competition is, of course, nothing new for U.S. farmers. As noted earlier, late nineteenth-century grain farmers faced lower prices due to a glut of crops from other areas of the world. Globalization since the end of World War II, as well as tariff-lowering treaties and organizations like the North American Free Trade Agreement (NAFTA) and the World Trade Organization, have only exacerbated the problem. Since NAFTA went into effect in 1994, annual U.S. agricultural imports have grown from roughly $27 billion dollars to well over $40 billion, a 50 percent increase, even while exports have stayed roughly even at $50 billion per year. As developing countries employ new technologies, new crops, and, most important, new and more effective distribution and marketing systems, these countries can use their lower labor costs to undersell U.S. farmers.

Some of the impact of international competition is mitigated by subsidies the federal government provides to U.S. farmers. In 1996, Congress passed the Freedom to Farm Act, which dramatically modified the agricultural subsidy program in place since the 1930s. Rather than tell farmers what and how much to grow, the federal government now allowed the decisions to be made by the farmer. At the same time, the bill was intended to allow the gradual phasing out of farm subsidies. But low crop prices in the late 1990s and early 2000s actually led to an *increase* in subsidies, which climbed from just over $7 billion in 1995 to more than $30 billion in 2004 (while high fuel prices cut into farm profits). In 2002, Congress passed the Farm Security and Rural Investment Act. Criticized by many as increasing farm subsidies dramatically and contributing to the national debt, the measure was designed to coordinate subsidies with the business cycle, increasing support at times when farmers faced increased economic hardship.

Mad Cow Disease and Genetically Modified Crops

In the late 1980s, cows in Great Britain were found to be infected with bovine spongiform encephalopathy (BSE), a disease that causes deterioration of brain tissue, leading to erratic behavior—giving rise to the popular name, "mad cow disease." Because BSE could be transmitted to humans through the ingestion of infected meat—leading to the often fatal human variant, Creutzfeldt-Jakob disease—the international community, including the United States, enacted an embargo against British beef. Scientists soon discovered that the disease was caused by nearly indestructible protein structures called prions, which were passed to the cows through the practice of feeding them the ground up offal of other infected cows. Britain not only put a stop to such practices—as did the United States and other industrialized countries—but destroyed most of its cattle herds. In 1993, an infected cow showed up in Canadian herds, leading to a U.S. embargo of beef from that country. The United States has largely escaped the problem to the time of this writing, as the Department of Agriculture has instituted strict testing. A few cases showed up in the early 2000s, leading to restrictions of U.S. beef imports by Japan and several other countries. In mid-2005, two cows in Washington state and Texas were found to be infected with the disease, but the Department of Agriculture assured consumers that meat from the cows did not enter the nation's food supply.

While government officials have done what they can to stop the spread of mad cow disease, they have openly encouraged the use of GM crops, particularly for staples like soybeans and corn, but also for vegetables such as tomatoes. GM crops take the ancient practice of selective breeding into the age of genetic research. Rather than simply breeding plants with sought-after qualities, such as insect resistance or productivity, GM developers restructure the genetic makeup of the plant, introducing genes from other species that give the modified plant desired qualities. Proponents of GM crops point to the benefits of such practices for the farmer, the consumer, and even the environment. Better insect resistance means less use of pesticides. Higher productivity means lower production costs and prices. And, in some cases, GM crops can offer things that traditionally bred crops cannot—for instance, higher levels of vitamins in grains such as rice.

Table 2. Genetically Modified Crops in United States, Percent Acreage of Total, 2001–04

Crop	2001	2002	2003	2004
Corn	26	34	40	45
Cotton	69	71	73	76
Soybean	68	75	81	85

Source: National Agriculture Statistics Service, U.S. Department of Agriculture.

Opponents say that GM crops have not been adequately vetted for potential harm to the environment. They point out that insect-resistant crops, which often achieve resistance through higher levels of toxins, are not only harmful to insect pests but also to those beneficial insects that pollinate plants. These toxins may also have adverse, long-term effects on other plant species and human health. Scientists and farmers, they say, just do not yet know the potential effects, and much more testing needs to be done before the crops are introduced on a mass basis. Organic farmers also worry that GM crops might cross-breed with their own, making it impossible to reassure consumers that organically grown crops are not genetically modified. There are also fears that GM-crop companies are creating planned crop obsolescence—that is, breeding plants whose seeds are infertile, forcing farmers to remain dependent on the companies for their annual seeds.

Despite these fears, GM crops—which were introduced in 1996—have spread rapidly around the world, with the greatest growth coming in the United States. While global acreage in GM crops was just over 167 million acres in 2003, more than 105 million of those acres—or about two-thirds—were in the United States. The use of GM crops has also produced a trade spat with the European Union (EU), where opposition from the public and farm community is greater. In 1998 the EU banned the importation of virtually all foods from GM crops, and in 2003 the United States filed a protest against with the World Trade Organization. No decision had been forthcoming as of early 2005.

CONCLUSION

North America has been an agricultural innovator since pre-Columbian times. Such basic foods and agricultural products as corn, tomatoes, and tobacco originated there, first domesticated by Native Americans. The arrival of Europeans in the seventeenth century not only introduced new crops such as wheat and rice but integrated North American agriculture into the global market. Over the subsequent centuries, the American farmer has been the envy of the world, producing increasing quantities of food with fewer people. Today, the United States is by far the world's largest agricultural producer and exporter.

But U.S. farmers at the beginning of the twenty-first century still face serious challenges. While the age-old problems of climate and the centuries-old problem of crop price fluctuations remain, new concerns have arisen—from the environmental impact of modern farming practices to global warming to greater competition from low-cost farmers in the developing world. In the past, U.S. farmers have thrived by employing the latest technology. Despite the promise of GM crops, however, some experts think this is not a sustainable strategy for several reasons. First, petroleum-intensive agricultural practices are threatened by declining oil reserves. Environmentally harmful practices may cut into U.S. agricultural productivity. And consumers, increasingly demanding pure foods, may turn away from GM crops.

James Ciment

REFERENCES

Beeman, Randal S., and James A. Pritchard. *A Green and Permanent Land Ecology and Agriculture in Twentieth Century Farming.* Lawrence: University of Kansas Press, 2001.

Carson, Rachel. *Silent Spring.* Boston: Houghton Mifflin, 1962.

Cochrane, Willard W. *The Development of American Agriculture: A Historical Analysis.* Minneapolis: University of Minnesota Press, 1993.

Danbom, David B. *Born in the Country: A History of Rural America.* Baltimore: Johns Hopkins University Press, 1995.

Drache, Hiram M. *History of U.S. Agriculture and Its Relevance Today.* Danville, IL: Interstate, 1996.

———. *Legacy of the Land: Agriculture's Story to the Present.* Danville, IL: Interstate, 1996.

Goodwyn, Lawrence. *Democratic Promise: The Populist Moment in America.* New York: Oxford University Press, 1976.

Hart, John Fraser. *The American Farm: How Farming Shaped the Landscape of America.* New York: B&N Books, 1998.

Hart, Kathleen. *Eating in the Dark: America's Experiment with Genetically Engineered Food.* New York: Pantheon Books, 2002.

Hurt, R. Douglas. *American Agriculture: A Brief History.* Ames: Iowa State University Press, 1994.

Spencer, Charlotte A. *Mad Cows and Cannibals: A Guide to the Transmissible Spongiform Encephalopathies.* Upper Saddle River, NJ: Pearson/Prentice-Hall, 2004.

WEB SITES

Environmental Protection Agency: www.epa.gov
Farm Aid: www.farmaid.org
U.S. Department of Agriculture: www.usda.gov

GLOSSARY

Bovine spongiform encephalopathy (BSE). A disease that results in deterioration in brain tissue, leading to erratic behavior in cows; it is caused by feeding cows the offal of infected cows.

Cotton gin. A 1793 invention by Eli Whitney that mechanically removed the seed from cotton, allowing for the vast expansion of U.S. cotton production and slavery.

Creutzfeldt-Jakob disease. The fatal human variant of BSE.

DDT. Dichlorodiphenyltrichloroethane, a synthetic pesticide invented in 1939. In 1972, after its deleterious effect on birds' health is discovered, DDT is banned in the United States.

Dead zone. A region in the Gulf of Mexico in which sea life has been largely killed off by pesticide and fertilizer runoff from the Mississippi River.

Genetically modified (GM) crops. Crops whose genetic makeup has been transformed by the introduction of genes from other species.

Global warming. The gradual warming of the Earth's climate caused by increases in heat-trapping carbon dioxide in the atmosphere.

Mad cow disease. Popular name for BSE.

Organic farming. Farming that does not employ synthetic fertilizers or pesticides.

Staple crops. Basic crops that supply most of the world's food; staple crops include wheat, rice, corn, soybeans, and potatoes.

Subsidies. A grant of money, property, or other support by the federal government to the private sector, including farmers.

DOCUMENTS

Document 1. Comparison of 1996 Freedom to Farm Act and 2002 Farm Security and Rural Investment Act

Federal subsidies have been a major part of the U.S. agricultural economy since the New Deal in the 1930s. Under legislation in place from the 1930s to the 1990s, these subsidies came with tight strings attached—Washington telling farmers what and how much they could grow. The Freedom to Farm Act of 1996 loosened those strings, allowing farmers a greater say in these decisions. In exchange, subsidies were supposed to be phased out. In 2002, however, Congress actually increased the amount of subsidies and continued them through at least 2007.

Direct payments for wheat, feed grains, upland cotton, rice, and oilseeds

1996 Freedom to Farm Act

Farmers who participated in the wheat, corn, barley, grain sorghum, oats, upland cotton, and rice programs in any 1 of the years 1991–95 could enter into 7-year *production flexibility contracts* (PFC) for 1996–2002 during a one-time enrollment period. An eligible farm's "payment quantity" for a given contract commodity was equal to 85 percent of its contract acreage times its program yield for that commodity. A per-unit payment rate (e.g., per bushel) for each contract commodity was determined annually by dividing the total annual contract payment level for each commodity by the total of all contract farms' program payment quantity. The annual payment rate for a contract commodity was then multiplied by each farm's payment quantity for that commodity, and the sum of such payments across contract commodities on the farm was that farm's annual payment, subject to any payment limits.

Total PFC payment levels for each fiscal year (FY) were fixed at: $5.570 billion in 1996, $5.385 billion in 1997, $5.800 billion in 1998, $5.603 billion in 1999, $5.130 billion in 2000, $4.130 billion in 2001, and $4.008 billion in 2002. Spending caps for each crop, except rice, were adjusted for prior-year crop program payments to farmers made in FY 1996 and any 1995 crop repayments owed to the government. The amount allocated for rice was increased by $8.5 million annually for FY 1997–2002. Allocations of the above payment levels were: 26.26 percent for wheat, 46.22 percent for corn, 5.11 percent for sorghum, 2.16 percent for barley, 0.15 percent for oats, 11.63 percent for upland cotton, and 8.47 percent for rice.

Oilseeds were not eligible for production flexibility contract payments.

2002 Farm Security and Rural Investment Act

Direct payments are available for eligible producers of wheat, corn, barley, grain sorghum, oats, upland cotton, and rice. New payments are established for soybeans, other oilseeds, and peanuts. (See peanut provisions for those provisions that apply uniquely to peanuts.)

To receive payments on covered crops (wheat, corn, grain sorghum, barley, oats, rice, upland cotton, soybeans, and other oilseeds), a producer must enter into an annual agreement.

Direct payments for the 2002 crop are to be made as soon as practicable after enactment of the Farm Act. For crop years (CY) 2003–07, payments are to be made no sooner than October 1 of the year the crop is harvested. Advance payments of up to 50 percent can be made beginning December 1 of the calendar year before the year when the covered commodity is harvested.

Payment rates specified in the 2002 Farm Act:

Crop	Payment Rate
Wheat	$0.52/bu[shel]
Corn	$0.28/bu
Grain sorghum	$0.35/bu
Barley	$0.24/bu
Oats	$0.024/bu
Upland cotton	$0.0667/lb
Rice	$2.35/cwt [hundredweight, or 100 pounds]
Soybeans	$0.44/bu
Other oilseeds	$0.008/lb

Since PFC payments for FY 2002 were made prior to enactment of the 2002 Farm Act, 2002 payments will be adjusted.

Counter-cyclical payments for wheat, feed grains, upland cotton, rice, and oilseeds

1996 Freedom to Farm Act

Supplemental legislation authorized Market Loss Assistance (MLA) payments for wheat, feed grains, rice and upland cotton for crop year (CY) 1998 through CY 2001. Payments were proportional to Production Flexibility Contract (PFC) payments. Payment levels were $2.857 billion in CY 1998, $5.5 billion in CY 1999, $5.465 billion in CY 2000, and $4.6 billion in CY 2001.

Oilseed payments provided in FY 1999 through FY 2001 were based on plantings in 1997, 1998, or 1999. Payment levels were $475 million in 1999, $500 million in 2000, and $424 million in 2001.

2002 Farm Security and Rural Investment Act

Counter-cyclical payments are available to covered commodities whenever the effective price is less than the target price. The effective price is equal to the sum of 1) the higher of the national average farm price for the marketing year, or the national loan rate for the commodity and 2) the direct payment rate for the commodity. The payment amount for a farmer equals the product of the payment rate, the payment acres, and the payment yield.

Target prices for counter-cyclical payments:

Crop	2002–03	2004–07
Wheat	$3.86/bu	$3.92/bu
Corn	$2.60/bu	$2.63/bu
Grain sorghum	$2.54/bu	$2.57/bu
Barley	$2.21/bu	$2.24/bu
Oats	$1.40/bu	$1.44/bu
Upland cotton	$0.724/lb	$0.724/lb
Rice	$10.50/cwt	$10.50/cwt
Soybeans	$5.80/bu	$5.80/bu
Other oilseeds	$0.098/lb	$0.101/lb

The Secretary shall make counter-cyclical payments for the crop as soon as practicable after the end of crop year for the covered commodity. A payment of up to 35 percent shall be made in October of the year when the crop is harvested. A second payment of up to 70 percent minus the first payment shall be made after February 1. The final payment shall be made as soon as practicable after the end of the crop year.

1996 Freedom to Farm Act

Participants could plant 100 percent of their total contract acreage to any crop, except with limitations on fruits and vegetables. Land had to be maintained in agricultural use. Unlimited haying and grazing and planting and harvesting of alfalfa and other forage crops were permitted with no reduction in payments. Planting of fruits and vegetables (excluding mung beans, lentils, and dry peas) on contract acres was prohibited unless the producer or the farm had a history of planting fruits and vegetables, but payments were reduced acre-for-acre on such plantings. Double cropping of fruits and vegetables was permitted without loss of payments if there were a history of such double cropping in the region. . . .

2002 Farm Security and Rural Investment Act

The 2002 Act planting flexibility provisions are the same as the 1996 Act, except wild rice will be treated the same as a fruit/vegetable. In general, fruit and vegetable violations on contract acres occur when harvested. Under the 1996 Act, the violation occurred when planted.

Source: Economic Research Service, U.S. Department of Agriculture.

FOOD AND DRUG SAFETY

Mad cow disease, the dangers of genetically modified foods, and deadly viruses such as SARS have captured newspaper headlines in recent years. While such stories represent legitimate threats to public health, the problems of unsafe foods and drugs are perhaps less sensational but more widespread. The Centers for Disease Control (CDC) estimate that there were roughly 76 million cases of foodborne illness annually in the United States in the early 2000s. Most are mild, but an estimated 325,000 persons are hospitalized and 5,000 die each year from these illnesses.

The situation is even worse in the developing world, where the incidence of infection is much higher and the consequences more dire. The World Health Organization (WHO) estimates that 20 million persons die each year from contaminated food and water, 2 million of whom are children under the age of 5. Food safety is not a negligible concern even in the developed world, but it is a serious matter among poorer nations.

Pharmaceutical drugs present their own set of dangers. Highly processed or artificially created, most modern drugs do not contain the bacteria, viruses, or parasites that are the main causes of foodborne disease. The dangers of drugs come, instead, from their side effects, that is, the harms they inflict as they fight an illness or treat its symptoms. Nearly all drugs inflict some form of harm, which is why they should be used with care. Even in the intensive testing environment of the United States, the Office of Drug Safety received reports of 370,000 adverse reactions to prescribed drugs in the year 2003; they classified 213,000 as serious. The office does not estimate the number of unreported adverse reactions, but it is safe to assume it runs into the millions.

CLASSIFICATION OF UNSAFE FOOD AND DRUGS

The dangers from food fall into three main categories. Foreign substances in foods can harm the human body. These substances can be chemical (pesticides, lead, arsenic) or organic (bacteria, viruses, parasites). Botulism, cholera, and giardiasis *are diseases caused by microorganisms*. These foreign substances may cause immediate sickness or death, as botulism does, or they may impair health over longer periods, as the buildup of lead in the body does.

A second category of danger involves the quantities or proportions of food eaten. Malnutrition from inadequate intake weakens the body's immune system and contributes to many illnesses. If the proportions of essential nutrients consumed are unbalanced, the person may have nutritional deficiency diseases such as beriberi, scurvy, and pellagra. Eating too much or improper types of food contributes to obesity, diabetes, and perhaps many forms of cancer.

The third category of danger involves food allergies. Foods that are beneficial to most people are poisonous to some; severe allergic reactions to peanuts, milk, wheat, corn, and other everyday foods are not rare.

Drugs, or medicines, have risks similar to those found in foods. Sometimes, albeit rarely, drugs may contain impurities that harm health. In 1982, Tylenol laced with arsenic killed seven persons in the Chicago area, an apparent act of product tampering. In 1988, a batch of tryptophan, an amino acid sold over the counter as a dietary supplement in the United States, contained a genetically engineered bacterium that killed 37 persons and permanently disabled 1,500 others. Another drug-related danger comes from contaminated needles used to inject illegal drugs; heroin users are at risk of contracting autoimmune deficiency syndrome (AIDS) and hepatitis this way. Even drugs that are pure and administered properly sometimes have severe adverse effects; thalidomide, for example, a drug prescribed as a tranquilizer in the 1950s and 1960s, causes birth defects in pregnant women. The proper dosage of

CHRONOLOGY

2800 B.C.E.   First extant written record of drug prescription is created in China.

ca. 500–400 B.C.E. Ancient Greek physician Hippocrates establishes first rational, as opposed to mystical, approach to medicine.

ca. 50–70 C.E.   Greek physician Dioscordes publishes *De Materia Medica*, five volumes prescribing drugs for various ailments; it is the first compilation of drug descriptions in the Western world.

1618   The Royal College of Physicians in London publishes the first pharmacopeia in the English language.

1674   Dutch biologist Antoni van Leeuwenhoek invents the microscope and becomes the first to see bacteria.

1796   English scientist Edward Jenner succeeds in developing the first safe smallpox vaccine.

1810   Canning process for preserving food is invented by French scientist Nicolas Appert.

1860   Britain passes first national law prohibiting adulteration of food.

1862   The Bureau of Chemistry, predecessor of the Food and Drug Administration, is founded within the Department of Agriculture.

1864   French microbiologist Louis Pasteur invents process of using heat to kill bacteria in food (pasteurization).

1870–1914   National and international food processing firms emerge in the United States and Europe.

1890   Widespread milk pasteurization begins in the United States.

1905   Drinking water is first chlorinated in Britain.

1906   Congress passes the Meat Inspection Act and Pure Food and Drugs Act to ensure the safety of the country's food and drug supplies.

1927   The Bureau of Chemistry is divided into two branches, the Bureau of Chemistry and Soils and the Food, Drug, and Insecticide Administration; the latter shortens its name to the Food and Drug Administration (FDA) in 1930.

1935   Protonsil, the first antibiotic, is discovered to fight staphylococcal infections.

1938   Congress passes the Food, Drug, and Cosmetic Act; among its provisions are requirements that drug companies provide scientific proof of the safety of new drugs; it also extends FDA control over cosmetics and therapeutic devices.

1944   Penicillin is first used to treat battlefield injuries.

1954   First widespread distribution of polio vaccines to American children occurs.

1958   Congress passes the Food Additives Amendment, requiring manufacturers to prove the safety of food additives; the so-called Delaney proviso of the law prohibits the approval of any food additive shown to cause cancer in animals or humans.

1962   The sleeping pill thalidomide is shown to cause major birth defects in Western Europe, and the FDA keeps the drug out of the United States.

1970   The Environmental Protection Agency (EPA) is established and takes over regulation of pesticides from the FDA.

1982   Tylenol laced with cyanide at Chicago-area supermarkets kills seven, resulting in stricter packaging rules and practices for food and over-the-counter drug products.

1994   Approximately 225,000 ice cream eaters are poisoned by *Salmonella enteridis* in the worst food poisoning case in American history. The first genetically modified food product, the Flavr Savr tomato, is made available to U.S. consumers.

1995   World Trade Organization establishes international sanitary regulations for food and drugs.

2003   The European Union passes the strictest rules on genetically modified food in the world.

drugs is also vital to safety; even beneficial drugs if taken in great enough quantities can be harmful or lethal. Finally, drug safety is complicated by the variability of human responses. Properly administered penicillin is beneficial for most persons, for example, but in some it causes a violent reaction or even death.

HISTORY

The advent of agriculture—that is, the raising of crops and breeding of livestock—began about 12000 B.C.E., laying the foundation of modern human civilization. Agriculture ensured a more predictable and greater supply of food, leading to gains in human population. But agriculture was not without its drawbacks, including declines in the quality of food and human health. For example, while meats contain all of the amino acids essential to human health, grains such as rice, wheat, and corn, do not. Moreover, repeated use of the same soil can deplete healthful minerals and vitamins in food. Both of these influences likely led to increases in diseases caused by deficiencies of essential nutrients. Also, agriculture-based societies brought human populations into more concentrated settlements around water supplies, resulting in closer contact with each other and with domesticated animals. These changes led to increasing transmission of illnesses and a decline in the average level of health. Anthropologists attribute widespread anemia in Europe, Asia, and America, even among people with adequate amounts of iron in their diet, to chronic bacterial and parasitic infection.

Use of drugs may go back as far as that of food, though no fossil record has yet been uncovered. In any event, poppy seeds, from which opium is derived, were found in a grave in Granada dating from 3000 B.C.E. Egyptian records from 1500 B.C.E. prescribe drugs for various ailments; the known use of drugs in China dates from about 1100 B.C.E. (although some attribute a book on drug prescriptions to Shen Nung, the Red Emperor, in 2800 B.C.E.) and in India from about 600 B.C.E. The conquering Spanish destroyed records of the native populations in the Americas, so little is known about their early drug use; quinine and nicotine, however, were brought to Europe from the New World after Columbus's voyages. In the first century C.E., Dioscorides, a physician from Anatolia (now part of Turkey), published a five-volume work prescribing medicines for various ailments. The prescriptions are so inaccurate by modern standards that it is impossible to weigh the

early benefits and harms from their use. Some drugs no doubt helped the afflicted; antibacterial molds and copper preparations, for example, probably helped fight wound infections.

The Reformation brought the spirit of science to food and drugs in Europe. The use of his remarkable microscopes enabled Antoni van Leeuwenhoek (1632–1723) to identify bacteria for the first time. Over the next two and a half centuries, scientists proved that microbes were the causal agents in many diseases as well as food spoilage, and they developed remedies. The effort involved brilliant discoveries from across Europe—Lazzaro Spallanzani (1729–1799) from Italy, Edward Jenner (1749–1823) from England, Louis Pasteur (1822–1895) from France, and Robert Koch (1843–1910) from Germany are among the best known, but many others also contributed. The principle of "spontaneous generation" was the focus of much debate during this period. Prior to the nineteenth century, most educated persons believed microbial pathogens came to life spontaneously in plants and animals. Microbiologists were eventually able to establish, through a series of ingenious experiments, that pathogens had to be transmitted from one organism to another. This insight was crucial for the control of foodborne diseases, indicating that quarantining contaminated organisms could prevent pathogens from affecting other organisms.

In 1618, the Royal College of Physicians in Britain issued a pharmacopoeia, a list of medicinal drugs and their chemical compositions, with instructions for testing purity and strength. The practice spread to the rest of Europe and to America. During the eighteenth and nineteenth centuries, new drugs were identified and known ones isolated. Joseph Priestly discovered nitrous oxide in 1772, although it was not used as an anesthetic until later. In 1785, digitalis was discovered as a treatment for dropsy, a swelling of the limbs. Opium was isolated from poppy seeds in 1806, quinine from cinchona in 1818, and salicylic acid (similar to aspirin) from willow bark in 1838.

Drugs that killed pain and prevented infection were crucial to the development of surgery. Nitrous oxide was first used in surgery in 1842 by a Georgia doctor named Crawford Long. Ether was used in Boston for dental surgery in 1846, and cocaine was used as a topical anesthetic for eye surgery in 1848. Oliver Wendell Holmes coined the term "anesthesia" to describe the effects of these new drugs. In 1853, British physician John Snow used chloroform to assist

Queen Victoria in childbirth, popularizing its use when the Queen sang its praises. In 1857, Joseph Lister identified bacteria as the cause of gangrene, a common consequence of surgery, and successfully used carbolic acid as an antiseptic in 1867.

Despite their benefits, drugs posed dangers. Patients often died from too much mercury, which was widely used to treat syphilis in the seventeenth century. Chloroform is toxic to the liver; opium is addictive in most people, even if used for only a few weeks. Arsenic compounds, though known to be poisonous, were commonly used to treat malaria because they were cheaper than quinine. The identification of pharmacological properties of drugs greatly improved medicinal treatments, but doctors and scientists were not able to eliminate their harmful effects, nor have the advances of modern science.

Diseases caused by a deficiency of nutrients were identified in the early eighteenth century. In 1747, when James Lind, a British naval surgeon, demonstrated through clinical trials that a deficiency of citrus fruit caused scurvy, the British admiralty (after a lag of 50 years) prescribed a regimen of lime juice for its sailors (known as "Limeys"). Cures for beriberi (caused by thiamin deficiency), pellagra (lack of niacin), anemia (lack of iron), osteoporosis (lack of calcium), and other deficiency diseases were discovered during the nineteenth and twentieth centuries.

Government regulation of foods and drugs may have been practiced in preliterate societies, but contemporary knowledge is limited to written records—such as kosher laws in the Hebrew Bible and the legal codes of Babylon that regulated the planting, growing, and harvesting of grain. Historically, however, most government regulation of food and drugs has been concerned with fraud—such as cheating on quantity or weight, substituting cheap for expensive ingredients, and making unjustified claims—although some laws, such as the mixing of fresh and spoiled butter, or the sale of unwholesome wine, were concerned with safety. In 1345, the mayor of London required parts of the Thames from which drinking water was drawn to be free of dung or other filth. The first national food law was passed in Britain in 1860, prohibiting adulteration. In 1872 the law made it a crime to mix "any injurious or poisonous ingredient" into food.

In America, Massachusetts passed a statute prohibiting the sale of unwholesome food in 1785, and over the next century and a quarter, most states enacted laws prohibiting adulteration. In 1906, Congress passed the nation's first two federal food and drug laws: the Meat Inspection Act and the Pure Food and Drugs Act. The former prohibited interstate traffic in meats that were "unsound, unhealthful, unwholesome, or otherwise unfit for human food," and provided for government inspections. The Pure Food and Drugs Act prohibited the "manufacture, sale, or transportation of adulterated or misbranded or poisonous or deleterious foods, drugs, medicines, and liquors," and likewise provided for government inspection of foods and prosecution of violators.

Neither of the measures was precipitated by an outbreak of poisoning. The Meat Inspection Act was largely a response to Upton Sinclair's novel *The Jungle,* in which he hoped to foment a socialist revolution by drawing attention to the fetid working conditions in the packinghouses. Instead, he raised concern about the safety of meat. "I aimed at the public's heart, and by accident I hit it in the stomach," he wrote. The Pure Food and Drugs Act was a response to sensational journalism and the politicking of Harvey Wiley, a government scientist who agitated against food adulteration. His campaign for safe food was politically effective, although he presented scant evidence that foods or drugs were unsafe.

By contrast, the expansion of the law in the Food, Drug, and Cosmetic Act of 1938—which, among other things, required drug manufacturers to provide scientific proof of their products' safety before putting them on the market—was precipitated by an outbreak of poisoning. In 1937, seventy-six persons died after taking sulphanilamide, a drug effective in fighting streptococcal infection. Death was caused by a manufacturer suspending the drug in ethylene glycol (antifreeze), a sweet-tasting but poisonous liquid. The deaths contributed to passage of a stronger law and more rigorous requirements for testing drugs.

Although the Pure Food and Drugs Act of 1906, the Harrison Narcotics Act of 1914, and the Food, Drug, and Cosmetic Act of 1938 established the main regulatory framework in the United States, the regulation of food and drugs has been modified and expanded over the years. The thalidomide deformities in Europe led Congress to pass the Kefauver-Harrison amendments in 1962, requiring companies to prove a drug was safe and effective before offering it to the public. In 1980, the Infant Formula Act empowered the FDA to regulate nutritional and safety standards for that product. In 1990, Congress required all packaged foods to bear a nutritional label. And the Bioterrorism Act passed in 2002 required the FDA to inspect foods more frequently and to devise methods for the rapid detection of intentionally adulterated foods. These laws, as extended, constitute the main federal regulation of drugs in the United States.

MODERN FOOD AND DRUG INDUSTRIES

The food and drug industries in the United States today are large, complex, and dependent on international trade. In 2004, the United States traded more than $100 billion worth of agricultural goods in international markets and exported more than $21 billion in medical and pharmaceutical preparations. Both industries consist of firms that operate for profit, consumers who exercise a large degree of autonomy in purchases, and regulators that exercise local, state, national, or supranational governmental authority. The scientists are vital to the food and drug industries and are employed by nonprofit organizations and universities, as well as firms and government agencies. All of these groups affect food and drug safety, but the primary influence is exerted by consumers. As purchasers of food and drugs, consumers want products that are safe. Of course, safety is not an absolute condition; consumers understand that there are risks, but they want those risks minimized. The demand for safe foods and drugs provides the impetus for taking precaution in the growth, processing, and distribution of these products. Consumer demand is also the rationale for regulators passing laws to govern the activities of food and drug firms, and it guides scientists' efforts to find safe cures for diseases and improvements in food safety.

Consumers

The incentive for companies to deliver safe foods and drugs is strong because large sums of money are at stake. American consumers spent $1.1 trillion on food in 2004. They spent an additional $1.4 trillion on medical care, $250 billion on drugs. Although profits vary from year to year, in 2000 farms earned $1.2 billion, food manufacturers $27 billion, and the healthcare industry about $26 billion. In 2004, food expenditures accounted for 14 percent of all consumer expenditures in the United States, compared to 6 percent for clothes, 14 percent for housing, and 12 percent for transportation. Medical expenditures accounted for 18 percent of consumer expenditures and drugs for 3 percent. Of the 2004 expenditures for food, about $55 billion went to imported foodstuffs.

As these statistics show, the food and drug industries in the United States are enormous. Although more money is being spent on food now than in the past, that money represents a smaller portion of the family budget. In 1930, 25 percent of consumer expenditures were for food. That percentage climbed to 34 percent during the war year of 1944, then gradually declined to 25 percent by 1960, 20 percent in 1980, and 14 percent by 2000. American consumers are spending increasing amounts of their food budget outside the home. In 1929, Americans spent 16 percent of their food budget eating out; by 1950 the figure had risen to 23 percent, and by 2001 to 41 percent. These trends reflect the growing wealth of U.S. citizens, the efficiency of the nation's prepared food industry, and the increased prevalence of the two-worker family, which leaves less time for preparing meals at home but creates more disposable income.

Opposite trends characterize drug and medical expenditures. Americans are consuming drugs in ever-greater quantities. In 1929, drugs constituted 0.8 percent of total consumer expenditures, compared to 2.5 percent in 2001. However, the percentage has grown rapidly of late. It took more than 50 years, from 1943 to 1997, for drug expenditures to climb from 1 percent to 2 percent of consumer spending, but in only 6 years it climbed from 2 percent to 3 percent. Even so, expenditures on drugs have climbed less rapidly than medical care expenses as a whole. Expenditures on medical care represented 4 percent of total consumer spending in 1930 but 17 percent in 2003. Of the many factors involved in this increase, some of the most important are an aging population, better and more expensive medical equipment, and higher drug research costs.

Businesses

The vast amounts of foods and drugs purchased in the United States are supplied by profit-seeking enterprises. Food industry companies undertake seven primary activities from plough to plate: growing and harvesting, processing, transporting, storing, wholesaling, retailing, and preparing (restaurants) of food. Safety is important in all stages, because contamination can take place anywhere along the chain. Farmers use pesticides, some of which are harmful; soil and water can contain poisonous chemicals or biological agents; animals can carry dangerous bacteria in their digestive tracts, as well as their hair, feathers, and skin, and these bacteria can enter the edible portions of the animal during slaughter and preparation; contaminants can enter foods while they are being transported (one of the largest outbreaks of salmonella poisoning in the United States was the result of careless transporting of ice cream); processing equipment can carry pathogens or harmful chemicals that are transferred to foods; finally, people who handle food at various stages of production as well as in the home can transmit diseases through improperly cleaned hands, hair, or clothes.

Each stage of the food industry is structured differently and thus has different associated food risks. In 2003, there were 2.127 million farms in the United States, with an average size of 441 acres. Although the trend is toward larger units (3.2 million farms had an average size of 352 acres in 1964), no small group of farmers dominates the production of wheat, corn, rice, pigs, cattle, poultry, or milk. Food is touched by many hands in the production process, leaving many opportunities for contamination. Offsetting this disadvantage is the gain that, should a batch of food contain poisonous chemicals or destructive bacteria, the number affected will not be large—a few hundred rather than a few hundred thousand.

The same is true of the trucking and restaurant businesses. Trucking and warehousing in America employed more than 2 million workers in 2004, and the wholesale trade at least another 7 million, perhaps half of whom handled food. More than 11 million workers were employed in nearly 1 million restaurants and bars, and almost half of all adults (46 percent) ate at a restaurant during the course of the average day. The opportunities for contamination are obviously large, but the chances that any particular case of contamination will affect large numbers is likely to be small.

Whereas the growth and harvesting of food products is dispersed among many firms, the manufacture of many kinds of food is not; most food manufacture is concentrated. One measure of economic concentration is the percentage of output produced by the four largest firms in an industry. The four largest U.S. firms refine 99 percent of the sugar, make 83 percent of the breakfast cereal, and process 53 percent of the butter and 32 percent of the ice cream. Animal processing is also concentrated. The four largest firms slaughter 41 percent of poultry in the United States and similar percentages of cattle and hogs. Contamination from a large manufacturing plant or slaughterhouse can affect many thousands

Table 1. Incidence of Infections from Foodborne Pathogens, 1996–2003*

Pathogens	1996–1998 Average	2003	National health objectives for 2010
Bacteria			
Campylobacter (per 100,000 persons)	21.7	12.6	12.3
Escherichia coli (per 100,000 persons)	2.3	1.1	1.0
Listeria (per 1 million persons)	4.9	3.3	2.5
Salmonella (per 100,000 persons)	13.5	14.5	6.8
Shigella (per 100,000 persons)	7.7	7.3	N/A
Vibrio (per 1 million persons)	2.4	3.0	N/A
Yersinia (per 1 million persons)	8.9	4.0	N/A
Parasites			
Cryptosporidium (per 1 million persons)	26.8	10.9	N/A
Cyclospora (per 1 million persons)	1.6	0.3	N/A

* Based on Centers for Disease Control's Foodborne Diseases Active Surveillance Network for nine states: California, Colorado, Connecticut, Georgia, Maryland, Minnesota, New York, Oregon, and Tennessee.
Source: Centers for Disease Control, Preliminary Morbidity and Mortality Weekly Report. FoodNet Data on the Incidence of Infection with Pathogens Transmitted Commonly Through Foods, Selected Sites, United States, 2003.

of persons, as happened with an outbreak of salmonella poisoning in 1994. A nationally branded ice cream maker had its ingredients shipped in tanker trucks. Although the company used pasteurized ingredients, they were shipped in tanks that had previously carried unpasteurized liquid eggs. *Salmonella entertidis*, a bacteria in the eggs, remained in the tanker trucks, infecting the ice cream. Despite the cleanliness of the plant itself, where no salmonella was found, contaminated ice cream was distributed nationally from a plant in Minnesota. An estimated 224,000 persons were poisoned from this source.

The danger of poisoning large numbers of customers, and the consequent decline of revenues and profitability, leads manufacturing firms to take precautions against contamination. Firms use sophisticated techniques to detect and eliminate harmful substances. Established techniques such as sampling and growing bacteria in a culture are used, but so are gene probes and other new methods designed to speed up detection. The design, use, and care of equipment, the materials and layout of the plant, the steps in processing, and the behavior of employees are subjected to close scrutiny by food companies.

These practices and improvements are often undertaken by firms that want to win customers and earn profits.

In addition to local building codes, health regulations, and national rules and inspections, a large community of private biologists, chemists, and engineers pay close attention to safety quite apart from regulators. Equipment is made from materials, such as stainless steel, that are easy to clean and disinfect. Gauges are mounted so that bacteria and viruses cannot collect in dead spaces. Even details like rubber O-rings are carefully specified, because moisture can collect and bacteria can grow around the edges. Buildings are constructed to discourage bird nesting; outside lights are placed away from the building because they attract insects; humidity is kept low to prevent molds; floors are kept dry; and administrative offices are separated from processing areas. Employees are required to wash their hands at specified times, to wear hats or nets over their hair, and to wear special clothing.

The management of food safety falls under a set of rules generally known as Good Manufacturing Practice. Good Manufacturing Practice incorporates the regulations established by local, state, and federal officials, but usually is more detailed in specifying the particular practices of a firm. The practices are explicitly set forth in company documents, which include the firm's safety goals, measurements to determine if the goals are being met, and controls put in place to ensure the safety of food.

Hazard Analysis Critical Control Point, first instituted in 1997 by the FDA's Center for Food Safety and Applied Nutrition, is a more recent approach to safety improvement. Hazard analysis consists of identifying potential hazards and the points at which those hazards can be effectively controlled. An investigation of the 1994 salmonella ice cream outbreak, for example, identified the tanker trucks as a critical point for controlling viral and bacterial poisoning. The analysts recommended that ingredients for ice cream be hauled in dedicated tankers, that the tanks and seals be checked at regular intervals for cracks or leaks, and that the inspections be documented and monitored by responsible managers. The company also identified another control point, at which the ice cream was ready to ship, and began inspecting finished ice cream for microorganisms. Had Hazard Analysis Critical Control Point been practiced before the outbreak, the poisonings would have been avoided.

Drug manufacturing, like food manufacturing, is concentrated among large firms. The four largest drug firms produce 62 percent of the drug output of the United States, as measured by revenues. One reason for concentration is the large expenditure needed to bring a drug to market. In the year 2000, it cost $400 million on average to research and develop a successful drug and another $400 million to bring it to market. Much of the money is spent screening drugs that do not succeed; only about 1 in 5,000 probed chemicals makes it to market. Successful drugs go through long and complicated processes to meet regulatory requirements. It takes more than 8 years for the average drug to meet regulatory approval.

Regulators

In the United States, government regulation of food and drugs is a patchwork of overlapping laws and authority that reflects the division of powers and the diversity of contending interests within the American system. Local governments—city, county, and state—establish safety regulations for restaurants, water supplies, and sewage systems. Local inspectors visit restaurants and issue citations or close those that violate safety codes. Local governments usually own the facilities that provide mass water and sewage services to communities, and they regulate the drilling and inspection of private wells and septic tanks. State governments usually regulate establishments, other than restaurants, that manufacture, store, and sell food at retail, although city and county governments sometimes perform this function. The U.S. Congress establishes regulations for food and drugs involved in interstate commerce. The FDA sets the rules for accurate labeling of foods, which are enforced by a number of agencies. The Department of Agriculture inspects eggs, grains, meat, and poultry. The FDA inspects other foods for chemical and biological agents. The Centers for Disease Control surveys outbreaks of food poisoning, and the Environmental Protection Agency enforces pesticide regulations. (Both the FDA and Centers for Disease Control are part of the Department of Health and Human Services.)

The budgets devoted to inspections and enforcement are substantial. For 2004, Congress budgeted $797 million to the Food Safety and Inspection Service of the Department of Agriculture to inspect meat, poultry, and eggs. The Animal and Plant Health Inspection Service, which looks for diseases before they enter the food supply, received a budget of $695 million for 2004. The FDA budget for 2004 was $1.7 billion.

The regulation of drugs falls to the FDA, which sets labeling rules and determines which drugs may be offered as over-the-counter medicines or as prescription-only from physicians. The FDA has long and costly procedures for approving new drugs for sale. Typically, a drug firm employs chemists, toxicologists, molecular biologists, statisticians, and computer modelers to scan the scientific literature for substances it hopes will be effective in treating a malady. Once the researchers identify or develop a substance, it is tested *in vitro*, that is, in an artificial environment such as a test tube, and *in vivo*, in laboratory animals such as mice. In these tests, researchers try to infer how the drug will influence the human body and how the body will influence the drug. Dosage, toxicity, absorption into the bloodstream, and effectiveness are of particular interest in these early studies.

Most potential drugs do not pass these first tests, but if a substance shows promise, it then moves to clinical trials, that is, testing in human subjects. These trials are conducted in specialized clinics (AIDS clinics, for example), in research hospitals, or sometimes in doctors' offices. To be approved, a drug must pass through three phases of clinical trials. In the first phase, healthy volunteers are subjected to a new drug, mainly to test for effectiveness and harmful effects. Subjects must be informed of the risks, and institutional review boards of competent professionals must approve the testing processes. The FDA may stop testing at any point in the process if it deems the drug too risky.

If a drug shows promise in the first phase, it moves into phase-two trials, which are conducted on patients. These trials use a small number of patients, not more than a few hundred, and are controlled—meaning that the treated patients are compared with a similar group that is not treated. The trials are closely monitored for effectiveness and safety. Only if a drug shows promise for effective treatment without harmful side effects does it move into phase three. In the third phase, the drug is usually tested in a few thousand patients to weigh the benefits against the risks to a general population.

If the benefits-to-risk ratio is acceptable, the testing firm applies to the FDA to approve the drug for sale either through prescription or over the counter. The FDA estimates that on average it takes 7 years to complete clinical trials and only about 20 percent of the drugs that enter clinical trials are approved. It takes another 18 months for the agency to review the application and approve a new drug.

Testing continues even after the drug is on the market. Phase-four trials study the long-term effects of drugs. If the long-term effects are sufficiently harmful, a drug will be taken from the market. Vioxx, a popular medication for arthritis, was removed from the market in late 2004 after it was discovered that long-term use could damage the heart.

Comprehensive testing provides additional knowledge about drugs, but also increases their cost and decreases their availability. U.S. tests are generally more stringent than their European counterparts, which means that many new drugs become available in Europe before they do in the United States. There is an inevitable tradeoff in the length and thoroughness of testing and the drugs' cost and availability. An agency that is very cautious about introducing only the safest drugs can damage the public health by holding valuable drugs off the market for too long. National regulation also sets a single standard for risk that all must accept, despite varying circumstances and individual tolerance for risk. A dying cancer patient may be willing to accept a great deal of risk in trying a new drug, whereas a healthy young adult may be willing to accept very little risk in taking a tranquilizer. In any case, complete knowledge about the undesirable effects of drugs, especially long-term effects, is unobtainable. For example, phenothiazine tranquilizers, approved for use by the FDA in the 1950s, had been in use for a decade before clinical reports of retinal degeneration appeared. The complexity of and variations in human biochemistry make it impossible to foresee all the potential effects of drug use.

Regulation of foods and drugs is increasingly international in scope. The World Trade Organization (WTO), established in December 1994, laid down rules governing food standards for international trade. The WTO's Sanitary and Phytosanitary Provisions represent an effort to harmonize national regulations and make all food regulations transparent. Among the WTO's goals is to promote trade in food and drugs without compromising their safety—no easy task. The United States, for example, permits the production and sale of genetically modified foods because the consensus of scientific opinion regards these foods as safe. The European Union (EU), however, does not permit their import because most Europeans think they are unsafe. U.S. firms claim this is an unfair restriction on trade, since scientific evidence does not support the EU policy. Although a dispute resolution body has ruled in favor of the United States, the EU is contesting the ruling. The result is a trade dispute that will eventually be settled through the rules and procedures of the WTO, although most experts expect the United States to win. Regardless of who prevails, the more important point is that international bodies are becoming increasingly involved in setting safety standards that were once the domain of national governments.

Drugs developed in the United States and Europe are often reproduced in poorer countries without the consent of the companies that developed the drugs. This enables governments or companies in poorer countries to sell the drugs more cheaply or even give them away. For example, Brazilian firms manufacture AIDS drugs, which the government distributes free of charge to fight the spread of that disease. Although the program has succeeded in slowing the spread of AIDS, the large pharmaceutical companies that developed the drugs claim it is unsafe. This dispute will also be settled by the WTO or through international negotiations. As of early 2005, the dispute had not been resolved. Brazil still refuses to pay what American drug companies are asking, but has offered to pay a much lower licensing fee—which it is allowed to do under WTO rules. Experts say it may take some time for the dispute to be resolved. Regardless of what happens, because so many foods and drugs are traded across borders, international rules and regulations are gaining in importance.

CONCLUSION

In the sweep of human history, much progress has been made in the fight against foodborne diseases and the search for safe and efficacious drugs. In the economically developed countries, typhoid fever, botulism, chronic infections, and deficiency diseases such as pellagra are much less prevalent today than they were as recently as the nineteenth century. Many other diseases that are not food related—smallpox, polio, pneumonia, tuberculosis, malaria, hookworm, gangrene, to name a few—have also been eliminated or substantially reduced thanks to the development of drugs. The credit for this progress goes to science, technology, education, economic progress, and the practice of good hygiene. Despite the progress in improving the chances for a long and healthy life in the industrial world, there is no room for complacency toward food and drug safety.

A striking aspect of foodborne disease in the world today is the emergence of new pathogens responsible for outbreaks. In the 1950s, four bacteria—*Staphylococcus aureus*, *Salmonella*, *Clostridium botulinum* types A and B, and *Shigella*—were the main foodborne pathogens in the United States. In the 1960s, *Vibrio cholerae* non-01, *Clostridium botulinum* type E, and hepatitis A were added to the list. In the 1970s, confirmed outbreaks were caused by *Vibrio parahaemolyticus*, *Vibrio cholerae* 01, *E. coli*, *Campylobacter jejuni*, and *Vibrio vulnificus*. In the 1980s, *Listeria monocytogenes*, new strains of *E. coli*, *Salmonella entertidis*, and Norwalk viruses caused outbreaks. The discovery of new pathogenic diseases is partly due to improved detection methods, but increased travel, changes in eating habits (eating out), new production methods (raising sedentary chickens), and the remarkable ability of pathogens to adapt (as demonstrated by the HIV and SARS viruses) are also factors. Adaptability of microorganisms means the fight against foodborne pathogens will be a long-running war with no final victory.

Genetically modified food is another area of concern today. Although the transfer of genetic material from one organism to another occurs naturally in evolution, cross-breeding and especially recombining genes in the laboratory has sped the process along. The danger is that the new genes will produce toxins when combined with existing genes. So far this danger has not materialized, but only continued vigilance will keep it in check. Biotech companies and regulatory bodies carefully monitor all genetically modified foods for toxins, allergens, and other dangers.

The main areas of concern with drugs are their expense, their failure at times to cure the intended illnesses or combat the symptoms, and their side effects. As already mentioned, false leads—the many attempts at producing new drugs that fail—and stringent regulations drive up the costs of drugs. In the United States, drugs are often out of the reach of ordinary citizens without health insurance, and those with insurance are finding their premiums ever more expensive, thanks in part to rising drug prices. Insurance companies, policymakers, and others are looking for ways to lower these prices without slowing research and innovation.

Despite huge amounts of money spent on drug research and the undeniable achievements of drugs in fighting diseases, results have been disappointing in some areas. For example, many types of cancer have been stubbornly resistant to drugs. The National Cancer Society estimates that, as of the early 2000s, roughly 1.3 million Americans are diagnosed annually, and between 500,000 and 600,000 die. Finally, despite the close scrutiny drugs receive from regulators, they still cause many serious side effects. One study estimated that in U.S. hospitals, 100,000 patients die each year from adverse reactions to drugs. Adverse reactions also cause serious illness, for which the prescription is often more drugs.

Food and drug safety is an even more critical problem in the developing world. Many diseases that are minor in the developed world wreak havoc in poor countries. Each year about 17 million persons, nearly all from developing countries, contract typhoid fever, mainly from contaminated food and water. Of these, about 1 million die. Cholera, another disease spread through contaminated food and water, has swept through the developing world in a wave of epidemics. One epidemic that started in Indonesia in the 1960s spread through East Asia, India, the Soviet Union, and Iran. In 1970 cholera reached West Africa, where the disease had not been experienced for 100 years and resistance was low, resulting in a high death toll. In 1991 the epidemic struck South America, then returned to India and Pakistan in 1992, via a slightly altered bacterium.

Malaria has been all but eliminated from the industrial countries, but in the developing world 300 million cases of malaria and more than a million deaths occur each year. Ninety percent of the deaths occur in sub-Saharan Africa, mainly among children. The reason for the high death rate is primarily economic. Poor populations cannot afford the insecticides and drugs that would control the disease. The economic problem is compounded by the evolution of mosquitoes and parasites resistant to existing treatment. Likewise AIDS, whose incidence and mortality rates are declining in industrial countries, is raging in Africa. Of the nearly 3 million deaths caused by AIDS in 2003, over two-thirds were in Africa. Poverty, ignorance of the disease, and lack of affordable medicine are the main reasons Africans have not combated AIDS successfully.

Foods and drugs will never be perfectly safe, but there is reason to be optimistic that they will become safer for more people. The greatest gains are to be had among the poorer countries of the world, where technology and hygienic practices of the developed world can be gradually applied. In the richer countries, advancing science and economic progress can

be expected to produce yet more effective methods of controlling pathogens and toxins.

Jack High

REFERENCES

Bailar, John C., III, et al. *Ensuring Safe Food: From Production to Consumption.* Washington, DC: National Academy Press, 1998.

Bean, N. H., P. M. Griffin, S. Goulding, and C. B. Ivey. "Foodborne Disease Outbreaks: 5-year Summary, 1983–1987." *Morbidity Mortality Weekly Report* 39 (SS-1)(March 1, 1990): 1–23.

Bulloch, William. *The History of Bacteriology.* New York: Oxford University Press, 1938.

Coppin, Clayton, and Jack High. *The Politics of Purity.* Ann Arbor: University of Michigan Press, 1999.

de Kruif, Paul. *Microbe Hunters.* New York: Harcourt Brace, 1926.

DiMasi, J. A., R. W. Hansen, and H. G. Grabowski. "The Price of Innovation: New Estimates of Drug Development Costs." *Journal of Health Economics* 22 (2003): 151–85.

Dittmer, Paul R. *Dimensions of the Hospitality Industry.* New York: John Wiley and Sons, 2002.

Folb, Peter I. *The Safety of Medicines: Evaluation and Prediction.* Berlin: Springer Verlag, 1980.

Hennessy, T. W., et al. "A National Outbreak of *Salmonella entertidis* Infections from Ice Cream." *New England Journal of Medicine* 334 (May 16, 1996): 1281–86.

Hill, Walter E., and Karen C. Jinneman. "Principles and Applications of Genetic Techniques for Detection, Identification, and Subtyping of Food-Associated Pathegenic Microorganisms." In *The Microbiological Safety and Quality of Food, 1813–1851,* ed. Barbara Lund et al. Baltimore: CTI Publications, 2000.

Hoffmann, Sandra, and Michael R. Taylor, eds. *Toward Safer Food: Perspectives on Risk and Priority Setting.* Washington, DC: Resources for the Future, 2004.

Hytt, P. B., and P. B Hutt, II. "A History of Government Regulation of Adulteration and Misbranding of Food." *Food, Drug, Cosmetic Law Journal* 39 (1984): 2–73.

Kerr, K. G., and R. W. Lacey. "Why Do We Still Get Epidemics?" In *Fifty Years of Antimicrobials: Past Perspectives and Future Trends,* ed. P. A. Hunter, G. K Darby, and N. J. Russell, 179–203. Cambridge: Cambridge University Press, 1995.

Kessler, David A., et al. "The Safety of Foods Developed by Biotechnology." *Science* 256 (1992): 1747–49.

Kiple, Kenneth, ed. *The Cambridge World History of Human Disease.* Cambridge: Cambridge University Press, 1993.

Kiple, Kenneth F., and Kriemhild C. Ornelas, eds. *The Cambridge World History of Food.* 2 vols. Cambridge: Cambridge University Press, 2000.

Lelieveld, Huub L.M. "Hygenic Design of Factories and Equipment." In *The Microbiological Safety and Quality of Food: 1656–1690*, ed. Barbara Lund et al. Gaithersburg, MD: Aspen, 2000.

Lloyd, W. Eugene, ed. *Safety Evaluation of Drugs and Chemicals*. New York: Hemisphere, 1986.

Nestlee, Marion. *Safe Food: Bacteria, Biotechnology, and Bioterrorism*. Berkeley: University of California Press, 2003.

Pearson, Kathy L. "Nutrition and the Early Medieval Diet." *Speculum* 72 (January 1997): 1–32.

Pennington, T. Hugh. *When Food Kills: BSE, E. coli, and Disaster Science*. New York: Oxford University Press, 2003.

Porter, Roy. *The Cambridge Illustrated History of Medicine*. Cambridge: Cambridge University Press, 1996.

Ray, Bibek. *Fundamental Food Microbiology*. New York: CRC, 1996.

Schlosser, Eric. *Fast Food Nation: The Dark Side of the All-American Meal*. Boston: Houghton Mifflin, 2001.

Unnevehr, Laurian, and Nancy Hirschorn. *Food Safety Issues in the Developing World*. Washington, DC: World Bank, 2000.

Weatherall, Miles. *In Search of a Cure: A History of Pharmaceutical Discovery*. New York: Oxford University Press, 1990.

Yount, Lisa. *Biotechnology and Genetic Engineering*. New York: Facts on File, 2000.

WEB SITES

Centers for Disease Control: www.cdc.gov
U.S. Department of Agriculture: www.usda.gov
World Health Organization: www.who.org
World Trade Organization: www.wto.org

GLOSSARY

Bacteria. The plural of bacterium, a one-celled organism that has no chlorophyll and multiplies by simple division. Bacteria assume three main shapes—spherical (cocci), rodlike (bacilli), and spiral (spirilla). Bacteria are responsible for many diseases, including Lyme disease, pneumonia, tuberculosis, and syphilis.

Botulism. A paralytic disease caused by toxins of *Clostridium botulinum*. The poisoning results mainly from improper home canning and can be fatal even in small doses.

Bovine spongiform encephalopathy (BSE). Popularly known as mad cow disease, BSE is caused by a virus similar to that which causes scrapie in sheep. BSE may be transmissible to humans through food in the form of Creutzfeld-Jakob disease, a deadly brain infection.

Campylobacteriosis. An infection of the intestinal tract caused by *Campylobacter coli* and *Campylobacter jejuni*, bacteria transmitted to humans through meat and poultry. It is the most common cause of infective diarrhea in developed countries.

Cholera. An acute bacterial infection caused by *Vibrio cholerae*, transmitted through food and water, and characterized by diarrhea, vomiting, and delirium.

Coliform. Shortened form of coliform bacillus, a rod-shaped bacterium found in the colon and fecal matter. A high coliform count in water means that it is unsafe to drink. An acceptable coliform count is 500 per hundred milliliters; the Ganges River in India has a coliform count of more than 150 million per hundred milliliters.

Drug. Any substance used as a medicine or an ingredient in a medicine.

Food. Any substance taken in by a plant or animal that enables it to live and grow. In this broad definition, water is considered a food; a narrower definition distinguishes solid food from drink.

Genetic engineering. The intentional alteration of genes or transfer of genes from one organism to another. Genetic engineering is commonly used to produce pest-resistant crops for humans and other animals. It is also used to alter the nutritional characteristics of crops, as in golden rice, which is rice that contains beta-carotene (vitamin A).

Mad cow disease. *See* Bovine spongiform encephalopathy (BSE).

Pellagra. A disease caused by a deficiency of niacin (vitamin B_6) and characterized by diarrhea, dermatitis, dementia, and, if not treated, death. Associated with a maize diet. With mortality rates of 70 percent, the disease caused widespread misery and death in Europe and America between 1730 and 1930.

Poison. A substance that causes illness or death when taken in small quantities.

Salmonellosis. A disease caused by any of the *Salmonella* bacteria. It is usually transmitted through eggs and meat that have been inadequately cooked. Characterized by vomiting and diarrhea and is generally self-limiting.

Scurvy. A chronic disease caused by lack of ascorbic acid (vitamin C) and characterized by weakness, anemia, and bleeding from the mucous membranes

Typhoid fever. A disease caused by *Salmonella typhi*, a bacterium that spreads from human to human through contaminated water or food. The disease is endemic in countries such as India, with poor facilities for sanitation.

Vaccination. The introduction of dead bacteria into the body to produce immunity to a disease. Edward Jenner used cowpox to vaccinate against smallpox.

Virus. An extremely small organism, or protein, that causes

disease. Smallpox and various strains of influenza are caused by viruses.

Vitamin. Any of various complex organic compounds necessary to the healthy functioning of the body but which the body does not produce in sufficient quantities to maintain health. Vitamins must be obtained from foods or supplements.

DOCUMENTS

Document 1. Excerpts from the Pure Food and Drugs Act, 1906

Numerous food and drug safety bills were introduced into Congress in the early 1900s, but all were defeated by industry lobbyists. Then, in 1906, muckraking journalist Upton Sinclair published his best-selling novel, The Jungle, *exposing the poor hygienic conditions in the nation's meatpacking industry. The uproar over the book goaded Congress into finally passing the Pure Food and Drugs Act in 1906. Along with the Meat Inspection Act of the same year, the legislation enacted the nation's first systematic federal regulations of food and drug safety.*

PURE FOOD AND DRUGS ACT OF 1906

AN ACT for preventing the manufacture, sale, or transportation of adulterated or misbranded or poisonous or deleterious foods, drugs, medicines, and liquors, and for regulating traffic therein, and for other purposes.

Be it enacted by the Senate and House of Representatives of the United States of America in Congress assembled,

SEC. 1. MANUFACTURE OF ADULTERATED FOODS OR DRUGS.
That it shall be unlawful for any person to manufacture within any Territory or the District of Columbia any article of food or drug which is adulterated or misbranded, within the meaning of this Act;

SEC. 2. INTERSTATE COMMERCE OF ADULTERATED GOODS.
That the introduction into any State or Territory or the District of Columbia from any other State or Territory or the District of Columbia, or from any foreign country, or shipment to any foreign country of any article of food or drugs which is adulterated or misbranded, within the meaning of this Act, is hereby prohibited.

SEC. 4. CHEMICAL EXAMINATIONS.
That the examinations of specimens of foods and drugs

shall be made in the Bureau of Chemistry of the Department of Agriculture, or under the direction and supervision of such Bureau, for the purpose of determining from such examinations whether such articles are adulterated or misbranded within the meaning of this Act.

SEC. 6. DEFINITIONS.
That the term "drug," as used in this Act, shall include all medicines and preparations recognized in the United States Pharmacopoeia or National Formulary for internal or external use, and any substance or mixture of substances intended to be used for the cure, mitigation, or prevention of disease of either man or other animals. The term "food," as used herein, shall include all articles used for food, drink, confectionery, or condiment by man or other animals, whether simple, mixed, or compound.

SEC. 7. ADULTERATIONS.
That for the purposes of this Act an article Shall be deemed to be adulterated:

IN CASE OF DRUGS:
FIRST. If, when a drug is sold under or by a name recognized in the United States Pharmacopoeia or National Formulary, it differs from the standard of strength, quality, or purity, as determined by the test laid down in the United States Pharmacopoeia or National Formulary official at the time of investigation.
SECOND. If its strength or purity fall below the professed standard or quality under which it is sold.

IN THE CASE OF FOOD:
FIRST. If any substance has been mixed and packed with it so as to reduce or lower or injuriously affect its quality or strength.
SECOND. If any substance has been substituted wholly or in part for the article.

SEC. 8. MISBRANDING.
That the term "misbranded," as used herein, shall apply to all drugs, or articles of food, or articles which enter into the composition of food, the package or label of which

shall bear any statement, design, or device regarding such article, or the ingredients or substances contained therein which shall be false or misleading in any particular, and to any food or drug product which is falsely branded as to the State, Territory, or country in which it is manufactured or produced.

SEC. 13. EFFECTIVE DATE.
That this Act shall be in force and effect from and after the first day of January, nineteen hundred and seven.

APPROVED, JUNE 30, 1906.

Source: The Statutes at Large of the United States of America, vol. XXXIV, Part I. Washington, DC: Government Printing Office.

Document 2. Excerpts from the World Trade Organization Agreement on the Application of Sanitary and Phytosanitary Measures, 1995

In 1995, the World Trade Organization adopted a measure on food safety called the WTO Agreement on the Application of Sanitary and Phytosanitary Measures (SPS Agreement). The accord was an attempt to prevent national food regulation from hindering international trade. In May 2003, the United States complained to the dispute settlement body that the European Union's refusal to admit genetically modified foods into EU nations violated the SPS Agreement.

Members,

Reaffirming that no Member should be prevented from adopting or enforcing measures necessary to protect human, animal or plant life or health, subject to the requirement that these measures are not applied in a manner which would constitute a means of arbitrary or unjustifiable discrimination between Members where the same conditions prevail or a disguised restriction on international trade;

Desiring to improve the human health, animal health and phytosanitary situation in all Members;

Noting that sanitary and phytosanitary measures are often applied on the basis of bilateral agreements or protocols;

Desiring the establishment of a multilateral framework of rules and disciplines to guide the development, adoption and enforcement of sanitary and phytosanitary measures in order to minimize their negative effects on trade;

Recognizing the important contribution that international standards, guidelines and recommendations can make in this regard;

Desiring to further the use of harmonized sanitary and phytosanitary measures between Members, on the basis of international standards, guidelines and recommendations developed by the relevant international organizations, including the Codex Alimentarius Commission, the International Office of Epizootics, and the relevant international and regional organizations operating within the framework of the International Plant Protection Convention, without requiring Members to change their appropriate level of protection of human, animal or plant life or health;

Recognizing that developing country Members may encounter special difficulties in complying with the sanitary or phytosanitary measures of importing Members, and as a consequence in access to markets, and also in the formulation and application of sanitary or phytosanitary measures in their own territories, and desiring to assist them in their endeavours in this regard;

Desiring therefore to elaborate rules for the application of the provisions of GATT 1994 which relate to the use of sanitary or phytosanitary measures, in particular the provisions of Article XX(b) (*1*);

Hereby agree as follows:

Article 1: General Provisions
1. This Agreement applies to all sanitary and phytosanitary measures which may, directly or indirectly, affect international trade. Such measures shall be developed and applied in accordance with the provisions of this Agreement.

Article 2: Basic Rights and Obligations
2. Members shall ensure that their sanitary and phytosanitary measures do not arbitrarily or unjustifiably discriminate between Members where identical or similar conditions prevail, including between their own territory and that of other Members. Sanitary and phytosanitary measures shall not be applied in a manner which would constitute a disguised restriction on international trade.

Article 3: Harmonization
1. To harmonize sanitary and phytosanitary measures on as wide a basis as possible, Members shall base their sanitary or phytosanitary measures on international standards, guidelines or recommendations. . . .

Article 4: Equivalence
1. Members shall accept the sanitary or phytosanitary measures of other Members as equivalent, even if these measures differ from their own or from those used by other Members trading in the same product, if the exporting Member objectively demonstrates to the importing Member that its measures achieve the importing Member's appropriate level of sanitary or phytosanitary protection. For this purpose, reasonable access shall be given, upon request, to the importing Member for inspection, testing and other relevant procedures.

Article 5: Assessment of Risk

1. Members shall ensure that their sanitary or phytosanitary measures are based on an assessment, as appropriate to the circumstances, of the risks to human, animal or plant life or health, taking into account risk assessment techniques developed by the relevant international organizations.

2. In the assessment of risks, Members shall take into account available scientific evidence; relevant processes and production methods; relevant inspection, sampling and testing methods; prevalence of specific diseases or pests; existence of pest—or disease—free areas; relevant ecological and environmental conditions; and quarantine or other treatment.

Article 11: Consultations and Dispute Settlement

2. In a dispute under this Agreement involving scientific or technical issues, a panel should seek advice from experts chosen by the panel in consultation with the parties to the dispute. To this end, the panel may, when it deems it appropriate, establish an advisory technical experts group, or consult the relevant international organizations, at the request of either party to the dispute or on its own initiative.

Source: World Trade Organization.

FOSTER CARE

Foster parents are adults licensed by the government—usually the state or county—to provide temporary homes for children whose biological parents are unable or unwilling to care for them. The period of time in which foster parents care for these children may be as short as a few months or extend over several years. They are usually, but not always, compensated by the government for some or all of the costs of raising these children.

Foster care, sometimes referred to as substitute care, takes place in foster family homes, boarding homes, institutional homes, or group homes when more than one foster child is being cared for. Foster care has a number of variants. Emergency foster usually occurs for very short periods when the child's well-being is immediately threatened; kinship foster care involves foster parents who are related to the child; and therapeutic foster care involves those trained to provide psychological or medical help for foster children who need such services.

HISTORY

The Elizabethan poor laws of the sixteenth century provided for outplacing of poor children whose families could not afford the expense of raising them. They were placed with families and taught a trade or profession, with the provision that the child be given food, clothing, and other necessities of life. These laws also set the principle of government responsibility for poor families, a legacy that continues today.

In Colonial Virginia, vestries (local church organizing bodies) were responsible for the poor, under the general supervision of the county courts. Vestries were empowered to indenture orphans and pauper children and to collect taxes for this purpose. Indentures were set periods of time, usually until the child reached maturity, during which the holder of the indenture, or contract, could use the child's labor. In return, he or she provided for the child's well-being and education. If the orphan did not have adequate inheritance to afford an education, the law required that he or she be bound out until age 21 to learn a manual trade. The law, as early as 1642, was enforced by the orphan's court, especially constituted for this purpose. Children of parents considered immoral or of "dissolute character" were subsequently bound out, or indentured, in keeping with the law of the day.

The history of orphan and pauper child outplacement in the United States has oscillated between the use of institutions (progressing from almshouses and orphan asylums to the residential treatment facilities of today) and foster home placement. Orphaned children without relatives to care for them in the early nineteenth century might be bound over to institutions called orphan asylums, auctioned into service, or incarcerated in almshouses until old enough to be indentured. Even then, institutional and foster care were closely related. Orphaned infants were, of necessity, placed in foster homes with wet nurses until weaned; as youths, they were placed in foster homes to do menial work or learn a trade. As early as the 1860s, the state of Massachusetts pioneered the practice of paying foster parents for the maintenance of children who would otherwise be institutionalized and were too young to be indentured.

The Civil War and the rapid influx of immigrants during the mid-nineteenth century left a disturbing number of orphans and destitute children wandering the country roads and city streets. Concerned citizens urged governments and philanthropic organizations to find ways to care for them. Individuals and charitable organizations known collectively as "child savers" led the movement that grew out of this concern. This also marked the beginning of conflict between proponents of institutional care and those favoring foster home placement.

The so-called father of the child savers was Charles

CHRONOLOGY

1601   Elizabethan Poor Law is enacted in England. The law established government responsibility for the poor, including children. It also defined who was eligible for service, thereby establishing residency requirements to receive aid.

1646   An act empowered the county justices in Virginia to bind out children of parents considered unfit to raise them. Binding out is synonymous with indenturing, an act of government, in contrast to apprenticing, an arrangement between the child's parents and the person to whom the child was apprenticed.

1853   Charles Loring Brace founds the New York Children's Aid Society and lays the groundwork for the "orphan trains" that transported thousands of New York City street children to the Midwest.

1886   Charles Birtwell becomes director of the Boston Children's Aid Society. During his tenure at the society, he refocused foster care on the needs of the child, not the foster family.

1909   First White House Conference on Children is held. Participants declared every child is entitled to a secure and loving home.

1912   The U.S. Children's Bureau is established by an act of Congress.

1921   The Sheppard-Towner Act is passed by Congress. The legislation authorized federal aid to states for maternity, child health, and welfare programs. The Supreme Court ruled the act unconstitutional in 1922.

1935   Social Security Act is enacted by Congress. This landmark social welfare legislation established Title V Child Welfare Services, aimed at rural children, and Aid to Families with Dependent Children.

1959   Henry Maas and Richard Engler publish *Children in Need of Homes*, which becomes the child advocate's handbook for reforming the foster care system.

1974   The Oregon and Alameda Projects identify permanency planning as the tool for reforming the foster care system.

1978   Indian Child Welfare Act is enacted by Congress, giving tribal councils jurisdiction and control over Native American children and their placements with foster and adoptive families.

1980   Adoption Assistance and Child Welfare Act introduces permanency planning and reasonable efforts concepts into law. Every child entering foster care would have a plan for return home, adoption, or long-term foster care, with judicial oversight. Agencies were directed to make reasonable efforts to return children to their biological parents, after which the agency could terminate parental rights.

1993   The Family Preservation and Family Support Program (PL 103–66) is enacted, giving child welfare agencies incentives to provide services to support biological families and reunify foster children with them. This act is renamed the Adoption and Safe Families Act on reauthorization in 1997.

1996   Personal Responsibility and Work Opportunity Reconciliation Act (PL 104–193), known as welfare reform, is enacted. This act abolished the 60-year-old Aid to Families with Dependent Children program, setting time limits for receipt of aid, and requiring that recipients find work. Its effects on the child welfare system remain undocumented, but are expected to be significant during difficult economic times.

1997   As part of its reauthorization, the Family Preservation and Family Support Program is renamed the Promoting Safe and Stable Families program.

1999   The Foster Care Independence Act (PL 106–169) is enacted, creating incentives for states to provide direct assistance to children aging out of the foster care system.

2002   The Promoting Safe and Stable Families Amendments are signed into law, extending the PSSF program through 2006 while creating a new state grant program to provide educational and training vouchers for youths as they grow too old for foster care.

2004   A Pew Charitable Trust study calls for an overhaul of the nation's foster care program, with greater accountability of courts and child welfare agencies, as well as more flexibility for the states to design programs to meet their particular needs and more reliable federal funding.

Loring Brace, a Protestant minister and founder of New York Children's Aid Society. Brace is known for settling thousands of the New York City children in Midwestern communities, principally in Indiana, Illinois, Iowa, Michigan, and Minnesota. Brace's Free Home Movement was both acclaimed and criticized for transporting children by train from the streets of New York to small towns in the Midwest, where they were placed in the care of farmers at auctions.

Criticisms leveled at the Free Home Movement varied from concern about the speed with which children were placed, the lack of supervision of children placed with foster families, and the lack of screening and investigation of foster families, to concerns that many of the children were incorrigibles who would run from their foster families, becoming wards of the state. Several persons in a position to observe testified against such charges; however, even these individuals were concerned about the looseness of the process and the potential for abuse of children.

It was later found that not all of the children were orphans. Brace's children included those voluntarily relinquished by impoverished families, resulting in parents being permanently separated from their children. Many of the immigrant children were Catholic or Jewish, and placing them in Protestant homes created a backlash among religious groups that some suggest sparked the creation of strong sectarian agencies that continue to provide child welfare services to this day.

The harsh reality of society's treatment of homeless children intensified discussions among charity professionals over the most prudent placement choices: foster family homes or orphanages. Beginning with Brace's Free Home Movement, one side argued the absolute superiority of foster families, while others argued the advantages of professionally operated institutions. Charles Birtwell, director of the Boston Children's Aid Society from 1886 to 1911, is credited with changing the course of foster care; he claimed each child is unique and the placement should fit the child—not the reverse.

Birtwell's new ideas strongly influenced the institutions versus foster care debate, which settled a century later on the general view that young children should be placed with families, and juveniles with behavioral problems should be placed in group homes and institutions. Today, child welfare agencies are pressured to use foster families and adoption as alternatives to institutional placement for all but the most difficult-to-place children, generally juveniles with emotional and behavioral problems or severely handicapping conditions.

In 1959, Henry Maas and Richard Engler published the controversial work, *Children in Need of Parents*, detailing problems in the foster care system. The book caused a stir among professionals and child advocates with its convincing claims that foster care had multiple harmful effects, particularly on young children. Foster care came increasingly under attack as detractors argued that the money states paid to keep children in substitute care could easily be spent to rehabilitate their families so they could remain at home. A series of research studies attempted to determine whether children were indeed harmed by substitute care, but most were inconclusive because of the research methods used.

Critics maintained that foster care was little more than a revolving door, that children were suffering emotional and psychological damage from repeated placements, and that the family was the best resource for its own children. Foster care "drift" (placement without a plan, for an indeterminate time) became the principal issue driving child welfare advocates to press for legislation limiting the time a child could remain in foster care without a specific plan for the future. The antidote to foster care drift was permanency planning, which subsequently became the cornerstone of seminal child welfare legislation, the Adoption Assistance and Child Welfare Act of 1980. The goal of permanency planning is to develop a plan, at the time the child is placed in substitute care, that clearly outlines the objectives for either returning the child to his or her parents, or, if that is not feasible, terminating parental rights as a precursor to adoption.

Currently, child welfare agencies seeking substitute homes for dependent children are encouraged to place them first with family members ("kinship placements"), then family foster homes, followed by group homes and institutions, in order of their restrictiveness and consideration of the child's age. Return to the biological family or, if not feasible, adoption are the preferred outcomes for foster children in America today. Such choices are tempered by the availability of placement options for children with difficult physical, emotional, and behavioral problems that, in many cases, are the result of abuse and neglect by a biological parent. Children exposed as fetuses to controlled substances or born with HIV/AIDS or fetal alcohol syndrome are among the great challenges foster agencies now face.

FOSTER CARE IN THE TWENTY-FIRST CENTURY

Foster parenting has had different meanings over time as its role has evolved into a contractual relationship with an agency of the state. Under institutional sponsorship, foster parents are surrogates for biological parents who are unable to, or prohibited by the court from, parenting their child. Not employees per se of the agency that licenses and supervises them, the foster family enters into an agreement that may be terminated by either party with minimal notice. Typically, a foster family is licensed to parent a specific number of children and may foster several children who are or are not biologically related to each other.

Some families make a lifetime commitment to foster parenting; others participate for only short periods of time. Agency contractual arrangements give no guarantee that a child will remain with a foster family for an extended period of time. Some children regularly come and go while others remain in one foster family home until they reach the age of emancipation. Various program initiatives have recently been designed to increase the stability of foster care placements and help children through the difficult transitions between placement and reunification. Among these are kinship placements and involving foster parents in working with the child's family toward reunification.

So-called subsidized guardianship and "fost-adopt" families have also found favor with child welfare agencies. Agencies that train and supervise foster families, both public and private, routinely enlist relatives of dependent children as foster families, but such kinship foster care has become more common in recent years. In most jurisdictions, adult relatives must undergo the same licensure that unrelated families do. This entails some period of training, criminal background checks, interviews with neighbors, friends and other family members, and employers, and home visits by an agency social worker to ensure the foster children will be living in a safe environment. The agency may or may not provide a stipend to kinship families, although this is generally encouraged.

Subsidized guardianship is an option for foster parents who wish to make a legal commitment to a child short of adoption. The agency pays the guardian a board rate much the same as with conventional foster care to help with child-rearing expenses; however, supervision of the foster family and child is no longer required. This is an attractive option for older children who do not wish to be adopted.

Fost-adopt homes are used when concurrent planning occurs. In this situation, the foster parents understand that reasonable efforts will be made to reunify the child with the legal family; however, if reunification becomes infeasible, the foster family agrees to adopt the child.

LEGISLATION

Until 1961, the U.S. federal government was minimally involved in funding foster care. Although not specifically addressing foster care, Title V §521 of the Social Security Act of 1935, Child Welfare Services, provided funding for homeless, dependent, and neglected children living predominantly in rural areas, through state plans approved by the U.S. Children's Bureau, then in the Department of Labor. In 1967, the law was changed to Title IV-B, Child Welfare Services. Congress authorized increased funding several years in the 1970s, encouraging the states to develop supportive, protective, and preventive services.

In 1961, Congress approved two temporary amendments creating Title IV-A of the Social Security Act. The Fleming Rule, as it was known, authorized 14 months of Aid to Dependent Children (ADC) funds for foster care when the child was removed from an unsuitable home, and a 1-year anti-recession measure providing matching federal funds to states for foster care. In 1962, ADC became Aid to Families with Dependent Children (AFDC), which focused on getting families off welfare. Also that year, Congress authorized prolonging the Fleming Rule indefinitely.

Another in the patchwork of foster care–related legislation was Title XX of the Social Security Act, enacted in 1974. This measure provided funding for social services to children and low-income families, including those on AFDC and Supplemental Security Income (SSI). It also stressed local-level planning and gave local agencies more discretion in using Title XX money. In 1981, however, the federal matching funds for social services were combined into a block grant to the states as part of the Omnibus Budget Reconciliation Act, and the funds for social services were significantly reduced.

A clear antifamily bias had crept into foster family care over the years. This bias was fueled by a number of elements in the child welfare system, includ-

Table 1. Total Federal Foster Care Expenditures, Title IV-E, Fiscal Year 1999–2000

Expenditure	Dollars (in millions)*
Maintenance payments	$1,955.38
Child placement services & administration	$1,751.92
Statewide automated child welfare information system (SACWIS)	$96.81
Training	$199.94
Total	$4,003.99

* Estimated dollars.
Source: Administration for Children and Families, Child Welfare League of America.

Table 2. Number of Children in Foster Care

Fiscal year	Entering FC during year	Exiting FC during year	In care last day of year
1999	289,721	247,181	565,265
2000	287,054	267,453	543,953
2001	295,194	268,720	542,764
2002	301,783	277,370	533,897
2003	297,308	281,472	523,085

Source: Administration for Children and Families, U.S. Department of Health and Human Services.

ing the overspecialization of foster care practices that led to supplanting the biological family rather than supporting its reunification. Children were remaining in foster care for longer and longer periods of time, and the number of children entering foster care was increasing significantly. Child advocates began pressuring for Congress to pass child welfare legislation to counteract these trends.

The result was the Adoption Assistance and Child Welfare Act of 1980. This legislation transferred Title IV-A to Title IV-E. The new title authorized foster care maintenance funding for AFDC and non-AFDC eligible children, and funding for preventive and restorative services. In addition, the law introduced several new concepts in child welfare, including permanency planning and "reasonable efforts." Reiterating the intention to make foster care temporary, it set time limits on care, including judicial oversight.

This seminal child welfare legislation set a new course for foster care that emphasized permanency planning goals for return home, adoption, long-term foster care, or emancipation. Reasonable efforts were to be made to return the child to his or her parents within a realistic time frame, after which the agency could proceed to terminate parental rights. The act also amended the Title IV-B Child Welfare Services provisions of the Social Security Act, changing the federal reimbursement for foster care and increasing the funding for prevention and reunification services.

The new law was followed by a decline in the number of children in foster care; the drop-off was short-lived, however, for a number of reasons. Although children did return home more rapidly under the new law, they also returned to foster care more often. The economy was stagnating, and the effects of crack cocaine and HIV/AIDS were alarming. As a result of these and other factors, the number of children coming into substitute care again began to increase.

In the 1990s, a series of laws were enacted by Congress to support biological, foster, and adoptive families. The first of these was the Family Preservation and Family Support Program, which became Part 2 of Title IV-B of the Social Security Act. The legislation was reauthorized in 1997, renamed Promoting Safe and Stable Families, and attached to the Adoption and Safe Families Act of 1997. Under this measure, states were required to allocate significant funds for family support, family preservation, family reunification, and adoption.

Congress enacted the Personal Responsibility and Work Opportunity Reconciliation Act, popularly known as welfare reform, in 1996. Although it does not directly address foster care, the act had implications for families vulnerable to child placement given the time limitations imposed on receiving benefits. AFDC was replaced with Temporary Assistance for Needy Families (TANF), a state-administered block grant. Income assistance under TANF is time-limited, unlike that under AFDC, leaving families potentially vulnerable to collapse after benefits are terminated. At this writing, empirical evidence is not sufficient to suggest that limiting benefits will increase foster care placements, but scholars in the field anticipate that problems would occur with a prolonged economic downturn or significant increase in unemployment.

The Adoption and Safe Families Act of 1997, intended to ensure the safety of children in foster care and promote adoption, refines aspects of the 1980 legislation, including its "reasonable efforts" provisions and time lines for foster care review (permanency planning). Adoptions have increased since the law's enactment, as have the number of children in foster care waiting to be adopted. The question remains: Are enough families willing to adopt children with family histories of controlled substance abuse or HIV/AIDS, especially when many have significant emotional and developmental problems?

Table 3. Age, Race, and Gender of Children in Foster Care, 2003

Category	Number	Percentage
Age		
<1	24,290	5.0
1–5	116,801	22.0
6–10	128,946	24.0
11–15	158,290	30.0
16–18	92,091	17.0
19+	10,321	2.0
Missing data	766	0.1
Race/Ethnicity		
White	243,796	49.4
Black	170,596	34.6
American Indian/Alaska Native	10,234	2.1
Asian-Pacific/Islander	4,763	1.0
Unknown	19,378	3.9
Multiple	13,313	2.7
Missing data	19,849	4.0
Other	11,568	2.3
Total	493,497	100.0
Hispanic	75,869	15.4
Non-Hispanic	321,875	65.2
Undetermined	70,029	14.2
Missing data	25,724	5.2
Gender		
Male	258,746	52.4
Female	234,572	47.6
Missing data	179	

Source: Child Welfare League of America.

Another important piece of legislation in this area is the Foster Care Independence Act of 1999. This measure addresses the preparation of foster children for emancipation from their foster families and the foster care system. It requires that states provide self-sufficiency services to foster children aged 18 to 21 years old. Before this law, there was no systematic effort to prepare children for independence when the state was no longer obligated to provide for them. In most jurisdictions, the age of legal emancipation is 18, although some agencies provide for extended dependency for developmentally disabled foster children.

LEGISLATION AFFECTING SPECIFIC POPULATIONS

Title 25 § 1901 U.S.C. recognizes "the special relationship between the United States and the Indian tribes and their members and the Federal responsibility to Indian people." The Indian Child Welfare Act, enacted in 1978, recognized that removing chil-

Figure 1. Permanency Plans for Children in Foster Care, 2003

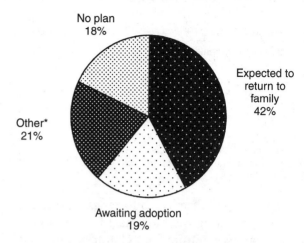

*Includes plans of child, in consultation with child welfare agencies or courts, for living with relatives, staying in long-term foster care, emancipation, or guardianship.
Source: Adapted from data on the Child Welfare League of America Web site, www.cwla.org.

dren of Native Americans from their parents for placement in non-Native American foster and adoptive homes and institutions endangered their cultural heritage. The law restored jurisdiction and control over their children to tribal authorities who have sole discretion regarding their disposition.

The Howard M. Metzenbaum Multiethnic Placement Act of 1994 prohibits discrimination in selecting foster and adoptive families for children of minority races and ethnic groups. It also seeks to ensure that agencies actively recruit potential foster and adoptive parents who reflect the racial and ethnic diversity of the children needing placement.

CONCLUSION

According to 2003 data from the Children's Defense Fund, a total of 581,000 children were part of the U.S. foster care system, 127,000 of whom were waiting for adoptive families. It is widely acknowledged that the U.S. foster care system is in trouble, but there is no consensus on remedies. Public child welfare agencies are understaffed and underfunded. Caseworkers do not have enough time to carefully supervise the children and families on their caseloads and must rely on the good will and good intentions of foster families to act responsibly on behalf of the children in their care. While it is fair to say many foster families fulfill these responsibilities, we cannot know the effects on children of those who do not; nor do we know the emotional and physical toll on children of moving from placement to placement, or the effects such moves will have on the child's future. In many respects, the circumstances of children in family foster care have not changed significantly over the last hundred years.

Janet R. Hutchinson

REFERENCES

Ashby, LeRoy. *Saving the Waifs: Reformers and Dependent Children, 1890–1917*. Philadelphia: Temple University Press, 1984.

———. *Endangered Children: Dependency, Neglect, and Abuse in American History*. New York: Twayne, 1997.

Barbell, Kathy, and Madelyn Freundlich. *Foster Care Today*. Washington, DC: Casey Family Programs, 2001.

Barbell, Kathy, and Lois Wright. *Family Foster Care in the Next Century*. New Brunswick, NJ: Transaction, 2001.

Barth, Richard P. *From Child Abuse to Permanency Planning: Child Welfare Services Pathways and Placements*. New York: Aldine de Gruyter, 1994.

Bartholet, Elizabeth. *Nobody's Children: Abuse and Neglect, Foster Drift, and the Adoption Alternative*. Boston: Beacon, 1999.

Bremner, Robert H. "Introduction, in Placing Out Children in the West." In *Children and Youth: Social Problems and Social Policy*, ed. Robert H. Bremner. New York: Arno, 1974.

Curtis, Patrick A., Dale Grady, Jr., and Joshua C. Kendall. *The Foster Care Crisis: Translating Research into Policy and Practice*. Lincoln: University of Nebraska Press in association with the Child Welfare League of America, 1999.

Duquette, Donald N., and Mark Hardin. *Guidelines for Public Policy and State Legislation Governing Permanence for Children*. Washington, DC: Administration for Children and Families, Administration for Children, Youth and Families, Children's Bureau, DHHS, 1999.

Fanshel, David, Stephen J. Finch, and John F. Grundy. *Foster Children in Life Course Perspectives*. New York: Columbia University Press, 1990.

Fein, Edith, Anthony N. Maluccio, and Miriam P. Kluger. *No More Partings: An Examination of Long-Term Foster Family Care*. Washington, DC: Child Welfare League of America, 1990.

Goldstein, Joseph. *The Best Interests of the Child: The Least Detrimental Alternative*. New York: Free Press, 1996.

Guerney, Louise F. "The Effectiveness of Foster Care as Supplementary Parenting." In *Child Nurturance: Volume 2, Patterns of Supplementary Parenting*, ed. Marjorie J. Kostelnik, Albert I. Rabin, Lillian A. Phenice, and Anne K. Soderman. New York: Plenum, 1982.

Hart, Hastings H. "Placing Out Children in the West, 1884." In *Children and Youth: Social Problems and Social Policy*, ed. Robert H. Bremner. New York: Arno, 1974.

Heger, Rebecca I., and Maria Scannapieco, eds. *Kinship Foster Care: Policy, Practice, and Research*. New York: Oxford University Press, 1999.

Kadushin, Alfred, and Judith A. Martin. *Child Welfare Services*. 4th ed. New York: Macmillan, 1988.

Kagan, Richard. *Turmoil to Turning Points: Building Hope for Children in Crisis Placements*. New York: Norton, 1996.

Maas, Henry S., and Richard E. Engler. *Children in Need of Parents*. New York: Columbia University Press, 1959.

Pelton, Leroy H. *The Reasons of Poverty: A Critical Analysis of the Public Child Welfare System in the United States*. New York: Praeger, 1989.

Pine, Barbara A., Robin Warsh, and Anthony N. Maluccio, eds. *Together Again: Family Reunification in Foster Care*. Washington, DC: Child Welfare League of America, 1993.

Tyler, Lyon G. "Education in Colonial Virginia: Part I, Poor Children and Orphans." *William and Mary Quarterly Historical Magazine 5*, 4 (April 1897): 219–23.

Wolins, Martin, and Irving Piliavin. *Institution or Foster Family: A Century of Debate*. New York: Child Welfare League of America, 1965.

WEB SITES

Administration for Children and Families: www.acf.dhhs.gov

Casey National Center for Resource Family Support: www.casey.org/cnc

Child Welfare League of America: www.cwla.org

Children's Bureau, Administration for Children, Youth and Families, Department of Health and Human Services: www.acf.hhs.gov/programs/cb

Children's Defense Fund: www.cdfactioncouncil.org

National Foster Parent Association, Inc.: www.nfpainc.org

GLOSSARY

Adoption. Legally taking another person's child as one's own.

Almshouse. An institution for housing the poor.

Boarding home. A home to which an agency or family pays a sum of money for the care of a dependent child.

Child savers. Individuals and organizations in the late nineteenth and early twentieth centuries that were dedicated to "saving" children from the vicissitudes of poverty and immorality.

Children's Bureau. Established by act of Congress in 1911, the Children's Bureau remains an advocate in the federal government for child welfare issues. It is part of the Administration for Children and Families, which is part of the Administration for Children, Youth and Families, in the Department of Health and Human Services.

Concurrent planning. Simultaneous planning for reunification of children with parents and adoption, if reunification becomes infeasible.

Dependent children. Children for whose care and nurturing the government pays.

Elizabethan poor laws. Enacted in 1601 during the reign of Queen Elizabeth I of England, these laws were designed to extend aid to the poor in either their own homes (indoor relief) or almshouses or workhouses (outdoor relief).

Emergency foster care. Foster families or institutions that accept children on short notice for short periods of time. They are used in emergencies when a child cannot remain with his or her family, and the disposition of the case is uncertain (also known as receiving and shelter care).

Fleming Rule. Legislation authorizing Aid to Families with Children, later Aid to Families with Dependent Children (Title IV-A of the Social Security Act of 1935); AFDC was eliminated in the 1996 welfare reform legislation.

Foster care. The act of providing for a child's needs as if the child were one's own. Can be an informal arrangement between parent and foster parent, or, more often, a formal arrangement between an agency and a trained, licensed family receiving a board rate for its services.

Foster care drift. Children placed in foster care without a plan for returning home, adoption, or emancipation.

Foster parent. An individual licensed by an agency to care for a child who has been removed from his or her biological family for cause.

Free Home Movement. Begun by Charles Loring Brace, director of the New York Children's Home Society, to relocate street children (known then as "street Arabs") to the rural Midwest.

Group home care. A congregate facility that organizes children into smaller living groups designed to emulate a family arrangement; also a single home with 8 to 12 children in residence.

Indenture. Binding out of a child or adolescent by the government to an individual who agrees to take responsibility for feeding, clothing, and training the child.

Institution. A congregate facility that provides room and board for a number of children; it is often contracted by a state or county, or owned by a sectarian or philanthropic organization.

Kinship foster care. Foster care by a family related to the foster child; also known as relative caregiver.

Long-term foster care. A foster home arrangement that is likely to be permanent until the child is emancipated.

National Foster Parent Organization, Inc. A nonprofit membership organization in the United States that focuses on legislative advocacy, training and education, publications, and networking among foster parents, state and local foster parent associations, and child welfare organizations.

Neglected child. A child whose physical, emotional, educational, or medical needs are not met by those into whose care the child is entrusted.

Orphan. A child whose parents are deceased.

Outplacement. Placement of a child in a family or institution other than the biological family.

Permanency planning. A case management model designed to remedy foster care drift by establishing time-limited plans for a child's return home, adoption, or emancipation.

Reasonable efforts. If, after reasonable efforts have been made in a time-limited service plan designed to assist parents in rebuilding their family to the point that the child can safely return home, the parents cannot ensure the child's safety and well-being, the court may terminate parental rights, freeing the child for adoption.

Reunification. Returning a child from substitute care to the legal family (also restoration).

Short-term foster care. A temporary foster care arrangement with the expectation that the child will shortly return home or be placed in another, longer-term arrangement.

Subsidized foster care. Foster care payments under Title IV-E of the Social Security Act to licensed foster care families. The foster child must come from a family eligible for the Aid to Families with Dependent Children program (AFDC, predecessor to TANF) under the rules that existed in July 1996.

Substitute care. The same as foster care.

Supplemental Security Income (SSI). Federal income supplement program, funded by general tax revenues, that provides assistance to aged, blind, and disabled people (including eligible children) with little or no income. Cash assistance may be used to meet basic needs for food, clothing, and shelter.

Temporary Assistance for Needy Families (TANF). A state-administered block grant for needy families and children developed under the Personal Responsibility and Work Opportunity Reconciliation Act of 1996.

Termination of parental rights. Legal action ending a parent's legal rights and responsibilities for his or her child.

Therapeutic foster care. Family or congregate care with specially trained caretakers skilled in working with chronically ill and handicapped children.

DOCUMENT

Excerpts from the U.S. Code regarding Foster Care, Title IV-E

The following are excerpts from the U.S. Code that pertain to foster care. Section 670 is the opening declaration by Congress that gives the purpose of the law—to enable the states to provide for the care of eligible children by authorizing appropriations for such assistance. Section 672 (c) (1) and (2) define foster family home and child care institutions as licensed, stressing the importance placed on formalizing and regulating the foster care industry. Part (h) (1) of the same section declares children in foster care eligible for federal assistance and permits the states to extend to them the same benefits given to children in needy families, including health, mental health, and dental care covered under the provisions of Title XIX of the Social Security Act.

Sec. 670. Congressional declaration of purpose; authorization of appropriations

For the purpose of enabling each State to provide, in appropriate cases, foster care and transitional independent living programs for children who otherwise would have been eligible for assistance under the State's plan approved under part A of this subchapter (as such plan was in effect on June 1, 1995) and adoption assistance for children with special needs, there are authorized to be appropriated for each fiscal year (commencing with the fiscal year which begins October 1, 1980) such sums as may be necessary to carry out the provisions of this part. The sums made available under this section shall be used for making payments to States which have submitted, and had approved by the Secretary, State plans under this part.

Sec. 672. Foster care maintenance payments program

(c) "Foster family home" and "child-care institution" defined

For the purposes of this part,

(1) the term "foster family home" means a foster family home for children which is licensed by the State in which it is situated or has been approved, by the agency of such State having responsibility for licensing homes of this type, as meeting the standards established for such licensing; and

(2) the term "child-care institution" means a private child-care institution, or a public child-care institution which accommodates no more than twenty-five children, which is licensed by the State in which it is situated or has been approved, by the agency of such State responsible for licensing or approval of institutions of this type, as meeting the standards established for such licensing, but the term shall not include detention facilities, forestry camps, training schools, or any other facility operated primarily for the detention of children who are determined to be delinquent.

(h) Aid for dependent children; assistance for minor children in needy families

(1) For purposes of subchapter XIX of this chapter, any child with respect to whom foster care maintenance payments are made under this section is deemed to be a dependent child as defined in section 606 of this title (as in effect as of July 16, 1996) and deemed to be a recipient of aid to families with dependent children under part A of this subchapter (as so in effect). For purposes of subchapter XX of this chapter, any child with respect to whom foster care maintenance payments are made under this section is deemed to be a minor child in a needy family under a State program funded under part A of this subchapter and is deemed to be a recipient of assistance under such part.

Once it became obvious to child welfare professionals that some children would remain in foster care until they reached eighteen, and that the states could not continue to support children in foster care beyond the legal age of emancipation (an exception being extended dependency for developmentally disabled youth), programs were needed to assist in the transition from foster family or institutional care to independence. Section 667, named after its sponsor, John H. Chafee, provides flexible funding to states so that they can provide education, training, job placement, and independent living arrangements for children likely to remain in foster care until they are 18 years old.

Sec. 677. John H. Chafee Foster Care Independence Program

(a) Purpose

The purpose of this section is to provide States with flexible funding that will enable programs to be designed and conducted—

(1) to identify children who are likely to remain in foster care until 18 years of age and to help these children make the transition to self-sufficiency by providing services such as assistance in obtaining a high school diploma, career exploration, vocational training, job placement and retention, training in daily living skills, training in budgeting and financial management skills, substance abuse prevention, and preventive health activities (including smoking avoidance, nutrition education, and pregnancy prevention);

(2) to help children who are likely to remain in foster care until 18 years of age receive the education, training, and services necessary to obtain employment;

(3) to help children who are likely to remain in foster care until 18 years of age prepare for and enter postsecondary training and education institutions;

(4) to provide personal and emotional support to children aging out of foster care, through mentors and the promotion of interactions with dedicated adults; and

(5) to provide financial, housing, counseling, employment, education, and other appropriate support and services to former foster care recipients between 18 and 21 years of age to complement their own efforts to achieve self-sufficiency and to assure that program participants recognize and accept their personal responsibility for preparing for and then making the transition from adolescence to adulthood.

Source: 42 U.S.C. 670, 672, and 677.

GAMBLING

An activity known to virtually every society in history, gambling remains a broadly controversial issue in contemporary American society. Many economists cite its debilitating effect on the financial well-being of individuals and communities; sociologists note the negative impact of compulsive gambling on individuals and families; criminologists say it attracts crime; and many in the religious community see it as sinful, an ungodly pursuit of money for its own sake. And yet, despite the breadth of condemnation, gambling in the United States has grown exponentially in recent years, both in revenues and geographic reach.

Gambling activity is defined by three elements: consideration, chance, and prize. A gambler places something of value (consideration) at risk (a chance event) to win something of greater value (the prize). Gambling—whether with cards, dice, slot machines, or the spin of the roulette wheel—is a zero-sum game, played within finite time limits. That is, for every winner, there is a loser, and the results are determined relatively quickly. (A note on terms: Although the gambling industry prefers the term "gaming," which carries less connotation of sin, the activity is referred to throughout this chapter as "gambling.")

INDUSTRY STATISTICS

The legal gambling industry in the United States today has developed largely since the end of World War II. The industry includes commercial and Native American casinos, government lottery games, race track and other pari-mutuel betting, charity games, and such other activities as Internet gambling (whose legality is being debated in legislatures and the courts).

Large amounts of money pass back and forth between the gamblers and the gambling operators, with the net results favoring operators. In 2002, nearly $900 billion was wagered in U.S. gambling facilities. The total amount of money put at risk by players is called the "gross gambling handle." Of that amount, however, the players were able to win back more than 92 percent—thus losing approximately $68.8 billion. The net amount of money lost by players is called "gross gambling revenues." Canadian gambling operations netted another $9 billion from players in 2002.

Of gross U.S. gambling revenues in 2002, about $28 billion came from commercial casinos and about $14 billion from Native American operations. Thus, commercial and Native American casinos together took in about 62 percent of net U.S. gambling revenues. Another $18.6 billion in revenues, or 27 percent, came from government lotteries. The remaining 11 percent came from pari-mutuel betting ($4 billion, mostly from horse and dog racing and jai alai) and charity and card room games ($3.6 billion).

In short, gambling in America is big business. Revenues by gambling operators exceed the combined revenues from ticket sales for live concerts, theater and movie performances (including video rentals), attendance at all professional sports games, and sales of all recorded music. Gambling revenues equal roughly 0.7 percent of the gross domestic product. The gambling industry provides money to state governments, through profits from state-run lottery

Table 1. Gambling in the United States: Establishment, Employees, and Payroll, 2002

Type of establishment	Number of establishments	Revenues (in $000s)	Number of employees	Payroll (in $000s)
Casino-hotels	1,807	$7,463,560	53,102	$1,122,890
Other establishments	394	12,717,661	108,721	2,603,104
Total	**2,201**	**$20,181,721**	**161,823**	**$3,725,994**

Source: U.S. Census Bureau.

CHRONOLOGY

1610   Horses are shipped to the British colony at Jamestown, and racing soon begins.

1665   An oval horseracing course is built on Hempstead Plain, Long Island, marking the start of the commercial racing industry in America.

1777   The Continental Congress initiates a lottery; four games are held to raise funds for the revolutionary armies of George Washington.

1780s–1830s Lotteries become an economic tool for financing civic projects in the new states.

1812   The first steamboat operates on the Mississippi River, Robert Fulton's *New Orleans*. Its appearance launches the era of riverboat gambling in the West; within a decade more than 60 riverboats are operating with gamblers on board.

1826   Thomas Jefferson supports the use of lotteries as a means for persons to dispose of their property in a respectable manner so that they can pay their bills. He calls lotteries a tax "laid on the willing only." His own lottery for the sale of goods at Monticello is unsuccessful.

1827   John Davis opens America's first complete casino, in New Orleans at the corner of Orleans and Bourbon Streets.

1832   At the high point of early lottery play, there are 420 lottery games in eight states. Scandals plague many of the games, however, leading to the prohibition of lotteries and other gambling in many locations.

1848   The gold strike in California marks a new trend: mining camp gambling halls. While opportunity brings prospectors to the West, reform pushes eastern gamblers in the same direction. San Francisco becomes a gambling center.

1868   Gambling activity regains momentum as the Louisiana Lottery begins; it enjoys great success as tickets are sold through the mail across the continent—but scandals and corruption continue to arise.

1892   An antigambling movement takes hold in Canada as Parliament bans most forms of gaming with revisions to the federal criminal code.

1895   Congress bans the transportation of lottery tickets in interstate or foreign commerce; as a result, the Louisiana Lottery is shut down.

1910   An era of antigambling reform seems nearly complete in the United States. Nevada closes its casinos, and legalized gambling in America, with the exception of a few horse race tracks, is dormant.

1931   The state of Nevada relegalizes casino gambling.

1935   Horse race betting legislation is approved in Illinois, Louisiana, Florida, New Hampshire, West Virginia, Ohio, Michigan, Massachusetts, Rhode Island, and Delaware.

1963–64 The legislature of New Hampshire authorizes a state-run sweepstakes game that becomes the first government lottery in the United States in the twentieth century.

1969   The Canadian Criminal Code is amended to permit lotteries to be operated by governments and charitable organizations. Soon many provinces have lotteries, and the door is opened for charities and governments to offer casino games.

1975–76 The Commission on the Review of the National Policy Toward Gambling meets and issues a report, the first of its type, affirming the notion that gambling activity, its legalization, and control are a matter for the jurisdictions of state governments.

1976   New Jersey voters authorize casino gambling for Atlantic City; casinos open doors 2 years later.

1978   High-stakes bingo games begin on the Seminole Indian reservation in Hollywood, Florida, signaling a new period of Indian gambling; in subsequent federal court litigation, the Indians retain the right to conduct games unregulated by the state.

1980   The American Psychiatric Association categorizes pathological gambling as a "disorder of impulse control."

1987	The U.S. Supreme Court upholds the rights of Indian tribes to offer unregulated gambling enterprises as long as operations do not violate state criminal policy; the case *California v. Cabazon* determines that any regulation of noncriminal matters must come from the federal government or be specifically authorized by Congress.
1988	The Indian Gaming Regulatory Act is passed by Congress in response to the *Cabazon* decision. The law provides for federal and tribal regulation of bingo games and for mutually negotiated Indian-state government schemes for the regulation of casinos on reservations.
	The voters of South Dakota authorize limited casino games for small casinos in the town of Deadwood.
1989	The Iowa state legislature approves riverboat casino gaming with limited betting on navigable waters in the state; boats begin operation in 1990.
	The Manitoba Lottery Foundation, a government-owned entity, opens the first year-round permanent casino facility in Canada; the Crystal Casino is located in the classic Fort Garry Hotel in Winnipeg.
1990	Riverboat casinos begin operation in Iowa; riverboat casinos are also approved by the Illinois State Legislature.
1996	Congress passes a law setting up a nine-person commission to study the social and economic impact of gambling on American society.
1999	The National Gambling Study Commission issues its report on the problems associated with gambling.
2004	Californians vote down two initiatives on gambling, one to expand slot machines to horse tracks and the other to tax Indian casino revenues; the latter is voted down, say experts, because it is seen as not generating enough revenue.

games or taxes. These revenues exceed $22 billion annually. Eleven commercial casino states received win taxes exceeding $4.6 billion in 2002. Nevada led the way with casino taxes approaching $700 million, or 40 percent of the state's general fund. Gambling activity is also responsible for approximately 1 million jobs in the American economy. Commercial casinos employ 400,000 workers, with another 450,000 jobs in businesses supported by casinos.

HISTORY

While gambling in America goes back to the pre-Columbian era, various forms have waxed and waned in popularity over the centuries and across the continent.

Lotteries

Gambling activity has been endemic to all North American societies. Native tribes played a variety of games involving dice and guessing, as well as contests of dexterity—archery, javelin throwing, and races that featured prizes. The crews that sailed with Columbus gambled with cards. Games of chance were popular among settlers of Jamestown as well; the first racehorses were shipped there as early as 1610.

In fact, the Jamestown Colony itself was the beneficiary of a lottery held back in England; investors in the Colony won permission to conduct four raffles in London between 1612 and 1615.

Almost from the beginning, clergy and civic leaders expressed concern about the effects of gambling on the sanctity, moral fiber, and work ethic of the Colonies. Colonial laws provided severe penalties for gambling. Nevertheless, after the Revolution, lotteries funded vital internal improvements in the new republic and private organizations, including several Ivy League colleges. But with the lotteries came corruption. By the 1830s, lotteries were rife with corruption, and reform movements to end the activity soon spread across the land. By the time of the Civil War, few lotteries survived.

Lotteries were revived in several southern states after the war, but these, too, soon fell into disrepute. Gambling was prohibited throughout the South during the late nineteenth century; the last state lottery was in Louisiana, which closed down as the twentieth century began. There were no other state-run lotteries anywhere in America until 1964, when New Hampshire introduced a sweepstakes game. The revenue it generated inspired other state legislatures, and by the early 2000s, lotteries were run in 39 states plus the District of Columbia. They also operated in every Canadian province and territory, permitted under a 1969 federal law.

Casinos

Gambling casinos emerged with the expansion of the Western frontier in the nineteenth century. Betting games were popular in port towns such as New Orleans, on riverboats along the Mississippi, and in mining camps of the Gold Rush period. As the West became more settled, however, and particularly as women and families moved in, gambling came to be frowned upon. With the Progressive Era at the turn of the twentieth century came a series of campaigns designed to eliminate vice from American life. The best-known of these movements was the banning of alcohol, but the period also saw growing sentiment to ban the companion vice of gambling. By the turn of the century, then, casinos were being closed down throughout the West, the last being in Nevada in 1909.

Inevitably, perhaps, Nevada was also the first state to make casinos legal again in 1931. In fact, it remained the only state with legal casinos until the opening of Resorts International in Atlantic City, New Jersey, in 1978. A decade later, South Dakota authorized small casinos in the frontier tourist town of Deadwood. Shortly after that, Iowa approved riverboat casinos, followed by others in succeeding years. By 2004, a total of eleven states had commercial casinos, operating under diverse rules and guidelines. Casinos were also operating in seven of Canada's ten provinces and the Yukon Territory. Under certain circumstances, various states and provinces also allow charities to raise funds by sponsoring gambling events on a limited, temporary basis.

Equally important to the spread of casino gambling in the United States was the U.S. Supreme Court ruling in *California v. Cabazon Band of Mission Indians* (1987). In that decision, the court ruled that federally recognized Native American tribes could run casinos and bingo halls even if those forms of gambling were prohibited in the states where the reservations were located. In 1988, Congress passed the Indian Gaming Regulatory Act providing regulations for tribal gambling. Today nearly thirty states have Native American casinos.

Horse Racing

The first horse races in settlements such as Jamestown were match races over straight short courses. The first oval course was laid out on Long Island in 1665, and racing soon became a popular pastime as tracks appeared throughout the Colonies. Horse racing remained popular for more than a hundred years, until the Civil War put a high demand on horses for military use. After that, it took decades for the sport to revive.

Only during the Great Depression of the 1930s was horseracing reestablished in many states, largely to provide employment and generate tax revenue. A new pari-mutuel betting system was put into place at that time, with all bets going to track operators. After subtracting shares for the track and the government, the balance of the money went to winning bettors. Today, a total of forty-one states have legal horserace betting; fifteen have dog racing. Every province in Canada permits horseracing, but none allows dog racing.

PROS AND CONS

The supporters of more legalized gambling emphasize the economic benefits. They point out that gambling employs thousands of people in good-paying jobs. Moreover, they argue that the government revenues gambling generates are devoted to "good causes." Ballot propositions pertaining to a proposed state gambling operation or lottery typically include a commitment to where the revenues will go. The beneficiaries can be quite diverse, ranging from primary and secondary schools and college scholarships to parks and recreation facilities, and even—in New Jersey—senior citizens to help in paying their utility bills. The proponents also suggest that people will always gamble anyway and legalization reduces illegal gambling. They also claim public support for gambling is widespread and governments should allow citizens do what they wish. The president of Harrah's Casinos has gone so far as to declare gambling a "fundamental" right of the people.

Opponents of gambling challenge the assumption that it generates jobs or significant revenues for government. Every dollar spent on gambling, they argue, would be taxed if it were spent in another economic sector. Gambling revenues have also been called regressive, because the activity is engaged in more frequently by members of lower income groups—who spend a higher percentage of their earnings—than higher income groups. Moreover, gambling has negative social costs, called "externalities." These include the behavior of persons addicted to gambling, everything from bankruptcy to divorce to suicide, and the higher incidences of crime, from drunk driving to racketeering, in communities with legalized gambling.

Gambling is also faulted for not producing a tangible economic product. As economist Paul Samuelson notes, "[gambling] involves simply sterile transfers of money or goods between individuals, creating no new money or goods. Although it creates no output, gambling does nevertheless absorb time and resources. When pursued beyond the limits of recreation, where the main purpose after all is to 'kill' time, gambling subtracts from the national income." Moreover, opponents also point out that money gambled is money not spent on other products. Thus, jobs created by the gambling industry are really only shifted from other economic sectors. This is especially the case if the gamblers are residents of the local area and not tourists, since this creates no net inflow of revenues into a given area.

PROBLEM GAMBLING AND ITS COSTS

Wherever gambling has existed, there have been problem gamblers. Stories of gambling among Native Americans tell of players who would wager all their possessions, even staking members of their families on a game. The nineteenth-century Russian novelist Fyodor Dostoyevsky recorded his self-destructive experiences at roulette in his 1866 novella, *The Gambler*. Sigmund Freud, the founder of modern psychoanalysis, recognized the problem of compulsive gambling and its destructiveness.

It was not until the 1970s, however, that the psychiatric community fully recognized the problem as a disease. In 1980, the American Psychiatric Association (APA) categorized pathological gambling as a "disorder of impulse control." Nevertheless, the precise definition of compulsive gambling continues to be debated. Some understand it is an extension of the normal human propensity to take risks. In any event, the APA designation has prompted many new studies of problem gambling, its prevalence in society, its costs, and its treatment.

Descriptions of pathological gambling converge around several factors. This kind of gambler, analysts say, becomes involved in increasingly negative behavior, betting more often and with more money as time passes. The pathological gambler cannot accept losing, which is interpreted internally as a loss of self and identity. To reestablish self-esteem, the

loss must be rectified immediately by trying to win back the money. Losses are also concealed from other people, including family, friends, coworkers, and employers, and the gambler becomes preoccupied with gambling at all times. When not gambling, he or she is reliving old experiences and craving future gambling. This gambler disregards the consequences of gambling, borrows money despite knowing that repayment is unlikely, lies to family and friends, and is often drawn into criminal behaviors, such as check forgery, embezzlement, or insurance fraud.

The first clinical attempt to learn how widespread gambling problems were was made by the federal Commission on Review of the National Policy Toward Gambling in 1975. In a nationwide survey conducted by the commission, 0.77 percent of respondents said they had a major problem with gambling. More recent studies have found even higher levels of problem gambling. In 1997, researchers at the Harvard Medical School conducted a meta-analysis of the over 125 studies into the prevalence of gambling in the United States, concluding that roughly 1.14 percent of the adult population in the country suffered from "clinically meaningful" levels of gambling pathologies, while 2.80 percent had "subclinical levels of gambling disorders." These seemingly low percentages translate into roughly 2.3 and 5.6 million adult Americans, respectively. A survey taken by the National Gambling Impact Study Commission in 1998 found that only 0.6 percent of the adult population were currently in a pathological state, while 3.6 percent were in a problem state. Meanwhile, the National Opinion Research Council found in 1999 that persons living within 50 miles of a casino were twice as likely to have a gambling problem as other persons.

Pathological and problem gamblers impose a wide range of burdens on family members, friends, coworkers, those with whom they have business relationships, and the general public. It has been estimated that one pathological gambler directly and adversely affects between ten and fifteen persons. Such gamblers are apt to borrow repeatedly from close associates and in many cases to steal. And when friends and family cannot help, society at large may have to bear the cost of welfare, clinical treatment, police services, or incarceration.

Several estimates have been made of the costs to society of compulsive gambling. Sociologists Henry Lesieur and Kenneth Puig found that roughly one-third of all cases of insurance fraud involve gamblers.

A recent study of members of Gamblers Anonymous in Las Vegas found that each compulsive gambler imposes costs of $19,711 annually on other people. The costs to society take the form of missed work, unemployment, bad debt, theft, criminal justice system expenses, civil suits, and welfare and health expenditures, among others. Less severe problem gamblers impose costs equal to an estimated 49 percent of the compulsive gamblers, or $9,658 per year.

While the proponents of gambling can certainly argue that only a small percentage of gamblers fall into the problem and compulsive gambler category, simple mathematics shows that American society suffers from their activity to the tune of something approaching $30 billion per year. It should be added that the figures cited here do not include a cost factor for suicide. More than one-fourth of troubled gamblers in the surveys indicated that they had attempted suicide.

The costs to society need not be so catastrophic in scope. Experts say they could be reduced if the number of problem gamblers were reduced and their problems were effectively mitigated. Experts in the field of gambling addiction say that the public needs to be educated about the problem of pathological gambling, including the symptoms, extent of the disease, and types of treatment. Educational efforts are needed, they say, in schools, the workplace, the media, and, most important, gambling facilities such as casinos and horse tracks. In addition, toll-free gambling problem hotlines need to be expanded.

Problem gamblers need money. Easy access to it for a serious problem gambler may be the equivalent of providing large quantities of alcohol to an alcoholic. Thus, say treatment professionals, credit card machines should not be placed in casinos, at racetracks, or in any location convenient for gamblers; automatic teller machines (ATMs) in or near gambling facilities should allow deposits only.

Experts also argue that treatment programs should be paid for by government and gambling operators. Counselor training should also be emphasized. As of 2004, fewer than 100 outpatient and 12 inpatient treatment centers for problem gamblers existed in the entire country. By contrast there were 13,000 facilities for alcohol and drug abusers.

ASSOCIATED CRIME AND ITS COSTS

When the notorious bank robber Willie Sutton was asked why he robbed banks, he replied, "That's where the money is." Perhaps the same characteristic explains why casinos and other gambling operations are a venue for crime as well. In identifying and explaining crime patterns, criminologists attach great importance to the factor of opportunity. Because gambling operations attract large sums of money, they say, criminal elements are likely to be attracted as well.

The gambling venue offers a myriad of potential crime victims. Persons walking in and out of a casino or racetrack carry excess cash. Winners are easily identified because they receive their payoffs in a public setting. Dealers may receive large cash tips, which they carry as they leave a casino or other gambling facility. Casinos and players can become victims of persons (or gaming entrepreneurs) who may use cheating schemes of one sort or another. The "cage" at a gambling hall is vulnerable to insiders who may skim from the facility's profits to line their own pockets or perhaps to make it appear that the facility won less money than it really did to avoid taxation. Organized crime elements seek financial gain by controlling the supply of materials going to a gambling facility—construction materials, goods, and labor. The criminal elements are sometimes secret unlicensed owners of facilities.

Gambling facilities may also be surrounded by a kind of ambient crime atmosphere. Loose money draws persons dealing in illegal drugs, loan-sharking, and prostitution. And because gambling operations can be highly profitable, prospective owners/operators may resort to illegal political influence, such as bribery, in an effort to secure a license for the facility. Over the course of the last several decades, a number of public officials have been convicted of felonies for receiving bribes in exchange for favors to gambling operatives. Officials ranging from county superintendents and state governor to U.S. senators have been indicted or driven from office because of gambling-related illegal activity.

Proponents of gambling take a contrary view. They advance the notion that the existence of legal casinos can reduce crime by raising employment levels in economically marginal areas. Lower unemployment, they say, means less crime. A number of studies have shown that crime rates do not go up after jurisdictions introduce gambling; others explain increases in crime by the fact that casino jurisdictions attract a large number of tourists and that non-gambling tourist attractions such as Disney World also experience increased levels of crime.

Moreover, proponents suggest that the introduction of legal forms of gambling can drive illegal gambling out of existence. This happened in Nevada when casinos were legalized in 1931. Illegal operators simply applied for and received a legal license to do exactly what they had been doing before. However, where the numbers of licenses are restricted and persons with illegal pasts are excluded, the simple process of legalization will not end illegal gambling. In fact, it can have the opposite effect, as the legal operation stimulates even greater demand for gambling; some of the new gambling will be captured by illegal operators, who may offer more convenient times and locations, better odds, and more appealing services (including illegal ones like prostitution).

While studies of crime and gambling jurisdictions have generated mixed findings, two comprehensive studies that examined all jurisdictions in the United States—those with gambling and those without—did find positive relationships. Criminologist Earl Grinols examined crime data from each of the 3,165 American counties (and parishes) from 1977 through 1996. According to his findings, the introduction of casino gambling into a county accounted for 7.7 percent of property crimes and 10.3 percent of violent crimes. For a county of 100,000 people or more, the study found that the presence of casinos accounted for 772 more larcenies, 357 more burglaries, 331 more automobile thefts, 12 more rapes, 68 more robberies, and 112 more aggravated assaults per year.

In a study of the state of Wisconsin, crime data from all eighty counties were examined for the years 1980 to 1995. Casinos were introduced into fourteen of the counties in 1992. The study found significant positive relationships between the presence of a casino and driving under the influence of alcohol, drug possession, forgery, possession of stolen property, and assault. Overall, serious crimes and arrests for lesser crimes were higher in counties with a casino than in those without. The annual cost of the additional crime was estimated at $51 million, or $17 for each adult in the state.

MORAL EQUATION: RELIGIOUS AND ETHICAL VIEWS

The opponents of gambling are often tied to religious groups, although not all religions are opposed to all gambling. Indeed, many churches and their affiliated organizations run gambling games (often bingo) to support their activities. Some proponents of legalized gambling point directly to the Bible in support of their cause. Indeed, both the Old and New Testaments include a number of scriptural references to the use of lots and dicelike objects, and not always in a negative context. Religious opponents of gambling, however, suggest that the use of lots in the Bible is not the same as the modern lottery today, as ancient priests used lots to discern the "will of God" rather than to pay gamblers. However, the one case in the Bible where dice were used for personal gain concerned Roman soldiers gambling for the robes of Christ at his crucifixion, and this was hardly an endorsement of gambling.

Some church groups interpret other passages of the Bible as admonishments against gambling. For instance, Isaiah (65:11–12) states, "But you who forsake the lord who set a table for fortune and fill the cups of mixed wine for destiny, I will destine you to the sword, and all of you shall bow down to slaughter." Other Old Testament passages suggest that gambling amounts to covetousness or stealing, which is condemned in the Ten Commandments (Exodus 20:15–17). Although the Commandments do not specifically condemn gambling, some biblical experts argue that the prohibition on stealing and covetousness also applies to gambling.

By no means do all Christian sects hold the same views on gambling. Two basic approaches are represented, with most interpretations falling somewhere on the continuum between outright endorsement of gambling in all forms and total condemnation of gambling in any form. Those who tend toward the condemnation end of the spectrum adhere to a deontological view of morality—that is, a philosophy based on a believer's duties and rights. By participating in gambling games, they believe, the actors are seeking unearned wealth and hoping for material gain at the expense of their fellow human beings. Hence, whatever the consequences of the activity in the short or long run, it is wrong in and of itself. United Methodists and Southern Baptists express this view. As the Social Principles of the United Methodist Church proclaim, "Gambling is a menace to society, deadly to the best interests of moral, social, economic, and spiritual life, and destructive of good government. As an act of faith and love, Christians should abstain from gambling. . . ."

Another view is based on a moral philosophy characterized as teleological—that is, one that focuses on consequences and end results. As L. M. Starkey writes in *Money, Mania, and Morals* (1994), "Catholic moralists agree that gambling and betting may lead to grave abuse and sin, especially when they are prompted by mere gain. The gambler usually frequents bad company, wastes much valuable time, becomes adverse to work, is strongly tempted to be dishonest when luck is against him, and often brings financial ruin upon himself and those dependent upon him." The Church reconciles gambling with the fact God has given people personal freedom. As *The New Catholic Encyclopedia* states, "A person is entitled to dispose of his own property as he wills . . ."; however, the passage continues, "so long as in doing so he does not render himself incapable of fulfilling duties incumbent upon him by reason of justice or charity. Gambling, therefore, though a luxury, is not considered sinful except when the indulgence in it is inconsistent with duty."

In the Catholic view, it is sinful for a person to gamble if the money used is not his or hers or if it is necessary for the support of others. The Church also condemns gambling behavior when it becomes compulsive or disruptive to family and social relationships. Moreover, the freedom to gamble implies a knowing freedom to enter into a fair and honest contract for play. Cheating at gambling is considered wrong, of course, but the Church also looks at the end result of the activity. If good consequences may follow, the gambling activity may be considered good in its own right. Hence, a limited stakes bingo game conducted honestly by Church members within the Church building to raise funds for a school or hospital is not bad.

On the question of legalization, Methodists and Baptists can almost always be counted on as opponents, while Catholic Church leaders will examine the particular circumstances involved. Advocates of legalized gambling raise another ethical consideration, which is that gambling at casinos, race tracks, and other legal venues is no different from investing in the stock market, buying an insurance policy, or indulging in any other government-sanctioned activity of the kind. All involve consideration, chance, and a prize. When state or local governments block gambling initiatives, gaming industry advocates call them hypocritical because they invest in pension funds, float bonds, and are otherwise involved in financial markets to fund operations and public projects.

Opponents to gambling say there are critical differences between the stock market and casino gambling. First, all business ventures—from opening a restaurant to buying a mutual fund—are inherently risky, with money put forward in hopes of greater gain. But those who believe in the free market system accept such risk as the price of creating wealth.

As for the stock market, by investing in shares, the purchasing public is saying it has confidence that certain products and services will be desired by others and meet the demands of the public. Buying a stock transfers money from individuals to entrepreneurs. If a stock performs well, the benefits lead to further economic development and growth. By contrast, they point out, the roulette wheel, craps table, blackjack game, lottery, and horserace are all zero-sum games. For each set of winning numbers, there is a larger number of losing numbers. The stock market, on the other hand, can be a positive-sum game, in which every player can be a winner. Indeed, during the 1990s a substantial majority—perhaps 90 percent or more—of investors were winners overall, depending on the length of their investments. They did not take their wins away from anyone else, their proceeds did not come from the holdings of other investors, and they did not gain at the expense of the companies in which they invested. They won because the companies in which they invested created wealth through their entrepreneurial activities.

Of course, a majority of people can lose in the stock market during times of economic crisis. But this points to yet another difference between traditional gambling and the securities market. In the casino, the game is finite in length. It comes to an end and someone has to pay at that moment. The stock market may be a kind of game, but the game is continuous and need end only when the investor *decides* to make his or her final sale. (Options trading, in which the investor attempts to predict the value of a stock at a specific moment in time is more like casino gambling.)

Insurance differs from gambling even more than the stock market. In fact, it is quite the opposite. In gambling, the bettor intentionally risks a sum of money. The goal of insurance, by contrast, is to *protect* the policyholder's assets and *mitigate* the risk of an event causing a loss of wealth—whether a fire or other natural disaster, theft, illness, or even death.

CONCLUSION

As old as civilization itself, and perhaps even more ancient than that, gambling is an essential aspect of the human spirit. It is a kind of ritualizing of the basic human need to take risks for gain. But the world's religions and governments have traditionally made distinctions between gambling and general economic risk-taking. One is considered a superfluous luxury and the other an economic necessity.

Gambling has had an uneasy existence throughout the course of American history. Widely accepted at times, particularly in regions where economic risk-taking was an inherent part of life, notably frontiers, gambling has also been sharply curtailed at other times, especially during periods when capitalism itself faced increased scrutiny and regulation. It is probably no coincidence that legalized gambling was nearly driven from existence during the first half of the twentieth century, when the modern regulatory state was erected in America.

Similarly, the general economic deregulation of the late twentieth century coincided with a vast expansion of legalized gambling. This may have been a result of larger sociological factors, such as a greater tolerance of risk in everyday life. Or the connection may be more prosaic. Periods of deregulation usually mean lower government revenues, and gambling provides a way to generate revenue through a form of voluntary taxation. But as opponents point out, the costs of gambling may outweigh the gains, as governments are forced to deal with the social pathologies connected with it. Regardless, gambling in America—its forms, popularity, and reach—no doubt will continue to evolve with the economic, social, and political character of the times.

William N. Thompson

REFERENCES

Albanese, Jay S. "The Effect of Casino Gambling on Crime." *Federal Probation* 49 (June 1985): 39–44.

American Gaming Association. *The Responsible Gaming Resource Guide.* Kansas City, MO: A.G.A, 1996.

Asbury, Herbert. *Sucker's Progress: An Informal History of Gambling in America.* New York: Thunder's Mouth, 2003.

Barker, Thomas, and Marjie Britz. *Jokers Wild: Legalized Gambling in the Twenty-First Century.* Westport, CT: Praeger, 2000.

Commission on the Review of the National Policy Toward Gambling. *Gambling in America: Final Report.* Washington, DC: U.S. Government Printing Office, 1976.

Eade, Vincent H., and Raymond H. Eade. *Introduction to the Casino Entertainment Industry.* Upper Saddle River, NJ: Prentice-Hall, 1997.

Findlay, John M. *People of Chance: Gambling in American Society from Jamestown to Las Vegas.* New York: Oxford University Press, 1986.

Grinols, Earl. *Gambling in America: Costs and Benefits.* Cambridge: Cambridge University Press, 2004.

Hakim, Simon, and Andrew J. Buck. 1989. "Do Casinos Enhance Crime?" *Journal of Criminal Justice* 17, 5 (1989): 409–16.

Lesieur, Henry R. "Costs and Treatment of Pathological Gambling." *The Annals of the American Academy of Political and Social Science* 556 (1998): 153–71.

Lesieur, Henry R., and Robert L. Custer. "Pathological Gambling, Roots, Phases, and Treatment." *The Annals of the American Academy of Political Science* 474 (1984): 146–56.

Lesieur, Henry R., and Kenneth Puig. "Insurance Problems and Pathological Gambling." *Journal of Gambling Behavior* 3, 2 (1987): 123–36.

Levinson, David. *Religion: A Cross Culture Encyclopedia.* Santa Barbara, CA: ABC-CLIO, 1996.

Longstreet, Stephen. *Win or Lose: A Social History of Gambling in America.* Indianapolis, IN: Bobbs-Merrill, 1977.

National Gambling Impact Study Commission. *Final Report.* Washington, DC: N.G.I.S.C., 1999.

National Opinion Research Center. *Gambling Impact and Behavior Study: A Report.* Presented to National Gambling Impact Study Commission, April 1, 1999.

Nibert, David. *Hitting the Lottery Jackpot: State Government and the Taxing Dreams.* New York: Monthly Review, 2000.

Ochrym, Ronald George, and Clifton Park. "Street Crime, Tourism, and Casinos: An Empirical Comparison." *Journal of Gambling Studies* 6 (Summer 1990): 127–38.

Pavalko, Ronald. *Risky Business: America's Fascination with Gambling.* Belmont, CA: Wadsworth/Thomson Learning, 2000.

Reith, Gerda. ed. *Gambling: Who Wins? Who Loses?* Amherst, NY: Prometheus Books, 2003.

Starkey, L. M. *Money, Mania, and Morals.* New York: Abington, 1994.

Thompson, William N. *Gambling in America: An Encyclopedia of History, Issues, and Society.* Santa Barbara, CA: ABC-CLIO, 2001.

Thompson, William N., Ricardo Gazel, and Dan Rickman. *The Economic Impact of Native American Gaming in Wisconsin.* Milwaukee: Wisconsin Policy Research Institute, 1995.

———. *Casinos and Crime: What's the Connection?* Mequon: Wisconsin Policy Research Institute, 1966.

Vogel, Jennifer. ed. *Crapped Out: How Gambling Ruins the Economy and Destroys Lives.* Monroe, ME: Common Courage, 1997.

Watson, Tom. *Don't Bet on It.* Ventura, CA: Regal Books, 1987.

WEB SITES

American Gaming Association:
www.americangaming.org
Gamblers Anonymous: www.gamblersanonymous.org
Responsible Gambling Council:
www.responsiblegambling.org

GLOSSARY

Cage. A secured room in a gambling establishment where money is kept and counted.

Gaming. A less pejorative term for gambling, favored by the gambling industry.

Gross gambling handle. Total amount of money gambled.

Gross gambling revenues. The amount of money gambled minus the amount of money paid back to gamblers as winnings; the earnings of those who run gambling operations.

Loan-sharking. Illegal lending of money, frequently by members of organized crime gangs, at exorbitant interest rates; problem gamblers often resort to loan sharks to obtain money after other legal sources refuse them.

Lottery. A game, often run by the government, in which numbers are drawn at random and those who pick those numbers share the amount bet after lottery operators deduct their share.

Pari-mutuel betting. A system of betting on horse and dog racing in which winners divide the total amount bet after management deducts its fees.

Pathological gambling. Defined as a mental illness by the American Psychiatric Society; more popularly known as compulsive gambling, its symptoms include an uncontrollable desire to gamble.

Problem gambling. Generally defined as a condition in which a person's gambling interferes to one degree or another with his or her professional or personal life.

Racketeering. Illegal business activities, often associated with gambling, that involves loan-sharking, extortion, bribery, and obstruction of justice.

Zero-sum game. A game in which one participant's gain is the other participant's loss.

DOCUMENT

Excerpts from *California v. Cabazon Band of Mission Indians*, 1987

In this landmark 1987 decision, the U.S. Supreme Court ruled that California state laws against gambling do not apply to Indian reservations located within the state, unless authorized by Congress. Citing precedents concerning Indian sovereignty, as well as the federal government's determination to provide economic opportunities for Native Americans, the Supreme Court opened the way for a vast expansion of gambling operations on Indian reservations throughout the country.

Justice [Byron] White delivered the opinion of the Court.

The Cabazon and Morongo Bands of Mission Indians, federally recognized Indian Tribes, occupy reservations in Riverside County, California. Each Band, pursuant to an [480 U.S. 202, 205] ordinance approved by the Secretary of the Interior, conducts bingo games on its reservation. The Cabazon Band has also opened a card club at which draw poker and other card games are played. The games are open to the public and are played predominantly by non-Indians coming onto the reservations. The games are a major source of employment for tribal members, and the profits are the Tribes' sole source of income. The State of California seeks to apply to the two Tribes Cal. Penal Code Ann. 326.5 (West Supp. 1987). That statute does not entirely prohibit the playing of bingo but permits it when the games are operated and staffed by members of designated charitable organizations who may not be paid for their services. Profits must be kept in special accounts and used only for charitable purposes; prizes may not exceed $250 per game. Asserting that the bingo games on the two reservations violated each of these restrictions, California insisted that the Tribes comply with state law. Riverside [480 U.S. 202, 206] County also sought to apply its local Ordinance No. 558, regulating bingo, as well as its Ordinance No. 331, prohibiting the playing of draw poker and the other card games.

The Tribes sued the county in Federal District Court seeking a declaratory judgment that the county had no authority to apply its ordinances inside the reservations and an injunction against their enforcement. The State intervened, the facts were stipulated, and the District Court granted the Tribes' motion for summary judgment, holding that neither the State nor the county had any authority to enforce its gambling laws within the reservations. The Court of Appeals for the Ninth Circuit affirmed, 783 F.2d 900 (1986), the State and the county appealed, and we postponed jurisdiction to the hearing on the merits. *476 U.S. 1168 . 4* [480 U.S. 202, 207]

I

The Court has consistently recognized that Indian tribes retain "attributes of sovereignty over both their members and their territory.". . . It is clear, however, that state laws may be applied to tribal Indians on their reservations if Congress has expressly so provided. Here, the State insists that Congress has twice given its express consent. . . . We disagree in both respects.

. . . We recognized that a grant to States of general civil regulatory power over Indian reservations would result in the destruction of tribal institutions and values. Accordingly, when a State seeks to enforce a law within an Indian reservation under the authority of Pub. L. 280, it must be determined whether the law is criminal in nature, and thus fully applicable to the reservation under 2, or civil in nature, and applicable only as it may be relevant to private civil litigation in state court.

The Minnesota personal property tax at issue in Bryan was unquestionably civil in nature. The California bingo statute is not so easily categorized. California law permits bingo [480 U.S. 202, 209] games to be conducted only by charitable and other specified organizations, and then only by their members who may not receive any wage or profit for doing so; prizes are limited and receipts are to be segregated and used only for charitable purposes. Violation of any of these provisions is a misdemeanor. California insists that these are criminal laws which Pub. L. 280 permits it to enforce on the reservations. . . .

We are persuaded that the prohibitory/regulatory distinction is consistent with Bryan's construction of Pub. L. 280. It is not a bright-line rule, however; and as the Ninth Circuit itself observed, an argument of some weight may be made that the bingo statute is prohibitory rather than regulatory. But in the present case, the court reexamined the state law and reaffirmed its holding in Barona, and we are reluctant to disagree with that court's view of the nature and intent of the state law at issue here.

There is surely a fair basis for its conclusion. California does not prohibit all forms of gambling. California itself operates a state lottery, Cal. Govt. Code Ann. 8880 et seq. (West Supp. 1987), and daily encourages its citizens to participate in this state-run gambling. California also permits parimutuel horse-race betting. Cal. Bus. & Prof. Code Ann. 19400–19667 (West 1964 and Supp. 1987). Although certain enumerated gambling games are prohibited under Cal. Penal Code Ann. 330 (West Supp. 1987), games not enumerated, including the card games played in the Cabazon card club, are permissible. The Tribes assert that more than 400 card rooms similar to the Cabazon card club flourish in California, and the State does not dispute this fact. Brief for [480 U.S. 202, 211] Appellees 47–48. Also, as the Court of Appeals noted, bingo is legally sponsored by many different organizations and is widely played in California. There is no effort to forbid the playing of bingo by any member of the public over the age of 18. Indeed, the permitted bingo games must be open to the general public. Nor is there any limit on the number of games which eligible organizations may operate, the receipts which they may obtain from the games, the number of games which a participant may play, or the amount of money which a participant may spend, either per game or in total. In light of the fact that California permits a substantial amount of gambling activity, including bingo, and actually promotes gambling through its state lottery, we must conclude that California regulates rather than prohibits gambling in general and bingo in particular.

California argues, however, that high stakes, unregulated bingo, the conduct which attracts organized crime, is a misdemeanor in California and may be prohibited on Indian reservations. But that an otherwise regulatory law is enforceable by criminal as well as civil means does not necessarily convert it into a criminal law within the meaning of Pub. L. 280. Otherwise, the distinction between 2 and 4 of that law could easily be avoided and total assimilation permitted. [480 U.S. 202, 212] This view, adopted here and by the Fifth Circuit in the Butterworth case, we find persuasive. Accordingly, we conclude that Pub. L. 280 does not authorize California to enforce Cal. Penal Code Ann. 326.5 (West Supp. 1987) within the Cabazon and Morongo Reservations. . . .

California and Riverside County also argue that the Organized Crime Control Act (OCCA) authorizes the application of their gambling laws to the tribal bingo enterprises. The OCCA makes certain violations of state and local gambling laws violations of federal law. The Court of Appeals rejected [480 U.S. 202, 213] appellants' argument, relying on its earlier decision. . . . The court explained that whether a tribal activity is "a violation of the law of a state" within the meaning of OCCA depends on whether it violates the "public policy" of the State, the same test for application of state law under Pub. L. 280, and similarly concluded that bingo is not contrary to the public policy of California.

The Court of Appeals for the Sixth Circuit has rejected this view. United States v. Dakota, 796 F.2d 186 (1986). Since the OCCA standard is simply whether the gambling business is being operated in "violation of the law of a State," there is no basis for the regulatory/prohibitory distinction that it agreed is suitable in construing and applying Pub. L. 280. 796 F.2d, at 188. And because enforcement of OCCA is an exercise of federal rather than state authority, there is no danger of state encroachment on Indian tribal sovereignty. . . . This latter observation exposes the flaw in appellants' reliance on OCCA. That enactment is indeed a federal law that, among other things, defines certain federal crimes over which the district courts have exclusive jurisdiction. There is nothing in OCCA indicating that the States [480 U.S. 202, 214] are to have any part in enforcing federal criminal laws or are authorized to make arrests on Indian reservations that in the absence of OCCA they could not effect. We are not informed of any federal efforts to employ OCCA to prosecute the playing of bingo on Indian reservations, although there are more than 100 such enterprises currently in operation, many of which have been in existence for several years, for the most part with the encouragement of the Federal Government. Whether or not, then, the Sixth Circuit is right and the Ninth Circuit wrong about the coverage of OCCA, a matter that we do not decide, there is no warrant for California to make arrests on reservations and thus, through OCCA, enforce its gambling laws against Indian tribes.

II

. . . This case also involves a state burden on tribal Indians in the context of their dealings with non-Indians since the question is whether the State may prevent the Tribes from making available high stakes bingo games to non-Indians coming from outside the reservations. Decision in this case turns on whether state authority is pre-empted by the operation of federal law; and "[s]tate jurisdiction is pre-empted . . . if it interferes or is incompatible with federal and tribal interests reflected in federal law, unless the state interests at stake are sufficient to justify the assertion of state authority." Mescalero, 462 U.S., at 333, 334. The inquiry is to proceed in light of traditional notions of Indian sovereignty and the congressional goal of Indian self-government, including its "overriding goal" of encouraging tribal self-sufficiency and economic development. . . .

These policies and actions, which demonstrate the Government's approval and active promotion of tribal bingo enterprises, are of particular relevance in this case. The Cabazon and Morongo Reservations contain no natural resources which can be exploited. The tribal games at present provide the sole source of revenues for the operation of the tribal governments [480 U.S. 202, 219] and the provision of tribal services. They are also the major sources of employment on the reservations. Self-determination and economic development are not within reach if the Tribes cannot raise revenues and provide employment for their members. The Tribes' interests obviously parallel the federal interests. . . .

The sole interest asserted by the State to justify the imposition of its bingo laws on the Tribes is in preventing the infiltration of the tribal games by organized crime. To the extent that the State seeks to prevent any and all bingo [480 U.S. 202, 221] games from being played on tribal lands while permitting regulated, off-reservation games, this asserted interest is irrelevant and the state and county laws are pre-empted. See n. 3, supra. Even to the extent that the State and county seek to regulate short of prohibition, the laws are pre-empted. The State insists that the high stakes offered at tribal games are attractive to organized crime, whereas the controlled games authorized under California law are not. This is surely a legitimate concern, but we are unconvinced that it is sufficient to escape the pre-emptive force of federal and tribal interests apparent in this case. California does not allege any present criminal involvement in the Cabazon and Morongo enterprises, and the Ninth Circuit discerned none. 783 F.2d, at 904. An official of the Department of Justice has expressed some concern about tribal bingo operations, but far from any action being taken evidencing this concern—and surely the Federal Government has the authority to forbid Indian gambling enterprises—the prevailing federal policy continues to support these tribal enterprises, including those of the Tribes involved in this case.

We conclude that the State's interest in preventing the infiltration of the tribal bingo enterprises by organized crime does not justify state regulation of the tribal bingo enterprises [480 U.S. 202, 222] in light of the compelling federal and tribal interests supporting them. State regulation would impermissibly infringe on tribal government, and this conclusion applies equally to the county's attempted regulation of the Cabazon card club. We therefore affirm the judgment of the Court of Appeals and remand the case for further proceedings consistent with this opinion.

It is so ordered.

Source: 480 U.S. 202 (1987).

GANGS

The term "gang" defies easy definition. In the contemporary context, the word is connected to a variety of phenomena—from loose-knit groups of alienated, criminal youth to a dangerous but exciting lifestyle promoted in media and advertising to sell music, video games, and movies.

For the purpose of this discussion, it is useful to define what gangs are not. To begin with, gangs are not the same as organized crime groups like the Mafia. Organized crime groups are capable of penetrating legitimate businesses and corrupting them; gangs are not. Organized crime groups have the capacity to corrupt and constrain public officials and the police; gangs do not. Second, gangs are not the equivalent of hate groups such as skinheads and neo-Nazis. While often engaging in criminal behavior, these groups have clear-cut political agendas—usually on the fringes of the radical right. Their criminal behavior often serves political ends. Gangs may occasionally adopt the rhetoric of ethnic pride, but typically they eschew overt political agendas and political activity.

Gangs do share certain characteristics with both Mafia organizations and hate groups. First, like organized crime groups, they engage in organized illegal activities, frequently drug dealing, to enrich both the gang and its individual members. And, like hate groups, they provide members with a sense of community and group identity and are often organized in opposition to other groups, usually other gangs rather than ethnic groups (though many are organized along ethnic lines).

What, then, *are* gangs? First, they usually consist of youths, mostly under the age of 30. Their organization consists of leaders who issue orders, a set of rules dictating members' actions and behavior, a set of symbols and colors defining membership, and a defined territory in which the gang operates, defending it against intrusion by rival groups. Criminal behavior, unlike that of organized crime groups, is not always connected with monetary gain. Initiation rites often include criminal behavior, and violence is often used in defending the gang's territory, not just to protect lucrative criminal enterprises from competing gangs, but as a matter of pride. Finally, gangs offer members a sense of belonging, group identity, and prestige—an appealing benefit for youths who often come from broken homes or abusive families.

1820s–1920s: ORIGINS

Gangs in America date back nearly two hundred years and are closely tied to the history of urbanization and immigration. The first gangs—as previously defined—appeared in the growing urban centers of the Northeast in the early and mid-nineteenth century. New York City was the most notorious center of early gang activity.

New York City experienced two distinct but equally large-scale influxes of newcomers, beginning in the 1920s and accelerating throughout the antebellum period: native-born Protestants migrated from rural areas of the United States, and Irish Catholic immigrants fled famine and English oppression in their island homeland. Together, these groups swelled the city's population with large numbers of unskilled, alienated, and impoverished young persons.

Many of these young adults—particularly the immigrant Irish—formed and joined gangs. Not only did the gangs instill a sense of community and pride in a population struggling to adapt to an alien and often hostile new home, but they provided practical benefits as well. At a time when signs proclaiming "no Irish need apply" for jobs were routine, the gangs offered a way to earn an income. One of the first gangs in the Five Points district—New York's most notorious antebellum slum—was the Forty Thieves, whose members were adept at picking pockets and fencing stolen goods. The success of the Thieves spawned other gangs with equally colorful names, like the Dead Rabbits, Dusters, Pug Uglies, Shirt

CHRONOLOGY

1820s–40s Rising tide of Irish immigration leads to the formation of urban gangs in several cities of the Northeast, particularly New York.

1863 New York City erupts in riots in July, as immigrant and poor communities protest unfair Civil War draft law; many gangs engage in attacks on African Americans and widespread looting.

1919 The Eighteenth Amendment to the Constitution is ratified, making the sale, transport, and possession of alcohol a crime; gangs thrived providing illegal alcohol until the amendment was overturned in 1933.

1943 White servicemen on leave from World War II attack Los Angeles zoot suiters, Mexican American gang members known for that particular style of dress; dozens of Latinos, but no servicemen, are arrested.

1950s Youth gang activity increases in many urban communities, becoming a major social issue in the press and among the public.

1960s The rise of protest movements from civil rights to antiwar impacts gang culture, leading to the rise of ideological gangs that combine politics with criminal activities.

1980s–90s The rising tide of drug activity—especially the introduction of crack cocaine—leads to a large increase in the number and size of gangs.

Tails, and Roach Guards. Like later gangs, those of early New York gangs not only had well-established territories but wore distinctive dress, often favoring stovepipe hats, striped pantaloons, and frock coats fashioned in the particular gang's style.

The gang wars of early New York began in earnest in the 1830s and 1840s, when the gangs in an area known as the Bowery (near Five Points) showed their distaste for other neighborhoods by establishing their own gang fighting units, among them the Atlantic Guards, Blue American Guards, and, the most famous, Bowery Boys. Warfare in these early years was relegated largely to fisticuff displays of aggression for territorial control. Although lacking the violent drama of modern gun battles, these fights were frightening events for the local citizenry. By the 1840s, the city of nearly 500,000 had an estimated 30,000 gang members. In response, New York established its first professional police force, numbering 800 officers, in 1845, largely to combat gang violence and crime. While the new police force did keep gangs in check, they were far from eliminated. Gangs were a major source of the violence during the New York City draft riots of 1863.

By the early part of the nineteenth century, gangs had spread to most large American cities, particularly those with many foreign immigrants or domestic migrants. The 1920s were pivotal to the history of gangs in modern America. Prohibition, with its potential for large profits in producing, smuggling, distributing, and selling illegal alcohol, turned many small-time youth gangs into major criminal organizations, like those of Dutch Schulz in New York and Al Capone in Chicago.

1930s–1940s: ETHNIC GROUPINGS

Although gangs of the 1930s and 1940s were still predominantly of European descent (Irish, German, Italian, or Polish), other ethnic groupings were beginning to appear. Increased numbers of Mexican and Puerto Rican immigrants appeared along with more African American migrants from the rural South. These new groups faced much the same poverty, segregation, discrimination, and hostility experienced by earlier Irish and Italian immigrants. They also engaged in many of the same criminal activities, both for profit and to defend their turf. These gangs also maintained the tradition of distinctive symbols and clothing.

Among the best-known gang styles of the period was the Mexican-American zoot suits of Los Angeles, although many nongang Chicanos also wore the outfit, which consisted of long coats and wide-brimmed hats. The zoot suiters, also known as *pachucos*, became targets of Anglo harassment. The open animosity, particularly among military men during World War II, toward zoot suiters seemed to center on their apparent unwillingness to fight for their adopted country, but they were also held in contempt because of the large amount of material used to make a zoot suit, given the wartime shortages.

In June 1943, a group of taunting sailors were attacked by a group of pachucos in Los Angeles. Later that evening, hundreds of sailors returned to retaliate. The fighting continued for thirteen nights in what became known as the 1943 Zoot Suit Riots. It is indicative of the times that the riots led to the arrest of pachucos only, while the more aggressive actions of sailors and civilians went virtually undeterred and unpunished. Both police and media accounts of the incident were heavily biased in favor of the men in uniform. Of the 115 arrests made, 95 were of zoot suiters. No deaths were reported; of 112 reported injuries, 94 were sustained by pachucos.

1950s–EARLY 1960s: NEW PROMINENCE FOR YOUTH GANGS

In the 1950s and early 1960s, a distinctive youth subculture emerged in America, with its own music, its own movies, and a strong sense of identity separate from childhood and adulthood. Much of this was the product of the nation's prosperity, which gave teenagers more leisure time and permitted them to put off the responsibilities of adulthood. This new prominence of the youth subculture also brought much greater awareness of youth-related problems, including gangs.

Youth gangs were becoming a major concern of law enforcement and the public at large. Some of this concern was exaggerated by lurid press accounts and films—such as *Rebel Without a Cause* (1955) and *West Side Story* (1961)—but some was about real developments. Gangs in the 1950s were more organized, and their struggles over turf became increasingly violent as fists and knives gave way to homemade "zip" guns, fashioned from automobile antennas. Gang conflicts also grew in size and complexity. Increasingly, gangs adopted military tactics, scouting out opponents' strengths and weaknesses before launching well-coordinated assaults. The changing face of gang members was also accelerating. The vast influx of Puerto Ricans to the mainland in the late 1940s and early 1950s—more than half a million by 1956—brought a new gang presence in the cities of the Northeast, particularly New York.

In response to escalating gang violence, Mayor Robert Wagner created the New York City Youth Board in 1957 to curb the establishment and growth of gangs. For the first time, social workers took to the streets to offer social services and counseling to current and potential gang-involved youth. Even as they met with gang members, they drew up reports on why youths joined gangs. Among their findings were that gang members

- made a reasoned choice to be a part of a group;
- chose to be a part of a group that offered them structure, cohesion, and a sense of camaraderie;
- participated in the gang to feel connected to a community and enhance their sense of self-worth;
- liked gangs for their clearly defined rules and responsibilities;
- followed leaders whom they respected;
- and found "warfare" appealing, understanding that violence was a normal part of gang life.

LATE 1960s–EARLY 1970s: IDEOLOGICAL GANGS

With the rise of various protest movements, from Black Power (the confrontational civil rights movement of northern ghettoes) to opposition to the war in Vietnam during the middle and late 1960s, new gangs arose, and old gangs were transformed, along ideological lines. According to noted gang sociologist Dan Korem, the "lure" of this kind of gang was not only the ideology itself but the justification it provided for criminal acts. But Korem also noted a deeper meaning to membership in the ideological gang than there had been in earlier "delinquent" gangs. Given their general oppression and the heightened political sensibility produced by the civil rights movement, ideological gangs tended to predominate among African Americans and, to a lesser extent, Puerto Ricans and other Latinos. Influenced by political militants such as the Black Panthers, ideologically oriented African-American gangs included the American Gangster Disciples of Chicago and the Vice Lords of New York. As one Vice Lord put it, "The militants came in and say why be a gangbanger [gang member who attacks members of other gangs] and kill each other when you can kill the honky [white person], and we began to see the enemy was not black."

Yet not all social unrest led to ideologically oriented gangs. The Watts race riot of 1965, initially a protest against police brutality, was a critical factor in the transformation of Los Angeles gang culture during the 1970s and 1980s. While black gangs of the 1950s and early 1960s formed for traditional reasons—lack of economic opportunities and alienation from society at large—the widespread looting and destruction of property during the riots led gang members to believe criminal activity could be more lucrative if better organized. The Crips and the Bloods, two of the major gang groupings of late twentieth-century Los Angeles, arose over turf fights in black high schools in the late 1950s and early 1960s. By the 1970s, the two had become major criminal organizations.

1970s–PRESENT: GANG CULTURE DIVERSIFIES

Several phenomena marked the history of gangs during the 1970s and 1980s: growth in number, immigration, and geographic dispersal. Law enforcement officials estimate that the number of gangs grew roughly tenfold from the 1970s to the 1990s, from just a few thousand to more than 20,000, as membership increased from about 100,000 to over 700,000.

At the same time, the rising tide of illegal drugs—particularly the crack cocaine epidemic of the late 1980s and early 1990s—presented new opportunities for gang recruitment and economic activity, as well as violence. By the 1980s, some gangs had become big businesses in their own right. In Chicago, Gangster Disciple leader Larry Hoover went so far as to create a corporate bureaucratic structure for his gang to engage in criminal activities, which he called "new concept" gangsterism.

Immigration was also a factor in the growth and diversification of gangs. The sheer number of immigrants led to a significant increase in gang membership and activity in the Latino community especially, and the rise of an entirely new ethnic gang culture—the Asian gang—in the period between the early 1970s and 2000s. Like immigrants before them, many Asians, particularly in the economically marginalized Chinese and Southeast Asian communities, joined gangs in hopes of improving their economic status, finding a sense of community in unfamiliar and dangerous neighborhoods, and earning self-respect in a culture that often discriminated against and looked down on both immigrants and youth.

By the late 1980s, another new gang phenomenon

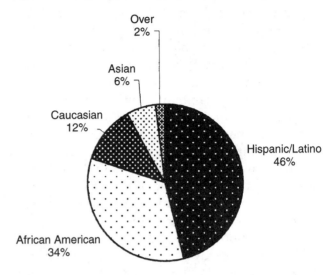

Figure 1. Gang Membership, by Race/Ethnicity, 1998

Over 2%
Asian 6%
Caucasian 12%
African American 34%
Hispanic/Latino 46%

Source: Department of Justice, National Criminal Justice Reference Service.

was emerging among middle-class youth—suburban gangs. Often alienated in suburban communities that offered little in the way of organized youth activities and influenced by the media's portrayal of the gangster lifestyle as dangerous but exciting, many suburban youth began to form their own gangs. These gangs generally eschewed contact with the ethnic and racial gangs of the inner city and, like the urban gangs before them, began with petty crime and small-scale drug trafficking. As with other gangs (if somewhat less pronounced), they adopted distinctive dress codes, rules of conduct, and leadership structures. By 2000, the Department of Justice's Office of Juvenile Delinquency Prevention estimated that roughly 200 U.S. cities with a population of 100,000 or more—including many large suburban communities—reported youth gang activity.

GOVERNMENT RESPONSE

The general trend in the postwar era has been away from earlier efforts to wean young people from the gang culture through counseling and other social services, to a more punitive approach. Indeed, between the 1960s and the 1990s, the growth of gangs and a rising crime rate led many politicians, law enforcement officials, and a majority of the public to conclude that earlier efforts had been too permissive and only empowered gangs.

States across the country began increasing the penalties for gang-related activities from graffiti to drug

Figure 2. Gang Membership, by Age, 1998

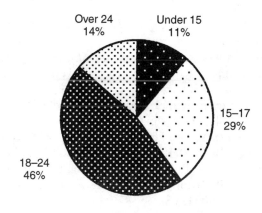

Source: Department of Justice, National Criminal Justice Reference Service.

trafficking. Some statutes specifically targeted gangs themselves. Illinois's 1992 Street Gang Terrorism Omnibus Prevention Act increased and expanded penalties for a host of activities related to street gangs, including any illegal acts associated with increasing gang membership, engaging in gang-related economic activity, or physically defending gang members. Street gang racketeering was made a Class I felony under the law, with penalties including extended jail terms, confiscation of property, and fines equal to the street value of weapons seized. The act also made it easier to prosecute gang members, allowing prosecutors to strike immunity deals with members who testified against their own.

Still, even as penalties became harsher, social conditions continued to encourage membership in gangs. As numerous studies have indicated, gang members come from broken homes more frequently than youths in general. Between 1970s and the 1990s, the number of children living in "mother only" households grew from roughly 10 percent to one-third in the general community and from about 30 percent to more than half among African Americans.

CONCLUSION

The evolution of gangs in America has seen a number of continuities and consistencies from the early nineteenth century to the present day. They have usually thrived in urban areas where economic opportunities are few or discrimination prevents certain members of the community from taking advantage of them.

But the appeal of gang membership has always been about more than economics. Many gang members have always come from broken homes, finding a sense of belonging and the structure and authority missing in their home lives. Gangs have often appealed to immigrants and other socially marginalized groups, unfamiliar with their new homeland or feeling unwelcome. Gangs, then, provide their members a sense of power and self-respect.

Gang activities have also been remarkably consistent over the centuries. Most have started out with petty illegal activity before developing into larger criminal enterprises. Gangs create a set of symbols indicating membership and fiercely defend their territory, both to protect their economic activities and to maintain respect. The more superficial aspects of gang membership have changed, however, including the particular ethnic groups involved, their specific criminal activities, and their sheer scale.

Charla Waxman

REFERENCES

Campbell, A. *The Girls in the Gang: A Report from New York City.* New York: Basil Blackwell, 1984.

Clark, R. *Crime in America: Observations on Its Nature, Causes, Prevention, and Control.* New York: Simon and Schuster, 1970.

Cloward, R. A., and L. E. Ohlin. *Delinquency and Opportunity.* Glencoe, IL: Free Press, 1960.

Cohen, A. K. *Delinquent Boys: The Culture of the Gang.* Glencoe, IL: Free Press, 1955.

Covey, Herbert C., Scott Menard, and Robert J. Franzese. *Juvenile Gangs.* Springfield, IL: C. C. Thomas, 1992.

Dawley, D. *A Nation of Lords: The Autobiography of the Vice Lords.* Prospect Heights, IL: Waveland Press, 1992.

Fleisher, M. S. *Dead End Kids.* Madison: University of Wisconsin Press, 1998.

Goldstein, A. P., and C. R. Huff. *The Gang Intervention Handbook.* Chicago: Research Press, 1993.

Hagedorn, J. M., and P. Macon. *Gangs, Crime, and the Underclass in a Rustbelt City.* Chicago: Lakeview Press, 1988.

Helmer, W. *Public Enemies: America's Criminal Past, 1919–1940.* New York: Checkmark Books, 1988.

Hernandez, A. *Peace in the Streets: Breaking the Cycle of Gang Violence.* Washington, DC: Child Welfare League of America, 1998.

Keiser, R. L. *The Vice Lords: Warriors of the Streets.* New York: Holt, Rinehart, and Winston, 1969.

Klein, M. W., C. L. Maxson, and J. Miller. *The Modern Gang Reader.* Los Angeles: Roxbury, 1995.

Knox, G. W. *An Introduction to Gangs.* Buchanan, MI: Vande Vere, 1993.

———, David L. Laske, and Edward D. Tromanhauser. *Schools Under Siege.* Dubuque, IA: Kendall/Hunt, 1992.

Kontos, Louis, David Brotherton, and Luis Barrios, eds. *Gangs and Society: Alternative Perspectives.* New York: Columbia University Press, 2003.

Korem, Danny. *Suburban Gangs.* Richardson, TX: International Focus Press, 1994.

Kotlowicz, A. *There Are No Children Here.* New York: Doubleday, 1992.

Lane, M. (1989). "Inmate Gangs." *Corrections Today* 51, 4: 98–128.

Leinwand, G., and C. West. *Problems of American Society: Crime and Juvenile Delinquency.* New York: Washington Square, 1968.

MaGillis, D., and ABC News. *Crime in America: The ABC Report.* Radnor, PA: Chilton Book, 1983.

Monti, D. J. *Wannabee Gangs in Suburb and Schools.* Cambridge, MA: Blackwell, 1994.

Nash, J. R. *Bloodletters and Badmen: A Narrative Encyclopedia of American Criminals from the Pilgrims to the Present.* New York: M. Evans and Company, 1995.

National Institute of Justice. *Research in Brief.* Washington, DC: U.S. Department of Justice, 1993.

———. *Street Gangs: Current Knowledge and Strategies.* Washington, DC: U.S. Department of Justice, 1993.

Padilla, F. M. *The Gang: An American Enterprise.* New Brunswick, NJ: Rutgers University Press, 1993.

Papachristos, A. V. *A.D., After the Disciples: The Neighborhood Impact of Federal Gang Prosecution.* Peotone, IL: New Chicago Press, 2001.

Saccente, D. (1993). "Rap to Street Gang Activity." *Police Chief* 60, 2: 28–31.

Sachs, S. L. *A Resource Guide for Parents and Professionals: Street Gangs Awareness.* Minneapolis, MI: Fairview Press, 1997.

Samenow, S. E. *Inside the Criminal Mind.* New York: Times Press, 1965.

Sanchez-Jankowski, M. *Islands in the Street: Gangs and Urban American Society.* Berkeley: University of California Press, 1991.

Scott, K. *Monster.* New York: Atlantic Monthly Press, 1993.

Spergel, I. "Violent Gangs in Chicago: In Search of Social Policy." *Social Service Review* 58 (1984): 199–226.

Thornberry, T. B., M. D. Krohn, A. J. Lizotte, and D. Chard-Wierschem. "The Role of Juvenile Gangs in Facilitating Delinquent Behavior." *Journal of Research in Crime and Delinquency* 30 (1993): 55–87.

Thrasher, F. M. *The Gang.* Chicago: University of Chicago Press, 1927.

———. *Third Impression.* Abridged. Chicago: University of Chicago Press, 1968.

Webb, M. *Coping with Street Gangs.* New York: Rosen, 1992.

Whyte, W. F. *Street Corner Society.* Chicago: University of Chicago Press, 1943.

Yablonsky, L. *Gangsters: Fifty Years of Madness, Drugs, and Death on the Streets of America.* New York: New York University Press, 1997.

Zimring, F. E. *American Youth Violence.* New York: Oxford University Press, 1998.

WEB SITE

National Criminal Justice Reference Service: www.ncjrs.org/gangs

DOCUMENT

Growth of Youth Gang Problems in the United States, 1970–1998, *Executive Summary*

According to this official report of the Office of Juvenile Justice and Delinquency Prevention, titled Growth of Youth Gang Problems in the United States, 1970–1998, *the number and geographic extent of youth gangs in the United States expanded "dramatically" in the nearly three-decade period under review.*

For many decades, communities in the United States have been troubled by criminal activities, including serious violent crimes, committed by youth gangs. The prevalence and seriousness of gang problems have fluctuated over time, with gang activity escalating during some periods and diminishing during others. The last three decades of the 20th century were characterized by a major escalation of youth gang problems throughout the Nation, accompanied by a substantial increase in gang studies, surveys, and reports. These reports conveyed a general impression that the number of localities experiencing gang problems had increased but failed to provide concrete, national-level information on the size of the increase, the localities involved, and their location. This information gap is filled by the present Report, which presents detailed information on the numbers and specific identities of gang problem localities, the size of these localities, rates of growth, and location by State and region of the cities, towns, villages, and counties that reported gang problems between the 1970's and late

1990's. Trend and rate analyses over a three-decade period were made possible by the availability of baseline data collected by the first national youth gang survey, conducted during the 1970's. Major findings of the Report are summarized below.

The number of localities reporting gang problems increased dramatically between the 1970's and 1990's. By the late 1990's, 3,700 identified localities in the United States—about 2,550 cities, towns, and villages and 1,150 counties, totaling the highest number ever reported—had reported the presence of gang problems. These figures represent a nearly tenfold increase in the number of cities and an elevenfold increase in the number of counties reporting gang problems during the study period.

In the 1970's, 19 States reported gang problems; by the late 1990's, all 50 States and the District of Columbia had reported gang problems. In the 1970's, the combined population of all cities reporting gang problems was about 25 percent of the population of all cities, and the population of all counties reporting gang problems was about 40 percent of the all-county population. By the late 1990's, the population of gang cities had risen to about 60 percent of all cities, and the gang-county population had risen to about 90 percent of the all-county population.

The States with the largest number of gang-problem cities in 1998 were California (363), Illinois (261), Texas (156), Florida (125), and Ohio (86). Of these, only two, California and Illinois, reported large numbers of cities with gang problems in the 1970's. The States with the largest number of gang counties in 1998 were Texas (82), Georgia (61), California (50), Illinois (42), and Florida (40), in that order; the South replaced the Northeast as the region with the most top-ranking States.

Nationwide, there was a substantial decrease in the concentration of gang cities in the higher ranking States as gang problems continued to spread to new States. In the 1970's, the top four States contained about three-quarters of all gang cities; in the 1990's, the percentage had fallen to about one-third. In the 1970's, only 8 States reported 5 or more gang cities; in the 1990's, all 50 States reported 5 or more. In the 1970's, gang counties were concentrated in a relatively small number of States, principally California and Texas. By the 1990's, gang counties were spread widely throughout the Nation. In the 1970's, only 6 States reported more than 5 gang counties; in 1998, 47 States reported more than 5. In 1998, gang-problem cities were concentrated in a relatively small group of counties, with the top-ranking, high-concentration counties containing more than 40 percent of all gang cities. Cook County, IL, reported the largest number of gang cities, followed by Los Angeles County, CA. Riverside and Orange Counties in California also reported high concentrations of gang cities.

The regional location of gang cities changed radically during the three-decade period. In the 1970's, the West ranked highest in the reported number of gang cities, and the South ranked lowest. By 1998, the South ranked second, with a 33-fold increase in gang cities since the 1970's. Traditionally, gang problems have been a big-city phenomenon, and this situation continued during the three decades prior to 2000. In the late 1990's, there were approximately 200 cities with populations of 100,000 or more, and every one of these large cities reported youth gang problems. Comparison of the numbers and percentages of gang cities in designated population categories in 1998 with the numbers and percentages of all U.S. cities shows that gang cities with more than 25,000 inhabitants (larger gang cities) made up 43 percent of all gang cities but contained 88 percent of their population. These larger gang cities made up 77 percent of the number of all larger cities, but 86 percent of their population, and 3 percent of the number of all U.S. cities, but 52 percent of their population.

Gang problems, however, were by no means confined to large cities. One of the best documented developments of this period was a striking increase in the growth of gang problems in the Nation's smaller cities, towns, and villages. The size of the average gang city population fell from 182,000 to 34,000, an 81-percent decline. The number of gang cities with populations less than 25,000 rose from 35 percent of all gang cities to 57 percent, and the population of gang cities smaller than 25,000 rose from less than 1 percent of the total U.S. city population to about 7 percent. The number of gang cities with 1,000 to 5,000 inhabitants increased more than 27 times, and the number of gang cities with 5,000 to 10,000 inhabitants increased more than 32 times.

Reasons for the striking increase in the number of gang-problem localities are discussed in this Report under seven headings: drugs, immigration, gang names and alliances, migration, government policies, female-headed households, and gang subculture and the media.

An analysis of projected growth rates of gang-problem cities provides a basis for predicting future trends in the number of gang cities. The data provide considerable support for a prediction that the rate of growth that prevailed during the later 1990's will decrease in the early 2000's and some support for a prediction that the actual number of gang localities in the United States will decrease.

Source: Walter B. Miller, *Growth of Youth Gang Problems in the United States.* (Washington, DC: U.S. Department of Justice, 2001).

GAY AND LESBIAN RIGHTS

Since the 1960s many industrialized nations have seen the rise of a social movement to protect the rights of lesbians and gays. Although groups in the United States had pursued justice for homosexuals through most of the twentieth century, it was not until 1969 that the debate over gay and lesbian rights became part of the American public dialogue. A riot by transvestites and homosexuals around the Stonewall Inn, a gay bar in New York City raided by police in June 1969, created the impetus for a full-fledged debate over gay and lesbian rights that continues today. Following the definition of gay and lesbian rights and the parameters of opposing viewpoints, this chapter presents a historical overview of the debate in American politics.

DEFINING GAY AND LESBIAN RIGHTS

The debate over gay and lesbian rights concerns the legal recognition and protection of homosexuality and the civil rights and liberties of homosexuals. On one side, gays and lesbians and their supporters argue that homosexuals face discrimination, harassment, and sometimes violence in American society simply because they are homosexual. This treatment violates their civil rights and liberties, which should be protected by the Constitution. To ensure protection of their rights and liberties, gays and lesbians have sought to persuade both the public and the government to enact policies banning various forms of discrimination against homosexuals. For example, many local and state governments have established policies that prohibit public and private employers from making hiring, firing, or promotion decisions based on an employee's sexual orientation. Some governments and private companies have gone further, providing insurance benefits for long-term partners of gay and lesbian employees who cannot legally marry in the United States and are therefore denied the benefits typically afforded to married employees.

Opponents of gay and lesbian rights argue that gays and lesbians already enjoy the rights and liberties all citizens are granted by the Constitution, state constitutions, and federal and state statutory law. Thus, they argue, gays and lesbians are asking for "special rights." Opponents further argue that homosexuality is not an immutable characteristic like race and ethnicity, and therefore should not be singled out in law. Homosexuality is seen as voluntary behavior that individuals can choose not to engage in; if homosexuals are discriminated against, they can stop the discrimination by not engaging in homosexual behavior.

The arguments made by opponents of gay and lesbian rights are also often intertwined with a religious conception of morality. Because many religious traditions define homosexuality as morally wrong, laws that single out homosexuals for protection are de facto endorsements of immoral behavior. Thus, opponents contend, gay rights laws may even encourage homosexuality. Finally, religious conservatives claim that banning discrimination against homosexuals infringes on freedom of religion by, in their view, allowing the government to determine what religious adherents may believe and practice in their faith.

As with many issues involving moral concerns about human behavior, both sides of this debate are often intractable, leaving no clear solution. However, if science uncovers evidence that sexual orientation is an innate characteristic, perhaps determined by our genes, some of the arguments made by opponents of gay and lesbian rights would be less convincing. Religious groups opposed to homosexuality would likely still object to gay rights based on moral grounds; nonetheless, gays and lesbians seeking to protect their rights have achieved some success.

GAY LIBERATION: 1969 TO 1980

Before 1969, the debate over gay and lesbian rights in the United States was frequently confined to dis-

CHRONOLOGY

1924 The first gay rights group in the United States is established by a Chicagoan named Henry Gerber.

1963 Lobbying by the Mattachine Society leads to members of Congress initiating hearings on the group and the introduction of a bill to revoke Mattachine's permit to raise funds in Washington, D.C. The bill, HR 5990, passes the House on August 11, 1964, but dies in the Senate. This marks the first vote on gay issues in Congress.

1968 Mattachine Society of New York successfully lobbies Mayor John Lindsay to issue an executive order forbidding city police from making arrests for "homosexual solicitation" without a signed citizen complaint.

1969 **June.** Police raid sets off riot at the Stonewall Inn in New York City.

1972 Gay delegates appear on the floor of the National Democratic Convention for the first time.

1973 **December.** American Psychiatric Association's board of trustees vote to remove homosexuality from its list of psychiatric disorders.

1974 **April.** Kathy Kozachenko becomes the first openly gay person to be elected to a public office in the United States, taking a seat on the Ann Arbor, Michigan, City Council.

May. First introduction of gay rights legislation in Congress, is sponsored by Bella Abzug and Edward Koch—New York Representatives.

1975 **July.** The U.S. Civil Service Commission drops its ban on lesbians and gays in civilian federal jobs.

1977 A ballot initiative to repeal a gay rights law in Dade County, Florida, sets off a wave of similar initiatives around the country in the years following.

November. Harvey Milk becomes the first openly gay man to be elected to the San Francisco Board of Supervisors.

1978 Gay conservatives in California rally to help kill the antigay Briggs Initiative. The gay Republican opposition in Los Angeles refers to itself as the Log Cabin Club.

1979 The first national March on Washington for Lesbian and Gay Rights draws more than 100,000 demonstrators.

1980 **June.** The Democratic Party adopts a plank insisting on protecting "all groups from discrimination," and opposing the ban on homosexual visitors and immigrants.

1981 What was sometimes called "gay cancer" first appears in U.S. urban areas; later becomes known as AIDS.

1982 **April.** The House Subcommittee on Health and the Environment, chaired by California Rep. Henry Waxman, holds the first federal hearing on Kaposi's sarcoma and related opportunistic infections associated with AIDS.

1983 **January.** America's largest blood banks issue a joint rejection of proposals to ban blood donations from gay males.

1984 **November.** Gerry Studds (D-MA), the first openly gay member of Congress, easily wins reelection after being forced out of the closet by a congressional investigation.

1985 **July.** A Minnesota judge denies custody of Sharon Kowalski, a paralyzed lesbian, to her lover; Kowalski's father is named conservator instead.

October. Rock Hudson dies a year and a half after being diagnosed with AIDS.

1986 The U.S. Supreme Court upholds Georgia's sodomy law in *Bowers v. Hardwick.*

1987 **March.** AIDS Coalition to Unleash Power (ACT UP) in New York is formed. Main slogan is Silence = Death. In its first major action, 250 activists block morning rush hour traffic on Wall Street.

May. Representative Barney Frank (D-MA) comes out of the closet, becoming the second openly gay member of Congress.

October. 500,000 attend the National March on Washington for Gay and Lesbian Rights.

1987   **October.** The House and Senate overwhelmingly pass the Helms Amendment, which forbids federal funding for AIDS education material that "promotes or encourages homosexuality."

1988   **March.** A dozen gay activists are ejected from the Presidential Commission on AIDS hearing after disrupting the testimony of William Dannemeyer (R-CA), who told the panel that AIDS was God's punishment for homosexuality.

1989   **March.** 3,000 protesters stage the largest AIDS demonstration yet in New York City in an attempt to "take over" City Hall to draw attention to the collapse of the city's hospital system; 200 are arrested.

1990   Queer Nation is founded in New York City by four gay men to attack homophobia and heterosexism, especially hate crimes against gays.

February. The U.S. Senate approves a hate crimes bill that includes crimes based on sexual orientation; President George H.W. Bush later signs it into law.

1991   Magic Johnson announces he is HIV positive in a live press conference on ESPN and CNN.

May 1. Case of *Baehr v. Lewin* (1993), later styled *Baehr v. Miike*, begins. Joe Melillo and Patrick Lagon joins two lesbian couples in filing suit against Hawaii to obtain marriage licenses.

September. AIDS activists from Treatment Action Guerrillas (TAG), an ACT UP-New York spin-off, cover the Arlington, Virginia, home of Senator Jesse Helms with a giant condom dropped from a helicopter.

1992   Gay political fund-raising achieves a historic milestone, raising at least $3.4 million toward the Democratic victory. Gay Republican organizing also peaks as Log Cabin Clubs are organized nationwide and openly gay delegates are present at the Republican convention.

February. University of Colorado, Boulder, football coach Bill McCartney sparks controversy by spearheading the antigay initiative, Amendment 2, which passes later that year.

1993   **May 5.** In *Baehr v. Lewin*, the Hawaii Supreme Court holds that a statute denying marriage rights to same-sex couples may violate the state constitutional equal rights provision.

September. Congress rejects President Clinton's attempt to end the ban on gays in the military and enacts the "don't ask, don't tell" policy.

1994   Unsuccessful petition drives for statewide antigay ballot initiatives in Arizona, Florida, Maine, Michigan, Montana, Nevada, Washington, and Ohio.

1995   **October.** In South Dakota, organizers announce the creation of Free Americans Creating Equal Status (FACES), the state's first gay political group, in Rapid City.

November. Barbara Kavanaugh becomes the first lesbian elected to the Buffalo, New York, city council.

1996   Congress passes and the president signs the so-called Defense of Marriage Act, which defines marriages as between a man and a woman for federal benefits purposes and allows states to refuse recognition of same-sex marriages performed in other states.

May 20. The U.S. Supreme Court upholds the Colorado Supreme Court's ruling and declares Amendment 2, the antigay ballot initiative, unconstitutional in *Romer v. Evans*. The high Court rules that the constitutional amendment violates homosexuals' equal-protection rights.

December 3. Case of *Baehr v. Lewin* (1993), now known as *Baehr v. Miike*, rules that the state could not demonstrate compelling interest to justify the statute defining marriage as only between a man and a woman. The ruling makes Hawaii the first state to recognize that gay and lesbian couples are entitled to the same privileges as heterosexual married couples.

1997   **February.** A pipe bomb covered with nails explodes in a crowded Atlanta gay bar, injuring several people. President Clinton condemns the act.

April. Ellen DeGeneres makes history by coming out as a lesbian as the lead character on the ABC television show *Ellen*. Some local affiliates choose not to run the show.

October. Virginia M. Apuzzo is appointed by President Clinton as the Assistant to the President for Management and Administration, making her the highest ranking openly LGBT official in history.

1998   **October.** National outcry erupts over the brutal murder of an openly gay college student, Matthew Shepard, in Wyoming.

1998 November. Tammy Baldwin wins her race for a U.S. House seat and makes history by becoming the first open lesbian elected to Congress, the first nonincumbent LGBT person elected to Congress, and the first woman elected to Congress from Wisconsin.

1999 New Hampshire repeals its 1988 ban on adoption by homosexuals.

December. The Vermont Supreme Court rules that the state must provide the benefits of marriage to same-sex couples by either allowing same-sex couples to marry or recognizing the relationship in some other manner.

2000 Vermont passes a historic law giving same-sex couples the right to form state-sanctioned civil unions and enjoy more than 300 benefits, rights, and responsibilities available to heterosexual married couples.

June. The U.S. Supreme Court rules that the Boy Scouts of America can ban homosexuals from their organization.

2001 May. After ten years of lobbying by LGBT groups, Maryland enacts a gay civil rights law.

July. Rhode Island joins Minnesota in banning discrimination against transgendered people.

2002 Minneapolis, Minnesota, elects two openly gay city council members.

August. Pennsylvania Supreme Court rules that gays and lesbians can adopt the children of their partners.

2003 June 27. In *Lawrence v. Texas*, the Supreme Court rules a Texas antisodomy law unconstitutional; in a sweeping statement, the court says that the government has no right to regulate the private sexual behavior of consenting adults; many in the gay and lesbian community see the ruling as a vindication of their full and equal citizenship rights.

November 18. In *Goodridge et al. v. Department of Public Health* the Massachusetts Supreme Judicial Court ruled that the state cannot bar "an individual from the protections, benefits and obligations of civil marriage solely because that person would marry a person of the same sex."

cussions of homosexuals' deviant status—or their treatment as deviants in American society. However, interest groups focused on protecting the civil rights and liberties of homosexuals existed as early as 1924. In the 1950s a number of relatively secretive homosexual groups formed on both coasts, creating what came to be known as the homophile movement. These early groups typically provided a safe space in which members could talk with other homosexuals, but some began initial efforts to protect the free speech rights of homosexuals and overturn government laws and regulations that specifically discriminated against them, for example, federal laws banning the employment of homosexuals and affecting the immigration rights of gays and lesbians.

During the 1950s, an early gay group, the Veterans Benevolent Association, worked with African-American groups to end the military's arbitrary use of undesirable discharges. Also in the 1950s, gay organizations successfully secured their right to mail material with homosexual content, challenging the U.S. Postmaster's 1954 ruling, following demands by members of Congress that a gay magazine (*ONE*) could not be sent through the U.S. mail. Gay groups challenged the decision, and the Supreme Court over-

ruled the Postmaster in 1958. Further, early homophile groups attempted to overturn state and local laws banning same-sex relations between consenting adults and to prevent police harassment of homosexuals in bars and bathhouses. Their successes, however, were limited to larger cities on the coasts and states that were revising their criminal codes in the 1960s.

Following the Stonewall riots in 1969, gays and lesbians developed a broader notion of gay and lesbian rights including both personal and societal liberation. Not only must hatred of homosexuals in society be stopped, but hatred by homosexuals of themselves as well. Gay liberationists believed that to stop their self-hatred homosexuals must publicly declare their homosexuality. This process came to be known as "coming out" or "coming out of the closet." Liberation activists set out to transform traditional notions of sex and gender by educating homosexuals and the larger public and by changing government policies to ensure that their civil rights and liberties were not violated.

But coming out to friends, family, and coworkers was not enough for some activists. The liberationists also believed gays and lesbians must take to the streets and the halls of government to make their existence known. Throughout the 1970s liberationists engaged in protest politics by marching in the streets, staging media events, and dogging elected officials about their stance on gay civil rights.

Other activists, labeled assimilationists by some, focused their attention on more mainstream political participation, taking part in political parties, forming interest groups, promoting litigation, and lobbying elected officials. Gay activists formed many new interest groups at the local, state, and national levels, and some, such as the National Gay (now Gay and Lesbian) Task Force and Lambda Legal Defense Fund, still operate today. Within the Democratic Party, gay activists increased their political muscle by forming caucuses and drafting platform planks supporting lesbian and gay civil rights.

But not all gay interest groups were purely assimilationist or liberationist. Hybrid groups, such as the Gay Activists Alliance (GAA) in New York City, combined protest politics with mainstream lobbying and political campaign participation. During the early 1970s, GAA directly lobbied politicians and conducted "zaps" (organized protests) outside the homes and offices of politicians during the group's initial attempt to pass a New York City ordinance banning discrimination against homosexuals.

Although the stigma attached to homosexuality remained largely unchanged throughout the 1970s, the gay movement began to build a list of impressive victories in government policy, private employment practices, and media depiction of homosexuality. Elected officials were becoming open about their sexual orientation, and openly gay and lesbian candidates were being elected for the first time. In cities such as San Francisco and New York, gays and lesbians were being appointed to government positions. Indeed, after gays helped elect George Moscone as mayor of San Francisco in 1975, Moscone appointed openly gay Harvey Milk to the city's Board of Permit Appeals, making Milk the first openly gay appointed official in the country. Milk subsequently used his position as a launching pad to campaign for and win an election to the San Francisco Board of Supervisors. Tragically, another supervisor murdered both Moscone and Milk on November 27, 1978. Milk's life and death helped reinvigorate the gay community, convincing a new generation of gays and lesbians to become involved in electoral politics.

Local governments across the country also began to adopt policies prohibiting discrimination based on sexual orientation in public employment, housing, and even private employment. State courts increasingly overturned archaic laws regarding sexual relations between adults, cross-dressing, and the civil liberties of homosexuals. State legislatures began repealing laws that banned homosexual relations, and legislators introduced bills to eliminate sexual orientation discrimination. By the late 1970s, even the U.S. Congress was holding hearings on issues related to homosexuals, and introduced the first bills prohibiting discrimination on the basis of sexual orientation. A federal policy barring gays from employment in the Foreign Service was lifted in 1977, the same year gay and lesbian activists were invited to the White House for the first time. The Internal Revenue Service ended a policy requiring homosexual education and charity groups to publicly state that homosexuality is a "sickness, disturbance, or diseased pathology" before they could obtain tax-exempt (501) status.

However, the successes of the gay movement also brought a political backlash. Believing that their religious values were under attack, conservative Christians began to exert their political muscle. By the late 1970s, gays and conservative religious groups were facing off in local and state battles with both sides claiming their rights were threatened. In Florida, Anita Bryant led a successful campaign for a 1977 ballot initiative to overturn Dade County's ban of sexual orientation discrimination. The national attention it received soon inspired other ballot contests in Eugene, Oregon, St. Paul, Minnesota, Seattle, Washington, and Wichita, Kansas; gay rights forces lost in every case but Seattle. And in California, a 1978 ballot initiative to prevent homosexuals from teaching in the public schools failed only because even conservatives such as Ronald Reagan viewed the measure as draconian.

AIDS AND THE CHANGING BATTLEGROUND

As the 1970s came to a close, the movement for gay and lesbian rights had made considerable strides. But with the rise of the religious right, the public shift to conservative values, and the outbreak of a new disease, the young social movement faced complex challenges.

In 1981 religious conservatives were celebrating the presidential inauguration of their chosen candidate, Ronald Reagan. At the same time, the freewheeling counterculture of gay liberationists was forced to confront what some called the movement's excesses as the first cases of "gay cancer," or gay-related immune deficiency (GRID), appeared in young gay men throughout the country. The disease came to be known as acquired immunodeficiency syndrome (AIDS) and disproportionately affected gay men and intravenous drug users, two groups already seriously stigmatized in society.

AIDS redefined both homosexuality and the gay movement. Religious conservatives saw it as a sign from God of the evils of homosexuality and used it as an opportunity to roll back policy victories of the gay movement and block further legal protections based on sexual orientation. In states across the country, fear over the spread of AIDS led to legislative efforts to criminalize and regulate the behaviors of persons with AIDS. In California, religious conservatives proposed a number of measures to stop the spread of the disease, including the quarantine of people with AIDS. The ballot measures all failed as gays and lesbians mobilized against them, but in many states gays were increasingly losing political battles.

At the national level, Democrats in Congress championed funding for AIDS research, education, and healthcare by 1985, even as President Reagan refused to publicly use the word AIDS. Interestingly, congressional action on AIDS appears to have been partly motivated by the increasing number of public figures who were declaring they had AIDS, were gay, or both. In fact, the first openly gay member of Congress was Rep. Gerry Studds (D-MA), who revealed that he was gay in July 1983 but continued to serve until 1996. The second member of Congress to reveal his sexual orientation was Rep. Barney Frank (D-MA), in May 1987. And although Rep. Frank's public declaration followed a personal scandal, he has continued to be reelected, gaining prominence in the House and the Democratic Party and serving as a national role model for gay and lesbian Americans.

By 1987 a few conservative members of Congress, including Senator Jesse Helms (R-NC), began to successfully attach amendments to AIDS funding bills that explicitly banned the use of federal funds to "promote homosexuality." Religious conservatives gained more ammunition against the gay movement in the late 1980s with the controversial museum exhibitions of Robert Mapplethorpe's homoerotic photographs, which was partially funded by taxpayers through the National Endowment for the Arts (NEA). At the behest of religious conservative groups, conservative members of Congress tried for several years to end or limit NEA funding, but succeeded only in slightly cutting its budget. Pro-gay Democrats in Congress joined forces with moderate Republicans and largely fended off the attacks by religious conservatives; nevertheless, all legislation seeking to protect gays from discrimination or hate crimes died in Congress during the late 1980s. These battles reinforced and expanded the increasingly partisan split on gay issues in Congress, with Democrats tending to support and Republicans tending to oppose gay rights.

The gay movement also had few litigation successes during the 1980s. State courts consistently ruled against homosexuals in child custody cases, allowed sodomy laws to stand, and upheld the rights of individuals and groups to discriminate against homosexuals on the basis of religious beliefs. The most important court decision from this period was in the 1986 Supreme Court *Bowers v. Hardwick* case. Gay litigation groups challenged Georgia's law banning homosexual sodomy under the constitutional right to privacy of sex acts in one's own home. Rejecting the right to privacy claims of a man convicted of illegal homosexual acts under this law, the Supreme Court ensured that similar laws would remain on the books throughout the country. The case still stands as the most significant legal defeat for the gay rights movement.

AIDS and the Republican presidents of the 1980s also provided a greater incentive for gays and lesbians to join and create more interest groups at the national and state level. Throughout the 1980s the number of gay groups grew steadily, with some focusing exclusively on AIDS issues. Further, by the late 1980s some of the new groups—AIDS Coalition to Unleash Power (ACT UP) and, later, Treatment Action Guerrillas (TAG), Queer Nation, and the Lesbian Avengers, for example—reintroduced radical protest tactics, calling for AIDS funding and an end to the cultural stigma attached to gays and lesbians. The attention-grabbing actions of these groups brought media coverage to the movement and helped mobilize a new generation of activists. But by the mid-1990s, most of their local chapters had disappeared.

New gay groups also formed at the state and local levels during the 1980s, and many were increasingly successful at securing legal protections for gays and lesbians. In 1982 Wisconsin became the first state to pass a law banning discrimination in public employment based on sexual "preference," but gay rights

legislation was being introduced on almost an annual basis in other states, such as Oregon, Maine,
New York, and California. Governors of several states
signed executive orders protecting state employees
from sexual orientation discrimination, including
New York, Washington, Oregon, and Ohio. The number of local ordinances banning sexual orientation
discrimination grew to one hundred by the end of
the decade, even though religious conservatives had
increasingly mobilized to defeat these measures.
When religious groups failed to block these policies,
they increasingly turned to the ballot box, ousted
elected officials who supported these policies, and
placed proposals on the ballot to repeal these policies. Indeed, more than twenty of these measures
were voted on during the 1980s; religious conservatives successfully repealed gay rights laws most of
the time, an Oregon state measure, several local
measures in California, and a city ordinance in Houston, Texas, among others.

THE GAY 1990s

When the 1990s began, the gay movement appeared
to be riding a favorable wave of public tolerance and
policy success. In 1990, a Democratic Congress and
Republican president enacted a hate crime policy
including sexual orientation and the Americans with
Disabilities Act, which protects persons with HIV/
AIDS from discrimination. In 1992 gay groups helped
elect gay-friendly candidates to Congress, and contributions of more than $3.2 million to the Demo-
cratic Party helped ensure the election of a
gay-friendly president, Bill Clinton. Gay rights legislation was also increasingly being passed in the states,
with Connecticut, Hawaii, Massachusetts, Minnesota, and New Jersey all providing legal protections
by 1993. Local governments continued to codify gay
rights, and more also began to adopt domestic partner policies for government employees, which allowed the committed partners of gays and lesbians
to obtain a variety of benefits such as health insurance that were usually reserved for the spouses of
married employees. Within the movement, groups
such as the National Gay and Lesbian Task Force
were addressing the concerns of bisexuals and
transgender individuals. Further, states and localities increasingly adopted policies that banned discrimination based not only on sexual orientation but
also on gender identity.

But even as gay activists celebrated these victo-

ries, religious conservatives redoubled their efforts
to protect traditional values. These groups increasingly attempted to repeal or prevent the passage of
gay rights laws through the ballot initiative process.
Nearly all their campaigns were successful, but the
key successes were in Cincinnati, Ohio, and Colorado. In 1992 a majority of Colorado voters supported Amendment 2, a referendum that sought to
repeal local gay rights laws and ban any new local or
statewide gay rights laws. The vote was a significant
victory for conservative religious groups, but the
Colorado Supreme Court soon overturned the election results; in 1996 the U.S. Supreme Court upheld
the earlier decision in *Romer v. Evans*, ruling Amendment 2 unconstitutional because it prevented homosexuals from using the political process to achieve
policy goals. In the Cincinnati case, voters in 1993
overwhelmingly passed a measure to repeal a 1992
gay rights law enacted by the city council. Mobiliz-
ing church members and the black community, conservatives argued that traditional religious values were
under fire. Gay groups challenged the election outcome in court, but the city council repealed the ordinance in 1995, making the challenges largely moot.
The lesson for the gay movement in these ballots
was that codified legal recognition of their civil rights
would lose in a popular vote.

Religious conservatives also won a major victory
against gay rights in 1993 when they soundly defeated President Clinton's effort to allow homosexuals to serve openly in the U.S. military. Candidate
Clinton had promised his gay supporters that he
would overturn the ban, but once in office President
Clinton attempted to convince Congress to repeal
the ban rather than issue an Executive Order. Religious conservatives overwhelmed members of Congress, voicing their support for the ban. Gay groups
were outgunned and arrived at the "Don't Ask, Don't
Tell" compromise that many argue is worse than the
original policy. Indeed, under the new policy discharges of homosexuals have generally increased
every year, reversing earlier trends.

The 1994 congressional elections brought more
conservatives to Washington, D.C., many of whom
had drawn their support from religious activists in
the Republican Party. With this shift in power, legislation supporting gay rights made little headway in
Congress through the remainder of the 1990s, and
gay groups had to spend most of their time defending against antigay rights legislation. However, new
opportunities were created for gays working within

Figure 1. Local Government Bans on Sexual Orientation Discrimination, 1972–2003

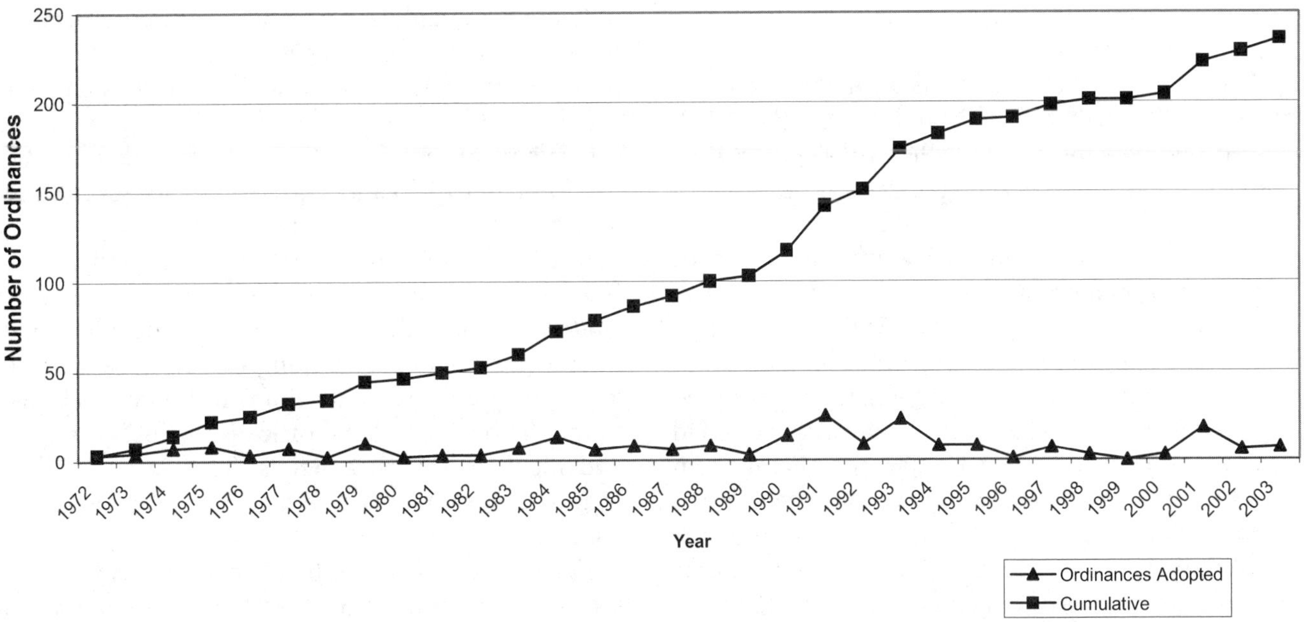

Source: Data compiled by the author from Raymond A. Smith and Donald P. Haider-Markel. *Gay and Lesbian Americans and Political Participation.* Santa Barbara, CA: ABC-CLIO, 2002; and historical data from the National Gay and Lesbian Task Force.

the Republican Party as a federation of local gay Republican groups established a national office in Washington, D.C., in 1993. Known as the Log Cabin Republicans, the new group formed a political action committee that raises tens of thousands of dollars per election cycle for Republican candidates and, by 1996, had six staff members and an annual budget of $700,000.

Throughout the 1990s, gays also faced an increasingly conservative Supreme Court. In *Dale v. Boy Scouts of America* (2000), the Court ruled that the Boy Scouts of America could ban homosexuals from their organization to maintain the moral objectives of the organization. However, President Clinton continued to support the gay movement, issuing official recognitions of gay pride month each June, signing an Executive Order in 1998 to ban discrimination against civilian federal employees on the basis of sexual orientation, and appointing 150 gays and lesbians to federal positions through two terms in office.

Same-sex marriage also became a significant gay rights issue in the 1990s. Although gays had tried to marry legally in the 1970s and 1980s, their efforts had always failed. Then, in 1993, a Hawaii Supreme Court ruling in *Baehr v. Lewin* (later *Baehr v. Miike*) argued that preventing same-sex marriage violated

the Hawaii constitution's ban on gender discrimination. Religious conservatives around the country were outraged by the case, claiming homosexuals would travel to Hawaii, get married, and try to force recognition of their marriages in their home states. In late 1994 and early 1995, a number of conservative groups formalized a national campaign to introduce legislation in all fifty states and the U.S. Congress to ban same-sex marriage. The organized effort manifested itself mainly through the National Campaign to Protect Marriage (NCPM), a coalition of groups such as the American Family Association, the Christian Coalition, Concerned Women of America, the Eagle Forum, Equal Rights Not Special Rights, the Family Research Council, Focus on the Family, and the Traditional Values Coalition.

These organizations helped distribute a video, *The Ultimate Target of the Gay Agenda. Same Sex Marriage,* to state legislatures, and many of them also engaged in independent actions promoting legislative bans on same-sex marriage. For example, Focus on the Family provided state legislatures with literature on same-sex marriage. In California, the national leader of the Traditional Values Coalition, the Rev. Lou Sheldon, presented an information session on legislation to ban same-sex marriage to Republican legislators and their staffs. Concerned Women of

America also distributed videos and information packets to California legislators on same-sex marriage and the case pending in Hawaii, targeting members of key committees.

The resulting national legislation on same-sex marriage, the Defense of Marriage Act (DOMA), passed overwhelmingly in 1996. Although DOMA allowed states to do as they pleased on the issue, it banned any federal recognition of same-sex marriages and permitted states to not recognize same-sex marriages performed elsewhere. State governments followed a similar path. By March 1998, all but two states had considered banning the recognition of same-sex marriages and twenty-eight had adopted such policies. By 2002 at least thirty-three states had passed similar laws, even though the threat from same-sex marriages in Hawaii never emerged. At the end of 1999, however, the Vermont Supreme Court ruled that the state must provide marriage benefits to same-sex couples by either allowing them to marry or recognizing the relationship in some other manner. This ruling led to the nation's first same-sex civil union law in 2000, which provided gay couples the right to form state-sanctioned civil unions and take advantage of nearly all the benefits, rights, and responsibilities available to heterosexual married couples.

Even facing a largely hostile Congress as the 1990s progressed, gay rights advocates achieved new victories in state and local public policy, political representation, and shifts in national public opinion. By the end of the 1990s more than two hundred local governments had adopted some form of legal protections for gays and lesbians and over eighty provided domestic partner benefits. In addition, a number of states and localities, including Minnesota and Boulder, Colorado, banned discrimination based on gender identity. Figure 1 shows the pattern of local antidiscrimination laws over time. Direct challenges to these policies began to decrease, and those that did reach the ballot were increasingly voted down. But religious conservatives in Maine repealed statewide gay rights laws twice in the late 1990s, even as local antidiscrimination ordinances were passed.

The 1990s also witnessed a tremendous increase in the number and scope of gay and lesbian officials in government positions. The first openly gay person to run for public office was Jose Sarria, who ran for the San Francisco Board of Supervisors in 1961. Sarria lost his race, but his effort inspired other gays and lesbians to run for public office. Throughout the

1970s and 1980s most of these candidates lost their races as well, and by 1987 the movement could claim only twenty openly gay or lesbian elected officials in the country, mostly in local government. By 1990, however, there had been a total of fifty openly gay officials, and in 1991 fifty-two openly gay elected officials were in office. By April 1998 this number had jumped to 146 and spanned twenty-seven states and the District of Columbia. In 2002 the number had risen to more than 200, but this was still a small fraction of the over 500,000 elective offices in the United States. Still, the 2002 figures included three openly gay members of Congress, forty-seven state legislators, and a scattering of other state-level positions; the rest were local officials, including mayors and local legislative officials. The city of Wilton Manors, Florida, even had a gay majority on its city council.

Furthermore, open lesbians increasingly began to seek elective office at the state and national level in the 1990s. They secured state legislative seats in California, Maine, Montana, New Mexico, New York, and Oregon. Indeed, some called 1998 the "year of the lesbian" as four lesbians ran for seats in the U.S. House and another ten ran for state legislative seats. The only lesbian House candidate to win her race was Rep. Tammy Baldwin (D-WI), who made history as the first lesbian and first nonincumbent gay person elected to Congress. In the 2000 elections only two lesbians ran for Congress, in addition to the first transgender candidate, but more than twenty lesbians ran for state legislative seats.

In addition to elected positions, gays and lesbians have also increasingly been appointed to various government positions. At the national level, President Carter was the first president to appoint an openly gay person to a national office, but appointments did not take off until President Clinton's administration in 1993. Clinton thanked the gay movement for its support by appointing 150 open gays and lesbians to positions in the executive branch. Although only five of these appointments required Senate confirmation, at least two were confirmed even over loud objections from religious conservatives. President George W. Bush had assured religious conservatives in the Republican Party that he would not appoint open homosexuals, but by August 2002 he had appointed seven open gays to his administration.

Most of the more than 200 gays and lesbians in local and state government have been fairly low profile, and without news coverage, often go unnoticed.

Figure 2. Support for Homosexual Civil Rights and Liberties, 1973 to 2001

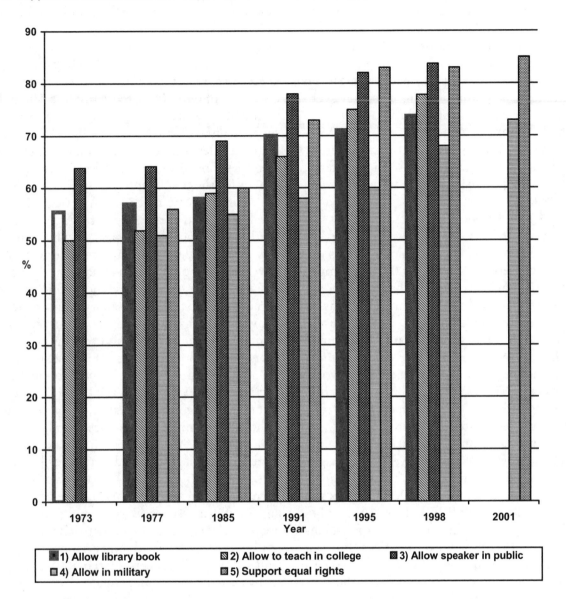

Notes: Data compiled from General Social Survey (GSS) and Gallup Poll questions asked of adults in the United States. The responses to each survey question are displayed as the percentage of respondents indicating a response supportive of gay civil rights and liberties.

The questions were stated as:

1. If some people in your community suggested that a book he wrote in favor of homosexuality should be taken out of your public library, would you favor removing this book, or not?

2. And what about a man who admits that he is a homosexual? Should such a person be allowed to teach in a college or university, or not?

3. And what about a man who admits that he is a homosexual? Suppose this admitted homosexual wanted to make a speech in your community. Should he be allowed to speak, or not?

4. Now I'd like to ask you about the hiring of homosexuals in specific occupations. Do you think homosexuals should or should not be hired for the following occupations: The armed forces?

5. As you may know, there has been considerable discussion in the news regarding the rights of homosexual men and women. In general, do you think homosexuals should or should not have equal rights in terms of job opportunities?

Source: Frank Newport. "Poll Releases, June 4, 2001, American Attitudes Toward Homosexuality Continue to Become More Tolerant." *Gallup News Service.* 2001.

Because some states still outlaw homosexual sex, these persons appointed by elected officials are admittedly breaking the law; nevertheless, some gays have been appointed to high-profile positions. For example, in 1998 Reform Party Minnesota Governor-elect Jesse Ventura tapped openly gay Steven Bosacker to lead his transition team. Bosacker eventually become Ventura's chief of staff in 1999, even though same-sex sexual relations were illegal in Minnesota at the time. Likewise, California Governor Gray Davis appointed at least thirty-seven high-level, open gays and lesbians to his administration between January 1999 and August 2002.

And although most local appointed positions are nonpaying, low-profile positions as well, gay and lesbian appointees do sometimes encounter serious opposition from conservatives. In July 2002, for example, when Nassau County executive Thomas Suozzi appointed openly gay William Borman to the Nassau County Human Rights Commission, Republicans on the Nassau County Legislature's Rules Committee voted against the proposed nominee citing his inexperience, even though Borman had spent years working on human rights issues. The Republican opposition was not enough to derail the nomination, however, and it passed the committee in a party-line vote.

Political representation of any group is certainly important, and does reflect how the debate over gay rights has evolved over time. But the evolving debate is perhaps most clearly reflected by changes in public opinion. By the late 1990s the public had become far more tolerant and supportive of lesbians and gays and their civil rights and liberties. Although many Americans still opposed hiring homosexuals for positions involving children, such as in the education system, Americans increasingly supported protecting gays and lesbians from discrimination. Figure 2 shows this trend over time. In the 1970s only small majorities supported allowing homosexuals to speak in public, allowing books on homosexuality in the public library, allowing homosexuals to teach in college or serve openly in the military, or providing equal rights to gays and lesbians. By the late 1990s support in all of these areas had increased, with the greatest support for a vague notion of equal rights.

But even as Americans have become increasingly supportive of gay and lesbian rights, opponents' arguments appear to fit with American attitudes toward homosexuals and the "rightness" of same-sex sexual relations. Though more tolerant of homosexuals as a group and less averse to the notion of same-sex sexual relations, most Americans still apparently object to homosexual behavior and oppose support of homosexuals. Figure 3 demonstrates this point by plotting average American attitudes about homosexuals. Survey respondents in this "feeling thermometer" are asked to state their emotional response to a group on a scale of 0 to 100; a score of 50 to 100 indicates favorable or warm feelings and a score from 0 to 50 suggests unfavorable or cold feelings. The American National Election Study has used feeling thermometer questions to access attitudes toward a variety of groups for the past twenty years. The mean scores in the figure indicate that most Americans have unfavorable or cold feelings toward gays and lesbians. Furthermore, across the years in which the survey was conducted, gays and lesbians have average scores lower than any other group except illegal immigrants.

Furthermore, Americans tend to oppose allowing homosexuals to teach elementary school children and allowing homosexual couples to marry legally. A Gallup poll from 1977 found that 65 percent of respondents opposed hiring a homosexual as an elementary schoolteacher. Though opposition had decreased to 40 percent by 2001, the level of opposition still suggests a rejection of gay employment rights under some circumstances. Gallup polls from 2000 and 2002 also suggest that majorities oppose same-sex marriage and civil unions for homosexuals akin to the civil union policy adopted in Vermont. Men tend to be slightly more opposed than women, and Republicans, conservatives, and frequent churchgoers are also more opposed to civil unions. This pattern is consistent with other national polls on gay rights and clearly reflects the religious, partisan, and ideological divide on the issue.

In June 2003, the Supreme Court reached a landmark decision concerning the rights of gays and lesbians. In *Lawrence v. Texas*, the court ruled six to three that Texas's antisodomy law was unconstitutional. The ruling reversed the court's own 1986 ruling upholding the constitutionality of a similar Georgia law. Writing for the majority, Justice Anthony Kennedy issued a sweeping statement against government laws regulating private sexual behavior between consenting adults. The ruling was hailed by many in the gay and lesbian community as vindicating their rights to full and equal citizenship. Conservatives, including dissenting justice Antonin Scalia, said the court was going along with the so-called homosexual agenda, and many feared the ruling would eventually call into questions laws against

Figure 3. American Attitudes Toward Gays and Lesbians, 1984–2000

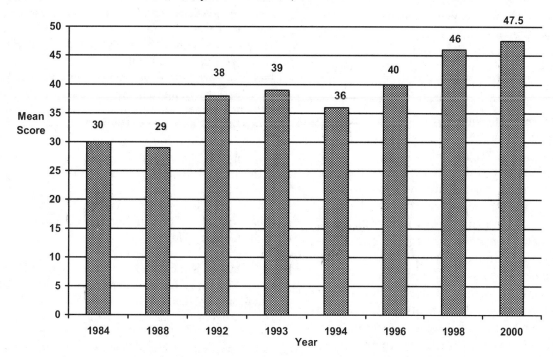

Note: Respondents were asked to state their feelings toward a group using a 0 to 100 scale, where a score of 50 to 100 indicates favorable or warm feelings and a score from 0 to 50 suggests an unfavorable or cold feeling with the following question: "How would you rate the following groups . . . gay men and lesbians, i.e. homosexuals?"
Source: Data compiled by the author from Alan S. Yang. *From Wrongs to Rights. Public Opinion on Gay and Lesbian Americans Moves Toward Equality, 1973–1999.* Washington, DC: National Gay and Lesbian Task Force, 1999; and American National Election Study (ANES).

homosexual marriage. Indeed, most national polls taken in July and August showed a reversal in the upward trend of favorable public opinion toward homosexuals and LGBT (lesbian, gay, bisexual, and transgender) equality. Responses to the question, "Do you think homosexual relations between consenting adults should or should not be legal?" showed that support for "legal" relations dropped from a record high of 60 percent in May 2003 to 48 percent in a July 2003 national poll of adults conducted by Gallup. In addition, the percentage of adults believing that homosexuality is an acceptable alternative lifestyle dropped from 54 percent to 46 percent in the same time period, and the percentage of the public who supported civil unions for homosexual couples dropped from 49 percent to 40 percent. Likewise, support for a constitutional ban on same-sex marriage increased from 41 to 52 percent.

The public opinion backlash against the Court's June decision may have been compounded by a November decision by the Massachusetts Supreme Judicial Court in *Goodridge, et al. v. Department of Public Health.* In a four to three decision, the court

said that "barring an individual from the protections, benefits and obligations of civil marriage solely because that person would marry a person of the same sex violates the Massachusetts Constitution." The court stayed its decision for 180 days to allow the legislature to determine how it would grant same-sex couples the rights and obligations of civil marriage. Although a slim plurality of Massachusetts voters supported the decision, national opinion toward homosexuals and LGBT equality continued to drop, and politicians in many states and the national government promised to promote legislation and constitutional amendments defining civil marriage as solely between a man and a woman. Nevertheless, the long-term impact of the *Lawrence* and *Goodridge* decisions will likely take some time to decipher.

CONCLUSION

The gay rights movement has experienced increasing policy successes and political representation during a time when the country faced serious questions concerning the HIV/AIDS epidemic and religious conservatives found a new voice in American politics. As with other culture war issues, such as the death penalty, abortion, and gun control, the gay rights debate often leaves little room for the political compromise needed in a democracy in which powers are divided across levels of government and political institutions. Furthermore, when religious morals are imposed and biological science offers no final answers on this issue, virtually any citizen can insist that he or she is "right."

Because both sides claim absolute values that cannot be compromised, the debate over gay and lesbian rights has become deeply entrenched in the American political landscape and will likely remain a contentious issue for some time to come. The parameters of the debate have clearly shifted over time, however, spreading across all levels of government and public life, not just in the streets, but also in courtrooms, legislatures, the executive branch, and the ballot box. The influx of gay characters into television shows and movies also exposes the public to issues surrounding homosexuality, even though a significant portion of the population apparently wants to avoid them. Clearly, advocates on all sides of this controversy can claim some victories and some defeats, but the nature of the policymaking process and society's shifting values will likely ensure that no one group can achieve absolute victory.

Donald P. Haider-Markel

REFERENCES

Adam, Barry D. *The Rise of a Gay and Lesbian Movement.* Rev. ed. New York: Twayne, 1995.

Bailey, Robert W. *Gay Politics, Urban Politics. Identity and Economics in an Urban Setting.* New York: Columbia University Press, 1999.

————. *Out and Voting II. The Gay, Lesbian, and Bisexual Vote in Congressional Elections, 1990–1998.* Washington, DC: Policy Institute of the National Gay and Lesbian Task Force, 2000.

Bull, Chris, and John Gallagher. *Perfect Enemies. The Religious Right, the Gay Movement, and the Politics of the 1990s.* New York: Crown, 1996.

Button, James W., Barbara A. Rienzo, and Kenneth D. Wald. *Private Lives, Public Conflicts. Battles over Gay Rights in American Communities.* Washington, DC: Congressional Quarterly, 1997.

Cain, Patricia A. *Rainbow Rights. The Role of Lawyers and Courts in the Lesbian and Gay Civil Rights Movement.* Boulder, CO: Westview, 2000.

Haider-Markel, Donald P. "Creating Change—Holding the Line. Agenda Setting on Lesbian and Gay Issues at the National Level." In *Gays and Lesbians in the Democratic Process. Public Policy, Public Opinion and Political Representation*, ed. Ellen D. B. Riggle and Barry Tadlock. New York: Columbia University Press, 1999.

————. "Redistributing Values in Congress. Interest Group Influence Under Sub-Optimal Conditions." *Political Research Quarterly* 52, 1 (1999): 113–44.

————. "Policy Diffusion as a Geographical Expansion of the Scope of Political Conflict. Same-Sex Marriage Bans in the 1990s." *State Politics and Policy Quarterly* 1, 1 (2001): 5–26.

Haider-Markel, Donald P., and Kenneth J. Meier. "The Politics of Gay and Lesbian Rights. Expanding the Scope of the Conflict." *Journal of Politics* 58, 2 (1996): 332–49.

Haider-Markel, Donald P., Mark R. Joslyn, and Chad J. Kniss. "Minority Group Interests and Political Representation. Gay Elected Officials in the Policy Process." *The Journal of Politics* 62, 2 (2000): 568–77.

Hertzog, Mark. *The Lavender Vote. Lesbians, Gay Men, and Bisexuals in American Electoral Politics.* New York: New York University Press, 1996.

Lindamen, Kara, and Donald P. Haider-Markel. "Issue Evolution, Political Parties, and the Culture Wars." *Political Research Quarterly* 55, 1 (2002): 91–110.

Newport, Frank. "American Attitudes Toward Homosexuality Continue to Become More Tolerant." *Gallup News Service* (June 4, 2001).

Rayside, David Morton. *On the Fringe. Gays and Lesbians in Politics.* Ithaca, NY: Cornell University Press, 1998.

Riggle, D. B., and Barry L. Tadlock. eds. *Gays and Lesbians in the Democratic Process.* New York: Columbia University Press, 1999.

Rimmerman, Craig A., Kenneth D. Wald, and Clyde Wilcox, eds. *The Politics of Gay Rights.* Chicago: University of Chicago Press, 2000.

Sherrill, Kenneth, and Alan Yang. "From Outlaws to In-Laws. Anti-Gay Attitudes Thaw." *Public Perspective* 11, 1 (2000): 20–31.

Shilts, Randy. *The Mayor of Castro Street. The Life and Times of Harvey Milk.* New York: St. Martin's, 1982.

Smith, Raymond A., and Donald P. Haider-Markel. *Gay and Lesbian Americans and Political Participation.* Santa Barbara, CA: ABC-CLIO, 2002.

Thompson, Mark, ed. *The Long Road to Freedom.* New York: St. Martin's, 1994.

Vaid, Urvashi. *Virtual Equality. The Mainstreaming of Gay and Lesbian Liberation.* New York: Anchor Books, 1995.

Yang, Alan S. *From Wrongs to Rights: Public Opinion on Gay and Lesbian Americans Moves Toward Equality, 1973–1999.* Washington, DC: National Gay and Lesbian Task Force, 1999.

WEB SITES

The Advocate: www.advocate.com
American Family Association: www.afa.net
Christian Coalition: www.cc.org
Gay & Lesbian Advocates & Defenders: www.glad.org
Gay and Lesbian Victory Fund: www.victoryfund.org
Human Rights Campaign: www.hrc.org

Lambda Legal Defense and Education Fund:
www.lambdalegal.org/cgi-bin/pages
Log Cabin Republicans: www.lcr.org/index.asp
National Gay and Lesbian Task Force: www.ngltf.org
Parents, Families and Friends of Lesbians and Gays:
www.pflag.org
PlanetOut.NewsPlanet: www.planetout.com/pno
Traditional Values Coalition: www.traditionalvalues.org
The Washington Blade: www.washblade.com

GLOSSARY

ACT UP. Protest group formed in 1987 in New York City to spark "direct action" on the AIDS epidemic. Formally named the AIDS Coalition to Unleash Power, the group was most active during the period 1987–93 when it grew to over 100 chapters.

The Advocate. Founded in 1967, this Los Angeles magazine is the major national print publication covering gay politics.

AIDS. Acquired immunodeficiency syndrome is a human biological disorder that severely inhibits the body's immune system. The syndrome is caused by the human immunodeficiency virus (HIV), which makes the body vulnerable to many diseases that a healthy immune system can typically cope with. The syndrome was first identified in the United States in 1981.

Amendment 2 (Colorado). In 1992, Colorado voters passed a referendum approving an amendment to the state constitution nullifying all laws in the state designed to protect people from discrimination on the basis of sexual orientation. A political firestorm and national boycott ensued, but the amendment was never enacted because it was blocked by the court system. Ultimately, the Supreme Court ruled in *Romer v. Evans* (1996) that Amendment 2 violated the Fourteenth Amendment guarantees of equal protection under the law.

Civil liberties. Constitutional protections protecting citizens from government.

Civil rights. Policies that protect individuals or groups from discrimination or arbitrary treatment by public or private organizations or persons.

Coming out. Or "coming out of the closet," involves an individual telling friends, family, and coworkers his or her sexual orientation.

Gay. A male individual who is primarily attracted, sexually and emotionally, to other males. Also a general term for all persons whose primary or secondary sexual and emotional attractions are toward others of the same sex.

Gay and Lesbian Alliance Against Defamation. Founded in 1985, GLAAD is a media-oriented activist organiza-tion working for "full, fair and accurate" representation of LGBT lives in film, television, print media, and other venues by opposing stereotyped or unbalanced representations.

Gay and Lesbian Victory Fund. Formed in 1991, GLVF recruits, trains, and provides qualified openly LGBT candidates with financial and technical support for campaigns.

Gay rights. Policies that protect homosexuals from discrimination by public or private organizations or persons, ensuring equal treatment.

GenderPAC. Founded in 1995 GenderPAC is a nonprofit group focused on eliminating gender stereotypes and ending discrimination and violence on the basis of how individuals look, act, or dress in terms of gender or sexual orientation.

HIV. Human immunodeficiency virus, which causes AIDS.

Homosexual. A person whose primary sexual and emotional attractions are toward persons of the same sex.

Human Rights Campaign (HRC). Formed in 1981 as the Human Rights Campaign Fund, HRC is the largest gay and lesbian organization in the country. HRC lobbies Congress, works with state and local groups, contributes money to campaigns for federal offices, and educates the public.

It's Time, America! Formed in 1994, this is the first national civil rights group seeking to secure and safeguard the rights of all transgendered and gender variant persons.

Lambda Legal Defense and Education Fund. Formed in 1973, Lambda is the nation's oldest and largest legal organization working for the civil rights of lesbians, gay men, and people with HIV/AIDS.

Lesbian. A female individual who is primarily attracted, sexually and emotionally, to other females.

Log Cabin Republicans (LCR). The nation's largest gay and lesbian Republican organization. Formed in 1993, LCR lobbies Congress and contributes to congressional campaigns.

National Gay and Lesbian Task Force (NGLTF). Formed

in 1973, NGLTF is the oldest continuously operating national LGBT group focused on eliminating prejudice, violence, and injustice against LGBT people at the local, state, and national level.

Public opinion. The aggregation of views of the mass populace, typically through random-sample survey techniques.

Public policy. Any action (or inaction) by government to address a perceived public problem.

Queer Nation. A radical direct-action group of the early 1990s. The group is perhaps best known for developing the confrontational political chant slogan "We're Here! We're Queer! Get Used to It!"

Transgender(ed). A general term describing persons who try to appear and behave in ways that reflect the opposite gender. The term encompasses transsexuals and transvestites, and transgendered persons can be heterosexual or homosexual.

Transsexual. Those persons who believe their biological sex does not reflect their gender identity and who subsequently attempt to alter their physical appearance to match their "correct" gender, using drugs as well as sexual reassignment surgery.

DOCUMENTS

Document 1. A Radical Manifesto: The Homophile Movement Must Be Radicalized!

August 28, 1969

Although written anonymously, this manifesto marks the end of the relatively conservative homophile movement and the beginning of the modern liberationist strain of the gay and lesbian movement. Written shortly after the Stonewall riots, the document clearly calls for the creation of a distinct homosexual subculture with its own ethics, but also links the struggle for homosexual civil rights to those of other oppressed groups.

l) We see the persecution of homosexuality as part of a general attempt to oppress all minorities and keep them powerless. Our fate is linked with these minorities; if the detention camps are filled tomorrow with blacks, hippies and other radicals, we will not escape that fate, all our attempts to dissociate ourselves from them notwithstanding. A common struggle, however, will bring common triumph.

2) Therefore we declare our support as homosexuals or bisexuals for the struggles of the black, the feminist, the Spanish-American, the Indian, the Hippie, the Young, the Student, and other victims of oppression and prejudice.

3) We call upon these groups to lend us their support and encourage their presence with NACHO and the homophile movement at large.

4) Our enemies, an implacable, repressive governmental system; much of organized religion, business and medicine, will not be moved by appeasement or appeals to reason and justice, but only by power and force.

5) We regard established heterosexual standards of morality as immoral and refuse to condone them by demanding an equality which is merely the common yoke of sexual repression.

6) We declare that homosexuals, as individuals and members of the greater community, must develop homosexual ethics and esthetics independent of, and without reference to, the mores imposed upon heterosexuality.

7) We demand the removal of all restriction on sex between consenting persons of any sex, of any orientation, of any age, anywhere, whether for money or not, and for the removal of all censorship.

8) We call upon the churches to sanction homosexual liaisons when called upon to do so by the parties concerned.

9) We call upon the homophile movement to be more honestly concerned with youth rather than trying to promote a mythical, non-existent "good public image."

10) The homophile movement must totally reject the insane war in Viet Nam and refuse to encourage complicity in the war and support of the war machine, which may well be turned against us. We oppose any attempts by the movement to obtain security clearances for homosexuals, since these contribute to the war machine.

11) The homophile movement must engage in continuous political struggle on all fronts.

12) We must open the eyes of homosexuals on this continent to the increasingly repressive nature of our society and to the realizations that Chicago may await us tomorrow.

Source: Donn Teal. *The Gay Militants.* New York: Stein and Day, 1971.

Document 2. Don't Ask, Don't Tell, Don't Pursue: Text of the Policy

This policy concerns the current (2003) armed forces policies concerning homosexual personnel. The document clearly reflects the compromise Congress reached following President Clinton's stated goal of lifting the military's ban on homosexuals serving openly in the military and the subsequent negative reaction from religious conservatives in Congress and the public at large. After this policy was adopted, discharges from the military for homosexuality actually increased in the 1990s compared to the 1980s.

Passed in Senate (63 to 33) on September 9, 1993
Passed in House (301 to 134) on September 28, 1993
1993 S. 1337; SEPTEMBER 16, 1993

SEC. 654. POLICY CONCERNING HOMOSEXUALITY IN THE ARMED FORCES.
(a) CODIFICATION.
1. Chapter 37 of title 10, United States code, is amended by adding at the end the following new section. 654. Policy concerning homosexuality in the armed forces

(a) Findings. Congress makes the following findings:
1. Section 8 of article I of the constitution of the United States commits exclusively to the congress the powers to raise and support armies, provide and maintain a navy, and make rules for the government and regulation of the land and naval forces.

2. There is no constitutional right to serve in the armed forces.

3. Pursuant to the powers conferred by section 8 of article i of the constitution of the United States, it lies within the discretion of the congress to establish qualifications for and conditions of service in the armed forces.

4. The primary purpose of the armed forces is to prepare for and to prevail in combat should the need arise.

5. The conduct of military operations requires members of the armed forces to make extraordinary sacrifices, including the ultimate sacrifice, in order to provide for the common defense.

6. Success in combat requires military units that are characterized by high morale, good order and discipline, and unit cohesion.

7. One of the most critical elements in combat capability is unit cohesion, that is, the bonds of trust among individual service members that make the combat effectiveness of a military unit greater than the sum of the combat effectiveness of the individual unit members.

8. Military life is fundamentally different from civilian life in that

(a) the extraordinary responsibilities of the armed forces, the unique conditions of military service, and the critical role of unit cohesion, require that the military community, while subject to civilian control, exist as a specialized society; and

(b) the military society is characterized by its own laws, rules, customs, and traditions, including numerous restrictions on personal behavior, that would not be acceptable in civilian society.

9. The standards of conduct for members of the armed forces regulate a member's life for 24 hours each day beginning at the moment the member enters military status and not ending until that person is discharged or otherwise separated from the armed forces.

10. Those standards of conduct, including the uniform code of military justice, apply to a member of the armed forces at all times that the member has a military status, whether the member is on base or off base, and whether the member is on duty or off duty.

11. The pervasive application of the standards of conduct is necessary because members of the armed forces must be ready at all times for worldwide deployment to a combat environment.

12. The worldwide deployment of United States military forces, the international responsibilities of the United States, and the potential for involvement of the armed forces in actual combat routinely make it necessary for members of the armed forces involuntarily to accept living conditions and working conditions that are often spartan, primitive, and characterized by forced intimacy with little or no privacy.

13. The prohibition against homosexual conduct is a longstanding element of military law that continues to be necessary in the unique circumstances of military service.

14. The armed forces must maintain personnel policies that exclude persons whose presence in the armed forces would create an unacceptable risk to the armed forces' high standards of morale, good order and discipline, and unit cohesion that are the essence of military capability.

15. The presence in the armed forces of persons who demonstrate a propensity or intent to engage in homosexual acts would create an unacceptable risk to the high standards of morale, good order and discipline, and unit cohesion that are the essence of military capability.

(b) Policy.
A member of the armed forces shall be separated from the armed forces under regulations prescribed by the secretary of defense if one or more of the following findings is made and approved in accordance with procedures set forth in such regulations.

1. That the member has engaged in, attempted to engage in, or solicited another to engage in a homosexual act or acts unless there are further findings, made and approved in accordance with procedures set forth in such regulations, that the member has demonstrated that-

(a) such conduct is a departure from the member's usual and customary behavior;

(b) such conduct, under all the circumstances, is unlikely to recur;

(c) such conduct was not accomplished by use of force, coercion, or intimidation;

(d) under the particular circumstances of the case, the member's continued presence in the armed forces is consistent with the interests of the armed forces in proper discipline, good order, and morale; and

(e) the member does not have a propensity or intent to engage in homosexual acts.

2. That the member has stated that he or she is a homosexual or bisexual, or words to that effect, unless there is a further finding, made and approved in accordance with procedures set forth in the regulations, that the member has demonstrated that he or she is not a person who engages in, attempts to engage in, has a propensity to engage in, or intends to engage in homosexual acts.

3. That the member has married or attempted to marry a person known to be of the same biological sex.

(c) Entry Standards and Documents.

1. The secretary of defense shall ensure that the standards for enlistment and appointment of members of the armed forces reflect the policies set forth in subsection (b).

2. The documents used to effectuate the enlistment or appointment of a person as a member of the armed forces shall set forth the provisions of subsection (b).

(d) Required Briefings.

The briefings that members of the armed forces receive upon entry into the armed forces and periodically thereafter under section 937 of this title (article 137 of the uniform code of military justice) shall include a detailed explanation of the applicable laws and regulations governing sexual conduct by members of the armed forces, including the policies prescribed under subsection (b).

(e) Rule of Construction.

Nothing in subsection (b) shall be construed to require that a member of the armed forces be processed for separation from the armed forces when a determination is made in accordance with regulations prescribed by the secretary of defense that-

1. The member engaged in conduct or made statements for the purpose of avoiding or terminating military service; and

2. Separation of the member would not be in the best interest of the armed forces.

(f) Definitions.

In this section.

1. The term 'homosexual' means a person, regardless of sex, who engages in, attempts to engage in, has a propensity to engage in, or intends to engage in homosexual acts, and includes the terms 'gay' and 'lesbian.'

2. The term 'bisexual' means a person who engages in, attempts to engage in, has a propensity to engage in, or intends to engage in homosexual and heterosexual acts.

3. The term 'homosexual act' means-

(a) any bodily contact, actively undertaken or passively permitted, between members of the same sex for the purpose of satisfying sexual desires; and

(b) any bodily contact which a reasonable person would understand to demonstrate a propensity or intent to engage in an act described in subparagraph (a).

Source: U.S. Code, Title 10, subtitle A, Part II, Chapter 37, Sec. 654.

GENETIC ENGINEERING

In 1953, American biologist James Watson and British biophysicists Francis Crick and Maurice Wilkins achieved a breakthrough discovery in human heredity that excited the biological community and raised public interest in the science of heredity, a science that still had, in the early post–World War II era, a taint of Nazi experiments in the breeding of a "superior race" of human beings.

In a momentous 900-word article published in *Nature*, Watson and Crick argued that deoxyribonucleic acid (DNA) has a structure, the now well-known double helix. This was of enormous importance to scientific understanding of the molecular components of heredity as they are tied to physics, biochemistry, medicine, and other disciplines. What these scientists had discovered was the internal cellular mechanics of passing hereditary traits from one generation to the next in species from human beings to oak trees or worms.

Moreover, the discovery of the structure of genetic information would open an investigation into how cells are created, function, and replicate. It would also reveal how inheritance is tied to specific genes. The discovery of DNA not only increased our understanding of how heredity works but allowed for the manipulation of that process. By the early twenty-first century, scientists were building on the discoveries of Watson, Crick, and Wilkins to manipulate the genetic makeup of organisms—creating genetically modified plants and animals and even cloning, or creating genetic copies of, creatures as complex as sheep and cattle.

A total of 30,000 to 80,000 genes make up the nucleus of each of the body's 10 trillion cells. There are also millions more bits of genetic information that do not code for the creation of anything; this so-called junk DNA nonetheless can be identified, mapped, and correlated with traits. Within the cells, DNA is organized in structures called chromosomes, which vary dramatically in size. Each human cell contains an arrangement of forty-six chromosomes (twenty-three from each parent, paired together). Altogether, some three billion "bits" of DNA (each a base pair of two to four amino acids) comprise the hereditary information, arranged in chromosomes, along the double helix.

But what is a gene? Genes contain instructions for creating proteins and enzymes that control the metabolism of cells. Within each cell, the gene's instructions facilitate the specific sort of metabolism appropriate to that cell's function. Though all cells in a given individual have pretty much the same genetic information combined when sperm penetrated an egg at conception, enormous specialization occurs among cells in the body. As a fetus develops from one fertilized cell to some 2 trillion cells at birth, the specialized metabolism of cells converts energy into organ systems and bodily structure.

Every cell of an organism has all of its genes, but only one or two genes are activated in each particular cell because of the astonishing complexity and fluidity of the system that allows genes to specialize. Bone cells, for example, become bone cells through enzymatic actions specified by genetic information. Instead of biological discord of toenail cells developing in the liver or eye cells in a paw, most organisms have cells perfectly suited to the organ or body part where they reside.

The work of twentieth-century scientists in the wake of Watson and Crick's discovery seemed to signal the end of the era of the crude genetics of pre–World War II eugenics labs, when researchers believed everything about a person was determined by inborn traits. Likewise, simple relationships between people's appearance and their heredity or family and social standing no longer withstood the scrutiny of scientific investigation in most universities. More important, all but the least sophisticated scientists and politicians jettisoned attempts to modify humans through simple actions, such as the "better marriages through time" imagined in eugenics. Conversely, appeals to natural law theory—that

CHRONOLOGY

1859   Charles Darwin publishes his theory of evolution, noting that characteristics that help a species survive are likely to be passed down to future generations.

1866   Austrian monk and amateur botanist Gregor Mendel maps how hereditary characteristics of organisms are passed on from one generation to the next; his discoveries go largely unnoticed in the scientific community.

1883   British scientist Francis Galton coins the word "eugenics" for the practice of using selective breeding to improve the human race.

1900   European botanists Carl Erich Correns, Erich Tschermak von Seysenegg, and Hugo de Vries independently obtain results similar to those of Mendel.

1930s–40s Nazi experiments in eugenics bring the field into international disrepute.

1953   British biophysicists Francis Crick and Maurice Wilkins and American geneticist James Watson discover the double helix structure of the DNA molecule.

1973   Molecular biologists Stanley Cohen and Herbert Boyer perform the first successful recombinant DNA experiment, inserting frog genes into the DNA of a bacterium.

1980   The first recombinant DNA drug, a form of human insulin, is marketed.

1990   The Human Genome Project, to map all of the genes in the human cell, is launched by the U.S. Department of Energy and the National Institutes of Health.

1997   British scientists clone Dolly the sheep, the first mammal to be cloned.

2001   President George W. Bush restricts research into embryonic stem cells, the cells found in embryos that can become other cells.

2003   Heads of the Human Genome Project announce that they have completed the project of fully mapping the human genome.

2004   California voters pass Proposition 71, approving a $3 billion bond issue to finance stem cell research.

is, that all people are born as blank slates and thus can be shaped entirely by experience—to explain individual differences faded with availability of more complex methods of investigating heredity. In other words, as science probed more deeply the mechanics of genetics, old ideas that inherited traits could be easily manipulated or, conversely, that they were insignificant in determining people's characteristics were increasingly seen as overly simplistic.

Organic laws would have to be much more complex, and critics of biotechnology would need much more knowledge of biology to oppose genetic innovation or use genetics for political purposes. Before the discovery of the DNA structure and its potential for genetic engineering, genetic innovation was opposed on the simple moral grounds that governments or institutions did not have the right to improve the race by selecting supposedly superior human beings. But the potential now existed to manipulate genes within a person, and simply manipulating undesirable inherited features such as a propensity for con-

genital deformities was not feasible. At the same time, one could not simply select mentally superior parents to produce mentally superior children—as some Nazi scientists had attempted. By contrast, those seeking to improve or repair humans through genetic medicine had the relationship between genotype (genetic makeup) and phenotype (physical appearance) to study in a variety of methods more difficult yet more systematic than imagined before World War II.

GENETIC SEWING MACHINE

The 1970s set the stage for the new technologies of genetic information. New procedures were created to find how genetic information operated within a cell and link that operation to a genetic pattern for the whole organism.

Perhaps the most important new technique was the *splicing* of genetic information. The splicing process takes genetic information from one source, mounts it atop a delivery mechanism, and inserts it into another cell, as with a genetic sewing machine. First, DNA is clipped out of the source chromosome. Second, a *vector*, or delivery mechanism, is constructed of special DNA typically taken from a virus. The delivery mechanism inserts the source DNA into the appropriate place on the helix of the destination cell, modifying its chromosomes. The modified cell begins to follow the instructions of the new DNA, duplicating a particular enzyme structure. As it duplicates itself, it begins churning out copies of the modified gene.

Using so-called restriction enzymes to cut DNA like a chemical razor blade, biologists of the 1970s were able to isolate and remove specific segments of genetic information. When molecular biologists Stanley Cohen and Herbert Boyer successfully implanted chromosomal information from one bacterium into another in the early 1970s, it was an important step toward using the new technologies of genetic information. They had catalyzed the process of genetic engineering, and soon human genetic information would be spliced into nonhuman cells, producing gallons of insulin and other useful compounds.

The production of human insulin by yeast cells was a stunning development in genetics. Many scientists and science writers in the early 1970s argued that genetic "codes" like those for insulin existed for every human function. More important, though, carving up bits of genetic information in this way opened an entirely new vista on the gene, allowing discrete analysis of the relationship between genes and the proteins or enzymes they typically make. The relationship between genes and traits could be studied outside as well as in its ordinary setting. Genes were kinds of building blocks ex vivo (into the body).

HISTORY

The dream of early genetic engineers in the 1960s and 1970s was that human, animal, or even plant DNA might be spliced into the DNA of a human being to cure hereditary diseases or improve human traits. Genetic therapy in human embryos could allow physicians to replace some or even most of someone's DNA before birth, preventing disease or improving human potential.

Technologies in the 1970s provided a way to splice the genetic information but gave only scant clues to the details of the connection between genetic information and animal function. A map of the human hereditary matrix was needed. The language of mapmakers—cartography—began to take shape in biology as scientists struggled to cope with the meaning of an organism's collective set of genes.

Some would call this map, or more properly the "land" it described, a *genome*, ascribing to the whole set of human genes some meaning much greater than the sum of its parts. Others were more apprehensive about such grand expeditions, arguing for a gene-by-gene examination of human and animal heredity, yet the resources and infrastructure necessary for this massive undertaking were not available. Dozens of facilities were needed, each specializing in a small segment of genetic information. Each of these facilities would need funding, and a structure would have to be created to coordinate and oversee the endeavor.

Support began to build for a major government-funded project to study human genetics. The U.S. Department of Energy took the lead in the 1980s, recruiting James Watson to oversee medical implications by establishing a National Center for Human Genome Research at the National Institutes of Health.

The mapping and sequencing of the human genome was underway. Scientists were embarked on what science journalist Matt Ridley described as the greatest scientific expedition of all time, sailing on in forty directions to chart the dimensions of heredity, with little more to guide them than computer and biological technologies that each knew was insufficient to the task.

GENOME PROJECT

Universities had to invent a new kind of geneticist, more akin to mathematicians and programmers than to biologists. In the 1980s Harvard's Walter Gilbert and Caltech's Leroy Hood predicted the prototype geneticist of the twenty-first century, the *molecular engineer*. Molecular engineers are capable of crunching tens of millions of bits of DNA as though they were nothing but numbers. It was becoming increasingly clear that the genetic makeup of organisms consisted of a variety of types of proteins in many different orders within the DNA, and which proteins are added, removed, or reordered could change the nature of the organism.

The engineer is engaged in projects rather than lifelong theoretical quests, and spends more time on research and entrepreneurship than on teaching, advising, and university service. He or she is just as likely to be an employee of a drug or computer company as a professor. Nonetheless, the engineer still needs the help of research biologists as it became clear that certain gene activities could be understood only in the context of the organism in which the gene existed. That is, organisms were the sum of their genetic parts but those genetic parts varied in activity given their specific environment, and only biologists could provide an understanding of that environment.

Genes are bounded by bookmarks of a sort, called introns and exons. Across the genome, processes called transcription and activation facilitate the "turning on" of the DNA between those bookmarks, allowing the gene to do its job, creating proteins or enzymes. That process is essential to all forms of genetic engineering sustainable in organic life, as are genes themselves. A single aberrant gene can cause many crucial cells to produce a lethal protein or fail to produce some enzyme the body needs. A "lethal gene," as Francis Collins, head of the U.S. human genome mapping effort, likes to call it, can kill a person. But the human body is infinitely more complex than single-gene diseases and defects would suggest.

FORMS OF GENETIC ENGINEERING

It is easiest to break genetic engineering into four types: the creation of compounds through gene splicing, invasive euphenic intervention, somatic cell intervention, and germ-line intervention. Different therapies using genetic materials or modifying human genetic makeup accomplish different purposes while working on problems for which varied nongenetic therapies are also available.

Gene Splicing

Compounds are created by splicing into bacterial cells some instruction for the human enzyme, hormone, antigen, or other protein that the body is failing to produce. The bacteria reproduce to provide the needed compound. Engineering of this kind has replaced animal insulin for many patients. These therapies are ex vivo, meaning they introduce new genetically engineered material into the body. The patient's cells are not required for the creation of the compound, because some human substances, such as insulin, are not patient specific. Thus, the patient's actual genetic information is not removed, altered, cultured in bacteria, or reinjected.

There seems to be no reason to object to the use

of such compounds. They do not alter the DNA of the person who donates the original DNA for cloning the insulin, nor the DNA of the person who receives the injection. Yet genetic engineering technologies allow scientists to make this somewhat radical leap to "cloning" the particular information for some human enzyme or compound. How do the realities of this noninvasive, nonmodifying genetic therapy relate to the arguments of ethicists Jeremy Rifkin or Paul Ramsey against any engineering of persons? The argument that humans have no right to "play God" with the basic genetic structure of the species is undercut by a technology that does not actually change that structure. Can one at least make copies of small bits of human biology and use them, without changing divine information? If genetic modifications upset the natural balance, what about the possibility of restoring natural balance in a diabetic's chemistry through genetic modification? Is the use of Humulin (genetically engineered human insulin) more unnatural than slaughtering thousands of cows for insulin or allowing unmedicated diabetics to die?

Cost is perhaps the essential issue concerning such engineering: Is it more effective and affordable than other diabetic therapies such as radical dietary change that may have a negative impact on other parts of the human body? Cloning an insulin-producing cell is critically distinct from cloning a person. Engineering these compounds neither advances nor retards the entirely different and much more problematic research concerning the reconstitution of "personhood" through genetic cloning.

Invasive Euphenic Intervention

Invasive euphenic engineering is distinguished here from the creation of compounds through engineering only to show that particular kinds of therapies have different delivery mechanisms. No genetic material is removed from the patient, and the patient's DNA is not the subject of an "editing procedure." Genetically engineered compounds are used in pinpoint surgical procedures, such as a modified herpes virus (infectious, easily eradicated, and carrying special affinity for unwanted cells), which enables the treatment of some cancers. The technique involves sophisticated engineering of viruses, enzymes, or bacteria, which are injected into the patient. An additional step may involve further invasive treatments: the infected cancerous cells are destroyed with an injection of the genetically engineered antiviral drug ganciclovir. The techniques, though, draw on the classic treatment methodologies for cancer and other diseases. The method is to destroy cancerous cells, rather than neutralize or reverse their mutations through modification of genes.

Other risks are associated with these invasive therapies, some of which deserve mention. First, there is the risk that modified viruses will revert to their "wild type" and become infectious. Modifications of viral cells occasionally have this outcome, a result of imperfect knowledge of virology and the process of cloning cells in the lab. Future generations of the cells, if they revert, could be dangerous and infectious. The patient with brain cancer could end up with both herpes and brain cancer, or worse. A related risk is the possible mutation of modified viral cells into dangerous new viral strains, which would be difficult to contain or treat. Both of these risks demand that scientists and clinicians work together on the development of invasive euphenic therapies.

Most scientists in the field agree caution is a wise posture toward both varieties of compound-creation engineering. The risks need to be studied and, in granting approval for human-subjects trials, the National Institutes of Health must pay careful attention to the emerging data on wild-type reversion. Given these risks, many potential genetic therapies may have to yield to safer alternatives. Yet progress in such modifications of viruses and compounds need not be cause for excessive fear or support for genetic determinism. The similarities between compound-creation genetic therapies and current nongenetic therapies are such that we need not fear the commodification of nature or dehumanization of illness.

Somatic Cell Intervention

Somatic cell therapies, such as cystic fibrosis inhaler trials conducted in centers around the United States, involve the deliberate modification of a patient's somatic (nonsex cell) genetic material. This simple description, however, is misleading. Gene therapies are of at least three types. Gene insertion involves the simple introduction of one or more copies of the normal version of a gene into the chromosomes of a diseased cell. In this case, no attempt is made to correct the disease. The goal is to implant replicating versions of DNA that can produce whatever antigen, chemical, or hormone is necessary to overcome a deficit or imbalance in the diseased cells. In simple

terms, the goal is to overwhelm the actions of cells containing defective genes with the actions of cells containing corrected genes. Such therapies simply internalize the delivery mechanism for engineered materials—insulin-producing cells are placed in the body—making insulin injection less necessary.

Gene modification would be the next step. Here the goal is to modify much of the material in the patient's cells. Such therapy would at times be in vivo, involving the patient's own cells. The cells would be extracted, modified, and reinserted. In most cases, though, ex vivo vector cells are sufficient. For example, in the case of the cystic fibrosis inhaler therapy, a flu virus (adenovirus) is engineered to carry genetic material that, when a patient "catches a cold," will modify the cells infected with the virus. Until the patient is able to develop immunity to the cold, lung function is improved. Improvements are not permanent and cannot be passed on through the germ-line cells, and there is a substantial risk that the virus will revert to wild type or just plain clog up the lungs of the already weak patient with cystic fibrosis.

The third variety of somatic cell genetic therapy involves in vivo modification of diseased, or causative, cells, for example, in fetuses in utero. Such therapies are entirely theoretical. Thus, while the principle is fairly simple, its application may be much less so. The theory is that through some delivery mechanism, a patient's somatic material can be slowly modified to express a correct (nondiseased) allele, or alternative form of the same gene. The patient would lose all expression for the disease and symptoms would cease.

All three varieties of somatic cell therapy share some technical problems. The first is the vector problem. Put simply, the modified viruses used to get the new DNA into the patient's cells have so far not been effective in transferring the genes. The viruses do not work in humans. The second problem is that even when better vectors establish good gene transfer rates, the body still eventually develops an immunity to the vector virus, and the whole therapy ends. Because no permanent change has been effected, the patient is not cured.

Germ-Line Intervention

Germ cell therapy—that is, therapy involving the modification of the genetic material passed on from one generation to the next—is seen by many as heralding a possible new eugenics. This therapy has the potential to modify the genetic makeup of future generations. Scientists could change the DNA of the sperm or egg to select for traits like great physical strength or mental capacity in the future human developing from that egg or sperm. The National Institutes of Health was so concerned with germ cell modification in the 1990s that it initially proposed adding a check-off box to its clinical trial application form for human gene therapies, which would have read: "Could this therapy be used to modify the germ cells?" An unsatisfactory response would have meant the death of the application. Though the box was never put into use, the rationale for dropping it was that virtually no somatic cell therapy could meet the test. Genetic modification of germ cells is identical to the second and third variety of somatic cell modification, with the additional element of the heritability of the modification by the patient's offspring.

Thus, germ-line therapies restrict the freedom or rights of a child that is actually born. The child is born "into the therapy," voiceless and unable to undo the therapeutic actions of others. In fact, they also restrict the kinds of children that can be born.

Yet stopping at the germ line to protect the freedom of the yet-to-be-born child may not be justified either. Such a moral distinction fails to account for nongenetic activities of parents, such as smoking during pregnancy, that have even greater impacts, including genetic consequences. Children cannot take back a whole set of parental actions. The only *unique* danger of germ-line engineering involves the possibility of complete control over the body that a child will inhabit. Yet the powers of genetic determination of social traits pale by comparison to the social power of parental activities.

There are ethical problems with germ-line therapy. While most would agree that it might be good to select out genes for inherited diseases, there is far less consensus on the idea of selecting for genes for higher intelligence or greater physical strength. Would this entrench the privileges of the rich who could afford such therapies? Would it lead to new forms of caste or racial prejudice? Most scientists and ethicists do agree that none of these problems has anything to do with the exaggerated claim that germ-line therapies will become eugenics, or decrease the value of life for patients with hereditary illness. Put plainly, none of these claims has any verifiable historical, biological, or political basis, making the oft-cited slippery slope from germ-line engineering to genetic enhancement seem less problematic or

different from arguments against gene therapy. The practical problems with germ-line engineering are sufficient to keep one engaged in the important philosophical issues: What diseases should be eliminated? How does one assess the causal relevance of a genotype to a disease, and the importance to the future of the loss of its expression? Who can afford such therapies, and will they be distributed fairly?

CONCLUSION

Answers to these questions depend on whether or not one sees genetic engineering as part of a range of options available to parents, society, and medical practice. Germ-line engineering is so expensive and risky that its implementation will depend on new medical advances. Moreover, in the present atmosphere of fear about research even remotely resembling eugenics, and where modification of germ cells is viewed as meddling in sacrosanct territory, government and medicine are reluctant to support such science.

While important, these considerations of the value of germ-line gene therapy are not necessarily *ethical*. Yet it is revealing that germ-line engineering may not be seen as competitive with other therapeutic options. Risks are clearly present for any approach to genetic engineering, yet the future of these scientific advances is not in doubt.

Glenn McGee, Vanessa Kuhn, Pasquale Patrizio,
and Claire Robertson-Kraft

REFERENCES

Adams, Mark B., ed. *The Wellborn Science: Eugenics in Germany, France, Brazil, and Russia.* New York: Oxford University Press, 1990.

Andrews, Lori B., and Dorothy Nelkin. *The Body Bazaar: The Market for Human Tissue in the Biotechnology Age.* New York: Crown, 2001.

Baxevanis, Andreas, and B. F. Francis Ouellette. *Bioinformatics: A Practical Guide to the Analysis of Genes and Proteins.* New York: John Wiley and Sons, 2001.

Bosk, Charles. *All God's Mistakes: Genetic Counseling in a Pediatric Hospital.* Chicago: University of Chicago Press, 1995.

Buchanan, Allen, Dan Brock, Norman Daniels, and Dan Wikler. *From Chance to Choice: Genetics & Justice.* New York: Cambridge University Press, 2000.

Burnham, Terry Jay Phelan. *Mean Genes: From Sex to Money to Food, Taming Our Primal Instincts.* New York: Penguin, 2001.

Cavalli-Sforza, L., P. Menozzi, and A. Piazza. *The History and Geography of Human Genes*. Princeton, NJ: Princeton University Press, 1994.

Dawkins, Richard. *The Selfish Gene*. 2nd ed. New York: Oxford University Press, 1989.

Doukas, D. J. "Primary Care and the Human Genome Project: Into the Breach." *Archives of Family Practice* 2, 11 (1993): 1179–83.

Doukas, D. J., and J. W. Berg. "Genetic Testing and the Family Covenant." *American Journal of Bioethics* 1, 3 (2001): 2–10.

Elston, Robert C., ed. *Biostatistical Genetics and Genetic Epidemiology*. New York: John Wiley and Sons, 2002.

Fletcher, Joseph. *The Ethics of Genetic Control: Ending Reproductive Roulette*. New York: Prometheus Books, 1988.

Frank-Kamenetskii, and D. Maxim. *Unraveling DNA: The Most Important Molecule of Life*. New York: Perseus, 1997.

Fukuyama, Francis. *Our Posthuman Future*. New York: Picador, 2003.

Kass, Leon R. *Toward a More Natural Science: Biology and Human Affairs*. New York: MacMillan, 1995.

Kay, Lily. *The Molecular Vision of Life: Caltech, the Rockefeller Foundation, and the Rise of the New Biology*. New York: Oxford University Press, 1992.

Keller, Evelyn Fox. *The Century of the Gene*. Cambridge, MA: Harvard University Press, 2001.

Khoury, Muin, et al., eds. *Fundamentals of Genetic Epidemiology*. New York: Oxford University Press, 1993.

Lewontin, Richard C. *The Triple Helix: Gene, Organism and Environment*. Cambridge, MA: Harvard University Press, 2001.

Long, Clarissa, ed. *Genetic Testing and the Use of Information*. New York: AEI, 1999.

Magnus, David, Arthur Caplan, Glenn McGee, eds. *Who Owns Life?* New York: Prometheus Books, 2002.

McGee, Glenn. *The Perfect Baby*. New York: Rowman and Littlefield, 2001.

Merz, J. F. "Patents Limit Medical Potential of Sequencing." *Nature* 419, 6910 (October 31, 2002): 878.

Merz, J. F., and M. K. Cho. "Disease Genes Are Not Patentable: A Rebuttal of McGee." *Cambridge Quarterly of Healthcare Ethics* 7, 4 (Fall 1998): 425–28.

Nelkin, Dorothy, and M. Susan Linee. *The DNA Mystique: The Gene as a Cultural Icon*. New York: W. H. Freeman, 1995.

Nightengale, Elena O., and Melissa Goodman. *Before Birth: Prenatal Testing for Genetic Disease*. Cambridge, MA: Harvard University Press, 1990.

Paul, Diane. *Controlling Human Heredity*. New York: Oxford University Press, 1989.

Pernick, Martin. *The Black Stork*. New York: Oxford University Press, 1999.

Phan L., D. J. Doukas, and M. Fetters. "Religious Leaders' Attitudes and Beliefs about Genetics Research and the Human Genome Project." *Journal of Clinical Ethics* 6, 3 (1995): 237–45.

Quaid, Kimberly, et al. *Early Warning: Cases and Ethical Guidance for Presymptomatic Testing in Genetic Diseases*. Indianapolis: Indiana University Press, 1998.

Ridley, Matt. *Genome*. New York: HarperCollins, 2000.

Robertston, John. *Children of Choice*. New York: Oxford University Press, 1994.

Sankar, P., and M. K. Cho. "Toward a New Vocabulary of Human Genetic Variation." *Science* 298 (2002): 1337–38.

Stock, Gregory. *Redesigning Humans: Our Inevitable Genetic Future*. New York: Mariner Books, 2003.

Tagliaferro, Linda, and Mark V. Bloom. *The Complete Idiot's Guide to Decoding Your Genes*. New York: Alpha Books, 2000.

United States Office of Technology Assessment Staff. *New Developments in Biotechnology: Patenting Life*. Washington, DC: Marcel Dekker, 1990.

Wade, Nicholas. *Life Script*. New York: Simon and Schuster, 2002.

Walters, Leroy, and Julie Gage Palmer. *The Ethics of Human Gene Therapy*. New York: Oxford University Press, 1997.

Watson, James D. *The Double Helix: A Personal Account of the Discovery of the Structure of DNA*. New York: Atheneum, 1968.

Wu, Cathy H., and Jerry W. McLarty. *Neural Networks and Genome Informatics*. London: Elsevier Health Sciences, 2000.

Young, Ian. *Introduction to Risk Calculation in Genetic Counseling*. New York: Oxford University Press, 1999.

Zweiger, Gary. *Transducing the Genome: Information, Anarchy, and Revolution in the Biomedical Sciences*. New York: McGraw-Hill, 2001.

WEB SITES

American Journal of Bioethics: http://bioethics.net
Human Genome Project: www.ornl.gov/sci/techresources/Human_Genome/home.shtml
National Institutes of Health: www.nih.gov

GLOSSARY

Biotechnology. The use of engineering principles in the life sciences; usually used in the context of gene modification.

Chromosome. A structure found in the nucleus of a cell, made up of DNA and proteins that contain genes.

Cloning. The reproduction of an organism by extracting and replicating DNA from a host cell.

Deoxyribonucleic acid (DNA). An acid within the nucleus of a cell that carries the cell's genetic information.

Double helix. The molecular structure of DNA.

Enzyme. A protein produced by an organism that acts as a biochemical catalyst.

Eugenics. The study of the hereditary improvement of the human race through selective breeding.

Gene. A unit of heredity consisting of a sequence of DNA.

Genome. The full set of genes of an organism.

Genotype. Genetic makeup of an organism.

Germ cells. The cells of the body involved in reproduction.

Germ line. The continuation of a set of genetic information from one generation to the next.

Germ line intervention. A medical procedure involving modification of the germ line.

Invasive euphenic intervention. A medical procedure in which genetically modified microorganisms are injected into a patient's body.

Junk DNA. Genetic code that has no apparent role in heredity.

Phenotype. The physical appearance of an organism.

Recombinant DNA. The DNA formed by combining DNA from different organisms.

Somatic cell intervention. A medical procedure involving the modification of somatic, or nonsex, cell material.

Splicing. Taking genetic information from one organism and inserting it into another organism.

Vector. A delivery mechanism constructed of DNA.

DOCUMENT

Excerpts, Press Release: International Consortium Completes Human Genome Project, 2003

Arguably the most important large-scale scientific project since the development of the atom bomb during World War II, the Human Genome Project was launched by the U.S. Department of Energy and National Institutes of Health in 1990. The aim was to map the full contingent of genes in the human body, the so-called human genome. In 2003, the heads of the U.S.-led international consortium announced they had completed the project, 2 years ahead of schedule. The following is the consortium's official press release announcing the completion.

BETHESDA, Md., April 14, 2003—The International Human Genome Sequencing Consortium, led in the United States by the National Human Genome Research Institute (NHGRI) and the Department of Energy (DOE), today announced the successful completion of the Human Genome Project more than two years ahead of schedule.

Also today, NHGRI unveiled its bold new vision for the future of genome research, officially ushering in the era of the genome. The vision will be published in the April 24 issue of the journal Nature, coinciding with the 50th anni-

versary of Nature's publication of the landmark paper by Nobel laureates James Watson and Francis Crick that described DNA's double helix. Dr. Watson also was the first leader of the Human Genome Project.

The international effort to sequence the 3 billion DNA letters in the human genome is considered by many to be one of the most ambitious scientific undertakings of all time, even compared to splitting the atom or going to the moon.

"The Human Genome Project has been an amazing adventure into ourselves, to understand our own DNA instruction book, the shared inheritance of all humankind," said NHGRI Director Francis S. Collins, M.D., Ph.D., leader of the Human Genome Project since 1993. "All of the project's goals have been completed successfully—well in advance of the original deadline and for a cost substantially less than the original estimates.". . .

The flagship effort of the Human Genome Project has been producing the reference sequence of the human genome. The international consortium announced the first draft of the human sequence in June 2000. Since then, researchers have worked tirelessly to convert the "draft" sequence into a "finished" sequence. Finished sequence is a technical term meaning that the sequence is highly accurate (with fewer than one error per 10,000 letters) and highly contiguous (with the only remaining gaps corresponding to regions whose sequence cannot be reliably resolved with current technology). That standard was first achieved for a human chromosome when a team of British, Japanese and U.S. researchers produced a finished sequence for human chromosome 22 in 1999.

The finished sequence produced by the Human Genome Project covers about 99 percent of the human genome's gene-containing regions, and it has been sequenced to an accuracy of 99.99 percent. In addition, to help researchers better understand the meaning of the human genetic instruction book, the project took on a wide range of other goals, from sequencing the genomes of model organisms to developing new technologies to study whole genomes. As of April 14, 2003, all of the Human Genome Project's ambitious goals have been met or surpassed.

When the Human Genome Project was launched in 1990, many in the scientific community were deeply skeptical about whether the project's audacious goals could be achieved, particularly given its hard-charging timeline and relatively tight spending levels. At the outset, the U.S. Congress was told the project would cost about $3 billion in FY 1991 dollars and would be completed by the end of 2005. In actuality, the Human Genome Project was finished two and a half years ahead of time and, at $2.7 billion in FY 1991 dollars, significantly under original spending projections.

"Never would I have dreamed in 1953 that my scientific life would encompass the path from DNA's double helix to the 3 billion steps of the human genome. But when the opportunity arose to sequence the human genome, I knew it was something that could be done—and that must be done," said Nobel Laureate James D. Watson, Ph.D., president of Cold Spring Harbor Laboratory in Cold Spring Harbor, N.Y. "The completion of the Human Genome Project is a truly momentous occasion for every human being around the globe."

Besides delivering on the stated goals, the international network of researchers has produced an amazing array of advances that most scientists had not expected until much later. These "bonus" accomplishments include: an advanced draft of the mouse genome sequence, published in December 2002; an initial draft of the rat genome sequence, produced in November 2002; the identification of more than 3 million human genetic variations, called single nucleotide polymorphisms (SNPs); and the generation of full-length complementary DNAs (cDNAs) for more than 70 percent of known human and mouse genes.

The International Human Genome Sequencing Consortium included hundreds of scientists at 20 sequencing centers in China, France, Germany, Great Britain, Japan and the United States. The five institutions that generated the most sequence were: Baylor College of Medicine, Houston; Washington University School of Medicine, St. Louis; Whitehead Institute/MIT Center for Genome Research, Cambridge, Mass.; DOE's Joint Genome Institute, Wal-

nut Creek, Calif.; and The Wellcome Trust Sanger Institute near Cambridge, England. . . .

All of the sequence data generated by the Human Genome Project has been swiftly deposited into public databases and made freely available to scientists around the world, with no restrictions on its use or redistribution. The information is scanned daily by researchers in academia and industry, as well as by commercial database companies providing information services to biotechnologists.

"From the beginning, one of the operating principles of the Human Genome Project has been that the data and resources it has generated should rapidly be made available to the entire scientific community," said Robert Waterston, M.D., Ph.D., of the University of Washington, Seattle. "Not only does the rapid release of data promote the best interests of science, it also maximizes the benefits that the public receives from such research."

In 1996, at a meeting in Bermuda, Dr. Waterston and John Sulston, Ph.D., then director of the Sanger Centre (now The Wellcome Trust Sanger Institute), led the International Human Genome Sequencing Consortium to adopt the so-called "Bermuda Principles," which expressly call for automatic, rapid release of sequence assemblies of 2,000 bases or greater to the public domain.

Scientists have been quick to mine this new trove of genomic data, as well as to utilize the genomic tools and technologies developed by the Human Genome Project. For example, when the Human Genome Project began in 1990, scientists had discovered fewer than 100 human disease genes. Today, more than 1,400 disease genes have been identified.

For scientists seeking to understand the role of genetics in human health and disease, the Human Genome Project's finished sequence represents a significant advance over the "working draft" that was announced in June 2000. The working draft covered 90 percent of the gene-containing part of the sequence, 28 percent of which had reached finished form, and contained about 150,000 gaps. The finished version of the human genome now contains 99 percent of the gene-containing sequence, with the missing parts essentially contained in less than 400 defined gaps.

These remaining gaps represent regions of DNA in the genome with unusual structures that cannot be reliably sequenced with current technology. These regions, however, appear to contain very few genes. Closing these gaps will require individual research projects and new technologies, rather than industrial-scale efforts of the Human Genome Project. The high-throughput sequencing of the human genome has thus reached its natural conclusion.

"This is the day that our planning group dreamed of," said Bruce Alberts, Ph.D., chairman of the 1988 National Research Council Committee on Mapping and Sequencing the Human Genome, which produced the original recommendations for the Human Genome Project. "And the quality of the sequence would have amazed us. In 1988, we weren't sure that accuracy rates of 99.9 percent were possible, and we were uncertain that continuity over distances of millions of base pairs could be achieved. . . ."

In addition to the improved accuracy, the average DNA letter now sits on a stretch of 27,332,000 base pairs of uninterrupted, high-quality sequence—about 334 times longer than the 81,900 base-pair stretch that was available in the working draft. Access to uninterrupted stretches of sequenced DNA can make a major difference to researchers hunting for genes, dramatically cutting the effort and expense required to search regions of the human genome that may contain small and often rare mutations involved in disease. . . .

The essentially complete version of the human genome sequence also represents a major boon to the growing field of comparative genomics: researchers are attempting to learn more about human genetic makeup and function by comparing our genomic sequence to that of other organisms, such as the mouse, the rat or even the fruit fly. . . .

The impact of the Human Genome Project, however, extends far beyond laboratory analysis. Under the guidance of Dr. Watson, the Human Genome Project became the first large scientific undertaking to dedicate a portion of its budget for research to the ethical, legal and social implications (ELSI) of its work. NHGRI and DOE each set aside 3 to 5 percent of their genome budgets to study how the exponential increase in knowledge about human genetic make-up may affect individuals, institutions and society. An example of how ELSI research has helped to inform public policy is the fact that more than 40 states in the United States have passed genetic non-discrimination bills, many based on model language that grew out of this research. These efforts will be even more crucial in the coming years as the results of genomic research begin to appear in the clinic.

"Achieving the goals of the Human Genome Project is a historic milestone. But this is no time to rest and relax," said Dr. Collins. "With this foundation of knowledge firmly in place, the medical advances promised from the project can now be significantly accelerated."

To spur such acceleration, NHGRI's "A Vision for the Future of Genomics Research" sets forth a series of "Grand Challenges" intended to energize the scientific community in using the newfound understanding of the genome to uncover the causes of disease and to develop bold new approaches to the prevention and treatment of disease. The plan was the outcome of more than a year of intense discussions with nearly 600 scientific and public leaders from government, academia, non-profit organizations and the private sector.

In the publication Nature, the challenges facing genomic research are depicted as a three-story house rising from the foundation of the Human Genome Project. The three floors, representing the three major thrusts of this new vision—Genomics to Biology, Genomics to Health and Genomics to Society—are interconnected by vertical supports, representing computational biology, ELSI, education, training, technology development and resources.

Many of the challenges in the vision are aimed at utilizing genome research to combat disease and improve human health. The recommendations include calls for researchers to work toward:

- New tools to allow discovery in the near future of the hereditary contributions to common diseases, such as diabetes, heart disease and mental illness.
- New methods for the early detection of disease.
- New technologies that can sequence the entire genome of any person for less than $1,000.
- Wider access to tools and technologies of "chemical genomics" to improve the understanding of biological pathways and accelerate drug discovery.

NHGRI and its partners in genome research have already begun tackling a number of these challenges. For example, in November 2002, a team of researchers from six nations launched the International HapMap Project, an effort to produce a map of common human genetic variations aimed at speeding the search for genes that contribute to cancer, diabetes, heart disease, schizophrenia and many other common conditions.

"The completion of the Human Genome Project should not be viewed as an end in itself. Rather, it marks the start of an exciting new era—the era of the genome in medicine and health," said Dr. Collins. "We firmly believe the best is yet to come, and we urge all scientists and people around the globe to join us in turning this vision into reality.". . .

Source: National Human Genome Research Institute, National Institutes of Health, 2003.

GENTRIFICATION

The discourse surrounding the issue of gentrification encompasses a number of interconnected debates and controversies. Academics, activists, and policy analysts, though, enter this discussion with sometimes very different definitions. The many definitions, the various understandings of what causes gentrification, and the polarized (good versus bad) views about the consequences of gentrification all reflect the controversial nature of this contemporary social issue. Beyond the academic, analytical posturing that often comes with discussions of gentrification, its controversial nature is evident in its material effects and the sometimes violent clashes that invariably define the pro- and anti-gentrification camps.

DEFINITION

Simon Velasquez Alejandrino, author of *Gentrification in San Francisco's Mission District: Indicators and Policy Recommendations* (2000), defines gentrification as the dramatic shifts in the demography, cultural flavor, and aesthetic quality of neighborhoods resulting when wealthy, usually white residents displace poor and minority residents, along with small local businesses, raising the housing costs. The Brookings Institute focuses more on the issue of class in its definition of gentrification as "the process by which higher income households displace lower income residents of a neighborhood, changing the essential character and flavor of that neighborhood." Urban anthropologist Neil Smith both clarifies and complicates the definition by calling gentrification "a dirty word."

Regardless of the precise definition or particular academic perspective, the process of gentrification comprises three essential elements: (1) the displacement of original neighborhood residents; (2) systematic upgrading of the neighborhood, especially its housing and businesses; and (3) a dramatic change in the character of the neighborhood.

Gentrification is a relatively new term, coined in the 1960s by the British sociologist Ruth Glass to describe the movement of London's middle class ("gentry") from expensive neighborhoods to deteriorating ones. As newcomers upgrade their homes and businesses open to cater to the new residents, housing values tend to increase, forcing out longtime residents who cannot afford them. Commercial real estate owners take advantage of the influx of financial capital by raising rents, further contributing to the displacement of lower-income residents. A similar process takes place in commercial business, as small, local shops cannot compete with the larger stores and chains coming to the neighborhood and are forced to close down.

Several structural indicators underlie the process of gentrification. Specific social, economic, and political circumstances typically foreshadow the onset of, are triggered by, or reflect the impact of gentrification in a particular community. Among these factors are (1) inordinate and rapid increases in both housing prices and rents; (2) exorbitant eviction rates; (3) significant growth in the number and commercial value of local businesses; (4) change in the neighborhood's racial or ethnic composition; (5) an increase in the number of harassment charges brought against landlords; (6) growth in turnover rates for both businesses and residences; and (7) a heightened level of private investment.

CAUSES

The discourse on gentrification among policymakers and social scientists inevitably divides over theories of why gentrification occurs in certain communities and not others. Academics, policy analysts, and community activists offer a variety of explanations, ranging from social-cultural arguments focusing on changing family structures to purely economic arguments, which focus on the balance (or imbalance) between jobs and housing. Regardless of ideological explanation or hypothetical policy solution, several factors are recognized as basic causes of gentrification: rapid job growth, a tight housing market, strong investment potential in a low-income neighborhood, a large rent gap, divestment, preference for downtown amenities, increased traffic and congestion, and shifts in public policy.

The relative importance of each factor is impossible to gauge, but rapid job growth is clearly an essential ingredient, as gentrification and the economy are directly correlated. As economic conditions improve locally and nationally, the life choices and social well-being of minorities, working families, and the poor often worsen. For example, when the San Francisco Bay Area—specifically Silicon Valley—experienced a dramatic increase in jobs (up 275,000) between 1992 and 2002, with an equally impressive wage increase (up nearly 5 percent during the same period), the city's Mission District and Bayview/Hunter's Point neighborhoods underwent rapid gentrification. In Atlanta, similarly, a massive increase in jobs within the city's central district created a market for downtown lofts, which allowed the young new professionals to walk to work but forced out many longtime, lower-income residents.

Another key ingredient of gentrification is a tight housing market. In downtown neighborhoods in the process of gentrification, real estate prices are exorbitant and with a limited supply of housing, jobs become more geographically removed from affordable housing. Moreover, a booming economy that draws better-paid workers into a particular community tends to worsen housing conditions for lower-paid residents, as the increased number of people living in the community tightens the already competitive market and raises rents and housing prices. From 1995 to 1997, for example, the nine counties in the Bay Area saw the creation of 300,000 new jobs but only 31,000 new homes were constructed. San Francisco itself saw a net gain of 52,000 new jobs from 1995 to 2000, during which time just over 8,000 new residential units were built. In cities across the country, the number of new homes were not nearly keeping pace with the increased number of jobs. In 1998 alone, San Francisco built only one new housing unit for every ten new jobs.

The constrained housing supply, of course, leads to higher real estate prices—and fewer people who can afford them. In July 1999, the California Association of Realtors reported that to buy a house in the Bay Area (with a median price of nearly $300,000),

a family needed an annual income of almost $80,000. Less than 6 months later, the required income topped $100,000, as the median price had risen to $368,950, more than double the national average. By the end of the year, only 17 percent of Bay Area families were able to afford a median-priced home. The majority of area residents were systematically priced out of the market, and those on the bottom (people of color and working families) were pushed to the fringes or out of the area entirely. Even with the nation's fifth-highest median annual income ($72,400), only 12 percent of the city's families could afford to purchase a median-priced home during the late 1990s. This reality, along with low vacancy rates, reflected the extent to which gentrification was making it difficult for people to find affordable housing.

In New York City, housing opportunities have not been much better. The median sale price for homes increased by 250 percent from 1968 to 1986, reflecting a first wave of citywide gentrification. For example, a building on the Lower East Side that sold for $5,709 in 1976 was sold in 1981, without renovation, for $202,600. The 1987 stock market crash brought the city's real-estate market back to earth, but the 1990s did not bring much in the way of affordable new housing. Many longtime residents were forced to traditionally cheaper areas such as the Lower East Side, Harlem, and Brooklyn, whose lower-income residents in turn were forced out. The median income of households on the Lower East Side hovered at just under $20,000 per year, but gentrification and the real estate boom of the 1980s and 1990s created conditions in which a family needed an annual income of more than $65,000 to afford the least expensive properties. The late 1990s saw a similar process in the East Village, where loft-style condominiums sold for more than $600,000 and former factories and warehouses were converted into rental spaces that went for as high as $3,000 per month for a 450-square-foot studio.

The lack of affordable housing in San Francisco, Manhattan, and other cities has forced many longtime residents to seek living quarters in more affordable neighborhoods. Record-high housing prices have forced residents of Washington, D.C., to gentrify several lower-cost neighborhoods as an alternative. Bay Area residents no longer able to live in Piedmont or Noe Valley, for example, purchased homes in Bayview/Hunter's Point, West Oakland, and the Mission District. The latter, the longstanding Latino community of San Francisco, took the brunt of this gentrification through the 1990s. As of the mid-1990s, the Mission District still offered homes at prices not available in other parts of the city, but by 2000 this was no longer the case.

A major issue related to investment and the cost of property is what Neil Smith calls the "rent gap." He argues that the gap between median incomes and median rents exacerbated constraints on a housing market, as well as the potential speculative gains. Specifically, Smith argues, a "rent gap" emerges when property owners and real-estate interests purposely divest from inner-city neighborhoods. At the particular moment when the difference between the value of property before and after renovation reaches its peak, investors and real-estate interests bring in more capital. The effect is to hasten gentrification by increasing the pace of renovation and driving up housing costs.

In the post–World War II era, suburbanization increased, facilitated by federal lending policies, construction of affordable homes, development of open space, and the "American dream" of private home ownership. Coupled with the movement of jobs into outlying areas, the period between the 1950s and 1980s saw the massive movement of people and capital out of downtown areas. With this mass exodus came a precipitous decline in the value of urban property. Gentrification tends to occur when investors see circumstances with a lucrative profit potential in a high-risk neighborhood. Housing speculation thrives in such an environment, leaving residents unwilling or unable to withstand the pressures to sell. As properties are sold and investors put more money into them, the value in a neighborhood increases further, feeding the process of gentrification.

Gentrification and divestment go hand in hand as the systematic decay of inner-city communities create the conditions for gentrification. As neighborhoods and the buildings in them age, property values tend to decline. Deterioration of inner-city communities is not inevitable or irreversible, but the failure to reinvest in a community, by upgrading or repairing the buildings, contributes to this process of declining property values. Investors are loathe to buy into neighborhoods where property values are declining and a large proportion of the population is poor people.

This divestment process has taken place in a number of American cities, especially in the years following World War II. During that period, the federal government encouraged suburbanization through federal homeowner loans, massive freeway construction, and middle-class tax breaks such as mortgage deductibility. In the cities, meanwhile, rising poverty rates led to higher crime rates, and in some cases urban rioting, which led many businesses—both commercial and manufacturing enterprises—to flee to the suburbs. The result of these processes was middle-class "white flight" from inner cities and decaying downtown business districts. As whites and the middle class moved to the suburbs, the tax base of inner cities collapsed, services were underfunded, and the infrastructure fell into disrepair. On the housing front, poor inner-city populations were unable to pay higher rents and landlords lost their incentive to upgrade or even maintain their properties.

This process began to reverse itself in the 1980s, as suburbanites began to rediscover the attractions of the inner city: interesting architecture, access to cultural venues, ethnic diversity, and freedom from the long, increasingly traffic-snarled commute from the suburbs. While some of the early "urban pioneers" were struggling creative types—musicians, actors, and various types of artists—they were soon followed by better-paid professionals, or Yuppies (young urban professionals), many of whom had no children but a lot of disposable income.

Many scholars and the media saw gentrification as a purely market-driven phenomenon, with higher rents and housing costs resulting from the financial choices of myriad newcomers to areas with fixed housing supplies. The role of local, state, and federal government in the process was often ignored. In fact, governments use a range of initiatives to revitalize neighborhoods, from investment and zoning policies to increased police patrols and anticrime programs. For example, Congress offered a $5,000 tax credit to first-time homebuyers as part of its plan to revitalize Washington, D.C. Similar programs in Atlanta and Cleveland lured former suburbanites back to the central city district. In San Francisco, hefty tax credits for live/work lofts played a significant role in the gentrification of the South of Market area (SOMA).

Another government intervention that stimulates gentrification is the federal Hope VI public housing revitalization program. Hope VI provides incentives and subsidies to encourage the demolition and replacement of large housing projects with single-family dwellings. While some of these dwellings are sold to lower-income people, lower-density housing, by definition, cannot provide enough residential units for the many poor people displaced by the destruction of large housing projects.

Similarly, the construction of transit facilities, sports complexes, convention centers, and other large city-owned ventures tends to promote investment, housing construction, and the eventual displacement of existing residents. In Washington, D.C., the Columbia Heights and Shaw neighborhoods, both examples of extreme gentrification, are in close proximity of a new subway station (Columbia Heights) and convention center (Shaw). Construction of sports complexes in Cleveland, Charlotte, and San Francisco has led to significant urban renewal and gentrification, as investors built homes to take advantage of rising property values and businesses to exploit increased foot traffic. In all cases, the end result has been the displacement of existing residents and a dramatic change in the character of surrounding neighborhoods.

The absence of rent-control laws is another public policy contributing to gentrification. In cities with no rent control, enabling landlords to raise rents indiscriminately and evict residents without cause, the likelihood of neighborhood transition increases. In Portland, Oregon, landlords are able to evict tenants without cause, merely to take advantage of changing market value. This has led to extensive gentrification within the city's African American neighborhoods on the east side.

Police activity is yet one more example of government policy that directly or indirectly results in gentrification. The criminalization of homelessness in New York, Los Angeles, and San Francisco, for example, reflects the extent to which local officials will go to pursue the apparently benign goal of "improving neighborhoods." In reality, measures intended to revitalize certain areas and attract investment may also drive the homeless from parks and street corners—in short, brutalizing the city's poorest residents.

CONSEQUENCES

Gentrification leads to an increase in tax revenues. Higher rents and property values draw families with higher median incomes and force those with lower incomes out. As the number of higher-income residents grows, so do business activity and ultimately tax revenues, which can be used to improve the urban infrastructure, thereby perpetuating the process of gentrification.

A related improvement gentrification elicits is a greater income mix and the dispersal of poor people to surrounding areas, including, ironically, some of the inner suburbs where earlier generations of whites and middle class fled. The arrival of middle-class and upper middle-class residents thus not only adds money to the city's coffer, but also displaces residents who required public welfare and health insurance, further enriching government coffers. This reality was captured by a community development director from Cleveland, who said in a Brookings Institute report, "I know it's not politically correct, but with an average poverty rate of 42 percent, what my target neighborhood needs is a little gentrification."

The influx of money benefits not only municipal government, but local businesses and landowners as well. In some cities, business owners have enjoyed greater success with the arrival of new residents. A *New York Times* article in 2001 recounted the story of Errol Joseph, a longtime dry cleaner in Harlem who profited tremendously from the influx of new, upwardly mobile residents. "'Four years ago, we closed for the summer. We weren't making it.' [Joseph] said, sitting at a sewing machine with a tape measure around his neck. 'Now, we're doing just fine.'"

Changes in a neighborhood's cultural fabric and street "flavor," a common consequence of gentrification, are not always positive. The Mission District in San Francisco has lost several of its cultural and historical landmarks, as well as a number of low-priced, longstanding ethnic restaurants, as a result of rapidly rising commercial rents. The history of Chicago's Wicker Park, located on the city's north side, is indicative of the effects of gentrification. During the 1980s, this neighborhood was home to primarily Latino and Eastern European working-class families, and was known for its inexpensive Mexican restaurants, furniture stores, and other affordable establishments. Over the decade, however, Wicker Park experienced a heavy influx of young artists and musicians, taking advantage of the low rents, cultural aesthetics, huge loft spaces, and neighborhood bars and restaurants. As in other communities, low-income artists served as the bridge, or transition population, between the working-class and yuppie communities. "Artists like certain kinds of buildings, big spaces and lofts within stimulating architecture," contends Nacho Gonzalez, a professor at the University of Illinois, Chicago. "They bring in galleries, cafés, rock clubs, and a certain night life, which attracts the gentrifiers." As artists saturate a community, businesses change accordingly, helping the real estate industry convert poor communities into yuppie havens.

The story of Urbis Orbis, a coffeehouse and theater in Wicker Park, further represents the story of gentrification within this neighborhood. Once a hangout for local artists and writers, it eventually closed because its owners could no longer afford the escalating rent. Down the block, at the corner of Milwaukee and Damne, stood a flatiron building known as the center of Wicker's Bohemian community, where artists could go months without paying rent for their huge loft-apartments. During the 1990s, this building was taken over by corporate realtors, who immediately raised rents without notice, emptying the building for wealthier tenants. On the same block, three-room flats now cost more than $500,000. Gone are reasonable rents and the small local businesses of the 1980s. Today, Wicker Park is less known for its community feeling and affordable shops than for its chic, expensive bars and restaurants. In less than 20 years, both the character and the residents of the neighborhood changed dramatically.

Despite the many "positives" of gentrification, all of which benefit city elites, a major consequence is displacement. Revitalization of neighborhoods through real-estate improvements and new businesses comes at the expense of low-income residents (primarily minorities) and local businesses. For example, rents in Portland's predominantly black neighborhoods increased 100 percent per year in the late 1990s, leading the northeast and southeast neighborhoods to become more and more white. Longstanding ethnic neighborhoods like Harlem, Boyle Heights, Roxbury, and the Mission have experienced not only an erosion of cultural institutions and businesses, but a displacement of their residents. Exorbitant rents, high tax rates, and outright eviction have forced these residents out of their own communities. While the literature and policy analysts talk about the positives and negatives of gentrification as an either/or phenomenon, it is clear that the positives inevitably devolve to the city's elite, while the poor, elderly, and people of color inordinately suffer the negatives.

RACE AND CLASS

Race is another issue defining the debate over gentrification. While not inherently a racial phenomenon, gentrification tends to take on a racial element. The reality of gaps in income and wealth, tied to historic and contemporary racist practices, results in a process of systematic displacement by whites of low-income residents of color. For example, San Francisco's Bay View/Hunter Point, a longtime African American community, saw an increasing number of higher-income Asian American newcomers during the 1990s. Their presence has led to rising rent costs as the African American residents were displaced. In some neighborhoods, however, gentrification is more of a class than a racial issue, as middle class African Americans—many of them or their parents having fled the same areas in decades past—return to the inner city, driving up housing costs and forcing poor blacks into ever less desirable neighborhoods.

FIGHTING BACK

While gentrification may seem like a self-perpetuating and irreversible process, individuals and organizations throughout the country are committed to fighting back. Indeed, every major U.S. city has a nonprofit organization dedicated to securing housing rights for the economically less fortunate. Some cities have a variety of organizations, including those dedicated to combating gentrification. In New York City, community groups have worked vigorously to maintain some form of rent control. The City Life/Vida Urban group, founded in the 1970s, organized a committee of New York landlords supporting affordable housing and opposing gentrification in the mid-1990s. Around the same time, the Anti-Displacement Project, an organization based in Springfield, Massachusetts, successfully lobbied for pro-tenant legislation and organized a series of public demonstrations. In Chicago, the Organization of the Northeast (ONE) has battled city officials and landlords over the need to maintain affordable housing within the uptown area. In addition to education campaigns, lobbying, and protests, ONE has actually bought properties to guarantee their affordability.

The Bay Area, like New York City, has been a hotbed of antigentrification activism. Embracing a wide range of strategies, from lobbying and electoral campaigns to protests and violence, activists have battled those who attempt to change neighborhoods through new residents and businesses. The Mission Yuppie Eradication Project, "a grassroots movement in San Francisco working to raise awareness about gentrification issues," has taken these efforts to a new extreme—attacking fancy cars, boycotting high-price establishments, spreading rumors about crime in certain neighborhoods, and taking other measures to make newly arrived, gentrifying, high-income residents want to move out.

Gentrification and the struggle to halt it have led to political wrangling and occasionally open confrontations among activists and their supporters, politicians, real estate developers, landlords, police, and incoming residents. The issue has polarized communities throughout the United States and, by all appearances, is likely to continue to do so in the decades to come.

David J. Leonard

REFERENCES

Abu-Lughod, Janet, ed. *From Urban Village to East Village: The Battle for New York's Lower East Side.* Cambridge, MA: Blackwell Publishers, 1994.

Alejandrino, Simon Velasquez. *Gentrification in San Francisco's Mission District: Indicators and Policy.* San Francisco: Mission Economic Development Association, 2000.

Blomley, Nicholas. *Unsettling the City: Urban Land and the Politics of Property.* New York: Routledge, 2003.

Bourne, Larry S., and David Ley. *The Changing Social Geography of Canadian Cities.* London: McGill-Queens University Press, 1993.

Castells, Manuel. *The Rise of the Network Society.* Cambridge, MA: Blackwell Publishers, 1996.

Fidel, K. "End of Diversity: The Long-Term Effects of Gentrification in Lincoln Park." *Research in Urban Sociology* (1992): 145–64.

Gale, D. E. *Neighbourhood Revitalization and the Postindustrial City: A Multinational Perspective.* Lexington, MA: Lexington Books, 1984.

Gibson, Timothy. *Securing the Spectacular City: The Politics of Revitalization and Homelessness in Downtown Seattle.* New York: Rowan and Littlefield, 2003.

Jacobs, Jane. *The Death and Life of Great American Cities.* New York: Random House, 2002.

Kennedy, Maureen, and Paul Leonard. *Dealing with Neighborhood Change: A Primer on Gentrification and Policy Choices.* Washington, DC: Brookings Institute, 2001.

Lang, Robert. *Edgeless Cities: Exploring the Elusive Metropolis.* Washington, DC: Brookings Institute, 2003.

Marcuse, Peter. "Gentrification, Abandonment and Displacement: Connections, Clauses and Policy Responses in New York City. *Journal of Urban and Contemporary Law* (1985): 195–248.

Muniz, Vicky. *Resisting Gentrification and Displacement: Voices of Puerto Rican Women of the Barrio.* New York: Garland Press, 1998.

Smith, Neil. *The New Urban Frontier: Gentrification and the Revanchist City.* New York: Routledge, 1996.

Smith, Neil, and Peter Williams, eds. *Gentrification of the City.* Boston: Allen and Unwin, 1986.

WEB SITES

California Association of Realtors:
http://car.org/index.html

Mission Yuppie Eradication Project:
www.infoshop.org/myep.html

Neighborhood Centre:
www.neighbourhoodcentre.org.uk/gent.html

San Francisco Bay Area Progressive Directory:
www.bapd.org/kgeion-1.html

Video Activist Network:
www.videoactivism.org/gentro.html

GLOSSARY

Abandonment. A situation where landlords are no longer able to collect enough rent to cover the costs of utilities, taxes, and maintenance and then abandon the building or land. Properties are rarely abandoned because of structural problems or unusability, but because they are no longer profitable.

Bohemian. A person, often an artist, who embraces a counterculture identity. Often attracted to inexpensive urban neighborhoods because of their large spaces, unique attributes, and cultural flavor, Bohemians play a significant role in the process of gentrification.

Deindustrialization. A shift in a nation's economy from one based on producing goods to one producing services. As the process occurs, the share of total jobs in manufac-turing industries declines dramatically, as employment within the service industry increases proportionally. Deindustrialization tends to occur when manufacturing companies are pressured to cut costs because of increased competition, regulation, or other demands, leading to manufacturing plants relocating to other communities or other countries, or automation of production processes. In the United States, deindustrialization has led to a dramatic decline in the availability of high-paying industrial jobs and the vitality of many urban communities.

Filtering. A model in which newer houses are occupied by upper middle-class and wealthy families, leaving their less desirable homes for poor families. In other words, better homes "filter" their way down the economic ladder, with the worst homes facing demolition.

No-cause eviction. Situation that allows a landlord to evict tenants for any reason, including a desire to raise rents. Portland, among other cities, has a no-cause eviction law on the books.

Owner move-ins. A means to avoid rent control or stabilization laws with landlords finding loopholes to allow increased rents. With owner move-ins landlords can evict a tenant so that they can move into the unit, only to move right out, allowing them to raise the rent or convert it to a condo. In San Francisco, owner move-ins increased by 300 percent from 1996 to 2000.

Redlining. Process in which certain neighborhoods are singled out, or redlined, by banks as a way to deny loans to otherwise qualified applicants.

Reinvestment. The integration of capital into a poor neighborhood, usually to upgrade its infrastructure and physical qualities.

Rent gap. "Disparity between the potential ground level and the actual ground rent capitalized under the present land use" (Smith). More specifically, the rent gap represents the disparity between the capital gain from property at a particular moment and the potential earnings through revitalization and reinvestment. When the rent gap is wide enough, or at its peak, gentrification will usually occur.

Revitalization. The process of upgrading the physical (enhancing housing or streets), commercial (creating new businesses and services), and social (increasing employment opportunities, reducing crime, improving sense of community) components of a particular neighborhood; improving the future prospects for a community's residents through public or private actions.

Sprawl. Geographic dispersion of human residential, business, and commercial development from urban and village centers along highways and in rural countryside, creating auto dependency, increased congestion, and excessive consumption.

Suburbanization. The development of communities and cities around large metropolitan city centers.

DOCUMENTS

Document 1. Why Is Affordable Rental Housing Being Lost?

The following is a brief article by Kristopher M. Rengert, the director of urban and metropolitan research at the Fannie Mae Foundation, a private company established by the federal government to provide financing to mortgage lenders. Rengert argues that gentrification, while raising the value of homes, is also responsible for rising rents and the lack of affordable housing for low-income individuals and families.

The growing concern over the preservation of affordable rental housing stems from a number of converging trends in U.S. housing markets. This article identifies the preconditions that often precipitate a loss of affordable rental housing, current trends that exacerbate such losses, and the populations and areas that are at greatest risk.

Essentially, there are two separate preconditions that threaten the preservation of affordable housing. The first involves cases where the market rate for rental housing units is or is expected to be substantially above the rents received by owners under the subsidy programs or under current conditions. Neighborhood gentrification is one cause of this scenario in which market rates for housing units increase as their neighborhoods become more attractive to higher-income households.

The other scenario results when owners are no longer willing or able financially to maintain properties utilizing the rental income streams from lower-income tenants. This scenario arises most frequently with aging properties in financially and socially distressed neighborhoods. In these cases, owners do not have the option of raising rents to improve their financial balance sheets and enable proper maintenance. Existing tenants are unable to pay higher rents and higher-income households are not attracted to the neighborhood or property in question. Property abandonment is frequently the ultimate outcome in many such cases, generally preceded by periods during which tenants live in substandard conditions as owners neglect property upkeep. Several current trends contribute to the focus of practitioners and researchers on the preservation of affordable housing. The first is the large stock of government-subsidized rental housing units in programs in which the subsidies have recently or will soon expire. Several million housing units face this situation, as Section 8, Section 236, and Section 221(d)(3) contracts began expiring in the early 1990s and will continue to expire over the next decade. In this situation, owners of housing units constructed using government subsidies requiring that they be rented to lower-income households become able to rent the same housing units at market rates. As described above, in some housing markets, these market rates are substantially higher than the rents paid by tenants under the subsidy programs, or higher than the Fair Market Rents assigned by the U.S. Department of Housing and Urban Development under the Section 8 program. Frequently, owners need to substantially improve their properties to make them attractive to higher-income renters, and the expected increased revenues from higher rents can be sufficient to warrant these investments.

In addition to the expiration of subsidies under the above-mentioned programs, substantial shares of public housing units are being eliminated via the HOPE VI program and not replaced by permanently affordable housing. This is a different issue than expiring subsidies of particular housing units that are then potentially leased at market rates unaffordable to lower-income households because the HOPE VI program demolishes the existing subsidized units and replaces them with new units. But the overall effect is the same—a reduction in the number of housing units available and affordable to lower-income households.

Another major trend contributing to the preservation issue is gentrification. Gentrifying neighborhoods experience increased rents as they become more attractive to higher-income households. As higher rents become widespread, owners of previously affordable units—in some cases, subsidized—gain incentives to raise rents to take advantage of new financial opportunities. In some cases they are able to pre-pay government-subsidized mortgages, freeing them to increase rents. In other cases, the gentrification of the neighborhood coincides with the "natural" expiration of the subsidization of their housing units, again freeing them to increase rents to current market levels. Owners of unsubsidized affordable rental units are generally free to raise rents as soon as the local housing markets make it possible. In all three scenarios the result is the same—gentrification results in a decrease in the number of rental housing units affordable to lower-income households. Neighborhoods undergoing gentrification that also contain substantial stocks of affordable housing—particularly affordable housing with rents held below market levels by expiring government subsidies—are especially in need of affordable housing preservation efforts.

The affordable housing stock is at risk in all states of the country, although typically the stock in metropolitan areas is at greatest risk. This is because the great and growing majority of U.S. households live in metropolitan areas and the bulk of government programs supporting the creation of affordable rental housing target metropolitan areas. As a result, the bulk of affordable housing units under expiring subsidy programs are concentrated in states with large metropolitan populations. For instance, the northeastern and midwestern regions of the country have concentrations of housing units constructed under the Section 8 program. California, Florida, and Texas also have concentrations of these units.

In addition to geographic concentrations, particular populations are at primary risk of loss of affordable housing. Residents of government-subsidized units are particularly likely to be elderly and/or handicapped. This fact raises a particularly troubling facet of the preservation issue—the populations most at risk of loss of their affordable housing include the most vulnerable and least mobile groups in society.

A number of tools have been developed to help preserve existing affordable housing units and help replace those that cannot—or in some cases, should not—be preserved. Two bipartisan commissions—the Millennial Housing Commission and the Commission on Affordable Housing and Health Facility Needs for Seniors in the 21st Century—made recommendations to Congress earlier this year in this regard, and the National Housing Trust has also championed efforts in this area. . . . The growing attention from these and other major national organizations for the preservation of affordable housing is heartening—a critical mass is assembling for recognizing and addressing this problem. Yet, realistically, the termination of government subsidies for literally millions of affordable rental housing units will require action by the federal, state, and local governments to ensure a future adequate supply of affordable rental housing. Unfortunately, the U.S. track record is rather dismal. Since housing conditions have been monitored in the United States, there have been large shares of the lower-income population residing in poor housing conditions or paying unaffordable rents. The growing movement to preserve affordable rental housing is an important effort to move beyond the historic patterns of housing distribution in the United States.

Source: Fannie Mae Foundation. *Housing Facts and Findings* 4, 4 (2002).

Document 2. Excerpt from the State of Oregon Rent Control Law

This excerpt provides a glimpse into Oregon's rent control laws, which reflect an attempt to minimize rent increases while preventing gentrification. It also illuminates the loopholes that allow property owners to circumvent rent control laws in an effort to secure market value by any means necessary.

91.225 Local rent control prohibited; exclusions; exceptions. (1) The Legislative Assembly finds that there is a social and economic need to insure an adequate supply of affordable housing for Oregonians. The Legislative Assembly also finds that the imposition of general restrictions on housing rents will disrupt an orderly housing market, increase deferred maintenance of existing housing stock, lead to abandonment of existing rental units and create a property tax shift from rental-owned to owner-occupied housing. Therefore, the Legislative Assembly declares that the imposition of rent control on housing in the State of Oregon is a matter of statewide concern.

(2) Except as provided in subsections (3) to (5) of this section, a city or county shall not enact any ordinance or resolution which controls the rent that may be charged for the rental of any dwelling unit.

(3) This section does not impair the right of any state agency, city, county or urban renewal agency as defined by ORS 457.035 to reserve to itself the right to approve rent increases, establish base rents or establish limitations on rents on any residential property for which it has entered into a contract under which certain benefits are applied to the property for the expressed purpose of providing reduced rents for low income tenants. Such benefits include, but are not limited to, property tax exemptions, long-term financing, rent subsidies, code enforcement procedures and zoning density bonuses.

(4) Cities and counties are not prohibited from including in condominium conversion ordinances a requirement that, during the notification period specified in ORS 100.305, the owner or developer may not raise the rents of any affected tenant except in a proportional amount equal to the percentage increase in the All Items Portland Consumer Price Index since the date of the last rent increase for the dwelling unit then occupied by the affected tenant.

(5) Cities, counties and state agencies may impose temporary rent controls when a natural or man-made disaster that materially eliminates a significant portion of the rental housing supply occurs, but must remove the controls when the rental housing supply is restored to substantially normal levels.

(6) As used in this section, "dwelling unit" and "rent" have the meaning given those terms in ORS 90.100.

(7) This section is applicable throughout this state and in all cities and counties therein. The electors or the governing body of a city or county shall not enact, and the governing body shall not enforce, any ordinance, resolution or other regulation that is inconsistent with this section.

Source: State of Oregon, Legislature. Statutes. 91.225.

GLOBAL WARMING

For the past two centuries, at an accelerating rate, the fossil-fuel effluvia of machine culture has been materially altering the basic composition of the Earth's atmosphere. Human-induced warming of Earth's climate is emerging as one of the major scientific, social, and economic issues of the twenty-first century, as the effects of climate change become evident in everyday life in locations as varied as small Pacific island nations and the shores of the Arctic Ocean.

"The risks of global warming are real, palpable, the effects are accumulating daily, and the costs of correcting the trend rise with each day's delay," warns Dr. George M. Woodwell, director of the Woods Hole Research Center in Massachusetts. Dean Edwin Abrahamson, an early leader in the field, comments: "Fossil fuel burning, deforestation, and the release of industrial chemicals are rapidly heating the earth to temperatures not experienced in human memory. Limiting global heating and climatic change is the central environmental challenge of our time."

To a certain extent, the greenhouse effect is necessary to maintain temperatures on Earth that sustain life as we know it. Without "infrared forcing" (popularly known as the "greenhouse effect"), the average temperature of the Earth would be about 33°C. (60°F.) colder than today's averages, too cold to sustain the Earth's existing plant and animal life. In other words, Earth's moderate degree of infrared forcing (along with its blanket of water) keeps the planet habitable. Perpetually cloudy Venus has an atmosphere in which carbon dioxide is the dominant element. The surface temperature on Venus, warmed considerably by runaway infrared forcing, is roughly 800°F. The planet Mars, with nearly no infrared forcing in its atmosphere, averages −53°C.

Evidence has been accumulating that sustained, human-induced warming of the Earth's lower troposphere has been in progress since about 1980, and accelerating during the 1990s. In 1997 and 1998, the global temperature set records for fifteen consecutive months; July 1998 averaged 0.6°F. higher than July 1997, an enormous increase if repeated year after year. The year 1998 was the warmest of the millennium, topping 1997 by one quarter of a degree Fahrenheit.

Michael Meacher, speaking as Great Britain's environment minister, has said that "Combating climate change is the greatest challenge of human history." Climate models indicate that, if the atmosphere's carbon dioxide level doubles over preindustrial levels, which is likely (at present rates of increase), before the year 2100 temperatures may rise 1.9 to 5.2°C (3.4 to 9.4°F), producing "a climate warmer than any in human history" within a century. "The consequences of this amount of warming are unknown and could include extremely unpleasant surprises."

The issue is at once very simple and astoundingly complex. Increasing human populations, rising affluence, and continued dependence on energy derived from fossil fuels are at the crux of the matter. The complexity of the problem is illustrated by the degree to which the daily lives of machine-age peoples depend on fossil fuels. This dependence gives rise to an array of local, regional, and national economic interests that cause tensions between nations negotiating to reduce greenhouse gas emissions. The cacophony of debate also reflects the strength and diversity of the established interests being assiduously protected. Add to the human elements of the problem the sheer randomness of climate (as well as the amount of time, variously estimated at 30 to 50 years, that passes before a given level of greenhouse gases is actually factored into climate), and the problem becomes sufficiently complex and intractable to (thus far) significantly impede any serious, unified human effort to fashion solutions.

The greenhouse effect is not a new concept to science. It has merely become more apparent today with rising temperatures and more sophisticated sci-

CHRONOLOGY

1712	Thomas Newcomen, an Englishman, develops a coal-burning steam engine.
1769, et seq.	James Watt, an Englishman, adapts Newcomen's steam engine to several industrial processes; the age of fossil-fueled energy consumption begins.
1820s	Jean Baptiste Fourier, a Frenchman, compares the Earth's atmosphere to a greenhouse.
1896	Svante A. Arrhenius, a Swedish chemist, publishes a paper, "On the Influence of Carbonic Acid in the Air upon the Temperature of the Ground," establishing the theory that atmospheric temperature is consistent with carbon dioxide levels.
1930s	G. S. Callendar, a British meteorologist, assembles worldwide weather records indicating that the Earth's atmosphere (near the ground) has warmed 0.4°C between the 1880s and the 1930s. A subsequent downturn in temperatures causes his research to be ignored.
1957	Roger Revelle and Hans Suess assert that human beings are carrying out "a large-scale geophysical experiment" by emitting increasing amounts of heat-trapping gases, including carbon dioxide, into the atmosphere.
1950s	Charles David Keeling assembles evidence that carbon dioxide levels are steadily rising in the Earth's atmosphere, from about 280 parts per million (ppm) in the 1880s, to 315 ppm in the 1950s. (By the year 2000, this level had reached 370 ppm.) Keeling develops the manometer, a device capable of measuring carbon dioxide levels and, after using it at several sites, discovers that CO_2 levels are generally the same worldwide, given annual cycle variations.
1979	Global warming becomes a political issue following a report by a group of well-known scientists to the Council on Environmental Quality, that "Man is setting in motion a series of events that seem certain to cause a significant warming of world climates unless mitigating measures are taken immediately." A warning published in the British scientific journal *Nature* (May 3) argues that the greenhouse effect could become "the most important environmental issue in the world."
1988	An unusually hot, dry summer in the United States brings publicity to global warming as scientist James Hansen warns Congress of its dangers. The summer of 1988 becomes the warmest on record to that date. (Worldwide weather records have been kept since the 1860s.)
1990	Intergovernmental Panel on Climate Change (IPCC), a body of 2,500 scientists, issues its first worldwide survey of global warming.
1995	The Intergovernmental Panel on Climate Change's *Second Assessment* strengthens its members' belief that human-generated use of fossil fuels is altering the world's climate.
1997	Kyoto Protocol is negotiated.
1998	A major El Niño brings the warmest year, globally, since worldwide weather records have been kept, eclipsing a number of record-warm years during the 1990s.
2000	George W. Bush is elected president of the United States; he repudiates the Kyoto Protocol as lacking a sound scientific basis.
	The IPCC's *Third Assessment* strengthens warnings of rapid warming during the twenty-first century; temperature rises of roughly 4 to 6°C are anticipated within 100 years.
2002	Global temperatures reach the second highest level on record, surpassed only by 1998's record.

entific tools for measuring and forecasting atmospheric processes. The atmospheric balance of "trace" gases actually started to change beyond natural bounds at the dawn of the industrial age, with the first large-scale burning of fossil fuels. It became noticeable in the 1880s and an important force in global climate change by about 1980. With the debate intensifying, scientific circles generally came to accept the idea that human activity is warming the earth in potentially damaging ways by 1995.

Table 1. Carbon Dioxide Levels in the Earth's Atmosphere

Year	Carbon dioxide (parts per million, ppm)
Glacial, preindustrial	200*
Interglacial, preindustrial	280
1750	270
1850	280
1957	315
1970	330
1980	340
1990	355
2000	370

* Range of 200 to 280 ppm for 20 million years.
Source: Adapted from Bruce E. Johansen, *The Global Warming Desk Reference.* Westport, CT: Greenwood, 2001.

RISING LEVELS OF GREENHOUSE GASES DUE TO FOSSIL-FUEL EFFLUVIA

Since the beginning of the industrial age roughly two centuries ago, an increasing human population has made more widespread use of fossil fuels to aid economic development as well as to augment human comfort, convenience, and financial profit. Combustion of oil, coal, and natural gas has been changing the atmospheric balance of carbon dioxide, methane, nitrous oxides, and other naturally occurring "trace gases," as well as chemicals created by industry, such as chloroflourocarbons (CFCs). Detectable increases in most of these gases, all of which retain heat in the atmosphere, date back to the mid-nineteenth century. The rise in greenhouse gas levels was small at that time, and the effects were difficult to separate from the climate's natural variability.

The Earth's atmosphere is composed of 78.1 percent nitrogen and 20.9 percent oxygen. All the other gases, including those responsible for the greenhouse effect, make up only about 1 percent of the atmosphere: carbon dioxide (CO_2) 0.035 percent; methane (CH_4) 0.0001 percent, and ozone 0.000001 to 0.000004 percent. Water vapor, which also retains heat in the atmosphere, plays a major role in the infrared forcing of the atmosphere. As the air warms, it holds more water vapor. The atmosphere holds 6 percent more water vapor with each 1°C rise in temperature.

Between 1850 and 2000, human combustion of fossil fuels has risen fiftyfold. According to contemporary observations, the carbon dioxide content of the atmosphere is increasing at an average of between 1.0 and 1.5 parts per million per year, with large annual variations. In some years, such as 1972 and 1988, atmospheric carbon dioxide rose 2.5 to 3.0 percent, while in 1973 it did not increase at all. Roughly two-thirds of the increase since industrialism began has occurred since 1950. In a century and a half of rapid industrialization, the proportion of carbon dioxide has risen from about 280 to 370 parts per million. By the year 2000, scientists had tested the composition of the atmosphere to approximately 60 million years in the past. The level of carbon dioxide today is believed to be as high as it has been in at least 20 million years.

Emission of carbon dioxide and other greenhouse gases is part of our everyday lives to the degree that our modes of transportation, production, and consumption are enabled by the combustion of fossil fuels. Roughly 80 percent of human industrial activity is fueled by energy that produces carbon dioxide (and often other greenhouse gases as well). These industrial processes also produce waste heat, and some manufactured goods (such as automobiles) produce waste heat and greenhouse gases as they are operated.

IPCC'S THIRD ASSESSMENT

The Intergovernmental Panel on Climate Change's (IPCC's) 2000 assessment, a summary of which was distributed to government officials worldwide in late October of that year, found that despite uncertainties, studies over the previous five years, including increasingly sophisticated computer modeling, showed "stronger evidence for a human influence" on the climate and more certainty that human-made greenhouse gases "have contributed substantially to the observed warming over the last 50 years."

The new assessment forecasts that if greenhouse emissions are not curtailed, the Earth's average surface temperatures may increase substantially more than previous IPCC estimates. The panel concluded that average global temperature increases ranging from 2.7 to as much as 11°F can be expected by the end of this century, if current trends in heat-trapping gas emissions continue. In its 1995 (second) assessment, the panel projected increases in a range of 1.8 to 6.3°F. The report based the higher temperature forecasts on more sophisticated computer modeling and an expected decline in sulfate releases into the atmosphere, especially from power plants, for environmental reasons. Sulfates tend to act as a cooling agent by reflecting the sun's radiation. "An increasing body of observations gives a collective picture of a warming world," according to the 2000 IPCC assessment.

FOREST FIRES AND GLOBAL WARMING

According to Robert C. Cowen of *The Christian Science Monitor,* "Forest fires have become a wildcard in the global-warming game." New research shows that, under the right circumstances, forest fires that burn on top of peat deposits can emit as much carbon dioxide as human activities. Indonesian fires polluted the air over Southeast Asia in 1997 and 1998, during a severe drought triggered by El Niño conditions. Susan Page at the University of Leicester in Great Britain, together with colleagues in England, Germany, and Indonesia, analyzed satellite photos and data gathered on the ground to estimate how much of the fire area's living vegetation and peat deposits were burned.

In a paper published November 7, 2002, in *Nature,* Page and colleagues reported that the CO_2 released by these fires was equivalent to 13 to 40 percent of the mean annual global carbon emissions from fossil fuels and, according to Cowen, "contributed greatly to the largest annual increase in atmospheric CO_2 concentration detected since records began in 1957." In Indonesia, nature and human activity combined to provide a massive subsurface fuel reservoir. Peat deposits in tropical forests had built up as vegetation died and decayed.

The work of Page and colleagues has major implications for climate-change modeling because, as they wrote in *Nature,*

> Tropical peatlands are one of the largest near-surface reserves of terrestrial organic carbon, and hence their stability has important implications for climate change. In their natural state, lowland tropical peatlands support a luxuriant growth of peat swamp forest overlying peat deposits up to 20 meters thick. Persistent environmental change—in particular, drainage and forest clearing—threatens their stability, and makes them susceptible to fire. This was demonstrated by the occurrence of widespread fires throughout the forested peatlands of Indonesia during the 1997 El Niño event.

The spread of human populations is aggravating the danger from fire. Scientists point out that, "In Indonesia, peatland fires are mostly anthropogenic, started by local (indigenous) and immigrant farmers as part of small-scale land clearance activities, and also, on a much larger scale, by private companies and government agencies as the principal tool for clearing forest, before establishing crops." During the abnormally long, El Niño dry season of 1997, many of these "managed" fires spread out of control, "consuming not only the surface vegetation but also the underlying peat and tree roots, contributing to the dense haze that blanketed a large part of Southeast Asia and causing both severe deterioration in air quality and health problems." Catastrophic events in small areas that release carbon locked away in peat or other rich reservoirs have to be taken into account. At the moment, no climate modeler knows how to do this. Yet, as Schimel and Baker have said, these events "can evidently have a huge impact on the global carbon balance."

"BIOTIC FEEDBACKS" AND ANTICIPATED WARMING

Certain attributes of global warming may amplify others, increasing temperatures more quickly than any single effect on its own. For example, significant warming could liberate large amounts of methane locked away under the ocean's surface in solid form into the atmosphere in gaseous form, increasing the severity of the greenhouse effect through processes scientists call "biotic feedbacks."

Such conversion of methane to gaseous form may have helped warm the Earth between 52 million and 58 million years ago, during the late Paleocene and early Eocene periods—the days of the dinosaurs. T. L. Hudson and L. B. Magoon have advanced a theory that, in the Gulf of Alaska at that time, "large amounts of sediment, eroded from freshly uplifted mountains, were deposited in deep water off the 2,200-kilometer coast of Alaska." The oceanic tectonic plate, subducting below the continental plate, generated heat, as well as producing hydrocarbons including liquid methane from organic matter in the sediment. According to Peter Clift and Karen Bice, writing in *Nature,* the methane may have subsequently turned to gas and bubbled into the atmosphere, "increasing greenhouse-gas concentrations [that] might [help] explain the higher global temperatures 58 to 52 million years ago." These authors believe that this process may have contributed significantly to the prolonged global warming at that time, but was probably too geographically isolated to have been its only cause.

M. L. Goulden and colleagues have provided additional evidence that the Earth's frozen reaches are already releasing additional greenhouse gases into the air. In their study of boreal forests, they found "clear evidence that carbon dioxide locked into permafrost several hundred to 7,000 years ago is now being given off to the atmosphere as warming climate melts the permafrost." Investigating black spruce forest, they found that carbon dioxide was being emitted into the atmosphere from well beneath the biologically active layer containing moss and tree roots. The same is frequently true for methane. According to Neil Davis, author of *Permafrost: A Guide to Frozen Ground in Transition* (2001), this "relict" carbon dioxide "represents a massive source since it is estimated that the carbon dioxide contained in the seasonally and perennially frozen soils of boreal forests is 200 to 500 billion metric tons, enough if all released to increase the atmosphere's concentration of carbon dioxide by 50%." Hence, it is possible that releasing carbon dioxide from melting permafrost during warming, or locking it into newly frozen soil during cooling, may accelerate climate change.

EXHAUSTION OF EXISTING CARBON "SINKS"

Other factors could accelerate warming. Researchers from the British Meteorological Office's Hadley Centre for Climate Prediction forecast land temperatures would rise by 6°C during the twenty-first century, 2°C more than the Centre's previous estimate. This projection resulted from a computer model forecasting accelerated global warming as warmer conditions reduce the amount of carbon dioxide absorbed by soil and vegetation. Michael Meacher, the British environment minister, called the research's implications "mind-blowing."

The oceans, soil, and vegetation now absorb more than half of the carbon dioxide emitted into the atmosphere. This study projects that by 2050 the soil and vegetation will stop absorbing the gas and start emitting it mainly because plant respiration is greater in warmer soils and drier conditions will damage the Amazonian rainforest. The new study indicates that, within a century, human society will experience a temperature rise unprecedented in its history; by the twenty-second century, if fossil fuel use is not sharply curtailed, the Earth may return to the climatic days of the dinosaurs. "We have had warmer periods in the past," said Geoff Jenkins of the Hadley Centre. "But the rate of warming is quite unprecedented."

As Peter M. Cox and colleagues have written, "climate-cycle feedbacks could significantly accelerate climate change over the twenty-first century." By the year 2050, according to their models, this "sink" will be exhausted as the biosphere itself begins to add carbon to the atmosphere. The result is that the warming will reinforce itself. By 2100, according to Cox and coauthors, the emission of carbon dioxide from land could become large enough to balance the oceans' ability to absorb it, further accelerating the warming.

WARMING SEAS

Because humankind is a narcissistic species, our focus regarding the implications of global warming is usually fixed on the third of the planet consisting of dry land. The other two-thirds of the Earth will be warming as well, however, with profound implications for the species that inhabit it, including a holocaust for coral reefs that has already begun.

According to Peter G. Brewer and his associates writing in *Science,* the chemistry of ocean water already is being changed by human-induced greenhouse gases in the atmosphere: "The invading wave of atmospheric CO_2 has already altered the chemistry of surface seawater worldwide, and over much of the ocean, this tracer field has now permeated to a depth of more than one kilometer." Given that the ocean is slowly warming, as its carbon dioxide level rises, its capacity as a carbon sink is probably being compromised.

The level of the world's seas and oceans has been rising slowly for much of the twentieth century, a millimeter or two a year, enough to produce noticeable erosion on 70 percent of the world's sandy beaches, including 90 percent of sandy beaches in the United States. The withdrawal of underground water and oil in some areas, such as the U.S. Gulf Coast between New Orleans and Houston, is causing the land to sink as the oceans rise.

Among the important results of warming seas will be coastal erosion, shoreline inundation with higher tide levels, higher storm surges, and saltwater intrusion into coastal estuaries and groundwater supplies. The World Wildlife Fund reported: "Scientific evidence strongly suggests that global climate change already is affecting a broad spectrum of marine species and ecosystems, from tropical coral reefs to polar ice-edge communities."

More than 20 percent of the world's population

lives within 30 kilometers of coastal areas. That portion of the population is increasing twice as quickly as the population as a whole. According to one estimate by the Natural Resources Defense Council, a one-meter rise in sea level could displace 300 million people around the world. Thirty of the world's largest cities lie near coasts and are vulnerable to a 1-meter rise in ocean level. Most of Australia's population lives in coastal cities. By 1990, more than 100 million people lived within 50 miles of coastlines in the United States.

A large number of the people who could be displaced by a modest rise in sea level are residents of broad river deltas such as the Mississippi near New Orleans, the Nile in Egypt, and the Ganges, which joins with several other rivers in Bangladesh. Half of Bangladesh lies less than 5 meters above sea level. A 1-meter sea-level rise in Bangladesh would displace about 10 to 20 percent of the country's human population, and cost at least 6 percent of gross national product (GNP). An ocean-level rise of 3 meters would affect 27 percent of the people, and cost roughly 15 percent of GNP.

In the twenty-first century, the phrase "environmental refugee" may become more familiar around the world. Lowland residents who could be forced from their homes by a 3-foot rise in sea levels over the next century include 26 million people in Bangladesh, 70 million to 100 million in China, 20 million in India, and 12 million in the Egypt's Nile Delta. In Egypt, a 1-meter sea-level rise could cost 15 percent of the country's GNP, including much of its agricultural base. A 14-inch rise in sea levels could flood 40 percent of the mudflats ringing Puget Sound, obliterating a significant habitat for shellfish and waterfowl.

These locations are only a few of a great many examples, because the Earth's junctures of seas and rivers have been important crossroads for human trade (as well as fertile farming areas) throughout human history. Many river deltas are densely populated and very vulnerable to even a small rise in sea level.

Forecasts of sea-level rise must contend with major uncertainties. Most projections do not indicate how much the increase hinges on what happens in Antarctica or how sudden some rises in sea level could be. William R. Cline called some of these estimates "innocuous," as he commented:

Consider sea-level rise, recently downgraded from one meter to about 40 centimeters for CO_2 doubling. The IPCC calculations are premised on no contribution to sea-level rise from the Antarctic, on grounds that its temperature remains in a range (below minus 12 degrees C) where warming increases rather than decreases glacier mass. (One reason is that warmer air is more moist, so it provides more snow for glacier buildup.) But warming of 10 degrees C or more would cause the Antarctic to move into the domain where it contributes to sea-level rise. If so, the increase in sea level would be much higher—particularly if the West Antarctic ice sheet [were to begin] to disintegrate.

A CORAL REEF HOLOCAUST

When an aquatic environment nurtures coral reefs, they are among the most productive, diverse ecosystems on earth. Sometimes called the rainforests of the sea, coral reefs cover much less than 1 percent of the world's ocean floors, but host more than a third of the marine species presently described by science as well as many species yet undocumented. Some of these organisms may provide new sources of anticancer compounds and other medicines. Coral reefs also protect shorelines from erosion by acting as breakwaters that, if healthy, can repair themselves.

Even small rises in water temperature destroy the ecosystem of a coral reef, leaving only a lifeless, bleached exoskeleton. By the early 1990s, an increasing number of the Earth's coral reefs were turning white, a sign of death from excessive heat. Most corals die at levels above 30 to 32°C. Bleaching results when symbiotic *zooxanthellae* algae are expelled from coral reefs. The algae provide reefs with most of their color, carbon, and ability to deposit limestone. Once bleached, the coral does not receive adequate nutrients or oxygen. If temperatures fall, the reefs may recover, but continued thermal stress will kill a large part of any given reef.

Pollution, disease, ultraviolet radiation, too much shade, and changes in the ocean's salinity also may contribute to coral bleaching. Warming seas is one among many human-induced changes that threaten coral reefs. Other problems include overfishing, coastal development, nutrient runoff from agriculture and sewage, and sedimentation from logging on streams that feed into coastal waters. By one estimate, 58 percent of the world's coral reefs were threatened by human activity by the late 1990s.

A scientific team led by Thomas J. Goreau plotted water temperatures at a number of locations in the tropical western Atlantic and Caribbean, finding slow rises beginning during the 1980s in such places as the Bahamas and Jamaica. In some cases, these temperature increases have been significant enough to dramatically accelerate the bleaching of coral reefs. The rate of bleaching correlates with general air temperature rises detected by global surveys of temperatures on land. The team concluded that "the fact that the high water temperatures of the late 1980s and mass coral bleaching have not been seen before in the Greater Caribbean during nearly 40 years of continuous study of coral reef ecosystems implies that temperatures have only recently exceeded tolerance limits of the corals." The authors cite similar results in Hawaiian waters and include an extensive list of references that detail exactly what is happening to coral reefs around the world.

Some areas, including the Cook Islands and several locations in the Philippines, have been afflicted with massive coral bleaching since 1983. In 1995, warming in the Caribbean produced coral bleaching for the first time in Belize, as sea surface temperatures surpassed 29°C (84°F). In 1997, Caribbean sea-surface temperatures reached 34°C. (93°F) off southern Belize, as coral bleaching was accompanied by the deaths of many starfish and other sea life.

The central barrier reef near Belize suffered a mass coral die-off following record high water temperatures in 1998. According to Richard Aronson, a marine biologist at the Dauphin Island Sea Laboratory in Alabama, this die-off represents the first complete collapse of a coral reef in the Caribbean Sea from bleaching. Aronson, working with colleagues at the Smithsonian Institution in Washington, D.C., wrote in an article in *Nature* that lettuce coral was the most abundant species living in the area until 1998. Later surveys showed that "virtually all living colonies had been bleached white at almost every depth investigated." Core samples from the corals indicate that such a mass bleaching is unprecedented for at least the last 3,000 years. The research team found that "complete bleaching was also evident in almost all . . . species down to the lagoon floor at 21 meters."

By the late 1990s, coral bleaching had become epidemic in many tropical seas and oceans around the world. A World Wildlife Fund report found that massive coral bleaching occurred during the 1990s, in response to unusually high water temperatures, particularly during the El Niño years of 1997 and 1998. Sites of large-scale coral mortality included the Pacific Ocean, Indian Ocean, Red Sea, and Persian Gulf, as well as the Mediterranean and Caribbean seas.

With more warming anticipated, the extent and severity of damage to coral reefs worldwide is expected to intensify. An Australian marine scientist, Dr. Terry Done, told Murray Hogarth of the Sydney *Morning Herald* that coral reefs are the "canaries in the coal mine." During 1998, large coral reefs up to 1,000 years old died, and in some parts of the world up to 90 percent of reefs have been devastated, Done said.

The International Society for Reef Studies concluded that 1997 and 1998 witnessed the most geographically widespread coral bleaching in the recorded histories of at least thirty-two countries and island nations. Reports of bleaching came from sites in all the major tropical oceans of the world, some for the first time in recorded history. The 1997–98 bleaching episode was exceptionally severe, as a large number of corals died. According to one study, parts of Australia's Great Barrier Reef have been so severely affected that many of the usually robust corals, including one over 700 years of age, were badly damaged or died during 1997 and 1998.

SEA-LEVEL RISE AND SMALL ISLAND NATIONS

The Alliance of Small Island States (AOSIS), including the Philippines, Jamaica, the Marshall Islands, the Bahamas, Samoa, and others, has been one of few voices at climate talks favoring swift, worldwide reductions in greenhouse-gas emissions. Their self-interest is evident: with warming already "forced," but not yet fully worked into the world's temperature equilibrium, many small island states will lose substantial territory and economic base in the next decades.

For every other country on Earth, competing economic interests drive climate negotiations. For the small island nations, the driving force is survival. "For us, it's a matter of death and life, whereas in terms of the citizens of the industrialized countries, [global warming] will affect their lifestyles basically, but not to the extent they will be disappearing," said Bikenibeu Paeniu, Tuvalu's prime minister. Sea-level rise provoked by global warming could imperil more than 3,000 small isolated islands, grouped into twenty-four political entities in the Pacific Ocean, with a population of about 5 million people in 800 distinct cultures. Many coral atolls also contain permanent areas of fresh water (lagoons), which are vulnerable to salinization as sea levels rise.

In no other place is global warming more urgent an issue, in a practical sense, than in equatorial Kiribati (pronounced "Kirabas"), a chain of coral atolls in the Pacific, near the Marshall Islands. Kiribati is a republic, a member of the United Nations, and home to about 79,000 people. Its land area, at any point, is no more than 2 meters above sea level. Additionally, the living corals that have raised the islands above sea level are threatened with demise. Ierimea Tabai, who became president of Kiribati after its independence from Britain in 1979, has said that "If the greenhouse effect raises sea levels by one meter, it will eventually do away with Kiribati. In fifty or sixty years, my country will not be here."

Kiribati's thirty-three islands, encompassing 277 square miles, are scattered across 5.2 million square kilometers (2 million square miles) of ocean, including three groups of islands: seventeen Gilbert Islands, eight Line Islands, and eight Phoenix Islands. Kiribati includes Kiritimati (formerly Christmas Island), the world's largest coral atoll (150 square miles). The surface area of the island of Kiribati, located roughly halfway between California and Australia, more than doubles at low tide.

During 1997, the area was devastated by El Niño, which brought heavy rainfall, a half-meter rise in sea level, and extensive flooding. About 40 percent of the atoll's coral were killed by overheated water, and nearly all of Kiritimati Island's approximately 14 million birds died or deserted the island.

WARMING AND THE SEA ICE LIFE CYCLE

Sea ice is fundamental to polar ecosystems. It provides a platform for many marine mammals and penguins to hunt, escape predators, and breed. Its edges and undersides provide vital surfaces for the growth of algae that form the base of the polar food web. In areas with seasonal ice cover, spring blooms of phytoplankton occur at ice edges as the ice cover melts, boosting productivity early in the season. With warming temperatures, sea ice is diminishing in both the Arctic and the Antarctic. As the area covered by sea ice diminishes, so does the food available to each higher level on the web, from zooplankton to seabirds. According to a World Wildlife Fund analysis, "Higher temperatures predicted under climate change will further diminish ice cover, with open water occurring in areas previously covered by ice, thereby diminishing the very basis of the polar food web." Satellite microwave data of perennial (year-round) arctic sea ice from 1978 through 2000 indicate that it is shrinking an average of 9 percent a year. At this rate, the Arctic will have no summertime ice by the late twenty-first century.

Polar bears, for example, "are often becoming shore dwellers rather than ice dwellers," with sometimes dire consequences for unwary tourists, according to Ron Kovic, wildlife manager in the Inuit province of Nunavut. The harbor ice at Iqaluit, on Baffin Island, did not form in 2000 until late December, five or six weeks later than usual. The ice also breaks up earlier in the spring—sometimes in May in places that once were icebound into early July. "In Western Hudson Bay, where warmer temperatures in the 1990s made for earlier ice melting in the summer and later formation in the fall, polar bears suffered," according to Richard A. Kerr, writing in *Science*. "For every week that the ice broke up earlier, bears came ashore 10 kilograms (22 pounds) lighter," said zoologist Ian Stirling of the Canadian Wildlife Service in Edmonton.

The Arctic's rapid thaw has made hunting, never a safe nor easy way of life, even more difficult and dangerous. Hunters in and around Iqaluit say the weather has been seriously out of whack since roughly the middle 1990s. Simon Nattaq, an Inuit hunter, fell through unusually thin ice and became mired in icy water long enough to lose both his legs to hypothermia, one of several injuries and deaths reported around the Arctic recently due to thinning ice.

Mountain glaciers also have shown copious evidence of warming during the last century, especially in the tropics. Qori Kalis, the largest glacier in Peru's Quelccaya ice cap, was retreating in 2002 at a rate forty-four times greater than from 1963 to 1978. In Bolivia, "the mass of glaciers and mountain snowcaps has shrunk 60% since 1978," raising a specter of water shortage for La Paz, home of 1.5 million people, as well as nearby El Alto, according to Forero. The snow and ice fields of Mt. Kilimanjaro, in Kenya, made famous by Ernest Hemingway, probably will melt by the year 2020; the last glacier in Montana's Glacier National Park will vanish, by some estimates, by 2050.

Recent measurements by aircraft using global positioning satellites and laser altimeters show that the 5000-square-kilometer Malaspina Glacier in Alaska is losing nearly a meter of thickness per year—the equivalent of 3 cubic kilometers of water. That glacier alone has ten times the water of all the glaciers

Table 2. Carbon Dioxide Emitted, per Capita, 2000

Country	Tons
Zaire*	0.03
Nigeria*	0.09
World average	3.85
France	7.04
Eastern Europe and Russia	7.19
European Union	9.06
Japan	10.16
Canada	16.32
Australia	17.31
United States	22.04

* Numbers for 1990.
Source: Bruce E. Johansen, *The Global Warming Desk Reference.* Westport, CT: Greenwood, 2001.

Table 3. Global Carbon Dioxide Emissions

Year	Gigitons (billion metric tons)
1850	0.1 ggt
1900	1.0 ggt
1940	1.5 ggt
1960	3.0 ggt
1970	5.0 ggt
1990	8.5 ggt
2000	9.5 ggt estimated

Source: R. L. Kane and D. W. South, "The Likely Roles of Fossil Fuels in the Next 15, 50, and 100 Years, With or Without Active Controls on Greenhouse-Gas Emissions." In *Limiting Greenhouse Effects: Controlling Carbon-Dioxide Emissions. Report of the Dahlem Workshop on Limiting the Greenhouse Effect, Berlin, September 9–14, 1990,* ed. G. I. Pearman, 193. New York: John Wiley and Sons, 1991.

in the Alps, which have shrunk to half their ice volume since the 1850s. The 300,000 visitors a year to Mendenhall Glacier, behind Juneau, Alaska, have witnessed its retreat at a rate that accelerated to 100 meters a year during 2000.

KYOTO PROTOCOL

The Kyoto Protocol, the first worldwide diplomatic effort to curtail the use of fossil fuels, was negotiated in the Japanese city of the same name in 1997. The protocol, in its original form, called on the world's industrialized nations to reduce their emissions of greenhouse gases to roughly 5 percent below 1990 levels by 2008 to 2012. This was an average; each country was given its own target. By 2002, the protocol was near its ratification target of countries responsible for 55 percent of the world's greenhouse gas emissions, with one very notable exception. The United States, which emits about one-quarter of humankind's greenhouse gases, refused to ratify the Kyoto agreement. Its opposition strengthened after George W. Bush became president, but the Senate had voted 95 to 0 against taking part even before that.

The Kyoto Protocol will be noted in history as an early attempt to recognize the seriousness of global warming, but it faces several problems. First, commercial aviation and the world's military forces are exempted from the pact's restrictions, as are many developing nations. Political figures in the United States have been quick to capitalize on what they believe to be bias against industrialized nations, while Third World diplomats argue that some countries

(e.g., Bangladesh) now emit less than 1 percent of the amount of greenhouse gas pollution per capita the United States emits. Many skeptical scientists also assert that reductions of 60 to 70 percent of greenhouse gas emissions are necessary to avoid significant and possibly destructive warming during and after the twenty-first century. To them, the 10 percent targets of the protocol are mere diplomatic window dressing.

The protocol will also face challenges as scientific knowledge evolves. For example, by 2002 scientists were coming to realize that, depending on the amount of moisture in soil, a plot of thick grassland may remove more carbon dioxide from the air than a forest of equal size. The protocol is built on assumptions supporting a complex system of emissions-trading arrangements that favor forests over other types of land use.

CONCLUSION

To avoid warming that will imperil the Earth's ecosystem, many scientists and policymakers endorse a paradigm shift in energy sources away from fossil fuels and toward renewable (or at least nonfossil) sources, including solar, wind, hydrogen, and nuclear power. Less ambitious plans call for the sequestration (burying) of greenhouse gases deep in the Earth or at sea. Other ideas, such as microwaving energy from plants in space, have been aired as well.

By 2002 all major auto makers were testing hydrogen-powered cars, and the European Union was preparing to fund millions of Euros worth of research aimed at changing the energy base of its member nations from fossil fuels to hydrogen. Denmark had become a world leader in wind-power technology with a system that gives each family a share in the industry. Even oil-dependent Texas had endorsed expanding wind energy.

Meanwhile, the proportion of carbon dioxide in the atmosphere has continued to rise, passing 370 parts per million shortly after the beginning of the third millennium, or about 35 percent higher than the level at the beginning of the industrial age. With a feedback loop of roughly 30 to 50 years, by the 1990s, a string of years with record-high global temperatures reflected an upsurge in fossil fuel usage worldwide during the two decades after World War II. As the human population slowly begins to switch energy paradigms, the "carbon clock" continues to tick.

Bruce E. Johansen

REFERENCES

Abrahamson, Dean Edwin. *The Challenge of Global Warming.* Washington, DC: Island Press, 1989.

Aronson, Richard B., William F. Precht, Ian G. MacIntyre, and Thaddeus J. T. Murdoch. "Coral Bleach-out in Belize." *Nature* 405 (May 4, 2000): 36.

Brewer, Peter G., Gernot Friederich, Edward T. Peltzer, and Franklin M. Orr, Jr. "Direct Experiments on the Ocean Disposal of Fossil Fuel C02." *Science* 284 (May 7, 1999): 943–45.

Bryant, Dirk, L. Burke, J. McManus, and M. Spaulding. *Reefs at Risk: A Map-based Indicator of Threats to the World's Coral Reefs.* Washington, DC: World Resources Institute, 1998.

Caldeira, Ken, and Philip B. Duffy. "The Role of the Southern Ocean in the Uptake and Storage of Anthropogenic Carbon Dioxide." *Science* 287 (January 28, 2000): 620–22.

Christianson, Gale E. *Greenhouse: The 200-Year Story of Global Warming.* New York: Walker, 1999.

Clift, Peter, and Karen Bice. "Earth Science: Baked Alaska." *Nature* 419 (September 12, 2002): 129–30.

Cline, William R. "Comments." In *Global Warming: Economic Policy Responses,* ed. Rudiger Dornbusch and James M. Poterba, 222–28. Cambridge, MA: MIT Press, 1991.

Connor, Steve. "Global Warming Is Blamed for First Collapse of a Caribbean Coral Reef." *The Independent* (London) (May 4, 2000): 12.

Cowen, Robert C. "One Large, Overlooked Factor in Global Warming: Tropical Forest Fires." *Christian Science Monitor* (November 7, 2002): 14.

Cox, Peter M., Richard A. Betts, Chris D. Jones, Steven A. Spall, and Ian J. Totterdell. "Acceleration of Global Warming Due to Carbon-Cycle Feedbacks in a Coupled Climate Model." *Nature* 408 (November 9, 2000): 184–87.

Davis, Neil. *Permafrost: A Guide to Frozen Ground in Transition.* Fairbanks: University of Alaska Press, 2001.

Edgerton, Lynne T., and the Natural Resources Defense Council. *The Rising Tide: Global Warming and World Sea Levels.* Washington, DC: Island Press, 1991.

Freeman, C., C. D. Evans, and D. T. Monteith. "Export of Organic Carbon from Peat Soils." *Nature* 412 (August 23, 2001): 785.

Gelbspan, Ross. *The Heat Is On: The High Stakes Battle Over Earth's Threatened Climate.* Reading, MA: Addison-Wesley, 1997.

Goreau, Thomas J., Raymond L. Hayes, Jenifer W. Clark, Daniel J. Basta, and Craig N. Robertson. "Elevated Sea-Surface Temperatures Correlate with Caribbean Coral Reef Beaching." In *A Global Warming Forum: Scientific, Economic, and Legal Overview,* ed. Richard A. Geyer, 225–62. Boca Raton, FL: CRC Press, 1993.

Gough, Robert. "Stress on Stress: Global Warming and Aquatic Resource Depletion." *Native Americas* 16, 3/4 (Fall/Winter 1999): 46–48.

Johansen, Bruce E. "Arctic Heat Wave." *The Progressive* (October 2001): 18–20.

———. *The Global Warming Desk Reference.* Westport, CT: Greenwood, 2001.

Kerr, Richard A. "A Warmer Arctic Means Change for All." *Science* 297 (August 30, 2002): 1490–92.

Keys, David. "Global Warming: Methane Threatens to Repeat Ice-age Meltdown; 55 Million Years Ago, a Massive Blast of Gas Drove Up Earth's Temperature 7C. And Another Explosion Is in the Cards, Say the Experts." London *Independent* (June 16, 2001): n.p. (in LEXIS).

National Academy of Sciences. *Policy Implications of Greenhouse Warming.* Washington, DC: National Academy Press, 1991.

Page, Susan E., Florian Siegert, John O. Rieley, Hans-Dieter V. Boehm, Adi Jaya, and Suwido Limin. "The Amount of Carbon Released from Peat and Forest Fires in Indonesia during 1997." *Nature* 420 (November 7, 2002): 61–65.

Radford, Tim. "World May Be Warming Up Even Faster; Climate Scientists Warn New Forests Would Make Effects Worse." London *Guardian* (November 9, 2000): 10.

Schimel, David, and David Baker. "Carbon Cycle: The Wildlife Factor." *Nature* 420 (November 7, 2002): 29–30.

WEB SITES

Global Warming Science, Strategies, Solutions from the Pew Center: www.pewclimate.org

Goddard Institute for Space Studies, NASA: www.giss.nasa.gov/edu/gwdebate

Intergovernmental Panel on Climate Change Publications Center: www.ipcc.ch/pub/reports.htm

National Center for Atmospheric Research Real-Time Weather Data: www.rap.ucar.edu/weather

Tyndall Centre for Climate Change Research, United Kingdom: www.tyndall.ac.uk

U.S. Global Change Research Information Office: www.gcrio.org/ipcc/qa/cover.html

World Wildlife Fund and Marine Conservation Biology Institute: www.worldwildlife.org

GLOSSARY

Anthropogenic. Caused (generated) by human activity.

Biotic feedbacks. Biological or geophysical processes that could accelerate warming of the atmosphere by releasing additional greenhouse gases into the atmosphere. For example, the warming of peat triggered by melting arctic permafrost could ignite fires that would increase atmospheric carbon dioxide levels. Also, the liquification and eventual gassification of methane deposits now stored in solid form under ocean surfaces.

Carbon cycle. The use of carbon (including carbon dioxide) by the Earth's natural systems, including air, soil, and oceans; the interchange of carbon between these venues.

Carbon sequestration. Burying of human-generated carbon in the oceans or deep in the Earth as a means of removing it from the atmosphere.

Carbon sink. An area such as a forest that absorbs more carbon dioxide, methane, or other greenhouse gases than it produces.

Carbon tax. A levy meant to increase the cost, and lower consumption, of fossil fuels.

Clathrates. Solid deposits of methane in the oceans that could turn to atmospheric gas in warming water. *See* "Biotic feedbacks."

Climate forcing. One of many influences on the Earth's climate. The greenhouse effect is said to be a "forcing" on the planet's overall climate, interacting with many other elements. *See* Infrared forcing.

Climate models. Forecasting tools, usually using computers, that estimate the results of several climate forcings on future climatic trends.

"Drunken forest." In Alaska, trees and telephone poles are caused to list at angles by melting permafrost.

Environmental refugees. People dislocated from their homes by environmental disruptions, including climate change.

Fossil fuels. Carbon-based fuels, the combustion of which produces greenhouse gases.

Greenhouse effect. Popular term for infrared forcing, the heating of the lower troposhere by heat-retaining gases, as in a greenhouse. *See* Infrared forcing.

Infrared forcing. The most widely used scientific term for the greenhouse effect, which produces global warming. *See* Greenhouse effect.

Intergovernmental Panel on Climate Change (IPCC). Scientific body charged by the United Nations with monitoring global warming on a worldwide basis.

Kyoto Protocol. International agreement, negotiated in 1997, intended to slow the consumption of fossil fuels and reduce atmospheric levels of greenhouse gases.

Methane burp. The gassification of solid methane deposits in the ocean, which could lead to increased atmospheric levels of the gas. *See* Clathrates; Biotic feedbacks.

La Niña. A cooling of equatorial waters in the Pacific Ocean that causes changes in temperatures and precipitation patterns worldwide. *See* El Niño.

El Niño or El Niño–Southern Oscillation (ENSO). A warming of equatorial waters in the Pacific Ocean that causes changes in temperatures and precipitation patterns worldwide. *See* La Niña.

Thermohaline circulation. "Rivers" of deep-water circulation driving ocean atmosphere circulation that can affect climate, notably in Europe.

Urban heat island. Combination of factors causing temperatures in cities to exceed those of the surrounding countryside, especially on calm nights.

Venus. Second planet from the sun where global warming has raised surface temperatures to 800°F.

DOCUMENT

Excerpts from the United Nations Framework Convention on Climate Change

In recent decades, scientists have warned of global warming, in which rising temperatures around the globe threaten increased severe weather and coastal flooding. Virtually the entire scientific community agrees that the key factor behind this warming is human behavior, specifically the increased production of hydrocarbon gases. Slowly, the world's politicians have begun to heed these warnings and recognize that global warming requires global solutions. The 2001 United Nations Framework Convention on Climate Change, signed in Bonn, Germany, builds on the earlier Kyoto Protocols of 1997.

The Parties to this Convention,

Acknowledging that change in the Earth's climate and its adverse effects are a common concern of humankind,

Concerned that human activities have been substantially increasing the atmospheric concentrations of greenhouse gases, that these increases enhance the natural greenhouse effect, and that this will result on average in an additional warming of the Earth's surface and atmosphere and may adversely affect natural ecosystems and humankind,

Noting that the largest share of historical and current global emissions of greenhouse gases has originated in developed countries, that per capita emissions in developing countries are still relatively low and that the share of global emissions originating in developing countries will grow to meet their social and development needs,

Aware of the role and importance in terrestrial and marine ecosystems of sinks and reservoirs of greenhouse gases,

Noting that there are many uncertainties in predictions of climate change, particularly with regard to the timing, magnitude and regional patterns thereof,

Acknowledging that the global nature of climate change calls for the widest possible cooperation by all countries and their participation in an effective and appropriate international response, in accordance with their common but differentiated responsibilities and respective capabilities and their social and economic conditions,

Recalling the pertinent provisions of the Declaration of the United Nations Conference on the Human Environment, adopted at Stockholm on 16 June 1972,

Recalling also that States have, in accordance with the Charter of the United Nations and the principles of international law, the sovereign right to exploit their own resources pursuant to their own environmental and developmental policies, and the responsibility to ensure that activities within their jurisdiction or control do not cause damage to the environment of other States or of areas beyond the limits of national jurisdiction,

Reaffirming the principle of sovereignty of States in international cooperation to address climate change,

Recognizing that States should enact effective environmental legislation, that environmental standards, management objectives and priorities should reflect the environmental and developmental context to which they apply, and that standards applied by some countries may be inappropriate and of unwarranted economic and social cost to other countries, in particular developing countries. . . .

Conscious of the valuable analytical work being conducted by many States on climate change and of the important contributions of the World Meteorological Organization, the United Nations Environment Programme and other organs, organizations and bodies of the United Nations system, as well as other international and intergovernmental bodies, to the exchange of results of scientific research and the coordination of research,

Recognizing that steps required to understand and address climate change will be environmentally, socially and economically most effective if they are based on relevant scientific, technical and economic considerations and continually re-evaluated in the light of new findings in these areas,

Recognizing that various actions to address climate change can be justified economically in their own right and can also help in solving other environmental problems,

Recognizing also the need for developed countries to take immediate action in a flexible manner on the basis of clear priorities, as a first step towards comprehensive response strategies at the global, national and, where agreed, regional levels that take into account all greenhouse gases, with due consideration of their relative contributions to the enhancement of the greenhouse effect,

Recognizing further that low-lying and other small island countries, countries with low-lying coastal, arid and semi-arid areas or areas liable to floods, drought and desertification, and developing countries with fragile mountainous ecosystems are particularly vulnerable to the adverse effects of climate change,

Recognizing the special difficulties of those countries, especially developing countries, whose economies are particularly dependent on fossil fuel production, use and exportation, as a consequence of action taken on limiting greenhouse gas emissions,

Have agreed as follows:

. . . The ultimate objective of this Convention and any related legal instruments that the Conference of the Parties may adopt is to achieve, in accordance with the relevant provisions of the Convention, stabilization of greenhouse gas concentrations in the atmosphere at a level that would prevent dangerous anthropogenic interference with the climate system. Such a level should be achieved within a time-frame sufficient to allow ecosystems to adapt naturally to climate change, to ensure that food production is not threatened and to enable economic development to proceed in a sustainable manner.

. . . In their actions to achieve the objective of the Convention and to implement its provisions, the Parties shall be guided, INTER ALIA, by the following:

1. The Parties should protect the climate system for the benefit of present and future generations of humankind, on the basis of equity and in accordance with their common but differentiated responsibilities and respective capabilities. Accordingly, the developed country Parties should take the lead in combating climate change and the adverse effects thereof.

2. The specific needs and special circumstances of developing country Parties, especially those that are particularly vulnerable to the adverse effects of climate change, and of those Parties, especially developing country Parties, that would have to bear a disproportionate or abnormal burden under the Convention, should be given full consideration.

3. . . . The Parties should take precautionary measures to anticipate, prevent or minimize the causes of climate change and mitigate its adverse effects. Where there are threats of serious or irreversible damage, lack of full scientific certainty should not be used as a reason for postponing such measures, taking into account that policies and measures to deal with climate change should be cost-effective so as to ensure global benefits at the lowest possible cost. . . .

4. . . . The Parties have a right to, and should, promote sustainable development. . . .

5. . . . The Parties should cooperate to promote a supportive and open international economic system that would lead to sustainable economic growth and development in all Parties. . . .

. . . In the implementation of the commitments in this Article, the Parties shall give full consideration to what actions are necessary under the Convention, including actions related to funding, insurance and the transfer of technology, to meet the specific needs and concerns of developing country Parties arising from the adverse effects of climate change and/or the impact of the implementation of response measures, especially on:

(a). . . . Small island countries;

(b). . . . Countries with low-lying coastal areas;

(c). . . . Countries with arid and semi-arid areas, forested areas and areas liable to forest decay;

(d). . . . Countries with areas prone to natural disasters;

(e). . . . Countries with areas liable to drought and desertification;

(f). . . . Countries with areas of high urban atmospheric pollution;

(g). . . . Countries with areas with fragile ecosystems, including mountainous ecosystems;

(h). . . . Countries whose economies are highly dependent on income generated from the production, processing and export, and/or on consumption of fossil fuels and associated energy-intensive products; and

(i). . . . Land-locked and transit countries.

Further, the Conference of the Parties may take actions, as appropriate, with respect to this paragraph.

9. . . . The Parties shall take full account of the specific needs and special situations of the least developed countries in their actions with regard to funding and transfer of technology.

10. . . . The Parties shall, in accordance with Article 10, take into consideration in the implementation of the commitments of the Convention the situation of Parties, particularly developing country Parties, with economies that are vulnerable to the adverse effects of the implementation of measures to respond to climate change. This applies notably to Parties with economies that are highly dependent on income generated from the production, processing and export, and/or consumption of fossil fuels and associated energy-intensive products and/or the use of fossil fuels for which such Parties have serious difficulties in switching to alternatives.

Source: United Nations Framework Convention on Climate Change, 2001.

GULF WAR SYNDROME AND OTHER VETERANS' ILLNESSES

Coined by *USA Today* reporter Bethany Kandel in a September 9, 1992, article, the term "Gulf War syndrome" soon became the catchall phrase for a myriad of seemingly unexplained medical symptoms first studied in a group of Operation Desert Storm veterans, Army reservists from Indiana, Illinois, and other midwestern states. Ill veterans complained of memory loss, personality changes, major gastrointestinal disorders, hair loss, fatigue, muscle and joint aches, dizzy spells, and shortness of breath. The initial Army study of less than 100 of the ill reservists blamed the ailments on stress, a theory immediately rejected by veterans and their family members, who argued that one or more environmental exposures during the 1991 Persian Gulf War was the root cause of their illnesses. This paradigm—veterans claiming that toxic exposures during the war led to illness and in some cases death, and the government asserting that the illnesses were stress-related—set the tone for the contentious debate over Gulf War syndrome (GWS) that continues to this day.

CAUSES

From the beginning of the controversy, a number of theories were put forward to explain the veterans' ailments: oil well fire pollution; indigenous parasites; experimental protective drugs and vaccines for chemical and biological warfare agents given prior to and during hostilities; specialized paint used on Coalition military vehicles; insecticides; insect repellants; and dust from expended, depleted uranium ammunition used by American tanks, infantry fighting vehicles, and A-10 Warthog ground attack aircraft. One explanation gained the most widespread currency outside of government circles: that Coalition bombing of Iraqi chemical and biological warfare sites had produced toxic fallout which, while not immediately fatal, had produced long-term health effects in tens of thousands of Desert Storm veterans unfortunate enough to be under the toxic clouds.

The epidemiological challenges in working retrospectively to establish an exposure-illness link were formidable. By its own admission, the Pentagon conceded that many medical records of Desert Storm veterans were either incomplete or missing. No effort had been made to monitor the types and concentrations of various drugs, vaccines, or toxic exposures while troops were in theater. Records regarding the number of personnel in theater during the war and their locations during air and ground fighting were either incomplete or not collated. Moreover, during the war, the Pentagon classified the use of nerve agent pretreatment medication (pyridostigmine bromide) as well as vaccines for anthrax and botulinum toxin. As a result, key exposure data were often cryptically abbreviated or completely absent from available patient records, further complicating diagnosis and treatment.

This last point was especially critical, as federal law requires that veterans who claim their military service has produced medical harm must prove a connection between an adverse event during their military service and their subsequent medical condition. As the Pentagon had, by its own admission, lost many Desert Storm veterans' medical records, the ill Gulf War vets faced a classic Catch-22: to prove their medical problems were service-connected, the veterans

Table 1. U.S. Gulf War Fatalities and Other Casualties, 2003

Condition	Number
Killed in action	148
Wounded in action	467
Died since war	6,000*
Contracted cancer and died since war	1,300*

* Estimated number.
Source: U.S. Department of Defense; Department of Veterans Affairs.

CHRONOLOGY

1961   Operation Shipboard Hazard and Defense (SHAD) is inaugurated, exposing U.S. Navy personnel to toxins to test the military's ability to withstand Soviet chemical attacks.

1962   The U.S. military begins dropping Agent Orange, a defoliant, on South Vietnam to eliminate jungle cover used by Communist insurgents; through the end of the U.S. phase of the war in 1972, some 19 million gallons of the substance, which included the chemical dioxin, later found to be a carcinogen, are used.

1984   Seven chemical companies reach a legal settlement in a class-action suit brought by 15,000 Vietnam veterans and their families, paying out $180 billion.

1991   President George H.W. Bush signs a bill granting permanent disability benefits to veterans suffering from various forms of cancer linked to Agent Orange. In Operation Desert Storm, the United States leads an international coalition to drive Iraq from Kuwait in the Persian Gulf War; soldiers are exposed to a number of potential carcinogens from Iraqi chemical weapons, oil fires, and depleted uranium weapons used by the U.S. military.

1992   Congress holds its first hearings into Gulf War veterans' illnesses and later passes the Persian Gulf War Veterans' Health Status Act to monitor Gulf War veterans for potential war-related illnesses.

1993   The National Defense Authorization Act directs the secretary of defense to establish a recordkeeping and health-monitoring system for Desert Storm veterans.

1995   President Bill Clinton creates the Presidential Advisory Committee on Gulf War Veterans' Illnesses.

1996   President Clinton expands disability benefits to Vietnam veterans suffering from diseases associated with Agent Orange.

1998   Citing health fears, a small number of U.S. military personnel refuse to take the vaccine against anthrax.

2003   The organization Vietnam Veterans of America files a class-action suit against the Pentagon for the 1960s-era Operation Shipboard Hazard and Defense (SHAD) tests.

needed records that no longer existed or lacked critical, relevant information.

Further complicating the tasks of the veterans and their medical providers was the fact that the vast majority of Pentagon-sponsored research over the years into the effects of chemical and biological weapons focused on the immediate, acute (and usually deadly) effects of exposures to agents such as sarin, soman, or tabun (the three nerve gases originally developed by the Nazis during World War II and subsequently weaponized by the Iraqi regime). Little prior research had been done on the effects of low-level exposures to various battlefield hazards, although what research had been done did describe neurological symptoms that were similar to some of those reported by ill Desert Storm veterans, a fact that veteran advocates and some nongovernment researchers keyed on in the early stages of the GWS controversy.

CONGRESS INVESTIGATES

The first congressional hearing into veterans' illnesses took place in September 1992, when the House Vet-

erans Affairs Committee convened to examine the issue, an act that was followed by passage of the Persian Gulf War Veterans' Health Status Act in November 1992. The law directed the Department of Veterans Affairs (VA) to establish its first Persian Gulf War registry and offer special health examinations for Desert Storm veterans in an effort to track the number who reported seemingly inexplicable illnesses. The Gulf War registry was modeled on one used for veterans exposed to Agent Orange and other herbicides during the war in Vietnam. Additionally, the National Defense Authorization Act for fiscal 1993 directed the secretary of defense to establish a recordkeeping and health-monitoring system for Desert Storm veterans exposed to oil well fire smoke and contamination, the first congressionally directed attempt to force the Pentagon to conduct medical studies to ascertain a link between environmental exposures during the war and potential health problems being reported by veterans.

Congressional interest intensified in the wake of the July 1993 announcement from the Czech ministry of defense that the chemical unit it deployed to

Saudi Arabia in 1991 had *repeatedly* detected sublethal levels of various chemical agents, including the nerve agents sarin and soman, during the Coalition air campaign against Iraq's weapons of mass destruction production and storage facilities. In September 1993, the Senate Committee on Banking, Housing, and Urban Affairs—using its jurisdiction under the Export Administration Act, which permitted the sale of chemically related materials to Iraq—released an initial staff report postulating that the veterans' illnesses were the result of exposures to a "cocktail" of poisonous substances, including chemical fallout from the wartime bombing. Pentagon officials categorically denied the possibility, dismissing both the Czech reports and the Senate report. Pentagon officials also asserted that existing scientific research indicated that sublethal doses of nerve agents had no known health effects in humans. House and Senate investigators, unconvinced by the Defense Department's stand, intensified their inquiries.

In May 1994, assuming a role normally taken by its Armed Services Committee counterpart, the Senate Banking Committee held the first major hearing involving testimony from officials of the Central Intelligence Agency (CIA). The CIA's role in the Gulf War syndrome controversy stemmed in part from its pre- and postwar assessments about the presence and potential release of Iraqi chemical agents, either deliberately through military action by Iraq, or indirectly through the Coalition bombing campaign or postwar demolition operations by Coalition troops in occupied Iraq. Agency officials categorically denied that any such agent releases had occurred, though by the fall of 1994, Pentagon officials were forced to concede that the Czechs' detections of low levels of Iraqi chemical agents were "valid," raising questions about the veracity of the CIA's testimony and its assessment of the improbability that the veterans' illnesses were the result of toxic exposures.

Separately, under pressure from both individual Desert Storm veterans and more established veterans organizations such as Vietnam Veterans of America, Congress directed its investigative arm, the General Accounting Office (GAO), both to monitor the Pentagon and VA response to the veterans' complaints and to investigate various aspects of the controversy. Between January 1992 and January 1995 (when Republicans regained control of the Congress), the GAO issued nearly a dozen reports highlighting both the Pentagon's prewar lack of preparedness to deal with chemical and biological warfare, and the slow, disjointed, and fundamentally unresponsive approach taken by Pentagon and VA officials to the medical problems reported by the veterans.

For their part, the Department of Defense (DoD) and Department of Veterans Affairs, with limited input and participation by the Department of Health and Human Services, formed the Persian Gulf (later known as the Military and) Veterans Health Coordinating Board (PGVHCB/MVHCB). The board was charged with both developing a set of working theories about the cause of the illnesses and managing the burgeoning federal medical research program dedicated to finding the cause of the illnesses and developing effective treatments. From the beginning, the PGVHCB/MVHCB was viewed with suspicion by Desert Storm veterans. In contrast to the statute governing the Congressionally Directed Medical Research Programs, which mandates patient advocates be placed on the peer-review panels that make research funding decisions, the PGVHCB/MVHCB remained a closed group of government officials with no representation from established veterans organizations allowed to watch, much less participate, in its decision-making process concerning research funding.

Belatedly responding to the ongoing controversy and intensifying press interest in the issue, President Bill Clinton in March 1995 signed Executive Order 12961, creating the Presidential Advisory Committee on Gulf War Veterans' Illnesses (known as the PAC). Composed of a dozen health experts and two Gulf War veterans, the PAC was charged with separately evaluating the DoD and VA response to the veterans' complaints as well as recommending what areas to focus existing and projected research on. From the beginning, Gulf War veterans charged the PAC with a bias toward stress causality; veterans also complained that DoD and VA representatives were routinely given an hour or more to make presentations before the committee, while veterans were restricted to 5-minute oral presentations, an imbalance that further fueled the hostility and suspicion of ill Desert Storm veterans. Only later would Desert Storm veterans and congressional investigators learn that the PAC's principal investigator on the chemical and biological exposure question, former United Nations weapons inspector Jonathan Tucker, had been specifically directed by PAC senior staff not to talk to government whistleblowers or some of the more outspoken veterans. Tucker ignored the directive and was subsequently fired by the committee in December 1995, an act that turned Gulf War veterans firmly against the panel.

VETERANS ORGANIZE

Even as they battled a federal government perceived as indifferent at best, ill Desert Storm veterans began to find their public voice through local, and later national, organizing efforts. The first national gathering of affected Gulf War veterans occurred in the summer of 1995 and led to the creation of an umbrella organization, the National Gulf War Resource Center (NGWRC), which received financial and logistical sponsorship from the more established Vietnam Veterans of America. NGWRC representatives rapidly became visible public spokespersons for their ailing comrades around the country, testifying before congressional committees and aggressively working both local and national media to publicize the plight of ill veterans and demand accountability for those Pentagon officials deemed responsible (at least in part) for the veterans' medical conditions.

One manifestation of the veterans' advocacy efforts that sometimes marred their effectiveness was the tendency for certain high-profile veterans or local groups to champion a specific theory of causality for the illness, and often the researchers who postulated those specific theories. The early tendency of veteran activists to favor one theory—and by implication, one researcher or group of researchers—over others divided along scientific lines what should have been a united advocacy effort aimed at finding both the causes of the illnesses and effective treatments.

Responding to the now more organized and vocal Gulf War veterans' advocacy community, the Republican-led House Government Reform Committee's National Security and Veterans Affairs subcommittee, chaired by Christopher Shays of Connecticut, launched a 19-month investigation of Pentagon, VA, and CIA handling of the Gulf War syndrome controversy. Only 3 months after Shays launched his oversight inquiry, DoD and CIA officials announced in June 1996 that a small number of Desert Storm veterans had likely been exposed to very low levels of the nerve agents sarin and cyclosarin from the destruction of thousands of Iraqi battlefield chemical rockets at the Khamisiyah Ammunition Storage Depot in southern Iraq. The dramatic policy reversal and subsequent admissions about the extent of both the information known about the Khamisiyah facil-

ity and the likely number of veterans exposed gave renewed credence to Pentagon critics who charged that an Iran-Contra style cover-up had been used to keep veterans in the dark about the incident.

While Pentagon and CIA officials went to great lengths to discount any adverse health effects for veterans exposed to sublethal doses of nerve agent, the revelations seemed to confirm the worst suspicions of veterans and their supporters in Congress: that the national security establishment had concealed the exposures out of concern that such an acknowledgment would directly tie the illnesses being reported by Desert Storm veterans to their service in the Gulf, and thus obligate the government to pay for their treatment, compensate them for their reduced physical condition, and remove the luster from a seemingly casualty-free war. Before the year was out, this author would reveal in congressional testimony that the CIA had deliberately excluded an examination of the testimony of veterans, as well as other key sources, from its own internal GWS investigation.

Moreover, research conducted more than 20 years earlier by the Stockholm Peace Research Institute (SIPRI) suggested that even sublethal exposures to chemical nerve agents could produce at least some of the symptoms reported by the veterans, including memory loss or other cognitive disorders. This author, in testimony before Congressman Shays's subcommittee in December 1996, also revealed that through research conducted at Brooks Air Force Base in Texas, Pentagon officials had known at least a year before the Gulf War that sublethal exposures to the nerve agent soman had produced cognitive and behavioral deficits in primates, contradicting both the sworn congressional testimony of Pentagon officials and the multiple public statements by DoD's public affairs office.

PENTAGON AND VA RESPONSE

As 1997 began, more than 100,000 Desert Storm veterans were on either the VA- or DoD-sponsored Gulf War registries, and the federal government's medical research program into the illness had grown into a multimillion-dollar endeavor. Despite this, congressional investigators continued to uncover evidence of bias in the VA/DoD-run medical research program.

A year after the Khamisiyah revelations, the GAO issued a 134-page report on the federal government's GWS medical research program which, according to congressional investigators, had not "systematically attempted to determine whether ill Gulf War veterans are any better or worse today than when they were first examined." The GAO also charged that "support for some official conclusions regarding stress, leishmaniasis [a parasite endemic to the Persian Gulf region], and exposure to chemical agents was weak or subject to alternative interpretations." The PAC also came in for criticism for its quick embrace of the "stress theory," and the GAO recommended an integrated, carefully planned approach to the medical research program, with emphasis on exploring toxic exposures among veterans and their potential health effects.

After nearly a dozen hearings that culminated in a report in November 1997, Congressman Shays's House Government Reform subcommittee harshly criticized the federal government's response to the veterans' concerns and conditions, charging that DoD and VA officials "did not listen to sick Gulf War veterans as to the causes of their illnesses" and that "there is no credible evidence that stress or [post-traumatic stress disorder] causes the illnesses reported by many Gulf War veterans." The CIA also came in for severe criticism, particularly after the agency acknowledged in April 1997 that it had in fact withheld numerous reports on the Khamisiyah facility from the veterans and their family members. By the end of 1997, however, media interest in the veterans and their plight also seemed to be ebbing.

During the first year of the controversy, 1992, only twenty-five stories mentioning "Gulf War syndrome" or "Gulf War illnesses" appeared in the print media. By 1994, the number of stories on the subject had exploded to 764. The media high-water mark for the issue was 1997, when 3,815 stories appeared in print. The number of stories devoted to the topic dropped to 2,031 in 1998, and declined each year thereafter. Even so, the controversial medical legacy of Operation Desert Storm was affecting Pentagon policy in often dramatic ways.

ANTHRAX VACCINATION CONTROVERSY

By early 1998, it was evident that the GWS controversy was having spillover effects on another controversial DoD initiative: the Anthrax Vaccine Immunization Program (AVIP). The AVIP was launched by the Pentagon ostensibly to protect American troops from a hypothetical Iraqi anthrax weapon threat. United Nations inspectors and U.S. govern-

ment officials believed at the time that Saddam Hussein's regime still possessed clandestine stockpiles of the deadly toxin. American intelligence officials also believed that Iran was seeking to weaponize anthrax. Critics charged that the vaccine, which had been given covertly to some 150,000 Desert Storm veterans 7 years earlier, was a potential culprit in causing GWS. Pentagon officials countered that no scientific studies supported this conclusion. The reality was that no such studies had been done, leaving the vaccine's safety and efficacy, as well as its potential role in GWS, open to question.

Beginning in the early spring of 1998, a small but growing number of American military personnel began refusing to take the newly mandated anthrax vaccine, as both the GAO and the Shays committee report had implicated the wartime vaccine as a potential GWS culprit. Although no major mutinies occurred over the refusals, the very fact that some veterans cited GWS-related concerns about taking the vaccine—and were willing to face court martial for their refusal—clearly showed that the Pentagon's public relations efforts to deny a link between Gulf War service and veterans illnesses had failed dismally. Moreover, revelations about the anthrax vaccine production plant's many citations for poor manufacturing practices raised further questions about the vaccine's safety, triggering a multiyear GAO investigation that validated critics' concerns.

OFFICIAL CRITICISMS OF THE PENTAGON AND VA

By 2000, the National Academy of Sciences Institute of Medicine (IOM) had completed its own preliminary review of the available scientific work on Gulf War illnesses and selected toxic exposures, including the nerve agent sarin. Based in part on exposure research on primates, the IOM concluded that "it is reasonable to hypothesize the occurrence of long-term adverse health effects from exposure to low levels of sarin." The IOM qualified its finding by noting there were no well-controlled studies of the effects of low-level nerve agent exposure in humans, leaving veterans, the Congress, and medical researchers without an ironclad answer to the exposure-illness nexus postulated by veterans but disputed by the Pentagon.

A major GAO report issued the same year concluded that the ongoing failure of the DoD and VA to properly manage the more than $200 million spent on Gulf War illness-related research had resulted in no definitive answers to the basic questions of what had made the veterans ill or whether they were any better or worse than when the research program began. Controversy also erupted within the Clinton-appointed Presidential Special Oversight Board (PSOB), a successor to the ill-fated PAC. At least one panel member and another key scientist resigned in protest, charging the panel director, former New Hampshire Senator Warren Rudman, with politicizing the research agenda to favor the "stress theory." Although Rudman angrily denied the charges, the resignations and subsequent negative publicity for the panel discredited its work.

In contrast, the most definitive work linking the illnesses to potential toxic exposures came from the University of Texas Southwestern Medical Center in Dallas. A team of researchers led by Epidemiology Department Chairman Dr. Robert W. Haley, using a specialized form of medical imaging known as magnetic resonance spectroscopy, found evidence of organic brain damage in a group of twenty-two ill Gulf War veterans compared to eighteen nondeployed Gulf War era counterparts. While small, the study was the first to pinpoint a potential physical marker for brain damage in Gulf War veterans. In earlier work beginning in 1994 and continuing today, Haley and his team theorized that, on the basis of the primate studies cited by the IOM, some—and perhaps most—of the cognitive and neuromuscular problems reported by sick Desert Storm veterans were likely the result of exposure to nerve agent fallout from the Coalition bombing of Iraqi chemical weapons sites.

Even as medical researchers continued to look for answers to the veterans' illnesses, the IOM issued a new report in October 2000 criticizing the Pentagon for failing to learn the appropriate lessons from the 1991 Persian Gulf War. In its report, the IOM urged that the federal government should immediately implement plans for protecting troops from environmental and other health hazards, because further delay could result in unnecessary risks to their health. The IOM found that "few concrete changes have been made at the field level to improve health protection for deployed service members." The IOM argued that for major deployments and those for whom there is an anticipated threat of chemical exposures, biological samples (such as blood and urine) should be collected from troops in the field. Given the fact that the DoD itself had commissioned the IOM study, its findings were yet another major embarrassment.

CHEMICAL AND BIOLOGICAL EXPERIMENTS

In the wake of the September 2001 terrorist attacks on the United States, fresh revelations about past U.S. government chemical and biological experiments on American troops surfaced, this time spotlighting a still largely classified program during the 1960s. Conceived in 1961 by Defense Secretary Robert McNamara, Project 112 was a $4 billion program designed ostensibly to determine the vulnerability of U.S. military equipment (and by implication, personnel) to the Soviet chemical and biological warfare threat. Pentagon officials released the first details of one Project 112 test, Operation Shipboard Hazard and Defense (SHAD), just 2 days after the World Trade Center and Pentagon terrorist attacks by al Qaeda. Veterans groups immediately charged that the timing of the release after a major national tragedy was designed to minimize coverage of the story, a charge Pentagon officials denied.

Over the next year, numerous SHAD veterans would come forward to tell about their exposure to toxic chemicals and being warned by the chain of command to remain silent about the incidents in the name of "national security." By the spring of 2003, Vietnam Veterans of America, acting on behalf of SHAD veterans, filed a federal lawsuit against former and current Pentagon officials for their role in denying the existence of Project 112 and related information relevant to the veterans' health claims. As of this writing, the case is pending.

As in the case of the Agent Orange and Gulf War syndrome controversies, the Pentagon once again maintained that no veterans had been harmed as a result of the experiments. A subsequent congressional inquiry raised questions about the claim, leading lawmakers to order the Pentagon to declassify all records associated with Project 112 tests so that the veterans and their medical caregivers could judge for themselves whether or not troops may have been harmed in the experiments, which included the use of the nerve agents sarin and VX.

POST–9/11 FIGHTING

The counterterrorist campaign in Afghanistan represented the first major combat deployment of American troops to the southwest Asian theater of operations since Desert Storm, and quickly questions were raised about whether the Pentagon had learned the necessary health lessons from the Gulf War and Bosnia deployment.

Section 765 of the 1998 National Defense Authorization Act required the Defense Department to conduct both pre- and postdeployment health examinations (to include mental health screenings and the drawing of blood samples) to accurately record the medical condition of members before their deployment and any changes in their medical condition during the course of deployment. As the first American troops began returning from Afghanistan, some veterans groups charged that DoD was ignoring the law and, in doing so, potentially setting the stage for a new "mystery illness" to plague yet another generation of veterans. Although DoD officials denied the charge, congressional investigators found ample evidence that despite the IOM's previous recommendations and the intent of the 1998 law, the Pentagon was not taking the necessary steps to document the pre- and postdeployment health of Operation Enduring Freedom veterans.

While Pentagon officials continued to receive regular criticism for their handling of the ongoing GWS, Project 112, and related controversies, the Department of Veterans Affairs began to show signs of listening to the veterans. A change long sought by Desert Storm veterans came in January 2002, when VA Secretary Anthony Principi established the Research Advisory Committee on Gulf War Veterans Illnesses (RACGWVI). The group's charter, established by legislation signed on November 11, 1998, stated that the panel would "provide advice and make recommendations to the Secretary of Veterans Affairs on proposed research studies, research plans and research strategies relating to the health consequences of military service in the Southwest Asia theater of operations during the Persian Gulf War."

Unlike previous government panels, this body contained both veterans and scientists known for their criticism of the existing Pentagon and VA postures on Gulf War illnesses. Moreover, the committee's primary focus was to determine what research should be funded and make recommendations to the Secretary of Veterans Affairs on ways to maximize delivery of effective treatments to ill Desert Storm veterans. In October 2002, Deputy VA Secretary Leo MacKay announced that the department would make available up to $20 million for research into Gulf War illnesses during fiscal year 2004, a figure twice the amount spent by the VA in any previous year. As of October 2002, the Departments of Defense, Health and Human Services, and VA had spent a combined $213 million on 224 research projects to answer the questions surrounding Gulf War illnesses.

Prior to Operation Iraqi Freedom and at the request of Deputy Secretary MacKay, the RACGWVI revisited many of the previous GAO and IOM recommendations regarding forced health protection and recommended urgent action by the Pentagon and VA on taking adequate physicals and biological samples before and immediately after major deployments. Whether the Pentagon will follow through on these latest recommendations remains to be seen.

In the wake of the second American war in Iraq, fresh questions about the health effects of the first Gulf War reemerged at a congressional hearing. On June 2, 2003, the GAO reported to Congress that the Pentagon and CIA modeling of the chemical fallout cloud from the Khamisiyah Ammunition Depot demolition in March 1991 was totally invalid, raising anew questions about the Pentagon's commitment to openly and honestly searching for answers to the veterans' illnesses.

Specifically, the GAO charged that the DoD models were not fully developed and validated for long-range environmental fallout; key assumptions were not accurate; plume height was underestimated; the modeling looked only at a single incident, not the effects of multiple bombings during the 6-week air campaign; and the field test at Dugway Proving Ground in Utah did not realistically simulate actual bombing conditions. Overall, Pentagon officials defended their methodology but conceded that some early models lacked sophistication. In their oral comments, GAO investigators maintained that exposure to nerve agents should be presumed for *all* veterans in theater since the federal government will never be able distinguish who was or was not exposed.

In late June 2003, the latest research results regarding Gulf War illnesses were presented to the Department of Veterans Affairs, providing further evidence of the potential harm from even low-level exposures to chemical agents. In one study, ill Desert Storm veterans demonstrated autonomic nervous system dysfunction on a broad range of tests. A second study showed that Gulf War-deployed veterans performed "significantly worse" on tests of attention, visuospatial skills, visual memory, and mood. Additionally, Gulf War-deployed veterans who used pyridostigmine bromide (an antinerve gas pill taken by an estimated 250,000 troops during the war) performed worse than their deployed comrades who did not use the drug. A third study demonstrated that low-level exposure to sarin nerve gas can cause delayed development of brain alterations that may be associated with memory loss and cognitive dysfunction in animals. Inexorably, science is providing answers to the causes of—and hopefully treatment strategies for—the malady known as "Gulf War syndrome."

CONCLUSION

What is less clear is whether the damage done to the federal government's reputation among veterans can ever be repaired. Decades of toxic exposure controversies—Agent Orange, Project 112, Gulf War syndrome—have soured many veterans since the Vietnam era on the value of the government's commitment to veterans. The failure of successive administrations—Republican and Democratic—to hold Pentagon, CIA, and VA officials responsible for their deceptions and blunders has eroded the trust of multiple generations of veterans and their families. How this new cynicism about government, and particularly military, service will impact military recruiting and retention—and thus the security of the United States—remains to be seen.

Perhaps the greatest irony of America's Gulf wars is that veterans who fought in the first war have struggled to prove they were harmed by Iraqi chemical agents the U.S. government claimed for years did not exist, even as a new generation of Persian Gulf veterans continues to search in vain for Iraqi chemical weapons the U.S. government claimed with certainty existed right up to the fall of Baghdad in April 2003.

Patrick G. Eddington

REFERENCES

Donnelly, Michael, with Denise Donnelly. *Falcon's Cry: A Desert Storm Memoir.* Westport, CT: Praeger, 1998.

Eddington, Patrick G. *Gassed in the Gulf: The Inside Story of the Pentagon-CIA Cover-up of Gulf War Syndrome.* Washington, DC: Insignia, 1997.

Hersh, Seymour M. *Against All Enemies: Gulf War Syndrome: The War Between America's Ailing Veterans and Their Government.* New York: Ballantine Books, 1998.

Johnson, Alison. *Gulf War Syndrome: Legacy of a Perfect War.* Brunswick, ME: MCS Information Exchange, 2001.

Matsumoto, Gary. *Vaccine A: The Covert Government Experiment That's Killing Our Soldiers—and Why GIs Are Only the First Victims.* New York: Basic Books, 2004.

Rostker, Bernard. *Depleted Uranium: A Case Study of Good and Evil.* Santa Monica, CA: RAND, 2002.

Wheelwright, Jeff. *The Irritable Heart: The Medical Mystery of the Gulf War.* New York: Norton, 2001.

WEB SITES

Congressionally Directed Medical Research Programs: http://cdmrp.army.mil

National Gulf War Resource Center: www.ngwrc.org

Office of the Special Assistant for Gulf War Illnesses: www.gulflink.osd.mil

U.S. Department of Veterans Affairs, Research Advisory Committee on Gulf War Veterans' Illnesses: www.va.gov/rac-gwvi

Vietnam Veterans of America: www.vva.org

GLOSSARY

Agent Orange. An herbicide widely used in the Vietnam War; Agent Orange contains dioxin, a known carcinogen.

Anthrax. An infectious and often highly fatal disease among mammals and human beings caused by the bacterium *Bacillus anthracis*.

Dioxin. A known carcinogen once used in herbicides like Agent Orange.

Gulf War syndrome. A variety of health conditions that many veterans say is the result of being exposed to toxins during the Persian Gulf War of 1991.

Nerve gas. Toxic chemicals such as sarin, soman, or tabun used in warfare to attack the nervous system of enemy troops.

Operation Desert Storm. The official military name for the 1991 conflict launched by the United States and allies to drive Iraq from Kuwait.

Operation Shipboard Hazard and Defense. A 1960s Defense Department program to test the military's ability to withstand a Soviet chemical attack by exposing naval personnel to a variety of toxins.

DOCUMENTS

Document 1. Excerpt from Persian Gulf War Veterans' Health Status Act, 1992

The Persian Gulf War Veterans' Health Status Act was passed by Congress in 1992 following that body's first hearings into complaints by veterans that they were suffering from a variety of ailments associated with their service in that conflict. The legislation established a registry to monitor veterans and offered free medical examinations to all Gulf War veterans.

§ 527. Evaluation and data collection

(a) The Secretary, pursuant to general standards which the Secretary shall prescribe in regulations, shall measure and evaluate on a continuing basis the effect of all programs authorized under this title, in order to determine their effectiveness in achieving stated goals in general, and in achieving such goals in relation to their cost, their effect on related programs, and their structure and mechanisms for delivery of services. Such information as the Secretary may consider necessary for purposes of such evaluations shall be made available to the Secretary, upon request, by all departments, agencies, and instrumentalities of the executive branch.

(b) In carrying out this section, the Secretary shall collect, collate, and analyze on a continuing basis full statistical data regarding participation (including the duration thereof), provision of services, categories of beneficiaries, planning and construction of facilities, acquisition of real property, proposed excessing of land, accretion and attrition of personnel, and categorized expenditures attributable thereto, under all programs carried out under this title.

(c) The Secretary shall make available to the public, and on a regular basis provide to the appropriate committees of the Congress, copies of all completed evaluative research studies and summaries of evaluations of program impact and effectiveness carried out, and tabulations and analyses of all data collected, under this section.

Source: U.S.C. Title 38, Part I, Chapter 5, Subchapters II, § 527.

Document 2. Executive Order 12961: Presidential Advisory Committee on Gulf War Veterans' Illnesses, 1995

In the years following the Persian Gulf War, thousands of veterans complained of a variety of medical conditions that they said were caused by their combat service. Increasingly, they also complained that the Department of Defense and the Department of Veterans Affairs were not taking these illnesses seriously or were denying that there were any connections to the war. In May 1995, President Bill Clinton established the Presidential Advisory Committee on Gulf War Veterans' Illnesses to investigate the accusations brought by the veterans against the government. The following is the text of the executive order establishing the committee.

By the authority vested in me as President by the Constitution and the laws of the United States of America, it is hereby ordered as follows:

Section 1. Establishment. (a) There is hereby established the Presidential Advisory Committee on Gulf War Veterans' Illnesses (the "Committee"). The Committee shall be composed of not more than 12 members to be appointed by the President. The members of the Committee shall have expertise relevant to the functions of the Committee and shall not be full-time officials or employees of the executive branch of the Federal Government. The Committee shall be subject to the Federal Advisory Committee Act, as amended, 5 U.S.C. App. 2. (b) The President shall designate a Chairperson from among the members of the Committee.

Sec. 2. Functions. (a) The Committee shall report to the President through the Secretary of Defense, the Secretary of Veterans Affairs, and the Secretary of Health and Human Services. (b) The Committee shall provide advice and recommendations based on its review of the following matters:

(1) Research: epidemiological, clinical, and other research concerning Gulf War veterans' Illnesses.

(2) Coordinating Efforts: the activities of the Persian Gulf Veterans Coordinating Board, including the Research Coordinating Council, the Clinical Working Group, and the Disability and Compensation Working Group.

(3) Medical Treatment: medical examinations and treatment in connection with Gulf War veterans' illnesses, including the Comprehensive Clinical Evaluation Program and the Persian Gulf Registry Medical Examination Program.

(4) Outreach: government-sponsored outreach efforts such as hotlines and newsletters related to Gulf War illnesses.

(5) External Reviews: the steps taken to implement recommendations in external reviews by the Institute of Medicine's Committee to Review the Health Consequences of Service.

During the Persian Gulf War, the Defense Science Board Task Force on Persian Gulf War Health Effects, the National Institutes of Health Technology Assessment Workshop on the Persian Gulf Experience and Health, the Persian Gulf Expert Scientific Committee, and other bodies.

(6) Risk Factors: the possible risks associated with service in the Persian Gulf Conflict in general and, specifically, with prophylactic drugs and vaccines, infectious diseases, environmental chemicals, radiation and toxic substances, smoke from oil well fires, depleted uranium, physical and psychological stress, and other factors applicable to the Persian Gulf Conflict.

(7) Chemical and Biological Weapons: information related to reports of the possible detection of chemical or biological weapons during the Persian Gulf Conflict.

(c) It shall not be a function of the Committee to conduct scientific research. The Committee shall review information and provide advice and recommendations on the activities undertaken related to the matters described in (b) above.

(d) It shall not be a function of the Committee to provide advice or recommendations on any legal liability of the Federal Government for any claims or potential claims against the Federal Government.

(e) As used herein, "Gulf War Veterans' Illnesses" means the symptoms and illnesses reported by United States uniformed services personnel who served in the Persian Gulf Conflict.

(f) The Committee shall submit an interim report within 6 months of the first meeting of the Committee and a final report by December 31, 1996, unless otherwise provided by the President.

Sec.3. Administration. (a) The heads of executive departments and agencies shall, to the extent permitted by law, provide the Committee with such information as it may require for purposes of carrying out its functions.

(b) Members of the Committee shall be compensated in accordance with Federal law. Committee members may be allowed travel expenses, including per diem in lieu of subsistence, to the extent permitted by law for persons serving intermittently in the Government service (5 U.S.C. 5701–5707).

(c) To the extent permitted by law, and subject to the availability of appropriations, the Department of Defense shall provide the Committee with such funds as may be necessary for the performance of its functions.

Sec. 4. General Provisions. (a) Notwithstanding the provisions of any other Executive order, the functions of the President under the Federal Advisory Committee Act that are applicable to the Committee, except that of reporting annually to the Congress, shall be performed by the Secretary of Defense, in accordance with guidelines and procedures established by the Administrator of General Services.

(b) The Committee shall terminate 30 days after submitting its final report.

(c) This order is intended only to improve the internal management of the executive branch and it is not intended to create any right, benefit or trust responsibility, substantive or procedural, enforceable at law or equity by a party against the United States, its agencies, its officers, or any person.

William J. Clinton
THE WHITE HOUSE,
May 26, 1995.

Source: The White House.

GUN VIOLENCE AND GUN CONTROL

Gun violence in America and efforts to control it have long historical roots. Yet the reality of both issues is more complex than the stereotypical views. While American violence through history has been rooted in guns, gun mayhem has been far more evident in large urban areas than in American frontier life, whose fanciful gun-toting, shoot-'em-up image was far less prevalent in real life than in Hollywood movies. And while many people assume gun control (regulations pertaining to gun ownership or operation imposed by some level of government) is an artifact of the late twentieth century, strict controls existed throughout American history, even before the Revolutionary era. In recent decades, the political and policy debate over gun control and gun violence has intensified, but the controls under consideration center on a set of relatively modest and limited changes.

EARLY GUN PRACTICES

Organized gun-related violence in America, in the form of military-style skirmishes and wars, pockmark American history, from the brutal Indian wars to the Civil War to various vigilante movements that have occurred throughout the nation's history. The focus of this essay, however, is gun violence at the individual level.

Gun possession in America extends back to its earliest settlements, in Jamestown and Plymouth, where guns were used for hunting and protection, providing the basis for the American gun culture. Yet guns were relatively rare in those nascent colonies and seldom associated with interpersonal violence. Most significant gun-related violence occurred between Native Americans and European settlers. Though guns were later a primary tool of war in early conflicts including the Revolutionary War, limited gun availability among the general population continued to be a severe problem; American military leaders, including General George Washington,

regularly complained that service-eligible males lacked not only working firearms, but the basic knowledge of their operation. This relative scarcity of guns in early America existed for several reasons: they were expensive, as they were mostly handmade by blacksmiths (the first gun factory in America did not begin operation until 1790) at a rate of perhaps a couple of dozen a year; they were made of iron, and rusted quickly without regular maintenance; they required parts and materials, like gunpowder, that were often difficult to obtain and deteriorated rapidly; they were cumbersome and dangerous to operate, requiring considerable skill to operate; and a well-maintained firearm, used periodically, could be expected to last no more than about 5 years. While some colonials hunted regularly for food and pelts, most were farmers who relied on agricultural produce and domesticated livestock for food. Many of the guns owned by citizens and the government were broken, rusted, or otherwise inoperable. Guns were also imported from Europe at substantial expense, but import became more difficult as the Revolution neared.

From the Colonial era through the end of the War of 1812, America relied substantially on citizen militias to defend its frontiers and fight its wars. Though supplemented by the Continental Army during the Revolution and a small professional army after the adoption of the Constitution of 1787, manpower derived primarily from ill-equipped and ill-trained citizen militias, who were expected, and even required, to own and supply the necessary firearms and accoutrements, as the government often lacked the resources to arm and equip a large army. Some militias did acquit themselves well in battle and maintained a high degree of skill, such as the Lexington and Concord "minutemen." Other militia units fought well when the battles were near their home areas. For the most part, however, the military record of these citizen militia units was poor. Their abysmal performance in the War of 1812 ef-

CHRONOLOGY

1775 **April 19.** Battle of Lexington and Concord, involving local militias, initiates the Revolutionary War.

1781 The Revolutionary War ends, and America wins its freedom from Great Britain.

1787 Shays's Rebellion is suppressed by militia forces.

The U.S. Constitution is written and sent to the states for ratification.

1789 The Constitution takes effect.

Twelve amendments to the Constitution, called the Bill of Rights, are approved by the First Congress and sent to the states for ratification; the Second Amendment protects the right of states to maintain militias and of militia members to "keep and bear arms."

1791 Ten amendments are ratified by the states and added to the Constitution as the Bill of Rights.

1792 Congress passes the Uniform Militia Act and the Calling Forth Act, which implement the militia system for national defense and assert the primacy of federal government power over the militias.

1794 The Whiskey Rebellion is suppressed by militia forces.

1812–14 The War of 1812 is fought against Britain. Because of their poor performance, this is the last major military conflict in which the U.S. relies on the old-style general militias.

1871 The National Rifle Association is formed by two Civil War veterans from New York to improve marksmanship skills.

1876 The first Supreme Court case in which the high court interprets the Second Amendment, *U.S. v. Cruikshank* states that the amendment does not apply to the states.

1886 Reaffirming *Cruikshank*, the Supreme Court rules in *Presser v. Illinois* that the Second Amendment does not afford citizens the right to form their own militias, as this power belongs solely to the government.

1894 In *Miller v. Texas*, the Supreme Court upholds a law prohibiting the carrying of dangerous weapons, saying that it does not violate the Second Amendment.

1897 The Supreme Court rules in *Robertson v. Baldwin* that a law barring the carrying of concealed weapons did not violate the Second Amendment.

1903 Congress passes the Militia Act, also known as the Dick Act, which for the first time recognizes the reserve or volunteer militias as the National Guard rather than unorganized or general militias. The act begins the process of consolidating federal control over old-style militias.

1911 The New York State legislature enacts the Sullivan Law, the first modern strict gun control law, which regulates the sale, possession, and carrying of handguns. Support for the law accelerated with the attempted assassination of the mayor of New York City.

1916 Congress passes the National Defense Act, implementing sweeping new federal control over the National Guard.

1919 Congress enacts the War Revenue Act, a revenue-raising measure that included a 10 percent federal excise tax on guns.

The Prohibition Unit, which becomes the Bureau of Prohibition, is the forerunner of the modern Bureau of Alcohol, Tobacco, and Firearms.

The Eighteenth Amendment to the Constitution is ratified, barring the "manufacture, sale, or transportation of intoxicating liquors" within and into the United States from other countries. Illegal efforts to meet continued demand for alcohol products spawn extensive bootlegging, cultivating the growth of organized crime.

1927 Congress passes a bill, titled "An Act Declaring Pistols, Revolvers, and Other Firearms Capable of Being Concealed on the Person Nonmailable and Providing Penalties," to prohibit the sale of handguns by private individuals through the mail.

1933 The Twenty-first Amendment to the Constitution is ratified, repealing alcohol prohibition.

1934 Congress passes the National Firearms Act, which restricts the manufacture, sale, and transfer of automatic weapons, sawed-off shotguns, and other exotic weapons such as cane guns.

1938 Congress passes the Federal Firearms Act, establishing a system of licensing for firearms dealers and regulating sales of guns to criminals.

1939   The Supreme Court rules in *Miller v. U.S.* that gun regulations in the National Firearms Act do not violate the Second Amendment, and the amendment pertains only to citizen service in a government-organized and regulated militia.

1963   **November 22.** President John F. Kennedy is assassinated in Dallas, Texas, with a rifle purchased through interstate mails. The assassination spurs national support for stronger gun control laws.

1968   **April 4.** Civil rights leader the Rev. Dr. Martin Luther King Jr. is assassinated in Memphis, Tennessee, by James Earl Ray.

June 5. U.S. Senator Robert F. Kennedy is assassinated in Los Angeles, California, by Sirhan Sirhan.

October 22. President Lyndon Johnson signs into law the Gun Control Act, banning the interstate shipment of firearms to individuals and strengthening other licensing and regulatory measures. Support for the bill was spurred by the assassinations of Martin Luther King Jr. and Robert F. Kennedy in the months before the bill's passage.

1972   The modern Bureau of Alcohol, Tobacco, and Firearms is transferred from the Internal Revenue Service to the Department of Treasury, where it is given bureau status.

Congress creates the Consumer Product Safety Commission. Just before enactment of the law, a provision is inserted by gun control foes to exempt firearms and ammunition from agency scrutiny, making guns virtually the only commodity available to consumers exempted from the law.

1974   Handgun Control Inc., the largest group advocating gun control, is formed by businessman Nelson "Pete" Shields. Originally founded as the National Council to Control Handguns, it changed its name to the Brady Coalition in 2001.

1981   **March 30.** President Ronald Reagan is wounded in an assassination attempt in Washington, D.C. After his recovery, Reagan continues to oppose stronger gun laws, a position he reverses after leaving office.

1986   Congress passes the Firearms Owners Protection Act, also known as the McClure-Volkmer bill, repealing some gun regulations enacted in 1968, notably allowing interstate sale of long guns and eliminating some recordkeeping requirements for licensed gun dealers.

1989   Loner Patrick Purdy kills five children and wounds twenty-nine others in a schoolyard massacre in Stockton, California, using an AK-47 assault weapon, and then shoots himself with a handgun he was also carrying. The mass shooting shocks the nation, spurring calls for a ban on assault weapons.

1991   George Hennard kills twenty-two people and himself, and wounds twenty-three others, in a shooting at a cafeteria in Killeen, Texas. The event strengthens support for gun control efforts.

1992   Federal law enforcement officials lay siege to the cabin of Randy Weaver in Ruby Ridge, Idaho, after he eludes capture. Two of his family members are killed, along with a federal agent. The incident rallies those who fear stronger gun laws and greater government power.

1993   Congress enacts the Brady Handgun Violence Prevention Act, which imposes a 5-business-day waiting period and background checks for handgun purchases. The waiting period is replaced by an instant check system in 1998.

April 19. Federal law enforcement officials storm the Branch Davidian compound in Waco, Texas, after a 51-day siege. Seventy-four Davidians died in the ensuing fire.

1994   Congress enacts the assault weapons ban, barring possession of nineteen named assault weapons, and several dozen copycat models.

1999   **April 20.** Two high school boys kill twelve students and a teacher at Columbine High School in Littleton, Colorado, before turning their guns on themselves. The killings shock the nation; in response, the U.S. Senate passes a gun control bill, but it dies in a conference committee after the House of Representatives fails to pass a comparable measure.

2000   A group of women concerned about gun violence organize the Million Mom March, held on Mother's Day in Washington, D.C., to support stronger gun laws. The first modern mass demonstration on behalf of gun control, the march attracted over 700,000 participants, making it one of the largest mass demonstrations ever held in the nation's capital.

2004   Congress allows the 1994 assault weapons ban to lapse. The original law had a 10-year sunset provision.

fectively ended the country's reliance on self-armed citizen militias and eligible males maintaining firearms at home.

Gun ownership became widespread in America only around the time of the Civil War, when millions of men learned to use firearms during military service. Technological improvements in gun manufacturing and standardization of ammunition also made guns safer to operate, more reliable, more prolific, easier to use, and less expensive. As early as the 1850s, gun manufacturer Samuel Colt aggressively marketed revolvers to the larger public, linking his guns through extensive advertising campaigns with romantic, idealized visions of the American West. Colt's innovations in the machine production of revolvers allowed a high-quality product to be produced in large numbers. By the end of the nineteenth century, the glut of handguns Colt and his competitors spawned began to prompt calls for the government to stem the rising tide of gun violence mostly in Eastern cities rather than in the Western frontier.

THE MYTH OF THE WILD WEST

A chief stereotype supporting the American ethos of guns-and-violence is the gun-toting frontier population of America's westward expansion. While the American West did witness gun violence, its extent and pervasiveness have been greatly exaggerated, beginning with the vivid stories of frequent wild shootouts dramatized, glorified, and invented by contemporary newspaper reporters and pulp fiction writers. In these tales of the nineteenth-century westward-bound settlers, storytellers created legends of armed citizens ready and willing to use their Winchesters, Smith & Wessons, Remingtons, and Colts to defend hearth and home against outlaws and Indians in an environment where the only reliable justice came from the barrel of a gun.

Such generalizations distort both the process by which the West was settled and the role guns played in that process. The settling and so-called taming of the West was primarily attributable to the homesteaders, ranchers, miners, tradesmen, businessmen, and others who drove out Native Americans, populated the region, worked the land, and established towns and cities. The major threats Western settlers faced were disease and starvation. In fact, gun-slinging cowboys played a relatively minor role in this process. As many historians of the West have noted, far more people died in shootouts in movies than ever

died in the real-life West. For example, at the height of lawlessness in the legendary Dodge City from 1876 to 1885, a total of only fifteen persons died violent deaths—an average of 1.5 per year. In Deadwood, South Dakota, in its most violent year, four people were killed. In the most violent year in Tombstone, Arizona, home of the celebrated gunfight at the OK Corral, only five people were killed. From 1870 to 1885, the total number of killings reported in the cowboy towns of Abilene, Caldwell, Dodge City, Ellsworth, and Wichita was forty-five, and only six of these were killed by six-shooters; sixteen killings were by police.

Outside populated areas, cowboys and other range riders who carried six-shooters almost never used them in Hollywood-style gunfights or to enforce some brand of Western justice. Even in the most violence-prone cattle towns, vigilantism and lawlessness were tolerated only briefly. As Western historians have noted, local business and other civic leaders quickly pushed for town incorporation to establish local police forces, which were supported by taxes levied against local bars, gambling establishments, and houses of prostitution. Prohibitions against carrying guns within city or town limits were immediately enacted and strictly enforced; guns were checked at some designated location, and usually reclaimed with a metal token for identification. As a consequence, few homicides occurred even during the heyday of gun violence in the 1870s, and most of these resulted from drunkenness and disputes over gambling. Most of the killing on the frontier took place in the Indian Wars between the U.S. Cavalry and Native Americans rebelling against harsh and duplicitous treatment at the hands of whites.

The gun disarmament routinely practiced in newly formed Western towns was well understood as a sign of civilization and an improvement in public safety, especially by local businesspeople who realized fear of violence and disorder drove away settlers and customers. Ironically, such strict gun control measures provoke more political heat and outrage in twenty-first century America than they did in the nineteenth century. Probably the single most important early cultural force responsible for spreading the gun-based Western mythology was William F. "Buffalo Bill" Cody's Wild West Show, seen by more than 50 million people over four decades at the end of the nineteenth and early twentieth centuries. The Western-style shootouts glorified in books and movies were all but unknown in the nineteenth century, as were the often-exaggerated or invented exploits of Western outlaws. One of the first feature films ever made, *The Great Train Robbery*, sent moviegoers ducking for cover when an outlaw in the 1903 film aimed his six-shooter at the camera and fired. From that day to this, movies and other forms of popular culture have maintained their fascination with guns and gun violence.

EARLY GUN CONTROLS

Government-enacted gun control policy extends back to the Colonial era. From that point through the early Federalist period, firearms possession was regulated in two primary ways. One type required eligible males to own guns for service in local militias. The lack of firearms among the general population was a primary concern for American leaders both during and after the American Revolution. In 1792, Congress passed the Uniform Militia Act, which required a militia-eligible man to "provide himself with a good musket or firelock, a sufficient bayonet and belt, two spare flints, and a knapsack, a pouch with a box therein to contain not less than twenty-four cartridges . . . each cartridge to contain a proper quantity of powder and ball." Within the next 2 years, all fifteen states passed similar measures, but the laws lacked enforcement power and were widely ignored. In addition, states often reserved the right to take or "impress" these guns if they were needed for defense.

The other type of early gun control law barred ownership by various groups including slaves, indentured servants, Native Americans, Catholics, other non-Protestants, non-property-owning whites, and those who refused to swear oaths of loyalty to the government. Laws barring distribution of guns to Native Americans were among the first such measures. As early as the 1600s, persons discovered selling guns to Indians could be subject to death. Pennsylvania went further than other states to take guns away from citizens deemed disloyal with the Test Act, passed in 1777, specifying disarmament of anyone refusing to swear an oath of allegiance to the government, referring specifically to "persons disaffected to the liberty and independence of this state." According to one historian, this law disarmed up to 40 percent of the state's adult white male population. Further, the government conducted periodic gun censuses before and after adoption of the Constitution in 1787. In 1803, for example, Secretary of War Henry Dearborn coordinated the most extensive and

thorough such gun census ever conducted till then, concluding that about 45 percent of all militiamen, or about a quarter of the white male adult population, had "arms." A similar census 7 years later produced similar results.

RISE OF GUN VIOLENCE AND MODERN GUN CONTROL

Two types of events spurred the frequent calls for tougher gun laws in the twentieth century: the spread and fear of gun-related crime, and the assassinations of political leaders and celebrities. Despite enduring popular support for tougher laws, new federal gun regulations have been infrequent and limited in scope.

The first push for gun control laws in modern times started during the Progressive era. A dramatic rise in urban crime, seemingly linked to the proliferation of handguns, prompted citizen groups, good government groups, newspaper editors, and other civic leaders to press for new regulations. In 1903, for example, the New York City Police estimated at least 20,000 citizens in the city regularly carried handguns. Gun crimes received extensive press coverage, and states and localities throughout the country banned the carrying of concealed weapons (a continuation of the gun-control tradition in the American West). The federal government did not intervene in early gun-control policies, based on the prevailing sentiment that gun regulatory decisions should be left to the states and localities. In several legal challenges, however, the U.S. Supreme Court upheld the constitutionality of such regulations.

Among the earliest and most sweeping of these new state laws was New York State's Sullivan Law of 1911. Spurred by spiraling urban violence and the attempted assassination of New York City Mayor William J. Gaynor in 1910, the Sullivan Law (named after the state senator who championed the bill) strictly regulated the sale, possession, and carrying of deadly weapons. In particular, pistol-carrying was licensed, and violation was elevated to a felony. To the present, New York state's handgun laws have remained among the toughest in the country.

The 1920s ushered in a new era of freedom, but also brought Prohibition and the concomitant rise of illegal alcohol production and smuggling (called bootlegging), which in turn accelerated the growth of organized crime. Alcohol bootlegging became highly profitable, attracting many to the criminal life. As rival criminal gangs jockeyed for control of the enormous illegal market, crime-related violence rose. At the same time, pressure on the national government mounted as more civic leaders demanded a coordinated federal response. An American Bar Association–commissioned study in 1922, for example, concluded that 90 percent of all murders nationwide were committed with handguns. The organization then endorsed a nationwide ban on the production and sale of handguns and handgun ammunition, except for law enforcement. As early as 1921, the U.S. Senate Judiciary Committee held hearings on a bill to bar the interstate shipment of handguns, with a few exceptions. Pushed every year from 1915 until 1924, the measure was always killed in committee. A similar fate met most other federal gun control efforts during this period.

By the late 1920s and early 1930s, crime had escalated and the Great Depression had set in; newspapers reported gangland killings and the growing popularity among gangsters of the Tommy gun, handheld machine guns developed for use in World War I. In mob-run Chicago, for example, bootlegger Hymie Weiss and his mob attacked rival Al Capone's gang headquarters in 1926, firing thousands of rounds into the building. Capone escaped, but he took revenge a few weeks later, killing Weiss and his accomplices. In 1926, within a single month 215 Chicago gangsters were murdered, and another 160 killed by the police. The public read with horror and fascination newspaper accounts of violent events from the St. Valentine's Day Massacre to the crime sprees of Bonnie and Clyde, Pretty Boy Floyd, and John Dillinger, as well as subsequent shooting deaths at the hands of government agents. Punctuating the country's gun crime worries, an unemployed anarchist fired five shots at President-elect Franklin D. Roosevelt in early 1933, as he visited Florida, narrowly missing him but fatally wounding Chicago Mayor Anton Cermak. The assassin had bought his .32 caliber revolver at a local pawnshop for eight dollars.

At the federal level, the first successful gun policy efforts were a 10 percent excise tax on guns enacted in 1919 and a 1928 law prohibiting the sale of handguns to private individuals through the mail. The rise of gangsterism and the 1932 election of Roosevelt, who unlike his predecessors was sympathetic to new national gun control efforts, boosted the prospects for new gun laws. The National Firearms Act of 1934 strictly regulated gangster-type weapons, including sawed-off shotguns and machine guns. Initially, the measure also included a system for registering hand-

guns, but gun control opponents stripped that provision from the bill. The Federal Firearms Act of 1938 established a licensing system for gun dealers, manufacturers, and importers.

America's involvement in World War II turned the nation's attention and resources to the war effort. After the war, millions of returning soldiers who had used guns for the first time in military service spawned a rise in gun ownership, mostly for hunting and sporting purposes. The relative prosperity and stability of the 1950s pushed crime issues—with the exception of juvenile delinquents, whom the public associated more with knives than guns—to the back burner.

No new federal gun control laws reached the president's desk until 1968, when a 5-year push for tougher laws culminated in enactment of the Gun Control Act. Momentum for new controls increased in the aftermath of the assassination of President John F. Kennedy in 1963. Lee Harvey Oswald had shot the president in Dallas, Texas, with a rifle purchased through interstate mail. By the mid-1960s escalating crime rates and the spread of urban disorder raised new fears about spiraling gun violence. Such fears peaked in 1968, as urban rioting continued and both civil rights leader Martin Luther King Jr. and Senator Robert Kennedy were assassinated. These two murders were the final impetus for passage of the Gun Control Act. The law banned interstate shipment of firearms and ammunition to private individuals; prohibited gun sales to minors; strengthened licensing and recordkeeping requirements for dealers and collectors; extended regulations to destructive devices such as land mines, bombs, and hand grenades; increased penalties for gun crimes; and regulated importation of foreign-made firearms. Blanket gun registration and licensing, backed by President Lyndon Johnson, were cut from the original bill.

The next major gun law enacted by Congress, the Firearms Owners Protection Act of 1986 (also called the McClure-Volkmer bill), rolled back many of the provisions of the 1968 law at a time when anti-control forces, led by the National Rifle Association (NRA), exerted their greatest influence over Congress and the presidency of Ronald Reagan. It allowed interstate sale of long guns (rifles and shotguns), reduced recordkeeping for dealers, limited government regulatory powers over dealers and gun shows (in particular, limiting inspections of gun dealers to one a year), and barred firearms registration.

Table 1. Crimes Committed with Firearms, 1973–2003

Year	Total firearm crimes[a]		Murders		Robberies		Aggravated assaults	
	Number	Rate	Number	Rate	Number	Rate	Number	Rate
1973	361,141	172.1	13,072	6.2	241,088	114.9	106,981	51.0
1974	326,235	154.3	13,987	6.6	197,257	93.3	114,991	54.4
1975	342,495	160.7	13,496	6.3	208,307	97.7	120,693	56.6
1976	307,252	143.1	11,982	5.6	179,430	83.6	115,841	54.0
1977	301,590	139.4	11,950	5.5	168,418	77.9	121,222	56.0
1978	307,603	141.1	12,437	5.7	170,152	78.0	125,015	57.3
1979	340,202	154.6	13,582	6.2	185,352	84.2	141,269	64.2
1980	392,083	174.0	14,377	6.4	221,170	98.1	156,535	69.5
1981	396,197	172.9	14,052	6.1	230,226	100.5	151,918	66.3
1982	372,477	160.9	12,648	5.5	214,219	92.5	145,609	62.9
1983	330,419	141.2	11,258	4.8	183,581	78.5	135,580	57.9
1984	329,232	139.4	10,990	4.7	173,634	73.5	144,609	61.2
1985	340,942	142.8	11,141	4.7	175,748	73.6	154,052	64.5
1986	376,064	156.0	12,181	5.1	186,174	77.2	177,710	73.7
1987	365,709	150.3	11,879	4.9	170,841	70.2	182,989	75.2
1988	385,934	157.0	12,553	5.1	181,352	73.8	192,029	78.1
1989	410,039	165.2	13,416	5.4	192,006	77.3	204,618	82.4
1990	492,671	198.1	15,025	6.0	233,973	94.1	243,673	98.0
1991	548,667	217.6	16,376	6.5	274,404	108.8	257,887	102.3
1992	565,575	221.7	16,204	6.4	271,009	106.2	278,362	109.1
1993	581,697	225.5	17,048	6.6	279,738	108.5	284,910	110.5
1994	542,529	208.4	16,314	6.3	257,428	98.9	268,788	103.2
1995	504,421	192.0	14,686	5.6	238,023	90.6	251,712	95.8
1996	458,458	172.8	13,319	5.0	218,579	82.4	226,559	85.4
1997	414,530	154.9	12,346	4.6	197,686	73.9	204,498	76.4
1998	364,776	135.0	10,977	4.1	170,611	63.1	183,188	67.8
1999	338,535	124.1	10,128	3.7	163,458	59.9	164,949	60.5
2000	341,831	121.5	10,179	3.6	166,807	59.3	164,845	58.6
2001	354,754	124.3	11,106	3.9	177,627	62.3	169,926	58.2
2002	357,822	124.1	10,808	3.7	177,088	61.4	169,926	58.9
2003	347,705	119.6	11,041	3.8	172,802	59.4	163,863	56.3

[a] Crimes included are murder, robbery, and aggravated assault.
Source: Federal Bureau of Investigation, U.S. Department of Justice.

Highly publicized incidents of mass shootings in the late 1980s and 1990s, combined with the election of control supporter Bill Clinton to the presidency, resulted in successful enactment of gun laws of limited scope. In 1989, the country's sensibilities were shocked when a drifter named Patrick Purdy opened fire with a Chinese-made AK-47 assault rifle on schoolchildren in a Stockton, California, playground. Within seconds, five children were killed and twenty-nine others wounded. Within weeks, thirty states began considering laws to ban assault weapons. Two years later, George Hennard opened fire in a cafeteria in Killeen, Texas, killing twenty-two people and himself. These and other such sensational killings encouraged new nationwide efforts to regulate guns, with primary focus on handgun waiting periods and regulation of assault weapons.

Yielding to public pressure, Congress enacted the Brady Law in 1993 and the Assault Weapons Ban in 1994. Named after President Reagan's press secretary, James Brady, who was seriously wounded in the 1981 assassination attempt against Reagan, the Brady Law required a waiting period of 5 business days for the purchase of a handgun (during which time local law enforcement authorities were to conduct background checks to weed out felons, the mentally incompetent, and others barred from handgun possession), increased federal firearms license fees, financed recordkeeping improvements, and called for implementation of an instant computerized background check to be instituted in 5 years. The National Instant Criminal Background Check System (NICS) was implemented in 1998, allowing hand-

Table 2. Percent of Murders, Robberies, and Aggravated Assaults in Which Firearms Were Used, 1973–2003

Year	All crimes		Murders		Robberies		Aggravated assaults	
	#[a]	%[b]	#	%	#	%	#	%
1973	818,460	44.1	19,510	67.0	382,680	63.0	416,270	25.7
1974	914,610	35.7	20,600	67.9	441,290	44.7	452,720	25.4
1975	970,190	35.3	20,510	65.8	464,970	44.8	484,710	24.9
1976	929,840	33.0	18,780	63.8	420,210	42.7	490,850	23.6
1977	946,480	31.9	19,120	62.5	404,850	41.6	522,510	23.2
1978	994,695	30.9	19,555	63.6	417,038	40.8	558,102	22.4
1979	1,102,550	30.9	21,456	63.3	466,881	39.7	614,213	23.0
1980	1,226,810	32.0	23,040	62.4	548,810	40.3	654,960	23.9
1981	1,240,370	31.9	22,520	62.4	574,130	40.1	643,720	23.6
1982	1,207,942	30.8	21,010	60.2	536,890	39.9	650,042	22.4
1983	1,159,060	28.5	19,310	58.3	500,220	36.7	639,530	21.2
1984	1,189,050	27.7	18,690	58.8	485,010	35.8	685,350	21.1
1985	1,240,100	27.5	18,980	58.7	497,870	35.3	723,250	21.3
1986	1,397,710	26.9	20,610	59.1	542,780	34.3	834,320	21.3
1987	1,392,890	26.3	20,100	59.1	517,700	33.0	855,090	21.4
1988	1,473,740	26.2	20,680	60.7	542,970	33.4	910,090	21.1
1989	1,551,540	26.4	21,500	62.4	578,330	33.2	951,710	21.5
1990	1,717,570	28.7	23,440	64.1	639,270	36.6	1,054,860	23.1
1991	1,805,170	30.4	24,700	66.3	687,730	39.9	1,092,740	23.6
1992	1,823,210	31.0	23,760	68.2	672,480	40.3	1,126,970	24.7
1993	1,819,390	32.0	24,530	69.5	659,760	42.4	1,135,100	25.1
1994	1,762,072	30.8	23,305	70.0	618,817	41.6	1,119,950	24.0
1995	1,701,321	29.6	21,597	68.0	580,545	41.0	1,099,179	22.9
1996	1,586,509	28.9	19,645	67.8	537,050	40.7	1,029,814	22.0
1997	1,539,943	26.9	18,208	67.8	498,534	39.7	1,023,201	20.0
1998	1,437,941	25.4	16,914	64.9	446,625	38.2	974,402	18.8
1999	1,341,586	25.2	15,533	65.2	409,670	39.9	916,383	18.0
2000	1,334,103	25.6	15,517	65.6	407,842	40.9	910,744	18.1
2001	1,346,120	26.4	15,980	69.5	422,921	42.0	907,219	18.3
2002	1,331,189	26.9	16,204	66.7	420,637	42.1	894,348	18.3
2003	1,287,826	27.0	16,503	66.9	413,402	41.8	857,921	19.1

[a] Number of crimes.
[b] Percentage of crimes committed with firearms.
Source: Federal Bureau of Investigation, U.S. Department of Justice.

gun sales to be completed as soon as the check inquiry is cleared. Dealers have up to 3 days to verify the applicant is eligible to purchase the handgun, although 95 percent of all purchases clear within 2 hours, according to the FBI. From 1994 to 2000, the Brady Law stopped about 600,000 handgun purchases, about 2.5 percent of all handgun purchases. Nineteen states still impose their own waiting periods regardless of when a potential sale clears. These periods range from a few days to several months.

In 1994, Congress enacted a ban on nineteen specified assault weapons, plus several dozen copycat models distinguished from other semiautomatic weapons by their distinctive military features, including a more compact design, short barrels, large ammunition clips, lighter weight, pistol grips or thumbhole stocks, flash suppressors, or telescoping stocks (traits that facilitate concealability and "spray fire"). The law also exempted from the ban 661 specifically named weapons. According to government studies, although assault weapons constituted only about 2 to 3 percent of all guns in America, they accounted for 6 to 8 percent of gun crimes. By 2001, four states and several localities had enacted their own assault weapons bans. The federal ban was imposed for a 10-year period that lapsed in 2004.

In 1997 and 1998 the country's attention was riveted by a series of seemingly inexplicable schoolyard shootings committed by school-age boys in small cities, towns, and rural areas around the country—Jonesboro, Arkansas; Springfield, Oregon; Pearl, Mississippi; Bethel, Alaska; Edinboro, Pennsylvania;

Johnston, Rhode Island; Pomona, California; Fayetteville, Tennessee; and West Paducah, Kentucky. The schoolyard mayhem reached its peak on April 20, 1999, when two high school boys shattered the relative security and placidity of Columbine High in Littleton, Colorado. Bringing four guns into the school, the boys killed twelve students and one teacher in less than 15 minutes; twenty-three others were wounded. As police closed in on 18-year-old Eric Harris and 17-year-old Dylan Klebold, the two turned the guns on themselves. The firearms had been purchased in 1998 by an 18-year-old friend. Three had been bought at a nearby gun show, and the fourth, also by a friend, at another gun show. All four purchases were conducted by private sellers who were therefore exempt from background check requirements. The friend who made the initial purchases was acting as a "straw buyer" for the boys, a practice outlawed in some states, but not in Colorado. In 2000, Colorado voters approved a referendum to close the so-called gun show loophole.

In the aftermath of the incident, national shock and outrage put unprecedented pressure on Congress to respond. U.S. Senate leadership yielded to national pressure, despite the opposition of Republican leaders to new gun control measures. After voting down some limited gun measures, the Senate reversed itself on May 20 and passed a bill requiring background checks at all gun show sales, flea markets, and pawn shops (closing the "gun show loophole"); revocation of gun ownership for those convicted of gun crimes as juveniles; tougher penalties for juvenile offenders who used guns in crimes and anyone who provided the guns; and sale of locking devices or boxes with all new handgun purchases while blocking legal immunity to those who sold guns to felons and banning the import of high-capacity ammunition clips (that hold more than ten bullets). Shifting national sentiments were reflected in the fact that the Senate had defeated attempts to require gun locks and ban the import of high-capacity clips the previous year.

The Senate-passed bill met a chilly reception in the House of Representatives, where Republican House leaders had long records of opposing stronger gun laws. After several weeks of bargaining and delay, the gun control package was defeated by a coalition of pro-control representatives who considered a compromise bill too weak, and anti-control representatives who opposed any new controls. A House-Senate conference committee convened to iron out their differences failed to act, killing the bill. The following Mother's Day in May 2000, some 700,000 protesters staged the so-called Million Mom March in Washington, D.C., in support of stronger gun laws and against gun violence.

The enduringly controversial nature of gun controls has prompted numerous lawsuits challenging their legality and constitutionality. A few of these challenges have succeeded, such as a 1997 Supreme Court ruling striking down the Brady Law requirement that local law enforcement officials conduct background checks (the court ruled that Congress had overstepped its power to regulate interstate commerce, on which the provision was based). From the nineteenth century to the present, however, no gun control law has ever been declared as violating the Second Amendment "right to bear arms," which the courts have consistently ruled protects a citizen's right to own guns only in connection with citizen service in a government-organized and regulated militia (a practice abandoned in the nineteenth century).

National gun control policy is implemented by the Bureau of Alcohol, Tobacco, Firearms and Explosives (ATF), which has had only limited success in fully enforcing national gun laws. Enforcement lapses have resulted from legislative restrictions on its authority, budget cutbacks, a tarnished reputation resulting from the 1993 confrontation with the Branch Davidian compound in Waco, Texas, and political opposition and criticism from the NRA.

CONCLUSION: THE LINKS BETWEEN GUN VIOLENCE AND GUN CONTROL

Considerable research has focused on the relationship between gun violence and various gun control measures. While this relationship is controversial, most agree on some principles. First, guns contribute significantly to the overall level, quantity, and harm associated with violence in America. On an annual basis, about 30,000 Americans are killed with guns each year, and 80,000 seriously injured. The largest number of gun deaths annually are suicide, followed by homicide and accident. Guns account for about two-thirds of all homicides and 60 percent of all suicides. (Gun suicides are especially problematic, because guns are more lethal than any other method of suicide.) An assault by an assailant carrying a gun is more likely to succeed but less likely to produce harm (as victims are intimidated by the presence of a gun). When harm does occur, however, it is more likely to be serious or fatal than that inflicted by other weapons. Gun assaults are three times more likely to result in victim death than assaults with the second-most frequently used weapon, knives. An estimate in 2000 concluded that gun violence cost the nation a total of $100 billion annually in direct and indirect costs, including medical costs and lost productivity.

Guns are not the sole cause of violence, however, and undoubtedly much gun-related violence would still occur if guns were not available. Yet control proponents argue that it is better that it occur without guns than with them. Gun control foes counter that guns in many situations actually reduce the extent of harm, because perpetrators are better able to control the crime situation. Further, guns can be "equalizers" when law-abiding citizens use them to deter or thwart crime. Control supporters counter that, regardless of their purpose for self-defense or defense of the home, the prevalence of guns causes harm when used in suicides, accidental shootings, or impulsive shooting incidents. And to serve as an equalizer for a potential victim, the gun must be kept handy and ready for use (i.e., loaded), storage practices that gun experts advise against as unsafe. Guns are also highly prized items for theft.

Gun control opponents claim the benefits of guns for self-defense outweigh their costs to society. Estimates of defensive gun uses (DGUs) vary, though most analysts believe guns are used in legitimate self-defense situations approximately 100,000 times per year. One anti-control analyst puts the annual DGU number as high as 2.5 million. Self-defense experts, however, note that a variety of alternatives to guns can increase an individual's safety, including improved home security, guard dogs, and a beefed-up police presence.

Most recent gun control efforts discussed here have focused on limited measures to impose stricter controls on handguns rather than long guns (rifles and shotguns). Estimates range from 200 million to 240 million guns in America, of which two-thirds are long guns and one-third handguns. The sheer number of guns, some believe, underscores the futility of any control measures. On the other hand, while long guns are twice as prevalent and generally easier to obtain than handguns, 80 percent of all gun crimes are committed with handguns, suggesting that efforts aimed at controlling handguns alone may yield benefits. Further, most guns used in crimes have a relatively short shelf life of 3 years or less because they are typically captured by authorities or disposed of by criminals. In addition, because most legitimate gun hunting and sporting activities are conducted with long guns, gun control supporters have focused primarily on handguns. But, building on the strict regulation of sawed-off shotguns and machine guns during the 1930s, recent control efforts are also aimed at newer, more harmful guns, such as assault weapons and .50-caliber sniper rifles.

Robert J. Spitzer

REFERENCES

Bellesiles, Michael A. *Arming America: The Origins of a National Gun Culture.* New York: Alfred A. Knopf, 2000.

———, ed. *Lethal Imagination: Violence and Brutality in American History.* New York: New York University Press, 1999.

Billington, Ray Allen. *Westward Expansion: A History of the American Frontier.* New York: Macmillan, 1974.

Bogus, Carl, ed. *The Second Amendment in Law and History.* New York: New Press, 2001.

Bruce, John M., and Clyde Wilcox, eds. *The Changing Politics of Gun Control.* Lanham, MD: Rowman and Littlefield, 1998.

Cook, Philip, and Jens Ludwig. *Gun Violence: The Real Costs.* New York: Oxford University Press, 2000.

Cornell, Saul. *Whose Right to Bear Arms Did the Second Amendment Protect?* Boston: Bedford/St. Martin's, 2000.

Davidson, Osha Gray. *Under Fire.* New York: Henry Holt, 1993.

DeConde, Alexander. *Gun Violence in America.* Boston: Northeastern University Press, 2001.

Diaz, Tom. *Making a Killing: The Business of Guns in America.* New York: New Press, 1999.

Dizard, Jan E., Robert Merrill Muth, and Stephen P. Andrews Jr., eds. *Guns in America.* New York: New York University Press, 1999.

Hofstadter, Richard, and Michael Wallace, eds. *American Violence.* New York: Vintage, 1970.

Karl, Jonathan. *The Right to Bear Arms.* New York: HarperCollins, 1995.

Kennett, Lee, and James LaVerne Anderson. *The Gun in America.* Westport, CT: Greenwood, 1975.

Kleck, Gary. *Targeting Guns.* New York: Aldine de Gruyter, 1997.

Larson, Erik. *Lethal Passage.* New York: Vintage, 1995.

Lott, John. *More Guns, Less Crime.* Chicago: University of Chicago Press, 1998.

Michel, Lou, and Dan Herbeck. *American Terrorist.* New York: Regan Books, 2001.

Nisbet, Lee, ed. *The Gun Control Debate.* Buffalo, NY: Prometheus Books, 1990.

Spitzer, Robert J. *The Right to Bear Arms.* Santa Barbara, CA: ABC-CLIO, 2001.

———. *The Politics of Gun Control.* New York: Chatham House, 2002.

Sugarmann, Josh. *Every Handgun Is Aimed at You.* New York: New Press, 2001.

Vizzard, William J. *Shots in the Dark.* Lanham, MD: Rowman and Littlefield, 2000.

Wills, Garry. *A Necessary Evil.* New York: Simon and Schuster, 1999.

Zimring, Franklin E., and Gordon Hawkins. *The Citizen's Guide to Gun Control.* New York: Macmillan, 1992.

WEB SITES

Brady Campaign to Prevent Gun Violence: www.bradycampaign.org.

Bureau of Alcohol, Tobacco, Firearms and Explosives: www.atf.treas.gov

National Rifle Association: www.nra.org

GLOSSARY

Alcohol, Tobacco, Firearms and Explosives, Bureau of (ATF). The federal agency charged with implementing national gun control laws.

Anti-Federalists. Those who opposed ratification of the Constitution of 1787, generally because of fears that it gave too much power to the national government, and too little to the states.

Assault Weapons Ban of 1994. A provision of the Violent Crime Control and Law Enforcement Act of 1994 that barred the possession of nineteen named types of assault weapons for 10 years. These are semiautomatic weapons that also possess at least two features of military-style weaponry.

Bill of Rights. The first ten amendments to the Constitution, added as a group in 1791 largely in response to the concerns of Anti-Federalists who feared the new and more powerful national government would usurp rights and liberties.

Brady Campaign to Prevent Gun Violence. Formerly known as Handgun Control Inc. (HCI) until 2001, the nation's largest gun control group was formed in 1974 to work for stronger gun laws. It grew in the 1980s and 1990s under the leadership of Sarah Brady, and seeks to counterbalance the power of the National Rifle Association.

Brady Handgun Violence Prevention Act of 1993. Also known as the Brady Law, after former Reagan Press Secretary James Brady (who was wounded during the 1981 assassination attempt against Reagan), this law imposed a national 5-business-day waiting period for purchase of a handgun. In 1998, under the terms of the law, the 5-day wait was replaced by a national instant background check system.

Columbine High School shootings. Two disgruntled high school boys entered Columbine High School in Littleton, Colorado, on April 20, 1999, with four guns and explosives. They killed twelve students and one teacher, wounded twenty-three others, and then killed themselves. The incident spurred renewed calls for stronger gun laws.

Defensive gun uses (DGUs). The use of guns by individuals to protect themselves from crime. Most estimates are about 100,000 such uses per year.

Federalists. Those who favored adoption of the Constitution of 1787, and generally stronger powers for the new national government.

Gun culture. The historical emotional attachment of some Americans to gun ownership and use, generally linked to hunting and sporting activities, but also to the romanticized frontier-militia tradition extending back to Colonial times.

Gun show loophole. A loophole allowing prospective gun purchasers to buy handguns at gun shows and flea markets without a background check, which would otherwise be required if the purchases were made from licensed gun dealers.

Handgun Control Inc. (HCI). *See* Brady Campaign to Prevent Gun Violence.

Militia Act of 1903. Law reorganizing the nation's militia system, separating the unorganized or reserve militia (the old-style general militia) from the organized militia, which under this act became the National Guard. Congress retained the right to mobilize the unorganized militia.

Militias. Part-time, amateur fighting forces called up by the government to service in times of military crisis, consisting of two types: unorganized or general militias that encompassed all eligible men between the ages of 18 and 45; and volunteer (also called organized or select) militias that trained on a more regular basis. Both dated from Colonial times. Last used in the War of 1812, the general militias' abysmal performance essentially ended the nation's use of such forces (in later wars, the nation instituted a military draft instead of calling up militias). Volunteer militias continued to operate until 1903, when Congress enacted the Militia Act, formally renaming such forces the National Guard, and bringing them under federal control. While some private individuals have formed groups they call "militias," only the government can create a militia.

Minutemen. Massachusetts militias formed to oppose the British Army in the American Revolution in the 1770s, so named because of the rapidity with which they could respond to a call-up.

National Rifle Association (NRA). Gun rights group formed in 1871 to improve marksmanship skills. The nation's oldest gun organization and staunchest opponent of stronger gun laws, the NRA has become one of the most influential and effective interest groups. Since the late 1970s, the organization has devoted more of its resources to political efforts to block new gun laws and repeal existing ones.

Second Amendment. "A well-regulated Militia, being necessary to the security of a free State, the right of the people to keep and bear Arms, shall not be infringed." This amendment was included in the Bill of Rights to reassure states' rights advocates and Anti-Federalists that the states would be able to maintain state-based militias under the new constitutional system that vested vastly expanded military powers in the hands of the national government under the Constitution of 1787.

Shays's Rebellion. An uprising of farmers in Massachusetts in January 1787, led by former Army captain Daniel Shays to protest foreclosure of debt-ridden lands. It underscored the national government's military weakness, and the unreliability of state militias in responding to emergencies.

Straw purchaser. An individual who buys guns on behalf of others who would not otherwise be able to make such purchases. Guns purchased by straw buyers account for a significant number of guns used in crimes.

Test Act of 1777. A Pennsylvania state law that barred gun ownership to citizens who refused to swear loyalty to the state.

Tommy gun. A handheld machine gun developed for use in World War I that became popular among gangsters in the 1920s and 1930s; they were strictly regulated by federal law in 1934.

Uniform Militia Act of 1792. A law passed by Congress defining militia service and stipulating that militia-eligible men maintain firearms and other military accessories should their services be required by the government.

Vigilantism. The belief that citizens have a right to take the law into their own hands if they believe they, or the nation, is at risk. Many individuals and groups, from the Ku Klux Klan to modern so-called militias, justify their extralegal activities with vigilantism.

War of 1812. The last major conflict fought with general (unorganized) militias. Their disastrous performance during the war effectively ended the use of these militias to meet military emergencies.

DOCUMENTS

Document 1. The Uniform Militia Act of 1792, 1 U.S. Stat. 271

The Uniform Militia Act, passed by Congress a year after adoption of the Bill of Rights, reveals what the country's leaders meant by a militia at a time when it was still considered the backbone of the American military. Congress intended the militias to be organized according to military principles; membership was limited not only to white males, but to those between 18 and 45 years old who were fit for service, underscoring the fact that white males over 45 and the infirm, though excluded from militias, were eligible to exercise other rights and freedoms. Militia men were to provide their own arms and other military accessories (since neither the states nor the national government could be relied on to provide them), and the militias were to be put to any use specified by the government. Thus, militias were not to be privately formed or operated, nor were they to be used against the government, as some modern commentators have suggested. The act, however, included no penalties against states or men who did not comply—another compromise resulting from continued tensions between Federalists and Anti-Federalists. The terms of this act were largely ignored. Aside from the general military and organizational failure of the old-style general militias, two nineteenth century developments put an end to the militia system described here: the military draft, and governmental issue of firearms, uniforms, and the other accoutrements of war. Congress finally revamped the old militia system in a series of enactments beginning with the Militia Act of 1903 (also called the Dick Act).

CHAP. XXXIII.—An Act more effectually to provide for the National Defence by establishing an Uniform Militia throughout the United States.

SECTION I. Be it enacted by the Senate and House of Representatives of the United States of America in Congress assembled, That each and every free able-bodied white male citizen of the respective states, resident therein, who is or shall be of the age of eighteen years, and under the age of forty-five years (except as is herein after excepted) shall severally and respectively be enrolled in the militia by the captain or commanding officer of the company, within whose bounds such citizen shall reside, and that within twelve months after the passing of this act. And it shall at all times hereafter be the duty of every such captain or commanding officer of a company to enroll every such citizen, as aforesaid, and also those who shall, from time to time, arrive at the age of eighteen years, or being of the age of eighteen years and under the age of forty-five years (except as before excepted) shall come to reside within his bounds; and shall without delay notify such citizen of the said enrolment, by a proper non-commissioned officer of the company, by whom such notice may be proved. That every citizen so enrolled and notified, shall, within six months thereafter, provide himself with a good musket or firelock, a sufficient bayonet and belt, two spare flints, and a knapsack, a pouch with a box therein to contain not less than twenty-four cartridges, suited to the bore of his musket or firelock, each cartridge to contain a proper quantity of powder and ball: or with a good rifle, knapsack, shot-pouch and powder-horn, twenty balls suited to the bore of his rifle, and a quarter of a pound of powder; and shall appear, so armed, accoutred and provided, when called out to exercise, or into service, except, that when called out on company days to exercise only, he may appear without a knapsack. That the commissioned officers shall severally be armed with a sword or hanger and espontoon, and that from and after five years from the passing of this act, all muskets for arming the militia as herein required, shall be of bores sufficient for balls of the eighteenth part of a pound. And every citizen so enrolled, and providing himself with the arms, ammunition and accoutrements required as aforesaid, shall hold the same exempted from all suits, distresses, executions or sales, for debt or for the payment of taxes.

SEC. 2. And be it further enacted, That the Vice President of the United States; the officers judicial and executive of the government of the United States; the members of both Houses of Congress, and their respective officers; all custom-house officers with their clerks; all postofficers, and stage drivers, who are employed in the care and conveyance of the mail of the post-office of the United States; all ferrymen employed at any ferry on the post road; all inspectors of exports; all pilots; all mariners actually employed in the sea service of any citizen or merchant within the United States; and all persons who now are or may hereafter be exempted by the laws of the respective states, shall be, and are hereby exempted from militia duty, notwithstanding their being above the age of eighteen, and under the age of forty-five years.

SEC. 3. And be it further enacted, That within one year after the passing of this act, the militia of the respective states shall be arranged into divisions, brigades, regiments, battalions and companies, as the legislature of each state shall direct; and each division, brigade and regiment, shall

be numbered at the formation thereof; and a record made of such numbers in the adjutant-general's office in the state; and when in the field, or in service in the state, each division, brigade and regiment shall respectively take rank according to their numbers, reckoning the first or lowest number highest in rank. That if the same be convenient, each brigade shall consist of four regiments; each regiment of two battalions; each battalion of five companies; each company of sixty-four privates. That the said militia shall be officered by the respective states, as follows: To each division, one major-general and two aids-de-camp, with the rank of major; to each brigade, one brigadier-general, with one brigade inspector, to serve also as brigade-major, with the rank of a major; to each regiment, one lieutenant-colonel commandant; and to each battalion one major; to each company one captain, one lieutenant, one ensign, four sergeants, four corporals, one drummer and one fifer or bugler. That there shall be a regimental staff, to consist of one adjutant and one quartermaster, to rank as lieutenants; one paymaster; one surgeon, and one surgeon's mate; one sergeant-major; one drum-major, and one fife-major.

SEC. 4. And be it further enacted, That out of the militia enrolled, as is herein directed, there shall be formed for each battalion at least one company of grenadiers, light infantry or riflemen; and that to each division there shall be at least one company of artillery, and one troop of horse: there shall be to each company of artillery, one captain, two lieutenants, four sergeants, four corporals, six gunners, six bombadiers, one drummer, and one fifer. The officers to be armed with a sword or hanger, a fusee, bayonet and belt, with a cartridge-box to contain twelve cartridges; and each private or matross shall furnish himself with all the equipments of a private in the infantry, until proper ordnance and field artillery is provided. There shall be to each troop of horse, one captain, two lieutenants, one cornet, four sergeants, four corporals, one saddler, one farrier, and one trumpeter. The commissioned officers to furnish themselves with good horses of at least fourteen hands and an half high, and to be armed with a sword and pair of pistols, the holsters of which to be covered with bearskin caps. Each dragoon to furnish himself with a serviceable horse, at least fourteen hands and a half high, a good saddle, bridle, mailpillion and valise, holsters, and a breast-plate and crupper, a pair of boots and spurs, a pair of pistols, a sabre, and a cartouch-box, to contain twelve cartridges for pistols. That each company of artillery and troop of horse shall be formed of volunteers from the brigade, at the discretion of the commander-in-chief of the state, not exceeding one company of each to a regiment, nor more in number than one eleventh part of the infantry, and shall be uniformly clothed in regimentals, to be furnished at their own expense; the colour and fashion to be determined by the brigadier commanding the brigade to which they belong.

SEC. 5. And be it further enacted, That each battalion and regiment shall be provided with the state and regimental colours by the field officers, and each company with a drum and fife, or bugle-horn, by the commissioned officers of the company, in such manner as the legislature of the respective states shall direct.

SEC. 6. And be it further enacted, That there shall be an adjutant-general appointed in each state, whose duty it shall be to distribute all orders from the commander-in-chief of the state to the several corps; to attend all public reviews when the commander-in-chief of the state shall review the militia, or any part thereof; to obey all orders from him relative to carrying into execution and perfecting the system of military discipline established by this act; to furnish blank forms of different returns that may be required, and to explain the principles on which they should be made; to receive from the several officers of the different corps throughout the state, returns of the militia under their command, reporting the actual situation of their arms, accoutrements, and ammunition, their delinquencies, and every other thing which relates to the general advancement of good order and discipline: all which the several officers of the divisions, brigades, regiments, and battalions, are hereby required to make in the usual manner, so that the said adjutant-general may be duly furnished therewith: from all which returns he shall make proper abstracts, and lay the same annually before the commander-in-chief of the state.

SEC. 7. And be it further enacted, That the rules of discipline, approved and established by Congress in their resolution of the twenty-ninth of March, one thousand seven hundred and seventy-nine, shall be the rules of discipline to be observed by the militia throughout the United States, except such deviations from the said rules as may be rendered necessary by the requisitions of this act, or by some other unavoidable circumstances. It shall be the duty of the commanding officer at every muster, whether by battalion, regiment, or single company, to cause the militia to be exercised and trained agreeably to the said rules of discipline.

SEC. 8. And be it further enacted, That all commissioned officers shall take rank according to the date of their commissions; and when two of the same grade bear an equal date, then their rank to be determined by lot, to be drawn by them before the commanding officer of the brigade, regiment, battalion, company, or detachment.

SEC. 9. And be it further enacted, That if any person, whether officer or soldier, belonging to the militia of any state, and called out into the service of the United States, be wounded or disabled while in actual service, he shall be taken care of and provided for at the public expense.

SEC. 10. And be it further enacted, That it shall be the duty of the brigade-inspector to attend the regimental and battalion meetings of the militia composing their several brigades, during the time of their being under arms, to inspect their arms, ammunition, and accoutrements; superintend their exercise and manoeuvres, and introduce the system of military discipline before described throughout the brigade, agreeable to law, and such orders as they shall from time to time receive from the commander-in-chief of the state; to make returns to the adjutant-general of the state, at least once in every year, of the militia of the brigade to which he belongs, reporting therein the actual situation of the arms, accoutrements, and ammunition of the several corps, and every other thing which, in his judgment, may relate to their government and the general advancement of good order and military discipline; and the adjutant-general shall make a return of all the militia of the state to the commander-in-chief of the said state, and a duplicate of the same to the President of the United States. And whereas sundry corps of artillery, cavalry, and infantry now exist in several of the said states, which by the laws, customs, or usages thereof have not been incorporated with, or subject to the general regulations of the militia:

SEC. 11. Be it further enacted, That such corps retain their accustomed privileges, subject, nevertheless, to all other duties required by this act, in like manner with the other militia.

APPROVED, May 8, 1792.

Source: 1 U.S. STAT. 271.

Document 2. Brady Bill (Public Safety and Recreational Firearms Use Protection Act)

Popularly known as the Brady Bill—after President Ronald Reagan's press secretary, James Brady, wounded in a 1981 assassination attempt, who, with his wife, lobbied heavily for the bill—the Public Safety and Recreational Firearms Use Protection Act was signed into law by President Bill Clinton in 1994. Passed despite heavy anti-gun control lobbying by the National Rifle Association and other pro-gun groups, the Brady Bill was the first major federal gun control legislation in many years, banning most types of semi-automatic weapons and requiring a 5-day background check for most handgun purchases.

Title XI Firearms
Subtitle A—Assault Weapons

SEC. 110101. SHORT TITLE.

This subtitle may be cited as the 'Public Safety and Recreational Firearms Use Protection Act.'

SEC. 110102. RESTRICTION ON MANUFACTURE, TRANSFER, AND POSSESSION OF CERTAIN SEMI-AUTOMATIC ASSAULT WEAPONS.

(a) RESTRICTION—Section 922 of title 18, United States Code, is amended by adding at the end the following new subsection:

(v)(1) It shall be unlawful for a person to manufacture, transfer, or possess a semiautomatic assault weapon.

(2) Paragraph (1) shall not apply to the possession or transfer of any semiautomatic assault weapon otherwise lawfully possessed under Federal law on the date of the enactment of this subsection.

(3) Paragraph (1) shall not apply to—

(A) any of the firearms, or replicas or duplicates of the firearms, specified in Appendix A to this section, as such firearms were manufactured on October 1, 1993;

(B) any firearm that—

(i) is manually operated by bolt, pump, lever, or slide action;

(ii) has been rendered permanently inoperable; or

(iii) is an antique firearm;

(C) any semiautomatic rifle that cannot accept a detachable magazine that holds more than 5 rounds of ammunition; or

(D) any semiautomatic shotgun that cannot hold more than 5 rounds of ammunition in a fixed or detachable magazine.

The fact that a firearm is not listed in Appendix A shall not be construed to mean that paragraph (1) applies to such firearm. No firearm exempted by this subsection may be deleted from Appendix A so long as this subsection is in effect. (4) Paragraph (1) shall not apply to—

(A) the manufacture for, transfer to, or possession by the United States or a department or agency of the United States or a State or a department, agency, or political subdivision of a State, or a transfer to or possession by a law enforcement officer employed by such an entity for purposes of law enforcement (whether on or off duty);

(B) the transfer to a licensee under title I of the Atomic Energy Act of 1954 for purposes of establishing and maintaining an on-site physical protection system and security

organization required by Federal law, or possession by an employee or contractor of such licensee on-site for such purposes or off-site for purposes of licensee-authorized training or transportation of nuclear materials;

(C) the possession, by an individual who is retired from service with a law enforcement agency and is not otherwise prohibited from receiving a firearm, of a semiautomatic assault weapon transferred to the individual by the agency upon such retirement; or

(D) the manufacture, transfer, or possession of a semiautomatic assault weapon by a licensed manufacturer or licensed importer for the purposes of testing or experimentation authorized by the Secretary. . . .

(b) DEFINITION OF SEMIAUTOMATIC ASSAULT WEAPON—Section 921(a) of title 18, United States Code, is amended by adding at the end the following new paragraph:

(30) The term 'semiautomatic assault weapon' means—

(A) any of the firearms, or copies or duplicates of the firearms in any caliber, known as—

(i) Norinco, Mitchell, and Poly Technologies Avtomat Kalashnikovs (all models);

(vi) SWD M-10, M-11, M-11/9, and M-12;

(vii) Steyr AUG;

(viii) INTRATEC TEC-9, TEC-DC9 and TEC-22; and

(ix) revolving cylinder shotguns, such as (or similar to) the Street Sweeper and Striker 12;

(B) a semiautomatic rifle that has an ability to accept a detachable magazine and has at least 2 of—

(i) a folding or telescoping stock;

(ii) a pistol grip that protrudes conspicuously beneath the action of the weapon;

(iii) a bayonet mount;

(iv) a flash suppresser or threaded barrel designed to accommodate a flash suppresser; and

(v) a grenade launcher;

(C) a semiautomatic pistol that has an ability to accept a detachable magazine and has at least 2 of—

(i) an ammunition magazine that attaches to the pistol outside of the pistol grip;

(ii) a threaded barrel capable of accepting a barrel extender, flash suppresser, forward hand grip, or silencer;

(iii) a shroud that is attached to, or partially or completely encircles, the barrel and that permits the shooter to hold the firearm with the non trigger hand without being burned;

(iv) a manufactured weight of 50 ounces or more when the pistol is unloaded; and

(v) a semiautomatic version of an automatic firearm; and

(D) a semiautomatic shotgun that has at least 2 of—

(i) a folding or telescoping stock;

(ii) a pistol grip that protrudes conspicuously beneath the action of the weapon;

(iii) a fixed magazine capacity in excess of 5 rounds; and

(iv) an ability to accept a detachable magazine. . . .

(c) PENALTIES—

(1) VIOLATION OF SECTION 922(v)—Section 924(a)(1)(B) of such title is amended by striking 'or (q) of section 922' and inserting (r), 'or (v) of section 922.'

(2) USE OR POSSESSION DURING CRIME OF VIOLENCE OR DRUG TRAFFICKING CRIME—Section 924(c)(1) of such title is amended in the first sentence by inserting, 'or semiautomatic assault weapon,' after 'short-barreled shotgun.'

(d) IDENTIFICATION MARKINGS FOR SEMIAUTOMATIC ASSAULT WEAPONS—Section 923(i) of such title is amended by adding at the end the following: 'The serial number of any semiautomatic assault weapon manufactured after the date of the enactment of this sentence shall clearly show the date on which the weapon was manufactured. . . .'

SEC. 110103. BAN OF LARGE CAPACITY AMMUNITION FEEDING DEVICES.

(a) PROHIBITION—Section 922 of title 18, United States Code, as amended by section 110102(a), is amended by adding at the end the following new subsection:

(w)(1) Except as provided in paragraph (2), it shall be unlawful for a person to transfer or possess a large capacity ammunition feeding device.

(2) Paragraph (1) shall not apply to the possession or transfer of any large capacity ammunition feeding device otherwise lawfully possessed on or before the date of the enactment of this subsection.

(3) This subsection shall not apply to—

(A) the manufacture for, transfer to, or possession by the United States or a department or agency of the United States or a State or a department, agency, or political subdivision of a State, or a transfer to or possession by a law enforcement officer employed by such an entity for purposes of law enforcement (whether on or off duty);

(B) the transfer to a licensee under title I of the Atomic Energy Act of 1954 for purposes of establishing and maintaining an on-site physical protection system and security organization required by Federal law, or possession by an employee or contractor of such licensee on-site for such purposes or off-site for purposes of licensee-authorized training or transportation of nuclear materials;

(ii) Action Arms Israeli Military Industries UZI and Galil;

(iii) Beretta Ar70 (SC-70);

(iv) Colt AR-15;

(v) Fabrique National FN/FAL, FN/LAR, and FNC;

(C) the possession, by an individual who is retired from service with a law enforcement agency and is not otherwise prohibited from receiving ammunition, of a large capacity ammunition feeding device transferred to the individual by the agency upon such retirement; or

(D) the manufacture, transfer, or possession of any large capacity ammunition feeding device by a licensed manufacturer or licensed importer for the purposes of testing or experimentation authorized by the Secretary. . . .

(4) If a person charged with violating paragraph (1) asserts that paragraph (1) does not apply to such person because of paragraph (2) or (3), the Government shall have the burden of proof to show that such paragraph (1) applies to such person. The lack of a serial number as described in section 923(i) of title 18, United States Code, shall be a presumption that the large capacity ammunition feeding device is not subject to the prohibition of possession in paragraph (1). . . .

(b) DEFINITION OF LARGE CAPACITY AMMUNITION FEEDING DEVICE—Section 921(a) of title 18, United States Code, as amended by section 110102(b), is amended by adding at the end the following new paragraph:

(31) The term 'large capacity ammunition feeding device'—

(A) means a magazine, belt, drum, feed strip, or similar device manufactured after the date of enactment of the Violent Crime Control and Law Enforcement Act of 1994 that has a capacity of, or that can be readily restored or converted to accept, more than 10 rounds of ammunition; but

(B) does not include an attached tubular device designed to accept, and capable of operating only with, .22 caliber rim fire ammunition. . . .

(c) PENALTY—Section 924(a)(1)(B) of title 18, United States Code, as amended by section 110102(c)(1), is amended by striking 'or (v)' and inserting '(v), or (w).'

(d) IDENTIFICATION MARKINGS FOR LARGE CAPACITY AMMUNITION FEEDING DEVICES—Section 923(i) of title 18, United States Code, as amended by section 110102(d) of this Act, is amended by adding at the end the following: 'A large capacity ammunition feeding device manufactured after the date of the enactment of this sentence shall be identified by a serial number that clearly shows that the device was manufactured or imported after the effective date of this subsection, and such other identification as the Secretary may by regulation prescribe.'. . .

SEC. 110201. PROHIBITION OF THE POSSESSION OF A HANDGUN OR AMMUNITION BY, OR THE PRIVATE TRANSFER OF A HANDGUN OR AMMUNITION TO, A JUVENILE.

(a) OFFENSE—Section 922 of title 18, United States Code, as amended by section 110103(a), is amended by adding at the end the following new subsection:

(x)(1) It shall be unlawful for a person to sell, deliver, or otherwise transfer to a person who the transferor knows or has reasonable cause to believe is a juvenile—

(A) a handgun; or

(B) ammunition that is suitable for use only in a handgun.

(2) It shall be unlawful for any person who is a juvenile to knowingly possess—

(A) a handgun; or

(B) ammunition that is suitable for use only in a handgun.

(3) This subsection does not apply to—

(A) a temporary transfer of a handgun or ammunition to a juvenile or to the possession or use of a handgun or ammunition by a juvenile if the handgun and ammunition are possessed and used by the juvenile—

(i) in the course of employment, in the course of ranching or farming related to activities at the residence of the juvenile (or on property used for ranching or farming at which the juvenile, with the permission of the property owner or lessee, is performing activities related to the operation of the farm or ranch), target practice, hunting, or a course of instruction in the safe and lawful use of a handgun;

(ii) with the prior written consent of the juvenile's parent or guardian who is not prohibited by Federal, State, or local law from possessing a firearm, except—

(I) during transportation by the juvenile of an unloaded handgun in a locked container directly from the place of transfer to a place at which an activity described in clause (i) is to take place and transportation by the juvenile of that handgun, unloaded and in a locked container, directly from the place at which such an activity took place to the transferor; or

(II) with respect to ranching or farming activities as described in clause (i), a juvenile may possess and use a handgun or ammunition with the prior written approval of the juvenile's parent or legal guardian and at the direction of an adult who is not prohibited by Federal, State or local law from possessing a firearm;

(iii) the juvenile has the prior written consent in the juvenile's possession at all times when a handgun is in the possession of the juvenile; and

(iv) in accordance with State and local law;

(B) a juvenile who is a member of the Armed Forces of the United States or the National Guard who possesses or is armed with a handgun in the line of duty;

(C) a transfer by inheritance of title (but not possession) of a handgun or ammunition to a juvenile; or (D) the possession of a handgun or ammunition by a juvenile taken in defense of the juvenile or other persons against an intruder into the residence of the juvenile or a residence in which the juvenile is an invited guest.

(4) A handgun or ammunition, the possession of which is transferred to a juvenile in circumstances in which the transferor is not in violation of this subsection shall not be subject to permanent confiscation by the Government if its possession by the juvenile subsequently becomes unlawful because of the conduct of the juvenile, but shall be returned to the lawful owner when such handgun or ammunition is no longer required by the Government for the purposes of investigation or prosecution.

(5) For purposes of this subsection, the term 'juvenile' means a person who is less than 18 years of age.

(6)(A) In a prosecution of a violation of this subsection, the court shall require the presence of a juvenile defendant's parent or legal guardian at all proceedings.

(B) The court may use the contempt power to enforce subparagraph (A).

(C) The court may excuse attendance of a parent or legal guardian of a juvenile defendant at a proceeding in a prosecution of a violation of this subsection for good cause shown. . . .

(b) PENALTIES—Section 924(a) of title 18, United States Code, is amended—

(1) in paragraph (1) by striking 'paragraph (2) or (3) of'; and

(2) by adding at the end the following new paragraph:

(5)(A)(i) A juvenile who violates section 922(x) shall be fined under this title, imprisoned not more than 1 year, or both, except that a juvenile described in clause (ii) shall be sentenced to probation on appropriate conditions and shall not be incarcerated unless the juvenile fails to comply with a condition of probation.

(ii) A juvenile is described in this clause if—

(I) the offense of which the juvenile is charged is possession of a handgun or ammunition in violation of section 922(x)(2); and

(II) the juvenile has not been convicted in any court of an offense (including an offense under section 922(x) or a similar State law, but not including any other offense consisting of conduct that if engaged in by an adult would not constitute an offense) or adjudicated as a juvenile delinquent for conduct that if engaged in by an adult would constitute an offense.

(B) A person other than a juvenile who knowingly violates section 922(x)—

(i) shall be fined under this title, imprisoned not more than 1 year, or both; and

(ii) if the person sold, delivered, or otherwise transferred a handgun or ammunition to a juvenile knowing or having reasonable cause to know that the juvenile intended to carry or otherwise possess or discharge or otherwise use the handgun or ammunition in the commission of a crime of violence, shall be fined under this title, imprisoned not more than 10 years, or both. . . .

Source: U.S.C. title IX, sec. 110101–110103, 110201.